DELPHI ACADEMY OF FLORIDA
1831 Drew St
Clearwater, FL 33765-2913
(727)447-6385

W9-APU-757

The Kingfisher

SCIENCE

ENCYCLOPEDIA

The Kingfisher
SCIENCE
ENCYCLOPEDIA

General Editor: Catherine Headlam

Kingfisher Books

NEW YORK

KINGFISHER BOOKS
Grisewood & Dempsey Inc.
95 Madison Avenue
New York, New York 10016

This one-volume edition
first published in the United States
in 1993. Originally published in
multiple volumes in 1991,
distributed by Encyclopedia Britannica.

2 4 6 8 10 9 7 5 3 1

Library of Congress Cataloging-in-Publication Data
Kingfisher science encyclopedia / general editor, Catherine Headlam.
p.   cm.
Includes index.
Summary: Presents articles on scientific and technological topics
arranged in alphabetical order.
1. Science——Encyclopedias, Juvenile. [1. Science—
—Encyclopedias.] I. Headlam, Catherine.
Q121.K55 1993
503——dc20   92–43209   CIP   AC

ISBN 1-85697-842-7

Printed in Italy

GENERAL EDITOR
Catherine Headlam

EDITORIAL DIRECTOR
Jim Miles

ASSISTANT EDITORS
Lee Simmons
Charlotte Evans

EDITORIAL ASSISTANT
Andrea Moran

CONSULTANTS
Professor Lawrence F. Lowery, University of California, Berkeley
Alison Porter, Education Officer, Science Museum, London

EDUCATIONAL CONSULTANTS
Terry Cash, Coordinator of a team of advisory teachers in Essex
Robert Pressling, Math Coordinator,
Hillsgrove Primary School, London

CONTRIBUTORS
Joan Angelbeck
Michael Chinery
John Clark
Neil Curtis
Gwen Edmonds
Andrew Fisher
William Gould
Ian Graham
William Hemsley
James Muirden
John Paton
Brian Ward
Wendy Wasels
Peter Way

DESIGN
Ralph Pitchford
Allan Hardcastle
Ross George
Judy Crammond

PICTURE RESEARCH
Tim Russell
Elaine Willis

PRODUCTION
Dawn Hickman

FOREWORD

When the 21st century dawns, science, mathematics, and accompanying technologies will be deeply interwoven within the fabric of all societies. The scientifically literate citizen of the next century will be the person who: knows that science, mathematics, and technology are interdependent human enterprises with strengths and limitations; understands key concepts and principles within the grand conceptual frameworks of science; is familiar with the natural world and recognizes both its diversity and unity; uses scientific knowledge and scientific ways of thinking for individual and social purposes.

Today's youngsters will be tomorrow's citizens and leaders. They will make decisions that will affect the quality of the world environment and the quality of life on this planet. To prepare for tomorrow, today's youngsters must have access to the knowledge of science early in their lives — when there is a budding interest and broad general curiosity about many topics. What better way to provide this knowledge than through a storehouse of scientific and technological information in the form of an encyclopedia written in a manner appropriate to beginning levels of interest? Never before has such a resource been provided. Prepared in the spirit and character of scientific inquiry and integrated with scientific values, *The Kingfisher Science Encyclopedia* provides more than facts. It invites youngsters to actively hypothesize by posing challenging questions, to collect and use evidence through suggested investigations, and to explore new topics that subsequently interrelate and extend ideas. It places a premium on the natural curiosity and creativity of youngsters. And it provides them with the challenges and issues that the future must face.

The contents of *The Kingfisher Science Encyclopedia* is the work of many people — those who compiled the information as well as those who discovered the ideas. It is a work of love and care for the purpose of contributing to an enlightened citizenry that will live most of its life in the next century.

Professor Lawrence F. Lowery
Graduate School of Education
and the Lawrence Hall of Science
University of California
Berkeley, California

SAFETY CODE

Some science experiments can be dangerous. Ask an adult to help you with difficult hammering or cutting and any experiments that involve flames, hot liquids, or chemicals. Do not forget to put out any flames and turn off the heat when you have finished. Good scientists avoid accidents.

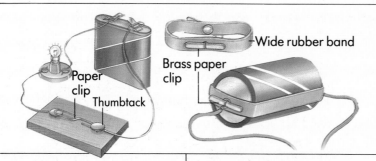

Paper clip

Thumbtack

Wide rubber band

Brass paper clip

ELECTRICITY
- Never use electricity from the outlet for experiments.
- Use batteries for all experiments that need electricity. Dispose of batteries carefully when they are used up and never heat them up or take them apart.

HEATING
- Tie back hair and be careful of loose clothes.
- Only heat small quantities of a substance.
- Always have an adult with you.
- Never heat any container with a top on it. Always point what you are heating away from you.
- Never hold something in your hands to heat it. Use a holder that does not conduct heat.

SAFE SOURCES OF HEAT
- Hot water from the faucet is a good source of heat.
- A hair dryer can be used to dry things. Always take care when using electricity near water.

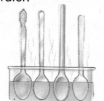

Sand

Metal tray

- For direct heat use a short thick candle placed in sand in a metal tray.

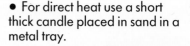

CHEMICALS AND QUANTITIES
- Only use a small amount of any substance even if it is just salt or vinegar.
- Never taste or eat chemicals
- Clean up all spillages immediately, especially if on your skin.
- Wash your hands after using chemicals.
- Always ask an adult before using any substance; many cooking or cleaning substances used at home are very powerful.
- Smell chemicals very carefully. Do not breathe in deeply any strong smells.
- Never handle chemicals with your bare hands. Use an old spoon and wash it very carefully after use.
- Label **all** chemicals.

SUN
- Never look directly at the Sun, especially when using a telescope or binoculars.

PLANTS AND ANIMALS
- Never pick wild flowers.
- Collect insects carefully so as not to harm them. Release them afterward.
- Be careful of stinging insects.

SAFE CONTAINERS
- Use plastic containers if an experiment does not require heating or strong chemicals.
- Use heat-proof glass or metal containers if you are using heat.
- Avoid using ordinary glass as it may shatter.

CUTTING
- Use scissors rather than a knife whenever possible.
- When using a knife keep your fingers behind the cutting edge.
- Put what you are cutting on a board that will not slip and will prevent damage to the surface underneath.

ABOUT *your* ENCYCLOPEDIA

This encyclopedia is very easy to use. All the entries are arranged in alphabetical order. You should find most of the information you want by first looking up the main entry word. If the subject you are looking for does not have its own entry, look in the Index at the back. Usually you will find some information about your subject in another article.

●

Throughout the encyclopedia you will find words printed in small capitals, like this: LASER. These words are cross-references. When you see one, you will know that there is a separate entry on the subject in your encyclopedia. That entry may have more information about the subject you are looking up.

●

Subject symbols appear next to each heading. These will help you to relate each entry to one or more of the branches of science, such as Chemistry ▨ or Technology ⚙. There are nine symbols in all.

●

Throughout the encyclopedia you will come across Special Feature entries. These take a large subject and look at it in more detail. Use them to help with a school project or to find out more about a particular branch of science. You will find a list of Special Features at the back of the encyclopedia.

●

In addition to the main text there are many See-For-Yourself panels with simple experiments for you to try. Use them to see-for-yourself how science works.

●

There are Fact Boxes and Milestones Boxes containing important facts and figures; Vocabulary Boxes which give the meaning of technical terms used in the main text; and Nugget Boxes which are full of fascinating and often surprising information.

●

Use your encyclopedia to discover a wealth of information about science, about how science works, and about scientists and their discoveries.

●

HOW TO GET THE MOST
from your ENCYCLOPEDIA

This encyclopedia contains many features to help you look up things easily or simply to have fun just browsing through. Every page is illustrated and there are Fact Boxes, Special Feature entries, and literally hundreds of cross-references to help you find your way around. Some of these features are shown here. We hope you will get a lot of enjoyment from exploring this encyclopedia.

- Subject symbols
- Fact Boxes
- Nugget Boxes
- Special Feature entries
- Cross-references

- Simple experiments and observations
- Vocabulary Boxes
- Biography Boxes
- Milestones

BIOGRAPHY BOXES give details about the lives and work of individual scientists, and appear on the same page as the subject for which they are known.

THE TEXT is arranged alphabetically and easy to read. Cross-references appear as SMALL CAPITALS or *see also* suggestions. Turn to these entries for more information on the subject.

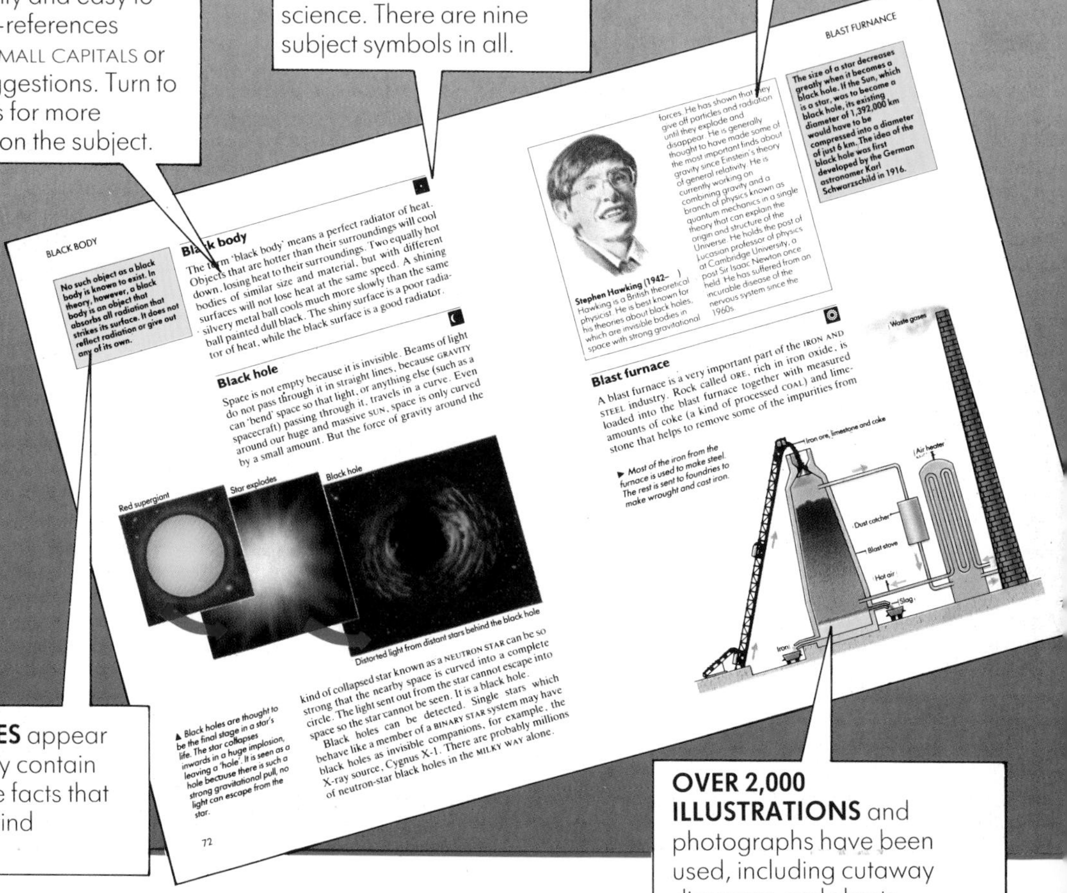

SUBJECT SYMBOLS allow you to relate an entry to one or more of the branches of science. There are nine subject symbols in all.

NUGGET BOXES appear throughout. They contain strange-but-true facts that you are sure to find fascinating.

OVER 2,000 ILLUSTRATIONS and photographs have been used, including cutaway diagrams and charts.

BLACK BODY

BLAST FURNACE

No such object as a black body is known to exist. In theory, however, a black body is an object that absorbs all radiation that strikes its surface. It does not reflect radiation or give out any of its own.

Black body
The term 'black body' means a perfect radiator of heat. Objects that are hotter than their surroundings will cool down, losing heat to their surroundings. Two equally hot bodies of similar size and material, but with different surfaces will not lose heat at the same speed. A shining silvery metal ball cools much more slowly than the same ball painted dull black. The shiny surface is a poor radiator of heat, while the black surface is a good radiator.

Black hole
Space is not empty because it is invisible. Beams of light do not pass through it in straight lines, because GRAVITY can 'bend' space so that light, or anything else (such as a spacecraft) passing through it, travels in a curve. Even around our huge and massive SUN, space is only curved by a small amount. But the force of gravity around the

Red supergiant   Star explodes   Black hole

Distorted light from distant stars behind the black hole

▲ Black holes are thought to be the final stage in a star's life. The star collapses inwards in a huge implosion, leaving a 'hole'. It is seen as a hole because there is such a strong gravitational pull, no light can escape from the star.

kind of collapsed star known as a NEUTRON STAR can be so strong that the nearby space is curved into a complete circle. The light sent out from the star cannot escape into space so the star cannot be seen. It is a black hole.
Black holes can be detected. Single stars which behave like a member of a BINARY STAR system may have black holes as invisible companions, for example, the X-ray source, Cygnus X-1. There are probably millions of neutron-star black holes in the MILKY WAY alone.

72

Stephen Hawking (1942–)
Hawking is a British theoretical physicist. He is best known for his theories about black holes, which are invisible bodies in space with strong gravitational

forces. He has shown that they give off particles and radiation until they explode and disappear. He is generally thought to have made some of the most important finds about gravity since Einstein's theory of general relativity. He is currently working on a branch of physics known as quantum mechanics in a single theory that can explain the origin and structure of the Universe. He holds the post of Lucasian professor of physics at Cambridge University, a post Sir Isaac Newton once held. He has suffered from an incurable disease of the nervous system since the 1960s.

The size of a star decreases greatly when it becomes a black hole. If the Sun, which is a star, was to become a black hole, its existing diameter of 1,392,000 km would have to be compressed into a diameter of just 6 km. The idea of the black hole was first developed by the German astronomer Karl Schwarzschild in 1916.

Blast furnace
A blast furnace is a very important part of the IRON AND STEEL industry. Rock called ORE, rich in iron oxide, is loaded into the blast furnace together with measured amounts of coke (a kind of processed COAL) and limestone that helps to remove some of the impurities from

▶ Most of the iron from the furnace is used to make steel. The rest is sent to foundries to make wrought and cast iron.

Waste gases

Iron ore, limestone and coke

Air heater

Dust catcher

Blast stove

Hot air

Slag

Iron

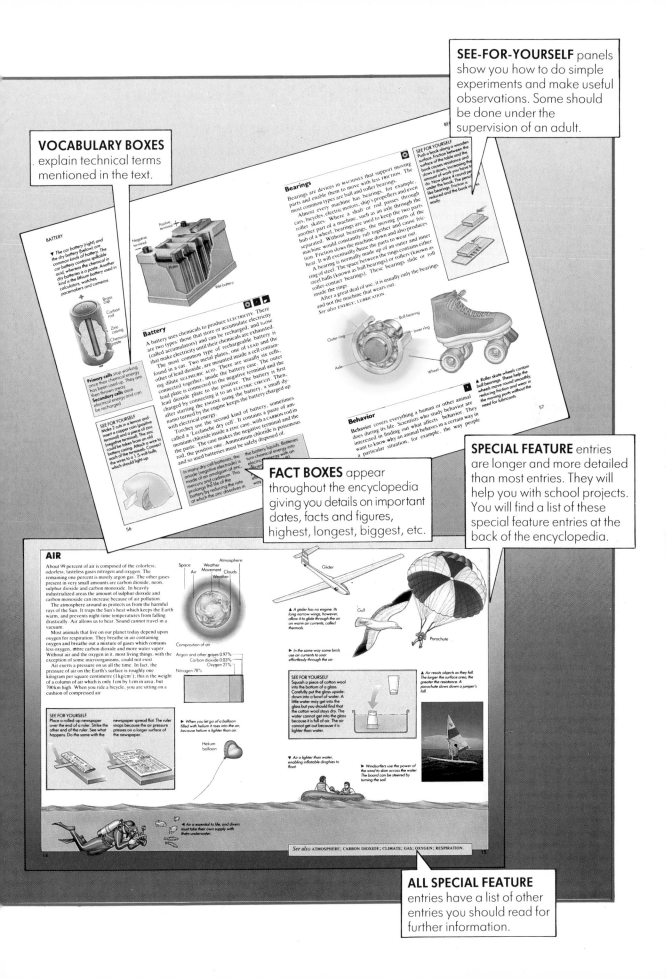

VOCABULARY BOXES explain technical terms mentioned in the text.

SEE-FOR-YOURSELF panels show you how to do simple experiments and make useful observations. Some should be done under the supervision of an adult.

SPECIAL FEATURE entries are longer and more detailed than most entries. They will help you with school projects. You will find a list of these special feature entries at the back of the encyclopedia.

FACT BOXES appear throughout the encyclopedia giving you details on important dates, facts and figures, highest, longest, biggest, etc.

ALL SPECIAL FEATURE entries have a list of other entries you should read for further information.

THE SUBJECT SYMBOLS

Each entry in this encyclopedia has its own easily recognized symbol opposite the heading. This symbol tells you at a glance which area of interest the entry falls into — is it Biography, Electronics, or Astronomy? Some entries fall into more than one subject area such as biochemistry which covers both Life Sciences and Chemistry. These entries have more than one subject symbol. Below are the nine subject areas we have used. At the back of the encyclopedia there is a list of all the articles divided into these subject areas.

ASTRONOMY
What are black holes, comets, and quasars? How did planets and galaxies form? How much of space have we discovered and explored?

BIOGRAPHY
The lives and discoveries of important scientists and inventors and their contribution to current knowledge.

CHEMISTRY
What are substances made of? How do they behave on their own or when in contact with other substances?

EARTH SCIENCES
How the Earth was formed and how it is still changing; its deserts, mountains, oceans, rivers, and weather.

ELECTRONICS
Explanations of devices based on electronic devices, such as televisions and computers; how they work and how they are used.

LIFE SCIENCES
The structure and behavior of living things; from microorganisms to the most complex plants and animals.

MATHEMATICS
How scientists use numbers and equations to analyze their experiments and to solve theoretical problems.

PHYSICS
Energy in the form of heat, light, sound, electricity, mechanics, and magnetism, and the effect it has on matter from atoms to whole planets.

TECHNOLOGY
From simple adhesives to jet engines; how science is used in industry and the home.

Abacus

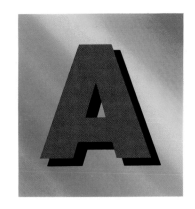

An abacus is a counting device used by ancient Greeks and Romans, and some modern Eastern traders, in which rows of beads represent NUMBERS. Calculations are made by sliding the beads along rods. Each row of beads has a different value. Different kinds of abacuses use different number systems. The five-bead abacus counts in ones, tens, and hundreds on the left, and five times these on the right. When four beads have been slid to the right, they are returned to the left and one bead is moved on the right to represent five, 50, or 500.

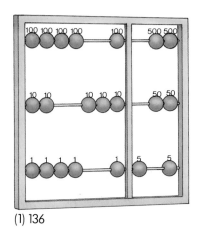

(1) 136

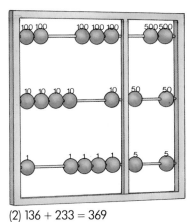

(2) 136 + 233 = 369

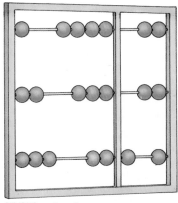

(3) 369 + ? = ?
▲ *Can you work out the missing numbers? Answer on page 3.*

Abrasives

When you rub sandpaper on a piece of wood to smooth it, you are using an abrasive. The tiny bits of sand in the sandpaper wear away the softer surface of the wood. Abrasives are used to smooth, grind, polish, sharpen, or cut other materials. Sand is the oldest abrasive. It was used to polish stone weapons and tools as early as 25,000 B.C. Quartz and pumice are abrasives that are found in the earth. Carborundum is made from a mixture of powdered coke and clay heated in a furnace. It is very hard and can be used to polish gemstones.

Abrasives are also used in homes. Scouring powders and creams are used to clean pots and bathtubs. Even toothpaste is a mild abrasive. It often contains finely powdered chalk.
See also HARDNESS.

▲ *Sand blasters blow quartz sand against stone walls to clean away dirt.*

Absolute zero *See* Kelvin

1

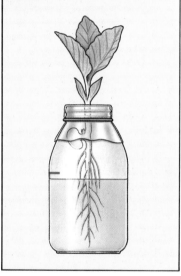

▼ *The funny sinking feeling in your stomach when going down a roller coaster is caused by the delay of your body in catching up with the acceleration of the car.*

Absorption

We generally use the word absorption to mean the soaking up of a LIQUID. Paper towels and sponges absorb liquids. In science, the word absorption is used in different ways. The roots of plants absorb water and other small MOLECULES from the soil. Animals' digestive systems break down food into simpler substances. These smaller molecules pass through the intestine walls and are absorbed into the BLOOD.

HEAT, LIGHT, and SOUND are absorbed too. Dark objects absorb more heat than pale objects. People in hot countries paint their houses in light colors so they will absorb less heat. The heat is reflected off the outside of the house and the people stay cool inside.
See also ACOUSTICS; DIGESTION; REFLECTION.

Acceleration

When an object accelerates, its speed increases. If the driver of a car presses down the accelerator pedal and increases the speed, we say that the car is accelerating. The faster the speed increases, the greater the acceleration. An object can only accelerate if a FORCE "pushes" or "pulls" it. When a rifle is fired, the bullet accelerates along the barrel, pushed by the exploding gases. Once it leaves the barrel it begins to slow down (*decelerate*). This is because the air holds it back and GRAVITY pulls it toward the ground.

If you drop a ball from the top of a building, it accelerates as it falls. This is because it is being pulled down by gravity. The surprising thing about gravity is that it pulls

Acid gases from automobile exhausts and factories

everything down with the same FORCE, no matter how heavy it is. It produces a constant acceleration of 32 feet (9.8 meters) per second per second. After one second the ball would be traveling at a speed of 32 feet (9.8 m) per second, and after two seconds its speed would be 64 feet (19.6 m) per second, and so on. Only AIR resistance slows it down as it falls. If there was no air resistance, a feather would fall as fast as a baseball.

You can feel the effect of acceleration slightly in an elevator. Astronauts have to undergo very high acceleration levels in the first few seconds of take-off. If the spacecraft accelerates too fast, the astronauts can feel sick.
See also MOVEMENT AND MOTION; VELOCITY.

Acid rain

Acid rain is caused by rain reacting with ACID gases, especially sulfur dioxide. These acid gases are waste GASES produced by factories, power stations, and cars. The waste gases rise into the air and react with the rain water. Rain is normally slightly acid but its reaction with acid gases makes it even more acid. This rain is what is known as "acid rain."

The WIND can carry the acid gases for long distances. Animal and plant life are threatened by acid rain as the rain slowly accumulates and increases the acidity of water in lakes, rivers, and soil. Acid gases in the air cause damage even when it is not raining. The 1990 Clean Air Act called for the reduction of air pollutants from many sources such as automobiles, power plants, and factories.
See also POLLUTION; PRECIPITATION.

▲ *This tree shows the damaging effect acid rain is having on woodlands in some parts of the world.*

Answers to Abacus question on page 1:
The number shown by the abacus is 437—four 100s, three 10s, one 5, and two 1s—and 68 has been added to 369.

▼ *Waste gases pollute the environment. They are carried in the air and fall to the ground, often far from their source, causing damage to aquatic life, trees, and other vegetation.*

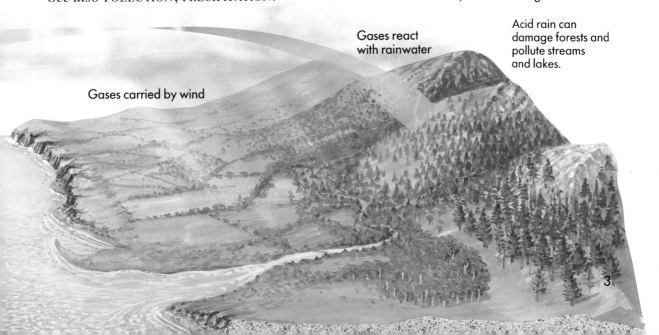

Gases react with rainwater

Acid rain can damage forests and pollute streams and lakes.

Gases carried by wind

3

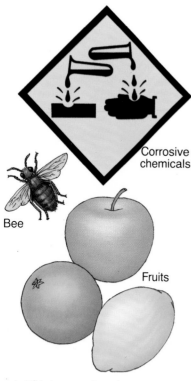

Corrosive chemicals

Bee

Fruits

▲ *This international warning symbol is found on vehicles carrying corrosive liquids. The residue left after a bee's sting is acid and can hurt, but the acid in fruit is fairly harmless.*

SEE FOR YOURSELF
Put a tablespoon of sodium bicarbonate (baking soda) onto the center of a dish. Pour some vinegar onto the bicarbonate. It starts to fizz as carbon dioxide is given off. This acid (vinegar) reacts with the bicarbonate to produce carbon dioxide.

Acids and Bases

The word "acid" comes from the Latin word *acidus*, which means "sour;" most acids have a sour taste. Some acids are poisons, some can cause serious skin burns, and others are quite harmless. Yet others are good to eat. We get citric acid from oranges and lemons. Our own bodies make acids to help us to digest our food.

One of the strongest and most important acids is SULFURIC ACID. It is used in enormous quantities in the manufacture of fertilizers, petroleum products, and iron and steel. The liquid in car batteries is dilute (watered down) sulfuric acid. Other strong acids are NITRIC ACID, used mainly in making fertilizers, drugs, and explosives, and HYDROCHLORIC ACID, used in the metal industries and in food processing.

Bases are substances that are the opposite of acids although, like acids, some bases are very reactive and corrosive such as lime (CALCIUM hydroxide) and CAUSTIC SODA. They are used in industrial processes. Magnesium hydroxide (the white powder or liquid we take to cure an upset acid STOMACH) is an example of a mild base. A base that can dissolve in water is called an alkali.

When an acid and a base are mixed in the right quantities, they neutralize each other (cancel each other out).

Some substances change color when they are put into an acid or base. These substances are called INDICATORS: LITMUS turns from blue to red in an acid solution and from red to blue in an alkaline solution.
See also CORROSION; pH.

Acoustics

The study of SOUND and how it travels is called acoustics. Sound waves travel in straight lines. Like LIGHT waves, they are absorbed or reflected by any objects that they may strike.

In a large room, sound waves are reflected back and forth from the walls and ceiling. Reflected sounds are ECHOES of the original sound. They may last for a few seconds before dying away completely. The sound waves that go directly to the listener are heard first, followed by sound reflected from around the room. Sound waves that bounce around are called reverberations. Good quality sound needs a little reverberation. More is needed for orchestral music, but not so much for

◄ *An anechoic chamber (left) is used to test the acoustics of a vehicle so that the noise it produces can be reduced. The panels in the walls and ceiling of the room absorb the sound, which is monitored (above).*

speech. An architect must pay careful attention to acoustics when the inside of a concert hall or theater is designed. The sound can be absorbed by the walls, the ceiling, the seating, and even the people. The architect must calculate whether a clear sound will reach every seat. There must not be too much REFLECTION or ABSORPTION of the sound.

The larger a hall is, the more difficult it is to make the acoustics equally good for all the audience. In many halls, sound reflectors hung from the ceiling help to spread the sound evenly.

The number of people in a hall can affect the acoustics. People are quite good absorbers of sound, especially in winter when they are wearing a lot of clothes.

There are two major fields in the study of acoustics: **Architectural acoustics** provides the right conditions for listening to speech and music; **Environmental acoustics** deals with the control of noise pollution. Other areas of acoustic study: design of stereo equipment and telephones; measurement and protection of hearing; use of sound in making measurements, and in processing materials.

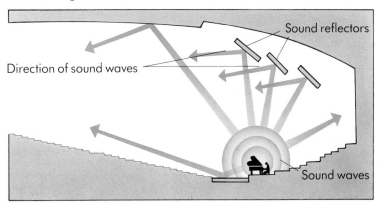

Direction of sound waves

Sound reflectors

Sound waves

▲ *Halls are designed so that the acoustics ensure that everyone in the audience hears the music in as perfect a form as possible.*

▲ *Sounds made by an orchestra or a loudspeaker bounce off the walls, floors, and ceiling. Ceilings in concert halls*

must be hard and low to ensure good sound quality. Sound panels reflect sound down onto the audience.

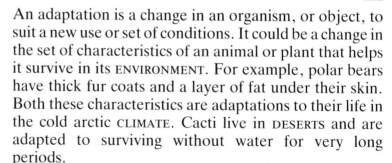

Kestrel

Puffin

Curlew

Hummingbird

Adaptation

An adaptation is a change in an organism, or object, to suit a new use or set of conditions. It could be a change in the set of characteristics of an animal or plant that helps it survive in its ENVIRONMENT. For example, polar bears have thick fur coats and a layer of fat under their skin. Both these characteristics are adaptations to their life in the cold arctic CLIMATE. Cacti live in DESERTS and are adapted to surviving without water for very long periods.

No two living things are born exactly the same; even identical twins have some differences. Often the differences are not important, but sometimes they can be important. This difference may improve the animal's chance of survival. It may live longer and have more offspring. After many generations, only individuals of that species with the useful variation are left. For example, giraffes with the longest necks will be able to reach and eat leaves from the highest branches. In a drought, when food is in short supply, giraffes with longer necks will be able to get more to eat than other giraffes and may be the only ones to survive and produce young. This is sometimes called "survival of the fittest" which is part of NATURAL SELECTION, first suggested by the naturalist Charles DARWIN. He noted that birds' beaks are different shapes so that they can eat different kinds of food. These changes occurred over a very long period of time by small adaptations.

See also EVOLUTION; GENETICS; LAMARCK.

◄ *Birds' bills suit their feeding habits. Birds of prey, such as the kestrel, have hooked bills to tear the flesh of prey. The sawedged bill of the puffin enables it to carry several fish at once. Wading birds, like the curlew, have long, slender bills to dig deep into the mud. A hummingbird's long bill allows it to reach nectar inside a flower.*

▶ *Eskimos (Inuit) have adapted to the Arctic climate. They have narrow eyes with folded eyelids to protect their eyes against the cold and a thick layer of flesh on their body.*

Adhesives

Adhesives are used to stick objects together. They can be made from natural materials such as bones, horns, and animal skin which can be boiled to make glue. Plants with a lot of STARCH, such as potatoes, can also be used to make glue. Liquid rubber is another example of a good natural adhesive.

Adhesives can also be made artificially (called synthetic adhesives). Synthetic adhesives are stronger than natural ones. Some, called *thermoplastics*, get soft when heated and hard again when cold. For example, synthetic resins (one kind of thermoplastic adhesive) are used to stick together the layers of glass that make the

◄ *This commercial adhesive is undergoing a bond strength test. The bonded surfaces are being forced apart and the adhesive is resisting. Surfaces must be absolutely clean for a successful bond.*

safety glass of car windows. Other *thermosetting* adhesives become very hard when heated. They are usually made by mixing two chemicals and heating the mixture to make a very strong bond. Some thermosetting adhesives are used to stick the layers of plywood together. Among the strongest adhesives of all are EPOXY RESINS. *See also* PLASTICS.

The "superglues" are capable of bonding all types of surfaces within seconds. Every care should be taken when handling such adhesives as they are extremely dangerous if they come into contact with the skin or eyes.

Adolescence

Adolescence is the time in our lives when we are no longer children, and yet we are not fully grown up. The length of adolescence varies because everyone is different, but it usually begins earlier in girls. It may start as early as 9 years and end as late as 24 years.

When a child reaches adolescence his or her body will begin to change in a number of ways. Both boys and girls will develop hair under their arms and in their pubic areas. A boy will develop a deeper voice and a beard will start to grow. A girl's breasts will start to develop and her hips will widen. Also, a girl will start to have monthly menstrual periods which mean that one day she will be able to have children.

Confused emotions are common during adolescence, not only because of HORMONE changes, but also because adolescents begin to depend less on their parents.

▼ *Boys and girls grow rapidly during adolescence. However, the rate differs between the sexes. Girls tend to gain weight and height about the age of 12 years, whereas boys tend to develop later, usually between 16 and 18 years.*

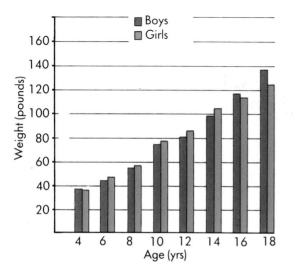

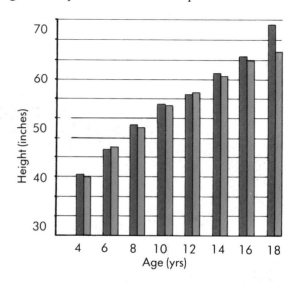

Aerodynamics

Aerodynamics is the science that deals with AIR moving against an object, like wind filling the sails of a boat; or something moving through the air, like an aircraft flying through the sky.

How does a kite fly? How does a glider soar through the air with no ENGINE? How does a jumbo jet weighing more than 700,000 pounds (350,000 kg) stay in the air? The answers to these questions come from aerodynamics.

The top surface of an aircraft's wing is curved, while the bottom is flatter. This shape is called an *airfoil*. As the plane cuts through the air, the air that flows over the top of the wing has to travel a greater distance than the air flowing underneath the wing, so it has to travel faster over the top. It is a scientific law, called Bernoulli's Principle, that air PRESSURE (or the pressure of a liquid)

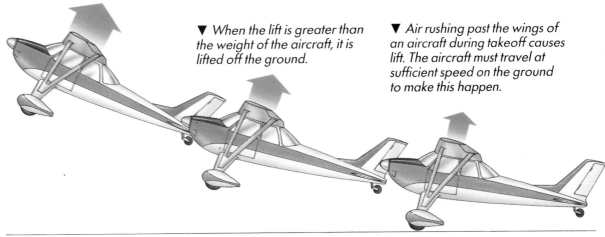

▼ When the lift is greater than the weight of the aircraft, it is lifted off the ground.

▼ Air rushing past the wings of an aircraft during takeoff causes lift. The aircraft must travel at sufficient speed on the ground to make this happen.

decreases when the flow of air (or liquid) speeds up. Because there is less pressure on the top surface of an aircraft's wing than on the bottom, the wing is pushed upward. This upward force is called *lift*, and the lift is greater the faster the aircraft flies.

But the aircraft is also held back by the resistance of the air. This resistance is called *drag*. The faster an aircraft flies, the more drag there is. Drag is a particular problem in designing high-speed planes because drag increases much faster than the speed of the plane. To reduce drag, all parts of the plane that are in contact with the air are STREAMLINED. Streamlining helps the air to flow smoothly over the plane.

Planes, cars, and trains are all designed with smooth,

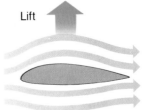

Lift

Wing shape: low drag

▲ The aerodynamic shape of an aircraft's wing.

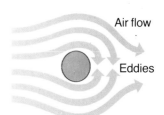

Air flow

Eddies

Round shape: medium drag

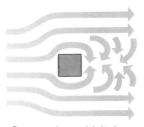

Square shape: high drag

▲ Angles or sharp curves on objects break up the airflow and cause eddies, or swirls of air, increasing drag.

◀ Wind tunnels are used to test new car designs. A car with a streamlined shape will go faster and use less fuel because it has low drag.

9

▲ *Modern trucks have specially designed cab roofs that direct the airflow up and over the load behind.*

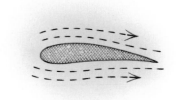
curved bodies to reduce drag. When they are being designed, models are tested in WIND TUNNELS where an airstream is blown over the model by a fan. Velocities of up to 20 times the speed of sound can be produced. If smoke is put into the wind tunnel, the designers can see how the air flows around the model. By making adjustments, the most efficient aerodynamic shape can be found.

Aerosol

An aerosol is a cloud of fine particles suspended in a GAS. The particles can be liquid, or solid as in smoke.

The term aerosol is often applied to the can that produces this spray. Aerosols are used to spray such products as paints and cosmetics. The contents of the can consist of the product to be sprayed and a liquefied gas under PRESSURE. The gas is called a propellant because it propels the product out of the can. When the button on the top of the can is pressed, a valve is opened and the product is forced out as a spray. The spray consists of the vaporized gas with the product suspended in it. An atomizer works by producing a fine spray of liquid particles without using a pressurized propellant.

Common propellants are CHLOROFLUOROCARBONS or CFCs. Over the years research has shown that CFCs are helping to create a hole in the OZONE LAYER. Steps have been taken to replace CFCs with less damaging propellants with less chlorine and fluorine in them.

Button released and valve closed

Button pressed down and valve open

Valve

Button

Nozzle

Aerosol spray

Pressure

Liquefied propellant and product

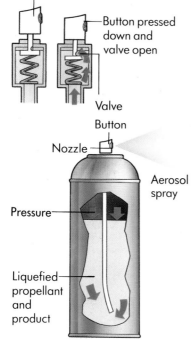

▲ *Pressing the button on an aerosol opens the valve. The pressure of the liquefied propellant forces the product up through the tube and out of the nozzle as a spray.*

Aging

As animals grow old, many changes take place in the way they function and in the way they look. Humans age more slowly than most other animals. People in the

◀ *Four generations are present in this family group. All are at different stages of the aging process.*

▼ *Trees are the longest living things on Earth. Bristlecone pines can live for up to 5,000 years.*

Bristlecone pine

industrialized countries generally live to about 70 years, with women outliving men on average by a few years. In poorer countries people generally have shorter lifespans. In the animal kingdom, elephants live for up to 70 years, horses 40 years, dogs 20 years, and mice about 4 years. These seem to be maximum ages. Some birds have longer lifespans. Parrots and eagles, for instance, can live for over 100 years.

As people get older, their SKIN becomes wrinkled and their HAIR gray. Their MEMORY may become poor and their EYES, EARS, TASTE, and sense of smell may deteriorate. But different people age at different rates. Two people 70 years old may be quite different in their strength and mental ability.

Over the last 100 years, doctors have become better at keeping people alive by curing and preventing disease. This means that there is an increasing number of elderly people in the population. But doctors still do not know what causes our bodies to wear out with the years.

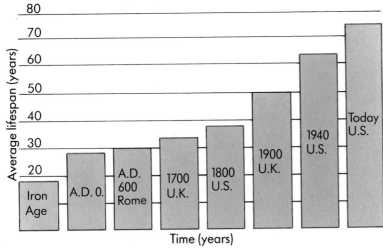

Average lifespan (years)

| Iron Age | A.D. 0. | A.D. 600 Rome | 1700 U.K. | 1800 U.S. | 1900 U.K. | 1940 U.S. | Today U.S. |

Time (years)

Aging is not simply a process of cells dying. Most cells keep renewing themselves, although not all cells have the same average life span. For example, skin cells only survive 19 days, whereas red blood cells last 3 weeks and bone cells can live for 25 years or more.

◀ *Better living conditions and advances in medicine are responsible for the increase in life expectancy over the centuries.*

11

AGRICULTURE

Agriculture is the world's largest and most important industry. It probably began about 10,000 years ago. Today it produces over 95 percent of the world's food and provides us with many kinds of oil and fiber. Nearly half of the world's work force is employed in agriculture, growing crops, or looking after farm animals. Sheep and goats were the first animals to be domesticated, but cattle are now the most important farm animals. There are over 12 billion of them in the world, providing us with meat, milk, and leather. In some countries, they are still used to pull carts and plows. Pigs and buffalo are the other major farm animals.

Cereals were the first cultivated crops, but about 100 different kinds of plants are now grown for food. People soon invented simple plows pulled by animals, but agriculture changed very slowly until about 100 years ago. Since then there have been tremendous advances in plant and animal breeding and in the use of fertilizers and pesticides, which have led to better crops. The great advances in engineering mean that today's farmers can use huge plows pulled by powerful tractors and all sorts of other machinery to help them harvest and move crops.

George Washington Carver (1864–1943)
Carver was an American educator and agricultural scientist. He worked to improve crop production and agricultural methods. He encouraged farmers of the southern states to grow soil-enriching peanuts and sweet potatoes. He discovered many uses for the new crops. From peanuts he made over 300 products, including soap and ink.

▼ About a third of the Earth's total land area is used for farming. About a third of this land is used to grow crops. The graph shows how world regions contribute to the world's total crop output.

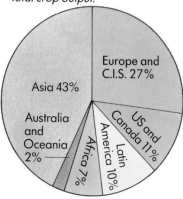

Europe and C.I.S. 27%
Asia 43%
Australia and Oceania 2%
Africa 7%
Latin America 10%
US and Canada 11%

▲ Because the environment within greenhouses can be controlled, they are useful for cultivating crops outside normal growing seasons.

◄ Some farming methods are slow and use much human and animal labor.

▶ The development of farm machinery means that several jobs can be done at once, speeding up production.

Brussels sprouts harvester

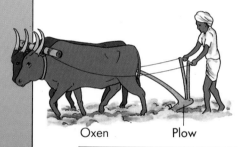

Oxen   Plow

See also BREEDING; CEREALS; FERTILIZERS; HORTICULTURE; HYDROPONICS; PESTICIDES.

AIDS

AIDS, Acquired Immune Deficiency Syndrome, is caused by a VIRUS named HIV. The AIDS virus attacks certain white blood cells that form an important part of the body's IMMUNE SYSTEM. This fights off viruses and bacteria when they enter the body. When these white blood cells are destroyed, the patient can become very ill with a disease which would not be serious in a healthy person. Because the body of a person with AIDS has lost its means of fighting disease, the patient can often die.

AIDS is passed from person to person in three main ways: by intimate sexual contact, by exposure to blood infected with HIV, and by transmission to a baby in an infected mother's womb. People most likely to catch AIDS are drug addicts who inject drugs into themselves and who share hypodermic needles. However, anyone can develop the disease through intimate sexual contact with somebody who has the HIV virus. People who have been infected with the HIV virus may not become seriously ill until years later.

AIDS was first identified in 1981. Since then it has become a serious problem throughout the world.

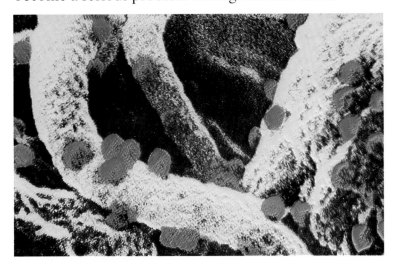

HIV Human Immunodeficiency Virus.
AIDS Acquired Immune Deficiency Syndrome.
Syndrome A combination of symptoms/signs showing that a condition/illness exists.

▼ *When the AIDS virus enters a white blood cell, the core of the virus breaks open and releases its genetic material. The virus DNA takes over the white blood cell which begins to make copies of the virus and then dies.*

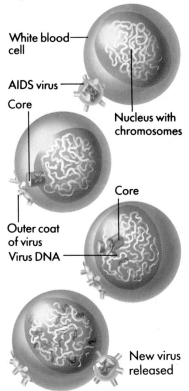

White blood cell

AIDS virus

Core

Nucleus with chromosomes

Core

Outer coat of virus

Virus DNA

New virus released

◄ *The AIDS virus travels in the bloodstream. It gets inside certain white blood cells whose job it is to fight off infection. The AIDS virus uses the white blood cell to produce many new viruses (red). These break out of the white blood cell and go on to infect more white blood cells, weakening the immune system.*

Air

Air is a mixture of GASES. The layer of air which surrounds the Earth is called the ATMOSPHERE. We cannot see or smell air, yet it is as real as the chair you are sitting on. Moving air can turn windmills, blow down large trees, and, if it is compressed, can break up solid concrete as in jackhammers. *See* pages 14 and 15.

AIR

About 99 percent of air is composed of the colorless, odorless, tasteless gases nitrogen and oxygen. The remaining one percent is mostly argon gas. The other gases present in very small amounts are carbon dioxide, neon, sulfur dioxide, and carbon monoxide. In heavily industrialized areas the amount of sulfur dioxide and carbon monoxide can increase because of air pollution.

The atmosphere around us protects us from the harmful rays of the Sun. It traps the Sun's heat, which keeps the Earth warm, and prevents nighttime temperatures from falling drastically. Air allows us to hear. Sound cannot travel in a vacuum.

Most animals that live on our planet today depend upon oxygen for respiration. They breathe in air containing oxygen and breathe out a mixture of gases which contains less oxygen, more carbon dioxide, and more water vapor. Without oxygen, most living things, with the exception of some microorganisms, could not exist.

Air exerts a pressure on us all the time. In fact, the pressure of air on the Earth's surface is roughly 15 pounds per square inch ($1\,kg/cm^2$). The air pressing down on your shoulders weighs about a ton, but because air presses on all sides you do not feel this weight. When you ride a bicycle, you are sitting on a cushion of compressed air in the tires.

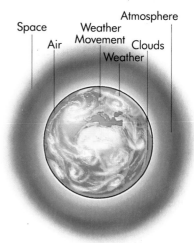

Composition of air

Argon and other gases 0.97%
Carbon dioxide 0.03%
Oxygen 21%
Nitrogen 78%

SEE FOR YOURSELF
Place a rolled-up newspaper over the end of a ruler. Strike the other end of the ruler. See what happens. Do the same with the newspaper spread flat. The ruler snaps because the air pressure presses on a larger surface of the newspaper.

▲ The air (top) cloaks the Earth in a layer we call the atmosphere. The movement of air is responsible for our weather patterns. The chart, (above) shows the gases that make up air.

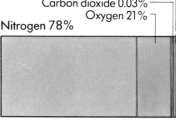

► When you let go of a balloon filled with helium it rises into the air, because helium is lighter than air.

Helium balloon

◄ Air is essential to life, and divers must take their own supply with them underwater.

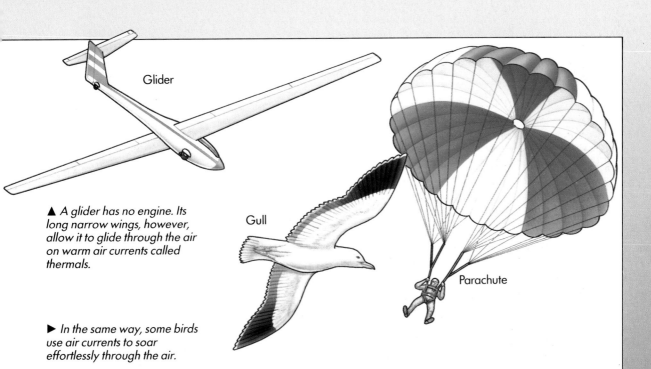

Glider

Gull

Parachute

▲ A glider has no engine. Its long narrow wings, however, allow it to glide through the air on warm air currents called thermals.

▶ In the same way, some birds use air currents to soar effortlessly through the air.

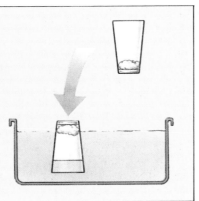

SEE FOR YOURSELF
Squash a piece of cotton into the bottom of a glass. Carefully put the glass upside down into a bowl of water. A little water may get into the glass but you should find that the cotton stays dry. The water cannot get into the glass because it is full of air. The air cannot get out because it is lighter than water.

▲ Air resists objects as they fall. The larger the surface area of the object, the greater the resistance. A parachute slows down a jumper's fall.

▼ Air is lighter than water, enabling inflatable life rafts to float.

▶ Windsurfers use the power of the wind to skim across the water. The board can be steered by turning the sail.

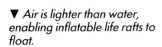

See also ATMOSPHERE; CARBON DIOXIDE; CLIMATE; GAS; OXYGEN; RESPIRATION.

The term air conditioning was first used in 1906 by Stuart Cramer, an American textile engineer. It was used to describe scientific systems that would clean, circulate, and control the temperature and humidity of air inside buildings. People have, however, been devising methods of "conditioning" the air for many hundreds of years. The ancient Egyptians hung wet mats inside their buildings through which the wind blew, evaporating the water and cooling the air.

Air conditioning

Air conditioning controls the moisture level, TEMPERATURE, and movement of AIR inside buildings. Air conditioning is responsible for the great drop in temperature that you notice when you walk into some offices, homes, or stores on a hot day. Outside it is hot and sticky but inside it is cool. An air conditioning unit uses fans to draw in air from the outside of the building. The air is then passed over a refrigerated HEAT EXCHANGER. The ice-cold grills of the heat exchanger take in the heat from the air so that only cold air is blown through the wide channels built into the ceiling or walls. Air conditioning can heat up air as well as cool it.

Air conditioning is not just available for large buildings; many homes in the United States have central air conditioning or small window units. Units can be made small enough to fit inside cars, making travel in even the hottest countries pleasantly cool. Air conditioning is used in many places where manufacturing processes need to be run at a steady temperature. Even small temperature changes can affect the size of METAL components, so air conditioning is essential.

See also CONTRACTION; EXPANSION; REFRIGERATION.

▼ *This is a central air conditioning system. All the conditioned air comes from one source. The liquid refrigerant removes the heat from the air,* *which is then blown through air ducts into the building. Used air is mixed with air from the outside, conditioned, and then returned to the building.*

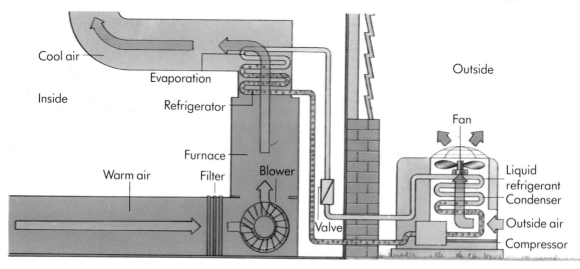

Cool air

Inside

Evaporation

Refrigerator

Furnace

Warm air

Filter

Blower

Valve

Outside

Fan

Liquid refrigerant

Condenser

Outside air

Compressor

Air cushion vehicle *See* Hovercraft

Air pollution

Much of the AIR we breathe is polluted and occasionally it may smell unpleasant. Pollution can cause irritation of the nose and throat, and lengthy exposure to some types of pollution may cause serious disorders.

Most air pollution comes from BURNING fuels. We burn fuels in industrial processes, in motor vehicles, in heating our homes, and in the production of ELECTRICITY (with the exception of nuclear power stations).

Smoke and SULFUR DIOXIDE come from burning coal.

These can affect people's LUNGS, causing bronchitis and other illnesses. In 1952, from December 5 to 9, 4,000 people died from heart and lung failure in dense fog in London. It was caused by smoke and unusual weather conditions. Other serious incidents of "smog" occurred in New York in 1966 and Donora, Pennsylvania, in 1948.

The exhausts of motor vehicles release several harmful GASES and are a major cause of air pollution. They also put LEAD into the ATMOSPHERE. Lead has become a major pollutant in areas of heavy traffic, and lead-free gasoline may eventually be the only kind available.

Cigarette smoke can pollute air at home and at work. Scientists have shown that cigarette smoke is not only damaging to the health of people who smoke but also to the health of nonsmokers who breathe other people's cigarette smoke.

So how can air pollution be controlled? Laws now insist that industries filter, destroy, or dilute polluting substances before they are allowed to escape into the air. Eventually we will be free from this type of pollution.

◄ *The unhealthy yellow haze hanging over this city is called smog and is made up of large numbers of tiny particles of factory smoke, exhaust fumes, and other pollutants.*

▼ *Carbon monoxide (CO) is one of the main types of air pollution. The diagram shows sources of the gas and percentages of the total given out. Motor vehicles account for 70 percent.*

Sources of carbon monoxide pollution (% of total)

Industrial processes 6.8%

Fuel combustion 10.3%

Miscellaneous 12.3%

(including solid waste disposal, chemical spray)

Transportation 70.6%

Roger Bacon (1214–1292)
An English monk and alchemist, Bacon became known as the founder of experimental science. He believed that doing experiments for yourself rather than just accepting what other people tell you was the way to learn about nature. His most important work was the *Opus Maius*, in which he wrote about the scientific method of learning. He did many experiments. He showed how rainbows are made by the effect of water-drops on sunlight, and how lenses could be used to help people with weak sight.

Alchemy

Most of our modern ideas about CHEMISTRY, our knowledge of ATOMS, MOLECULES, ELEMENTS, and COMPOUNDS and so on, date back only to about 1700. Before that time, the makeup of substances was a mystery. The people who tried to uncover the mystery were called alchemists and their field of study, alchemy.

Alchemy mixed magic with science, secret semi-religious rituals, and philosophy. It was based on ancient Chinese, Indian, and Greek theories about the natural world. In the Middle Ages, Arabs trading with China passed on knowledge of alchemy to Egypt and then into Europe, where many people studied it.

Some alchemists were cheats and tricksters, but others, such as Roger Bacon, were serious researchers who laid the foundations for chemistry and MEDICINE.

The alchemists believed in ARISTOTLE's view that everything in the UNIVERSE was made up of four elements, earth, air, water, and fire. They believed that if they could change the balance of these elements, they could turn one substance into another and, particularly, turn lead into gold. They tried without success. They also searched unsuccessfully for a medicine that would prolong human life, perhaps forever. They did, however, discover ALCOHOL and many natural substances that could be used to make DRUGS.

▶ The Alchemist *painted by Joseph Wright in 1771 shows Hennig Brand, his face lit by the glow of his new discovery, phosphorus.*

Alcohol

Alcohols are members of a group of chemical compounds that contain atoms of CARBON, HYDROGEN, and OXYGEN. All alcohols are liquids. We usually think of alcohol as an ingredient of beer, wine, and spirits. But this is really only one of the many types of chemicals called alcohols, most of which are important in industry. The majority of alcohols are used as SOLVENTS (substances that dissolve other substances). Methanol, or wood alcohol, is very poisonous and is used for making plastics, paints, and varnishes. Ethanol, or ethyl alcohol, is the alcohol present in alcoholic drinks. It is produced naturally by FERMENTATION, in which YEAST acts on sugar to make ethanol and carbon dioxide. Ethanol is used as an ingredient in flavorings, detergents, and perfumes. It is also mixed with gasoline to improve its OCTANE rating. Different alcohols are also used as solvents for sticky substances called resins, making cosmetics and lotions. Ethylene glycol, a poisonous alcohol, is an ingredient of ANTIFREEZE which prevents the coolant liquid in automobile engines from freezing.

If sweet fruit or vegetable juice is left in a warm place it begins to froth, giving off a gas – carbon dioxide. What is left is a solution of alcohol. This process – fermentation – is speeded up if some yeast is added. Wine and beer are made by fermenting fruit and vegetable juices, and if they are bottled at the right time, some of the bubbles of carbon dioxide are trapped in the drink to make it fizzy.

▼ *All these products contain an alcohol compound.*

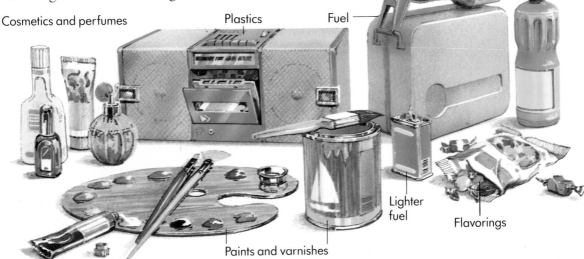

Cosmetics and perfumes

Plastics

Fuel

Detergents

Lighter fuel

Flavorings

Paints and varnishes

Algebra

Algebra is a branch of MATHEMATICS. It links together the other branches of mathematics into a single subject. Algebra was developed from its origins by the Arabs over a thousand years ago. In its simplest form, algebra is like ARITHMETIC but uses letters and symbols to stand for numbers. For example, we know that $2+5=7$ and that $5+2=7$. So we can say that $2+5=5+2$. If you take any

The Persian poet Omar Khayyam, who lived in the 11th century and who wrote a famous poem called the *Rubaiyat*, spent most of his time in the study of algebra. His work on algebra was known throughout Europe, but few people knew about his verses.

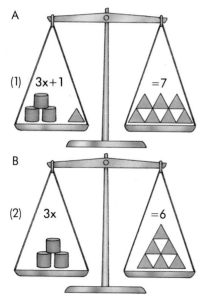

A

(1) 3x+1 =7

B

(2) 3x =6

▲ *Equations are like scales. The sides must always balance. Can you find the value of x, represented as a cylinder in the diagram? Answer on page 23.*

Allergies can be caused by a variety of different substances. Dust, pollen spores, mold, animal hairs, and cigarette smoke may cause respiratory allergies such as asthma, hay fever, and an all year-round nasal allergy known as perennial rhinitis. Certain foods may produce allergic reactions. Chocolate and cheese may be the cause of some allergic headaches, whereas cow's milk, gluten, and shellfish may provoke digestive disorders, such as stomachache and sickness.

▶ *Skin tests are used to find out which substance is causing an allergy. Small doses of common antigens are injected just below the skin. The skin will usually become red where the substance to which the person is allergic has been injected.*

two numbers, you can add them together either way and get the same answer. To show that this is true for any pair of numbers, we can let a stand for one and b stand for the other. Then we can write, $a+b=b+a$. Another example is $a\times b=b\times a$ (or $ab=ba$, for short). Algebra can solve problems by employing letters to stand for unknown values.

Alkali *See* Acids and Bases

Allergy

An allergy is when your body reacts against a substance which is actually quite harmless. Allergies usually develop after you have been exposed to a substance several times. At first, the body tolerates the substance, but after a time, it becomes sensitive to it. Then every time you encounter this substance, called an ANTIGEN or allergen, the body tries to destroy it. It does this by releasing chemical substances including histamines, which can cause an uncomfortable allergic reaction like hay fever. Drugs, called antihistamines, that prevent the production of histamines, are used to treat allergies.

Hay fever is the most common form of allergy. It is caused by breathing in clouds of pollen which are released by grass and other plants during the spring and summer months. For most people, this does no harm at all, but for people who are sensitive to pollen, it causes symptoms similar to a streaming cold, with sneezing, and red watery eyes.

We can develop allergies to many different things and some people are allergic to foods such as strawberries or

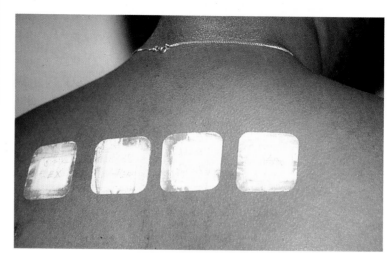

milk. Another form of allergy causes an irritating SKIN rash called dermatitis. This type of allergy is caused by the skin rubbing against a material which contains the antigen. For example, many people are allergic to the NICKEL plating on zippers, jewelry, and buckles used on clothes.

Alloy

An alloy is a mixture of two or more METALS, and sometimes, a metal and a nonmetal. They are most commonly produced by heating and melting the substances together. The first man-made alloy we know of was bronze (a mixture of COPPER and TIN), which was widely used to make items such as pots and pans, swords and spears, as long as 6,000 years ago. Two other well-known alloys are brass (copper and ZINC) and steel (IRON and CARBON).

Today there are thousands of alloys, each produced for some special purpose. There are those that have high tensile strength (they can resist great WEIGHT or PRESS-

▲ Bronze was often used to make tools, weapons, helmets, and ornaments. The shield and dagger date from the 1st century B.C; they were dredged up from the River Thames in London.

◀ Special aluminum alloys have been developed for use in aircraft manufacturing, because aircraft parts must be strong and light.

URE without breaking), those that can withstand very high temperatures such as the alloy of tungsten and thorium used in the filaments of light bulbs, and those that have a strong resistance to acids.
See also AMALGAM; CONDUCTION.

Alpha particles *See* Subatomic particles

Alternating current *See* Electricity

Alternator *See* Generator

Bronze was so important in history that there is a period of history called the Bronze Age. This is because bronze is harder than copper on its own and therefore had many more uses.

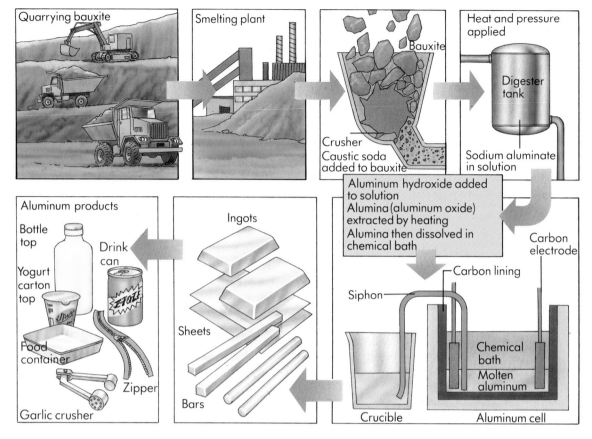

Quarrying bauxite

Smelting plant

Bauxite

Crusher
Caustic soda
added to bauxite

Heat and pressure applied

Digester tank

Sodium aluminate in solution

Aluminum hydroxide added to solution
Alumina (aluminum oxide) extracted by heating
Alumina then dissolved in chemical bath

Carbon electrode

Carbon lining

Siphon

Chemical bath

Molten aluminum

Crucible

Aluminum cell

Aluminum products

Bottle top

Yogurt carton top

Drink can

Food container

Zipper

Garlic crusher

Ingots

Sheets

Bars

▲ Aluminum production has two main stages. Alumina is extracted from bauxite and smelted to obtain aluminum.

▼ Drink cans are made from aluminum because it is light and does not corrode easily.

Aluminum

Aluminum is a lightweight, silver colored, metallic ELE-
MENT. It readily reacts with the oxygen in the air to form
a surface coating of aluminum oxide called alumina.
This coating preserves it from further CORROSION or
wear. Aluminum is the most common METAL in the
Earth's crust, and a large number of things are made out
of it, from saucepans, aluminum foil, and drink cans to
tanks and the fuselage of aircraft.

Although it is common, aluminum is difficult and
costly to get at because it only occurs in COMPOUNDS and
never as pure aluminum. It is extracted from a mineral
called bauxite, using electrical power.

Aluminum can be easily bent, it can be hammered
into different shapes, and drawn out into thin wires. It is
a good conductor of electricity and can be mixed with
other metals to form very strong ALLOYS. Aluminum is
present in plants such as tea, and is used in drugs such as
aspirin. Many doctors fear that too much aluminum can
affect the brain and may cause illness in elderly people
and newborn babies.

Amalgam

An amalgam is a special form of ALLOY. It is a mixture of METALS, in which one of the metals is MERCURY. Mercury is a most unusual metal because it is a liquid, bright silver in color, and very heavy. Most common metals, apart from iron and platinum, can be combined with mercury to form amalgams. Amalgams have many uses. Silver/mercury amalgams are sometimes used in dentistry for fillings. Mercury/tin amalgams were once used to coat the backs of mirror glasses.

Mercury is used in the extraction of gold from gold ORE. The rock is crushed and mixed with mercury to form a gold/mercury amalgam. It is then heated to burn off the mercury to leave the gold behind. This method causes major ecological problems because mercury is highly toxic and the waste can poison rivers.

Answer to Algebra question on page 20:
The original equation was 3x+1=7. The second illustration shows that if we take 1 from each side 3x=6. If you divide each side by 3, x=2.

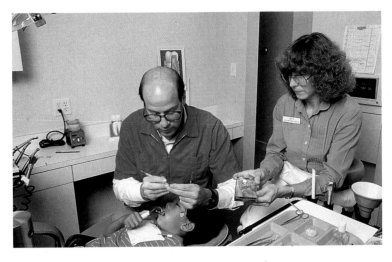

◀ Amalgams have been used for filling teeth cavities since the 19th century. Today, hard plastic material the color of teeth is more commonly used.

NH₃

▲ Ammonia is one of the most important compounds of the element nitrogen. It contains three atoms of hydrogen to each one of nitrogen.

Amino Acids *See* Protein

Ammonia

Ammonia is a colorless GAS with a sharp smell that irritates the eyes and nose. It is a chemical COMPOUND consisting of one ATOM of nitrogen and three atoms of hydrogen. Ammonia is lighter than air and burns in pure oxygen with a dull yellow flame. It does not burn in air. Ammonia becomes liquid at −28°F (−33.4°C) and when it turns back into a gas again it takes in a large amount of HEAT from its surroundings. This makes liquid ammonia very useful as a cooling agent in REFRIGERATION equipment. Ammonia in solution is used for cleaning and

▲ Ammonia is often used in the manufacture of fertilizers. It contains nitrogen, which is important for plant growth.

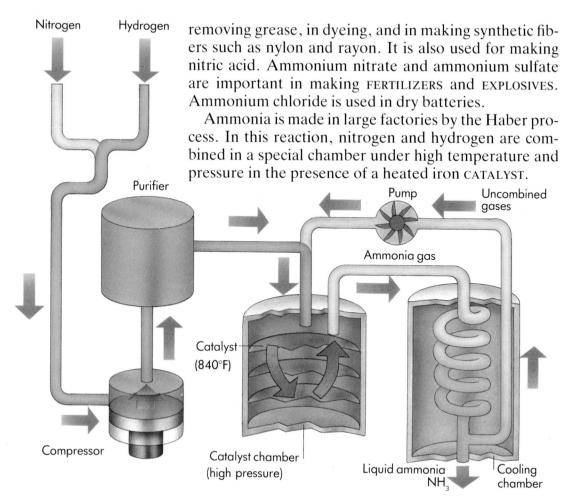

Nitrogen   Hydrogen

Purifier

Pump   Uncombined gases

Ammonia gas

Catalyst (840°F)

Compressor

Catalyst chamber (high pressure)

Liquid ammonia NH_3 Cooling chamber

removing grease, in dyeing, and in making synthetic fibers such as nylon and rayon. It is also used for making nitric acid. Ammonium nitrate and ammonium sulfate are important in making FERTILIZERS and EXPLOSIVES. Ammonium chloride is used in dry batteries.

Ammonia is made in large factories by the Haber process. In this reaction, nitrogen and hydrogen are combined in a special chamber under high temperature and pressure in the presence of a heated iron CATALYST.

▲ Ammonia is made commercially by the Haber process. A catalyst is used because it speeds up the reaction between nitrogen and hydrogen without itself being used up. Not all the nitrogen and hydrogen combine and any uncombined gases are reused.

Ampere

The ampere is the scientific unit for the strength of an electric current. It is usually shortened to amp. A 100-watt electric light bulb, for example, uses almost 1 amp of current. Scientific instruments often use current measured in microamps (millionths of amps).

Meters which are used to measure electric current are called *ammeters*.

See also FUSE; MAGNETISM.

André Ampère (1775–1836)

Ampère was a French physicist. He is famous for his work with electricity and magnetism. Ampère discovered that parallel electric currents attract each other if they move in the same direction, and repel each other if they move in opposite directions. He discovered that electricity produces magnetism and that when electricity is passed through a coiled wire it acts like a magnet. The unit used to measure the size of an electric current was named ampere, or amp, in his honor.

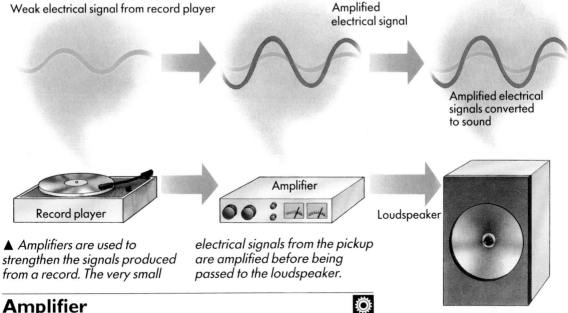

Weak electrical signal from record player

Amplified electrical signal

Amplified electrical signals converted to sound

Record player

Amplifier

Loudspeaker

▲ *Amplifiers are used to strengthen the signals produced from a record. The very small* *electrical signals from the pickup are amplified before being passed to the loudspeaker.*

Amplifier

Amplifiers are devices for increasing the power of electrical signals. They are found in electrical equipment such as radios, televisions, and record players. A guitarist in a band will use an amplifier to increase the tiny electrical sound signals from the guitar's pickups and from the MICROPHONE so that they are powerful enough to drive speakers that can fill a stadium with SOUND.

Deep SPACE PROBES such as *Voyager* and SATELLITES in orbit around the Earth send back signals that are so weak that the information cannot be understood until the signal strength has been amplified many times.
See also ELECTRICITY; HI-FI; LOUDSPEAKER.

Lee De Forest (1826–1906)
This American inventor pioneered wireless telegraphy and radio broadcasting. He invented a vacuum tube that amplified electrical signals, which was to be significant in the development of radio and television communication.

Analog

An analog is an object or quantity that is similar to another object or quantity. The voltage passing through the TEMPERATURE sensor in an electric THERMOMETER rises and falls smoothly with the temperature change. The sensor current is an electrical analog of the temperature and so it can be used to measure the temperature.

Biologists also use the word analog to describe similarities between living creatures. The legs of a fly are "analogous" to the legs of a cow, because both serve the same purpose. They both support the weight of the animal, but they have very different structures.
See also DIGITAL.

▲ *An ordinary clock is an analog device.*

Different methods are used to find out what substances are made of.

Electronanalysis is used to find out about substances by the way they react to an electric current.

Chromatography is a technique that may be used to separate a substance into its component parts before it is analyzed.

Spectrometry can be used to find out what a substance is by examining the spectrum of light it gives off.

Analysis, chemical

Chemical analysis is the process used to find out the exact makeup of a substance. The substance has to be examined in very great detail using a number of different methods. There are two main types of analysis: qualitative and quantitative. *Qualitative analysis* is used to discover which ELEMENTS or groups of elements make up the substance under examination. *Quantitative analysis* is the process of measuring the amounts, or proportions of the elements in the substance. In qualitative analysis, a sample of the substance may be heated to see what is given off, it may be held in a flame (a flame test), or it may be dissolved in water and treated with various agents to find out how it reacts. In quantitative analysis, once the ingredients of a substance are known, they must be measured, using extremely accurate measuring devices. Analysis is of great importance in diagnosing DISEASE, preparing medicines, and testing for POLLUTION or acidity levels in soil or air.

Flame Test
Flame tests are used to identify chemical elements by seeing which color they give off when held in the flame of a Bunsen burner. The substance under test is burned on the end of a piece of platinum wire or asbestos. The flame burns a distinctive color and so the element can be identified.

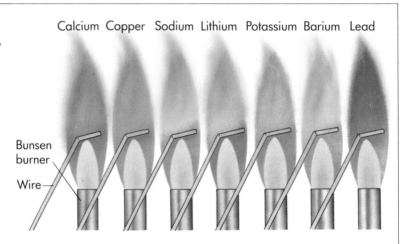

Calcium Copper Sodium Lithium Potassium Barium Lead

Bunsen burner

Wire

Adults have 206 bones in their bodies (children have more but some fuse together as they grow). These bones make up the skeleton, which has three main functions. It protects important organs, such as the heart, lungs, and the brain. It allows the person to stand upright, and provides attachment points for the muscles.

Anatomy

Anatomy is the study of the structure of living things. By knowing how organisms are constructed, we are able to discover and understand how they work. Doctors study the structure of the human body including the SKELETON, MUSCLES, blood vessels, and NERVES as well as all the internal organs so they know how the body functions in health and illness. Zoologists and veterinarians study the anatomy of other animals. Botanists study plant anatomy, the structure of plants including the FLOWERS,

STEMS, LEAVES, and ROOTS as well as all the complex internal systems.

See also BOTANY; MEDICINE; PHYSIOLOGY; ZOOLOGY.

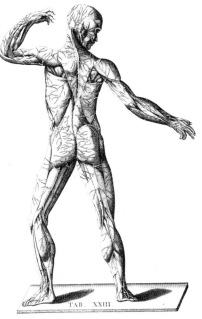

▲ *This 16th-century anatomical drawing suggests positions for a human's nerves and muscles.*

◄ *Plant anatomy has been studied for centuries. This drawing of the nutmeg dates from 1795.*

Anemia *See* Blood

Anemometer

An anemometer is an instrument which is used in METEOROLOGY to measure the speed of the WIND. It is usually mounted on a mast and positioned so that the wind blows freely around it. The most common type has three or four cone-shaped cups at the end of arms that rotate as the wind blows. The faster the wind blows, the faster the cups rotate. Wind speed can be measured by the number of REVOLUTIONS per minute.

Anode *See* Electrolysis

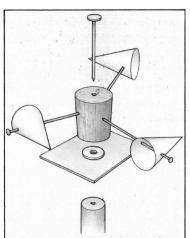

SEE FOR YOURSELF
Make 3 cardboard cones. Push a pin through each of the cones and into a cork. Next insert a long nail through the cork, a metal washer, and a piece of cardboard and fix to the top of a wooden pole. The wind will make the cups rotate. The faster they rotate, the stronger the wind.

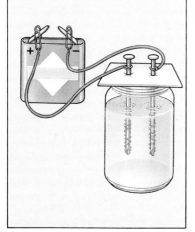

▲ *This black fly has been greatly magnified. It uses its antennae to detect danger.*

▶ *Antennas transmit and receive different kinds of radio waves.*

Anodizing

Anodizing is a process in which a protective coating of an oxide is placed on a metal. This is done by putting the metal, usually ALUMINUM, into a special liquid and passing an electric current through the liquid. By anodizing metal, it is possible to produce a surface on it that cannot be scratched or rubbed off.

There are other benefits of anodizing metal. It makes the metal resistant to CORROSION. Anodized metal is used in aircraft, trains, and ships. One common use for anodizing is in making aluminum window frames. Aluminum is light and strong, but it turns white and dull when exposed to the damp. Anodizing coats it with a very hard layer of oxide less than 0.0004 inch (0.01 mm) thick, so that the surface still stays bright.
See also ELECTROLYSIS.

Antenna

An antenna is a long thin growth on the head of an insect, snail, or shellfish, used to sense the world around the animal. Antennae (the plural of antenna) usually occur in pairs. The end of each antenna carries organs for sensing touch, taste, or smell.

In a RADIO or TELEVISION system, an antenna transmits or receives radio waves. At the transmitter it turns electrical signals into radio waves. At the receiver it turns radio waves back into electrical signals. The antenna may be made from a length of wire, a metal rod, or a branched structure of metal struts. Its shape depends on the signal it is designed to receive. A dish-shaped antenna is used to receive very weak signals. The

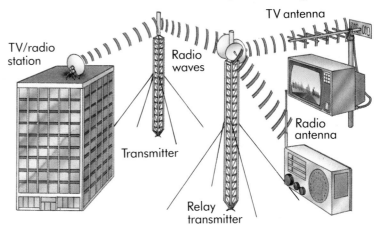

dish acts like a mirror and reflects radio signals inward toward a small antenna at the center of the dish, called the FOCUS. From there the signals are amplified and passed to a receiver. The biggest dish antenna, 1,000 feet (305 m), across, used by astronomers to receive radio signals from distant stars, was built in a natural valley near Areceibo in Puerto Rico in 1963.

Antibiotics

Antibiotics can be used to treat many diseases in both animals and humans. These drugs attack MICROORGANISMS such as the bacteria which are the cause of infections such as tonsillitis and boils. Antibiotics work well against bacteria, but have almost no effect against VIRUSES which are the other common cause of infection.

Antibiotics work by damaging the bacteria as they reproduce and do not usually damage human cells.

Alexander Fleming (1881–1955)
Fleming was a British bacteriologist. In 1928 he noticed that a spot of green mold stopped the growth of some bacteria he was cultivating. The antibiotic drug penicillin was developed from this mold. Fleming won the 1945 Nobel Prize for Medicine, which he shared with Ernst Chain and Howard Florey, the scientists who developed the use of the drug.

◄ *This dish contains bacteria. The circles contain different antibiotics. Four antibiotics have killed the bacteria around them, but the other two have not.*

Bacteria have a rigid cell wall, which gives them a firm shape and protects them from the body's defenses. They reproduce by dividing and re-forming their cell walls as two new cells. The antibiotics hinder this process. This may either kill the bacteria or weaken them so that the body's IMMUNE SYSTEM can easily destroy them.

The first antibiotics were discovered by accident and extracted from tiny fungi called molds. Penicillin, from the fungus *Penicillium*, was the first of these. Many different antibiotics are now available. They are all produced from living things.

See also MEDICINE; REPRODUCTION.

In 1941, a British policeman became the first person to be treated with the antibiotic penicillin. The patient was suffering from bacterial blood poisoning and after a dose of penicillin, he started to make a recovery. Despite his initial recovery, he died because there was not enough penicillin available to kill all the infectious bacteria.

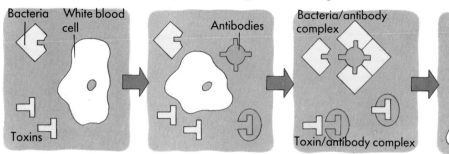

1 Bacteria invade the blood and produce toxins. They both infect the blood.

2 In defense, white blood cells produce antibodies, which recognize the antigens.

3 The antibodies attack the antigens and capture them by locking onto them.

4 White blood cells engulf the bacteria and toxins, break them up and digest them.

▲ *The steps taken by white blood cells to defend the body against infection.*

SEE FOR YOURSELF
Float an ice cube in a bowl of water. Place a matchstick on top of the ice cube and sprinkle some salt around it. Salt causes the ice on each side of the matchstick to melt. This is because salt water freezes at a lower temperature than ordinary water. No salt falls under the matchstick and so the stick stands out on a ridge of ice.

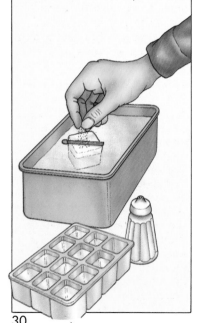

Antibodies and Antigens

An antibody is produced by the body to fight against invading organisms or substances which could be harmful. Antibodies are PROTEINS which are produced in great numbers in the body by some white blood cells. An antibody is able to recognize an antigen (the substance it is to attack). The antigen may be part of the cell wall of a bacterium, part of a VIRUS, or it could be a chemical substance which has entered the system.

An antibody MOLECULE is shaped so that it can attach itself firmly to the antigen like a key entering a lock. The antigen becomes covered with a mass of antibodies, which makes it harmless. It is then either broken down or consumed by scavenging white blood cells.

Once the body has learned how to deal with a particular type of invading organism by producing antibodies to attack it, it can produce antibodies again very quickly if the same organism enters the body. In this way, we become immune to an INFECTION, which normally prevents us from catching the same infection again.

See also ALLERGY; BLOOD; IMMUNE SYSTEM; VACCINATION.

Antifreeze

Antifreeze is a substance that is added to a liquid to lower its FREEZING POINT. Many antifreezes also raise the BOILING POINTS of liquids. The most common liquid used as an antifreeze is the ALCOHOL ethanediol (ethylene glycol). Antifreeze is used in deicing compounds and refrigerants. It is most commonly used in the water cooling systems of motor vehicles.

An engine runs at very high temperatures and needs

to be cooled, usually by water which is circulated through the system. It is necessary to add antifreeze to the water to prevent the water FREEZING in cold temperatures. When water freezes it expands in volume, and if this happens in a pipe or the engine block of a vehicle, it can cause the metal to split or crack, ruining the engine. *See also* MIXTURES.

Antihistamines *See* Allergy

Antimatter

Antimatter is MATTER made up of SUBATOMIC PARTICLES that are exactly the same as the particles commonly found, except that they have the opposite charge. They are called antiparticles. An ELECTRON, for example, is an ordinary particle which has a negative charge. Its antiparticle, a kind of antielectron called a POSITRON, is the same as the electron in every way except that it carries a positive charge. If you think of an ordinary ATOM, it is made up of PROTONS, NEUTRONS, and electrons. An antiatom would be made up of antiprotons, antineutrons and positrons. Antimatter was first described in 1930 before anyone had discovered or produced it. Antiparticles can be produced using a PARTICLE ACCELERATOR.

Antiseptics

Antiseptics are substances which kill or prevent the growth of germs (DISEASE-producing organisms) on body surfaces. They have to be mild enough not to irritate the SKIN or membranes. There are many different

> **Disinfectant** A liquid that destroys or inhibits the activity of germs on non-living things.
> **Infection** An illness caused by disease-carrying organisms.
> **Septic** A condition caused when bacteria rot or decay living matter.
> **Septicemia** A disease caused by contamination of the bloodstream by infectious bacteria.

▲ *This carbolic acid spray was the first successful antiseptic used in hospitals. Previously, antiseptics such as wine, tar, turpentine, and mercury had been used to kill germs, but they often harmed the patients.*

Joseph Lister (1827–1912)
Lister was a British surgeon who radically changed surgical practice with the introduction of antiseptics. They reduced the risk of bacterial infection during surgery. Lister's antiseptic solution of carbolic acid was used to clean wounds and surgical cuts and to scrub surgeons' hands. Lister believed that infection was caused by airborne dust particles, so he also sprayed the air with carbolic acid. The equipment was heated to a high temperature to make it bacteria free. His discoveries met with initial resistance but had become widely accepted by the 1880s when he introduced antiseptic catgut ligatures. Ligatures are the strong threads used to sew surgical wounds together. He also devised new operations and invented several surgical instruments.

It is believed that divers first used snorkels, made of hollow reeds, in about A.D. 100. Independent breathing devices for diving, which were the forerunners of the Aqualung, were tested during the late 1800s and early 1900s.

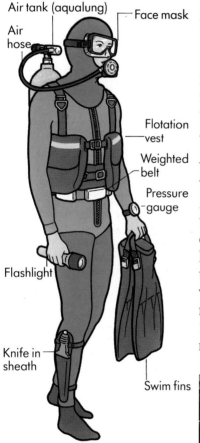

Air tank (aqualung)

Air hose

Face mask

Flotation vest

Weighted belt

Pressure gauge

Flashlight

Knife in sheath

Swim fins

▲ Aqualungs are essential equipment for divers. The one shown here is an open circuit system, where the air is exhaled into the water instead of being reused.

► The invention of scuba equipment has provided the diver with greater freedom and range.

chemicals that are used as antiseptics, including some ALCOHOLS. The many different kinds of antiseptic products available include mouthwashes, soaps, creams, and ointments.

The most common use for antiseptics is in the first-aid treatment of wounds. If you graze yourself, you may use an antiseptic, diluted with water, to clean away dirt from the area of the wound and kill any germs on the surface of the skin. Surgeons use antiseptics to scrub their hands and to prepare the patient's skin before an operation so bacteria will not cause an INFECTION.

Antiseptics were introduced into surgery in the late 1860s by Joseph Lister and the number of deaths resulting from infection fell dramatically. In modern operating rooms, surgical instruments are sterilized by heat under pressure in an autoclave.
See also MEDICINE; STERILIZATION.

Aqualung

An Aqualung is a metal tank, full of compressed AIR, that can be easily strapped to the back of a diver. This enables him or her to breathe underwater for up to an hour at a time. The air in the tank passes through a pipe to the mouthpiece. A demand valve releases the air only when the diver breathes in so that he or she can breathe normally. The first Aqualung was successfully tested in 1943 by Jacques Cousteau. It is often called scuba equipment, (self-contained underwater breathing apparatus).

Even with an Aqualung it is rare that a diver goes below about 100 feet (30 m) because of problems caused by the enormous PRESSURE of the water on the diver's body. Water pressure is greater than ATMOSPHERIC pressure and increases with depth. If a diver comes to the surface too quickly after a deep dive, the nitrogen in his or her blood, which has been compressed, bubbles in the bloodstream causing an agonizing and dangerous condition called the "bends." This is avoided by rising slowly to allow the body to release the nitrogen slowly.

Archimedes

Archimedes (*c*.287–212 B.C.) was a Greek mathematician and inventor who lived in Syracuse, Sicily. He made some important basic scientific discoveries.

His most famous invention was the Archimedean screw, a rotating device for raising water or grain. In places where pumps are not available, these are still used

▲ *Archimedes, a Greek mathematician and inventor tested his ideas by experimentation.*

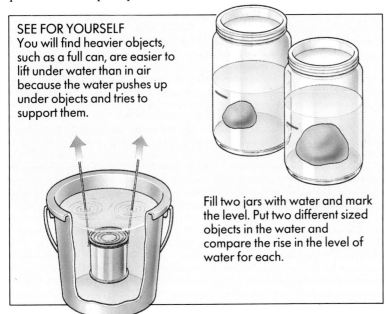

SEE FOR YOURSELF
You will find heavier objects, such as a full can, are easier to lift under water than in air because the water pushes up under objects and tries to support them.

Fill two jars with water and mark the level. Put two different sized objects in the water and compare the rise in the level of water for each.

▼ *The Archimedean screw has been in use for centuries. It is used to lift water from a low to a high level. One end of the screw is placed in the water. As the handle is turned, the screw inside the cylinder revolves and the water is carried upward. The casing must fit tightly to prevent leakage.*

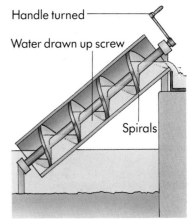

Handle turned

Water drawn up screw

Spirals

to lift water for irrigation. He also worked out the laws of LEVERS and PULLEYS. One well-known story about Archimedes says that one day he got into a bath and it overflowed. He jumped out and ran through the town shouting "Eureka!" (Greek for "I have found it!"). He had suddenly realized how to measure the volume of gold in the king's crown. If he put it into a container full to the brim with water, the water that overflowed would be the same volume as the crown. *See also:* FLOTATION.

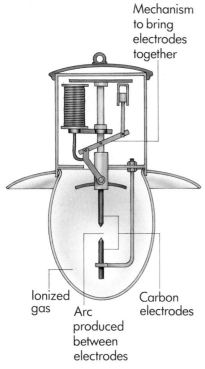

Mechanism to bring electrodes together

Ionized gas

Arc produced between electrodes

Carbon electrodes

▲ *The arc lamp was one of the earliest electric lights.*

▶ *Arc lamps are used where bright light is needed, such as on this 1948 film set.*

▲ *Aristarchus, a Greek astronomer who lived on Samos in around 300 B.C.*

Arc lamp

An arc lamp produces a very bright light when an electric current jumps, or arcs, across the space between two CARBON rods called electrodes. The tips of the carbon rods become white hot and begin to burn away. A mechanism keeps the burning tips of the rods the right distance apart. The first lamp of this kind was invented by Thomas Wright in 1845. In 1856, Frederick Homes, tried using an electric GENERATOR to power arc lamps for use in lighthouses. A high-intensity carbon-arc lamp for military searchlights was patented in the United States in 1915 by Elmer Sperry.

Carbon-arc lamps have now been superseded by other forms of lighting such as sodium-arc and mercury-arc lamps for powerful outdoor lighting.
See also ELECTRIC ARC; ELECTRICITY.

Aristarchus

Aristarchus was a Greek astronomer who was born about 300 B.C. He is believed to be the first person who thought that the EARTH revolved around the SUN. In those days the Earth was considered fixed at the center of the UNIVERSE. Almost two thousand years later, scientists realized Aristarchus was right.

Before TELESCOPES had been invented, Aristarchus made important observations with the naked eye. For example, by observations he proved that the Sun must be much farther away than the Moon. He also tried to measure the length of the year to an accuracy of one minute.

His opinion that the Earth moves around the Sun

made him unpopular, and he risked being arrested for teaching false beliefs. But he is remembered as one of the very first "scientists" (people who try to show that an idea must be supported by observed evidence).
See also COPERNICUS; GALILEO; SOLAR SYSTEM.

Aristotle

Aristotle (384–322 B.C.) was a Greek philosopher and scientist. He was a pupil of the famous Greek philosopher Plato. Aristotle was keen on observing and cataloging what he saw in nature. Most Greeks of the time believed that the basic facts about the world could be discovered by thinking about them rather than by observation and EXPERIMENTATION as the modern scientist does. Aristotle also pondered mathematical and astronomical problems, ethics (right and wrong), politics, and law.

Aristotle's reputation grew after his death. This probably slowed down scientific progress. For example, believing him to be right in suggesting that all heavenly bodies move in circles, astronomers tried in vain for 17 centuries, to explain the PLANETS' movements.

▲ Aristotle, the Greek thinker, is also regarded as the first great biologist. He thought everything was made up of four main elements: earth, fire, air, and water and their properties: dry, hot, cold, and wet.

▼ Aristotle divided the animal world into different categories, depending on how the animals' offspring were produced.

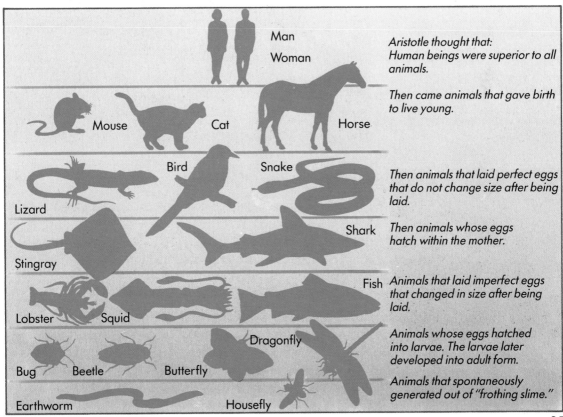

Man
Woman

Aristotle thought that: Human beings were superior to all animals.

Then came animals that gave birth to live young.

Mouse   Cat   Horse

Bird   Snake

Then animals that laid perfect eggs that do not change size after being laid.

Lizard

Shark

Then animals whose eggs hatch within the mother.

Stingray

Fish

Animals that laid imperfect eggs that changed in size after being laid.

Lobster   Squid

Dragonfly

Animals whose eggs hatched into larvae. The larvae later developed into adult form.

Bug   Beetle   Butterfly

Earthworm   Housefly

Animals that spontaneously generated out of "frothing slime."

Arithmetic is used to solve problems using numbers. It comes from a Greek word *arithmetike, arithmos,* meaning number and *techne,* meaning art or skill. Different number systems have been developed by different civilizations. The most common system is the one in which objects are counted in groups of 10. This is known as the decimal system, or base 10 arithmetic.

▶ *Arithmetic has been used since ancient times to solve mathematical problems. This Egyptian papyrus dates from 1650 B.C. It was copied from an even older papyrus written between 1849 and 1801 B.C. It is full of problems for students, exactly like those we do in school today.*

Arithmetic

Arithmetic is a branch of MATHEMATICS that helps us to use NUMBERS to solve problems which may be practical ones, such as how large the area of a field is, or more complex sums. Arithmetic lets us use numbers in four ways. We can add them together, take one away from another one, multiply them together, or divide one by another. These separate actions are known as addition, subtraction, multiplication, and division.

Arithmetic involves working with parts of numbers, such as fractions, DECIMALS and percentages, and measures to find out lengths, areas, and volumes. The Babylonians were among the first to use arithmetic about 4,000 years ago. They counted in sixties. The Hindus invented the system that we now use, called Arabic numerals because the Arabs brought them to Europe.

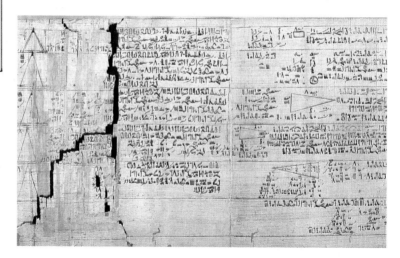

Arsenic

Arsenic is a semi-metallic chemical ELEMENT with three solid forms: gray arsenic, yellow arsenic, and black arsenic. Gray arsenic is the most stable form. It is shiny in appearance, quite a good conductor of heat and electricity, but it breaks easily. At 1135°F (613°C) gray arsenic sublimes (the solid form turns into a vapor without becoming a liquid first). Arsenic is usually extracted from the rocks in which it is found by roasting the rocks in air. The arsenic combines with the oxygen in the air, and this oxygen can later be removed. Arsenic is very poisonous and if taken in small doses over a long period it can cause cancer. Since ancient times arsenic has been

▲ *This picture shows a crystal cluster of arsenic trisulfide. It was once thought to contain gold because of its color.*

used in making poisons, medicines, and artists' colors. Today, it is used mainly in insecticides, rat poisons, and weed killers, in LASERS, TRANSISTORS, and other electrical devices, and for toughening alloys.

Artery *See* Circulation

Artesian well

An artesian well is a borehole in a layer of porous rock such as sandstone, limestone, or CHALK. Artesian wells are found throughout most of the world because large amounts of WATER soak into the Earth's surface.

Water collects in areas of high rainfall and flows down into the porous rock layer. If it is sealed above and below by layers of clay or impermeable rocks (that do not let water through), the water then accumulates in the porous layer (the water table). The water lower down in the sealed rock layer (an aquifer) is under PRESSURE from the water above. When a hole is drilled, the pressure will force water to the surface. Sometimes water is drawn from the aquifer faster than it is replaced. In this case, the pressure drops and water cannot be raised to the surface without pumps. Today, pumps are often used.

Permeable A material such as sandstone that allows air, water, or other fluids to pass through it.
Impermeable A material that does not allow water or other fluids to pass through.
Water table The highest level in the porous layer of ground that is filled (saturated) with water.
Aquifer A layer of porous material such as rock, sand, or gravel filled with ground water.

▼ *Pumps are used to draw water up from the artesian well when the water table is low. The name "Artesian" comes from a region in France called Artois. The oldest artesian well in Europe is believed to have been dug there in 1126. Below is an artesian well showing how water collects between layers of rock.*

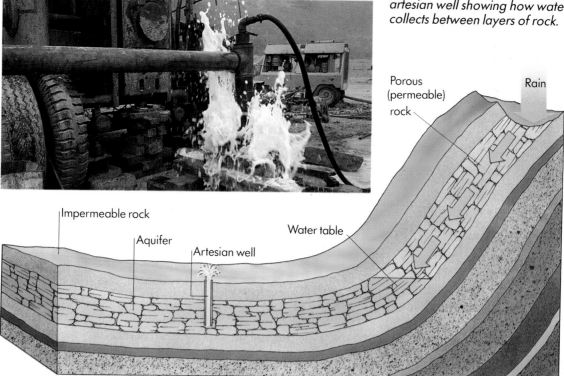

Impermeable rock

Aquifer

Artesian well

Water table

Porous (permeable) rock

Rain

Answer to Arithmetic question on page 36:
On the 11th square there will be 1,024 grains of rice, too many to fit on a chessboard square. By the 21st square there will be over a million.

▶ When playing tick-tack-toe a computer assesses all possible moves at each stage. It assigns each move a value; +1 for a win, 0 for a draw, and −1 for a loss. Each move is then tried out and the one that gives the best score is taken. The computer's moves (X) are mapped out on the right.

▼ Here a computer is being used to test an autopilot, a device which can fly an aircraft.

Arthritis *See* Joints

Artificial intelligence

Artificial intelligence is the performance by COMPUTERS of tasks that seem to require INTELLIGENCE. It is as if the computer can think for itself, but we know that any computer can only follow a series of operations laid down in programs written by computer programmers. Research

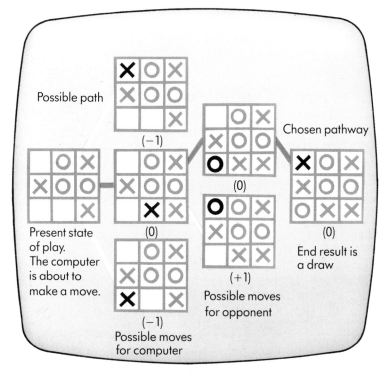

Possible path

(−1)

Chosen pathway

(0)

Present state of play. The computer is about to make a move.

(0)

End result is a draw

(0)

Possible moves for opponent

(+1)

(−1)
Possible moves for computer

in this area concentrates on getting computers to solve problems. This has led to the development of computers that can, for example, calculate where best to drill for oil, how to diagnose medical conditions, and even how to fly aircraft. In order to make these decisions, the computer has to be given vast amounts of information.

Experiments are under way to link cameras with computers so that they can identify shapes. Sound links will enable computers to recognize human speech so that instructions can be spoken to a computer instead of entering them through a keyboard. The whole area of "expert systems," where computers can help us to make important decisions by analyzing masses of information quickly and accurately, already plays an important part in industrial development.

See also COMPUTER LANGUAGES; COMPUTER MEMORY.

Asbestos

Asbestos is a soft and threadlike MINERAL noted for its resistance to BURNING. It is extracted from certain rocks. It was once used for a variety of purposes, including fireproofing clothes and as an insulating material. Now its use is severely limited because the fibers that it produces and releases into the air can damage the LUNGS if they are breathed in for a long time. This fatal disease is called asbestosis.

See also INSULATION, THERMAL.

Asteroid

An asteroid is a tiny PLANET that revolves around the SUN. Most of them can be found in the wide gap between the orbits of MARS and JUPITER. The largest, Ceres, is 620 miles (1,000 km) across, but most are much smaller.

Some asteroids have unusual orbits. Chiron is further from the Sun than SATURN. Others come inside the Earth's orbit, and may pass near us. The closest recorded encounter happened on March 22, 1989, when a tiny asteroid, now called 1989 FC, passed at less than twice the distance to the Moon.

Most asteroids are thought to have formed when specks of dust orbiting the Sun in a vast cloud formed small clumps, which collected together and grew in size.

There are so many asteroids that naming them is difficult. Most commemorate people, but No. 3568 has been named after the computer character code ASCII!

▲ *This is what an apollo asteroid may look like. All asteroids whose orbits cross the Earth's orbit are called apollo asteroids. The name comes from the first asteroid discovered to have this orbit.*

▼ *Most known asteroids orbit the Sun in a belt between Mars and Jupiter. Asteroids are also called minor planets.*

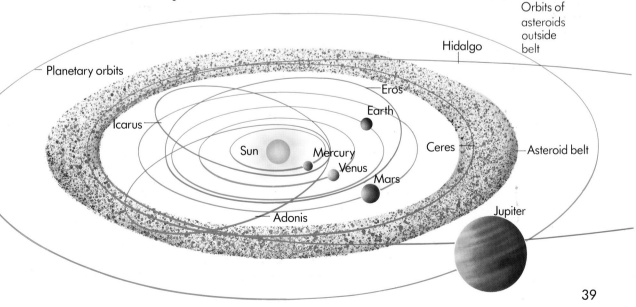

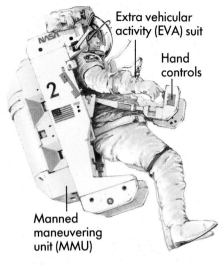

Extra vehicular
activity (EVA) suit

Hand
controls

Manned
maneuvering
unit (MMU)

▲ *Bruce McCandless was the first astronaut ever to use an MMU. For work outside the spacecraft, an astronaut wears an EVA suit.*

Astronaut

An astronaut is someone who is trained .to travel in space. More than 200 people have been launched into space since the Soviet pilot Yuri Gagarin made the first orbit of Earth on April 12, 1961 and began the age of SPACE EXPLORATION.

Astronauts must be extremely fit to survive the tremendous force of lift-off, which makes the body feel as if it is being squashed. An astronaut is trained to operate spacecraft controls and carry out complicated tasks in difficult conditions. These tasks could include performing experiments for scientists on the ground, launching new SATELLITES, or even rescuing damaged ones for repair.

In space, everything in the cabin is weightless. This affects the human body, which is used to fighting GRAVITY. Muscles are not used as much, and they will begin to waste away without regular exercise. Keeping astronauts healthy (SPACE MEDICINE) is important. Eating and drinking present problems since water breaks up into floating droplets, and a haze of crumbs and debris would form. Therefore an astronaut has to squeeze food into his or her mouth from squeeze bottles and suck liquid through a straw.

Underneath the EVA suit

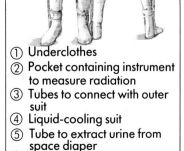

① Underclothes
② Pocket containing instrument to measure radiation
③ Tubes to connect with outer suit
④ Liquid-cooling suit
⑤ Tube to extract urine from space diaper
⑥ Tubes containing water

Space food

Plastic
tube

▲ *An astronaut's food must be easy to eat and store, as well as nutritious. Food is freeze-dried and the astronaut only needs to add water to make it ready to eat.*

▶ *A view of Earth that astronauts see from space.*

Some Famous Astronauts
April 12, 1961 Yuri Gagarin first orbits the Earth.
June 16, 1963 Valentina Tereshkóva first woman in space.
July 21, 1969 Neil Armstrong and Edwin Aldrin make first moon landing.
July 15, 1975 Vance Brand, Donald Slayton, Thomas Stafford, Alexei Leonov and Valery Kubasov in first international space mission.
April 12, 1981 John Young and Robert Crippen make first Space Shuttle flight.

ASTRONOMY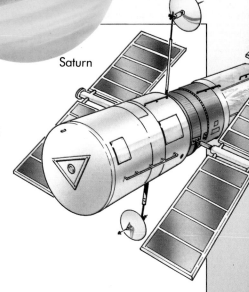

Saturn

The Earth is a tiny speck in space. If you imagine it shrunk down to a diameter of a twenty-fifth of an inch (1 mm), the Sun's nearest neighboring star would be 1,800 miles (3,000 km) away. The remotest visible galaxies are so distant that the light they send out takes about 10 billion years to reach us, even though light can travel to the Moon in just over a second.

Astronomers survey this huge volume of space. Our nearest star, the Sun, sends out light and heat to make life on Earth possible. It also shines on the other eight major planets and numerous other tiny bodies (over 50 satellites, thousands of asteroids or "minor planets," and possibly a million comets) in the Solar System.

In our galaxy, there are 100 billion stars. Some, the "dwarfs," are much dimmer than the Sun, while the "giants" are far brighter. Many stars are in clusters containing from 50 to 100,000 members, and there are also vast clouds of gas and dust, known as "nebulae," in which new stars are being born. Millions of other galaxies, some smaller and some larger than our own, can be detected. They are moving apart like particles in an explosion, suggesting that the universe started with a "big bang."

▲ The Hubble Space Telescope can send us detailed pictures of distant objects because it is above the Earth's atmosphere.

Milestones
270 B.C. Aristarchus teaches that the Earth orbits the Sun.
1608 Lippershey invents the telescope.
1600s Kepler proposes that the planets' orbits are ellipses.
1687 Newton publishes theory of gravity.
1838 Bessel measures the distance to a star.
1920 Distant galaxies are discovered to be flying away at great speeds.
1929 Hubble demonstrates that the universe is expanding.
1963 Background radiation, thought to be from the Big Bang, is discovered.
1990 Light recorded from farthest ever point.

▲ A radio telescope collects and records radio waves that come from objects in space.

SEE FOR YOURSELF
By using a pair of binoculars you can make your own astronomical observations at night. NEVER look at the Sun. Record what you see at the same time every evening. Keep the electric light off so that your eyes grow accustomed to the dim light. Use a flashlight covered with red see-through paper so you can see to write.

◄ These astronomers lived in Turkey in the Middle Ages.

See also ASTEROID; BIG BANG THEORY; BIG CRUNCH; BLACK HOLE; COMETS; GALAXY; NEBULA; PLANETS; SOLAR SYSTEM; STARS; UNIVERSE.

► *The atmosphere is held close to the Earth by gravity. It is divided into various layers according to differences in temperature. The troposphere, in which we live, contains more than 75 percent of the atmosphere. Nearly all the clouds, rain, and snow occur in this layer. The stratosphere extends up to 30 miles (48 km) above the Earth. Clouds are rare and aircraft usually fly in this layer above the weather disturbances in the troposphere. The ozone layer is between the stratosphere and the mesosphere. The mesosphere extends to 50 miles (80 km) above the Earth. Above this lies the thermosphere where the air is very thin. Over 99.99 percent of the atmosphere lies below it. The lower part of the thermosphere, the ionosphere, reflects radio waves back to Earth so signals can be sent around the world. The exosphere begins about 300 miles (480 km) above the Earth and fades away into space.*

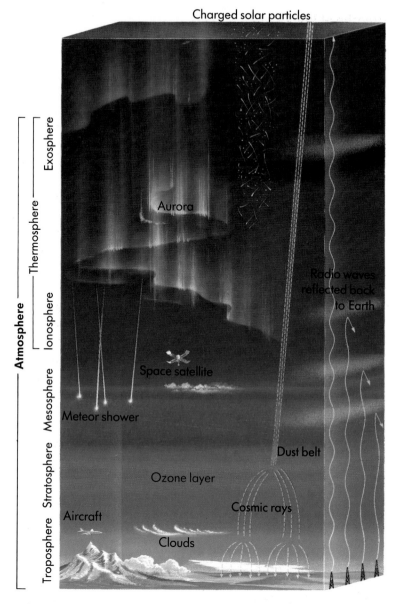

Charged solar particles

Aurora

Radio waves reflected back to Earth

Space satellite

Meteor shower

Dust belt

Ozone layer

Cosmic rays

Aircraft

Clouds

Atmosphere — Exosphere — Thermosphere — Ionosphere — Mesosphere — Stratosphere — Troposphere

The mixture of gases in the atmosphere has taken over 4.5 billion years to evolve. About 99 percent of the atmosphere is made up of nitrogen and oxygen. The gases in the remaining one percent are argon, carbon dioxide, and tiny amounts of hydrogen, ozone, methane, carbon monoxide, helium, neon, krypton, and xenon. The amount of water vapor depends on temperature and humidity.

Atmosphere

The atmosphere is a band of gas known as AIR, surrounding the Earth. It extends from the Earth's surface into outer space. It is made up of about 78 percent nitrogen, 21 percent oxygen, and 1 percent other gases.

The atmosphere also exerts PRESSURE. Atmospheric pressure is produced by the weight of air at the top of the band as it presses down on the air below. It presses onto the surface of Earth with a force of about 14.7 pounds per square inch (1 kg per square cm). We do not notice this pressure though it is present all the time.

The atmosphere becomes thinner and harder to

breathe at high altitudes. This is because less air is pressing down from above. Traces of atmosphere can be detected for thousands of miles into space, but even at the height of Mexico City (7,200 ft/2,200 m) some athletes in the 1968 Olympics suffered from breathlessness.

As well as becoming thinner, the higher atmosphere is cold. At the height of Everest (29,028 ft/8,848 m) the air temperature is −58°F (−50°C). For both these reasons aircraft need to be airtight and supplied with their own oxygen as well as being insulated against the cold.

The atmosphere protects us by blocking out dangerous RADIATION from the SUN and space. For example, a layer of oxygen called the OZONE LAYER cuts out invisible light (ULTRAVIOLET) that could cause fatal sunburn. *See also* BAROMETER; BOILING POINT.

> Scientists have worked out that if the carbon dioxide content of the Earth's atmosphere rose to 0.06 percent (double its normal level), the overall temperature would rise. This would cause the ice caps to melt, resulting in flooding of low areas.

Atom

An atom is a minute unit of MATTER. Atoms are so tiny that about a million of them would fit onto the period at the end of this sentence. Everything around us is made up of atoms. Atoms contain even tinier particles called PROTONS, NEUTRONS, and ELECTRONS. These have different arrangements in different chemical ELEMENTS. There are 92 chemical elements existing in the UNIVERSE, each of which is made up of only one kind of atom. Hydrogen and oxygen are two examples. *See* pages 44 and 45.

Atom bomb *See* Hydrogen bomb

Atomic energy *See* Nuclear energy

Atomic number

The atomic number of a chemical ELEMENT gives us the number of positive charges or PROTONS there are in the atomic nucleus (or how many negative ELECTRONS there are spinning around it). The number is the same for both, so the ATOM has no charge. Carbon, for example has six protons and six electrons. Its atomic number is six.

The atoms of the 92 naturally occurring elements can be placed in order by arranging them according to their atomic numbers. The atomic number determines an element's position in the PERIODIC TABLE. Elements with atomic numbers greater than 92 can be created artificially. Lawrencium has an atomic number of 103.

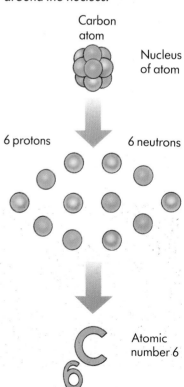

▼ Every element has its own atomic number. The atomic number is the same as the number of protons. The nucleus of a carbon atom has six protons and six neutrons, and so has an atomic number of six. It also has six electrons spinning around the nucleus.

Carbon atom

Nucleus of atom

6 protons   6 neutrons

Atomic number 6

ATOM

More than 2,000 years ago the Greeks argued about the makeup of matter. One group of philosophers, known as the atomists, believed that if you kept cutting something into smaller and smaller pieces, you would eventually get a tiny piece you could not cut. (The Greek word *atom* means "uncut.") The theory of the atom did not catch on until John Dalton developed his atomic theory. The discovery of the electron in 1897 proved that atoms are cuttable.

Atoms are made up of a system of tiny particles. Every atom has a nucleus, which contains protons and, except hydrogen, neutrons, with electrons spinning around it. A proton has a positive electrical charge, an electron has a negative charge, and a neutron has no charge at all. Each atom making up the same element has the same number of protons and electrons, so it is neither positive nor negative. An atom is made up of a large amount of empty space, but electrons travel at such a high speed that it makes an atom appear to behave like a solid (in the same way as a propeller blade turning at very high speed both looks solid and repels objects thrown against it). Individual atoms of the same or different elements can join together by sharing electrons to form molecules and also compounds.

▼ *If an atom were the size of your little finger nail, then your hand would be large enough to hold the Earth.*

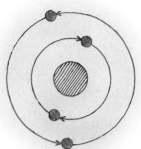

Bohr's model of the atom

Niels Bohr (1885–1962)
Bohr was a Danish physicist who contributed greatly to the development of modern nuclear physics. For his work on the structure of the atom he won the 1922 Nobel Prize for Physics. In 1943 he worked as an advisor to scientists developing the nuclear bomb.

◄ *Atoms are so small that they need to be magnified many times in order to be seen. The first pictures of individual atoms were taken in 1970 with an electron microscope, like the one pictured here.*

A tiny speck of dust, which is only just visible to the human eye, contains about 1000 million million (or a million billion) atoms.

Milestones in the study of the atom
400s B.C. Democritus gives the name atom to the basic particle.
1750 Boscovich believes atoms are made up of even smaller parts.
1803 Dalton proposes that each element has its own particular type of atom.
1911 Rutherford proposes that most of the mass of an atom is concentrated in a small nucleus consisting of protons, which is surrounded by electrons traveling at great speed.
1932 Chadwick discovers that the nucleus contains neutrons.
1938 Nuclear fission is discovered.
1971 Quarks identified. Shown to be smaller than protons and neutrons.
1988 Positron (antielectron) microscope in use.

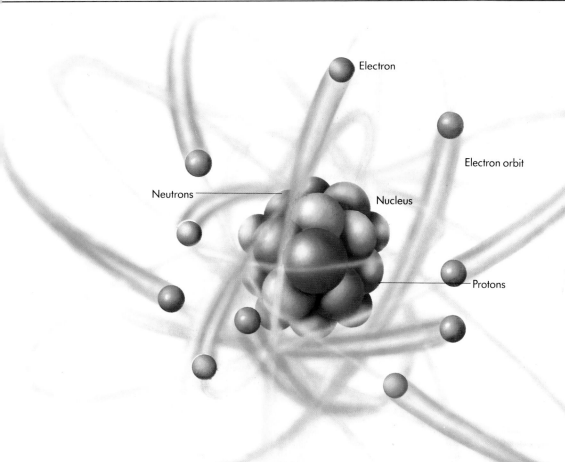

Electron

Electron orbit

Neutrons

Nucleus

Protons

▲ *Electrons constantly change their positions as they whizz around a nucleus of protons* *and neutrons, making billions of trips in one millionth of a second.*

▼ *An atom's nucleus contains energy that can be released to produce nuclear energy. The blue glow in the core of a nuclear reactor is produced by the atoms.*

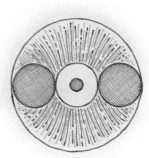

Dalton's model of the atom

John Dalton (1766–1844)

Dalton was an English chemist. He is best known for his atomic theory to explain the structure of matter. It became one of the foundations of modern chemistry. He was first to calculate the weights of the atoms of several elements. He worked out a table of atomic weights of elements, but it was later found to be inaccurate.

See also ANTIMATTER; COMPOUNDS; ELEMENT; ELECTRON; ION; MOLECULE; NEUTRON; PROTON; SUBATOMIC PARTICLES.

Jons Berzelius (1779–1848)
Berzelius was a Swedish chemist. He classified different substances by calculating their atomic weights. By 1818 he had accurately calculated the atomic weights of 45 elements and suggested a new way of naming the elements by using the first letter or letters of their names, e.g. O = oxygen. Combinations of elements are represented by putting the letters together, e.g. CO_2 = carbon dioxide, one carbon atom joined to two oxygen atoms.

Atomic weight

Atoms are so small and light (there are approximately 17,000 billion trillion hydrogen ATOMS in an ounce) that it is not strictly possible to weigh them. Therefore chemists use a RATIO of the average mass of the atoms of an ELEMENT instead of a very small unit of weight. Carbon which has an atomic weight of 12, has been used as the reference point since 1961. An atomic weight is really the mass of an atom relative to that of one twelfth of a carbon atom. The term relative atomic mass is very often used as an alternative to atomic weight.

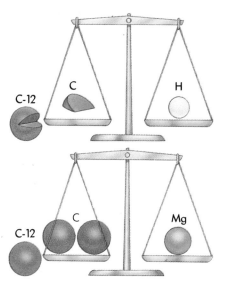

◀ *The reference element carbon has an atomic weight of 12. Hydrogen (H) is one twelfth the weight of a carbon-12 atom and so its atomic weight is one. Magnesium (Mg) is the weight of two carbon atoms and so its atomic weight is 24.*

▲ *The brilliant light displays of auroras are most common at the poles during intense sunspot activity.*

Aurora

Auroras are glows of light, hundreds of miles above the Earth's surface. They are seen when electrically charged atomic particles, sprayed off the SUN's surface, collide with atoms in the Earth's atmosphere and make them release energy in the form of flashes of light.

The Sun sends out a steady stream of particles, but these do not normally cause auroras. However, once in a while a tremendous explosion, or *solar flare* occurs at a SUNSPOT. This sends a fountain of particles into space in a burst that usually lasts for just a few hours.

Electrically charged particles are magnetic, and when they reach the magnetic field that surrounds the Earth some are pulled down toward the Earth's magnetic poles (close to the North and South poles). This is why auroras are strongest when observed from the arctic and antarctic.

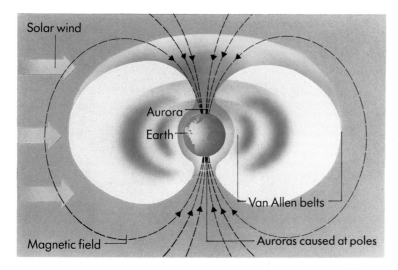

Solar wind
Aurora
Earth
Van Allen belts
Magnetic field
Auroras caused at poles

◄ Solar winds are streams of electrically charged particles sprayed from the Sun. As they come near Earth some are trapped and pulled toward the poles by the Earth's magnetic field. Here they join particles in the Van Allen belts, two zones of electrically charged particles that surround the Earth. During intense sunspot activity the solar wind can disrupt the belts, striking particles and releasing energy in the form of light, creating auroras. The auroras in the Northern Hemisphere are called the aurora borealis (northern lights) and those in the Southern Hemisphere, aurora australis (southern lights).

The most common color in an aurora is green, but displays occurring very high in the sky may be shades of red or purple.

See also MAGNETISM; VAN ALLEN BELTS.

Automation

Automation is the use of machines to perform a wide variety of tasks. Automatic systems are especially useful for performing repetitive tasks. For example, robots are used on production lines to assemble car parts. Used in this way, machines can be extremely efficient, since some tasks can be performed more cheaply by machines than by human workers. Electronic cash registers make an instant record of each item as it is sold and are able to place orders for new stock before an item runs out. Machines can also be used for decision making, for example, to regulate the flow of vehicles through sets of traffic lights.

▼ Some robots are very basic, like this mobot. It has flexible arms that are used for lifting and moving dangerous substances.

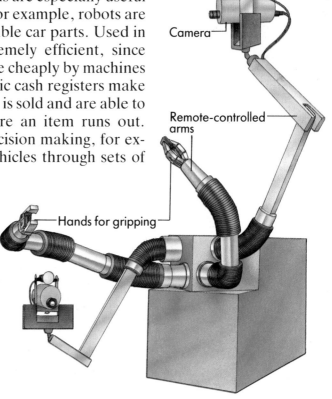

Mobot
Camera
Remote-controlled arms
Hands for gripping

An early example of automation was James Watt's flyball governor. Two balls were attached to a shaft that rotated at engine speed. When the engine speeded up, the balls were thrown farther out. As they moved out, they controlled a steam inlet valve to the engine, allowing less steam in and slowing the engine.

▶ *Most robots are used in factories. They are often used for jobs such as welding, because they can be programmed to be very accurate.*

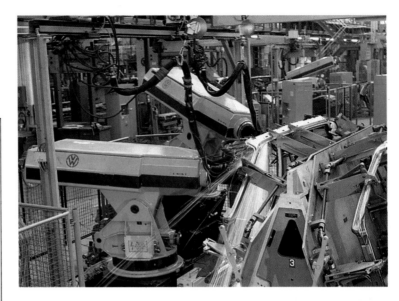

The earliest known example of automation is a water clock that is thought to have operated in Egypt in about 200 B.C. The water clock consisted of a large tank full of water which was set up so water could flow out of a hole near the bottom of the tank and into a glass jar. On the jar was a scale marked off into the hours of the day. You could tell what time it was by looking at the level of water in the jar. As the level of water in the tank dropped, the water pressure decreased. You would normally expect the drop in water pressure to cause the water to flow more slowly into the jar, which would affect the accuracy of the clock. To prevent this, the drop in water level triggered a device that made the size of the hole in the tank larger to keep a constant flow of water into the jar.

An automatic system depends on information about the output and input of the system so it can regulate its performance. This is known as FEEDBACK. The system compares the actual output with the required output. If these are not the same, a device called a *controller* decides what to do to correct the error. The idea of a controller can be illustrated by thinking of a THERMOSTAT in a water heater. For example, say that the required temperature of the water is 150°F (65°C). The thermostat continually compares the temperature of the water as it heats up with the setting of 150°F (65°C) on the thermostat. When the temperature of the water reaches the required point the thermostat switches the burner off. As the water starts to cool down the thermostat detects a fall in the temperature and switches the burner on again. In many systems COMPUTERS are used to control the various stages of an automated process.

Average Also called the arithmetic mean. The mean of a number of objects is like the idea of the balancing point, or center of gravity.
Median The middle value in a group of numbers arranged in increasing order.
Mode The mode of a group of numbers is the number that occurs most frequently.

Average

The average of a set of quantities is the value that is most typical of that set. The value obtained by adding all the quantities in the set and dividing by the number of quantities is the *arithmetic mean*. For example, there are five children aged 13, 12, 10, 6 and 4. What is the average, or mean, of their ages? It is 9, 13+12+10+6+4=45 and 45 divided by 5 is 9. This is only one type of average. Others are also important, especially in STATISTICS. The *median* of a set of values is the middle value in the set. If our numbers, 13, 12, 10, 6 and 4, were points out of 15 in a

Average height for the group (Mean)

test, the median would be the middle number 10. The *mode* is the number that appears most often in a set of numbers. Suppose ten children take a test. The points they get out of 20 are: 18, 17, 15, 15, 13, 12, 12, 12, 9 and 6. The most frequent mark is 12, so 12 is the mode.

▲ *To get the mean height of a group of people add all the heights together and divide the total by the number of people in the group.*

SEE FOR YOURSELF
Fill some differently shaped glasses with water. You can now work out the average amount of water contained in each glass. First pour the water from each of the glasses into a measuring pitcher. Next look to see how much water is in the pitcher. Do this by looking at the scale on the side of the pitcher. Then divide this figure by the number of glasses. You may need a calculator to do this. The resulting figure is the average.

Median height

▲ *To find the median height of the group, arrange everybody in order of size. The median height is the height of the person in the middle.*

Mode height

▲ *The mode of the group is the most common height in the group.*

Avogadro, Amedeo

▼ *Avogadro, known for his work in chemistry and physics.*

Amedeo Avogadro (1776–1856) was an Italian physicist. He is famous for his gas law, known as Avogadro's law, which states that when each one of a set of identical glass jars is filled with a different GAS, at the same TEMPERATURE and PRESSURE, they each contain the same number of MOLECULES of gas. To discover the actual number of molecules requires the use of Avogadro's number. It is usually written as 6.0220×10^{23} which is a short way of writing 602,200,000,000,000,000,000,000. This is about the number of molecules of any gas, including AIR, that would be contained in 6 gallons (22.7 liters).

▶ *Babbage worked on his second calculating machine, the Analytical Engine, from 1835 to 1848, but never finished it.*

▲ *Babbage spent much of his life developing two kinds of calculating machines.*

▼ *Baird is considered to be the "father" of television.*

Babbage, Charles

Charles Babbage (1792–1871) resigned as Professor of Mathematics at Cambridge University, England, to work on designing a mechanical calculating machine. Despite the invention of logarithms, the need for accurate and complicated calculations had outgrown the existing simple machines, such as the ABACUS.

Babbage's aim was to use sets of GEARS that moved each other to produce columns of figures. These figures would then be printed out automatically.

His Difference Engine, as he called it, was never finished, but the beautifully machined parts can be seen in the Science Museum, London. He abandoned it for the Analytical Engine, which was intended to solve algebraic problems as well as do direct calculations, but he could not find enough money to complete it. He is now respected as a computing pioneer born before his time.

Bacon, Roger *See* Alchemy

Baird, John Logie

Baird (1888–1946) was a Scottish engineer. In 1924 he became the first person ever to transmit a television picture by RADIO waves. He was also the first to transmit a picture across the Atlantic (in 1928), and in the same year he transmitted color television pictures. Baird's first television apparatus, set up in his attic workshop at Hastings, England, included some old boxes, the front LENSES from a number of bicycle lights, bits of wood, darning needles, string, and sealing wax. This crude CAMERA transmitted a blurred image of a cross to a receiver at the other end of the attic.

Despite improvements made by Baird, in 1937 the British Broadcasting Corporation chose for its broadcasts a rival system that used a CATHODE-RAY TUBE. *See also* ELECTROMAGNETIC RADIATION.

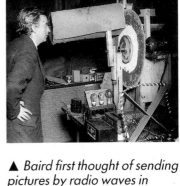

▲ *Baird first thought of sending pictures by radio waves in 1923. His mechanical scanning television system failed commercially, but he continued to experiment with picture transmission until his death.*

Balance *See* Scales and Balances

Balancing point

The balancing point of an object is the point at which it balances. The whole WEIGHT of the object appears to be concentrated in one spot. This point is called the CENTER OF GRAVITY. If a regular shaped object such as a can is tipped slightly it will fall back onto its base when released. If the can is tipped too far beyond its balancing point, which is in the middle, this causes the can to become unstable and it will fall over.

Not all objects have their balancing point in the middle. An irregularly shaped object such as a bus is designed to tilt over at a large angle without becoming unstable. This is done by making the chassis (the frame to which the engine and wheels are attached) of the bus very heavy which moves the balancing point, its center of gravity, lower down. *See also* EQUILIBRIUM.

Baird kept improving his television system. Before World War II he gave a demonstration of TV in natural colors and just before he died it is said he had constructed a system for stereoscopic TV. He also invented an instrument called the "Noctovision" for seeing in the dark.

If a person stands up in a rowboat the balancing point is raised. Any slight disturbance is likely to cause the boat to tip over. The lifeboat has been designed with a low balancing point so that it can ride rough seas without being overturned. If it does happen to be overturned it will quickly right itself again.

SEE FOR YOURSELF
Tape a heavy weight into the corner of a box. Close the box, place it on a table and push it gently off the edge with the weight on the table side. You would normally expect an unweighted box, with its balancing point in the middle, to fall over the edge when it is about halfway off the edge of the table. By taping the weight in the corner of the box you have altered the weight and its even distribution throughout the box. This has moved the balancing point toward the corner. You can, therefore, push more than three-fourths of the box off the table before it falls over the edge.

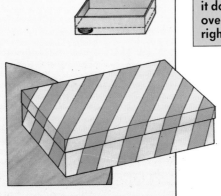

Ballistics

Ballistics is a branch of engineering that studies the movement of bodies (called projectiles) which have been projected into the air. It is concerned mainly with: the path, or trajectory, of bullets fired from cannons and small arms; the free fall of bombs dropped from an aircraft; and the trajectory followed by a ROCKET or guided MISSILE once its engines have been turned off and it is acted upon only by the pull of gravity.

Interior ballistics investigates what happens to a bullet as it travels along a gun or rifle barrel, or a missile as it is fired from a launcher. *Exterior ballistics* examines the projectile in flight and its path to its target, and *terminal ballistics* studies how the projectile affects its target.

Projectile An object or body that is projected, or thrown, forward and continues in motion under its own inertia.
Missile A self-propelled object that is directed at a target.
Trajectory The path an object follows as it moves through air under force.

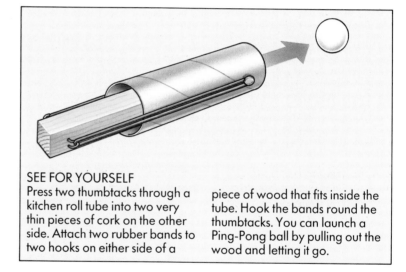

SEE FOR YOURSELF
Press two thumbtacks through a kitchen roll tube into two very thin pieces of cork on the other side. Attach two rubber bands to two hooks on either side of a piece of wood that fits inside the tube. Hook the bands round the thumbtacks. You can launch a Ping-Pong ball by pulling out the wood and letting it go.

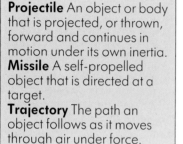

▼ *In November 1783, a Montgolfier brothers' balloon made its first free flight with people on board. It took off from the center of Paris, France.*

Balloon

Balloons are bags or sacks filled with a GAS. They are usually made from a nonporous material so the gas remains inside the balloon. If the balloon is filled with a gas that is lighter than AIR, such as HELIUM, the balloon will float upward. In hot air balloons, a gas burner is used to heat the air (hot air is lighter so the balloon rises). Balloons usually have a basket or other container attached to them to carry passengers. Ballooning is a popular pastime and sport.

Unmanned balloons are used for scientific research. Special balloons, carrying instruments, are sent into the upper ATMOSPHERE to measure and record information about temperature, wind, humidity, and pressure.

▲ As ballooning becomes a more popular sport, the colorful sight of the sky filled with hot air balloons is more common.

Sometimes balloons are used to carry advertisements for particular products or services.

Cut the shape above out of paper, or glue one square and four rectangles of paper together.

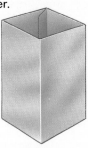

Glue the long sides of the paper shape together to make it into a balloon.

Place a short candle in a jar and light it carefully. Put the balloon over the jar and as the air inside heats up, the balloon will rise.

Bar code

A bar code is a series of black bars of different thicknesses with spaces between them. You will find bar codes printed onto the packaging of most goods that are bought in stores.

The width of the white spaces between the lines on a bar code is interpreted as a number by a scanner which is passed over the code. The number, which identifies the product, is then passed to a COMPUTER. In supermarkets and other large retail outlets low-powered LASER beam scanners are linked to a computerized cash register. The computer matches the current price of the item to the coded number and prints a description of the goods and its price onto the cash register receipt. With this system an accurate analysis of goods sold can be made and goods can be restocked before they sell out. Light pen scanners are used in some libraries to read the bar codes

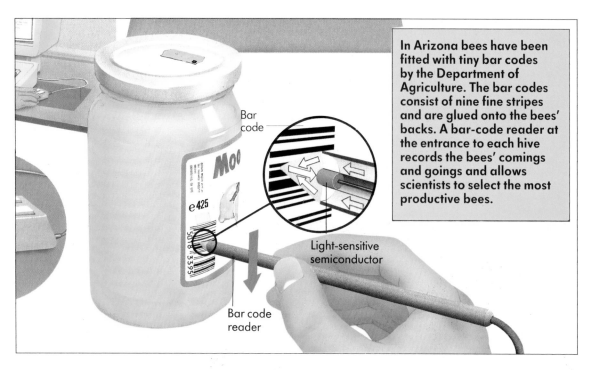

In Arizona bees have been fitted with tiny bar codes by the Department of Agriculture. The bar codes consist of nine fine stripes and are glued onto the bees' backs. A bar-code reader at the entrance to each hive records the bees' comings and goings and allows scientists to select the most productive bees.

▲ Nowadays bar codes can be found on many products, since they provide an up-to-date record of stock in stores.

▼ It is difficult to see the intestine on an X-ray unless a "barium meal" has been taken. A barium meal absorbs X-rays and so the intestine shows up clearly.

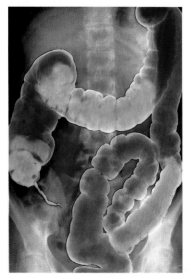

that are now being used to code library books. The light pen sends the code to a computer which matches the book's unique number to the coded number of the borrower, recording which books are being taken out or returned. These systems can also issue reminder notices when borrowed books become overdue for return.

See also AUTOMATION; OPTICAL CHARACTER RECOGNITION.

Barium

Barium is a soft, heavy, silvery white metallic element that readily reacts with other elements to form useful COMPOUNDS. Barium sulfate occurs in nature in the MINERAL barytes. Chemists make pure barium for laboratory work by passing an electric current through melted barium chloride. Barium compounds are used in paints, ceramics, special glass, liquid muds used in drilling oil wells, and for purifying chemical solutions and alloys.

Barium compounds that dissolve in water are poisonous, but barium sulfate, which is extremely insoluble, is harmless. When a doctor wishes to X-RAY a patient's digestive passage, the patient has to drink a barium "meal" (a preparation of barium sulfate and water). The X-rays cannot pass through the barium sulfate, so when the photograph is developed, the intestines show up as a clear outline.

Barometer

A barometer measures the PRESSURE of the ATMOSPHERE. This is the FORCE exerted on everything at the Earth's surface by the weight of the atmosphere. Changes in atmospheric pressure affect the WEATHER. By measuring these changes, barometers help forecast the weather.

Mercury barometers are used in weather stations. Atmospheric pressure on a reservoir of mercury causes the mercury to move up a long thin glass tube (with the air sucked out of it) until it cannot be pushed any higher. Usually this is when it is about 30 inches (760 mm) high. Variations in atmospheric pressure cause the liquid in the tube to rise or fall by small amounts which can be read off a scale.

See also METEOROLOGY.

Evangelista Torricelli (1608–1647)
Torricelli was an Italian mathematician and physicist. He discovered the principle of the barometer. He put a long mercury-filled glass tube, closed at one end, upside down in a cup of mercury. The air pressure on the surface of the mercury in the cup held the column of mercury in the tube at a height of 30 inches (760 mm). The weight of the column of mercury was equal to the pressure of the atmosphere.

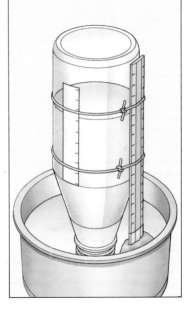

Mercury barometer

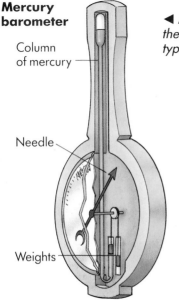

Column of mercury

Needle

Weights

◀ *Mercury barometers are the most sensitive and accurate type of barometer.*

▼ *The vacuum chamber of an aneroid barometer expands or contracts as the air pressure changes, causing the needle to move.*

Aneroid barometer

Dial
Needle
Spindle
Lever
Vacuum chamber

▼ *The car battery (right) and the dry battery (below) are common kinds of batteries. The car battery contains spillable acid, whereas the chemical in dry batteries is a paste. Another kind is the lithium battery used in calculators, watches, pacemakers, and cameras.*

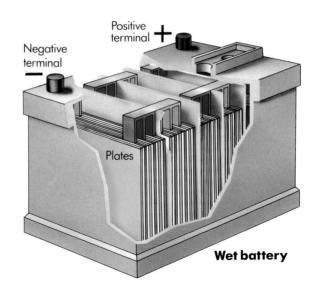

Negative terminal

Positive terminal

Plates

Wet battery

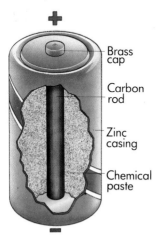

Brass cap

Carbon rod

Zinc casing

Chemical paste

Dry batteries stop working once their chemical energy has been used up. They are then thrown away.
Storage batteries store electrical energy and can be recharged.

SEE FOR YOURSELF
Make 2 cuts in a lemon and insert a copper coin (positive terminal) and a piece of aluminum (negative terminal). The aluminum could be taken from an old can. Connect a low-voltage flashlight bulb by two pieces of wire to make the circuit. The lamp may light up.

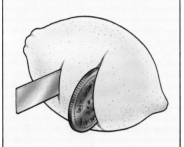

Battery

A battery uses chemicals to produce ELECTRICITY. There are two types: those that store or accumulate electricity and can be recharged, and those that make electricity until their chemicals are exhausted.

The most common type of rechargeable battery is found in a car. Two metal plates, one of LEAD and the other of lead dioxide, are mounted inside a cell containing dilute SULFURIC ACID. There are usually six cells, connected together, inside the battery case. The outer lead plate is connected to the negative terminal and the lead dioxide plate to the positive. The battery is first charged by connecting it to an ELECTRIC CIRCUIT. Then, after starting the ENGINE by using the battery, a small dynamo turned by the engine keeps the battery charged up with electrical energy.

Flashlights use the second kind of battery, sometimes called a dry cell. It contains a paste of ammonium chloride inside a ZINC case, with a CARBON rod in the paste. The case makes the negative terminal and the rod, the positive one. Ammonium chloride is poisonous and so used batteries must be safely disposed of.

In many dry cell batteries, the negative electrode is made of an amalgam of zinc, mercury, and cadmium. This prolongs the life of the battery by reducing the rate at which the zinc dissolves in the battery liquids. Batteries turn chemical energy into electrical energy with an efficiency of about 90 percent. This is the most efficient but most expensive way of producing electricity.

Bearings

Bearings are devices in MACHINES that support moving parts and enable them to move with less FRICTION. The most common types are ball and roller bearings.

Almost every machine has bearings, for example, cars, bicycles, electric motors, ship's propellers, and even roller skates. Where a shaft or rod passes through another part of a machine, such as an axle through the hub of a wheel, bearings are used to keep the two parts separated. Without bearings, the moving parts of the machine would constantly rub together and cause friction. Friction slows the machine down and also produces heat. It will eventually cause the parts to wear out.

A bearing is normally made up of an outer and inner ring of steel. The space between the rings contains either steel balls (known as ball bearings) or rollers (known as roller-contact bearings). These bearings slide or roll inside the rings.

After a great deal of use, it is usually only the bearings and not the machine that wear out.
See also ENERGY; LUBRICATION.

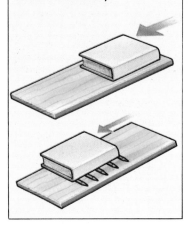

SEE FOR YOURSELF
Push a book along a wooden surface. Friction between the surface of the table and the book causes resistance and slows it down, increasing the amount of work you have to do. Now place four round pencils under the book. The pencils act like bearings. Friction is reduced and the book moves easily.

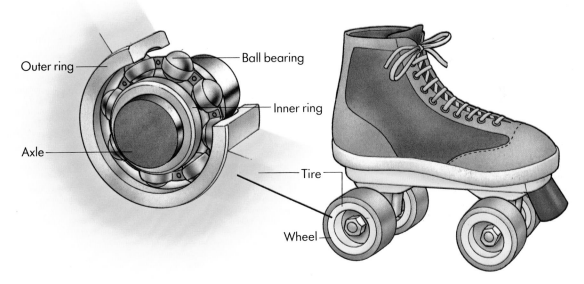

Outer ring — Ball bearing — Inner ring — Axle — Tire — Wheel

▲ *Roller skate wheels contain ball bearings. These help the wheels move around smoothly, reducing friction and wear in the moving parts without the need for lubricants.*

Behavior

Behavior covers everything a human or other animal does during its life. Scientists who study behavior are interested in finding out what affects it. They want to know why an animal behaves in a certain way in a particular situation, for example, the way people behave in

▲ In crowds people tend to copy one another, rather than act as individuals.

▼ Grebes have an elaborate courtship dance. The male crouches as he approaches the female, wings outstretched. Then a headwagging display begins. They often carry weeds in their beaks as they stretch their necks and sway. Finally the male will give the female a fish. This is instinctive behavior.

groups, how they sit or look at each other, or why some people shriek when they see a spider.

Behavior has been divided into three main types: reflex, instinctive, and learned behavior. *Reflex actions* are not planned or decided beforehand. If you accidentally touch a hot object, you pull your hand away without thinking. *Instinctive behavior* is behavior that does not have to be learned. A young bird that has never seen another bird build a nest, does not have to be taught how to build one. Behavior can be changed by LEARNING (*learned behavior*). Many animals will run away when they hear a loud bang. But if the bangs are repeated often enough, the animal grows used to the noise and ceases to run away. It has changed its behavior.

People's behavior is more complicated than the behavior of other animals. It is often difficult to separate instinctive behavior from learned behavior. For example, a person might inherit from his parents the capability to become a brilliant violinist, but without a violin and training he or she can never play the violin well. *See also* GENETICS; PSYCHOLOGY AND PSYCHIATRY.

Bell, Alexander Graham

Alexander Graham Bell (1847–1922) was born and educated in Scotland but lived for most of his life in the United States. Before he left Scotland, Bell began teaching deaf children using a code of symbols invented by his father. His interest in the human voice, and the realization that speech produces SOUND waves vibrating in air, led him to become the first person to successfully transmit speech by means of electrified wire. In 1876, he announced the world's first workable TELEPHONE. It had certain disadvantages; it had to be moved quickly from mouth to ear and the sound was very faint even when the speaker shouted. The American inventor EDISON

▲ *Alexander Bell, teacher of the deaf and inventor of the telephone.*

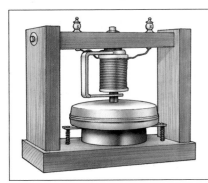

The First Bell Telephone
Alexander Graham Bell's telephone worked by changing sound produced by the human voice into electric current. This current could then be transmitted along a wire and changed back into sound at the other end. The telephone was invented while

Bell and his assistant Watson were trying out a new transmitter for sending several telegraph messages at once. The first words were transmitted by accident. Watson heard Bell call from another room that he had spilled acid on his clothes.

soon produced a much more powerful and successful telephone. In 1880, Bell brought out the *gramophone* which was an improved version of Edison's *phonograph*, a machine which recorded speech and played it back.

Though Bell will always be associated with the invention of the telephone, he would rather have been remembered as a teacher of the deaf.

Benzene

Benzene is a sweet-smelling, colorless LIQUID used for the industrial manufacture of several materials such as polystyrene, synthetic rubber, and nylon. It is also used in detergents and dyes. Benzene belongs to a class of chemicals called HYDROCARBONS. Each molecule of it contains six ATOMS of hydrogen and six atoms of carbon arranged in a ring formation. This is known as a benzene ring and is found in many other chemical compounds, including aspirin and the explosive TNT. Benzene is poisonous and can cause cancer. The British physicist

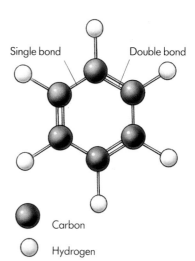

Single bond   Double bond

Carbon

Hydrogen

▲ *The benzene ring consists of six atoms of carbon and six atoms of hydrogen.*

August Kekulé, the German chemist, had a daydream in which he saw benzene atoms twisting and turning like snakes. One of the snakes seized its own tail. This gave Kekulé the idea that benzene is a ring of atoms.

Michael FARADAY discovered benzene in 1825. It was originally prepared by heating coal tar and changing its vapor into liquid. Large quantities of benzene are now extracted from PETROLEUM.

See also BOND, CHEMICAL; CHEMISTRY; PLASTICS.

Bessemer, Henry *See* Iron and Steel

Beta particles *See* Subatomic particles

Big Bang theory

The Big Bang theory explains the origins of the UNIVERSE in terms of a "big bang" that caused the galaxies to start moving apart at great speeds 15 billion years ago. It must have been hotter and denser than we can imagine, a raging chaos of atomic particles. But physicists have calculated that in just *three minutes* these particles had turned into all the hydrogen ATOMS that now make up 90 percent of the universe. As the hydrogen cloud expanded, it began to break up into separate clouds. These eventually became galaxies of stars like our own Milky Way galaxy, still moving apart from the Big Bang.

The universe may expand for ever, or it may eventually stop expanding and then collapse inward. But, it is predicted that before this, in about 5 billion years the Sun will heat up, and burn the Earth.

See also COSMOLOGY; UNIVERSE.

▼ *Some scientists believe that the universe was created about 15 billion years ago in an explosion they call the Big Bang. Matter was formed in the tremendous heat that followed and galaxies were created.*

Big Crunch theory

If all the GALAXIES in the UNIVERSE were stationary, their GRAVITY would attract each other and they would finally come together in a huge "implosion." The study of COSMOLOGY shows that the galaxies are moving apart from the BIG BANG, but is their gravity strong enough to slow down their outward flight and eventually pull them back together?

The force of gravity of a body depends on its MASS. The galaxies do not contain enough mass to pull them back together, but there may be "invisible" matter (single atoms) in the spaces between the galaxies. If this "invisible" matter adds up to several times the material in the galaxies themselves, the extra gravity could reverse the expansion and eventually cause a "big crunch."

▼ The galaxies are still expanding, but the Big Crunch theory suggests that one day they will stop. Gravity will pull them together until they collide and implode.

Implode To collapse violently inward because of external pressure.
Explode To burst violently outward as a result of internal pressure.

Some astronomers predict that in about 70 billion years time the galaxies will start moving together again. If this happens all the matter in the Universe will eventually come together in a big crunch. At this point there would be another big explosion, which would probably result in another Universe similar to the existing one.

61

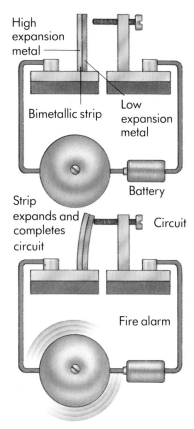

High expansion metal

Bimetallic strip

Low expansion metal

Battery

Strip expands and completes circuit

Circuit

Fire alarm

▲ *This fire alarm system uses a bimetallic strip. When the strip heats up and bends, the electrical circuit is completed and the bell rings.*

▼ *The binary system is shown in cell division. Cells divide into two at each stage, until the egg is a mass of cells. This can be seen clearly in frog spawn.*

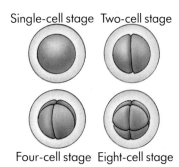

Single-cell stage   Two-cell stage

Four-cell stage   Eight-cell stage

Bimetallic strip

A bimetallic strip is made from pieces of two different metals stuck together along their length. When the strip is heated, each metal expands by different amounts. The strip forms a curve with the metal which expands more on the longer (outside) edge. The larger the temperature change the greater the amount of bending, so the strip is a sort of THERMOMETER.

They can be used in THERMOSTATS to help control TEMPERATURE. They are also used to turn on and off the flashing light of a car indicator. The electric current lights the light and also heats a bimetallic strip, which bends away from the contact and breaks the electrical circuit. This turns off the light and stops the heating, the strip cools and straightens, remakes the circuit and turns the lamp on again.

See also ELECTRICITY; EXPANSION.

Binary numbers

The binary number system uses only two digits: 0 and 1. With a binary number the digit on the right has the value one, the next digit going left is two times larger and the next is two times larger again. So, reading from right to left, the first place has a value of 1, the second of 2, the

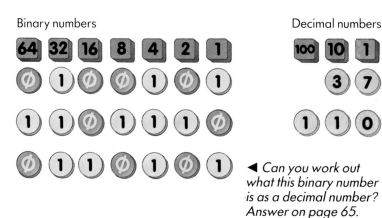

Binary numbers

Decimal numbers

◄ *Can you work out what this binary number is as a decimal number? Answer on page 65.*

third of 4, the fourth of 8, the fifth place of 16, and so on, doubling each time. Following this system, the binary number 101 means one 4, no 2s, and one 1 which when added together is 5 in the DECIMAL system. In COMPUTERS, binary numbers are used to code information by setting the many tiny electrical switches either on or off.

See also MATHEMATICS; NUMBERS.

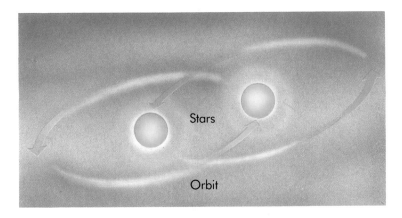

Stars

Orbit

◄ *Binary stars are pairs of stars which are born together. The force of gravity holds them close so that they orbit around each other. Binary stars are often different in shape and brightness from each other.*

Binary stars

Binary stars, sometimes known as double stars, are pairs of stars that revolve around each other and are held together by GRAVITY. The closer a pair of stars are, the faster they revolve. Some binary stars are almost touching, and go around each other in a few hours. Others are separated by hundreds of times the diameter of the SOLAR SYSTEM and may take a million years to orbit each other. About a quarter of all the stars in our Milky Way GALAXY have at least one companion in space. The star *Castor* in the constellation *Gemini* is really six stars!

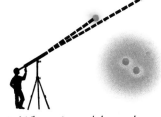

▲ *When viewed through a telescope a pair of stars may appear close together, although one may be many thousands of miles in front of the other. These are called optical double stars.*

Binocular vision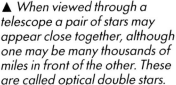

Binocular vision is the type of vision many animals have, in which each EYE sees a single object from a slightly different direction. If you move your head from side to side an object will appear to move slightly against other objects in the background. This is called PARALLAX and

► *Animals can judge distances better if their eyes are in front, because they have a larger area of binocular vision.*

Owl

Human

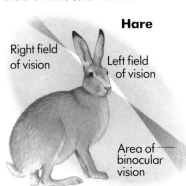

Hare

Right field of vision

Left field of vision

Area of binocular vision

◄ *Animals with eyes at the side of their heads can see all the way around, although they only have a small area of binocular vision.*

▶ In this breathing experiment, biochemists are able to examine the chemical changes that take place during respiration.

Antoine Lavoisier and the Marquis de Laplace were among the first scientists to carry out experiments in biochemistry. They demonstrated that animal respiration was chemically similar to combustion (burning). Lavoisier also demonstrated that food gives the body energy.

it helps animals to judge how far away an object is. Some animals with binocular vision, including humans, have eyes on the front of their heads giving them *stereoscopic vision*. The brain builds up a three-dimensional picture from the two eyes, enabling the animal to judge distance and depth accurately. The amount the eyes have to FOCUS on an object tells the brain how far away it is.

Biochemistry

The science of biochemistry, in which the methods of the chemist are used to find out about biological processes going on in living things, is a very complex and very important one. All plants and animals are made up of chemical COMPOUNDS and it is the task of the biochemist to discover the structure of these substances and work out what part they play in keeping the plant or animal alive. Carbohydrates, proteins, lipids (fats and oils), and nucleic acids such as DNA, which are all essential for cell building, are just some of the chemical molecules that are subjects of study by biochemists. They have used their knowledge in medicine, where GENETIC ENGINEERING is used to make vaccines against VIRAL DISEASES such as mumps. Biochemists are also working to find cures for such DISEASES as CANCER and AIDS.

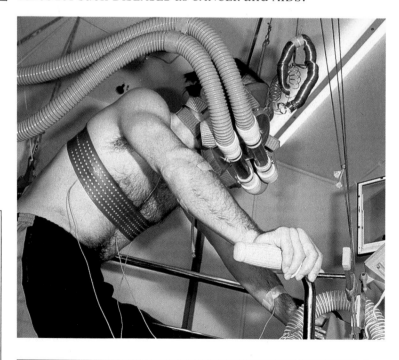

Biodegradable *See* Pollution

Biological control

Biological control is the system of killing pests with their natural enemies instead of with poisonous PESTICIDES. It is less damaging than spraying poison everywhere, as long as these enemies will not attack other organisms when they have got rid of the pests. Insects, fungi, and

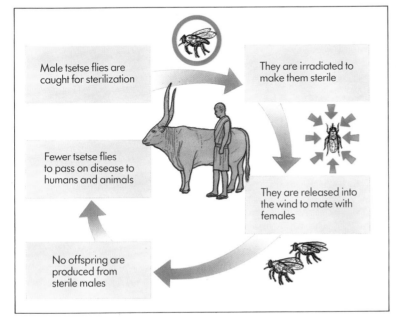

Male tsetse flies are caught for sterilization

They are irradiated to make them sterile

Fewer tsetse flies to pass on disease to humans and animals

They are released into the wind to mate with females

No offspring are produced from sterile males

▲ Tsetse flies like this are the cause of many problems in Africa, because they carry parasites and spread disease.

Answer to Binary question on page 62:
110101 is 53—one 32, one 16, one 4 and one 1 added together to give 53.

◄ Various attempts have been made to control tsetse flies. The method shown here uses radiation to sterilize males.

several larger animals have all been used to control pests. A small American moth successfully controlled the prickly pear cactus, which spread rapidly through Australia after being introduced from the United States. On the other hand, large toads were introduced from Hawaii to try and control the sugar cane beetle in Australia. They did not eat the beetles, they ate lots of other animals and many birds died when they tried to eat the poisonous toads. The toads have now become serious pests and the cane beetle still damages the sugar cane.

Biology

Biology is the study of living things. It is one of the three major divisions of science, with PHYSICS and CHEMISTRY. There are about two million known living species, and it is clearly impossible for a biologist to study them all. For this reason, biology is subdivided into several more specialized sciences each concerned with a particular form of life or activity. *See* pages 66 and 67.

SEE FOR YOURSELF
Look for a branch of a small tree or shrub that is covered with aphids. Find a ladybug and gently lift it onto the infested branch. You will notice that the ladybug will attack the aphids and eat them. This is a natural form of pest control.

BIOLOGY

The word biology is derived from Greek and means "knowledge of life." Originally, biologists studied the structure or anatomy of animals and plants, and tried to describe their relationships with each other. It was soon realized that some types of living organisms were closely related and could be grouped into families. Study of the anatomy of animals and humans led quickly to the development of surgery and to medicine becoming a science in its own right.

Specialized biologists are now more interested in how living organisms work and behave. Some of the most important work in biology is directed toward finding out how cells work. This type of study could lead to prevention or cure of many diseases. Biologists have learned how to manipulate and alter the genes inside the cell. The genes control how an organism lives and grows.

The study of genetics has enabled the development of new types of cultivated plants which are healthier and produce larger crops than the original types. Similarly, farm animals are bred to grow faster and reach a larger size, or produce more milk or wool.

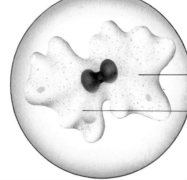

► Amoebas are single-celled animals. They have no particular shape and are made up of cytoplasm inside a thin membrane. They split into two to make new amoebas.

Cell membrane

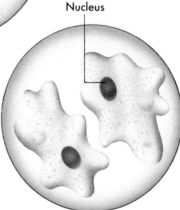

Amoeba cells dividing

Nucleus

BRANCHES OF STUDY
Anatomy Study of the structure of organisms
Botany Study of plants
Genetics Study of genes
Microbiology Study of microscopic organisms
Physiology Study of functions in living organisms
Zoology Study of animals

▲ Biologists study the growth of plants in plant breeding experiments. Plant tissue such as this can be grown from a single plant cell in a special mixture containing salts, vitamins, and growth substances.

SEE FOR YOURSELF
You need a narrow wooden-framed box with two glass sides. Make airholes in the top. Fill three-fourths of the box with several layers of different types of soils. Put leaves on the surface and add three or four earthworms. After a few days, the different layers of soil become mixed as the worms burrow up and down through them. The leaves will be pulled down and eaten.

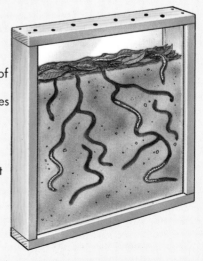

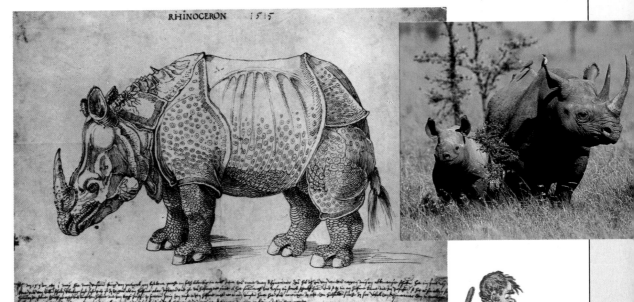

▲ *Compare the photograph of the rhinoceroses with this drawing made by Durer who had never seen a rhinoceros.*

▶ *When cowpox was used as a vaccination for smallpox in 1796, some people thought they would turn into cows.*

Milestones
1000 B.C. Ancient Egyptians study anatomy.
1300–1600 The importance of experimentation and observation is realized.
1735 Linnaeus classifies animals according to structural similarities. System still used today.
1800s Schlieden and Schwann show that the cell is the basic unit of life.
1859 Darwin publishes *On the Origin of Species*, which describes the theory of evolution and the principle of natural selection.
1953 Watson and Crick propose DNA structure.
1970s Biologists discover genetic engineering.

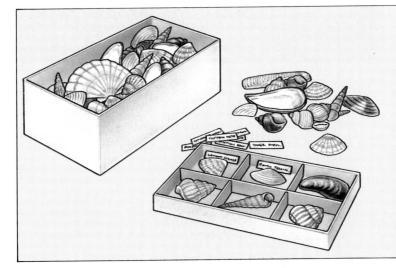

SEE FOR YOURSELF
Collect and classify different types of shells. Try to find out the name of each one. You can do this by looking in a book about shell identification, which you should be able to find in your local library. Make a box with separate compartments in it. Choose the best example of each shell type, put it into a compartment and label it with its name.

See also ANATOMY; BIOCHEMISTRY; BIOPHYSICS; BIOTECHNOLOGY; BOTANY; GENETICS; MEDICINE; PHYSIOLOGY; ZOOLOGY.

▲ *Deep within the ocean, where sunlight cannot reach, fish such as the angler fish use bioluminescence to find food or to attract a mate.*

▶ *Sometimes the sea appears to be lit by a strange light. The light actually comes from luminescent organisms including certain bacteria and fungi. Many squids are also luminescent. The light comes from the chemical processes that go on in the cells of these plants and animals.*

The chemical process used by animals to produce bioluminescence has been copied by scientists to produce cold lights that are used for emergency lighting and also in the glowing bracelets and necklaces that are often sold in fairgrounds. These lights glow brightly until the light-producing chemicals inside them are used up.

Bioluminescence

Bioluminescence is the production of light by living organisms, such as fireflies, glowworms, and many animals that live in the sea. The lights are produced by CHEMICAL REACTIONS in various parts of the animals' body. In these reactions, OXYGEN is combined with a substance called luciferin, and ENERGY is given out in the form of light. Unlike our electric lights, the lights give out almost no heat. The animals turn their lights on and off by altering the amount of oxygen reaching them. Some fungi and bacteria produce glowing light, but it is not yet clear how.

Fireflies (a kind of beetle) are found in many parts of the world. Some flash while resting on trees or on the ground, and others, while flying. The lights bring the males and females together for mating. Many deep-sea fish produce light to find their way or to attract prey.

Biophysics

Biophysics is a mixture of BIOLOGY and PHYSICS, in which scientists use the methods of the physicists to investigate living things. Biophysics is particularly important in investigating the way the human body works. The motion of the BLOOD being pumped around the body, the action of the HEART and other MUSCLES, and blood pressure are all processes and activities that can be explained by means of physics. The physical process of DIFFUSION, for example, is used to explain the exchange of gases between the blood and cells and the blood and the lungs.

◀ *Biophysics has taught us much about the function of the human body. Research into muscle movements has helped in the development of artificial limbs.*

An important area of biophysics is the detailed study of the structure of molecules in living things. One of the best known achievements in the field of biophysics was in 1953 when Francis Crick and James Watson constructed a model of the DNA (deoxyribonucleic acid) molecule. DNA is the hereditary material of life. The cells of living things contain DNA strands grouped together in chromosomes. The combination of DNA molecules determines the shape and form of offspring.

The effects of LIGHT, SOUND, PRESSURE, and other forces on living things, are also examined by biophysicists.

See also MOVEMENT AND MOTION.

Biotechnology

Biotechnology is the use of living things to make or change products. Its use dates from the first fermented drinks, such as wine and beer, made by people thousands of years ago. Microscopically small organisms such as bacteria can process some materials more efficiently than normal industrial methods.

Some fuels can be made by bacteria. For example, bacteria feeding on household waste produce a gas called METHANE. Methane burns easily and so it can be

---

SEE FOR YOURSELF
Add two tablespoons of live yogurt to a pint of milk and gently heat them together. This process causes the milk to ferment. The bacteria in the yogurt turns the lactose (milk sugar) in the milk into lactic acid, which makes the milk thicken. The result is yogurt.

One of the first examples of biotechnology can be traced back to 1916. A liquid called acetone (now also known as propanone) was needed to make explosives during World War I. The British Admiralty powder department found that it was possible to ferment grain by special bacteria, which enabled it to be converted into several substances, including acetone.

used as a fuel. At least five species of bacteria make cold water form ice crystals. This fact is being used to develop a quick test to identify food infected by salmonella, the bacteria which causes FOOD POISONING. The ice-producing part of a bacteria is transferred into a VIRUS that attacks salmonella. If ice forms when food is chilled this means the virus is inside salmonella. Similar tests for other food-spoiling bacteria are being developed. In the 1970s, the new field of GENETIC ENGINEERING provided scientists with a way of altering genetic material (the living material inside every cell of the body that controls GROWTH and development).

See also FERMENTATION; GENETICS; MICROORGANISMS.

Birth

Birth is the series of events that carry a baby from inside its mother's body to the outside world. A baby mammal develops in a muscular bag called the womb inside its mother's body. Birth begins when HORMONES in the mother's blood tell the muscles of the womb to start to contract and push the baby toward the womb's opening. In humans, we call this process labor, probably because it is hard work for the mother. As the contractions strengthen, the baby's head bursts the bag of fluid that protected it while it was inside its mother, and further contractions push the baby out of the mother's body.

Birth occurs in egg-laying animals when the offspring emerge (hatch) from the egg to begin life independently from their parents.

See also EMBRYO; REPRODUCTION.

▼ The female kangaroo gives birth to a tiny baby (a joey), which develops in its mother's pouch. There, the joey attaches itself to a teat and feeds on its mother's milk for several months.

Kangaroo

Teat

Joey in pouch

▶ A rabbit feeds its young (called kits or kittens) for only a few weeks after birth.

Bit and Byte

A bit is the smallest piece of information that a COMPUTER can process and a byte is a group of eight bits operating together as a single unit.

The word bit is formed from "binary digit." A bit can only have one of two values, zero or one. Every character (letter, number, or symbol) on a computer keyboard can be represented by a group of eight bits, a byte. For example, the letter A is represented by 01000001 and the number 8 by 00111000. Every character typed into a computer, or sent to another device such as a printer is represented in this way according to a standard code called American Standard Code for Information Interchange, or ASCII (pronounced askey).

> A byte is a space in the computer's memory that is occupied by one character. A group of four bits, or half a byte, is called a **nibble**.

Bitumen

Bitumen is a thick, sticky liquid or solid. It is brownish or black in color, consisting of HYDROCARBONS and the substances derived from them. There are various types of bitumen. Many types burn easily and are valuable as fuels. Some bitumen is produced by the DISTILLATION of crude oil. We also get it from naturally occurring MINERALS, such as bituminous (soft) coal, tar, asphalt, PETROLEUM, and naphtha. Bituminous sands, a major source of crude oil, contain up to 13 percent of bitumen. Bitumen is used in making oil, waterproof coating, electrical insulation, and in road building.

▲ Asphalt, a type of bitumen used to coat the surface of roads, wears well, is weatherproof, and is unharmed by most salts and acids.

Male seahorse

Young

Pouch

▶ The female seahorse lays its eggs in the male's pouch. They are released when they have developed. After a day, the young can look after themselves.

Parrot

◀ A young bird is born as an egg, which hatches after a few weeks. The mother feeds it until it can fly and feed itself.

Chick hatching from egg

71

Black body

The term "black body" means an object that absorbs all radiation that falls on it. It does not reflect radiation or give out any of its own. No perfect black body really exists. If a dull black surface is illuminated with light, almost all the light will be absorbed. In fact, it is because no light is reflected to our eyes that the surface appears black. A surface covered with lampblack will absorb about 97 percent of all light striking it.

Black hole

Space is not empty because it is invisible. Beams of light do not pass through it in straight lines, because GRAVITY can "bend" space so that light, or anything else (such as a spacecraft) passing through it, travels in a curve. Even around our huge and massive SUN, space is only curved by a small amount. But the force of gravity around the

Red supergiant

Star implodes

Black hole

Distorted light from distant stars behind the black hole

▲ Black holes are thought to be the final stage in a star's life. The star collapses inward in a huge implosion, leaving a "hole." It is seen as a hole because there is such a strong gravitational pull, no light can escape from the star.

kind of collapsed star known as a NEUTRON STAR can be so strong that the nearby space is curved into a complete circle. The light sent out from the star cannot escape into space so the star cannot be seen. It is a black hole.

Black holes can be detected. Single stars which behave like a member of a BINARY STAR system may have black holes as invisible companions, for example, the X-ray source, Cygnus X-1. There are probably millions of neutron star black holes in the MILKY WAY alone.

forces. He has shown that they give off particles and radiation until they explode and disappear. Hawking is generally thought to have made some of the most important finds about gravity since Einstein's theory of general relativity. He is currently working on combining gravity and a branch of physics known as quantum mechanics in a single theory that can explain the origin and structure of the universe. He holds the post of Lucasian professor of physics at Cambridge University, a post Sir Isaac Newton once held. Hawking has suffered from an incurable disease of the nervous system since the 1960s.

Stephen Hawking (1942–   )
Hawking is a British theoretical physicist. He is best known for his theories about black holes, which are invisible bodies in space with strong gravitational

A star becomes much smaller when it turns into a black hole. If the Sun, which is a star, was to become a black hole, its existing diameter of 865,000 miles (1,392,000 km) would have to be compressed into a diameter of just 4 miles (6 km). The idea of the black hole was first developed by the German astronomer Karl Schwarzschild in 1916.

Blast furnace

A blast furnace is a very important part of the IRON AND STEEL industry. Rock called ORE, rich in iron oxide, is loaded into the blast furnace together with measured amounts of coke (a kind of processed COAL) and limestone that helps to remove some of the impurities from

▶ Most of the iron from the furnace is used to make steel. The rest is sent to foundries to make wrought and cast iron.

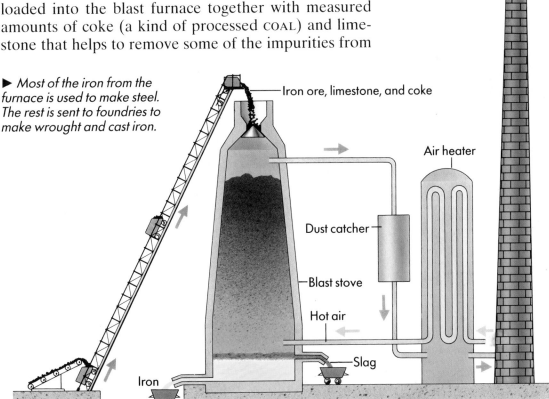

Waste gases

Iron ore, limestone, and coke

Air heater

Dust catcher

Blast stove

Hot air

Slag

Iron

the molten iron. Inside the furnace hot, dry air, at high PRESSURE, is blasted in through the bottom causing the coke to burn. This raises the temperature toward the bottom of the furnace to a point where the oxygen in the iron oxide reacts with CARBON MONOXIDE from the coke and the iron melts. Every three or four hours the molten iron is run off. The impurities (known as slag) floating on the surface of the iron are removed and the molten iron then flows into molds (known as pigs) to form large bars of "pig" iron that can be processed to make steel.

▲ *Blast furnaces are lined with firebrick that can withstand extremely high temperatures. When the lining wears out, the furnace must be shut down so that the lining can be replaced. The lining can last up to three years with 7,000 tons of iron and steel being processed each day.*

Bleaching

Bleaching is the process of removing the color from something. Sunlight is a very good bleach. This was a fact well known to the ancient Egyptians, who brightened and whitened their cloth by exposing it to the Sun. We still bleach textiles today, to prepare them for dyeing or to remove a DYE from them. Industrial bleaching is a chemical process using a bleach based on SODIUM chlorate. This compound breaks down in use to release OXYGEN, which is a very good bleaching agent. Almost all flour for baking used to be bleached, but now unbleached flour is available. In the home, bleaches are used for cleaning and brightening clothes and also as a disinfectant.

In the 17th century in Europe, oil of vitriol (sulfuric acid) was used to bleach the hair. It is now more sensibly used in car batteries. Today hydrogen peroxide is the main ingredient in products made for bleaching hair. It is also widely used to bleach cotton cloth.

Safety with bleach
Always handle bleach with great care. Bleach contains dangerous chemicals, which can be harmful to health if swallowed. Make sure you wear rubber gloves to protect your skin and, if necessary, safety goggles to protect your eyes. Wipe up any spillages immediately.

SEE FOR YOURSELF
Take an old colored T-shirt, roll it up and tie it tightly with string in about 4 or 5 places. Add a solution of bleach to a bowl of water. Put the T-shirt into the bowl and leave for 30 minutes. Take it out of the solution and rinse it in cold water. Untie the strings and rinse again. The bleach has removed the color from the parts of the T-shirt not covered by strings.

BLOOD

Blood is the vital life-sustaining liquid that is found in the bodies of all large animals. It is pumped around the body by the heart through a network of arteries, veins, and capillaries. The kidneys control the amount of water in the blood and expel, as urine, the waste products of the body. The blood carries oxygen and food materials from the digestive system to the body tissues.

In humans about 20 percent of body weight is blood and other fluids not included in the body cells. The basis of blood is a straw-colored liquid called plasma, in which the food materials, waste products, hormones, etc. are dissolved. Plasma can pass through the cell walls. It has millions of blood cells floating in it which have two main functions: carrying oxygen and fighting disease. In vertebrates, blood is red because of flat disk-shaped red cells or erthrocytes. These contain hemoglobin, which absorbs oxygen in the lungs, and releases it all over the body. The disease-fighting cells are known as white cells or leucocytes. Some attack invading germs and clear away dead cells, others produce antibodies that kill the germs and destroy their poisons. Blood platelets are very small cells which make the blood clot.

In humans, everyone belongs to one of four blood groups (A, B, O, and AB). The letters indicate the presence or absence of particular substances in the blood. Some blood groups cannot be mixed; if they are, the blood sticks together.

◄ *This test tube shows the parts of blood after they have been separated in a centrifuge, an instrument that spins the blood sample at high speed.*

Plasma

White blood cells and platelets

Red blood cells

1 Hemoglobin
2 Hemoerythrin
3 Hemocyanin
4 Chlorocruorin

▲ *Animal blood is not always red. Different blood pigments have different colors. Hemoglobin is the most common. Hemocyanin is bluish and is found in some invertebrates.*

◄ *The three types of blood cells found in human blood. Red blood cells are doughnut-shaped, white blood cells are round, and platelets are disk-shaped. Anemia is a condition in which the number of red blood cells falls below normal. The shortage of oxygen causes tiredness and weakness.*

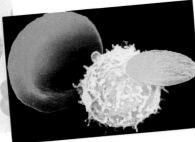

▲ *White blood cells have a nucleus, unlike red blood cells. Here, the nucleus of the white blood cells has been stained purple.*

▼ *During a blood transfusion a patient must be given the right blood group. This table shows which blood groups can be mixed.*

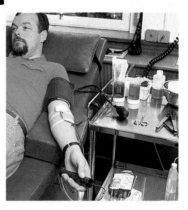

	Blood group	Antigens on red cells	Antibodies in plasma	Can receive blood type
	A	A	B	A and O
	B	B	A	B and O
Universal recipient	AB	A and B	none	A, B, AB, O
Universal donor	O	none	A and B	O

▲ *Donated blood is stored in blood banks for use in transfusions.*

See also AIDS; ANTIBODIES AND ANTIGENS; CIRCULATION; HEART.

▲ *Doctors analyze pictures of organs in a patient's body using the computerized tomography system.*

Body scanner

A body scanner is a machine used in MEDICINE to produce pictures of the inside of the body. There are two basic types of scanner. The first uses a process called computerized tomography (CT). A thin beam of X-RAYS is fired through the body at different angles. The results registered by X-ray detectors are analyzed by a COMPUTER which adds up all the individual results to make a picture of a slice through the body. The second type of scanner uses a process called magnetic resonance (MR). Hydrogen particles in the body move a minute amount in a magnetic field and then give out a field of their own. This can be detected by sensors in the MR scanner and, as in a CT scanner, analyzed by computer to produce a picture of a slice through the body.

Bohr, Niels *See* Atom

Boiling point

The boiling point of a substance is the TEMPERATURE at which it changes from a LIQUID to a GAS or VAPOR. Boiling occurs because the MOLECULES which make up the liquid move around more quickly as the temperature rises, until they escape from the liquid into the gas. Lighter molecules move around faster than heavier ones and some sorts of molecules stick together in liquid more strongly than others. This means that the boiling points of different substances can be very different.

See also EVAPORATION; FREEZING POINT; MELTING POINT.

▲ *When a pan of water boils water vapor is released. The water vapor is only visible when it condenses and is called steam.*

▶ *The boiling point of a liquid depends on air pressure. Air pressure decreases with altitude so water, which normally boils at 212°F (100°C), boils at 162°F (72°C) at 10,000 feet (3,000 m) above sea level.*

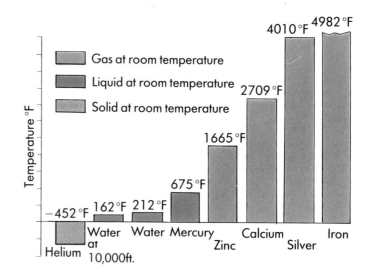

Bond, chemical

Chemical bonds hold together the atoms in compounds, and these bonds cannot easily be broken. There are two main types of bond: *ionic bonds* and *covalent bonds*. An atom is made of a positively charged nucleus, around which circle negatively charged electrons. Ionic bonds are made by the transfer of electrons from one atom to one or more other atoms. For example, the elements sodium and chlorine bond together to form the compound sodium chloride (common salt). When the two elements are brought together, each sodium atom loses a single electron to a chlorine atom, and becomes positive. The chlorine atom, having gained an electron, becomes negative. Positive and negative bodies attract each other, so the sodium and chlorine atoms become bonded together to make sodium chloride. In covalent bonding, two or more atoms join by *sharing* pairs of electrons. For example, carbon atoms and oxygen atoms combine by sharing electrons to make carbon dioxide.

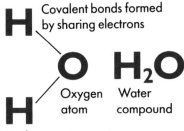

▲ *In ionic bonding* (top) *one atom takes an electron from another atom. In covalent bonding, electrons are shared.*

Bone

Bone is the very hard, living material that makes up the SKELETONS of most vertebrates. The skeleton holds our bodies together and supports our weight. Bones also protect important organs. There are 206 bones in the adult human body. The largest is the femur, which runs from the hip to the knee. Bones contain tiny living CELLS, which is why bones can mend themselves. The cells produce a tough PROTEIN called collagen which gives the bones their strength, and they secrete calcium and phosphorus salts which give the bones their hardness.

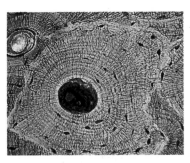

◀ *The skeleton which supports humans is made up of two kinds of bones: the long bones, which are mainly in the arms and the legs, and the short bones in, for example, the skull and the spine. This bone cell is part of the compact bone tissue forming the solid, outer part of the femur or thigh bone.*

Linus Pauling (1901–)
A U.S. chemist, Linus Pauling won the 1954 Nobel Prize for Chemistry for his work on chemical bonding. He calculated the energies needed to bind atoms in a molecule, the distances between the atoms, and the angles at which bonds form. Also he won the Nobel Prize for Peace in 1962.

Botany

Botany is the study of plants. *See* pages 78 and 79.

BOTANY

Botany is a very important branch of biology covering the study of plants. Only plants can manufacture food from simple materials, using the energy of the Sun, so every food chain begins with a plant, and every animal on Earth, including people, depends on plant life for its food. Plants also recycle the air that we breathe, absorbing much of the carbon dioxide and giving out the oxygen that we need. We get many of our clothes and medicines from plants; trees provide timber which is needed for houses, furniture, and making paper. Much of the world's population relies on wood for fuel, for warmth, and cooking.

The Greeks began the serious study of plants over 2,000 years ago, but it was not until microscopes were invented that people really began to learn how plants are constructed. Today more powerful microscopes and advances in biochemistry have enabled us to discover more about what goes on inside plants. It was only in the 18th century that a Swedish naturalist named Linnaeus started to name plants systematically. Now we know that there are over 300,000 species of plants in the world. Not surprisingly, botany is divided into many branches, and botanists usually specialize in one branch or another. Many work in agriculture and horticulture, helping us to grow better crops.

▲ Many plants produce spores (top) *which can develop into new plants. In ferns* (bottom), *the spores are held under the leaves.*

SEE FOR YOURSELF
Draw pictures of several plants. Carefully copy the shape of flower petals and leaves. Write the name of the plant and where you found it by each drawing. You can find most of the names of plants in a field guide or other plant book. See if you can label the parts of the flowers. Look under FLOWER in this encyclopedia if you need help with this.

small flower

short fruit

stalked

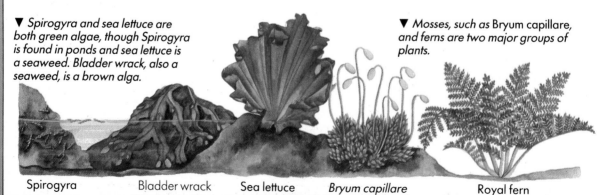

▼ *Spirogyra and sea lettuce are both green algae, though Spirogyra is found in ponds and sea lettuce is a seaweed. Bladder wrack, also a seaweed, is a brown alga.*

▼ *Mosses, such as Bryum capillare, and ferns are two major groups of plants.*

Spirogyra   Bladder wrack   Sea lettuce   *Bryum capillare*   Royal fern

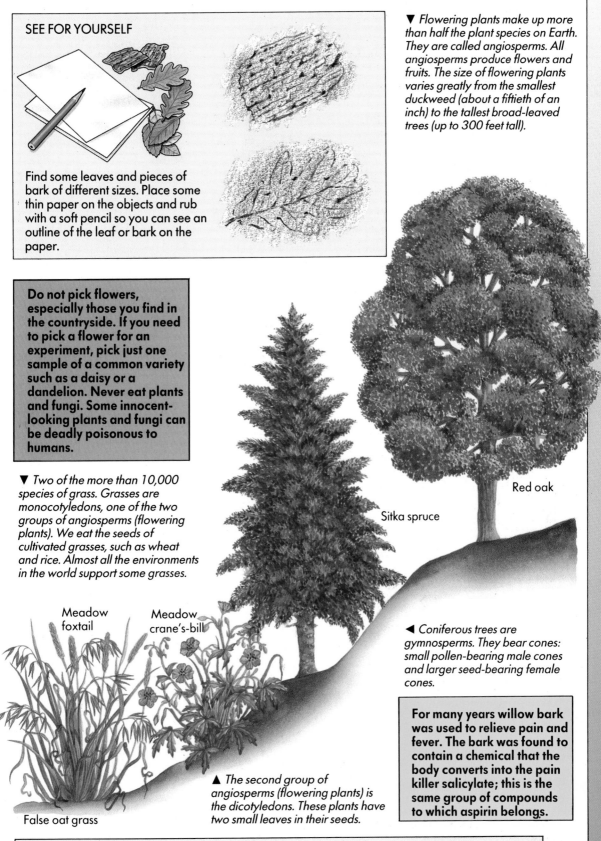

SEE FOR YOURSELF

Find some leaves and pieces of bark of different sizes. Place some thin paper on the objects and rub with a soft pencil so you can see an outline of the leaf or bark on the paper.

▼ *Flowering plants make up more than half the plant species on Earth. They are called angiosperms. All angiosperms produce flowers and fruits. The size of flowering plants varies greatly from the smallest duckweed (about a fiftieth of an inch) to the tallest broad-leaved trees (up to 300 feet tall).*

Do not pick flowers, especially those you find in the countryside. If you need to pick a flower for an experiment, pick just one sample of a common variety such as a daisy or a dandelion. Never eat plants and fungi. Some innocent-looking plants and fungi can be deadly poisonous to humans.

▼ *Two of the more than 10,000 species of grass. Grasses are monocotyledons, one of the two groups of angiosperms (flowering plants). We eat the seeds of cultivated grasses, such as wheat and rice. Almost all the environments in the world support some grasses.*

Red oak

Sitka spruce

Meadow foxtail

Meadow crane's-bill

◄ *Coniferous trees are gymnosperms. They bear cones: small pollen-bearing male cones and larger seed-bearing female cones.*

For many years willow bark was used to relieve pain and fever. The bark was found to contain a chemical that the body converts into the pain killer salicylate; this is the same group of compounds to which aspirin belongs.

▲ *The second group of angiosperms (flowering plants) is the dicotyledons. These plants have two small leaves in their seeds.*

False oat grass

See also AGRICULTURE; BIOLOGY; CHLOROPHYLL; COTYLEDON; CYTOLOGY; HORTICULTURE; LEAVES; MICROSCOPE; ORGANISM; SPECIES; ZOOLOGY.

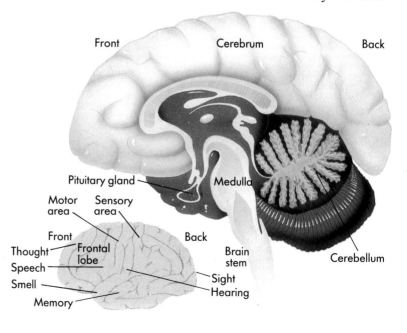

▲ *Tycho Brahe, the astronomer who observed the planets.*

The brain contains more than 10 billion neurons with complex pathways linking our senses, our movements, and memory. The signals transmitted through these routes enable us to eat, walk, lift loads, speak, make decisions, and so on.

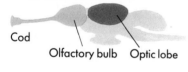

Cod

Olfactory bulb   Optic lobe

Frog

Horse

▲ *The brains of lesser-evolved animals have clearer functional divisions than the human brain. The olfactory bulb is associated with smell, and the optic lobe with sight.*

▶ *The largest area of the human brain is the cerebrum, which controls conscious feeling and voluntary movements. (Right) Different areas of the cerebrum control the various different functions.*

Boyle, Robert *See* Chemistry

Brahe, Tycho

Tycho Brahe (1546–1601), a Danish astronomer, lived before the TELESCOPE was invented and made the most accurate observations with the naked eye ever known. Like most astronomers of the time, he was employed by his king as an astrologer who had to cast horoscopes, but his real interest was the movement of the PLANETS. He believed that the planets orbit the Sun, but he also thought that the Sun orbits the Earth and that our planet was the center of the UNIVERSE. Brahe set out to prove this by observing the positions of the planets.

After his death the observations reached the hands of Johannes KEPLER, who was studying the same problem. Brahe's naked eye observations helped Kepler prove that the Earth also revolves around the Sun, and that the planets move in ellipses, not circles.

Brain

The brain is the largest and most important part of an animal's nervous system. In vertebrates, the brain is held in place and protected by the skull. The brains of invertebrates are generally much simpler and are often no more than swellings of NERVES at the head end.

The brain's function is to control the body. It uses

Front   Cerebrum   Back

Pituitary gland   Medulla

Motor area   Sensory area

Front   Back

Thought   Frontal lobe
Speech   Brain stem
Smell   Sight
    Hearing
Memory

Cerebellum

information from sense organs such as the EYES and the EARS. It then decides what action is needed and sends messages through the nerves to the MUSCLES or GLANDS. The brain can also store information for use at a later date. In other words, it can learn and remember things. Most animals can learn, but humans are better at learning because their brains are relatively larger than those of other animals. Our brains have also developed language for communication and for expressing ideas.
See also INSTINCT; LEARNING; SENSES.

Brass *See* Alloy

Breathing

All animals need OXYGEN to burn up food and produce ENERGY in their bodies. This is called respiration, and the process of getting the oxygen into the body is called breathing. Land-living vertebrates breathe with LUNGS, which are filled with air and then emptied again by

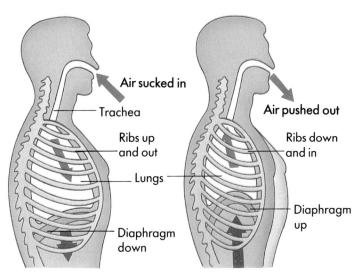

Air sucked in
Trachea
Ribs up and out
Lungs
Diaphragm down

Air pushed out
Ribs down and in
Diaphragm up

muscular movements of the chest and throat. In the lungs, the oxygen from the air passes into the animal's BLOOD and is then carried around the body. Fish breathe with GILLS which take oxygen from water that has been sucked in through the mouth. Insects breathe through tiny holes called spiracles that are found in a line on each side of the body. The air is carried right into the insect's body by a network of slender tubes. Active insects like wasps often also use bellowlike movements of their bodies to pump the air along.

Neuron A nerve cell in the nervous system.
Cerebellum This controls muscles and balance.
Medulla This controls involuntary activities such as breathing.
Cerebral hemisphere The cerebrum is divided into left and right hemispheres connected in the middle by bundles of nerve fibers.

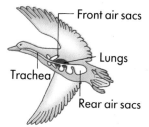

▲ Birds breathe using a system of air sacs as well as lungs.

Front air sacs
Lungs
Trachea
Rear air sacs

◄ Breathing in humans is assisted by the diaphragm. It contracts (moves down) when we breathe in, and is relaxed when we breathe out.

SEE FOR YOURSELF
Push a balloon through the top of a plastic bottle. Tape the balloon's mouth tightly around the neck of the bottle. Cut the end off the bottle and tape a piece of balloon over the bottom. Pull the rubber down to give the effect of the diaphragm contracting. The pressure in the bottle falls and the balloon is filled with air.

Bos primigenius
Ancestor of modern cattle

Aberdeen Angus
Domestic descendant

▲ *Modern cattle have been bred so that they produce more meat and less fat.*

▶ *Breeders have developed varieties of strawberry plants that can produce large, juicy, disease-resistant fruit throughout the summer and autumn months.*

▼ *Shafts of sunlight show up the particles of dust and smoke in the air. Particles are struck by fast-moving, invisible molecules of gases in the air, which cause them to move about at random. This is called Brownian motion.*

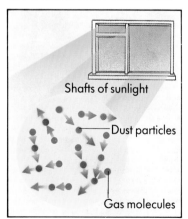

Shafts of sunlight

Dust particles

Gas molecules

Breeding

Breeding means producing offspring. People have controlled the REPRODUCTION of plants and animals so that they develop features that we consider useful. A Jersey cow, for example, can produce at least 10 gallons of milk every day, but a wild cow can produce only about one gallon of milk in a day (enough to feed its calf). Jersey cows give so much milk because dairy farmers in the past have carefully picked out those cows that gave the most milk, and allowed only these cows to mate and produce calves. By repeating this process year after year, the farmers eventually produced the Jersey breed. By selecting only animals or plants with particular features, people have bred hundreds of horses, garden flowers, and crops, and can produce varieties of plants that are resistant to various diseases.

Cultivated strawberry plant

Wild strawberry plant

Bridges *See* Construction

Bronze *See* Alloy

Brownian motion

Brownian motion is the continual random movement of microscopic particles suspended in a LIQUID or GAS. The particles move as if being hit by the fluid. In fact, that is just what is happening. Molecules in the fluid constantly move around and bump into the particles, causing them to move. The hotter the fluid is, the faster the particles vibrate because the molecules are moving faster too. The movement is in any direction, and this is why particles of a material will, in time, spread evenly throughout a fluid. Dust, smoke, and smells spread through air in this way. Brownian motion was discovered by Robert Brown (1773–1858), a Scottish botanist and physicist, while studying the motion of pollen grains in water in 1827. Brownian motion was seen as positive evidence of the existence of ATOMS and MOLECULES.

Bubbles

A bubble is a spherical region of GAS, such as AIR, found inside a liquid or surrounded by a thin film of liquid. Water with detergent in it forms thin films well because the detergent molecules tend to line themselves up with one end pointing in and the other, out, making the surface of the liquid more stable. Soap bubbles are shaped by the balance between the outward PRESSURE of the gas inside and the inward force of SURFACE TENSION which tends to make the surface shrink. The thickness of the liquid layer is due to the detergent molecules and is the same for bubbles of different sizes; COLORS can be seen because of the DIFFRACTION of light through the layer.

SEE FOR YOURSELF
Mix 2 tablespoons of liquid soap with 6 tablespoons of water. Make different sized bubble frames out of thin wire. Dip a frame into the solution and blow through it gently.

◀ Diffraction of light on the surface of a bubble makes colored patterns.

Bunsen burner

The bunsen burner produces a flame by burning NATURAL GAS from a small metal pipe. The TEMPERATURE and intensity of the flame can be adjusted by controlling the air supply. Since its invention in 1850 by the German scientist Robert Wilhelm Bunsen (1811–1899), it has provided an instant and efficient source of heat for scientific experiments. It is a familiar item in laboratories around the world.

See also BURNING; COMBUSTION; INSTRUMENTS, SCIENTIFIC.

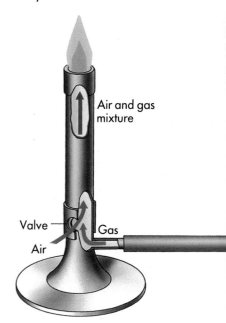

Air and gas mixture

Valve

Gas

Air

▲ With the air valve open, the gas flowing through a bunsen burner burns completely and produces a flame that is very hot, about 2,700°F (1,482°C).

Buoyancy

Buoyancy is the name given to the upward FORCE exerted on an object when it is in a liquid or gas (a fluid). This force acts on an object whether it floats or sinks. Pick up a heavy stone under water and you will find it lighter than when you lift it out of the water. Whether a body floats or sinks depends on its density. If two bodies of different materials weigh the same, the smaller one is the denser of the two. Fluids have density too. If two fluids occupy the same space, the one that weighs more is the denser. If a solid body is immersed in a fluid, it pushes some of the fluid aside. If the solid is denser than the fluid, it will sink. Archimedes' principle says that if something is immersed in a fluid, the buoyant force is equal to the weight of the fluid it pushes aside.
See also ARCHIMEDES; FLOTATION.

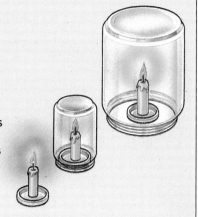

▼ *In laboratories, technicians test different materials to find the temperatures that the materials must be heated to before they burst into flames and burn.*

Burning

Burning is the common word for what chemists call COMBUSTION. It produces light and heat. If light and heat are not produced, the process is called OXIDATION. Oxygen is usually needed for burning, although oxygen itself does not burn — it reacts chemically with the fuel to give out chemical energy. Very rapid burning is called an explosion. Controlled burning of FUEL containing HYDROCARBONS such as oil, coal, and natural gas helps to produce energy for heating and the production of ELECTRICITY.
See also ENERGY; OXIDATION AND REDUCTION.

Butane *See* Propane

Cable television *See* Television

Caffeine

Caffeine is a chemical COMPOUND of carbon, nitrogen, hydrogen, and oxygen. It is an odorless, crystalline SOLID, slightly bitter to the taste and is SOLUBLE in water and alcohol. Caffeine occurs naturally in small amounts in tea, coffee, cacao (chocolate tree), and cola nuts but can also be made artificially. Caffeine speeds up the blood CIRCULATION and the working of the nervous system. In small doses, it is not thought to have ill effects, but when taken in excess it can cause nervousness, loss of sleep, headaches, and digestive trouble.

Cola drinks contain caffeine (about 2 percent) from the cola nut, a nut from the tropical cola tree. In South America and Africa the nuts are chewed to fight fatigue. An average cup of coffee may contain four-thousandths of an ounce of caffeine, a harmless amount on its own but too much if you drink 20 cups a day.

Calcium

Calcium is a softish, silvery white metallic ELEMENT that reacts readily with water or oxygen. It makes up 3.6 percent of the Earth's crust and is found in nature as COMPOUNDS. Calcium carbonate forms limestone, CHALK, and marble. Calcium sulfate occurs as gypsum. Pure calcium, used in certain ALLOYS, is obtained by passing an electric current through molten calcium chloride. Calcium and its compounds have many industrial uses. Among the most important compounds are calcium oxide (lime); calcium chloride; calcium fluoride, and calcium sulfate (used in CEMENT and plaster). Calcium compounds, present in green vegetables and milk, are essential for strong bones and teeth.

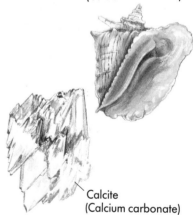

Seashell
(Calcium carbonate)

Calcite
(Calcium carbonate)

▲ The mineral calcium carbonate forms the shells of mollusks and other sea animals, as well as the pearls of oysters and eggshells. It also makes up 4 to 6 percent of the Moon.

◄ Under an electron microscope calcium sulfate crystals appear as needlelike structures. They form part of the "fur" found on the inside of kettles in hard water areas.

The first true electronic calculator was produced in Britain by the Bell Punch Company in 1963. It had a display 8 inches wide, which is as wide as this book. It could perform four functions: addition, subtraction, multiplication, and division.

Calculator

A calculator is an electronic device used for calculations. It consists of a set of numbered keys and a display that shows which keys have been pressed as well as the answers to the calculations. Inside the calculator is an INTEGRATED CIRCUIT that can perform calculations much more quickly than a person. Some calculators are almost as small and thin as credit cards. The simplest calculators can carry out simple ARITHMETIC functions (addition, subtraction, multiplication, and division). More advanced calculators can perform other functions. Some can be programmed like a COMPUTER. Up to 10,000 instructions may be executed during every second a calculator is in use. The first electronic calculators were sold in 1971. Most of them were made in Japan.

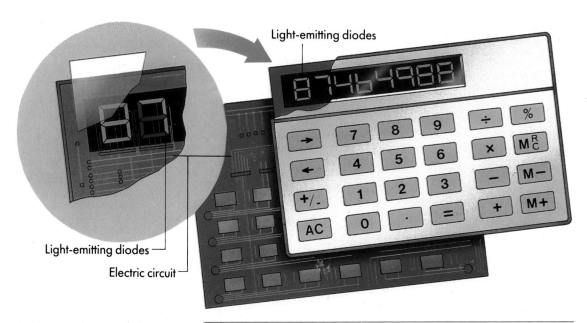

Light-emitting diodes

Light-emitting diodes

Electric circuit

▲ Most modern pocket calculators use silicon chips and have a light-emitting diode display. This calculator can add, subtract, multiply, and divide as fast as we can press the keys. More advanced calculators can also do more difficult scientific calculations.

Calendar

Calendars are used to measure and record the passage of TIME. For thousands of years most calendars were based on either the observation of the phases of the MOON or the Earth's orbit around the Sun. Julius Caesar introduced the Julian calendar in 46 B.C., which is the basis of the one we use today. It had a 365-day year, with one extra day added every fourth, or leap, year because the solar year, the time the Earth takes to go around the Sun, is about 365¼ days. This was inaccurate because the calendar year was about 11 minutes longer than the solar year. The difference soon became noticeable, reaching 10 days in 1582. Pope Gregory dropped the extra 10 days in that year, instructing that October 5 should become October 15. He said leap years should not happen on centenary years except for multiples of 400, which is why the year 2000, unlike 1900 and 1800, will be a leap year.

Calorie *See* Joule

Camcorder *See* Video camera

Camera

A camera is a device for taking photographs. It has an opening called an aperture in one side to let light in and light-sensitive FILM on the opposite side to register the image. A LENS in front of the aperture focuses the light into a sharp image on the film. The earliest cameras made in the 19th century were large and heavy. They were called plate cameras because they used copper or, more commonly, glass plates coated with chemicals to register the image. A photograph was taken by removing the lens cap to let light enter the camera for perhaps 30 seconds and then replacing the cap. People had to stay still for a long time to have their photographs taken.

Most modern cameras use rolls of film instead of plates, but disk cameras use disks of film. Film is usually taken out of the camera and developed with chemicals to

◄ *The 20 days in the Aztec month are represented in the inner ring of this calendar stone.*

A 13-month year is one of the proposals for the reform of the present calendar. Each month would be exactly 4 weeks long. An extra month called Sol would be placed between June and July. A "Year Day" at the end of the year would not belong to a week or month, and every four years a "Leap-Year Day" would be added before July 1.

SEE FOR YOURSELF
Paint the inside of a box and its lid black. Cut out a square from the side and stick tracing paper or photographic paper over the opening, the "screen." Make a small hole, the "viewer," in the opposite side of the box. Point the "viewer" at a well lit object.

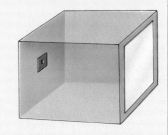

An upside down image of the object appears on the screen. Light rays from the object travel in straight lines and cross as they pass through the hole.

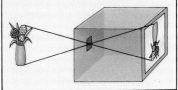

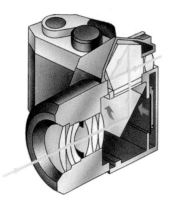

▲ *When a photograph is being taken by an SLR camera, seen here in cross section, the mirror lifts up, the shutter opens to expose the film and closes again. The light makes an upside down picture of the image on the film. The film is wound on and later developed and made into negatives from which prints are made.*

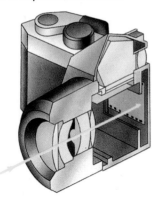

▲ *In a camera, the light passes through the lens, then through the diaphragm, which is adjusted to let in the correct amount of light.*

SLR cameras with automatic shutter releases and automatic film winders can take several pictures every second. The fastest camera in the world, used in scientific research at London's Imperial College of Science and Technology, can process 33 billion images every second.

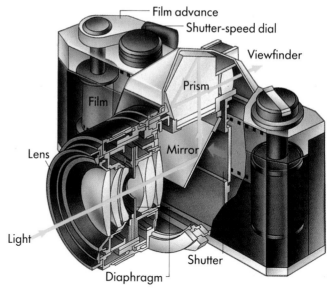

▲ *In a Single Lens Reflex (SLR) camera there is a mirror which reflects the image seen through the lens up to the viewfinder.*

reveal the images on it. The exception is the instant picture camera, for example a POLAROID CAMERA, which produces photographs that develop by themselves. All but the simplest cameras allow the photographer to control the amount of light that enters the camera by changing the size of the aperture and the length of time that the shutter is open (the shutter speed).

A very popular type of camera is the Single Lens Reflex (SLR). Light entering the lens of an SLR camera is reflected by a mirror up to the top of the camera where it is reflected again to emerge through the eyepiece. This enables the photographer to see the same image that will form the picture on the film. Other cameras have a separate lens and viewfinder.

See also DAGUERREOTYPE; FOCUS; PHOTOGRAPHY.

Camouflage

Camouflage is an ADAPTATION of many animals that makes them difficult to be seen. Some animals hide from their enemies and others from their prey. Camouflage usually involves colors and disruptive markings, which help the animals to blend in with their backgrounds so that they are not noticed. Many caterpillars are green and very difficult to see when they are sitting on leaves, while many moths that rest on tree trunks have barklike patterns on their wings. Even big animals like antelopes are camouflaged. Their backs are dark but underneath

◄ Some World War I ships had disruptive stripes to break up their outlines against the sea.

▲ The zebra's stripes are disruptive markings which make it less obvious to its grassland predators.

they are usually very pale. This counteracts the shadows caused by the overhead Sun, making the animals look flat, helping them to merge into the background. Chameleons, flatfishes, and shrimps change colors to match different backgrounds. Stick insects take their camouflage further and actually look like twigs. This is called protective resemblance. The animals' enemies can see them, but take no notice because they are deceived. *See also* NATURAL SELECTION.

▲ The leaf insect is the same color as leaves. It has leaflike markings on its wings, which help camouflage it from predators.

Cancer

Cancer is a disease of the body CELLS in which their functioning and REPRODUCTION is uncontrolled. When a cell turns cancerous or malignant, it will not work properly, and it divides rapidly to produce more cells. A collection of cancerous cells is called a tumor. These cells are able to break away and are carried in the blood to other parts of the body, where they continue to grow.

◄ Radiation therapy is used to destroy cancer cells with X-rays or particles from radioactive elements such as cobalt-60.

Tumor A buildup or mass of tissue where the reproductive process of the cells is abnormal.
Benign tumor A tumor that does not spread into the surrounding healthy tissues of the body.
Malignant tumor A tumor that invades. It increases in size and eventually destroys surrounding healthy tissue.

Carcinogen A cancer-causing substance. It attacks normal cells, and may eventually cause some of them to turn cancerous.
Carcinoma Cancer that starts to grow in tissue that forms the skin and linings of inner organs.
Sarcoma Cancer that starts to grow in the tissue that forms the body's supporting structures, such as the bones and the cartilage.

Usually, cells are replaced as they become old and inefficient. The development of these new cells is controlled so that the new cells are identical to the old ones. In cancer, so many abnormal cells are produced that they interfere with normal body functions and if untreated may cause very severe illness or death.

The causes are not clear, but chemicals such as tar from cigarettes and many other substances are known to change normal cells into cancer cells. Cancer can be treated by surgery, by very powerful DRUGS, or by radiation which damages the affected cells. Though people still die from cancer, many are surviving due to the improvement and success of modern treatments.

Canning

Canning is the most common way of preserving food. The food is sealed inside a METAL can of ALUMINUM or thin STEEL and then heated to over 212°F (100°C). This kills any MICROORGANISMS that might spoil the food. Since the can is heated after sealing, no new organisms can affect the food before the can is opened.

▼ The filling and sealing of cans is generally done by machines. Modern commercial machines are able to fill up to 1,200 cans in one minute.

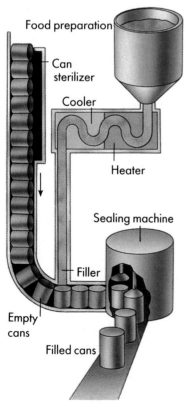

Food preparation
Can sterilizer
Cooler
Heater
Sealing machine
Filler
Empty cans
Filled cans

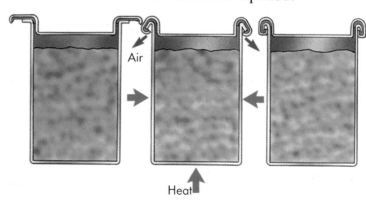

Air

Heat

▲ After being filled up with the prepared food, some of the air is removed from the can. It is then sealed and heated to destroy microorganisms before being rapidly cooled.

In 1809, a Frenchman named Nicholas Appert successfully preserved food by sealing it inside a glass container. The containers were easily broken and unsuitable for packaging food. The following year Peter Durand, an Englishman, produced the first TIN cans which were used for food storage. Foods of many different kinds are canned in canning factories. The first canning factory was opened in 1819 in the United States and soldiers in the Civil War (1861–1865) ate canned food.

Capacitor

Capacitors store electrical charge. The simplest capacitor consists of two metal plates separated by an electrical INSULATOR called a dielectric. If each plate is connected to a battery terminal, a positive charge is stored on one plate and a negative charge on the other. The amount of charge the device can store for a given voltage difference is called the *capacitance*; for the capacitance to be large, the plates have to be large and close together.

Capacitors can smooth the flow of a fluctuating current and variable capacitors are used in circuits that tune

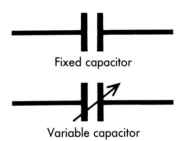

▲ *The standard symbols for fixed and variable capacitors are used in circuit diagrams. Variable capacitors have movable plates.*

◀ *Capacitors are just one of the components of electric circuits. They can block the flow of a direct current, but allow an alternating current to flow through them.*

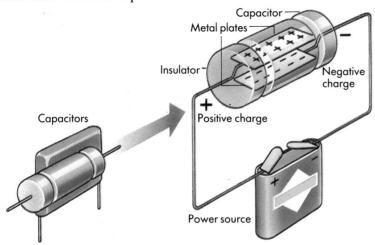

a radio or television to the desired station. They can also block the flow of a direct current and allow an alternating current to pass.

See also CIRCUIT, ELECTRIC; ELECTRICITY.

Capillary action

Capillary action is the process which causes LIQUID in the soil to rise up through the roots and stems of plants and water to seep through a paper towel. If one end of a narrow tube is placed in water, the water rises up the tube; the narrower the tube the higher the water will rise. This is caused by an attraction between the MOLECULES at the surface of the liquid and the molecules of the glass of the tube. It is called SURFACE TENSION. The liquid rises until the weight of the liquid balances the surface tension.

When liquid molecules at the surface attract each other more than they do the wall of the tube, surface tension causes the liquid to be depressed. Mercury acts like this. It sinks in a narrow glass tube.

SEE FOR YOURSELF
Split the stem of a flower, such as a carnation. Place one end of the stem into a jar of colored water and the other end into plain water. The flower "sucks up" the water through narrow tubes in its stem. The capillary action overcomes the pull of gravity.

$$C_nH_{2n}O_n$$

▲ *Many carbohydrates have this general formula. The n stands for a number; for example, in glucose the n is 6 – glucose has the formula $C_6H_{12}O_6$.*

Common Sources of Carbohydrates:
Sugars: syrup, candy, cake, chocolate, ice cream, ketchup, fruit, cola.
Starches: potatoes, bread, cake, flour, spaghetti, rice.
Fiber: corn, branflakes, fruit, vegetables, brown rice, nuts.

Carbohydrate

Carbohydrates are chemical COMPOUNDS containing only the elements carbon, hydrogen, and oxygen. There is little carbohydrate present in the body, and we obtain this important food substance from plants. The various SUGARS are carbohydrates and are an important source of ENERGY in our food. They are easily absorbed from the digestive system where they are converted into glucose and fructose, which release energy when broken down by oxygen. Starch is also a carbohydrate but must be broken down by digestive ENZYMES into simpler sugars before it can be absorbed. This process begins in the mouth, with the enzymes in the saliva. If you chew a piece of bread for a few minutes, you will notice that it begins to taste sweet. This happens because the starch in the flour used to make the bread is gradually being converted by enzymes into sugar. A carbohydrate called CELLULOSE, commonly known as fiber, helps to keep the bowels healthy. It consists mostly of the cell walls remaining in plant foods. These cannot be digested, and pass through the system almost unchanged.

Rice

Polished rice grains

Sugar beet

Sugar

Sugar cubes

Sugar cane

Potatoes

Bananas

Fries

Spaghetti

Bread

Flour

Pasta

Wheat

▲ *Carbohydrates are formed in green plants during photosynthesis and are a vital source of fuel for both plants and animals. About half the food we eat should be made up of carbohydrates.*

Carbon cycle

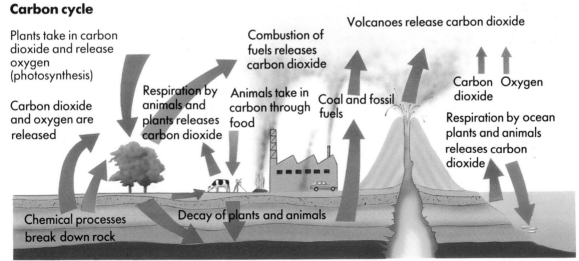

Plants take in carbon dioxide and release oxygen (photosynthesis)

Carbon dioxide and oxygen are released

Respiration by animals and plants releases carbon dioxide

Combustion of fuels releases carbon dioxide

Volcanoes release carbon dioxide

Animals take in carbon through food

Coal and fossil fuels

Carbon dioxide Oxygen

Respiration by ocean plants and animals releases carbon dioxide

Chemical processes break down rock

Decay of plants and animals

Carbon

Carbon is an important nonmetallic ELEMENT. It is found naturally in both the pure form and in combination with other elements. Carbon occurs in three forms: the DIAMOND, graphite, and amorphous carbon which has a nonregular structure. In the diamond, the carbon atoms are arranged regularly in a framework called a lattice, and in graphite, in layers. Amorphous carbon includes wood or animal CHARCOAL and carbon black (a soot). Apart from the diamond, most forms of carbon are black. Typical carbon compounds include calcium carbonate (limestone), CARBON DIOXIDE, and HYDROCARBONS, such as COAL and PETROLEUM products. Burning coal without air produces coke used in BLAST FURNACES.

Compounds containing carbon, hydrogen, and certain other elements make up the tissues in all plants and animals and are studied in ORGANIC CHEMISTRY.

▲ The carbon cycle is a constant exchange of carbon between the atmosphere and plants and animals. Carbon dioxide is taken in by plants during photosynthesis. These plants are in turn eaten by animals. Carbon dioxide is given out during respiration.

▼ Carbon has two crystalline forms, the diamond and graphite. The diamond is the hardest natural substance and graphite is one of the softest.

Diamond

Graphite

Carbon dating

Carbon dating is a technique for discovering the age of an object that was once alive. Recent fossils can be dated by this method. It is also called radiocarbon or carbon-14 dating.

The nucleus of a carbon atom usually contains 12 particles (the MASS NUMBER), six protons and six neutrons. Sometimes carbon atoms with a mass number of 14 are formed. Carbon-14 is radioactive because it is unstable and breaks down, or decays, very slowly into other

For more than 40 years many scientists believed that the "missing link" between modern humans and apes had been found. Parts of a skull and jawbone thought to be more than 250,000 years old were found at Piltdown in Sussex, England, between 1908 and 1912. Carbon dating of the skull in 1955 showed that the Piltdown man was a hoax.

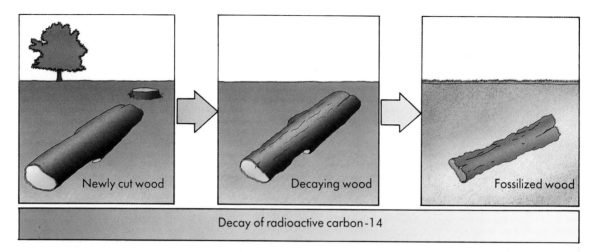

Newly cut wood

Decaying wood

Fossilized wood

Decay of radioactive carbon-14

▲ *The age of an archeological object can be estimated by measuring the amount of carbon-14 it contains. This is because carbon-14 decays constantly. After 70,000 years it will have decayed almost completely.*

CO₂

▲ *Carbon dioxide is a compound of two parts of oxygen to one of carbon. The bubbles in carbonated drinks are carbon dioxide. Also, because things cannot burn in carbon dioxide, it is used in fire extinguishers.*

ELEMENTS. It has a HALF-LIFE of 5,730 years. Carbon-14 in the ATMOSPHERE is taken in by plants which are eaten by animals. When plants or animals die, the carbon-14 inside them begins to decay at a constant rate. The age of a once living object can therefore be discovered by measuring the amount of carbon-14 it still contains.

Carbon dioxide

Carbon dioxide is a colorless, odorless GAS. It makes up less than one percent of the Earth's ATMOSPHERE and is found in the atmospheres of other PLANETS, notably Mars and Venus. Carbon dioxide is formed when compounds called carbonates (containing CARBON and OXYGEN) are heated or treated with an acid and also when coal, oil, wood, and other carbon compounds are burned. Animals produce carbon dioxide and release it into the air when breathing out. Plants convert carbon dioxide into oxygen by PHOTOSYNTHESIS. Carbon dioxide absorbs heat and traps it near the Earth's surface. *See also* GREENHOUSE EFFECT.

SEE FOR YOURSELF
Make a hole in a cork. Push a tube through it. Put some sodium bicarbonate (baking soda) and vinegar into the bottle and quickly cork it. Collect the gas that is formed by placing an upside down jar over the end of the tube. Move the upside down jar over a small flame. The flame goes out because it cannot burn in the carbon dioxide that is produced.

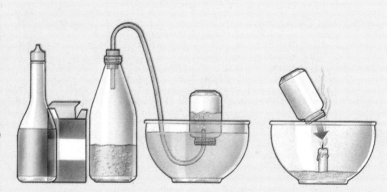

Carbon fibers

Carbon fibers are light, very strong, silklike fibers of pure carbon made by stretching and heating textile fibers. They can stand very great strains without breaking and keep their strength even at high TEMPERATURES. Compared with the steel used in making aircraft, carbon fibers are about a quarter of the WEIGHT but twice as strong. They are used chiefly for reinforcing plastics, ceramics, and metals, especially turbine blades.

▲ Individual carbon fibers are combined with plastic to give a composite material that is both strong and light.

◄ The aerospace industry is one of the largest users of materials containing carbon fibers. This Beechcraft aircraft is unusual because its body is made from layers of carbon fibers with other materials in between.

Carbon monoxide

Carbon monoxide is a colorless, tasteless, odorless, and extremely poisonous GAS. It is given off when CARBON is burned in a restricted air supply. When oxygen is plentiful, the much less dangerous CARBON DIOXIDE is formed. People who accidentally breathe in carbon monoxide can lose consciousness. Traffic fumes and cigarette smoke contain carbon monoxide, and in busy streets there may be a dangerous buildup of carbon monoxide in the atmosphere. Carbon monoxide is used in certain industrial processes, such as the separation of iron and other metals from ORES.

▲ Carbon monoxide is a compound of carbon and oxygen. It has half as much oxygen as carbon dioxide. It is formed when substances containing carbon are burned in a very small air supply.

Carver, George Washington *See* Agriculture

▶ *Portable cassette recorders contain all the components needed to enable cassettes to be played, including the cassette drive, speakers, and an amplifier.*

▼ *Modern microelectronics has made it possible to build radio cassette players that are small enough to be carried in a pocket. The cassette players do not have speakers, so you need to use headphones to listen to the sound.*

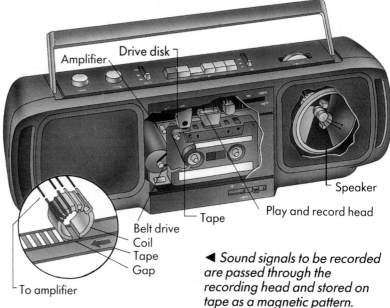

Amplifier · Drive disk

Speaker

Play and record head

Tape

Belt drive
Coil
Tape
Gap

To amplifier

◀ *Sound signals to be recorded are passed through the recording head and stored on tape as a magnetic pattern.*

Cassette recorder

A cassette recorder is a machine used to record SOUND and play it back through a LOUDSPEAKER or headphones. The sounds are recorded on a strip of flexible plastic tape wound onto tiny reels housed in a cassette. Most cassette tapes are coated with iron oxide. The particles of iron oxide normally lie randomly, pointing in different directions. To record sound, it is first changed into an electric current by a MICROPHONE. The current changes the strength of the magnetic field produced by a recording and playback head. As the tape travels past the head, the changing magnetic field makes the magnetic particles in the tape line up together. To listen to the recording, the tape is rewound. As it passes the head again, the magnetic particles in the tape produce currents in the head which are amplified into the original sound.

Cast iron

Cast iron is the general name given to various ALLOYS of IRON. It is a poor quality yet strong type of iron. Each type of cast iron has its own composition and qualities and is made up of varying amounts of iron, carbon, silicon, and smaller amounts of manganese, phosphorus, and sulfur. It contains so much carbon that it is too brittle to be worked into shape by FORGING. It is only possible to shape cast iron in its liquid state when it can be formed into objects using molds, a process called CASTING. Cast iron is used for decorative ironwork and objects such as car engines, which need to be strong.

The Chinese produced cast iron as early as the 6th century B.C., but it did not reach Europe until the 12th century A.D. In the 19th century it formed the basis for the very first skyscrapers. The most famous cast iron building was the Crystal Palace. It was designed by Joseph Paxton for the Great Exhibition of 1851 in London.

◀ *Iron must be heated in a furnace to very high temperatures so that it becomes liquid. It can then be poured into molds for casting.*

SEE FOR YOURSELF
Pour some Jell-O® mixture into a mold. When the Jell-O has set, place the bottom of the mold in a bowl of hot water for a few seconds. Turn the Jell-O mold over onto a plate. Tap it and lift the mold off the Jell-O, which appears cast in the shape of the mold.

Casting

Casting is the process used to shape objects by pouring a liquid into a mold and letting it harden. It is used to produce objects in plastic, iron, steel, aluminum, and ceramics.

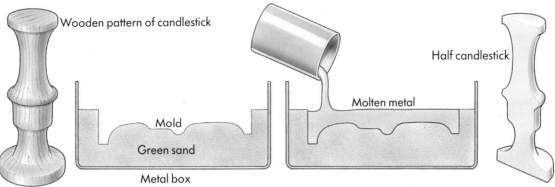

Wooden pattern of candlestick

Half candlestick

Mold

Molten metal

Green sand

Metal box

The first stage is to make a model of the object to be cast. This may be of wood or some other material. Some articles may need to be cast in more than one piece. The model is then placed in a special molding box called a flask. Molds for objects with spaces in the middle have a small hole through which the material can be poured.

▲ *The casting process is made up of three stages. A model, or pattern, of the finished object is made. A mold is made by packing sand around the pattern and then removing the pattern to leave a hollow. Finally the molten metal is poured in.*

Metal objects are usually cast in sand molds. Damp sand is packed tightly around the model to fill the space between it and the walls of the flask. The model is then removed and the molten metal is poured into the mold. Once the metal has cooled and hardened, the mold is broken open to reveal the cast object.

Catalysts in plants and animals are called enzymes. They are protein molecules that speed up the chemical reactions without which life would be impossible. Enzymes break down substances into simpler substances. A single enzyme molecule can perform its entire function a million times a minute. The human body has over 1,000 kinds of enzyme. Enzymes in the digestive system, for example, break down food for use in the body.

Catalyst

A catalyst is a substance that speeds up a reaction between two other substances without itself being changed or used up by the reaction. Catalysts are very important in the industrial production of certain chemical substances. The process by which they work is known as catalysis. In most CHEMICAL REACTIONS there are several possible sequences of steps through which the reactions can proceed. Catalysts take part in some or all of these steps. They help reactions to take place more quickly and more efficiently than they otherwise would; for example, heated IRON is used as a catalyst that speeds up the combination of hydrogen and nitrogen in the industrial manufacture of AMMONIA. Chemicals called ENZYMES are catalysts that speed up and encourage complicated chemical reactions in all animals and plants.

SEE FOR YOURSELF
Put a sugar cube into a glass of carbonated drink. This causes the drink to fizz up violently. This is an example of a physical catalyst. The sugar provides lots of sites for bubble formation on the sharp sugar crystals, which dramatically increases the number of bubbles of carbon dioxide inside the glass.

Catalytic converter

A catalytic converter is designed to reduce the amount of harmful gases pumped into the ATMOSPHERE by vehicle engines. The converter is a METAL case containing a metal or CERAMIC honeycomb coated with a precious metal such as platinum, palladium, or rhodium which is the CATALYST. A honeycomb is used because it enables a

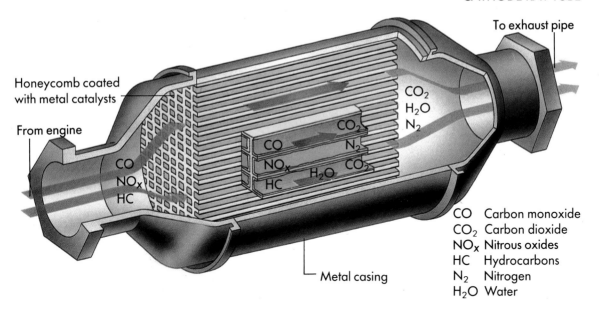

To exhaust pipe

Honeycomb coated
with metal catalysts

From engine

CO_2
H_2O
N_2

CO_2
N_2

CO
NO_x
HC

CO
N_2
NO_x
HC
H_2O
CO_2
CO_2

Metal casing

CO	Carbon monoxide
CO_2	Carbon dioxide
NO_x	Nitrous oxides
HC	Hydrocarbons
N_2	Nitrogen
H_2O	Water

very high surface area to be packed into a small volume. The converter is fitted to the vehicle's exhaust pipe. As the engine's exhaust gases flow through the honeycomb, the catalyst produces CHEMICAL REACTIONS among the gases that change the harmful ingredients (carbon monoxide, oxides of nitrogen, and hydrocarbons) into water vapor and carbon dioxide. A converter works most efficiently when the mixture of fuel and air supplied to the engine is carefully monitored and adjusted by a computerized engine management system.

▲ *All new cars will eventually be required by law to have pollution reducing catalytic converters fitted to their exhausts.*

Cathode *See* Electrolysis

Cathode ray tube

A cathode ray tube is a tube, usually made of glass, from which most of the air has been removed and inside which a beam of ELECTRONS is produced. The beam comes from an electron gun made of a piece of heated METAL kept at a negative voltage. This repels the electrons which are emitted from the surface and a series of positive grids accelerates them to a high speed. The piece of hot metal is known as the cathode after the negative electrode in ELECTROLYSIS.

Very narrow beams of electrons can now be produced. If the far end of the tube is covered with luminescent paint, the beam then produces a small spot of light. Electric deflecting plates or magnetic deflecting rings are used to bend the beam, so the spot traces an image. The paint continues to glow for a short time after

William Crookes (1832–1919)
Crookes was a British physicist and chemist. In 1861, he discovered the element thallium. His studies on electrical discharges in vacuum tubes resulted in the Crookes tube, an early cathode ray tube, in 1880. He found that "cathode rays" cast shadows and traveled in straight lines, which could be deflected by a magnet. He believed that cathode rays were made up of negatively-charged particles (electrons).

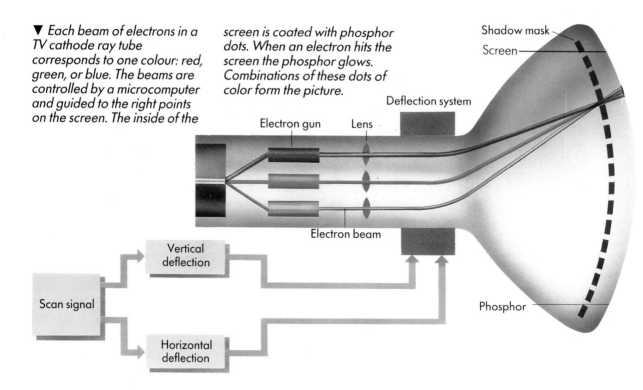

▼ *Each beam of electrons in a TV cathode ray tube corresponds to one colour: red, green, or blue. The beams are controlled by a microcomputer and guided to the right points on the screen. The inside of the screen is coated with phosphor dots. When an electron hits the screen the phosphor glows. Combinations of these dots of color form the picture.*

Shadow mask
Screen
Deflection system
Electron gun
Lens
Electron beam
Phosphor
Scan signal
Vertical deflection
Horizontal deflection

the spot has moved on, so our eyes do not see the movement. This is how pictures are produced by a TELEVISION or an OSCILLOSCOPE. Color pictures can be made by using luminescent paints which glow different colors. The first cathode ray tube was made by William Crookes in 1880.

See also COLOR; LUMINESCENCE.

NaOH

▲ *This is the chemical formula for sodium hydroxide or caustic soda. Sodium hydroxide is often produced by the electrolysis of sodium chloride or salt. It is also called lye and is used as an oven cleaner.*

Caustic soda

Caustic soda is sodium hydroxide, a chemical compound formed from SODIUM, HYDROGEN, and OXYGEN. Caustic soda is a very dangerous compound. "Caustic" means "burning" and caustic substances will burn or eat away other substances, especially organic materials, including human body tissues. Caustic soda should never be allowed to come into contact with the skin, mouth, or any other part of the body. In laboratories, where necessary, it should be handled with great care. Caustic soda is a strong alkali. It is used to make soap and is an efficient drain cleaner because it attacks grease and other waste matter blocking pipes.

Cavendish, Henry *See* Hydrogen

CELL

A cell is the smallest living unit which is able to carry out all the basic functions of life: growth, metabolism, and reproduction. Some simple organisms consist of a single cell, while most plants and animals are constructed from huge numbers of cells, adapted to perform particular functions. But even in these multicellular organisms, the individual cells are capable of growing, feeding, and reproducing.

A typical cell consists of *cytoplasm*, a watery, jellylike material, surrounded by a thin membrane which helps to give the cell its shape but allows various substances to pass through. Oxygen and food substances enter the cell in this way, and waste products are removed. Plant cells also have a cell wall, made of cellulose, which can sometimes be very thick and so gives the plant its shape. Vertebrate animals are supported by a hard skeleton produced by bone cells.

The nucleus is a dense body within the cytoplasm containing the chromosomes and genes which govern the cell and the way it works. It can be seen under a microscope.

Most of the chemical reactions that power and maintain the body take place in the cell. Small structures called organelles are present in the cytoplasm, and these tiny chemical factories produce hormones, enzymes, and other substances which are released for use in the cell and elsewhere in the body.

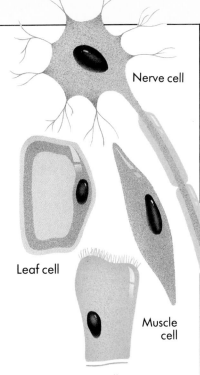

Nerve cell

Leaf cell

Muscle cell

Skin cell

▲ A human consists of many millions of cells. Nerves and muscles, for example, are made up of specialized cells.

◄ Animal cells contain a number of different organelles that carry out the chemical processes required for life. Lysosomes contain enzymes that can help white blood cells break down harmful bacteria.

▼ Plant cells have a cell wall made of cellulose which animal cells do not. Vacuoles are fluid-filled cavities, common in plant cells.

Animal cell

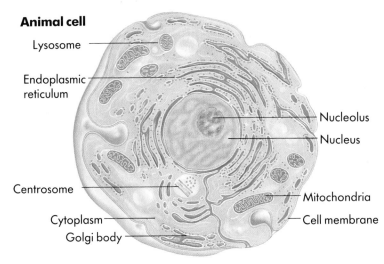

- Lysosome
- Endoplasmic reticulum
- Nucleolus
- Nucleus
- Centrosome
- Mitochondria
- Cytoplasm
- Cell membrane
- Golgi body

Plant cell

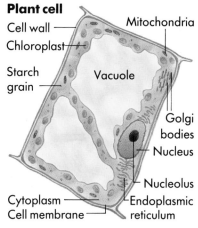

- Cell wall
- Chloroplast
- Mitochondria
- Starch grain
- Vacuole
- Golgi bodies
- Nucleus
- Nucleolus
- Cytoplasm
- Endoplasmic reticulum
- Cell membrane

Centrosome This contains the centrioles that are important in cell division.
Endoplasmic reticulum These contain the units where protein is made.
Golgi bodies Involved in the secretion of cell products and may also help in protein manufacture.
Mitochondria Tiny rod-shaped structures with a tightly-folded inner membrane where glucose is broken down to keep the cell supplied with energy.

See also BIOLOGY; BONE; CELL DIVISION; CELLULOSE; CHROMOSOMES AND GENES; CYTOLOGY; GENETICS; MICROSCOPE; NUCLEUS, CELL; OXYGEN; REPRODUCTION.

Cell division

Cells divide when they have grown larger than is necessary for them to carry out their normal function, or when they reach the end of their lifespan. Cell division is seen most easily in simple microscopic animals, for example the amoeba, which is a single cell. When ready to divide, it simply splits in half, dividing the contents of the CELL equally. Most simple plants and animals divide like this. In more complex organisms, a process called *mitosis* is used, which makes sure that the information in the genes is shared equally between the new "daughter" cells. All this material is in the cell nucleus, stored on threadlike CHROMOSOMES. The chromosomes are in pairs, and during cell division these pairs are separated and move to opposite sides of the cell. The cell now divides into two, and the chromosomes are doubled again. A similar process called *meiosis* takes place when the body produces sperm and eggs, except that in this case, the chromosomes are not doubled until after FERTILIZATION. All the cells in the body are able to divide except for nerve cells, which last throughout life.

▼ *Meiosis is the process by which male and female sex cells are formed. It produces cells with only half the number of chromosomes. This means that when a male and female sex cell combine during sexual reproduction, the new cell that is formed will have the normal number of chromosomes. Both animal and plant cells divide in the same way. 1 Bodies in the cell called centrioles move to opposite sides of the cell. The chromosomes appear as long threads in the nucleus. 2 A structure called a spindle starts to form from the centrioles. 3 The chromosomes become shorter and fatter and pair up. 4 Each chromosome copies itself and divides into two strands called chromatids joined*

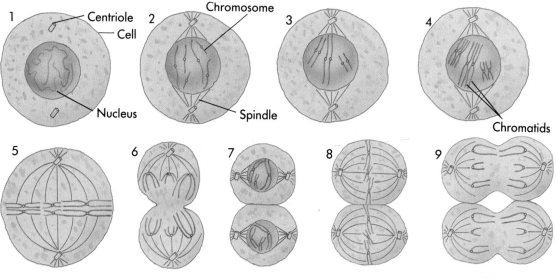

at the center. *5 The chromosomes become arranged across the middle of the cell. 6 The pairs of chromosomes split apart and go to opposite sides of the cell, and the cell divides once. 7 A resting period follows before the cycle is repeated, 8 and 9. This time the pairs of* chromatids split apart and move to opposite sides of the cell, and the cells divide again *10. Each one of the four new cells has half the number of chromosomes that were in the original cell. At fertilization, two cells fuse together so the embryo has a full set of chromosomes.*

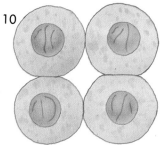

Cellular radio and telephones

Cellular RADIO and TELEPHONES are used for COMMUNI-CATION. Telephones are connected by cable, and cord-less telephones allow the user to move only a few yards

▼ The cellular telephone network area is divided up into cells. When a cell phone user makes a call, a radio signal is sent to the nearest base station. This is sent to the nearest mobile telephone exchange. The call is then directed to either another telephone network or to another telephone.

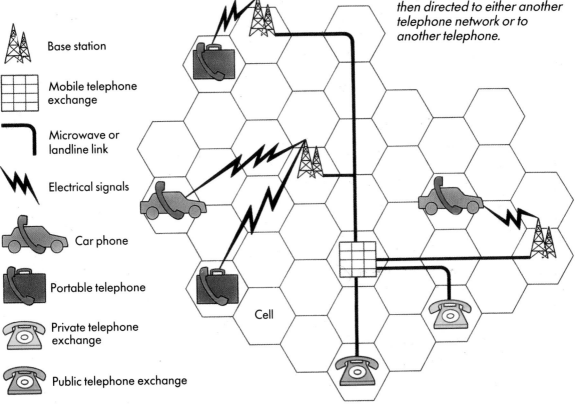

Base station

Mobile telephone exchange

Microwave or landline link

Electrical signals

Car phone

Portable telephone

Private telephone exchange

Public telephone exchange

Cell

from the base station. A cellular phone can be used almost anywhere. The country is covered by a grid of radio cells, areas where a particular radio channel or transmitting FREQUENCY is used. A relay station in each cell handles transmissions from all the telephones in that cell. If the telephone user moves into another cell, a new relay station takes over. Because the cells are small, the same small number of radio channels can be used again and again. The second generation cellular telephone network uses only 40 channels. They are all DIGITAL and suffer less from interference than the earlier analog sys-tems. Cellular telephones have rapidly increased in numbers in the United States, growing from zero in 1983 to three million in 1990.

▼ With a compact cellular telephone you can make and receive calls anywhere within the cellular network.

Celluloid *See* Plastics

▶ *This greatly magnified criss-cross pattern of fibers is of cellulose microfibrils. They form a large part of the surface of a leaf.*

▼ *The cell wall of a plant cell is made up mainly of cellulose, which gives a plant its firm structure.*

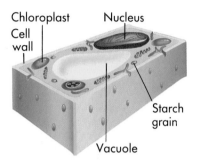

Chloroplast   Nucleus
Cell
wall
                    Starch
                    grain
        Vacuole

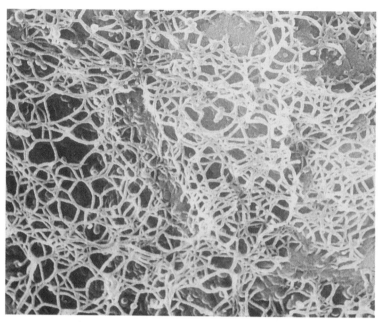

In the 1850s chemists first dissolved wood pulp and cotton fibers to obtain the cellulose in them. Fibers of cellulose were first made in 1855 by Georges Audemars of Switzerland. Unfortunately, the chemical process he used turned the cellulose into nitrocellulose, a powerful explosive. Fabrics made from it burst into flames very easily.

▲ *Anders Celsius (1701–1744), a Swedish astronomer, suggested that temperature should be measured on what we now call the Celsius scale.*

Cellulose

Cellulose is a CARBOHYDRATE and is an important part of plant CELLS, where it makes up most of the material in the cell wall. It is a very tough substance, made up from long molecules which are laid down in a crisscross pattern, giving strength and rigidity to the cell. Cotton and linen fabrics consist almost entirely of cellulose, which is naturally formed in long fibers. *Viscose* is a form of processed cellulose commonly used to make fabrics and clothes. Humans are unable to digest cellulose, which makes up most of the fiber in our diet. However, animals such as sheep, cattle, and rabbits have specially adapted digestive systems. This allows them to use the cellulose that they obtain from the grass they eat. Bacteria in their digestive systems break down the cellulose into simpler SUGARS, which are easily absorbed.

Celsius

The Celsius scale is one of the systems for measuring TEMPERATURE. It is named after Anders Celsius and is sometimes called the Centigrade scale. On this scale the normal FREEZING POINT of water is at 0 degrees and the normal BOILING POINT at 100 degrees. It is the standard scale for measuring temperature in countries which use the METRIC SYSTEM. To convert a temperature in degrees Celsius to a temperature in FAHRENHEIT, multiply by nine and divide by five, then add 32 (to reverse the conversion, subtract 32, multiply by five and divide by nine).

The choice of zero degrees on the Celsius scale is only made out of convenience, because WATER is such a common substance on the Earth. The fundamental scale of temperature is the KELVIN scale, in which water freezes at 273.16 K. The zero temperature on the Kelvin scale is called absolute zero, $-459.67°F$ $(-273.15°C)$.

Cement

In the CONSTRUCTION industry, cement is made from limestone and clay. These are mixed together and roasted. The dry "clinker" produced is mixed with a material called gypsum (calcium sulfate) and ground into a fine powder. This cement is mixed with sand and water to make mortar for sticking bricks together. It is also mixed with sand, gravel, and water to make concrete. Cement and water react together chemically, making

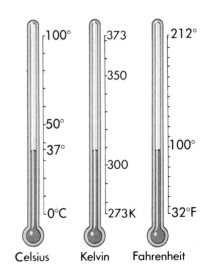

▲ Normal body temperature in humans is 37°C on the Celsius scale, 310 K using the Kelvin scale and 98.6°F on the Fahrenheit scale.

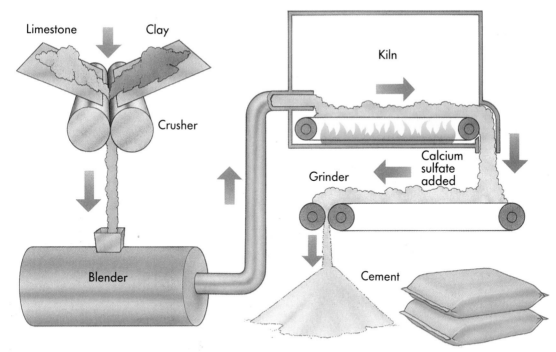

the mortar or concrete harden. After this, water does not affect it.

The ancient Romans used cement and concrete similar to the kind we use today. Many of their buildings and bridges still exist. To make their cement they used a volcanic ash called *pozzolana*, which they mixed with lime and water.

▲ Cement is made by mixing crushed limestone and clay. This mixture is heated to 2,550°F (1,400°C) in a rotating kiln, cooled, and ground to a fine powder. When mixed with water it becomes a solid mass.

105

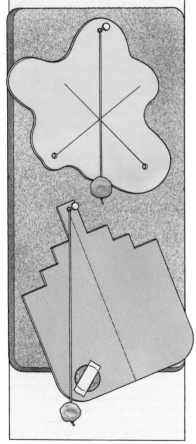

Center of gravity

The force of GRAVITY acts on all parts of an object, but it is often helpful to think of it as a FORCE applied at a single point. This point is called the center of gravity; you can think of it as the average position of all the particles that make up the body. It is also known as the center of mass. If an object is balanced or hung so it does not fall over, the BALANCING POINT must be exactly below the center of gravity so that the gravitational force and the supporting force exactly cancel each other out and do not cause the body to turn and fall over. If the center of gravity is not over the balancing point of an object, the object is not stable and will turn and fall over.

Centrifugal force

Centrifugal force occurs when an object is spinning fast. It is the FORCE that appears to push everything to the outside of the spinning circle, but in fact it is a reaction to the *centripetal force* which is acting toward the center of the circle. You can see the centrifugal effect when you whirl an object on a string around your head. You are pulling the object toward you with the string. The force you are creating pulling inward is the centripetal force. The object is reacting to the centripetal force and seems to be pulling outward away from you. If the centripetal force stops (for example, if you let the string go) the centrifugal force also stops and the object will fly off in a

▶ *Part of the excitement of this fairground ride comes from being pulled up and away from the center of rotation. This is because of the centrifugal force.*

straight line, following the direction it was moving at the time you let the string go.

It is because of the centrifugal force that a bucket of water can be whirled around in a circle without spilling. You can feel the centrifugal force yourself in a car going round a corner or in amusement park rides.

There is another force, called the Coriolis force; you can feel it trying to pull you to one side if you walk toward the center of a merry-go-round while it is turning. This force is an important influence on the airflow in the ATMOSPHERE.

Centrifuge

A centrifuge is a machine used to spin substances at a high speed. Scientists often use centrifuges to separate particles from a liquid or to divide a mixture of liquids into its different ingredients. The mixture is placed in a tube which pivots so that when the machine starts to move, the tube can swing out horizontally. The CENTRIFUGAL FORCE tries to push the mixture away from the center of the centrifuge. The heavier particles or liquid move further outward (toward the bottom of the mixture). When the centrifuge is stopped, the materials stay in this unmixed state. Blood and other biological samples are often separated by centrifuge. The fastest centrifuges, called ultracentrifuges, spin at up to 200,000 revolutions per minute. Large centrifuges are used to test military pilots and ASTRONAUTS who have to be able to withstand high accelerations.

SEE FOR YOURSELF
Put a marble into a can. Move the can in a circular motion. The marble will move up the side of the can and spin around the walls. This is the effect of centrifugal force which causes objects traveling at speed to move up and outward. Passengers in a car going around a corner at speed feel a pull to the outer edge of the corner in the same way as the centrifugal force acts on the marble.

▼ *Laboratory centrifuges are used to separate substances. A type of centrifuge is used to train astronauts. They are whirled around so they experience the same forces as when a rocket blasts off.*

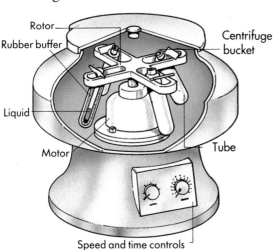

Rotor
Rubber buffer
Liquid
Motor
Centrifuge bucket
Tube
Speed and time controls

Laboratory centrifuge

Astronaut in centrifuge

▲ *This softball bat has a very strong ceramic coating. The ceramic will not split, chip, or wear away so the bat will last longer than a wooden one.*

▶ *New ceramic engine casings are very strong and can withstand high temperatures. They are lighter than ordinary metal casings.*

Nutrients in Cereals:
Carbohydrates, for energy; **Protein**, for growth and maintenance of bones, skin, and muscles; **Calcium**, for growth and maintenance of bones and teeth; **Iron**, for the blood; **Vitamin A**, for development of skin and bones; **Vitamin C**, for the development of tissue, ligaments, and tendons; **Vitamin B$_1$**, used to break down starches and sugars in the body; **Vitamin B$_2$** and **Niacin**, used by the body to break down food into useful substances.

Ceramics

Ceramics are hard, brittle materials made mainly from clay. When the clay has been molded or shaped, it is heated in a kiln until it hardens. Ceramics are resistant to the action of water and most chemicals. They also have a high resistance to electric currents and so they can be used in electrical systems as INSULATORS. There are several different types of ceramic materials. Enamels and POTTERY AND PORCELAIN are examples. Heavy clay ceramics include bricks, underground drain pipes, and roofing tiles used in construction. Some ceramics with a particularly high MELTING POINT are used to make the bricks that line furnaces and also parts of spacecraft that have to withstand high temperatures.

Ceramics have been replaced in many cases by PLASTICS that are more resistant to damage and can be molded into more complicated shapes. However, research has resulted in new ceramics and manufacturers of car and aircraft engines are experimenting with ceramic parts that wear out more slowly than metal and can stand very high temperatures.

Cereals

Cereals are large grasses which are cultivated for their nutritious SEEDS (grain). They provide the staple food for people in nearly every part of the world. The grain is rich in energy-giving STARCH and also contains valuable amounts of PROTEIN, VITAMINS, and dietary fiber (as you

World map of cereal production

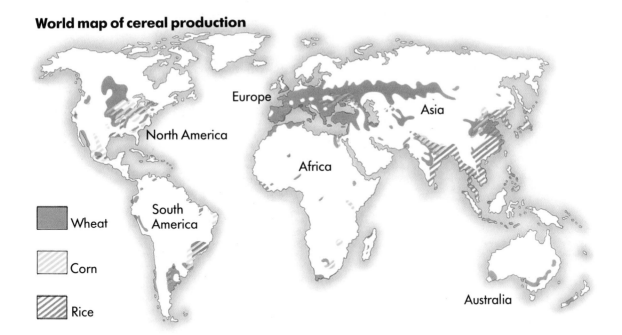

Wheat

Corn

Rice

will see from your breakfast cereal box). The carbohydrate content of cereals ranges from 60 to 80 percent. Cereals provide about 90 percent of all protein eaten by the world's people. Wheat, rice, and corn are the most important cereals. Between them they cover over half of the world's cultivated land and yield about 1,000,000,000 tons of grain every year. Not all this is for human food; much of it goes to feed cattle and other livestock. Other important cereals include barley, oats, rye, sorghum, and millet.

Grains are used industrially to manufacture malt, beer, starch, liquors, and oils. Oil extracted from the grain germ is refined for salad or cooking use.

Cereals have been cultivated for about 10,000 years and now look very different from the wild grasses from which they are descended. Early farmers gradually increased the size and quality of their crops simply by sowing seed from the biggest and best plants every year, and plant breeders have made further huge improvements during the 20th century using modern HORTICULTURE and BREEDING techniques.

The main cereal-producing states in the United States are: Nebraska, Kansas, North and South Dakota, Texas, Montana, Iowa, Washington, and Illinois. People in the United States eat over 20 billion servings of breakfast cereal yearly.

See also AGRICULTURE; GENETICS; HEREDITY.

▲ *Wheat is the most important cereal grain in the world followed by corn. Rice is the staple diet of over half the world's population.*

▼ *Barley, oats, and corn are the main food crops where wheat and rice crops are poor.*

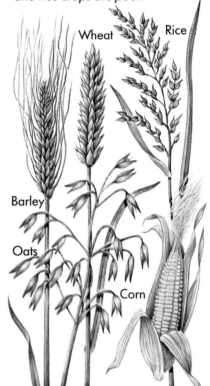

Wheat

Rice

Barley

Oats

Corn

▶ *The large circle marks the underground path of the Large Electron-Positron collider at CERN in Switzerland.*

▼ *Chalk started to be formed millions of years ago. As sea animals and plants died, they sank to the bottom of the sea and formed a layer of calcium deposits. In places where the sea receded these deposits formed the land. Millions of years of erosion and land movement mean that some of this chalk is now exposed.*

CERN *See* Particle accelerator

Chain reaction *See* Nuclear energy

Chalk

Chalk is a soft, powdery, white rock, consisting of CAL-CIUM carbonate. Like limestone rocks, it is mostly formed from the fragments of countless millions of tiny sea creatures that were deposited on the ocean floor during the Cretaceous period (about 135–90 million years ago). The Cretaceous period got its name from the Latin word for chalk, *creta*. A chalky soil indicates that the land was once almost certainly under the sea, for example, the land and cliffs of much of southern England, Normandy in France, Texas and Kansas in the United

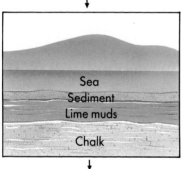

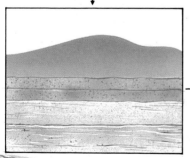

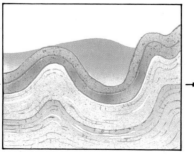

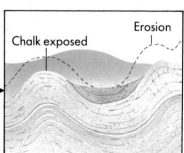

States. Chalk deposits in western Kansas contain preserved skeletons of extinct flying reptiles, birds, and fish. Chalk is best known as a writing material (though writing chalk is usually calcium sulfate). It has many other uses, notably in the manufacture of CEMENT and FERTILIZERS. Large quantities of whiting, which is washed chalk, are used in paints, putty, and polishing powders. Many toothpastes have chalk in them.

Charcoal

Charcoal is a form of CARBON. It is a black, brittle substance and is found in two forms: wood charcoal and animal charcoal. These are made by burning wood or bone in an oven that contains little or no air. In this process, hydrogen and oxygen are driven off, leaving the charcoal, together with some impurities. Wood charcoal in some cases burns well and is used as a fuel. Activated charcoal is a purified form of charcoal that is used for removing unwanted colors, flavors, and smells from things. It absorbs them because it has large spaces between its atoms.

$$CaCO_3$$

▲ Calcium carbonate is the main compound in chalk. It is a white, crystalline mineral.

During the Roman period, charcoal and wood were the only fuels available for use in the iron, tin, and copper-making industries. The wood used for producing charcoal at this time included maple, birch, plum, ash, and oak.

Analysis of prehistoric pigments shows that Stone Age people used charcoal as a cosmetic.

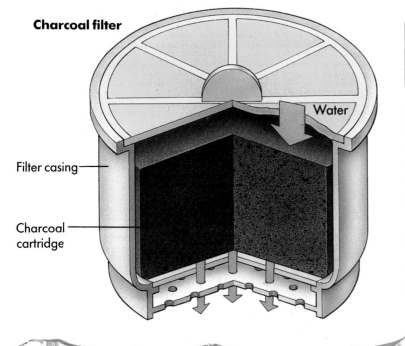

Charcoal filter

Water

Filter casing

Charcoal cartridge

◄ Charcoal is an effective filter. It is used in water purification systems. The water is passed through a container full of charcoal which absorbs, like a sponge, the impurities and chemicals in the water.

▼ Many countries have dramatic chalk landforms. These cliffs are in southern Britain — the White Cliffs of Dover.

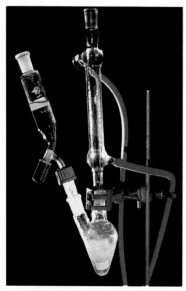

▲ *Chemical reactions are carried out and measured using a variety of complicated looking apparatuses.*

▼ *Bread rising and the digestion of food are chemical reactions just like experimental reactions in a laboratory. The reaction below produces a solid compound. The blue solids show that there is copper in the solution of copper sulfate. If more ammonia is added a further reaction takes place to give a slightly different compound with a darker color.*

Charles, Jacques *See* Gas

Chemical reactions

A chemical reaction is a process in which one set of chemical substances, known as the reactants, are changed into another substance or set of substances, called the products. In a chemical reaction, BONDS between atoms are broken and re-formed. The products of a reaction usually have different chemical properties (appearance and behavior) from those of the original reactants. For example, when the gases hydrogen and oxygen are ignited together with a flame, they explode and form the liquid water. Reactions such as that one between hydrogen and oxygen can be very fast. Others, such as the rusting of iron, are very slow. Many reactions take place over a measurable period of time. Chemists use chemical equations and CHEMICAL SYMBOLS to show what happens in a reaction. The formation of water from hydrogen and oxygen looks like this:

$$2H_2(g) + O_2(g) \rightarrow 2H_2O(l)$$

This shows that the gases (g) hydrogen and oxygen produce the liquid (l) water. Some reactions are reversible, which means that the reactants produce products that then recombine to produce the original reactants.

Heat will speed up a slow reaction; so will the use of a CATALYST. Light can also cause a chemical reaction; for example, light causes silver salts on photographic film to change when a photograph is being taken.

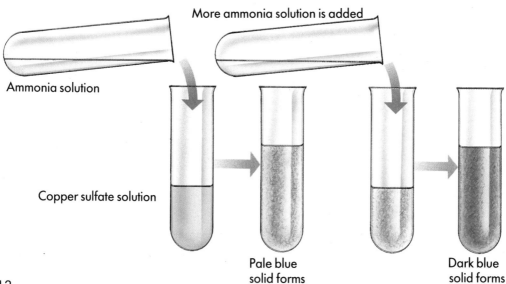

More ammonia solution is added

Ammonia solution

Copper sulfate solution

Pale blue solid forms

Dark blue solid forms

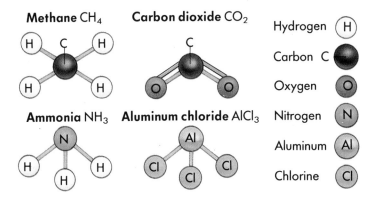

Methane CH_4

Carbon dioxide CO_2

Ammonia NH_3

Aluminum chloride $AlCl_3$

Hydrogen H

Carbon C

Oxygen O

Nitrogen N

Aluminum Al

Chlorine Cl

◀ *These are just some of the symbols used to stand for chemical elements. These symbols are used in chemical formulas to show combinations of elements.*

Chemical symbols

A chemical symbol is a single alphabetic letter or a pair of letters that stands for a chemical ELEMENT. Symbols are used in chemical equations and formulas and in a chart showing the PERIODIC TABLE. All the elements up to lawrencium (which has an ATOMIC NUMBER of 103) have internationally agreed symbols to go with their names. The symbol is either a capital letter (e.g. C for carbon, H for hydrogen or S for sulfur) or a capital letter followed by a small letter (e.g. Al for aluminum, Ba for barium, or Ca for calcium). Usually the small letter in a two letter symbol is the second letter of the element's name, as in the above examples, but often different letters are chosen to avoid confusion. Thus calcium has the symbol Ca, but cadmium has Cd, and the radioactive element californium has Cf. Some elements have symbols formed from their Latin names (e.g. iron has the symbol Fe, from *ferrum*; lead has Pb, from *plumbum*). The names of certain elements have been changed, but the symbols are made up from the older names. Thus sodium has the symbol Na, from natrium, the old name for sodium. The element tungsten used to be called wolfram and still has the symbol W. The Scottish chemist Thomas Thomson was the first to use letters for chemical symbols in an article written in 1801.

See also entries for most of the elements mentioned.

Sand and salt are both chemical compounds which chemists call silica (silicon oxide) and sodium chloride. They have the chemical formulas SiO_2 and $NaCl$. From the chemical symbols we can see that a molecule of silica is made up of a silicon atom combined with two oxygen atoms and that each salt molecule contains a sodium atom combined with a chlorine atom.

The more recently discovered elements have been named after important scientists or places where research has been carried out.

Am = Americium
Es = Einsteinium
Fr = Francium
Lr = Lawrencium
Md = Mendelevium
No = Nobelium

Chemistry

Chemistry is the scientific study of ELEMENTS and the COMPOUNDS that they make with other elements. Chemists work to describe the properties of the various substances: what they are like, how they behave, how they are affected by HEAT and PRESSURE, how they react with other substances. *See* pages 114 and 115.

About four million different chemicals have been identified. This is being added to at a rate of over 5,000 every week.

CHEMISTRY

Ever since our earliest ancestors began using fire one-and-a-half million years ago, we have been able to produce and control chemical reactions to help us to observe, investigate, and change the properties of substances. The ancient Greek philosopher Democritus thought that substances consisted of atoms, but Aristotle considered that all substances were different combinations of four elements (earth, air, water, and fire) and that one substance could be changed into another by adjusting the balance of these elements. The medieval alchemists also believed this, but in the 16th and 17th centuries alchemy gave way to modern chemistry. Chemists realized that substances that could not be changed or broken down into other substances were the real elements. A modern atomic theory was developed and various laws were discovered about the way substances behave and how they combine. Today, chemical substances of all kinds are mined or manufactured, used for research, and for the production of detergents, dyes, cosmetics, drugs, food additives, glass, paints, paper, and plastics.

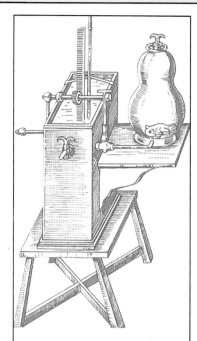

Robert Boyle (1627–1691)
Boyle was an Irish scientist. He founded the study of chemistry as a separate science and aimed to "improve natural knowledge by experiment." He is known for his experiments on gases and was the first chemist to isolate and collect a gas. He formulated Boyle's Law: a volume of gas at a constant temperature varies inversely with the pressure applied to the gas. He showed that air is absorbed in the process of combustion and that only one part of air, oxygen, is necessary for breathing.

SEE FOR YOURSELF
Remember to take care when handling any chemical and that any compound, even salt, can be harmful in a large enough quantity. This is a simple experiment you can do yourself. Make a hole in a cork and push a tube through it. Place some baking soda (sodium bicarbonate $NaHCO_3$) and some vinegar (weak acid) into a bottle and quickly cork it. Place the tube in a bowl of water and watch the reaction produce bubbles of carbon dioxide gas.

Many of the discoveries made by chemists have resulted in the production of new substances from carbon compounds that have been of huge value to humans. These have included antibiotics, vitamins, hormones, and drugs for medicine; pesticides for agriculture; dyes, and a wide range of artificial materials such as plastics and rubbers for the manufacturing industries.

Antoine Lavoisier (1743–1794)
Lavoisier was a French chemist. He explained the role of oxygen in combustion. By carefully weighing and analyzing materials after burning, he showed that burned materials are heavier than unburned materials. This was because of the addition of a gas, discovered by Scheele and Priestley. Lavoisier named it oxygen.

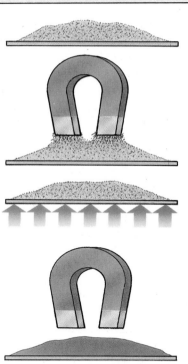

▲ Experiments are an interesting and fun part of a chemistry lesson. An electric current will flow through some solutions and when it does the circuit is completed and the bulb will light. Electrical conduction in solutions is called electrolysis.

▼ A polymer is a giant molecule formed from many small units. A nylon molecule is an example of a polymer. It is formed from carbon, nitrogen, hydrogen, and oxygen. Models are made of molecules to show how the different atoms are joined together.

▲ When iron is mixed with sulfur, it can be removed again using a magnet. If, however, the mixture of iron and sulfur is heated, a chemical reaction takes place forming iron sulfide which is not attracted to the magnet.

Nylon molecule

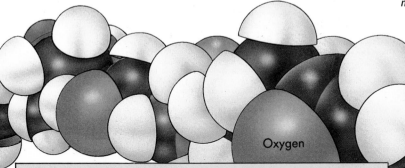

Carbon

Nitrogen

Hydrogen

Oxygen

Milestones in Chemistry
c.3500 B.C. Smelting metal and making glass.
c.400 B.C. Democritus proposes an atomic theory.
1661 Boyle introduces modern idea of elements.
1766 Cavendish discovers hydrogen.
1770s Scheele and Priestley discover oxygen.
1828 Wöhler makes first synthetic organic substance from inorganic compounds.
1869 Mendeleyev and Lothar Meyer devise periodic law.
1913 Bohr proposes a model of the atom.
1916 Lewis describes electronic bonding between atoms.
1953 DNA and RNA found to affect heredity.
1980s Chemists work to develop a chemical cell that produces hydrogen fuel by the chemical breakdown of water.

See also ATOM; CHEMICAL REACTION; INORGANIC CHEMISTRY; MOLECULE; ORGANIC CHEMISTRY; PERIODIC TABLE.

▲ *During World War I, chlorine gas was the first method of chemical warfare to be used. The first attack caught many troops unprepared. Gas masks were eventually issued to troops to reduce the number of people suffering from severe respiratory problems.*

▶ *Chlorine gas is manufactured by passing an electric current through a solution of sodium chloride in water. Liquid chlorine is made by putting the gas under pressure. Because chlorine is so poisonous, the equipment has to be carefully sealed.*

By the end of the 1990s, refrigerators will be manufactured without the use of chlorofluorocarbons. Many aerosol products are now produced without CFCs and alternative substances, such as hydrocarbons, carbon dioxide, and nitrous oxide are now used to create the propellant forces.

Chlorine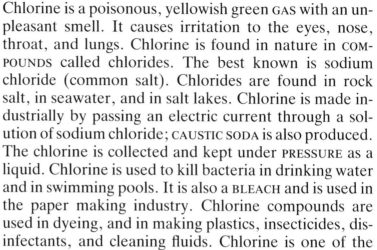

Chlorine is a poisonous, yellowish green GAS with an unpleasant smell. It causes irritation to the eyes, nose, throat, and lungs. Chlorine is found in nature in COMPOUNDS called chlorides. The best known is sodium chloride (common salt). Chlorides are found in rock salt, in seawater, and in salt lakes. Chlorine is made industrially by passing an electric current through a solution of sodium chloride; CAUSTIC SODA is also produced. The chlorine is collected and kept under PRESSURE as a liquid. Chlorine is used to kill bacteria in drinking water and in swimming pools. It is also a BLEACH and is used in the paper making industry. Chlorine compounds are used in dyeing, and in making plastics, insecticides, disinfectants, and cleaning fluids. Chlorine is one of the HALOGENS, or salt-producing nonmetallic elements.

Chlorofluorocarbons (CFCs)

Chlorofluorocarbons, or CFCs, are chemical COMPOUNDS of CHLORINE, fluorine, and CARBON. They are similar to HYDROCARBONS, but instead of HYDROGEN atoms being bonded to the carbon atoms, the carbon atoms are bonded to atoms of chlorine and fluorine (HALOGEN gases). CFCs have many industrial uses. They are used under pressure to propel AEROSOLS from cans. They are also used in refrigerators to help cooling agents circulate and are produced in the manufacture of PLASTIC foam for containers. CFCs are very stable over long

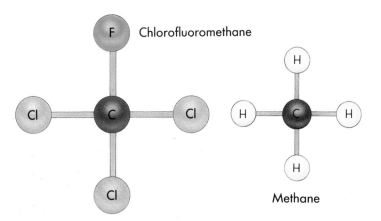

Chlorofluoromethane

Methane

◀ *Chlorofluorocarbons have chlorine (Cl) and fluorine (F) atoms bonded to the carbon (C) atom instead of the hydrogen (H) atoms in hydrocarbons. Methane (CH_4) is the simplest hydrocarbon.*

periods but eventually they give up their chlorine atoms and release them into the environment. Chlorine reacts with the protective OZONE LAYER in the atmosphere to form chlorine oxide. This reaction has begun to destroy the ozone layer. Conservationists fear that CFCs may destroy it altogether. Many countries no longer allow the use of CFCs and have signed international agreements to ban their use.

Chlorophyll

Chlorophyll is the PIGMENT in plant CELLS that gives them their green COLOR. Most plant cells do not produce chlorophyll unless they are exposed to light. Chlorophyll is essential for PHOTOSYNTHESIS. It absorbs energy from the Sun's light and uses it to help the plants make food from carbon dioxide and water. Chlorophyll is a MOLECULE which is made up of mostly carbon and hydrogen, with a single atom of magnesium surrounded by nitrogen in its center. It is contained in tiny chloroplasts which are located mainly in the LEAVES but may also occur in stems. In some leaves there are other pigments. In autumn, chlorophyll is not produced as much and the other pigments are more noticeable as the fall colors.

SEE FOR YOURSELF
Using a paper clip, attach a piece of paper to the edge of a large leaf. After a few days a pale patch will appear under the paper. This is because light is prevented from reaching the cells that make chlorophyll, the substance that makes plants green.

▶ *Chlorophyll is found mainly in chloroplasts in the palisade cells in the leaves of plants. The pile of sheetlike membranes (or lamellae) inside the chloroplasts is called a granum. They hold the chlorophyll molecules and enzymes in the best position for trapping light energy from the Sun.*

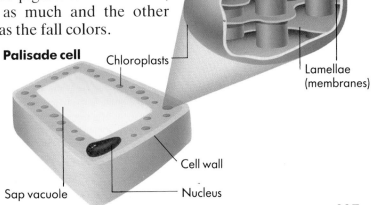

Palisade cell

Chloroplasts

Granum

Lamellae (membranes)

Cell wall

Nucleus

Sap vacuole

117

Useful Cholesterol

Cholesterol and its by-products are secreted through the oil glands of the skin to act as a lubricant to soften the skin. It also provides a protective coating for the hair and skin. Sheep's wool is covered with a coating containing lanolin, which is made up of substances containing cholesterol.

Cholesterol

Cholesterol is a fatty material (a FAT or lipid) that exists in all animal tissues. The human body makes its own cholesterol but also takes in extra amounts of it in such foods as butter, eggs, fatty meats, and liver. The membranes of CELLS contain cholesterol. It is used to make bile salts that help in digestion and to produce certain HORMONES. Most cholesterol is produced by the LIVER and is carried through the BLOOD to other cells by substances called lipoproteins. The presence of large amounts of certain types of cholesterol in the blood has been linked to certain diseases, for example arteriosclerosis (hardening of the arteries), which develops when fatty deposits due to cholesterol collect on the inner walls of arteries, making them narrow. Blood clots can block these narrow passages and cause a heart attack.

Artery

Muscle

Wall swells

Fatty streak appears

Cholesterol builds up in fatty streak

Cholesterol build-up continues

Artery narrows

▲ *Diseases such as arteriosclerosis (hardening of the arteries) develop when fat deposits containing cholesterol, collect on the inner walls of the blood vessel. This causes the arteries to narrow. Blood clots can easily block these narrowed vessels. Heart attacks can result if the blockage occurs in the arteries close to the heart.*

Chromatography

Chromatography is used to separate the different substances in a mixture of liquids or gases. It is an important technique used in chemical ANALYSIS. It is used to separate small amounts of substances, such as pollutants in air; to separate and measure the quantities of two or more substances produced by a CHEMICAL REACTION; and to remove impurities from substances. In *liquid column chromatography*, a tube is filled with absorbent material and a sample of the mixture is poured in at one end. Another liquid called an eluant is then poured in which

◀ *This machine analyzes the chemical makeup of mixtures of gas and liquid samples. The samples are placed in numbered tubes. Results are given in the form of a chromatogram, a printout of concentrations of the parts making up the mixture.*

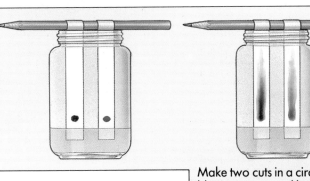

SEE FOR YOURSELF
Tape two strips of blotting paper to a pencil. Hang the strips in a jar so that the end of each strip is in the water. Put a blob of different colored washable ink on each strip above the level of the water. The paper absorbs the water and the different colors making up the blobs are dissolved at different speeds.

Make two cuts in a circle of blotting paper and bend the strip into a jar of water. Put a blob of ink in the center of the circle. As the water is absorbed by the paper it dissolves the ink. Rings of color are formed as the ink is split into its parts.

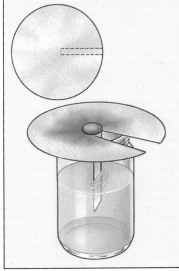

washes through the absorbent material. The different substances in the mixture are absorbed by the material at different rates as they are carried through by the eluant, each substance forming a distinct layer. *Thin layer chromatography* works in a similar way, except that the absorbent material is in the form of a thin film. In *gas chromatography*, used for analyzing a gas mixture, helium is used as an eluant to carry the different gases in the mixture through a column of absorbent material.

Chromium

Chromium is a hard bluish-white metallic ELEMENT that resists CORROSION and becomes shiny when polished. It occurs as chromite, which is a COMPOUND of chromium, iron, and oxygen. Chromium was discovered in the late 1790s and now has a wide range of industrial uses. It is used to plate other metals, for example, on car bumpers. In the aircraft industry, its compounds are used to ANODIZE aluminum. Chromium, also often called chrome, is added to steel to make it hard and corrosion resistant. Steel containing more than 10 percent of chromium is called STAINLESS STEEL. Chromium compounds have distinctive colors and traces of these give rubies and emeralds their attractive red and green colors. Lead chromate and other compounds are used in paints and dyes. Chromium dioxide is used in magnetic recording tape.

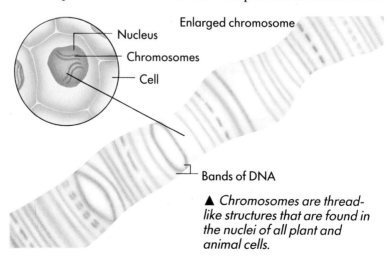

▶ *The black layer in this rock is the ore of chromium. Chromium is unusual as it only has one ore.*

Thomas Hunt Morgan (1866–1945)
An American zoologist and geneticist, he won the Nobel Prize for Physiology in 1930 for his work linking chromosomes and heredity. His experiments with the fruit fly *Drosophila* showed that the genes, the units of heredity, were carried on the chromosomes. He later showed that the position of the genes on the chromosome controlled inherited characteristics.

Chromosomes and Genes

Inside the nucleus of every living CELL there are a number of microscopic threads called chromosomes. These chromosomes carry all the information necessary for the proper development of the cells and the whole body. They are the "plans" from which the cells work. Each kind of plant or animal has its own particular number of

Enlarged chromosome
Nucleus
Chromosomes
Cell
Bands of DNA

▲ *Chromosomes are thread-like structures that are found in the nuclei of all plant and animal cells.*

August Weismann (1834–1914)
Weismann was one of the founders of the science of genetics. He realized that something in the germ cells contained in the sexual organs was passed on to the next generation, controlling their heredity. He found that inborn characteristics of both parents, such as height and eye color, were combined in their offspring but that acquired characteristics were not inherited. He showed that offspring of mice which had had their tails cut off were born with normal tails.

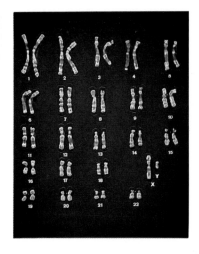

▲ Humans have 23 pairs of chromosomes in most of their cells. Males and females differ only in the sex chromosome of the 23rd pair. A female's sex chromosomes would look like XX, instead of XY in the male.

chromosomes. They occur in pairs. Humans have 22 pairs in each normal cell plus two extra chromosomes, sex chromosomes, which decide the body's sex.

The chromosomes are made largely of chains of DNA molecules. Parts of these chains are genes, and there may be hundreds of them on a chromosome. Each one controls one or more features in the body by determining what PROTEINS are made in the cells. Proteins are the major materials of living cells.

Although we all have the same number of chromosomes in our cells, we have slightly different genes, and so we look different. When plants and animals reproduce, chromosomes and genes from both parents are mixed together.

See also CELL DIVISION; GENETICS; HEREDITY; NUCLEIC ACIDS.

Among plants, many new species have arisen because the number of their chromosomes has changed. This occurs during cell division when the chromosomes fail to separate properly. Occasionally whole sets of chromosomes fail to separate; for example, the wheat used in bread flour has 42 chromosomes while its ancestors had 14 and 28 chromosomes.

Cinematography

Cinematography is filmmaking. A motion picture FILM is actually a long strip of thousands of still photographs. The film strip is wound onto a reel, and the reel fitted to a projector. The film threads through the projector and each picture, or frame, is projected onto the screen. The pictures appear so rapidly (24 frames per second) that they merge together into smooth, lifelike movement. The images on the film are made by a special camera. It works like a still CAMERA, except that it takes 24 pictures every second on a continuous strip of film.

The first moving pictures or movies were made by the

Different Genes
Organisms inherit two forms of the same gene for each characteristic. These forms may be identical or they may be different. If they are different then one form may be **dominant** — its effect will be seen — or it may be **recessive** — its effect will be hidden. Only if both forms of a gene, such as blue eye color, are recessive will the organism show the recessive characteristic.

121

► *This explosion is one of the many stunning visual effects created for the film* Indiana Jones and the Last Crusade.

SEE FOR YOURSELF

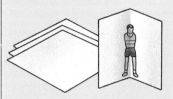

You need four sheets of thin cardboard or paper measuring about 8 inches square. Fold each piece of paper or cardboard down the center. Draw a picture of a person without arms.

Trace this picture onto the center of each piece of paper. Now draw in the arms on the body as shown in the illustration. Arrange the pictures so that each of the two pictures with the arms outstretched at the side are placed between the other two.

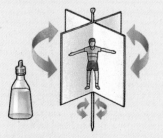

Glue the backs of the pictures to a knitting needle. Spin the needle. The speed makes it look as if the still pictures are joined and the arms are moving as in cinematography.

inventor Thomas Alva EDISON. They were shown in a machine called a Kinetoscope. However, only one person at a time could see the film. The French Lumière brothers were the first to make a film projector that allowed a number of people to see the film together.

The earliest movies were silent. Sound recording had been invented but there was not yet a successful way of keeping the sound in step with the pictures, called synchronization. The first Hollywood movie with synchronized sound, a "talkie," was *The Jazz Singer*, starring Al Jolson. It was shown for the first time in 1927. Color film only became available in the 1930s. Most films have been made in color since the 1950s.
See also PHOTOGRAPHY.

Circuit breaker

A circuit breaker is a device that stops an electric CIRCUIT working in the event of an abnormal or dangerous situation. A sudden increase in the electric current can damage electrical equipment or start a fire. Most electrical equipment in the home and office and its users are protected from dangerous electrical faults by FUSES. In a fuse, a thin wire heats up and melts, cutting off the power supply. A new fuse must be fitted before the equipment will work again. Modern circuit breakers use ELECTRONIC sensors to detect faults and switch the power off. The power can be switched on again by pressing a switch on the circuit breaker to reset it.

Circuit, electric

An electric circuit is a loop of electrical CONDUCTORS through which a current of ELECTRONS can flow. You can think of a current as a flow of water; in just the same way as water can be pumped around a circuit of pipes and made to drive water wheels, an electric current is driven around a circuit and made to light bulbs or run motors. The electrical equivalent of a pump is the BATTERY, which uses chemical ENERGY stored within it to drive the electric current. Just as the pump has to overcome friction to force water through the pipes, the battery has to overcome electrical RESISTANCE to make a current flow in the circuit. If the current has to flow through several resistances (light bulbs can be used as resistances), one after the other, then the battery is not able to make so much current flow; the resistances are said to be in series. If the resistances are arranged so that some of the current flows through one and some through another, they are said to be in parallel.

Circuits with batteries work with direct current; the flow of current is always in the same direction. Most mechanical GENERATORS generate an alternating current which flows alternately in opposite directions. The electric sockets in houses are connected through large electrical circuits to the generators in power stations, and carry an alternating current.

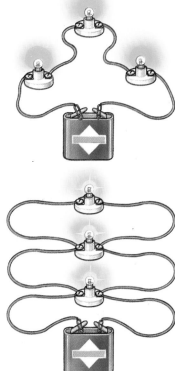

▲ The bulbs in the top circuit are wired in series; the bulbs are all sharing the power so they are dim. The bulbs in the bottom circuit are wired in parallel; each bulb has its own connection to the battery and so is not dim.

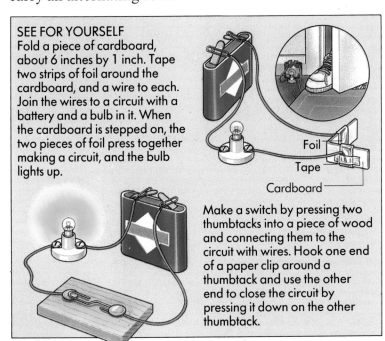

SEE FOR YOURSELF
Fold a piece of cardboard, about 6 inches by 1 inch. Tape two strips of foil around the cardboard, and a wire to each. Join the wires to a circuit with a battery and a bulb in it. When the cardboard is stepped on, the two pieces of foil press together making a circuit, and the bulb lights up.

Foil
Tape
Cardboard

Make a switch by pressing two thumbtacks into a piece of wood and connecting them to the circuit with wires. Hook one end of a paper clip around a thumbtack and use the other end to close the circuit by pressing it down on the other thumbtack.

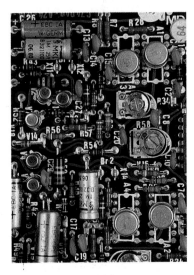

▲ Electrical circuits in appliances are made up of different components, attached to a circuit board.

William Harvey (1578–1657)
Harvey was an English physician. He was the first to accurately describe the circulation of the blood. He showed that blood moves around the body in only one direction along arteries and veins.

Circulation

Circulation is the process in which BLOOD is moved around an organism's body by the HEART so that cells and organs in every part of the body can receive oxygen and food substances from the blood, and waste materials can be carried away. Blood also contains chemical messengers called HORMONES which can activate or switch off certain body processes as required. Humans have a double circulation. Blood leaving the right side of the heart is pumped through the LUNGS, where it picks up oxygen and releases carbon dioxide and water vapor. This oxygenated blood then returns to the left side of the heart, and is pumped around the body until it comes back again to the right side of the heart. Blood always leaves the heart through arteries, passes through microscopically small capillaries, then returns along veins.

▶ The blood is pumped from the heart into arteries and circulates through veins back to the heart.

Fish

Gills
Heart
Liver
Gut
Kidneys
Tail

Human

Veins — Arteries
Head
Lungs
Heart
Liver
Intestines
Kidneys
Limbs

Deoxygenated blood   Oxygenated blood

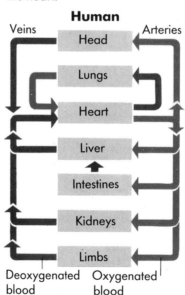

▲ The arrows show the path of the blood through the fish and human circulatory systems.

◀ The earthworm has five hearts to circulate its blood. In snails, blood flows from vessels into open spaces between organs. It moves through these spaces to return to the heart.

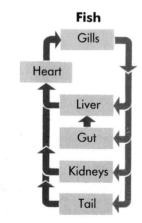

Shell
Lung
Snail
Heart   Sinus

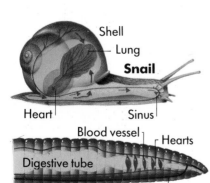

Blood vessel — Hearts
Digestive tube
Earthworm Nerve cord

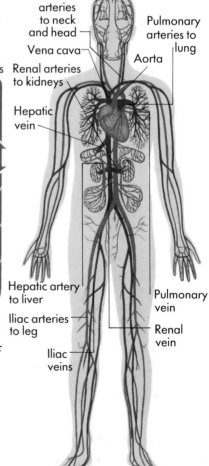

Carotid arteries to neck and head
Vena cava
Renal arteries to kidneys
Hepatic vein
Pulmonary arteries to lung
Aorta
Hepatic artery to liver
Iliac arteries to leg
Iliac veins
Pulmonary vein
Renal vein

CLASSIFICATION

There are over a million kinds of animals and nearly half a million kinds of plants, so it is essential to have some way of classifying them or arranging them into groups so that we can refer to them easily. Look at the plants and animals around you and you will probably see several ways of classifying them. You might decide to group the flowers according to their colors. This is an easy way to do it, but it is not a very satisfactory way because it would put red and white tulips in separate groups when they clearly belong together. Classifying by color is an artificial classification and it tells us nothing about the structure or the biology of the flowers. Biologists use natural systems of classification, in which the members of each group have similar structures and are related to each other.

In the present day classification system, species of animals that are closely related are grouped into a genus (plural genera). Genera with similar characteristics are grouped into families. Families, in turn, are grouped into orders; orders into classes; and classes into phyla. Finally, related phyla are placed into kingdoms. Plants are classified in the same way, although the major groups are often called divisions instead of phyla. Aristotle was one of the first people to attempt to classify animals and plants in this way, but the Swedish naturalist Linnaeus laid the foundations of modern classification in the 18th century.

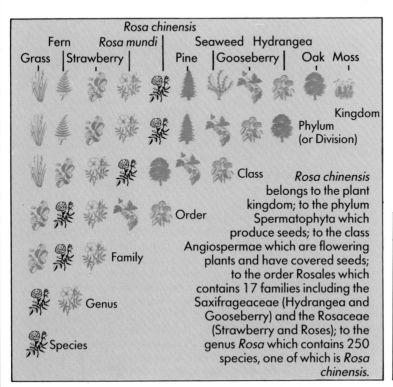

Rosa chinensis

Fern   Rosa mundi

Grass | Strawberry | Seaweed Hydrangea

Pine | Gooseberry | Oak   Moss

Kingdom

Phylum (or Division)

Class

Order

Family

Genus

Species

Rosa chinensis belongs to the plant kingdom; to the phylum Spermatophyta which produce seeds; to the class Angiospermae which are flowering plants and have covered seeds; to the order Rosales which contains 17 families including the Saxifrageaceae (Hydrangea and Gooseberry) and the Rosaceae (Strawberry and Roses); to the genus *Rosa* which contains 250 species, one of which is *Rosa chinensis*.

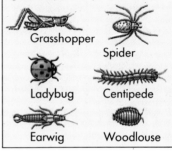

► Organisms are named using a binomial (two name) system introduced by Linnaeus. The first name is the genus and the second, the species name. Even the common housefly is named like this — *Musca domestica*.

◄ Different levels of classification of the plant kingdom showing how one plant species *Rosa chinensis* can be separated from other plants.

Panthera leo (lion)

Panthera tigris (tiger)

▲ These two cats belong to the same genus, *Panthera*, but are different species.

See also BIOLOGY; BOTANY; LINNAEUS; MICROBIOLOGY; MICROORGANISMS; ZOOLOGY.

The **Arthropoda** is the largest animal phylum, and includes arachnids, crustaceans, and insects among others. They have an external skeleton and jointed appendages.

The **Mollusca** is the second-largest phylum. They are soft-bodied animals and most have a shell to protect them. They include snails, bivalves, and octopuses.

Aves

Mammalia

The class **Mammalia** contains the mammals. They are warm-blooded animals with hair. Offspring are fed on milk from the mother.

The class **Aves** contains the birds, separated from all other animals by their feathers. All birds hatch from eggs and have wings but not all can fly.

Arachnids

Snails

Octopuses

Bivalves

Crustaceans

Insects

The class **Reptilia** contains the reptiles, which are scaly, cold-blooded animals and include lizards, snakes, crocodiles, and turtles.

The phylum **Annelida** are limbless animals whose soft bodies are divided into segments. They include the earthworms and their relatives.

Annelida

The phylum **Coelenterata** are a group of soft-bodied animals, most of which live in the sea. They include jellyfish, sea anemones, and corals.

Coelenterata

Amphibia

Reptilia

The class **Amphibia** contains cold-blooded animals that spend part of their lives in water and part on land. They include frogs, toads, and newts.

Fish belong to several classes in the phylum **Chordata**. They all live in water, swim with fins, and almost all breathe through gills.

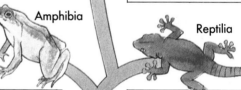

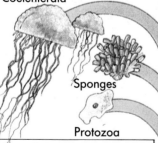

Sponges

Protozoa

The phylum **Protozoa** contains microscopic animals, each consisting of only a single cell. There are more than 30,000 different kinds of protozoa.

Echinoderms

Fishes

THE ANIMAL KINGDOM

The animal kingdom is divided into about 30 major groups. Animals with one or more of the same body characteristics are separated into major groups called phyla. Animals with backbones, called vertebrates, plus a few other creatures, belong to the phylum Chordata. They include the lancelets, fish, amphibians, reptiles, birds, and mammals. All the other phyla contain more than 950,000 species of animals without backbones, called invertebrates. Among these phyla are the annelids, mollusks, arthropods, and the echinoderms (starfish and sea urchins). Not all scientists agree about the number of phyla, since some animals do not fit neatly into phyla. The velvet worms, for example, are neither annelids nor arthropods and so can be put into a phylum of their own.

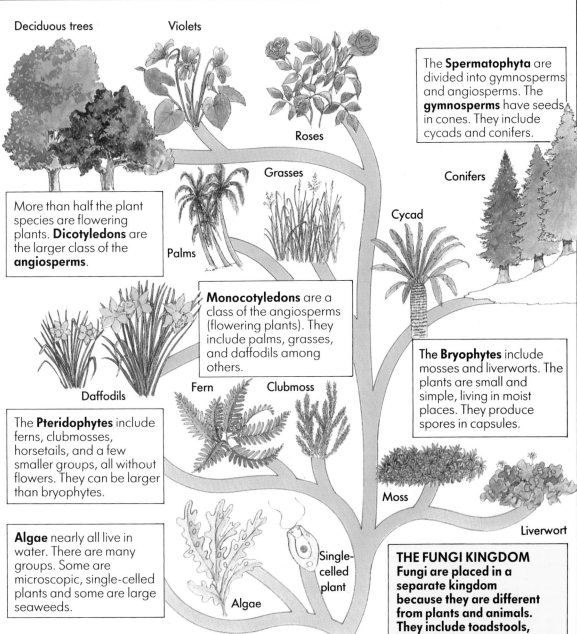

Deciduous trees

Violets

Roses

The **Spermatophyta** are divided into gymnosperms and angiosperms. The **gymnosperms** have seeds in cones. They include cycads and conifers.

Grasses

Conifers

More than half the plant species are flowering plants. **Dicotyledons** are the larger class of the **angiosperms**.

Palms

Cycad

Monocotyledons are a class of the angiosperms (flowering plants). They include palms, grasses, and daffodils among others.

The **Bryophytes** include mosses and liverworts. The plants are small and simple, living in moist places. They produce spores in capsules.

Daffodils

Fern

Clubmoss

The **Pteridophytes** include ferns, clubmosses, horsetails, and a few smaller groups, all without flowers. They can be larger than bryophytes.

Moss

Liverwort

Algae nearly all live in water. There are many groups. Some are microscopic, single-celled plants and some are large seaweeds.

Algae

Single-celled plant

THE FUNGI KINGDOM

Fungi are placed in a separate kingdom because they are different from plants and animals. They include toadstools, yeasts, and molds. They live almost anywhere in the soil, water, and air. They do not produce their own food, since they have no chlorophyll, so they take nutrients from the animals, plants, or decaying matter on which they live. They reproduce by spores sexually or asexually.

THE PLANT KINGDOM

Several systems are used to classify the 450,000 or so kinds of plants that belong to the plant kingdom. The main divisions, or phyla, of the plant kingdom are the Algae, Bryophyta, Pteridophyta, and the Spermatophyta. The spermatophytes make up the largest phylum, consisting of over 350,000 different species which reproduce by way of seeds. There are two kinds of seed-bearing plants, the gymnosperms, or "naked seed" plants, and the angiosperms, or "covered seed" plants. The angiosperms, which include all of the flowering plants, are divided into two classes, the monocotyledons, plants with one seedleaf, and the dicotyledons, plants with two seedleaves. The other phyla do not produce flowers and all reproduce by scattering particles called spores.

Chinese fire clock 3000 B.C.

Italian monastery clock 1400s

Pendulum clock

Quartz watch

Digital alarm clock

Mechanical watch

▲ *There have been ways of measuring time for many thousands of years. At first clocks were only accurate to the nearest hour but now they can measure seconds precisely.*

▶ *Mechanical watches and some small mechanical clocks are regulated by a balance wheel and spring. The wheel spins one way and then the other. It makes an arm rock back and forth, which allows the escape wheel to move round one step at a time. The escape wheel is driven by the clock's mainspring, which slowly unwinds.*

Climate

The climate of a particular region of the world describes the average WEATHER conditions over a long period of time — at least 50 years. These conditions include the average TEMPERATURE, rainfall, air PRESSURE, HUMIDITY, hours of sunshine, and wind speed and direction in that region. *See* pages 132 and 133.

Clocks and Watches

Clocks and watches are designed to show the passage of TIME. Clocks usually stand on their own and watches are strapped to the wrist. Time was probably first measured several thousand years ago by observing the position of the Sun in the sky. Water clocks and sandglasses, or hour glasses, used changing levels of water or sand in a container to measure time. Candles burn at a constant rate and can be used to measure time. Sundials use the movement of shadows cast by the Sun. The first mechanical timepieces were made in China in the 8th century.

All mechanical timepieces need a source of power. Before electric power, clocks used springs or weights. Many modern clocks and watches are powered by batteries. Digital watches have no moving parts. Instead of hands, the time is shown by numbers on a tiny screen. *See also* LIQUID CRYSTAL DISPLAY; MEASUREMENT.

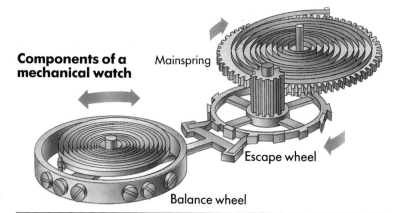

Components of a mechanical watch

Mainspring

Escape wheel

Balance wheel

Clones

Clones are living creatures reproduced or copied from a single CELL, without sexual REPRODUCTION or meiosis taking place. This means that the new organisms are physically and genetically identical to the "parent" cell. Identical twins are produced naturally in this way, when the EGG cell splits after FERTILIZATION and separates into two separate EMBRYOS, sharing identical genes. It is possible to produce cloned animals in the laboratory.

Cloning is a commercial process often used in plant BREEDING, where flowers or crop plants are produced in huge numbers from a single cell taken from a plant with the desired characteristics. This process results in a population with identical genes, and this is not always good; in the case of plants, some varieties with useful properties could die out without passing on their genes.

Closed circuit television *See* Television

Cloud

A cloud is a mass of tiny droplets of water floating in the AIR sometimes at a great distance from the Earth's surface. Water VAPOR is water in the form of a GAS and, under normal conditions, it is invisible. If you boil a kettle, for example, the water vapor that is produced cannot be seen at first. It is only when the vapor cools and condenses into drops of LIQUID water that you see the steam.

All air contains water vapor from EVAPORATION of lakes, ponds, rivers, and seas. Almost 500 million tons of water pass between the Earth and the air every year.

Warm air can hold more water vapor than cool air before the water condenses. As air rises, it becomes

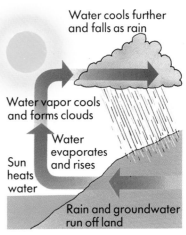

▲ Clouds are formed from water that has evaporated from oceans, rivers, lakes, or from moist soil and plants. The evaporated water cools as it rises. When it has cooled enough, the vapor condenses and forms clouds.

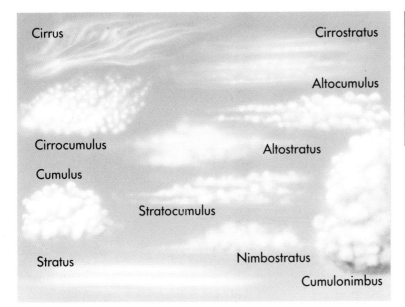

Cirrus
Cirrostratus
Altocumulus
Cirrocumulus
Altostratus
Cumulus
Stratocumulus
Stratus
Nimbostratus
Cumulonimbus

"Mother of pearl" clouds are not often seen. When they do occur they appear at great height and provide one of the most beautiful displays in the sky. They have a rainbow colored marbled texture, which is continually changing.

◀ Different types of clouds are seen at various heights above the Earth. Clouds that appear as layers or sheets are called stratus clouds. Those that appear as piled up white masses are known as cumulus clouds, and high, wispy clouds are called cirrus clouds.

Despite the fact that coal is not as important as it was, coal-burning power plants still produce almost two-thirds of the world's electricity.

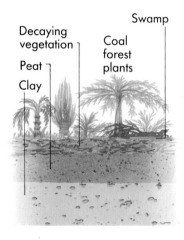

Decaying vegetation

Swamp

Coal forest plants

Peat

Clay

▲ *The remains of dead plants in prehistoric forests became peat which was gradually buried and subjected to great pressure. After many thousands of years the peat turned into coal.*

▶ *Coal deposits deeper than 200 feet (60 m) are normally mined underground. Shaft mines have access passages which run straight down from the surface to the coal seam. The coal is taken to the surface using a hoist.*

cooler so that, eventually, the air becomes saturated with water vapor. If the saturated air continues to rise and cool, the water vapor condenses into drops of liquid water. If the cloud gets even colder the drops of CONDENSATION become large enough to form rain. These are the clouds you see in the sky. If a mass of air falls, however, it gets warmer and so holds more water vapor. There are different clouds defined and named after their shape and height in the ATMOSPHERE.

Coal

Coal is a black or blackish rock, consisting chiefly of CARBON. There are two main kinds, anthracite or hard coal, and bituminous or soft coal. It is one of the main FOSSIL FUELS, formed during the Carboniferous period (about 350–250 million years ago) from the rotting vegetation of tropical forests. This became overlaid by other rocks and gradually turned into coal. Most coal is found in bands or seams at varying depths under the ground. When we burn it we are releasing the Sun's ENERGY, stored for millions of years in the partly fossilized vegetable matter.

Coal was the most important fuel of the INDUSTRIAL REVOLUTION and also the chief domestic FUEL. In the last 50 years, coal has largely been replaced by other fossil fuels. But many of its by-products are still used in detergents, antiseptics, dyes, pesticides, and medical drugs.

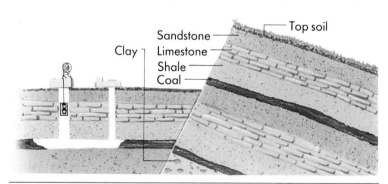

Top soil

Sandstone

Clay

Limestone

Shale

Coal

Cockerell, Christopher *See* Hovercraft

Cold

Something is cold when its TEMPERATURE is lower than its surroundings. Things that feel cold to us have a temperature lower than our body temperature. When objects are cold, the MOLECULES in them are moving around more slowly than in hotter objects. The molecules in hotter objects tend to bump into the molecules in a colder one, causing the cold object to heat up. For this reason it is difficult to keep an object very much colder than its surroundings.

Cryogenics is the study of low temperatures and their effects. It has helped scientists to perform experiments at only a few millionths of a degree above absolute zero, which is as cold as it is possible to get since all molecules stop moving at absolute zero.

See also CONDUCTION, HEAT; EVAPORATION; HEAT.

Colloids

A colloid is halfway between a SOLUTION and a SUSPENSION. In a colloid, particles of MATTER measuring between about a ten-millionth of an inch and a thousandth of an inch in diameter are evenly scattered throughout liquid or gas.

Smoke is a colloid in which microscopic solid particles are dispersed in the air. This kind of colloid is also known as an AEROSOL. Other colloids include dairy products like butter, the cytoplasm of CELLS, and fluids found inside our body tissues. An EMULSION is a colloid in which droplets of a liquid are scattered evenly in another liquid. In a FOAM, a gas (usually air) is dispersed in a liquid. A paste is a concentrated mixture in which solid particles are dispersed in a liquid. An example of a typical paste is toothpaste.

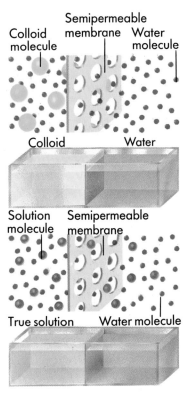

▲ The particles in a colloid such as cream are larger than those of a true solution such as food coloring and water. The colloid particles cannot diffuse through a membrane into the water on the other side of the container, but the particles of a true solution can, turning the clear water pink.

◄ Milk is a colloidal dispersion of fats in water. During cheese-making the milk is separated into curds (the solid milk fats lumped together) and whey (the liquid). The curd is then packed into molds for pressing into cheese.

CLIMATE

Temperature and rainfall are the most important factors determining the climate. If you look at a map of the world's climates or even at separate maps of average rainfall and temperature, you can see that there is a rough pattern. The different climates seem to occupy bands running horizontally across a map with north at the top and south at the bottom. There is another factor which affects climate; the distribution of land and sea. This is because continental areas heat up and cool down more quickly than the sea, which tends to have a moderating effect on the weather pattern of an area.

Warm air holds far more water than cold air. Close to the equator, air is warmed by the Sun and holds a lot of water evaporated from the oceans. As it rises, the water condenses into clouds and falls as rain so this area tends to be hot and wet. Further north or south at the tropics, the air which has risen and circulated from the equatorial area is falling again. As the air falls it warms up so it can hold more water at the tropics. Here, the world's hot, dry deserts occur because there is very little rain.

The Sun's rays heat the atmosphere only a little. It is the heat reflected back from the Earth that has the most warming effect. In the polar regions, the Sun's rays must travel much farther through the air before reaching the ground and they lose a lot of the Sun's warmth on the way. The air is so cold at the poles that what water there is falls as snow. These are the coldest parts of the world. The climate of areas between these three main climatic zones tends to be more variable, and the presence of mountains, forests, or large cities can affect it.

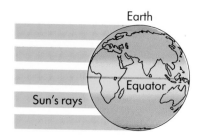

▲ Every place on Earth has its own climate. Regions near the equator, where the Sun shines directly overhead, have a hotter climate than those farther away.

▼ The Earth can be roughly divided into six climatic zones. Within each zone there are variations due to altitude and latitude.

- Polar climate
- Mountain climate
- Cold forest climate
- Mid-latitude (temperate) climate
- Dry (desert) climate
- Tropical rainy climate

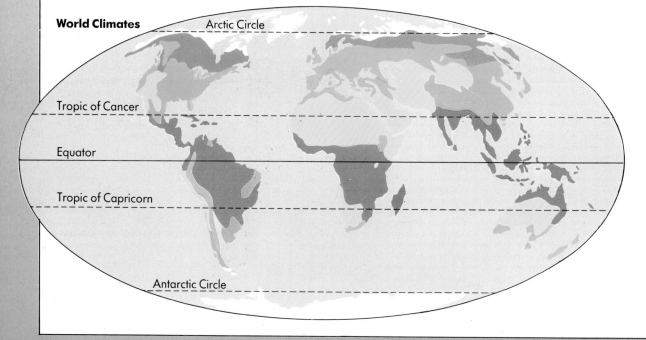

World Climates

Arctic Circle

Tropic of Cancer

Equator

Tropic of Capricorn

Antarctic Circle

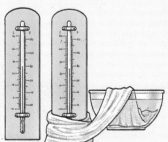

▲ Dry, sandy deserts are often intensely hot by day and cold by night.

◄ A freezing desert, the Antarctic, has the most severe climate in the world.

Climatic Zones

Polar climate: Always cold (average temperature below 50°F/10°C), brief chilly summer, little precipitation.

Mountain climate: Affected by altitude, cooler and wetter than the climates of neighboring areas.

Cold forest climate: (also called subarctic) Short, cool summer (four months at 50°F to 70°F/10°C to 20°C) and long, cold winter, light to moderate precipitation.

Mid-latitude (temperate) climate: Moderately warm summer and mild, cool winter (eight months, average temperature 50°F to 70°F/10°C to 20°C), moderate precipitation in all seasons.

Dry (desert) climate: Hot to cold, great changes in daily temperature except in coastal areas, little precipitation.

Tropical rainy climate: Always hot and wet (temperatures above 70°F/20°C), heavy precipitation throughout the year.

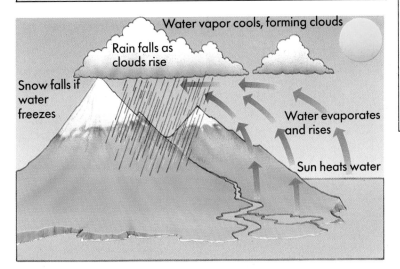

Water vapor cools, forming clouds

Rain falls as clouds rise

Snow falls if water freezes

Water evaporates and rises

Sun heats water

SEE FOR YOURSELF

Place two thermometers outside. Wrap a damp cloth around the bulb of one thermometer and put the end into water. When humidity is low the difference between the two thermometer readings will be greater than when humidity is high, because water from the cloth evaporates quickly and cools the thermometer.

◄ The Sun heats the surface of the sea. Hot air containing water vapor rises rapidly. As it rises the air cools and the vapor condenses to form water droplets, which develop into clouds. The droplets fall to the Earth as rain. If the water droplets freeze they fall as snow.

See also CELSIUS; CLOUD; CYCLONE; DESERT; EVAPORATION; FRONT, WEATHER; HEAT; METEOROLOGY; PRECIPITATION; SUN; TEMPERATURE; WEATHER; WIND.

COLOR

Light is a wave, a form of electromagnetic radiation. Different colors are made up of light with different wavelengths. The longest wavelength of light that we can see is red light and the shortest wavelength is blue light. Different substances in the world around us give off light of different colors because they are different chemically, and it seems that animals have evolved the ability to see various colors to help them tell these different substances apart.

There are special cells in your eye, called cones because of their shape, which can distinguish light of different colors when it falls on them. Some animals, such as dogs, do not have any cones in their eyes so we believe that they do not have color vision. The cones work well only in quite strong light, so in the near dark everything looks the same color.

Some animals that are active at night (owls, for example) have developed the ability to see light with wavelengths longer than those of red light. Similarly, some insects such as bees can distinguish markings on flowers that give off ultraviolet light. This has a shorter wavelength than the blue we can see.

Light with a shorter wavelength carries more energy than light with a longer one. When an object gives out heat by radiation, the wavelength of the light becomes shorter as the object becomes hotter so it glows first red, then white, then blue. Astronomers use the color of the light from the Sun and from other stars to find out their temperatures.

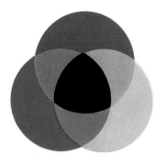

▲ When mixing pigments, the primary colors are yellow, blue, and red.

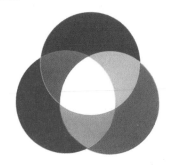

▲ When mixing lights, the primary colors are red, green, and blue. All three together make white light.

	Ultraviolet	Visible spectrum	Infrared
Cats and dogs	Bees	Humans	Owls

▲ Not all animals can see light from the same part of the spectrum.

SEE FOR YOURSELF
Try mixing colored lights. Use three flashlights covered with red, green, and blue see-through plastic. Green and red mix to make yellow; blue and green mix to make turquoise, and red and blue make purple.

Spin a disk painted with the colors of the spectrum. As the disk spins you see white as the different colors merge together.

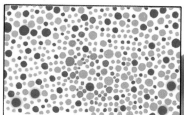

Color-blindness is the inability to tell some colors apart. If you have normal color vision you should see the number 6.

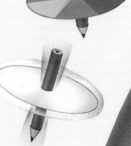

White light can be split into the colors of the spectrum using a prism. The colors it is made up of are red, orange, yellow, green, blue, indigo, and violet. A rainbow is a spectrum of light.

See also CAMOUFLAGE; ELECTROMAGNETIC RADIATION; EYE; LIGHT; PRISM; RAINBOW; SPECTRUM; WAVELENGTH.

Combustion

Combustion is a chemical process in which substances react together in a fast CHEMICAL REACTION accompanied by HEAT and LIGHT in the form of a BURNING flame. Combustion may also be accompanied by an EXPLOSION. In combustion, one of the reacting substances is usually the gas OXYGEN, and chemists commonly use the term combustion to mean the OXIDATION of a substance through burning. In some kinds of burning, no light is given off. If a fuel combines slowly with oxygen, heat alone is given off. This is what happens when iron rusts, but the burning is so slow that you can't even feel the heat being given off. Fire is fast combustion, rusting is slow combustion, but the total amount of heat given out is always the same. There are many industrial applications of combustion and, of course, in the INTERNAL-COMBUSTION ENGINE.

▲ A match is struck against the rough surface of the side of the matchbox. This makes the head of the match get hot and the match lights because the head contains substances that combust when they get hot.

◄ The temperature in the combustion chamber of a solid-propellant rocket, such as those used to launch the Space Shuttle, ranges from 3,000°F to 6,000°F (1,600°C to 3,300°C).

Some substances can burst into flames without anything being done to set them alight. This is called spontaneous combustion and is caused by slow oxidation. Damp coal sometimes begins to burn without being ignited. The same thing can happen to piles of oily rags.

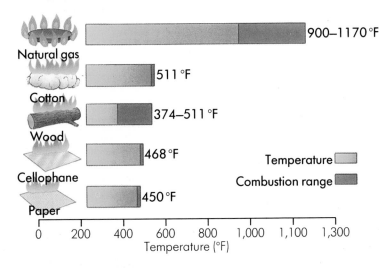

Natural gas — 900–1170°F

Cotton — 511°F

Wood — 374–511°F

Cellophane — 468°F

Paper — 450°F

Temperature ▭
Combustion range ▭

Temperature (°F)
0   200   400   600   800   1,000   1,100   1,300

◄ Every burnable substance has a particular temperature to which it must be heated before it combusts. The lower the temperature, the more easily the substance will catch fire. Some substances will burn at a range of temperatures.

135

The closest approach to Halley's comet occurred in 1986. It was by the European Space Agency's Giotto spacecraft, which came to within 335 miles (539 km) of the comet's core before its cameras stopped working because of the dust. Giotto revealed that the comet's core is a very black peanut shaped body about 10 by 2½ miles (15 by 4 km) in size.

Comet

A comet is a member of the SOLAR SYSTEM, orbiting the SUN. The solid part of a comet, the nucleus, is very small (a few miles across) but the cloud of gas and dust boiling away from the nucleus, the tail, can stretch out millions of miles. Comets are believed to be leftover particles from the beginning of the Solar System, when most of these particles collided with each other to build up the planets. The comet nuclei, containing crumbly rock par-

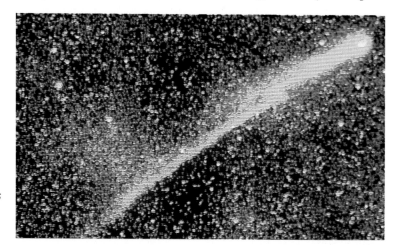

▶ Particles of gas and dust are swept outward into a tail behind a comet as it approaches the Sun. When a comet moves away from the Sun, its tail leads.

▼ Comets are not normally seen until they are within the orbit of Jupiter. By then the Sun has melted some of the ice they contain. Gases and dust are given off which reflect light well and make the comets more visible.

ticles trapped in frozen liquid, were left. If their orbits take them near the Sun, the heat turns the outer ice to vapor and the solid particles are released as dust. In their frozen state far from the Sun, comets are invisible. Each time a comet passes near the Sun it pours some more of its nucleus into space. Eventually it "dies" and becomes just an orbiting rock.

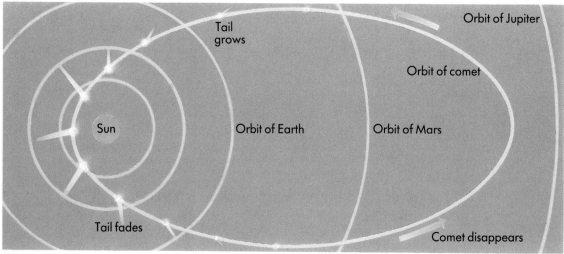

COMMUNICATIONS

Communication means exchanging ideas and information. For example, a dog warns another dog not to come closer by showing its teeth and snarling. Some moths find a mate by releasing a chemical that other moths can detect. Humans have developed language and then writing. This enables us to express complicated ideas and information.

Technology has given us new ways of communicating. Telecommunications give us almost instant communication with people and machines long distances apart. Computers can exchange information automatically through the telephone. Newspapers, radios, television, and the movies enable information to be communicated to millions of people.

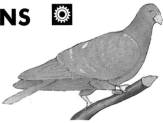

▲ Carrier pigeons are bred specially to carry messages over long distances. The message is tucked under a ring attached to one of its legs.

▲ Around 5,000 years ago, pictorial messages were inscribed on stone, leading to writing.

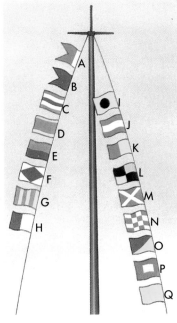

▲ International signal flags are used by ships at sea. Each flag represents a letter of the alphabet and has also an internationally recognized meaning.

▲ A fax machine enables people to send letters and documents to each other within a matter of seconds.

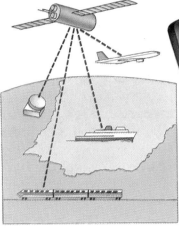

▲ Communications satellites are used to transmit and relay information around the world.

▲ In the future, everybody may have a compact personal telephone.

SEE FOR YOURSELF
Make your own telephone. Push the ends of a piece of string through two paper cups, knot

the ends and pull tight. When you speak into one cup, the sound travels along the string.

See also BEHAVIOR; CELLULAR RADIO AND TELEPHONES; COMPUTER; RADIO; TECHNOLOGY; TELECOMMUNICATIONS; TELEGRAPH; TELEPHONE; TELEVISION.

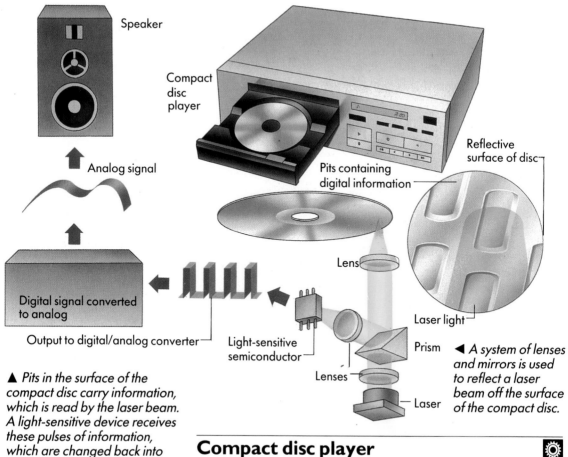

Speaker

Compact disc player

Analog signal

Digital signal converted to analog

Output to digital/analog converter

Light-sensitive semiconductor

Pits containing digital information

Reflective surface of disc

Lens

Laser light

Lenses

Prism

Laser

▲ *Pits in the surface of the compact disc carry information, which is read by the laser beam. A light-sensitive device receives these pulses of information, which are changed back into the original, recorded sound.*

◄ *A system of lenses and mirrors is used to reflect a laser beam off the surface of the compact disc.*

Compact disc player

A compact disc player is a machine used to play music recorded on a special type of disc. Unlike a vinyl record, a compact disc has no grooves. Music is recorded on the disc as tiny pits etched into a layer of ALUMINUM. The aluminum is protected by sealing it inside a clear layer of smooth PLASTIC. The music on the disc is played by directing a LASER beam onto the disc. The beam is reflected back to a detector by the smooth aluminum, but not by the rough surface of the pits. As the disc spins at high speed and the laser beam scans across the disc surface, the detector produces a series of pulses representing the pattern of pits etched into the disc. The player's electronic circuits change the pulses back into a copy of the original music.

The speed of the disc varies. When the laser is reading tracks near the center, the disc spins at its maximum speed, 500 revolutions per minute (rpm). As the laser moves to the edge, the speed reduces to 200 rpm so that information is read at a constant rate. The laser never actually touches the disc, so it should not wear out.

The laser beam in a compact disc player must be very fine to read only one track of the disc at a time. The tracks are only 1.6 micrometers apart. (A micrometer is a millionth of a meter or about 0.00004 of an inch.) The pits are only 0.5 micrometers wide and 1 to 3 micrometers long. The laser produces an intense, but invisible, infrared beam measuring only 1 micrometer across at its focus.

Compass

A compass points in a particular direction on the EARTH's surface; usually it shows north. The earliest and most common kind of compass, first used by Chinese sailors around A.D. 1100, worked by detecting the magnetism produced within the Earth. If a metal needle is magnetized and suspended so that it is free to turn it will point on a line which runs approximately north to south. The Earth's magnetic field changes with time, and so does the direction of this "magnetic north."

Other types of compass which do not use the Earth's magnetic field are now in use, including the GYROCOMPASS and inertial navigation systems which use LASERS.

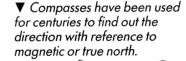

▼ Compasses have been used for centuries to find out the direction with reference to magnetic or true north.

An early European compass

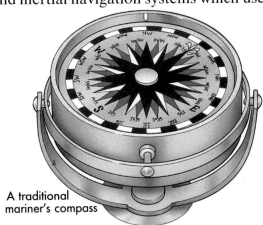

A traditional mariner's compass

SEE FOR YOURSELF
Place a small piece of cork in the center of a saucer of water. Magnetize a steel needle by running a magnet along it from the eye to the point several times. Carefully place the needle on top of the cork. The needle and cork will spin around to point to magnetic north. Magnetic north is actually 1,000 miles from the geographic North Pole.

Compound

A chemical compound is a substance consisting of ATOMS of two or more different ELEMENTS, held together in identical MOLECULES by means of chemical BONDS. In water, two parts of hydrogen combine with one part of oxygen. So one molecule of water contains two atoms of

▲ *Most elements do not exist on their own but as compounds with other elements. The colors visible in this rock are compounds of iron and niobium. Niobium is a rare metal which is often used with steel to make alloys that are resistant to high temperatures.*

Tools driven by compressed air have several advantages. They are light in weight; there is no risk of electric shock; they do not give off sparks or fumes, so they are useful in places such as mines where the air has to be kept pure or is flammable. They can even be used by divers underwater.

▶ *This industrial compressor uses compressed air to power heavy duty construction tools. Compressors are used for jobs such as breaking up concrete or paving, drilling, pile driving, sand-blasting, and tunneling. A compressor works on the same principle as a pump. A piston moves back and forth inside a hollow cylinder, which compresses the air and forces it into a hollow chamber. A pipe or hose connected to the chamber channels the compressed air to the tools.*

hydrogen and one of oxygen. This relationship, discovered by John Dalton (1766–1844), enables chemists to write down formulas in CHEMICAL SYMBOLS that show the composition of a compound. The formula for water is H_2O. There is a huge number of both natural and artificial compounds. Apart from water, the most familiar compounds include salt (sodium and chlorine, NaCl) and sugar (carbon, hydrogen, and oxygen, $C_6H_{12}O_6$). Compounds are different from MIXTURES because in a mixture the atoms of the different elements do not combine chemically and are not present in fixed proportions. Elements in a mixture can usually be separated easily; those in a compound cannot.

See also CHEMISTRY; POLYMER; SALTS, CHEMICAL.

Compressor

A compressor is a machine used to increase the PRESSURE of AIR above its normal or atmospheric pressure. Compressed air is used in a wide range of activities. The outside of buildings are often cleaned by ABRASIVES in a process called sandblasting where sand, in a jet of air from a compressor, strips away the surface layer of dirt coating the stone. Compressors are used to fill with compressed air the tanks that underwater divers need.

A variety of tools can be powered by compressed air. The drills used to dig holes through concrete and roads are powered by air from large compressors. All sorts of vehicles are painted, not with brushes, but by spraying the paint onto the metalwork. The jet of air that carries the paint from the spray gun to the vehicle is provided by a compressor.

See also PNEUMATICS.

Computer

A computer is a machine that processes information (data), at great speed according to a set of instructions (a computer program). Different programs in various COMPUTER LANGUAGES are used to process data in different ways, though the computer is performing the same simple operations. *See* pages 142 and 143.

Computer graphics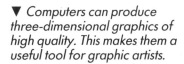

Computer graphics are pictures produced by a COMPUTER. They may appear on the screen or be printed on paper. Almost all computer games use graphics, and business, scientific, and engineering programs are using more graphics now. This is because drawings and color can give the computer user more information, more quickly than hundreds of words. The use of graphics in Computer Aided Design (CAD) can help in designing objects from shoes to spacecraft. In some cases, the design computer is also linked to manufacturing machinery: Computer Aided Manufacture (CAM). When an agreement is made on the design, the system can produce samples and finally the finished product. The most powerful computers can produce lifelike images that are used in television commercials or parts of movies.

▼ *Computers can produce three-dimensional graphics of high quality. This makes them a useful tool for graphic artists.*

▲ *This effect was achieved by transferring a photograph into a computer animation system and drawing it onto a grid of tiles.*

▼ *Engineers use computers in the design of more efficient vehicles. Small changes can be made to the design, and their effects observed, without having to redraw the whole object and make a new model for testing.*

COMPUTER

The first electronic computer, Colossus, was built in Britain in 1943. It used 1,500 electron tubes, each the size of a small bottle and it needed a team of trained operators. The tube was replaced by the transistor in the 1950s. It was a tiny fraction of the size of a tube. Computers became much smaller and the miniaturization has continued ever since. Computers are now built from integrated circuits, or chips, each chip containing up to several hundred thousand components. The most advanced chip is the microprocessor. It contains a computer's Central Processing Unit (CPU), its control, and calculating parts.

Computers affect almost every aspect of our lives. A person traveling on an aircraft has the seat booking made by computer. The aircraft was probably designed and built with the aid of computer controlled machinery and many of the aircraft's systems are controlled and monitored by computers. Before and during the flight, the crew is supplied with weather reports prepared with the aid of computers.

Many of the letters sent and received every day are prepared on a type of computer called a word processor. If a person has to go to the hospital, appointment details and some records are stored on computer files. All sorts of personal and business records are kept on computers.

Computers are also very good at creating lifelike images. Aircraft simulators enable pilots to train without leaving the ground. In a simulator, the detailed scene the pilot sees through the aircraft's windows is created by a computer. The computer's ability to process large amounts of data very quickly is used in scientific research to analyze the results of experiments.

▲ *This computer was used in 1952 to predict the results of the presidential election.*

▲ *A modern portable computer.*

▼ *Some of the devices that can be used to input information into a computer are: a joystick, often used when playing games; a mouse for drawing computer graphics; and a keyboard. Disk drives are used for both inputting information and storing it.*

▼ *Computers store data and programs on RAM and ROM memory chips. The central processing unit (CPU) is the heart of a computer system. Input devices such as a keyboard, and output devices, such as a visual display unit,* and a printer are used to communicate between the computer and the user.

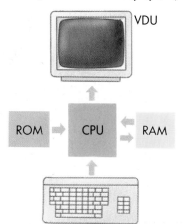

VDU

ROM → CPU ⇄ RAM

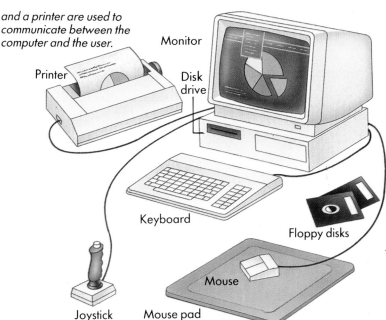

Monitor

Printer

Disk drive

Keyboard

Floppy disks

Mouse

Joystick   Mouse pad

▲ Most home computers can store the rules of computer games and display detailed colored graphics. Games also have special sound effects to make them more exciting.

▲ A microcomputer can be programmed to enable you to play chess against it. The memory keeps a record of all the moves made.

▲ The resolution of modern computer (and television screens) allows graphics programs to produce very realistic animation.

▶ Modern, fast, and powerful computers still take up quite a lot of space though they are much less bulky than the old-fashioned tube computers. The central processing unit is contained in the upright structures.

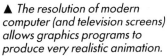

▼ A light pen is a device used to input information into a computer. This is done by holding the pen to the screen.

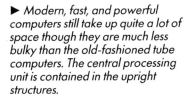

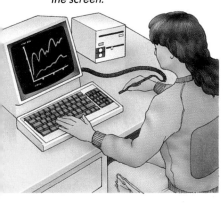

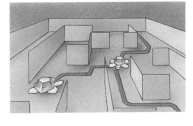

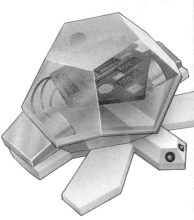

▶ This mechanical turtle is a robot that moves under computer control. It is used to help teach children about computers; for example, the turtle can be programmed to find its way around a maze (above).

See also HARDWARE; LANGUAGE TRANSLATION BY COMPUTERS; MAGNETIC TAPE; MICROCHIP; MICROPROCESSOR; SOFTWARE.

Program The sequence of instructions given to a computer to make it perform a particular task.
BASIC The initials stand for Beginners' All-purpose Symbolic Instruction Code. This programming language was developed in the 1960s and is one of the most widely used computer languages in the world.
Logo A program language specially designed to allow young children to program using a device called a turtle.
Fortran A program language, first introduced in the 1950s, which is used for scientific work. The name comes from "formula translation."

Computer languages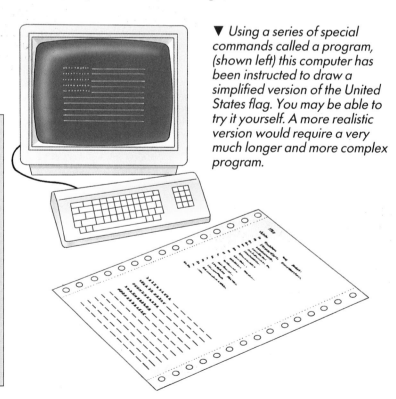

Computer languages enable people to communicate with COMPUTERS. Computers can only process information in the form of a series of NUMBERS. This is practically impossible to understand. A computer language translates the computer operator's instructions into the "machine code" that the computer uses and translates the computer's coded responses back into words that the human operator can understand.

There are many different computer languages designed to do different work. One of the most popular is BASIC (Beginners' All-purpose Symbolic Instruction Code) because it is easy to learn. Another, Pascal (after the 17th-century French mathematician, Blaise Pascal) was developed as a language for teaching. COBOL (Common Business Oriented Language) is used for writing financial programs. Logo uses simple instructions to control a "turtle." The turtle may be a small ROBOT that travels across the floor, connected to the computer by cable, or it may be a drawing on the screen. When the robot moves it draws a line. Logo teaches children how to analyze a problem, write a program to solve it, and correct any mistakes, or "bugs," in it.

▼ Using a series of special commands called a program, (shown left) this computer has been instructed to draw a simplified version of the United States flag. You may be able to try it yourself. A more realistic version would require a very much longer and more complex program.

A BASIC program
```
LIST
5 FOR ROW = 1 TO 5
10 FOR STAR = 1 TO 10
15 PRINT "*";
20 NEXT STAR
25 FOR STRIPE = 1 TO 20
30 PRINT "=";
35 NEXT STRIPE
40 PRINT
45 NEXT ROW
50 FOR ROW = 1 TO 5
55 FOR STRIPE = 1 TO 30
60 PRINT "=";
65 NEXT STRIPE
70 PRINT
75 NEXT ROW
RUN
```

Computer memory

Computer memory is like a set of pigeon holes. Each has an address. The address is a number that identifies it. Here it can store one unit of information. The COMPUTER is made up of various INTEGRATED CIRCUITS, or chips. Some form the computer's memory. Other chips control how information flows into and out of the computer.

There are two types of memory, Read Only Memory (ROM) and Random Access Memory (RAM). ROM stores programs that tell the computer how to process data and control its various parts. RAM is a temporary data store. Data in RAM is lost when the computer is switched off. The memory is connected to the computer's Central Processing Unit (CPU) by a data bus, an address bus, a read line, and a write line. A bus is a connection with several paths or wires so that several signals can be sent along it at the same time.

To store data, the CPU sends a signal along the write line to tell the memory that it wants to store (or write) data. It then sends the address where the data is to be stored on the address bus. The CPU sends the data on the data bus to the memory, where it is stored as electrical charges. To obtain data from (or read) the memory, the CPU sends a signal on the read line and then the address on the address bus. A copy of the contents of the address is sent to the CPU.

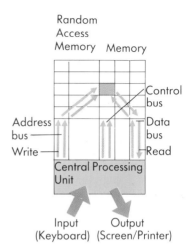

▲ Computers connect their three parts with links called buses down which data can be passed. Two types of computer memory are shown, RAM and ROM. Information can be put in or taken out of the RAM memory. The ROM memory has the computer's operating instructions on it and can't be changed.

Concentration

The concentration of a substance is the amount of that substance that exists in relation to something else. For example salt dissolves in water and the more salt you add the more salty the water will be. The salt is the SOLUTE, water the SOLVENT. The more solute there is dissolved

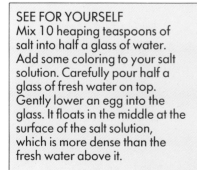

SEE FOR YOURSELF
Mix 10 heaping teaspoons of salt into half a glass of water. Add some coloring to your salt solution. Carefully pour half a glass of fresh water on top. Gently lower an egg into the glass. It floats in the middle at the surface of the salt solution, which is more dense than the fresh water above it.

SEE FOR YOURSELF
The steam from a boiling kettle escapes from the hot water inside into the colder air outside and forms water vapor. Put on a glove and hold a spoon in the steam. Tiny drops of water condense from the vapor and form on the spoon. These collect together and fall off the spoon as larger water drops.

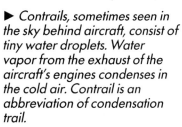

▶ Contrails, sometimes seen in the sky behind aircraft, consist of tiny water droplets. Water vapor from the exhaust of the aircraft's engines condenses in the cold air. Contrail is an abbreviation of condensation trail.

in the solvent, the higher the concentration of the solution. The concentration of a solute in a solvent is at its highest when the solution is SATURATED. The concentration of a solution is usually expressed as a percentage and indicates how many units of solute are dissolved in 100 units of solvent. The higher the concentration of a substance the greater the number of MOLECULES of that substance in a particular volume.
See also DIFFUSION; OSMOSIS.

Concrete *See* Cement

Condensation

Condensation is the process by which a GAS or a VAPOR forms a LIQUID when it is cooled. The cooling causes the gas molecules to slow down, so the forces of attraction between them make them stick more closely together. As they become closer together they become a liquid. For example, water vapor which evaporates during cooking often condenses on the inside of the lid of the saucepan, and some of the water vapor in the air in a room can condense on the cold windows. Mist, fog, and CLOUDS are produced when air that contains a lot of water vapor is cooled and the water condenses into very small droplets. If the droplets are large enough they fall to the ground as rain. Condensation is important in industry for purifying substances and in DISTILLATION, where a liquid is condensed and collected.
See also BOILING POINT; PRECIPITATION.

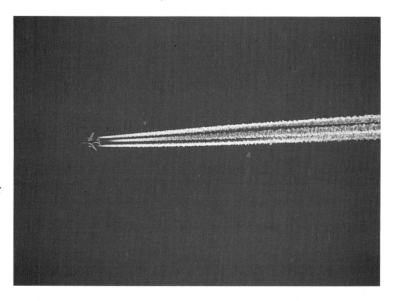

Condenser *See* Capacitor

Conduction, heat

Heat conduction (or thermal conduction) is the process by which HEAT travels through a material. This happens in all materials because MOLECULES in the hotter parts vibrate more quickly than molecules in the colder parts; the molecules that move more quickly bump into the more slowly moving ones and transfer ENERGY to them. This means that heat tends to travel through the material or substance from the hot parts to the colder parts. The best conductors of heat are METALS, since the ELECTRONS that carry electric current can also carry energy from hot parts to cold parts. Gases are by comparison poor

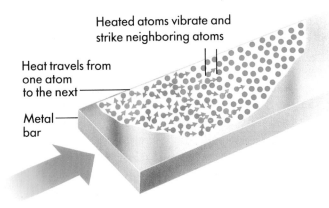

Heated atoms vibrate and strike neighboring atoms

Heat travels from one atom to the next

Metal bar

conductors, since the molecules that make them up are relatively far apart and do not collide very often. In a gas or a liquid, CONVECTION, which involves heat being carried by the circulation of the fluid, tends to carry more heat than conduction unless prevented from doing so by restricting movement of the fluid. Heat can also be transferred by RADIATION, which does not require any material to travel through.
See also INSULATION, THERMAL; THERMODYNAMICS.

Conductors, electric

Electric conductors are MATERIALS that can carry an electric current. The best conductors are METALS, because in these the ELECTRONS can move freely through the material, carrying the current. As the electrons move, they strike the ATOMS and make them vibrate; this interferes

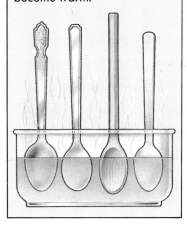

SEE FOR YOURSELF
Put four spoons made out of different materials into hot water. See which spoon handles get warm. Metal spoons get warm because the metal conducts heat. Wooden and plastic spoons do not conduct heat and so do not become warm.

◀ *Heat flows from the hot part of an object to the cold part. The rapidly moving atoms in the hot part strike the less energetic atoms in the cold part and speed them up.*

▼ *Current moves through materials that conduct electricity. Copper makes one of the best conductors and so is used to make wires and electrical connections. This diagram shows a section through a wire.*

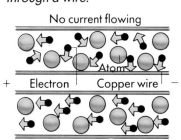

No current flowing

+ Electron   Copper wire −

Current flowing

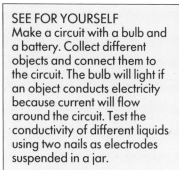

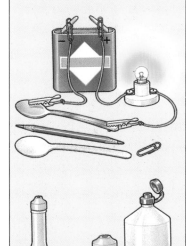

Gustav R. Kirchhoff (1824–1887)
Kirchhoff was a German physicist. In 1845, he worked out a set of laws called Kirchhoff's laws. These laws made it possible to calculate the amount of current flowing at any point in a network of electric conductors. He also showed that alternating current in an electric conductor with no resistance travels at the speed of light. With the German chemist Robert Bunsen he developed the modern spectroscope. They used the spectroscope and a prism specially designed by Kirchhoff to analyze substances. In 1860, they showed that when metal compounds are heated in a flame, each gives off a spectrum of colors particular to the metal. It was by using this technique that Kirchhoff and Bunsen discovered the elements caesium and rubidium.

The spectroscope also enabled astronomers to identify the elements that make up a star by studying the spectral lines in the star's light.

with the current flow and causes the material to heat up. This is electrical RESISTANCE. Good conductors have low resistance. Today the best conductors are not familiar metals like COPPER but are synthetic materials made from HYDROCARBONS.

Materials in which the electrons are not free to move separately are known as INSULATORS. Electrical conduction in solid insulators involves the movement of whole atoms and is much more difficult. There is also a class of materials, known as SEMICONDUCTORS, in which the electrons are almost, but not quite, free to move.

Conservation

A quantity is said to be conserved if, no matter how complicated the system, it does not change. For example, in CHEMICAL REACTIONS the total number of ATOMS of every ELEMENT is conserved; when hydrogen is burned in oxygen to form water, there are just as many hydrogen and oxygen atoms in the water at the end as there were in the starting materials.

It used to be thought that, since all substances are made up of atoms, the total amount of MASS present would also be conserved. However, the theory of RELATIVITY tells us that mass is a form of ENERGY and that it can be converted into other forms, for example, heat. It is the total energy, not just mass, which is conserved. This effect is too small to be measured in chemical reactions but is important to NUCLEAR ENERGY.

Conservation, environmental

Conservation is the management of the ENVIRONMENT, in all aspects, in such a way that its quality and natural RESOURCES are maintained. It does not necessarily mean that particular forms of wildlife, habitats, or climates, for example, should be protected and preserved unchanging for ever. Conservation recognizes that any natural system is constantly changing. Although humans evolved as part of the Earth's natural environment, our activities are often very damaging on a large scale. It is, therefore, necessary for humans to manage the environment, and the effects they have upon it, wisely. This means, for example, that, in world terms, a wide variety of animals and plants should be preserved, that resources such as MINERALS or ENERGY should be used sparingly, and that POLLUTION should be reduced.

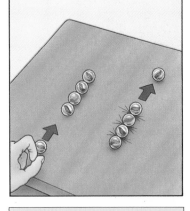

SEE FOR YOURSELF
Place four marbles in a row. Take another marble and roll it into the end of the row of marbles. The impact of the marble causes energy to be transferred between the marbles in the line. The marble at the end is propelled forward but the other marbles do not move. Since the energy is conserved, the energy of the moving marble is transferred to the marble at the end of the row and it moves.

People are becoming more aware that we must conserve our environment before it is too late. A number of United Nations agencies coordinate conservation on a worldwide basis. Mediterranean nations have agreed to work together to clean up the water of the sea and prevent oil spills. African and Asian countries are establishing national parks.

◀ Paper is just one of a number of products that can be recycled and turned into new paper goods. Waste paper is collected and stored as bales before being transported to a mill to be processed. Other products that can be recycled include aluminum cans and glass.

▼ Different constellations can be seen in the skies of the Northern and Southern Hemispheres. The 12 constellations which the Sun passes through in the course of a year are known as the signs of the zodiac.

Constellation

People usually think of a constellation as a group of stars, such as the bright stars of Ursa Major (the Great Bear). It is really one of the areas, arbitrarily named by astronomers, that fit together to make up the sky. Con-

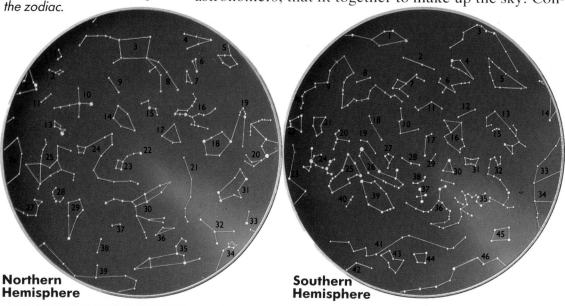

Northern Hemisphere

Southern Hemisphere

Main constellations of the Northern Hemisphere	
1 Equuleus	29 Boötes
2 Delphinus	30 Ursa Major
3 Pegasus	31 Gemini
4 Pisces	32 Cancer
5 Cetus	33 Canis Minor
6 Aries	34 Hydra
7 Triangulum	35 Leo
8 Andromeda	36 Leo Minor
9 Lacerta	37 Canes Venatici
10 Cygnus	38 Coma Berenices
11 Sagitta	39 Virgo
12 Aquila	
13 Lyra	
14 Cepheus	
15 Cassiopeia	
16 Perseus	
17 Camelopardus	
18 Auriga	
19 Taurus	
20 Orion	
21 Lynx	
22 Pole or North star	
23 Ursa Minor	
24 Draco	
25 Hercules	
26 Ophiuchus	
27 Serpens	
28 Corona Borealis	

Main constellations of the Southern Hemisphere			
1 Cetus	13 Sagittarius	25 Puppis	36 Centaurus
2 Sculptor	14 Aquila	26 Carina	37 Crux
3 Aquarius	15 Corona Australis	27 Volans	38 Musca
4 Piscis Austrinus	16 Pavo	28 Chamaeleon	39 Vela
5 Capricornus	17 Octans	29 Apus	40 Pyxis
6 Grus	18 Dorado	30 Triangulum	41 Hydra
7 Phoenix	19 Pictor	Australe	42 Sextans
8 Fornax	20 Columba	31 Ara	43 Crater
9 Eridanus	21 Lepus	32 Scorpio	44 Corvus
10 Hydrus	22 Orion	33 Serpens	45 Libra
11 Tucana	23 Monoceros	34 Ophiuchus	46 Virgo
12 Indus	24 Canis Major	35 Lupus	

stellations are all different shapes and sizes. Some constellations contain very few bright stars, for example, the largest constellation, Hydra (the Water Sanke), is so dim that few people know of it, but everyone has heard of the smallest, Crux (the Southern Cross).

Many of the constellations were named before 2000 B.C. by Babylonian astronomers. The oldest are the 12 forming the zodiac. By A.D. 150, when the Greek astronomer Ptolemy published his famous star catalog, he listed 48. No more were added until explorers began to sail south and saw parts of the sky invisible from Europe and the Mediterranean. The total number is now 88.

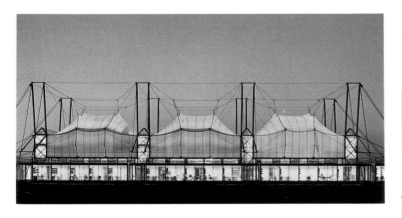

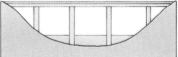

◀ The building of complicated elaborate structures has been made possible by advances in construction technology.

Beam bridge

Cantilever bridge

Arch bridge

Suspension bridge

▲ Examples of some of the most common types of bridge design.

Construction

Construction, or building, has changed the world around us. Construction engineers build the biggest structures in the modern world: the major road systems, bridges, tunnels, dams, skyscrapers, and power stations. Concrete and STEEL are among the most commonly used MATERIALS.

Every structure has a natural FREQUENCY called its resonant frequency. Any structure that vibrates at its resonant frequency may shake so violently that it tears itself apart. Engineers must be careful that the flow of wind or water around a structure does not cause resonant vibration. Models of proposed structures are tested in WIND TUNNELS to ensure this does not happen. Analysis of structures by COMPUTER helps to predict problems.

Some shapes are particularly strong. Tubes and triangles are the strongest. Steel structures such as bridges and ELECTRICITY pylons are composed of steel struts bolted together to form hundreds of triangles. This is the most efficient way of spreading forces evenly throughout the structure. Tunnels and the legs of oil rigs are often tubular because this shape resists bending.

SEE FOR YOURSELF
Using pipecleaners and straws, experiment with a variety of different constructions. The pipecleaners can be bent to form different joints to join the straws. You could try making the construction illustrated. The crisscross pattern gives it extra strength. Try using your construction to support a weight.

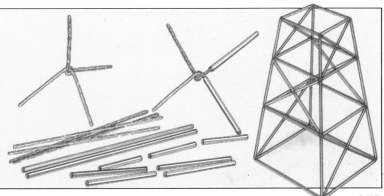

There is a great deal of evidence to support the idea that the North and South Poles were once in very different positions in relation to the continents. Fossils discoveries have shown that western Europe once had tropical life, and forests once grew in what is now Antarctica. Scientists predict that a shift in the Earth's axis could upset the balance of the Earth and cause the continents to move to new positions — but very slowly.

▼ The major land masses on the Earth's surface are called continents.

Continent

A continent is any one of the seven main land masses of the world: Europe, Asia, North America, South America, Africa, Australasia, and Antarctica. The arctic region is not a continent because it consists largely of water, some of which is frozen. Less than one-third of the EARTH's surface area is occupied by the continents; the rest is OCEANS and the smaller areas of land.

The Earth's crust beneath the continents is thicker and more complex than that beneath the oceans. Continental crust is, on average, about 20 miles (35 km) thick although where major MOUNTAIN chains, such as the Himalayas, occur, the crust may be up to 30 miles (50 km) thick. And, whereas oceanic crust is made up of largely basaltlike rocks, the continents are mainly granite overlain by various SEDIMENTARY and METAMORPHIC rocks. Most scientists now believe that the continents are still growing.

See also PLATE TECTONICS.

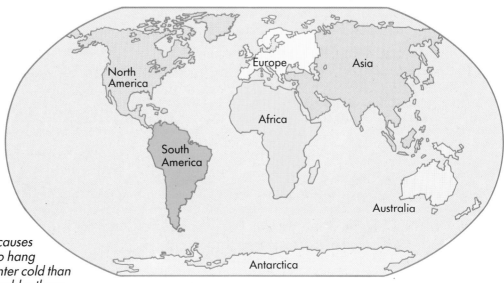

North America

Europe

Asia

Africa

South America

Australia

Antarctica

▼ Contraction causes electric cables to hang higher in the winter cold than in summer. The cables therefore appear low in the summer.

Contraction

Contraction is the name given to the shrinking or decrease in volume of a substance. This can happen due to the substance becoming colder. As the substance cools, the MOLECULES that make it up vibrate less and the forces of attraction between them are able to bind them together more closely, so the substance shrinks slightly. Contraction also occurs in GASES due to changes in PRESSURE, normally because of increases in pressure.

The ability of materials to expand and contract has to be taken into consideration by the CONSTRUCTION industry when choosing MATERIALS. Unless the design allows for contraction it can produce distortion or cracking in the structure, which would make it unsafe. Large road bridges, for example, have EXPANSION joints which are clearly visible.

Convection

Convection is the process in FLUIDS in which, because of changes in DENSITY, the LIQUID or GAS rises or falls. For example, if a liquid is heated the liquid near the HEAT source warms up first and expands. It becomes less dense, therefore, and tends to rise and cold fluid comes in to take its place. The rise of the hot fluid and the fall of the cold fluid transports heat from one place to another. Heat also travels by CONDUCTION and RADIATION, but these do not involve the movement of the material itself as does convection.

Convection is important in heating and insulating homes. Radiators and central heating furnaces warm a room by producing convection currents which distribute the heated air around. Double glazing windows helps prevent heat from escaping from a room because the narrow space between the two panes of glass is not big enough for convection to develop and transport heat. Convection also occurs in the ATMOSPHERE; rising currents of warm air can allow birds to soar for a very long time without flapping their wings at all.

See also EXPANSION; THERMODYNAMICS.

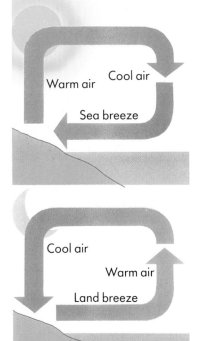

▲ Sea breezes are caused by convection currents. During the day, the land heats up more quickly than the sea. Air over the land becomes warmer and rises. Cooler air from the sea moves in to take its place. At night, the land cools down more quickly than the sea. A convection current is formed in the opposite direction to the daytime current. Warm air over the sea rises and cool air from the land moves in to take its place.

◄ The hang glider is carried across the sky on a current of air, a convection current.

▲ The feat of juggling needs excellent coordination. A continuous flow of information (feedback) is sent to and from the hands and brain.

Coordination

Coordination is the combination of mind and MUSCLES which allows animals to move smoothly and without injury. This happens automatically, once it has been learned as a young animal, for example, a child. A young child cannot coordinate mind and muscles sufficiently to catch a ball, but this skill is learned rapidly.

Each movement we make involves a very complex set of instructions sent from the BRAIN to the muscles, and further signals which are returned to the brain, telling it how far the muscle has moved, and when it has completed the activity. All of this involves millions of electrical signals passing to and from the brain. It also uses REFLEXES, which involve the muscles and a part of the nervous system outside the brain, and so can take place very rapidly. A blink is a reflex, and so is the rapid movement of your finger away from a hot object. Most movement is controlled by automatic coordination. We do not have to think about how to walk, because this skill has been learned and the body coordinates it. All we need to do is to decide where to walk, and how fast to move. If you try to learn a new skill such as gymnastics, you need to practice all over again until the body can coordinate the movements automatically.

See also GLANDS; HORMONE; LEARNING; NERVES.

Copernicus, Nicolaus

Nicolaus Copernicus (1473–1543), a Polish canon or priest, proposed that the SUN and not the EARTH is at the center of the UNIVERSE. This was dangerous teaching at a time when the Bible was believed to prove that the Earth is the central and most important body of all. Like ARISTARCHUS 1,800 years earlier, it made him unpopular.

He published his theory in a book which very few people bought or read, but the fact that it existed was enough to start others discussing the theory. However, proof did not come until the century after Copernicus died. His theory was not completely accurate. First, he believed that the planets move in circles instead of ellipses. Second, he thought that the stars are dim objects not much farther off than the outermost planet then known, Saturn. In other words he thought that the Sun was really at the center of the universe instead of being an average star in a huge GALAXY.

▲ Nicolaus Copernicus proposed that the Earth and the planets rotate around the Sun.

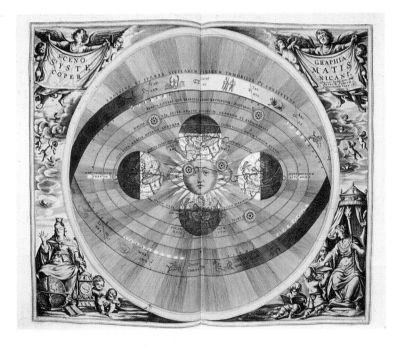

▼ The copper ore is crushed to small pieces. Water is mixed with it and it is ground by a ball mill into fine particles to form a slurry. The slurry is heated in a furnace to separate the copper. A converter purifies the molten copper. During the electrolytic refining process an electric current causes chemical reactions, which produce copper metal that is over 99.9 percent pure. The final processing stage consists of melting and casting the copper metal into cakes, billets, bars, and ingots.

Copper

Copper is a soft reddish brown solid metallic ELEMENT found free in nature and also in copper-bearing minerals in combination with other elements. It may also be found in ores containing lead, zinc, gold, platinum, and nickel. Copper has been important to human development since before 3000 B.C. Although too soft for most purposes, it can be mixed with other METALS to form very strong ALLOYS, such as brass and bronze. Pure copper is a good CONDUCTOR of ELECTRICITY and is therefore used for electrical wiring. Copper piping is used for plumbing, and copper-nickel alloy is used in coinage. Copper is malleable (can be easily shaped or beaten) and extremely ductile (can be drawn out without breaking). Copper is extracted from its ores and pure copper is refined by ELECTROLYSIS.

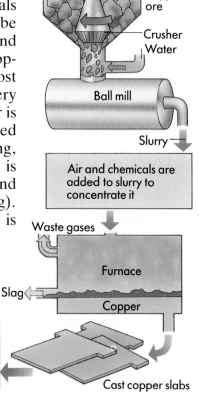

Copper ore

Crusher

Water

Ball mill

Slurry

Air and chemicals are added to slurry to concentrate it

Waste gases

Furnace

Slag

Copper

Cast copper slabs

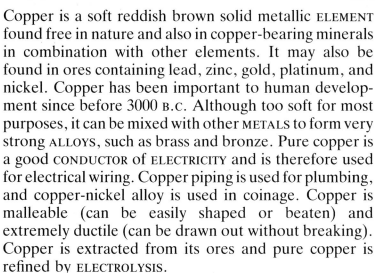

Ornaments

Ingot

Bar

Billet

Cake

Wire

Pipes

Electrolytic refining

Kitchenware

▲ *The Sun's corona cannot normally be seen because of the Sun's brightness. The corona is only visible during an eclipse when the Sun is covered by the Moon.*

Some metals, such as steel, are often coated with a thin layer of a second metal to improve their resistance to corrosion. This is carried out by the process of electroplating, which is an application of electrolysis. Bathroom faucets are coated with chromium and cutlery with silver, nickel, or chromium.

Corona

When the Moon passes completely in front of the SUN during an ECLIPSE, and the blinding light of the Sun is obscured, a glowing halo shines out. This is the corona, the Sun's atmosphere. The visible part spreads for over 600,000 miles (960,000 km) above the surface, but it continues invisibly further into space. Unlike our ATMOSPHERE, which is held to the Earth by GRAVITY, it is pouring off into space at a speed of about 250 miles (400 km) per second. These clouds of atoms pass the planets and race toward the stars. This movement is the *solar wind*.

Corrosion

Corrosion is the chemical process by which a material such as METAL is tarnished or destroyed by the action of a liquid (usually an ACID, an alkali, or water) or a gas (usually oxygen). Rust is a form of corrosion in which iron, exposed to damp air or to water containing impurities, undergoes OXIDATION. The red iron oxide formed is flaky and crumbles away. The surface of an aluminum pan also turns into an oxide, and if scratched or attacked by acid it too can flake away. When an acid or alkali corrodes the surface of a metal, it may eat holes where it reacts with the metal. Oxidation in a dry atmosphere usually causes general tarnishing. Corrosion under moist conditions or when a metal lies under water is caused by ELECTROLYSIS, with one part of the metal forming an anode and another a cathode. Air pollution by gases such as sulfur dioxide and nitrogen dioxide, which produce ACID RAIN, are sources of corrosion. Painting or electroplating metal helps to protect it.

SEE FOR YOURSELF
Take two iron nails and paint one of them. Place both nails in a shallow tray. Put the tray outside. After a few days the unpainted iron nail goes rusty. After a few months rust spots appear through the paint on the painted nail. Rust is the most common form of corrosion; it forms on iron and steel that has been exposed to moist air or water.

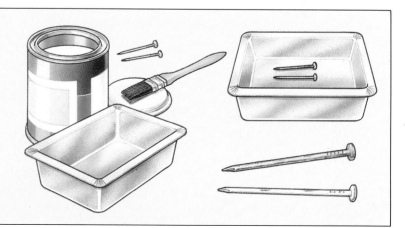

Cosmetics

Cosmetics are materials applied to the body to beautify it. People have used paints and sweet-smelling oils on their bodies for thousands of years. Mirrors and jars of cosmetic materials from 4,000 years ago in Egypt can be seen in museums. Cosmetics were brought to England by Crusaders returning from wars in the East, and Queen Elizabeth I increased their popularity in the 16th century. A worldwide cosmetics industry developed in the 20th century. Most cosmetics are used by women, but some men use them too. Modern cosmetics contain FATS, oils, and scents extracted from animals and plants. Some are artificial materials made in laboratories. Powders usually contain talc, chalk, kaolin, and various pigments. Cake makeup consists of powder mixed with dry gum. Lipsticks are melted oils mixed with dyes and hardened in molds.

The ancient Egyptians used cosmetics of all kinds. They edged the underside of the eye with green paste made from ground malachite, a copper ore. They outlined the eyes with a mixture of ground ants' eggs. Henna was used as a hair dye and to dye the fingernails, the soles of the feet, and the palms of the hands. Some Egyptians also used rouges, whitening powders, bath oils, and lipstick.

Deodorant · Handcream · Raspberries · Wool (lanolin) · Perfume · Camomile · Coconut · Hair gel · Shampoo · Cucumber · Rouge · Lipstick · Lip pencil · Soaps · Rose

▲ Some cosmetic products and their natural ingredients.

▼ When primary cosmic rays meet atmospheric particles they are broken down into secondary rays.

Cosmic rays

Cosmic rays are not rays at all. They are atomic particles from space. Most of them are PROTONS, tiny charged particles usually found inside ATOMS. These particles move almost as fast as light and are so small they cannot be seen, but their effects can be detected, since they break up any atom they strike. The RADIATION produced by cosmic rays can be dangerous but fortunately, our ATMOSPHERE shields us from most cosmic rays, although the particles known as neutrinos have so much ENERGY that they pass right through Earth! Some cosmic rays come from the Sun, but most come from exploding, dying stars called SUPERNOVAS or from distant GALAXIES.

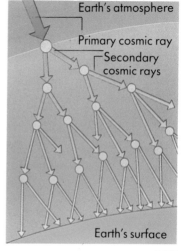

Earth's atmosphere

Primary cosmic ray

Secondary cosmic rays

Earth's surface

Fred Hoyle (1915–)
A British cosmologist who with others proposed the Steady State theory. This states that the universe has always existed and that new matter is constantly being created to fill the space left as the universe expands. Hoyle also writes science fiction.

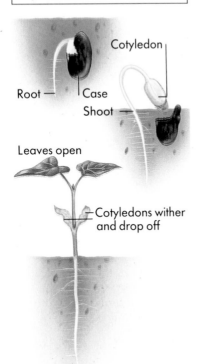

Cotyledon

Root — Case

Shoot —

Leaves open

—Cotyledons wither and drop off

▲ The cotyledon, the seedleaf, is a storage organ for the food needed by the plant during germination and early growth stages.

Cosmology

Cosmology is the study of the nature of the UNIVERSE and its beginning and ending. Until the 17th century, most people believed that everything beyond the Earth's surface was "unknowable." The breakthrough came when KEPLER proved that the planets move around the Sun in elliptical orbits, and NEWTON showed how GRAVITY explained why they moved as they did. These discoveries showed that "Earth-based" laws of geometry and physics seem to work in space too.

At the beginning of the 20th century, the universe

> **Milestones in Cosmology**
> **1700s and 1800s** Astronomers contradict the simple explanation of the universe and show that stars are not distributed evenly throughout the universe.
> **1916** Albert Einstein publishes his general theory of relativity, which brings about a rethinking of space, time, and gravity.
> **1920s** Edwin Hubble studies the speed of galaxies' motion. Using the Doppler effect he determines that all galaxies began moving away from one another 10 to 20 billion years ago.
> **1965** Astronomers show that the universe is full of weak radio waves.
> **1980s** Stephen Hawking's work supports the theory that the universe began in a big bang. He also explains what happens when a star collapses and becomes a black hole.

was proved to contain countless galaxies in addition to our own. The BIG BANG theory became generally accepted about 25 years ago. It says that the universe began with a huge explosion 10 to 20 billion years ago. Before that there was the Steady State theory which said that new galaxies formed to fill in the spaces left as the older ones moved apart. Some things, such as the cause of the Big Bang, may remain "unknowable," but cosmologists have begun to understand some apparently baffling problems about the universe.

Cotyledon

Inside every SEED there is a miniature plant or EMBRYO, waiting until the conditions are right for it to grow. Many seeds also contain food for the embryo until it is big enough to establish itself in the soil and make its own food. Cotyledons, or seedleaves, are the initial food source for the plant. They absorb and digest food from the storage tissue of the seed. Most flowering plants

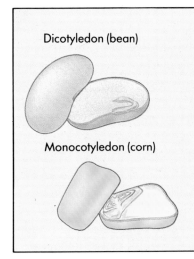

Dicotyledon (bean)

Monocotyledon (corn)

SEE FOR YOURSELF
Soak a bean and a corn seed in water for a while. Carefully peel the protective coat off the bean and open it up. There are two cotyledons. Look for the tiny plant (embryo) inside. Peel the seed coat off the corn seed. You will find the embyro under the seed coat. The corn seed has just one cotyledon. The grasslike plants which are monocotyledons include all important cereal crops, such as barley, oats, wheat, and rice.

have two cotyledons in their seeds but narrow-leaved plants, like grasses and onions, have only one cotyledon. The seeds of pine trees and other conifers contain up to 15 cotyledons. In some plants, such as peas, the cotyledons do not appear as leaves. They stay inside the germinating seeds and gradually shrivel as their food reserves are used up by the growing seedlings.

▲ *Flowering plants with only one seedleaf, such as the bluebell (top), are called monocotyledons. Plants such as the bean (bottom) with two seedleaves, are called dicotyledons.*

Coulomb

The coulomb is the unit in which electric charge is measured in SI UNITS (International System of Units). It is named after a French scientist, Charles-Augustin de Coulomb (1736–1806), who was the first to measure accurately the forces between objects with an electric charge. He found that like charges repel each other, and unlike charges attract each other.

Electric charge moves when an electric current flows in a circuit; the SI unit of electric current, the AMPERE, corresponds to one coulomb (1 C) of charge passing each point in the circuit every second.

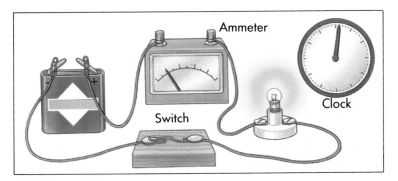

Ammeter

Switch

Clock

◄ *The coulomb (C) is the unit of charge. It is the amount of charge that passes a given point in an electric circuit in one second (shown on the clock) when a steady current of one ampere (shown on the ammeter) is flowing through the circuit. When one coulomb of charge takes one second to flow past a point in a circuit, then the current in that circuit is one ampere (1 A).*

Products from cracking oil
The main products of cracking are fuels: gasoline, aircraft fuel, diesel fuel, and fuel oil. Chemicals derived from oil include detergents, plastics, cosmetics, drugs, fertilizers, and animal foods.

Cracking

Cracking is an important process in the refining of gasoline and other FUELS. Crude oil is broken down into different products by a process called fractional DISTILLATION; the oil is heated to a very high temperature and different products (fractions) are drawn off as they vaporize. The heavy oils, those with the highest boiling point, are then cracked. Cracking breaks down the large HYDROCARBON molecules into smaller molecules and this greatly increases the quantity of useful products that can be produced from oil.

There are two main types of cracking: thermal cracking, in which the large molecules break down in the presence of high temperature and pressure; and the more

During the early 1970s the demand for oil rose annually by almost 8 percent. The annual increase in demand has now fallen below 3 percent. World consumption of oil is nearly 70 million barrels daily. It is estimated that the total world demand for energy in all its forms rises by about 3.7 percent every year.

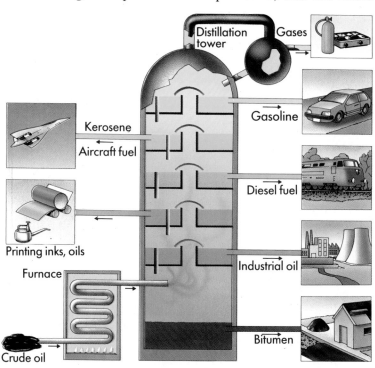

▶ Fractional distillation is based on the principle that different products boil at different temperatures. Crude oil is heated in a furnace to temperatures as high as 725°F (385°C). The oil becomes vapor and passes into a distillation tower. As the vapor rises it cools and condenses and can then be drawn off. Each fraction will condense at a different temperature. Gasoline condenses at about 75°F (24°C) but the heavier oils have condensing points as high as 600°F (316°C). The lightest fractions with the lowest condensing points rise to the top.

efficient catalytic cracking, in which the thermal cracking process is speeded up by the presence of a CATALYST, usually a compound of aluminum, silicon, and oxygen. The catalyst is not used up by the reaction and can be used again.

Crick, Francis *See* DNA

Crookes, William *See* Cathode ray tube

Crystals

A crystal is a small piece of a SOLID that has a regular three-dimensional shape. The plane (flat) faces are arranged in a regular order and meet each other at definite angles. All crystals have an orderly shape due to the internal arrangement of the atoms, ions, or molecules making up the solid. The shapes vary but they can be classified into six three-dimensional geometric patterns or systems. Most solids have a crystalline structure, for example, ROCKS and MINERALS, METALS, salt, and sugar. Crystals usually occur as a result of a process called crystallization. This may happen when molten rocks cool down and solidify. It also occurs when a SOLUTION of a crystalline solid is allowed to EVAPORATE slowly, or when extra amounts of a crystalline solid are added to a SATURATED SOLUTION of the solid.

Calcite

Pyrite

Gypsum

Sulfur

Zircon

Rhodonite

SEE FOR YOURSELF
Find some old jars. Carefully pour some hot water into one of the jars. Take some table salt, sugar, alum, or borax and stir it into the hot water until no more will dissolve. Pour the mixture into a clean jar and leave it for a while. Crystals will form. Pick out one of the best crystals. Make up some more of the same solution in a clean jar. Attach the crystal to a thread and suspend it from a pencil into the new solution. Watch the crystal as it continues to grow. Try different substances to get different shaped crystals.

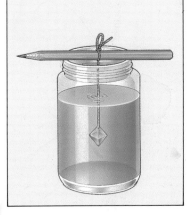

◄ There are six main "systems" (types) of mineral crystal shape. These are based on the size, shape, number, and angle of the faces of each crystal. The scientific study of crystals is called crystallography. Scientists measure the angles between crystal faces and analyze the symmetrical arrangements of the surfaces.

Curie, Marie and Pierre

Pierre Curie was born in Paris in 1859. He carried out early research into MAGNETISM, and in 1894, while teaching at the Sorbonne university in Paris, he met Marie Sklodowska, a Polish student. They were married the following year. They began research together in Paris

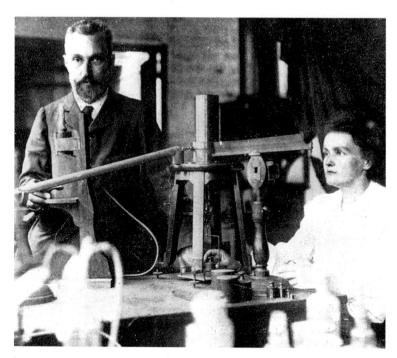

▶ *The Curies working in their laboratory. They first conducted experiments on the radioactivity of radium in 1898.*

To obtain a hundredth of an ounce of radium, the Curies had to refine about 7 tons of pitchblende! It is a strange fact that this precious element is now only of historic interest. Nearly all of its original medical and other uses have been taken over by other, cheaper and more easily obtainable substances.

The name radium comes from the Latin *radius*, meaning ray. The Curies named polonium after Poland, Marie Curie's homeland. In 1944 a new radioactive element was discovered in the U.S.A. and it was named curium (atomic number 96) after the Curies.

into RADIOACTIVITY; they found that the element thorium is radioactive, and then in 1898 discovered two new radioactive elements, polonium and RADIUM. They shared the Nobel Prize for Physics in 1903 with Henri Becquerel, the discoverer of radioactivity. Pierre was killed in a road accident in 1906, but Marie carried on working and succeeded in isolating pure radium in 1910; for this she was awarded a second Nobel Prize, for Chemistry, in 1911. Marie died in 1934 from CANCER, probably brought on because she had worked for so long with radioactive materials without protection.

Her daughter, Irene, married Marie's assistant Frederic Joliot. They continued working and in 1935 they too were jointly awarded the Nobel Prize for Chemistry. Both died of cancer, Irene in 1956 and Frederic in 1958.

▶ *At one time radium was widely used in the treatment of cancer, but this role has been taken over by cobalt-60. It was also used in fluorescent paint for watch dials. Polonium was the first radioactive element to be isolated. Its discovery in 1898 marks the beginning of the atomic age. It is an extremely dangerous substance.*

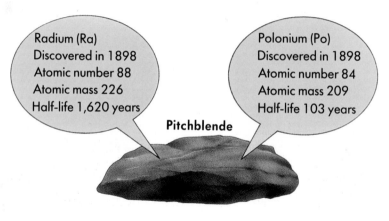

Radium (Ra)
Discovered in 1898
Atomic number 88
Atomic mass 226
Half-life 1,620 years

Polonium (Po)
Discovered in 1898
Atomic number 84
Atomic mass 209
Half-life 103 years

Pitchblende

Current *See* Electricity

Cuvier, Georges *See* Paleontology

Cyclone

A cyclone is a tropical HURRICANE. These cyclones are fierce storms bringing with them torrential rain and extremely strong winds with speeds of up to 200 mph (300 km/h). They can lead to widespread destruction.

In METEOROLOGY, however, a cyclone is a system of low atmospheric PRESSURE in which the winds blow in a counterclockwise direction in the Northern HEMISPHERE and a clockwise direction in the Southern Hemisphere. In fact, the air mass moves from an area of high pressure to an area of low pressure, toward the center of the cyclone. Because the EARTH is spinning, the moving air is pushed sideways so that it actually moves clockwise or counterclockwise.

Cyclones are also known as depressions or lows, and the air pressure in a deep depression can fall as low as 940 millibars (mb) while that in a high pressure area or anticyclone may rise to more than 1,060 mb. Even outside tropical areas, cyclones are often associated with stormy weather, which may not last very long.

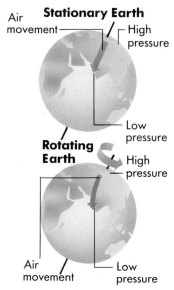

▲ Cyclones move in curved paths because of the rotation of the Earth.

▼ Warm air rises from the center of a cyclone (the eye of the storm). Winds spiraling inward toward the center of the cyclone reach such great speeds that they blow around the center in complete circles.

▼ *The cell has been observed in greater degrees of detail, using increasingly powerful microscopes. The early optical microscope developed by Anton van Leeuwenhoek could magnify objects by about 250 times. Modern electron microscopes can magnify objects by up to 1,000,000 times. Scientists can observe the cell's structure and see that cells contain vacuoles of liquid in their cytoplasm (a watery jelly-like material). Nucleoli in the nucleus are important in making protein. Mitochondria are the cell's power producers. Plant cells have chloroplasts which contain the green chlorophyll used in photosynthesis.*

Cytology

Cytology is the study of CELLS and how they work. This very important science has led to the understanding of GENETICS and the causes of many DISEASES. Cells were first described in 1663 by the English scientist Robert Hooke, who examined and drew plant cells which he observed under a MICROSCOPE. It was not until the 1800s that Henri Dutrochet was able to point out that all plants and animals were built from cells. Most of the advances in knowledge of cell structure and function followed the development of effective microscopes. The introduction of the ELECTRON MICROSCOPE in the 1930s allowed even the smallest details of the internal and external structure of cells to be examined in enormous detail. This has contributed to understanding of the detailed workings of CELL DIVISION and genetics.

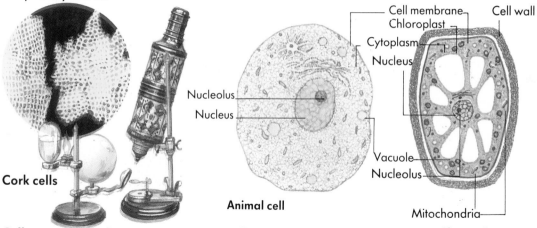

Cork cells

Cells seen through an early optical microscope

Nucleolus
Nucleus
Animal cell

Cells seen through a powerful optical microscope

Cell membrane
Chloroplast
Cytoplasm
Nucleus
Cell wall
Vacuole
Nucleolus
Mitochondria
Plant cell

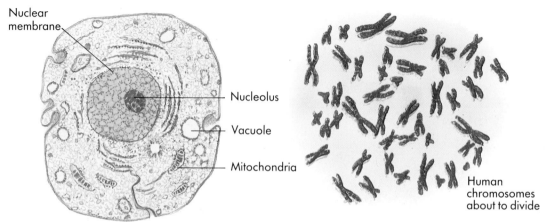

Nuclear membrane

Nucleolus
Vacuole
Mitochondria

Animal cell seen through an early electron microscope

Human chromosomes about to divide

Nucleolus magnified by a powerful electron microscope

Daguerreotype

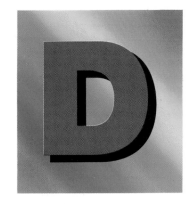

A daguerreotype is a photograph produced by the first commercial PHOTOGRAPHIC process, called the daguerreotype process. It was invented in 1839 by the French painter Louis J.M. Daguerre. He used a silver-plated sheet of copper made light-sensitive by exposure to the fumes from heated crystals of iodine. The plate was loaded into a camera and the photograph taken by removing the lens cap for several minutes. The image was developed in mercury and a solution of either sodium chloride or sodium thiosulfate.

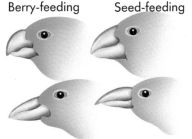

◄ The daguerreotype was one of the first kinds of photograph.

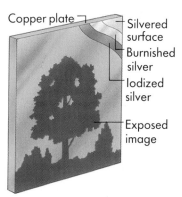

▲ Daguerre's process involved treating a sheet of silver-plated copper with iodine to make the silver plating sensitive to light.

Dalton, John *See* Atom

Darwin, Charles

Charles Darwin was born in England in 1809 and became one of the world's most famous naturalists. He was the first person to give a workable explanation of EVOLUTION. During a five-year voyage around the world, he studied animals and plants in many countries and he was impressed by their great variety. He observed what he called the struggle for existence, with each organism struggling to get food and avoid being eaten, and he realized that only those individuals best fitted or suited to their surroundings could survive. Here was an explanation for the great variety of plant and animal life throughout the world: conditions vary enormously from place to place and living things have gradually changed to suit these different conditions and habitats. On his

Berry-feeding   Seed-feeding

Cactus-feeding   Insect-feeding

▲ Darwin noticed that there were many species of finch on the Galapagos Islands. He believed that these had adapted gradually from one species to eat different foods.

165

▲ Humphry Davy invented a safety lamp that saved many thousands of miners' lives. He did not patent his invention so that it could be widely copied and used.

▼ Davy surrounded the safety lamp's flame with a wire gauze. This cooled the flame and prevented it passing through the gauze to the explosive gases. The middle lamp has a "bulls eye" lens to give a beam from the dim light produced.

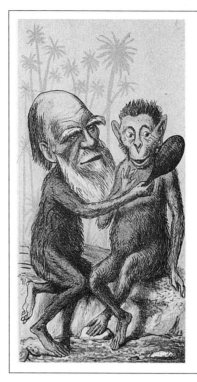

The Theory of Evolution
Darwin developed the theory of evolution gradually. His observations during the voyage on HMS *Beagle* and other expeditions contributed to his ideas. He published his theory in *On the Origin of Species* in 1859. At first the theory met with great opposition — especially among religious leaders — and Darwin was ridiculed in cartoons because people mistakenly thought he had said that human beings are descended from monkeys. Today a modified version of Darwin's theory is widely accepted. There are still people who are not able to believe in the theory of evolution.

return home, he set about collecting more evidence and in 1859 he published his ideas in his famous book called *On the Origin of Species by Means of Natural Selection*. Darwin's ideas met a lot of opposition at first, but were gradually accepted by most people and are still the basis of the theory of evolution today. Darwin died in 1882 and was buried in Westminster Abbey, in London.

Davy, Humphry

Humphry Davy (1778–1829) was an English scientist, best remembered for his invention of the miner's safety lamp in 1815. His lamp prevented the explosion of air containing METHANE, or firedamp, a gas once common in coal mines. The lamp's flame was protected by a fine wire mesh to separate it from the explosive gases.

Davy was born and educated in Cornwall, England. When he left school, he went to work for a doctor. He gave this up and took charge of a laboratory in Bristol where he studied the effects of gases on people. He discovered that nitrous oxide (laughing gas) could be used as an anesthetic. Later, in London, he studied how electricity is stored in batteries. He also discovered that materials could be separated into their ELEMENTS by passing an electric current through them.

Daylength

The length of the day changes during the year except close to the equator. It is longest at midsummer and shortest at midwinter. This is because the axis of the EARTH is tilted. People in the hemisphere tilted toward the SUN see it pass higher across the sky between sunrise and sunset, and so their day is longer. The daylength affects the BEHAVIOR of all animals and plants: birds begin to lay their eggs in spring not the fall, and not all plants flower at the same time of the year.

Long-day plant

Petunia

Grown during long days   Grown during short days

Short-day plant

Chrysanthemum

Grown during long days   Grown during short days

▲ *The amount of daylight plants receive affects how they grow and flower. Short-day plants begin to flower when daylength is short. Long-day plants flower when daylength is long.*

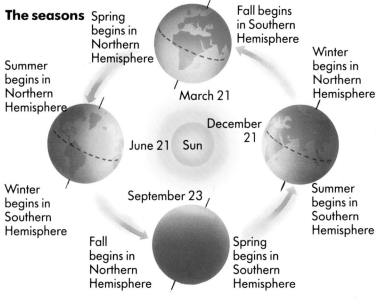

The seasons

Spring begins in Northern Hemisphere

Fall begins in Southern Hemisphere

Summer begins in Northern Hemisphere

Winter begins in Northern Hemisphere

March 21

December 21

June 21   Sun

Winter begins in Southern Hemisphere

September 23

Summer begins in Southern Hemisphere

Fall begins in Northern Hemisphere

Spring begins in Southern Hemisphere

The difference in daylength also depends upon the LATITUDE. The "midnight Sun" occurs at latitudes greater than 67° north or south at mid-summer. Try measuring the changing height of the Sun during the year. One way is to measure the length of the shadow cast by a stick, post, or other fixed object at noon each day.

◄ *The length of daylight changes during the year in all parts of the world, except the equator, where there are approximately 12 hours of daylight every day of the year. Day and night lengths are equal everywhere in the world on the two equinoxes, about March 21 and September 23.*

SEE FOR YOURSELF
Make a chart to record your observations of daylength. Over a week write down the time the Sun rises in the morning, the time the street lamps come on in the evening (though this is not natural time), and the time the Sun goes down at night. Compare your observations of daylength at different times of the year.

Decibels at sound source

- 150 Rocket take-off
- 140 Pain threshold
- 130 Jet aircraft
- 120
- 110 Thunder
- 100
- 90 Heavy traffic
- 80
- 70 Orchestra
- 60
- 50 Conversation
- 40
- 30 Whispering
- 20 Leaves falling
- 10 Hearing threshold
- 0

▲ *The lower threshold of human hearing is usually taken as around zero to 10 on the decibel scale. The sound of ordinary conversation can carry quite far and noises such as coughing (if not smothered) can be nearly as loud as a range of musical instruments. Sounds above 120 decibels are likely to damage our hearing.*

The ancient Egyptians used a decimal system. The unit one was represented by a single line, and tens, hundreds and thousands by hieroglyphic symbols.

Decibel

The decibel (dB) is the SI UNIT which measures the loudness of a sound, or its sound pressure level. It is named after the American inventor Alexander Graham BELL. A sound of 30 dB carries ten times more power than a sound of 20 dB. The sound of someone speaking a yard away is about 50 dB, while that of traffic in a street is about 75 dB. People who are exposed to more than 80 dB regularly for long periods of time, risk permanently damaging their hearing. Beyond 140 dB, it is probable that the eardrums will burst.

Decimal

The word decimal describes the system based on powers of ten that we use for writing down NUMBERS. We use the numerals 0 to 9 to represent numbers through a place-value system. That is, each numeral stands for a number that has ten times the value of the place to its right. So 7,285 stands for seven thousands, two hundreds, eight tens (eighty), and five ones.

We also use decimal to describe a type of fraction. Decimal fractions are not written down like ordinary fractions. The common fractions $^3/_{10}$ and $^7/_{100}$ become 0.3 and 0.07 as decimal fractions. In common fractions the top figure is the numerator, the lower figure the denominator. Common fractions can be changed into decimal fractions by dividing the numerator by the denominator (*see* box below).

Decimal fractions

Decimal fractions can be made from ordinary fractions by dividing the denominator into the numerator. A decimal fraction can be thought of as a fraction of 10. For example $^1/_2$ is the same as $^5/_{10}$ or 0.5.

A fraction $\dfrac{1}{2}$ — Numerator, — Denominator

A decimal fraction **0.5**

$$^1/_8 = 1 \div 8 = 0.125$$

Deforestation

Deforestation is the felling of all trees, usually over a wide area, in a region which was previously natural forest. Deforestation takes place without plans to plant more trees. It may be carried out to supply wood for the timber trade, or, more usually, to provide agricultural land for an increasing local population.

Trees are often cut down on steeply sloping land so that they bring down more trees further downhill as they fall. Deforestation on steep slopes is very damaging to the ENVIRONMENT because once the soils have been exposed to running water, they are quickly washed away leading to severe soil EROSION. In tropical rainforests, the soil is very low in nourishment, so that when the trees are removed and the land farmed without replenishing the nutrients, the soils are soon exhausted.

◄ *Every year many thousands of trees are cut down and the ground cleared by being burned. Here farmers are burning the cloud forest in the Ecuadorean Andes. The cleared ground will probably be used as pasture for livestock.*

Dehydration

When something is dehydrated, it has had the water removed from it. Dehydration is used principally in preparing convenience foods such as dried soups, coffee, tea, mashed potatoes, milk and dairy products, and medical items such as serum. These products are dried, usually FREEZE-DRIED, and can be reconstituted by adding water. Dehydrated items are light, compact, and easy to transport. If kept dry, they stay fresh for months.

In MEDICINE, dehydration is a condition in which water and salt are lost from the body. Water is essential for life, and all living things contain a lot of water. Mild

▼ *If the pattern of rings in a wooden object matches that of a tree it is fairly certain that the wood used in the object was growing at the same time as the tree. This way the article can be dated.*

dehydration can be cured by drinking lots of liquid. Severe dehydration needs immediate medical attention because rapid loss of water and salt causes the HEART to beat faster, lowering the BLOOD pressure. This may bring about a state of shock, and even death.

Dendrochronology

Dendrochronology is a method of dating past events by looking at tree rings. Every year a tree trunk adds a new ring of wood just under the bark. These annual rings are easy to see when a tree has been cut down, and if you count the rings, you can find out the age of the tree. The wood produced in the spring and early summer consists of wide, thin-walled CELLS, but the autumn wood consists of narrower cells with thick walls, so the growth rings are easy to see. It is not necessary to cut trees down to find their age; scientists drill tiny holes in the trunks and take out slim cores so they can count the rings.

The rings can tell us much more than just a tree's age. Trees put on more wood in wet years than they do in dry years, so we can discover what the weather was like at particular times of the tree's life. We can also investigate the ages of old wooden buildings and ships.

▶ *Each ring of a tree is a result of one year's growth and reflects the growing conditions over a period of time.*

Density

The density of an object is the MASS, or amount of material, that it contains per unit of volume. It is expressed in pounds per cubic foot or grams per cubic centimeter. Because most materials expand or contract when the TEMPERATURE changes, their density depends on the temperature. This is particularly true for gases such as air, which expand a lot when their temperature is raised so that their density decreases. Hot-air balloons can fly because the density of the hot air inside the balloon is less than the density of the surrounding cold air. This is an example of the law of FLOTATION: a body will float in a FLUID if its density is less than that of the fluid.

The density of a solid body can be found by measuring its volume and its mass and finding the RATIO of the two. The density of pure water is 1 gram per cubic centimeter (62.4 pounds per cubic foot). Checking the density of a fluid can help indicate whether it is pure or whether something else, such as water, has been added to it because pure substances have a precise density.
See also ARCHIMEDES; CONTRACTION; EXPANSION.

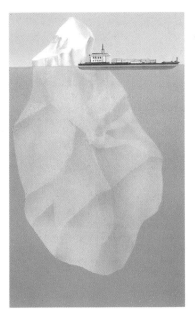

▲ *An iceberg floats because the density of ice is less than the density of water. But seven-eighths of it remain under water.*

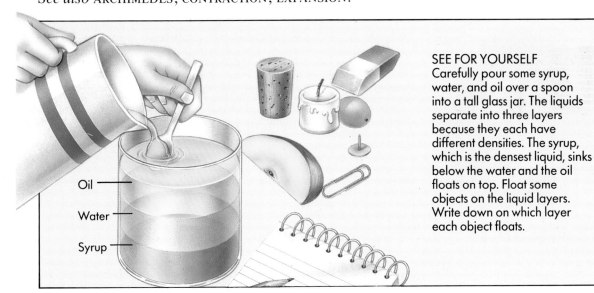

Oil

Water

Syrup

SEE FOR YOURSELF
Carefully pour some syrup, water, and oil over a spoon into a tall glass jar. The liquids separate into three layers because they each have different densities. The syrup, which is the densest liquid, sinks below the water and the oil floats on top. Float some objects on the liquid layers. Write down on which layer each object floats.

Desalination

Desalination is a process for producing fresh water by removing salt from seawater. Two methods are used. The simplest is DISTILLATION. Seawater is heated until it evaporates. The VAPOR passes over a cool surface. This makes it condense back into a liquid in the same way as

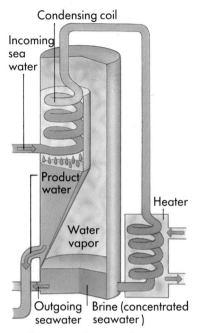

▲ *Seawater is heated up and passes into a chamber where it evaporates. The water vapor produced condenses to give fresh water.*

▲ *René Descartes' work advanced several areas of science.*

▶ *Apart from his other studies, Descartes also investigated the natural sciences. This illustration shows the coordination of the senses. He thought that a visual stimulus traveling from the eye to the pineal gland stops attention being given to the olfactory stimulus (smelling the rose).*

water vapor in the air of a warm room condenses as droplets on a cold window. Salt in the seawater does not rise with the vapor. The water condensed from the vapor is therefore fresh. The second method, developed in the 1970s, involves the use of POLYMERS. The large molecules of some polymers are used like a kitchen sieve to trap the salt molecules in seawater and allow only fresh water to pass through. Water produced by desalination is used for irrigating crops or for drinking in places where fresh water is scarce but seawater is plentiful, such as the Middle East.

Descartes, René

René Descartes (1596–1650) was a French philosopher, mathematician, and natural scientist who invented analytical GEOMETRY and was the first philosopher to describe the UNIVERSE as he saw it in terms of mind and matter. He worked out laws of motion. Descartes rejected the idea that everything we observe is false or a dream by saying that, because we have thoughts, we exist. His Latin motto, *"cogito, ergo sum"* (I think, therefore I am), is famous. It means that because we have thoughts, we exist. Descartes' approach to science was to question everything. He worked out things for himself from the beginning. Born at La Haye, in France, Descartes was brought up as a Jesuit, traveled widely, and fought in several wars. From 1628 to 1649 he lived in the Netherlands. He died on a visit to Sweden in 1650.

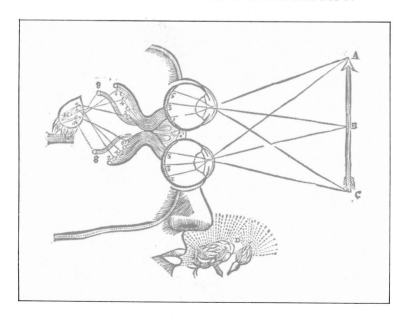

Desert

A desert may be defined as an area where the average annual rainfall is less than 10 inches (25 cm). Because the vast majority of plants and animals need a plentiful supply of water to survive, the wildlife of a desert may be sparsely distributed, very specialized, or even absent.

Most people picture a desert as an area, such as the scorching Sahara or central Australia, where daytime temperatures may soar to almost 120°F (50°C) and where there are only dunes and sandstorms as far as the eye can see. But a desert need not be hot. If the tempera-

ture is so low that there is a permanent frost and little PRECIPITATION falls, even as snow, this, too, would be a desert. The Gobi Desert in eastern Asia is an example of a cool desert but the Antarctic may also be regarded as a desert because the water there is locked up as ice.

Some animals and plants are adapted to survive in deserts. They either avoid the harsh conditions by adapting their lifestyles or they have specialized body forms. Kangaroo rats burrow into the soil to avoid the heat and cactuses store water in their fleshy stems.

Plants and animals that live in deserts have evolved various ways of surviving with very little water. Many desert plants have a waxy covering on their stems and leaves to prevent water escaping from them. Some, such as cacti, are covered in spines to prevent animals from eating them as a source of moisture. Many desert animals are nocturnal — that is, they are active only at night when it is cooler. They sleep in the shade during the day. Their kidneys filter wastes from their blood but return almost all the water to their bodies, so that they pass very little urine.

◄ *The rainfall in desert areas is very unpredictable. It may not rain for a number of years and then the average annual rainfall of 10 inches (25 cm) may fall in a couple of hours. The desert cannot absorb a great quantity of water and most of it will run off or will evaporate.*

World deserts
Sahara Northern Africa 3.5 million square miles (9.1 million km²).
Australian Desert Australia 600,000 square miles (1.5 million km²).
Arabian Desert Arabia 500,000 square miles (1.3 million km²).
Gobi Mongolia, China 500,000 square miles (1.3 million km²).
Kalahari Southwestern Africa 200,000 square miles (520,000 km²).
Chihuahuan USA and Mexico 140,000 square miles (360,000 km²).

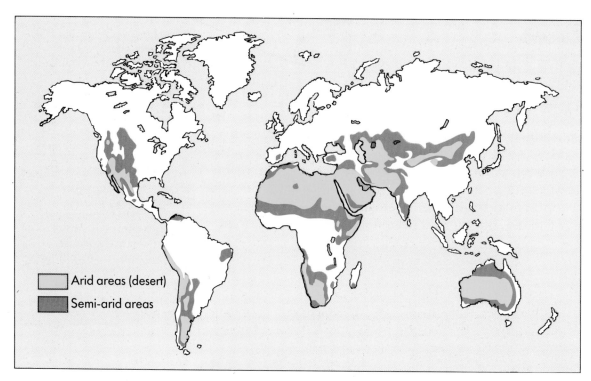

▲ About one-seventh of the Earth's land surface is covered with desert. Most are located around the Tropics.

Legend:
Arid areas (desert)
Semi-arid areas

Threatened areas

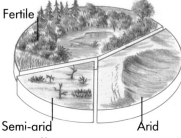

Fertile

Semi-arid   Arid

▲ Inefficient irrigation, over-cultivation, overgrazing, and forest clearance are the four main causes of desertification. It spreads from regions where the land was once fertile and affects neighboring land.

▶ Poor irrigation methods used on land that drains badly lead to an increase in the level of salts in the water as the water table rises. As the salts reach the surface, they poison the plants and they die.

Desertification

Desertification is the process by which an existing DESERT spreads across an area which was formerly moist and fertile or by which a new desert is actually formed.

There are two main causes of desertification: a natural change in the CLIMATE may take place as a result of a major shift in the Earth's weather patterns; or poor management of a delicate natural system, mainly by bad farming practices, may lead to soil EROSION, drying, and eventual desertification. On many occasions, it is a mixture of both factors which leads to the formation of desert. The best known modern example of desertification and its consequences for wildlife and the local human population is in the Sahel region in West Africa on the edge of the Sahara Desert. Recently, the desert conditions have been spreading into the Sahel.

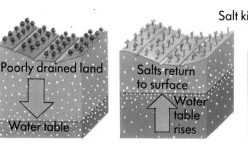
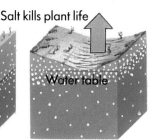

Poorly drained land

Water table

Salts return to surface

Water table rises

Salt kills plant life

Water table

174

Detergents *See* Soaps and Detergents

Dewar, James *See* Vacuum bottle

Diamond

Diamond is a type of nearly pure CARBON that has been crystallized under extremely high pressures and temperatures. Diamonds are comparatively rare in nature and, in gem quality, they are often regarded as the most beautiful of all gemstones. Diamond is the hardest known naturally occuring substance and is also extremely resistant to attack by ACID or alkali. Diamonds have many important industrial uses for cutting or grinding other hard substances. It is now possible to produce so-called "industrial diamonds" relatively cheaply but the best gem quality stones still come from natural sources in South Africa, Zaire in central Africa, and parts of Russia and central Asia.

▲ Diamonds have been valued throughout history for their beauty and for their extreme hardness. The uncut diamond (top) can be cut and polished to produce a sparkling gem.

◄ Diamonds are used on the cutting edges of drilling bits for oil wells. Diamonds are also used in industry for cutting and grinding hard materials.

Dielectric *See* Insulators, electric

Diesel engine

A diesel engine is a type of INTERNAL-COMBUSTION ENGINE which generates POWER by burning a heavy oil called diesel. The first diesel engine was built in 1897 by the German engineer, Rudolf Diesel. It works by sucking air into a cylinder and compressing it with a piston. As the air is compressed its TEMPERATURE rises. When a carefully measured amount of FUEL is sprayed into the cylinder, the air inside is so hot that the fuel immediately

The world's largest diamond, the Cullinan, named after its discoverer, was mined in the Transvaal region of South Africa in 1905. It was part of a diamond which originally weighed 3,106 carats (about 1½ pounds). It was presented to King Edward VII of England in 1907 and then cut into the famous "Star of Africa" diamond as well as over one hundred separate stones, some of which form part of the British Crown Jewels.

▶ *Diesel engines have several advantages over gasoline engines. They do not need an electrical ignition system; they use cheaper fuel; and they do not need a carburetor. Diesel engines also have a greater ability to convert the stored energy in the fuel into mechanical energy, or work.*

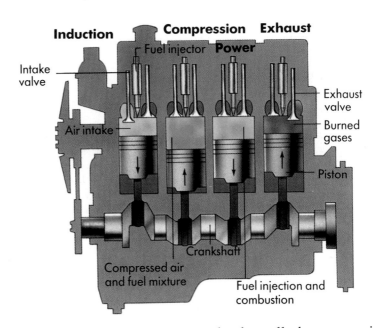

Induction   **Compression**   **Exhaust**

Fuel injector   **Power**

Intake valve

Air intake

Exhaust valve

Burned gases

Piston

Crankshaft

Compressed air and fuel mixture

Fuel injection and combustion

Rudolf Diesel, the inventor of the engine, disappeared mysteriously while crossing the English Channel in a German ship in 1913.

Wave Interference
When two waves meet they join together.

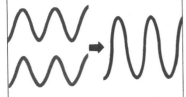

If two waves meet so that the crests of both run together a larger wave will result.

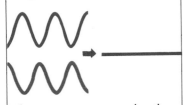

If two waves meet so that the crests of one wave run together with the troughs of the other, the two waves cancel each other out.

ignites. Diesel engines can also be called compression-ignition engines. The burning mixture expands rapidly and forces the piston down again. The next time the piston rises, it pushes the exhaust gases out of the cylinder through a valve. The up and down motion of the pistons is converted into the rotary motion of a shaft to drive the vehicle's wheels around. Diesel engines are now used by almost all commercial vehicles and an increasing number of cars. Diesel-powered vehicles are popular because their engines have lower running costs, partly because diesel is less expensive than gasoline and partly because diesel engines are more efficient.

Diffraction

Diffraction describes the spreading out of waves — light, sound, and water — when they pass through a small opening or slit. If the opening is very large compared with the WAVELENGTH of the waves, the waves travel straight on. However, if the opening is about the same size as the wavelength, the shape of the waves beyond the slit is changed; they spread out (they are diffracted). White light is made up of a mixture of different colors or wavelengths. If white light is sent through a narrow slit, the long waves (red) spread out more than the short ones (blue). To separate the various wavelengths sharply, scientists use a *diffraction grating* — thousands of very fine lines scratched closely together on a metal mirror. Light is sent through a narrow slit onto the grating. The

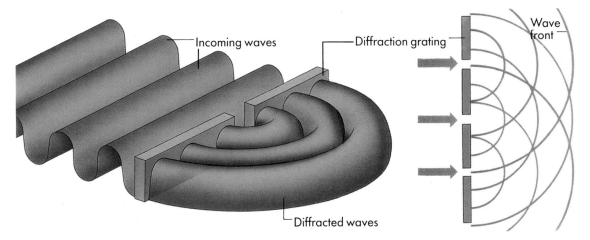

Incoming waves — Diffraction grating — Wave front

Diffracted waves

different wavelengths of light are diffracted at different angles to form a spectrum on a screen. By measuring the positions of the spectrum lines, scientists can calculate the wavelength of each radiation.

Diffraction effects mean that objects smaller than the wavelength of light can never be seen.

▲ A diffraction pattern results when waves spread out after passing through small openings in a barrier.

Diffusion

Diffusion is the natural chemical process by which the ATOMS or MOLECULES of one substance become mixed with those of another. Diffusion is caused by the ordinary natural motion of the atoms or molecules and, unlike stirring or shaking, does not depend on an external FORCE. In gases and liquids, but not in solids, molecules are relatively free to move about at random so it is easy for the molecules of one gas or liquid to be diffused throughout another gas or liquid. If you put a drop of perfume in one corner of a room you will soon be able to smell it at the other side of the room. The vapor

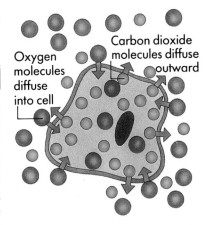

Oxygen molecules diffuse into cell

Carbon dioxide molecules diffuse outward

▲ In cells, carbon dioxide diffuses outward and oxygen inward to where the concentration is lower.

SEE FOR YOURSELF
You need two bowls. Put cold water in one bowl and hot water, in the other. Put one or two drops of ink onto the surface of the water in each bowl. The ink diffuses through the hot water more quickly than through the cold water. This is because of the greater movement of hot water molecules caused by heat energy.

Why doesn't the stomach digest itself? This is an important question, because meat is digested in the stomach. The stomach juices contain hydrochloric acid as well as digestive enzymes. This acid could quickly eat through the stomach wall. The stomach protects itself with a lining of sticky mucus. If this lining is damaged, the digestive juices attack the stomach lining, causing an ulcer.

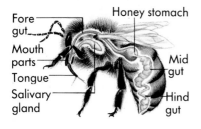

Fore gut
Honey stomach
Mouth parts
Mid gut
Tongue
Salivary gland
Hind gut

▲ Bees carry nectar in a special stomach, called a honey stomach, which is located in the abdomen.

▼ Digestion starts in the mouth and stomach but most of it takes place in the small intestine.

molecules diffuse quickly through the air in the room. *See also* BROWNIAN MOTION; OSMOSIS.

Digestion

Digestion is the process in which animals break down food into simple substances. These are then ABSORBED into the BLOOD and carried around the body and used to build new CELLS and to provide ENERGY. In humans, the first stage of digestion takes place in the mouth, where the food is broken into small pieces and mixed with saliva, which softens them for swallowing. The ENZYMES in the saliva change the insoluble STARCH into soluble SUGAR molecules. The food is swallowed and passes down the esophagus into the STOMACH, where it is mixed with more enzymes and hydrochloric acid. It is broken down into a creamy liquid which passes into the small INTESTINE. Alkaline digestive juices produced by the PANCREAS and bile from the LIVER are added. As the part-digested food moves on, further enzymes are added. Some split the sugars into even smaller molecules, while others act on the fats and proteins. Eventually, all the molecules that will dissolve are small enough to pass into the tiny BLOOD vessels in the lining of the intestine. The remaining waste material that cannot be digested (known as roughage) passes to the large intestine and out of the body through the anus as solid feces.

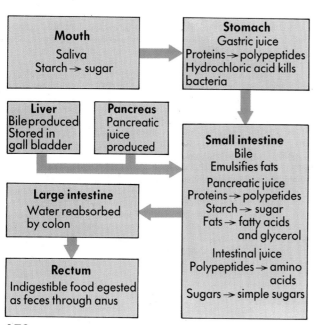

Mouth
Saliva
Starch → sugar

Stomach
Gastric juice
Proteins → polypeptides
Hydrochloric acid kills bacteria

Liver
Bile produced
Stored in gall bladder

Pancreas
Pancreatic juice produced

Small intestine
Bile
Emulsifies fats
Pancreatic juice
Proteins → polypetides
Starch → sugar
Fats → fatty acids and glycerol
Intestinal juice
Polypeptides → amino acids
Sugars → simple sugars

Large intestine
Water reabsorbed by colon

Rectum
Indigestible food egested as feces through anus

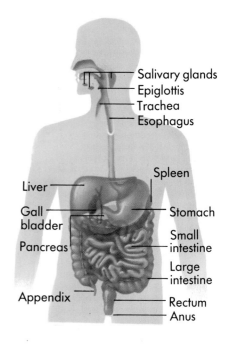

Salivary glands
Epiglottis
Trachea
Esophagus
Spleen
Liver
Gall bladder
Stomach
Pancreas
Small intestine
Large intestine
Appendix
Rectum
Anus

Digital

A digital system is one in which information is represented by electrical pulses instead of smoothly changing electrical signals which are ANALOG. The pulses represent NUMBERS and the numbers can represent any form of information including speech, music, pictures, and

▼ Analog signals from the telephone are changed into a series of digits in binary code. In this form, signals are less likely to be distorted or noisy. To hear the sounds, the digital signals are changed back to analog.

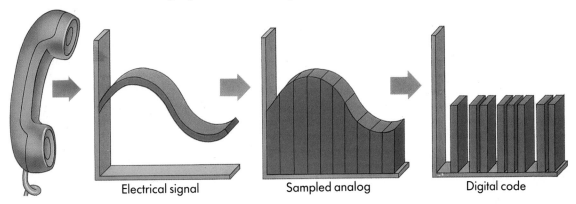

Electrical signal   Sampled analog   Digital code

printed text. Digital systems do not use the same DECIMAL counting numbers that we do. Instead they use a BINARY code with only two numbers: zero and one. (Numbers can also be referred to as digits.) This is an easy system for computers to handle because even the simplest electronic circuits can have two states or conditions; off or on (zero or one). Converting information into binary code is called *digitization*. Morse Code is similar to digital communication, but has three states, dot (short), dash (long), and off.
See also BIT AND BYTE; COMPUTER.

Dimensions *See* Measurement

Diode

A diode is an ELECTRONIC component. An electric current can flow through it in one direction only. It can change alternating current (AC), which flows in one direction and then in the opposite direction, into a current flowing in one direction only, called direct current (DC). This is called *rectification* and it enables portable electrical products such as radios or tape recorders to be powered either by batteries (DC) or from the AC main electrical supply.

Direct current *See* Electricity

▼ Electronic equipment uses semiconductor devices called diodes to allow an alternating current (AC) to flow in only one direction (from blue to red). It is then a direct current (DC). Each of these circuits has four diodes arranged rather like a maze. No matter which way the current comes from the AC source, it always leaves the group of diodes in the same direction (red).

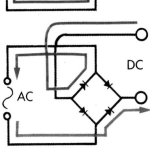

DISEASE

A disease is any form of ill health that can be described and recognized by the symptoms it causes. Usually we think of diseases as infections caused by attacking bacteria or viruses, when the damage they cause to the body, or poisonous substances they produce, make us feel ill. The body's reaction to infections of this type is usually to increase the temperature, and to produce disease-fighting substances which can themselves make us feel sick. Diseases caused by bacteria, such as boils and infected wounds are readily treated by antibiotics, but viruses are not affected by antibiotics, and the body has to fight off the infection itself. Protection against viral diseases, such as measles, mumps, and rubella, can be given by vaccination. Vaccination also protects against dangerous bacteria like the one causing tetanus.

Many serious diseases are caused by processes in the body working incorrectly. Some of these are inherited. Diabetes is a common disease, which is caused by the pancreas failing to make sufficient insulin, so sugar levels in the body are affected. Cancer occurs when the process controlling cell division gets out of control, and the cells multiply to produce a tumor.

▲ Moldy grapes, diseased because of a fungus, are used in this case to produce a sweet wine.

Contagious A contagious disease can only be passed on by touching someone or something with the disease.
Infectious An infectious disease can be transmitted in many ways.

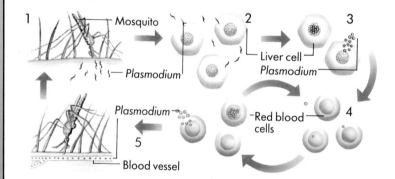

◄ Malaria is caused by a parasite called a plasmodium, transmitted by mosquitos **1**. Following a bite from an infected mosquito, the parasite attacks and reproduces inside the person's liver cells **2**. After several days, new plasmodia **3** spread to the blood **4** where they may infect further mosquitos **5**.

The Plague

The plague is a serious disease, which appears in various forms. It is passed to humans mainly by infected fleas and rats. In the 1300s the plague, or Black Death, killed about one quarter of Europe's population.

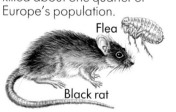

Disease	Signs and Symptoms	Treatment
Tonsilitis	Sore throat, swollen tonsils	Antibiotics
Diabetes	Thirst, damage to vision, unconsciousness	Drugs or insulin injection
Measles	Runny nose, cough, rash	Vaccination to prevent
Chicken pox	Red itchy spots followed by scabs	No treatment; it clears up
Athlete's foot	Itchy scaling between toes	Anti-fungal drugs
Rubella (German measles)	Fever, swollen glands, rash	Vaccination to prevent

See also ANESTHETIC; ANTIBIOTICS; BODY SCANNER; INFECTION; IMMUNE SYSTEM; PATHOLOGY; VACCINATION; VIRUS AND VIRAL DISEASES.

Display

A display is a form of BEHAVIOR used by an animal to attract a mate or to frighten a rival or enemy. When a peacock spreads his beautiful fan of feathers, he is putting on a courtship display. By showing off in front of a female, he encourages her to become his mate. Many male animals display bright colors to the females in this way, and some sing or dance as well. Threat displays are used to frighten other animals. For example, a male cichlid fish puffs out its gills to scare off other male cichlids that come too close to its mate. Australia's frilled lizard defends itself by erecting a large frill around its neck and opening its mouth very wide. Although it is harmless, it looks very fierce.

South American bush cricket

▲ A sudden display can frighten off an attacker. The South American bush cricket can suddenly flash its pair of eye spots if its "dead leaf" camouflage fails to protect it.

Dissolve *See* Solution

Distillation

Distillation is the process of separating a LIQUID from a SOLUTION or mixture by vaporization and CONDENSATION. In simple distillation, the solution or mixture is boiled in a vessel or flask, and the vapor is directed into a condenser, where it cools and becomes a liquid. This whole apparatus is called a still. The substances originally dissolved in the liquid remain behind in the flask. Different kinds of distillation are used in industry. The most important of these are *fractional distillation* and *flash distillation*. Fractional distillation separates liquids

◀ Birds defend their territories in several ways. Sometimes a threatening position or warning call is enough but at other times the birds may fight. Normally a bird fights with a combination of its beak, legs, or wings, but will sometimes fly at the predator's head and call loudly. These Japanese cranes have a spectacular display.

▶ *If a solution of salt in water is boiled, the liquid you get by condensing the vapor is pure water. Crystals of salt are left behind in the flask.*

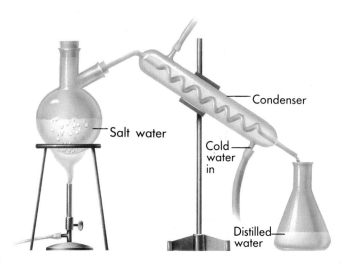

Condenser

Salt water

Cold water in

Distilled water

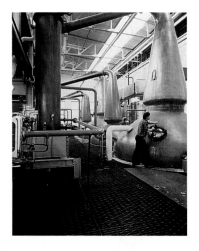

▲ *Distilling is done in a still. These are column stills and are used in the production of whiskey.*

that boil at different temperatures. This is the method used to distil alcoholic liquors such as whiskey and to refine crude oil. Flash distillation does not make use of heat to vaporize the liquid. Instead, liquid in a vessel at high PRESSURE passes into one of lower pressure. Part of the liquid turns quickly into vapor and is condensed. In another process called rectification, part of the condensed vapor flows back into the still to make the remaining vapor even purer. Rectification is very important in oil and PETROLEUM refining.

DNA

DNA is the abbreviation for deoxyribonucleic acid, the MOLECULE that makes up the CHROMOSOMES AND GENES. DNA is found in the nucleus of a CELL and contains the instructions coded to pass on characteristics from one generation to the next, and to make the

James Watson (1928–) and Francis Crick (1916–)
In 1953, they discovered the structure of DNA (deoxyribonucleic acid) the substance that transmits genetic information from one generation to the next. They showed the shape of the molecule and worked out how the individual components of DNA were joined together. Watson (right) and Crick won a Nobel Prize for their work, which changed the science of genetics.

molecules needed for growth and development. DNA is composed of two spiral and interlocked threads, a double helix. The genetic information is stored on the threads in a code of four types of molecules. Just as a large number of words can be made from only a few letters, so DNA can make lots of different instructions from a few building blocks. DNA can reproduce itself by splitting into two halves, as in CELL DIVISION. Each thread can copy the missing thread to regenerate the double helix.

Each DNA molecule is built up from 100,000 to 10 million atoms. If the DNA fails to copy properly during REPRODUCTION, by accident or because of damage, a MUTATION results. Mutations alter the working of some cells and are often lethal, but they can be an advantage; this is the basis for EVOLUTION.

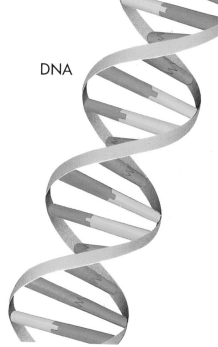

DNA

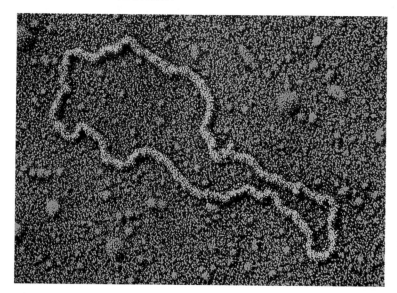

▲ Chromosomes contain deoxyribonucleic acid (DNA). DNA is made up of two long strands coiled around each other into a double helix.

◄ A plasmid of bacterial DNA. A plasmid is a molecule of DNA that can exist apart from a chromosome. It can reproduce on its own.

Doppler effect

The Doppler effect is the name given to the change you hear or see in the FREQUENCY or WAVELENGTH of a wave when the source which produces the wave is moving. If the source is moving toward you, the frequency increases, so the wavelength decreases, and if it is moving away from you then the frequency decreases and the wavelength gets longer. You notice this effect in the SOUND you hear when a car passes you. The sound made by its engine seems to drop in pitch because as the car approaches it is moving in the same direction as the sound wave coming from the engine. The sound waves

To make a red traffic light appear green, you would have to drive toward it at a speed of about 37,000 miles (60,000 km) per second! The change in the frequency (color) of the light waves given out by the traffic lights would be caused by the motion of the driver in relation to the traffic lights.

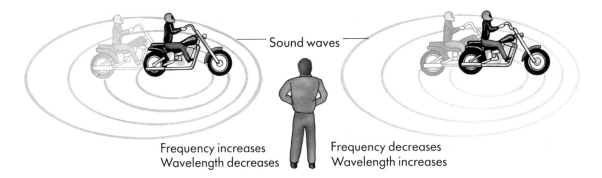

Sound waves

Frequency increases
Wavelength decreases

Frequency decreases
Wavelength increases

▲ *The pitch of the sound made by a motorcycle seems to get higher as it approaches an observer and lower as it moves away. This is caused by the movement of the source of the waves in relation to the observer. It is called the Doppler effect.*

are pushed closer together, giving a higher frequency and a higher-pitched sound.

Once the car has passed you and is moving away, the sound waves are spaced farther apart, giving a lower frequency, and a lower note. The effect is important in astronomy; the light reaching us from distant GALAXIES has its wavelength changed: it undergoes RED SHIFT. This is because the galaxies are moving very rapidly away from us.

Double star *See* Binary star

Dreams

▼ *The graphs compare the length and type of sleep for humans, chimpanzees, and cats. Note the different periods of REM (rapid eye movement) sleep, when dreaming occurs.*

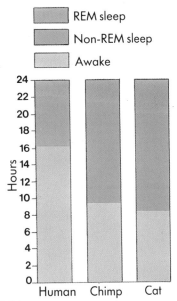

REM sleep
Non-REM sleep
Awake

Hours

24
22
20
18
16
14
12
10
8
6
4
2
0

Human   Chimp   Cat

Everyone has dreams each night, but they are usually forgotten before waking. During sleep we go through several stages, and while we are most lightly unconscious, dreaming takes place. When this happens the muscles are relaxed and the eyes move rapidly beneath the eyelids (called rapid eye movement or REM). If you wake up at this moment, you will remember the dream, otherwise you will slip into another form of sleep and the dream will be forgotten. This cycle of dreaming is repeated several times during the night. The function of dreams is uncertain. Often it feels as though a vivid dream must have some purpose, but many scientists believe that dreams are simply a way for the brain to dispose of unwanted information. Certainly some nightmares are very frightening, causing the heart to race. Some psychoanalysts believe that the content of dreams is very important and can give insights into a person's mind. Sigmund FREUD was the first psychoanalyst to make a detailed study of dreams. He believed that many dreams indicated memories that were deliberately being hidden or repressed, causing emotional problems.

Drug

A drug is a substance which when taken, produces an effect on the body. Most drugs are used as medicines, but some are taken because of the effects they have on the mind. Some mind altering drugs are perfectly legal, such as the stimulant CAFFEINE which is contained in coffee and tea. Nicotine and alcohol are also drugs with a powerful effect on the BRAIN. The effects of drugs are studied by pharmacologists, who must ensure that drugs for medical use are safe. Medical drugs are classified according to their effects. Tranquilizers calm the mind; hypnotics help people to go to sleep; ANTIBIOTICS fight infection; antidepressants are used against depression; and antiarthritics help arthritic people. Most drugs are given as tablets or gelatin capsules, but when a quick response is needed they can be given in an injection. Recently, drugs have been developed which are absorbed slowly through the skin from a special adhesive patch. Other drugs can be given in the form of a suppository which is inserted into the rectum. Some drugs continue to work for several weeks after being injected. These are used to treat serious mental illness, as a birth control drug, or to cause farm animals to put on weight quickly. Illegal drugs such as heroin and cocaine were originally used for medical purposes, before their addictive effects were known.

▲ Up until the beginning of the modern drug industry after 1800, the doctors and pharmacists themselves prepared almost all the drugs they sold.

Tobacco, coffee, and even tea were thought to be dangerous drugs when they were first introduced. It is now known that smoking tobacco can increase the risk of cancer and heart disease. Drinking too much strong brewed coffee can cause symptoms of caffeine poisoning. Alcohol, another drug, has been consumed by humans for as long as history records. It can also be damaging to health if consumed in large quantities. The introduction of all these drugs would not be allowed today if modern methods of testing were applied to them.

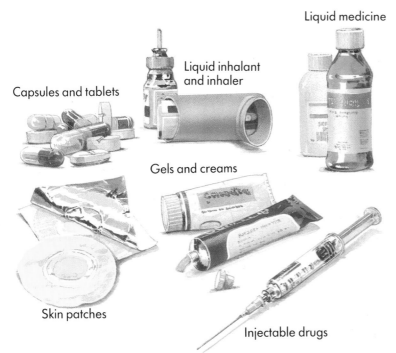

Capsules and tablets

Liquid inhalant and inhaler

Liquid medicine

Gels and creams

Skin patches

Injectable drugs

◀ Various types of drugs are used to treat illness and diseases. They are introduced into the body in various ways, swallowing, inhalation, or injection through the skin.

▲ *Vaporized dry ice (carbon dioxide) is being poured onto someone's hands. It is often used in theaters to make special effects.*

Gold is one of the most ductile of all metals. It can be drawn into a very fine wire or hammered into sheets so thin that light can pass through the metal. An ounce of gold can be drawn into a wire more than 40 miles (65 km) long.

Dry ice

Dry ice is solid CARBON DIOXIDE. It is formed when carbon dioxide turns directly from a GAS into a SOLID at a temperature of −109.3°F (−78.5°C). Because it is so cold, dry ice must be handled with extreme care in order to avoid frostbite. Dry ice is usually prepared by cooling carbon dioxide under high PRESSURE. It looks like snow but can be made into blocks by compressing the flakes. Dry ice is very important for cooling or refrigerating foods and medicines. It is also used to simulate fog and steam effects in television or stage plays because it rapidly sublimes (turns back to a gas without becoming liquid) at ordinary room temperature.

Ductility

A material is said to be ductile if it can be permanently distorted or bent without cracking or fracturing. For example, most METALS are ductile but glass is not. For a material to be ductile, the ATOMS that make it up must be able to slide past each other without causing the material to break apart; this is possible for metals because the forces between the atoms do not depend very much on the position of the atoms.

In many nonmetals, the chemical BONDS between the atoms depend on them being in particular positions relative to each other and at specified angles to the other atoms. Therefore, trying to move one set of atoms past another tends to break the bonds and to cause the material to crack or fracture.

See also FORGING; MALLEABILITY.

▶ *Many metals, including aluminum, gold, iron, copper, and silver are ductile. This means that they can be drawn into wire, and hammered or rolled into various shapes without breaking.*

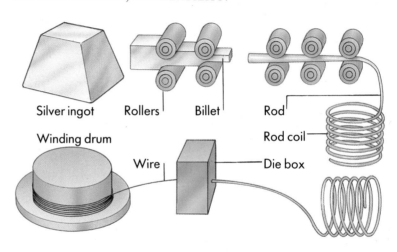

Silver ingot   Rollers   Billet   Rod

Winding drum

Wire

Rod coil

Die box

Dye

A dye is a COMPOUND that gives a long-lasting, distinctive COLOR to textiles (fibers, yarns, and fabrics); food; paper and ink; plastics; wood; and many other materials. A dye works by having its molecules absorbed by the material. For example, textiles are placed in a dyebath containing a SOLUTION of the dye and take up the dye MOLECULES. The most permanent dyes are those whose molecules form chemical BONDS with the molecules of the material being dyed. Some dyed fabrics fade in sunlight or through washing. A material's color-

William Perkin (1838–1907)
William Perkin discovered aniline dyes, which were the first dyes to be made in the laboratory; previously, all dyes were made from animals and plants. He made his first dye, called mauvene, by accident when trying to find a way of making the drug quinine. He was only 18 years old, and the law had to be changed so that he could take out a patent on his discovery. The introduction of synthetic dyes was disastrous for farmers who grew dye plants such as madder and indigo, and many of them went out of business.

SEE FOR YOURSELF
Try dyeing some old pieces of cotton cloth with natural dyes. For red, try beetroot, cherries, and red cabbage; green, try spinach; brown, try onion skins, tea, and coffee. Take the leaves or fruit of plants and cover with boiling water. Leave for 15 minutes. Pour the liquid through a filter to make the colored liquid that can be used for dyeing.

fastness (its ability to retain the color) can be improved by adding a substance called a "mordant" to the dyebath. Mordants bond the dye molecules to the fabric. People have been dyeing textiles and other materials for 5,000 years. Before the late 19th century, natural dyes from plants, such as madder (bright red) and indigo (deep, dark blue), were used. In the 20th century, new synthetic dyes have been made. A major class of dyes are the azo dyes which produce an intense color when two colorless organic compounds react together. They are used with acrylic, cotton, nylon, and rayon.

Dynamite *See* Explosives

Dynamo *See* Generator

▲ *Some of the large vats of dye used for coloring leather in the Moroccan leather industry.*

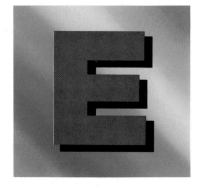

Ear

Ears are the organs through which animals hear SOUNDS. Sounds are caused by vibrations that spread through the air as sound waves. Our ears collect these waves. The human ear, like that of any mammal, has three main regions. The outer ear, which is the part that you can see, is a funnel that collects the sounds and passes them along a canal to the eardrum. This drum vibrates when the sounds hit it and the vibrations are passed on to three tiny bones, the hammer, the anvil, and the stirrup, collectively called ossicles. They amplify the sounds and carry them across an air-filled gap called the middle ear. A narrow tube called the Eustachian tube connects the

Frogs and many lizards have their eardrums on the surface of the head and have no outer ear. Fish have no eardrums at all, and no middle ear. They can, however, pick up sounds or vibrations in the water through another organ, the lateral line.

▶ *The human ear has three main sections: outer, middle, and inner. The semicircular canals of the inner ear give us our sense of balance. The auditory nerve, which sends sound signals to the brain can be clearly seen.*

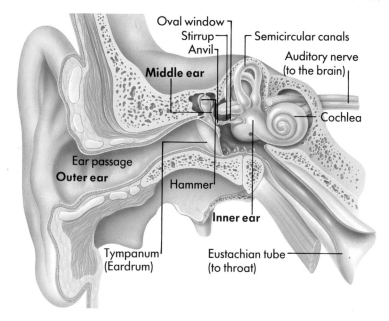

Oval window
Stirrup
Anvil
Middle ear
Semicircular canals
Auditory nerve (to the brain)
Cochlea
Ear passage
Outer ear
Hammer
Inner ear
Tympanum (Eardrum)
Eustachian tube (to throat)

The ear is such a complicated mechanism that it is not surprising that problems can occur, and cause deafness or hearing problems. If the eardrum is broken, temporary deafness will result until it has regrown. Defects can also occur in the bones of the middle ear and in the sensitive cochlea. As long as some hearing remains, a hearing aid can restore much of the ability to hear sounds.

middle ear to the throat and ensures that the PRESSURE inside the middle ear is the same as that on the outside. It is the movement of air through this tube to equalize the pressure which causes your ears to pop. The ossicles carry the vibrations to the inner ear. From here, sounds pass into a spiraling liquid-filled tube called the cochlea, where highly sensitive CELLS pick up the vibrations and NERVES carry the electrical signals to the brain, where the sounds are identified. The inner ear also contains three semicircular canals that help us to keep our balance. Each canal is filled with fluid and as you move your head the fluid moves. If you spin around and around or knock your head, the delicate balance of the fluid in the canals is disturbed and you will feel dizzy.

Earth

The Earth is a PLANET which, together with eight other planets, orbits a single star that we call the SUN. The Sun and its planets make up the SOLAR SYSTEM, which is located in space on one of the arms of a GALAXY that we can see as a faint band of light across the night sky. *See* pages 190 and 191.

Earthquakes

An earthquake is a series of shock waves that pass through the EARTH. These cause further movements, and result from a break in the rocks deep in the Earth's crust. The crust is made up of a number of plates which are able to move. Earthquakes mostly occur at the edges of plates and may be associated with volcanic activity.

In 1906, when a movement took place in the San Andreas Fault system along the western seaboard of California, there was a severe earthquake causing widespread damage and a fire leading to the deaths of 500 people. In 1989, the fault moved again and there was another quake, but the damage was much less severe.

Earthquakes are occurring all the time, but few of them cause widespread destruction. The severity of earthquakes is measured by the Richter scale. Scale 1.5 is the smallest quake that can be felt; a quake of 4.5 causes some damage; and an earthquake of 8.5 or more is devastating. Less than twenty earthquakes a year measure over 7 on the Richter scale.

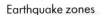

Earthquake zones

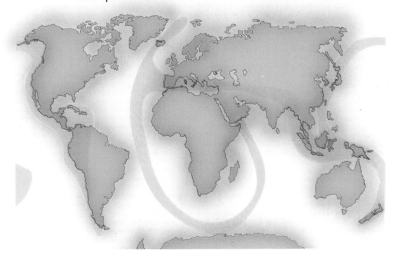

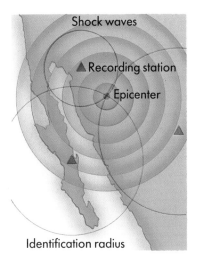

Identification radius

▲ The point on the Earth above the source of an earthquake is called the "epicenter." The source of an earthquake, the "focus," may occur in rocks up to 300 miles (500 km) below the surface of the Earth. Earthquakes are the result of rock movements under stress. Vibrations from the earthquake radiate outward from the focus.

Over a thousand earthquakes with a magnitude of two on the Richter scale occur every day. Earthquakes can be measured on other scales as well, such as the Modified Mercalli scale. In 1985 an earthquake hit Mexico City and measured 8.1 on the Richter scale and between 8 and 9 on the Modified Mercalli scale (8 = chimneys and monuments fall, buildings move on foundations; 9 = heavy damage to buildings, large cracks open in the ground). The Mexico City earthquake killed 7,200 people and injured thousands more.

◄ Regions of the world where most earthquakes occur, lie along the edges of crustal plates, continents, and along chains of islands.

EARTH ❄

The planet on which we live is not completely round. In fact, it bulges a little at the equator and is flattened at the poles, a shape known as an oblate spheroid. We can look at our world as a series of balls, one within the other, rather like the skins of an onion. First, there is the planet itself, the geosphere, the outer, rocky part of which is called the lithosphere. On it live the plants and animals which go to make up the biosphere. Surrounding these, there is the envelope of air known as the atmosphere which, in turn, is divided into a number of layers from the lowest, the troposphere, through the stratosphere and mesosphere, to the thermosphere, which is also called the ionosphere at a height above 50 miles (80 km) from the Earth's surface. It is in the troposphere that our weather conditions occur.

The inside of the Earth (the geosphere) is also made up of layers. At the center is a solid inner core made up of an iron-nickel alloy under pressure. Surrounding this is a liquid outer core composed mainly of nickel and iron but with a certain amount of some lighter material such as silicon or sulfur. Within the next layer, the mantle, the material rises and falls as a result of heating and cooling of the material. These movements are thought to be what causes the processes of continental drift and plate tectonics. The rocky crust varies generally in composition and is made up of a wide range of rock types.

Flat Earth?
Until about 500 years ago, many people thought that the Earth was flat. They feared that if a ship sailed too far to the east or the west, it would topple over the edge. Then the early voyages of discovery showed that the Earth is round. When Columbus set sail in 1492, he was seeking a new way of reaching Asia and India by sailing west from Europe, and hoping to go right around the world. Instead he discovered America.

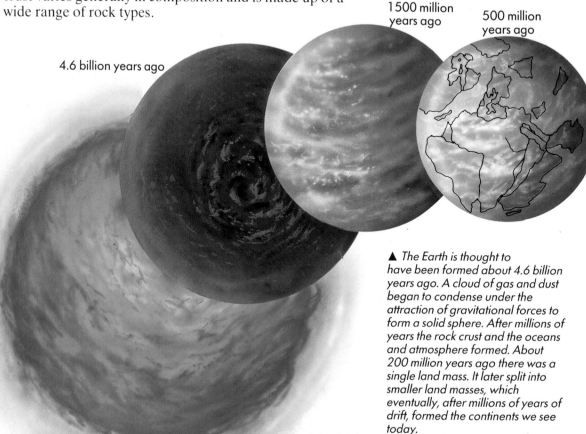

4.6 billion years ago

1500 million years ago

500 million years ago

▲ The Earth is thought to have been formed about 4.6 billion years ago. A cloud of gas and dust began to condense under the attraction of gravitational forces to form a solid sphere. After millions of years the rock crust and the oceans and atmosphere formed. About 200 million years ago there was a single land mass. It later split into smaller land masses, which eventually, after millions of years of drift, formed the continents we see today.

190

Crust

Mantle

Outer core

Core

◀ The Earth's crust varies in thickness from about 5 miles (8 km) under the oceans to about 25 miles (40 km) under the continents. The inside of the Earth is divided into three parts, the mantle, the outer core, and the inner core. The mantle is solid rock about 1,800 miles (2,900 km) thick. The outer core is about 1,400 miles (2,250 km) thick.

Water 71%

Land 29%

More than two-thirds of the Earth's surface is covered by water. The land areas make up only 29 percent.

▲ The Earth, which people once thought to be flat, can now be seen in satellite pictures to be roughly shaped like a ball. Water covers about 71 percent of the Earth or 140 million square miles (361 million km²). Land covers about 29 percent or 57 million square miles (149 million km²).

200 million years ago

100 million years ago

Today

▼ The Earth spins around its axis, which tilts about 23° from the vertical. This tilt and the Earth's motion around the Sun causes the change of seasons. The northern half of the Earth tilts toward the Sun in summer and away from the Sun in winter (below).

23°

EARTH FACTS AND FIGURES
World population 5.4 billion
Circumference 25,000 miles (40,075 km)
Diameter at the equator 7,927 miles (12,757 km)
Diameter through the Poles 7,900 miles (12,713 km)
Distance from Sun 93 million miles (150 million km)
Age About 4.6 billion years

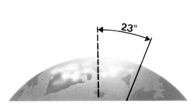

Spring

Summer   Sun   Winter

Fall

See also ATMOSPHERE; CONTINENT; ELEMENTS; GEOGRAPHY; GEOLOGY; HEMISPHERE; MOON; PLATE TECTONICS; POLLUTION; SOLAR SYSTEM.

Eastman, George *See* Photography

Echo

An echo is the SOUND produced when sound waves are reflected from an object. Clapping your hands and listening for the echo from your surroundings is like shining a flashlight and looking at the light waves that are reflected from objects around you. There is a delay between clapping your hands and the echo; this is because it takes the sound waves a certain amount of time to travel through the air from your hands to the object and back again. You do not notice the same effect when you shine a light because light travels so much more quickly than sound. This time delay can be measured and used to work out the distance to the object reflecting the sound; ships and SUBMARINES use this effect in SONAR equipment to measure the depth of the water and to look for features on the seabed. Similarly, bats that cannot see well use high-pitched sound waves to build up detailed pictures of their surroundings which enable them to "see" objects around them in the dark.

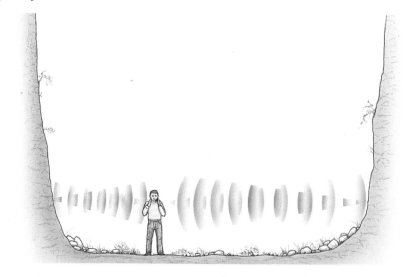

▲ Bats make high-pitched sounds while flying, which bounce off objects in the form of echoes. These give the bats information about the direction and distance of objects.

The speed of sound in air is approximately 1,085 feet per second (331 m/s). The distance to a surface that reflects an echo can therefore be estimated from the time that passes between the making of a sound and the reception of the echo.

► Echoes are produced when sound waves bounce off a nearby surface. Sound waves striking surfaces at different distances return to the person at different times.

Eclipse

When the Sun or Moon goes into eclipse, its bright surface turns dark. An eclipse of the Sun (*solar eclipse*) occurs when the Earth passes into the Moon's shadow; an eclipse of the Moon (*lunar eclipse*) is seen when the Moon passes out of the sunlight into the Earth's shadow.

Solar eclipses occur at new moon, although usually

Total eclipse

Moon

Umbra | Earth

Penumbra

Partial eclipse

the Moon "misses" the Sun altogether. Even if the Moon does cross in front of the Sun, most places on the Earth only see a partial eclipse. This is because the Moon is only just large enough to cover the Sun completely, and the shadow it casts on the Earth (which is where the eclipse appears total) may be only a few dozen miles wide. A total eclipse is the only time when the Sun's faint atmosphere or CORONA can be seen, but the view only lasts for seven minutes.

When the Moon passes into the Earth's shadow it does not usually disappear altogether. The Earth's atmosphere shines like a brilliant reddish halo around the black planet, and this light is enough to make the eclipsed Moon glow with a coppery tint. A total lunar eclipse can last for more than an hour.

▲ During a solar eclipse the Moon casts a very small black shadow or "umbra" on the Earth. This is the only place where a solar eclipse is total. In the large "penumbra" around it, observers see a partial eclipse.

Total Solar Eclipses in the 1990s
November 3, 1994 South America, South Atlantic Ocean
October 24, 1995 Southeast Asia
March 9, 1997 Mongolia, eastern Siberia
February 26, 1998 Central America, Central Pacific Ocean
August 11, 1999 Europe, Middle East, North Atlantic.

By 31 December 1999, the 20th century will have witnessed 228 solar and 147 lunar eclipses.

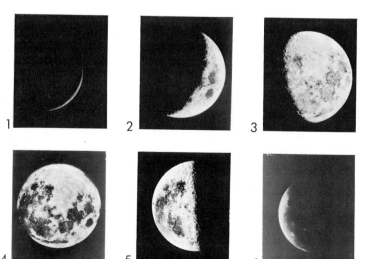

◀ Some stages in the progress of a lunar eclipse. It can take up to 6 hours for the Moon to pass completely through the Earth's shadow. A total eclipse can last for up to 1 $^3/_4$ hours.

193

ECOLOGY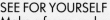

Ecology is the study of animals and plants in their natural surroundings and how each species fits into its ecosystem. Ecologists try to find out why plants and animals live in some places and not in others, and to discover exactly what conditions they need to survive. They also try to discover how much space animals need and they study food chains to find out how the plants and animals are linked together. It is important to understand these things when trying to conserve wildlife in nature preserves, and also when trying to assess how human activities might affect wildlife. Almost all organisms are specialized for their habitat and interrelationships with other animals and plants. They may be unable to adapt if their ecosystem is disturbed or destroyed.

For example, ecologists warned that widespread killing of snakes in Thailand could damage the rice crop, but the killing went on. Now the rice is being eaten by rats. The snakes had previously kept the rats under control.

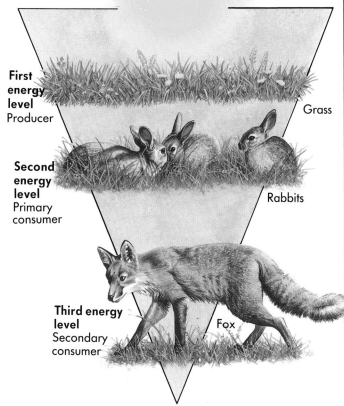

First energy level
Producer

Second energy level
Primary consumer

Third energy level
Secondary consumer

Grass

Rabbits

Fox

▲ In a food chain at the first level, producers such as green plants are eaten by herbivores. These primary consumers are, in turn, eaten by carnivores, which are secondary consumers. Each organism in the food chain feeds on, and obtains energy from, the previous level. This is the way energy is transferred from level to level.

SEE FOR YOURSELF
Make a frame and put it down at random several times in different fields or gardens. List the plants and insects found in each square of the frame. You could also use a field guide to try to identify what you find.

Monkey

Giraffe

Gerenuk

Dik dik   Eland   Elephant   Warthog

▲ Ecologists study how communities of animals and plants interact with one another and with the nonliving elements of their environments. Also of importance to ecologists are the different roles each of the species plays in its environment.

See also CONSERVATION, ENVIRONMENTAL; ECOSYSTEM; ENDANGERED SPECIES; ENERGY; EVOLUTION; FOOD CHAIN; RESOURCES.

Ecosystem

An ecosystem is a community of plants and animals occupying a certain area, together with the SOIL and other nonliving materials. It can be as small as a water-filled hole in a forest tree, or as big as the forest itself. In a perfect ecosystem all the components are balanced: the plants provide all the food and OXYGEN needed by the animals, and all the waste products are recycled to produce new plant material. Changes are always taking place in such an ecosystem, but the numbers of organisms stay roughly the same. Many of the world's natural ecosystems have taken hundreds or thousands of years to reach a balanced state and, given a stable CLIMATE, they would remain balanced for thousands more years were it not for human interference.

SEE FOR YOURSELF
You can create a simple ecosystem yourself by setting up an old fish tank with some insects and small animals, for example, from a pond. Use water and different kinds of vegetation in the environment. Place a lid on the tank, with air holes in it. Do not make the holes too large otherwise the insects will climb out.

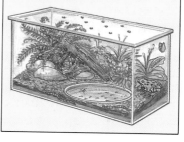

Sunlight

Kestrel preys on bird

Bird eats caterpillar

Caterpillar feeds on leaf

Fungi decompose leaf litter

Magnified root showing root tip and root hairs

Falling leaves decompose (break down) and the nutrients pass into the soil

Bacteria break down nutrients

Edison, Thomas Alva

Thomas Alva Edison (1847–1931) was responsible for over 1,000 inventions. He was born in Milan, Ohio. When he was only ten years old, he set up his own chemistry laboratory in his basement. In the 1860s he worked as a TELEGRAPH operator in the United States

▲ The Sun's energy is harnessed by plants and passed on to animals when they feed. The energy from the decomposition of dead animals is absorbed by plants through their roots.

195

▲ *Thomas Edison the inventor.*

and Canada. In 1876, the profits he made from selling telegraphic printers he had invented, enabled him to set up a laboratory. A year later, he invented the *phonograph*, a type of record player that used wax cylinders instead of disks. His first recording was of himself saying the rhyme "Mary had a little lamb." In 1879, he demonstrated the first successful electric LIGHT BULB. He also discovered that he could cause electricity to flow from the bulb's glowing filament onto a metal plate inside the bulb. This is known as the Edison Effect. It later led to the invention by other people of the radio tube.

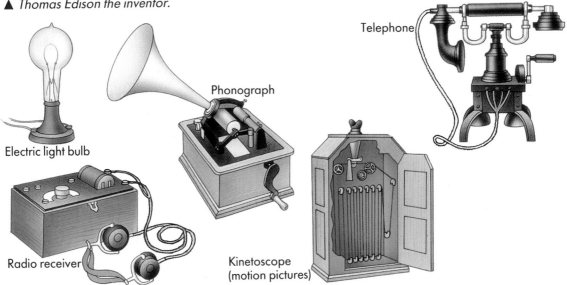

Telephone

Phonograph

Electric light bulb

Radio receiver

Kinetoscope
(motion pictures)

▲ *Most of Thomas Edison's inventions and patents were modifications of already existing inventions. His improvement on Bell's telephone enabled conversations to be held over distances of 100 miles (160 km) or more, instead of just a few yards. However, the phonograph was completely new and original and the kinetoscope was the first machine to produce moving pictures. A hundred and fifty feet of film revolved on spools and the person looked through an eye hole to see the pictures move. Edison took out a total of 1,097 patents.*

Efficiency

The efficiency of a process or a machine is equal to the *useful* ENERGY output divided by the energy that has to be put in to drive it. It is often expressed as a percentage; for example, 50 percent efficiency means that half the energy that is put in comes out in a useful form. The total could never be more than 100 percent; the *total* energy output will always be equal to the total input, since energy is conserved, but a lot of the output will be in a form that is not useful. For example, in a car ENGINE some of the energy in the gasoline goes into producing HEAT and vibrations in the engine, some goes into FRICTION, and some into heating the exhaust gas, rather than into driving the wheels. The overall efficiency is usually around 30 percent. The efficiency of a power plant converting chemical energy stored in coal into electrical energy is about 40 percent.

Egg

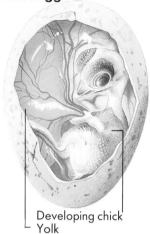

Hen's egg

Developing chick
Yolk

▲ *The chick of a hen starts to hatch out of its egg about 21 days after the egg has been laid. By this stage its feathers and claws are fully formed.*

An egg is produced by a female animal. It is a single CELL, called an ovum (plural "ova"), and it contains a supply of food known as the yolk. Most eggs are surrounded by one or more protective membranes, the outer one of which often forms a hard shell. After FERTILIZATION by a male sex cell or sperm, the ovum divides into more cells and becomes an EMBRYO which grows by feeding on the yolk. Some eggs contain very little yolk and it is soon used up. These eggs hatch quickly. Birds' eggs have lots of yolk and a store of water in the albumen (the white in a hen's egg). Baby birds can grow quite large before they need to leave their eggs. The eggs sold in stores for us to eat are usually unfertilized, and so they have no embryos inside them.

Every kind of animal produces eggs, but they do not all lay eggs. Female mammals, including people, produce very small eggs which they keep inside their bodies. The embryos that grow from these eggs get food from their mothers' bodies until they are ready to be born. *See also* REPRODUCTION.

◀ *There are many kind of eggs. A slug lays its eggs in groups. The eggs are enclosed in capsules filled with a nourishing fluid.*

Duckbilled platypus

▲ *The duckbilled platypus is one of only two mammals that lays eggs. The other is the spiny anteater, or echidna. This kind of mammal is called a monotreme. After they hatch, the young are fed on the mother's milk, like all other mammals.*

Einstein, Albert

Albert Einstein (1879–1955) was a physicist who was born in Ulm, Germany; he left Germany for the United States in 1933, and became a U.S. citizen in 1940. He is most famous for developing the theory of RELATIVITY, out of which came the famous equation $E = mc^2$. In 1905

► *Albert Einstein delivered many lectures about his theories. Most of his theories were explained by using long and complex calculations.*

Einstein is one of the famous scientists whose name has been given to a chemical element. As well as the 92 naturally occurring elements there are several synthetic ones which only exist during experiments. In 1952 an element with the atomic number 99 was discovered in the United States and called Einsteinium.

he suggested that light is absorbed in the form of packets of ENERGY, now called photons; for this he received the Nobel Prize for Physics in 1921. Also in 1905 he developed the special theory of relativity and later, in 1915, he arrived at the general theory of relativity. These theories are the basis for all our ideas about the history and structure of the UNIVERSE.

Einstein's work on photons helped to found QUANTUM THEORY, although he disagreed with some of the later work on this subject.

Elasticity

Elasticity is the change of shape or size of an object when a FORCE is applied to squash it or stretch it. The change is only temporary; when the force is removed, the object goes back to its original shape or size. For example, if

SEE FOR YOURSELF

Fix a thumbtack to a piece of board and hook a rubber band around it. Attach an empty cup to the rubber band. Put marbles one at a time into the cup. Mark the amount the rubber band stretches. Take out the marbles. The band returns to its original shape. If you load the cup until the elastic limit is reached, the band will stretch out of shape and break.

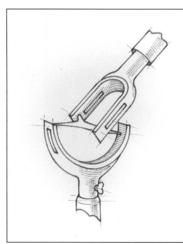

Robert Hooke (1635–1703)
Hooke was a British scientist. He was one of the first scientists to study elasticity. He was interested in the elastic behavior of springs. This led him to the development of Hooke's law. The law states that the amount an elastic body stretches out of shape is in direct proportion to the force acting on it. He also invented the universal joint (*left*), used to change the direction of a rotating shaft.

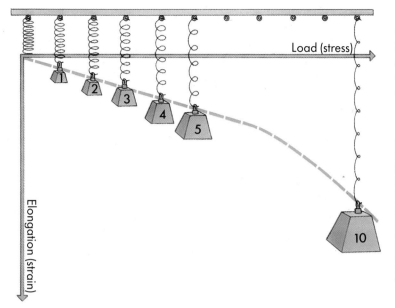

Load (stress)

Elongation (strain)

◀ *Every material has its characteristic "elastic limit." If the strain on the material is too great, the material will remain deformed when the stress has been taken away* **10**.

Elastic A material is elastic if it can return to its original shape after it has been compressed, or stretched.

Plastic A material is plastic if it can be molded or formed into a different shape.

you lie down on a bed the springs inside change shape under the force of your weight, but when you get up again, the bed goes back to its original shape. But bed springs will not go on returning to their original shape if too large a force is put on them for too long. Many MA-TERIALS can undergo in addition to these temporary elastic changes, a permanent, or plastic, change of shape if the distorting force is large enough. Mechanical structures, such as buildings, which may experience distorting forces are usually carefully designed so that each part behaves elastically, not plastically.

Electric arc

An electric arc is the very intense HEAT and LIGHT which is produced when an electric current is passed from one CONDUCTOR to another through air or some other gas. Normally gases do not conduct ELECTRICITY, but if a large enough voltage is applied it can tear charged ELECTRONS out of the molecules and propel them through the gas, carrying the electric charge with them. The charged molecules or ions which are left behind are speeded up by the ENERGY of the voltage, causing the temperature of the gas to rise dramatically.

Electric arcs are used to provide an intense source of light in ARC LAMPS. They are also used in arc welding, where an arc is created between a welding tool and the metal surfaces to be joined together; this melts the pieces and creates a very strong joint when they cool.

▼ *In arc welding a current called an electric arc is formed between an electrode and the metals to be welded. The metals are welded as a result of the intense heat produced by the electric arc.*

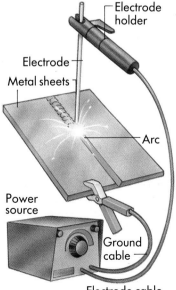

Electrode holder

Electrode

Metal sheets

Arc

Power source

Ground cable

Electrode cable

An electric car may not produce dirty exhaust gases, but the power that recharges the batteries is made in a power station. The power is mostly generated from fossil fuel, which produces polluting gases. So electric vehicles may reduce air pollution in the streets where they run, but generating power to recharge their batteries does still cause some pollution.

Electric vehicle

An electric vehicle is one whose power comes from an electric motor instead of a gasoline or DIESEL ENGINE. Electric vehicles have several advantages. They are almost silent, they do not produce the harmful exhaust gases that gasoline engines do and they do not need a supply of poisonous FUEL that catches fire easily. They have not become a commercial success, mainly because they are slower than gasoline-powered vehicles and cannot travel far without recharging their heavy BATTERIES. An ordinary vehicle can stop at a gas station and fill its fuel tank in a minute or two. It can take several hours to recharge an electric vehicle's batteries. Electric power has been successful in a few vehicles such as delivery trucks and golf carts. These vehicles need not travel at high speed and after work they can be left plugged in to a power supply so that their batteries are recharged for the start of work next morning. Future electric cars will have lighter and more efficient batteries to give them higher speeds and greater range (distance traveled between battery charges).

▶ A close-up of the batteries in the engine compartment of an electric car. At the moment, an electric vehicle is capable of a maximum speed of about 50–55 mph (80–90 km/h), batteries last 2 years and take about 5–6 hours to recharge. Research continues to design a lightweight battery that will have long life, require minimum maintenance, and withstand numerous rechargings.

Between 1896 and 1939, 565 different types of electric car were registered but none of them was successful. Recently a car has been developed which uses an electric battery in town but switches to a diesel engine for longer distances. This, today, is a more practical design than a fully electric car.

Electricity

Electricity is used to light and heat homes and to power motors in cars, trains, and factories. These uses all take the ENERGY in the electric current and convert it to other forms. Today, electricity is also used to power ELEC-TRONIC equipment. *See* pages 202 and 203.

Electrocardiograph

An electrocardiograph is an instrument designed to record the electrical activity of the HEART. Electrodes placed on the chest detect electrical signals produced by the NERVES that control the heart muscles. These signals are amplified and used to operate a pen recorder. The recorder's trace, called an electrocardiogram or ECG, is used to detect some abnormalities in the heart's behavior. If any problems are discovered by analysis of an ECG, it may be possible to treat them with DRUGS or surgery before they lead to more serious problems, such as a heart attack. If a heart attack has already occurred, an ECG can show how the heart is damaged.

A few electrocardiograms (ECGs) are taken while a patient is exercising. ECGs taken during exercise can show a difference between the blood supply and the amount of oxygen needed by the heart muscle. They may also show that the heart rate and the amount of oxygen needed by the heart rise so much that the circulatory system cannot meet the demand.

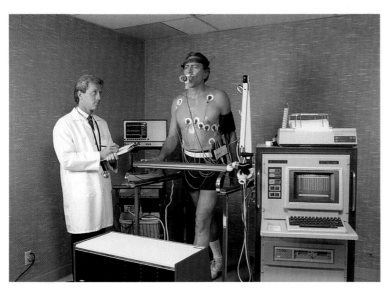

◄ Electrocardiographs are machines used to check the health of the heart. This patient is being monitored for stress. Electrodes attached to the body measure heart beat. Breathing is monitored by a computer. Both patterns are displayed on a screen.

▼ A trace from an electroencephalograph (EEG) measuring the electrical activity of the brain shows the change in the pattern of the brain waves when the eyes are open and when they are closed.

Electroencephalograph

An electroencephalograph is an instrument designed to record the electrical activity of the BRAIN. Electrodes placed on the scalp pick up tiny electrical signals associated with brain activity. They are amplified and used to operate a pen recorder. The trace, called an electroencephalogram or EEG, is used to study brain waves and detect brain abnormalities such as epilepsy where the brain produces large amounts of electricity. The brain produces different types of brain waves according to what it is doing. Their FREQUENCY decreases as the body goes to sleep. Brain waves detected by an EEG range in frequency from one cycle per second (one hertz or 1 Hz) during deep sleep to 18 Hz when awake.

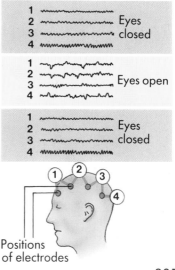

Positions of electrodes

201

ELECTRICITY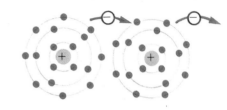

Electrical processes all involve the flow of electric charges, which come in two types, positive and negative. The electrons in atoms carry negative charge and the nuclei of atoms carry positive charge. Electrons are very much lighter than atoms and are easier to move around, so most charges arise because electrons are moved from one place to another. An electric current is a flow of electric charge. Electricity is not used up, the amount of electric charge never changes. It just moves from one place to another.

Electric currents are driven by an electromotive force or emf. This is often driven by a battery, in which case the force arises because it is chemically more favorable for the electrons to be in one terminal of the battery than the other; there is a potential difference between the two terminals. This current is called direct current or DC because it flows in only one direction. Michael Faraday discovered that a changing magnetic field also drives a current. A dynamo changes the magnetic field through a coil of wire by spinning the coil in the field so that at one time the field passes through the coil in one direction and at a later time in the other. The field alternately increases and decreases, so an alternating emf is produced which drives the current first one way and then the other. This is called an alternating current or AC.

Electricity can also be produced naturally and the most dramatic natural occurrence is lightning.

▲ *Electrons orbit around the nucleus of each atom. They carry a tiny negative charge. Electricity flows along a wire when electrons jump from one atom to the next.*

▼ *In a circuit, the potential difference of the cell or battery drives the flow of electricity by making the electrons jump from one atom to the next. The atoms remain fixed, only the electrons move.*

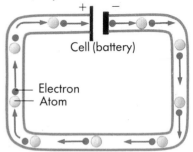

Cell (battery)

Electron
Atom

▶ *Direct current (DC) flows in one direction only. Alternating current (AC) changes its direction of flow at regular intervals. The first half of the AC graph shows current in one direction and the second half in the other direction.*

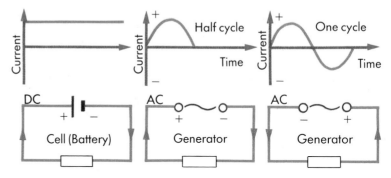

Alessandro Volta (1745–1827)
Volta was an Italian scientist. In 1794, he explained why a frog's leg twitched when its muscles were touched with two different metals. Volta showed that this was because an electric potential difference was produced between the two metals. Potential difference is set up when there is a difference in charge between two points. He then went on to make the first battery in 1800.

▼ *Plotting a graph of current against time gives the frequency at which the current alternates. In this case the frequency is 50 cycles per second ($50 \times 0.02 = 1$). Frequency is measured in hertz and so, here, the frequency is 50 Hz.*

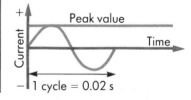

Peak value

1 cycle = 0.02 s

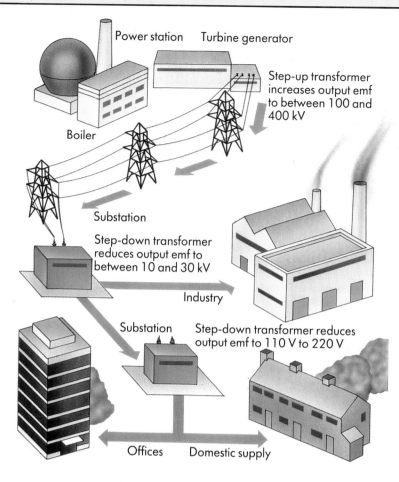

Power station   Turbine generator

Step-up transformer
increases output emf
to between 100 and
400 kV

Boiler

Substation
Step-down transformer
reduces output emf to
between 10 and 30 kV

Industry

Substation   Step-down transformer reduces
output emf to 110 V to 220 V

Offices   Domestic supply

▲ Can you imagine life without
electricity? What would this city
look like at night if there was no
electricity?

WARNING
Never experiment with
electricity from the electric
outlet. You can receive a
shock which can kill. Always
use batteries.

▲ Electricity generated at a power
station is usually distributed at high
voltage and low current. Step-up
transformers convert the output of
the generators to the high voltage
required for distribution. The
voltage is the pressure or force
which drives the electricity along
the wire. Transformers (at
substations) reduce the voltage to
make it suitable for use in factories
and homes.

▶ Electricity supplied to the home is
first fed into a meter which records
the amount used. The amount of
current flowing is monitored by a
fuse box. If the current passing
through a fuse gets too great, the
fuse blows and breaks the circuit.
Household appliances are
operated from power points
around the home.

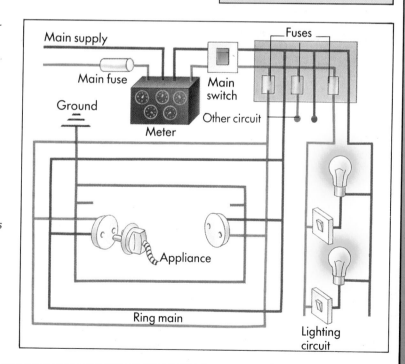

Main supply

Fuses

Main fuse

Ground

Main
switch

Other circuit

Meter

Appliance

Ring main

Lighting
circuit

See also AMPERE; AMPLIFIER; BATTERY; CIRCUIT, ELECTRIC; GENERATOR; MOTOR,
ELECTRIC; STATIC ELECTRICITY; VOLTMETER; WATT.

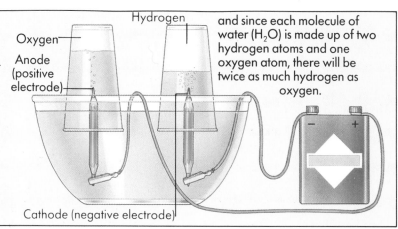

SEE FOR YOURSELF
Sharpen two pencils at each end and attach a wire to one end of each. Connect the other ends of the wires to a 6-volt battery. Put the pencils in a bowl of water and add a tablespoon of vinegar to make the water conduct electricity. Fill two glasses with water and turn them upside down underwater over the pencils. Electrolysis splits up the water into hydrogen and oxygen,

Oxygen

Anode (positive electrode)

Hydrogen

and since each molecule of water (H_2O) is made up of two hydrogen atoms and one oxygen atom, there will be twice as much hydrogen as oxygen.

Cathode (negative electrode)

▼ *This large disklike electromagnet is suspended on chains and manipulated by a crane. It is used to separate and lift iron and steel objects from among waste.*

Electrolysis

Electrolysis is the process of separating the ELEMENTS of a COMPOUND by passing an electric current through a SOLUTION or liquid form of the compound. Electrolysis is used to break down water into the two gases, hydrogen and oxygen, from which it is formed. It can also be used to extract METALS from solutions or melted forms of metallic compounds. For instance, SODIUM is extracted by electrolysis from molten sodium chloride. The main industrial uses of electrolysis are in refining or purifying metals and ELECTROPLATING objects. In electrolysis, the direct electric current from a battery passes between two solid electrical conductors called electrodes placed in the solution to be broken down or electrolyzed. The solution is called an electrolyte and it conducts electricity between the electrodes. The negative electrode is called the cathode and the positive electrode is called the anode. Since the current is a flow of ELECTRONS, the surface of the cathode has an excess of electrons and attracts positively charged IONS in the liquid. At the anode, from which electrons are being drawn away, negatively charged ions collect. When a solution of a metallic compound is electrolyzed, positive metal ions attracted to the cathode are deposited on its surface. This is how objects are gold or silver plated.

Electromagnet

An electromagnet is a magnet that, rather than being permanent, produces the MAGNETISM because of the flow of electric current through a wire. The magnetic effect of electric current was first noticed by the Danish scientist

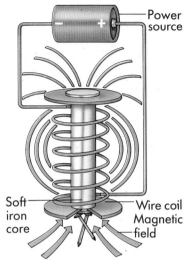

Power source

Soft iron core

Wire coil
Magnetic field

▲ *Electric current flows through a conductor and produces a magnetic field.*

Hans Oersted. Electromagnets are usually made from a piece of wire coiled many times to increase the magnetic effect. Such a coil of wire is often called a solenoid. The magnetic field produced by a solenoid can be increased by placing a core made of a magnetic material, such as iron, inside it. The current flowing in the solenoid causes the iron to become temporarily magnetic and add to the total magnetic field.

Electromagnets are useful because the magnetic effects that they produce can be controlled by changing the current through the solenoid. For example, electromagnets are used to guide the electron beam in the CATHODE RAY TUBE of a TELEVISION set; the current in the solenoids is controlled by the signal received from the antenna and the changing magnetic field that this produces sends the beam to different parts of the screen. Electromagnets are also found in many LOUDSPEAKERS; the changing magnetic field, produced by the change of current in the solenoid, moves the surface of the loudspeaker in and out to produce sound waves.

SEE FOR YOURSELF
Wind a length of insulated wire many times around a nail to make what is called a solenoid. Connect the ends of the wire to the terminals of a battery. Try picking up small metal objects with the electromagnet. As the electricity flows through the tight coils of wire, it creates magnetic forces from one end of the coil to the other. The nail is turned into a magnet because the force causes all the magnetic particles in the nail to line up.

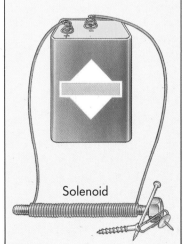

Solenoid

Oliver Joseph Lodge (1851–1940)
Lodge was a British physicist. He carried out experiments to produce and detect the electromagnetic radiation predicted by Maxwell in 1864. In 1881, he became professor of physics at Liverpool University, where he carried out his experiments on electromagnetic waves and later worked to improve the reception of radio signals. In 1900, he became the first principal of Birmingham University, and retired in 1919 because he wanted to study "psychic phenomena." He strongly opposed Einstein's theory of general relativity in its early years.

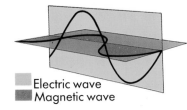

Electric wave
Magnetic wave

▲ *Electromagnetic radiation is made up of electricity and magnetism. It consists of an electric and a magnetic field at right angles to each other.*

▼ *The electromagnetic spectrum ranges from long wavelength radio waves through light waves to short wavelength gamma rays. Gamma rays are used in the treatment of cancer, ultraviolet rays in fluorescent lights, and microwaves are used to cook food.*

Electromagnetic radiation

Electromagnetic radiation is a WAVE MOTION of the electric and magnetic fields. Unlike other waves, such as water or SOUND waves, it does not need any material through which to travel. Hans Oersted discovered that an electric current produces a magnetic field, while Michael FARADAY found that a change in a magnetic field causes an electric current to flow. When James Clerk Maxwell wrote down these laws in mathematical form, he realized that this meant that even in empty space, a pattern or wave of changing electric and magnetic fields could travel along. He calculated the speed at which such a wave would travel and it turned out to be exactly the speed of LIGHT, so he suggested that light is a form of electromagnetic radiation.

There is a whole SPECTRUM of different types of electromagnetic radiation, with different FREQUENCIES and WAVELENGTHS. Radio waves can have wavelengths of several miles, while MICROWAVES have wavelengths of a few millimeters or centimeters. The wavelength of INFRARED RADIATION is between a few thousandths and a few tenths of a millimeter and that of the light which we can see (known as visible light) is a few ten thousandths

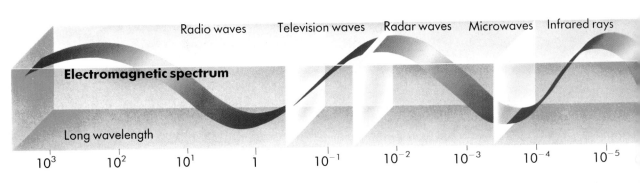

Radio waves   Television waves   Radar waves   Microwaves   Infrared rays

Electromagnetic spectrum

Long wavelength

10^3 10^2 10^1 1 10^{-1} 10^{-2} 10^{-3} 10^{-4} 10^{-5}

of a millimeter. The wavelengths of X-RAYS are a few millionths of a millimeter, while waves of even shorter wavelength, called gamma rays, are produced as a form of RADIOACTIVITY from the nuclei of atoms.

Electromotive force *See* Electricity

Electron

An electron is a SUBATOMIC PARTICLE that carries a negative electric charge. In an ATOM, electrons travel around a nucleus made up of positively charged PROTONS, and NEUTRONS which have no charge. An electron's motion is random, but it is kept at a set distance from the nucleus by its ENERGY. An electron's "orbit" is therefore equivalent to its energy level (or shell). The number of electrons in an atom's outermost shell determines the atom's behavior. If the shell is full, the atom is unreactive but if it is not full, BONDS can be formed by sharing, or losing, or gaining electrons to or from other atoms.

Robert Millikan (1868–1953)
Millikan was a United States physicist. He won the Nobel Prize for Physics in 1923 for being the first scientist to measure the charge of an electron. He did an experiment, known as the oil-drop experiment, in which he was able to measure the amount of an electric force, and the size of an electric field acting on a charged droplet of oil. From this he calculated the size of the charge carried by an electron. During the 1920s Millikan researched into cosmic rays and showed that they come from space.

John Joseph Thomson (1856–1940)
Thomson was a British physicist. He won the Nobel Prize for Physics in 1906 for his discovery of the electron. In 1895, he investigated the rays produced when an electric current passed through a vacuum in a glass tube. The rays came from the negative end of the tube (the cathode) and were called cathode rays. He showed that the rays consisted of particles (electrons) which were negatively charged and are found in every atom.

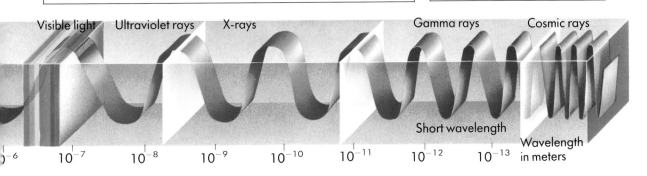

Visible light   Ultraviolet rays   X-rays   Gamma rays   Cosmic rays

Short wavelength

Wavelength in meters

10^{-6} 10^{-7} 10^{-8} 10^{-9} 10^{-10} 10^{-11} 10^{-12} 10^{-13}

▶ *Electrons travel at great speed around the central nucleus of an atom. They are arranged in energy levels called shells. When atoms combine to form molecules, electrons in the outermost shell are transferred from one atom to another or are shared between atoms.*

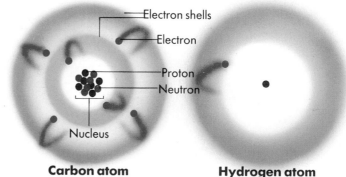

Carbon atom   **Hydrogen atom**

Electrons are fundamental particles and cannot be split into anything smaller. The diameter of an electron is less than 0.001 times that of a proton, and its mass is $\frac{1}{1836}$ that of a proton.
See also POSITRON.

Transmission electron microscope

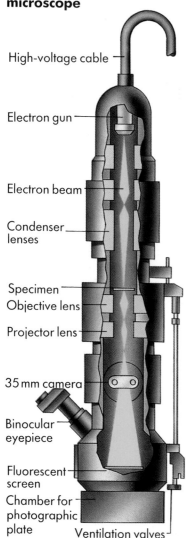

High-voltage cable

Electron gun

Electron beam

Condenser lenses

Specimen
Objective lens

Projector lens

35 mm camera

Binocular eyepiece

Fluorescent screen

Chamber for photographic plate

Ventilation valves

▲ *Electrons from an electron gun are passed through the item being observed, to a fluorescent screen. A magnifier enlarges the image.*

Electron microscope

An electron microscope is an instrument used for producing greatly magnified images of specimens. Light MICROSCOPES magnify a specimen by passing its image through a series of LENSES to an eyepiece. An electron microscope does not use light at all. The specimen is sealed inside the microscope and air sucked out to form a vacuum. A beam of ELECTRONS is fired through the specimen. The beam is then focused by ELECTROMAGNETS, the electrical equivalent of an optical microscope's lenses. The focused image is formed on a screen at the bottom of the microscope. The image can be viewed directly, displayed on television monitors, or photographed to give an electron photomicrograph. Electron microscopes can magnify objects up to several million times and show CELLS, viruses, and even MOLECULES.

Vladimir Kosma Zworykin (1889–1982)

Zworykin was a Russian-born American physicist and electronics engineer. He is most famous for his work in developing and perfecting the electron microscope. He is also known for his contribution to advances in radio and television. He helped develop the television camera and picture tube. By 1929, his television camera had replaced the mechanical system developed in Britain by Baird.

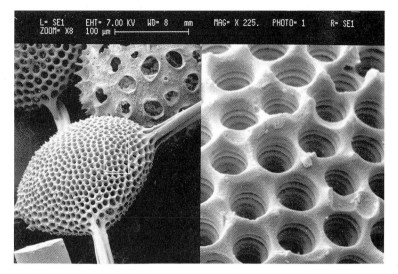

L= SE1   EHT= 7.00 KV   WD= 8   mm   MAG= X 225.   PHOTO= 1   R= SE1
ZOOM= X8   100 μm

◄ *Seen with the aid of an electron microscope a single-celled animal called Radiolaria (left) is full of holes. On the right it is magnified a further eight times. Electron microscopes have become important research tools in biology.*

They can do this because the WAVELENGTH of the electron is much smaller than that of light, allowing greater resolving power. The first electron microscope, with a magnification of only 400, was built in 1932 by two German engineers, Ernst Ruska and Max Knoll.

Electronics

Almost every device and machine we use in our everyday lives and in business and industry depends on electronic circuits. Electronics is so widespread today because the electronic components that circuits are made from have become much smaller and much less expensive than in the past. *See* pages 210 and 211.

Electroplating

Electroplating uses an electric current to put a metallic coating onto the surface of a METAL object or other material that conducts ELECTRICITY. We electroplate objects to protect them from CORROSION and to improve their appearance. The object to be electroplated is cleaned and placed in a SOLUTION of a compound of the metal with which it is to be coated. It is then connected to a BATTERY and becomes the cathode, or negative electrode in an ELECTROLYSIS process. As the electric current flows, positive metallic ions are drawn to the object to be plated and a metal coating builds up. Coatings of copper, gold, silver, and zinc can be applied to objects by the electrolysis of solutions of the metals.

SEE FOR YOURSELF
Put two old metal spoons into a solution of copper sulfate. Connect the spoons to battery terminals. The spoon connected to the negative terminal is the cathode and the spoon connected to the positive terminal is the anode. A coating of copper forms on the cathode. The electric current acts on the metallic ions in the solution. These ions are attracted to the cathode and deposited on the spoon's surface.

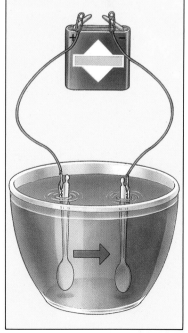

ELECTRONICS ⎯⋀⋁⋀⎯

Electronics is an important branch of science and technology concerned with the devices controlling the motion of electrons, tiny particles of matter. An electric current is simply a flow of electrons. Tiny devices called electronic components can affect the way electrons and therefore electric currents flow through them. There are many different types of electronic components, including diodes and transistors. Each affects the electric current flowing through it in a different way.

When components are connected together to form a circuit, they can be made to do a useful job. For example, the electronic control system in a washing machine operates the motors, pumps, heater, and valves at the correct times to produce the different washing cycles.

Today, complete electronic circuits can be made small enough to fit on a single silicon chip and lots of chips can be connected together to form even more complex electronic circuits. Electronic components including chips are usually linked together by fixing them to a printed circuit board, sometimes called a card. The circuit board is drilled with lots of holes to take the wire leads of the components. The components are connected together by a pattern of metal tracks printed on the board. The printed circuit allows electric currents to flow along the tracks between the components. Printed circuits are found in computers, cars, microwave ovens, airplanes and spacecraft.

▲ Silicon chips can be used to control the flow of current by acting like switches. These switches are called logic gates. Different kinds of logic gates are known as AND, OR and NOT gates and pass on, or change the electrical 0s and 1s that go through them. This arithmetic circuit will take two binary digits (in this case 1 + 1) and add them together, coping with any carrying that has to be done. The binary digit 1 is decimal 1 and so 1 + 1 is binary 10 or decimal 2.

Circuit board and components

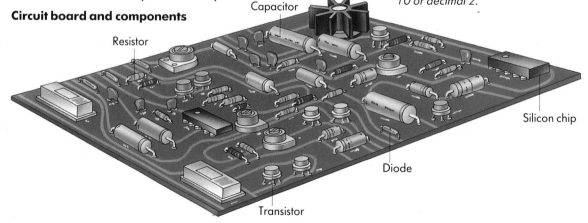

Capacitor

Resistor

Silicon chip

Diode

Transistor

Diode Allows electricity to flow in one direction only — from the cathode, negative terminal, to the anode, positive terminal. It converts alternating current to direct current.

Resistor Resists the flow of current. Resistors add a known electrical resistance to a circuit.

Capacitor Accumulates and stores electric charge. It consists of two conducting surfaces separated by an insulator.

Transistor Amplifies electric current passing through it or switches current on or off in response to a controlling signal.

Silicon chip A tiny wafer of silicon semiconductor material processed to form an integrated circuit of a component for use in electronic machines.

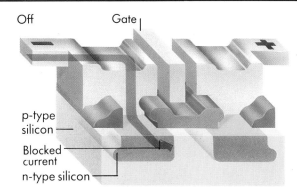

Off   Gate

p-type
silicon

Blocked
current

n-type silicon

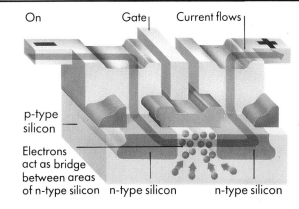

On   Gate   Current flows

p-type
silicon

Electrons
act as bridge
between areas
of n-type silicon   n-type silicon   n-type silicon

▲ *Silicon chips can control the flow of current by acting like switches, or transistors. When the switch is "off" (left), the current is blocked. When the switch is "on" (right), the current flows.*

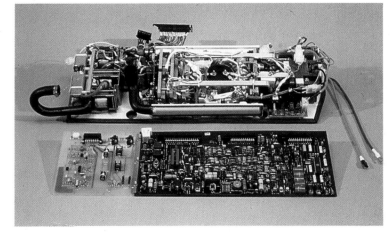

▶ *Printed circuit boards are found in all sorts of things. Most printed circuit boards are made from stiff materials, such as fiberglass.*

▲ *Electronic circuits are built with such tiny components that they have to be greatly magnified when being designed.*

Remote
control
television

Checkout till

Automobile
dashboard
display

◀ *Microelectronics are used in remote control units that enable you to change channels and turn the television set on and off without touching it.*

▼ *Microprocessors are now used in the manufacture of a wide variety of products that were once mechanical.*

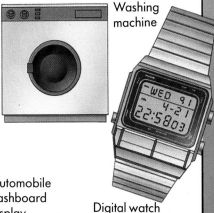

Washing
machine

Digital watch

See also CALCULATOR; CAPACITOR; COMPUTER; DIODE; INTEGRATED CIRCUIT; LOGIC; MICROPROCESSOR; RESISTANCE, ELECTRIC; TRANSISTOR.

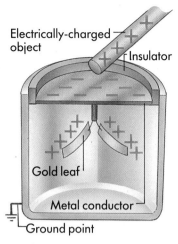

Electrically-charged object

Insulator

Gold leaf

Metal conductor

Ground point

▲ *If an electrically charged object touches the conductor the gold leaf strips become charged and spread apart.*

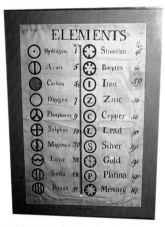

▲ *This is John Dalton's chart of the chemical elements. He was the first to use letters of the alphabet as symbols for elements.*

Electroscope, gold leaf

An electroscope is a scientific INSTRUMENT used to detect electrical charges or STATIC ELECTRICITY. The gold leaf electroscope consists of a metal rod with a metal cap at one end and one or two pieces of thin gold leaf at the other end. The end of the rod attached to the gold leaf is usually housed in a glass case so that the leaf can be seen clearly and is also screened from air movements. When an object carrying an electrical charge touches the metal cap, some of the charge travels down the rod to the gold leaf. In a one-leaf electroscope, the end of the rod and the leaf both acquire the same positive or negative electrical charge. Like charges repel each other so the gold leaf is bent away from the rod. In a two-leaf electroscope, the leaves, which normally hang vertically, separate, repelled by the like charges.

Element, chemical

A chemical element is a substance in which all the ATOMS in it are of the same kind. Elements cannot be broken down into simpler substances, but in certain nuclear reactions one element can be changed into another. Substances in which elements combine with each other are called COMPOUNDS. For instance, the compound sodium chloride (salt) is a combination of two elements, sodium and chlorine. Only two elements are LIQUID at room temperature: they are bromine and mercury. Every other element is either a SOLID or a GAS.

A total of 103 elements are known and recognized internationally, but since 1964 various teams of scientists

Elements in Ancient Times

Ancient scientists thought that there were only four elements: earth, water, fire, and air. These, in turn, gave rise to the properties of dry, wet, hot, and cold. We now know that elements are substances that cannot be split into others. Some, such as gold, copper, iron, and sulfur, have been known for thousands of years. Then from the 1700s onward chemists began to discover many more elements. Now there are 103.

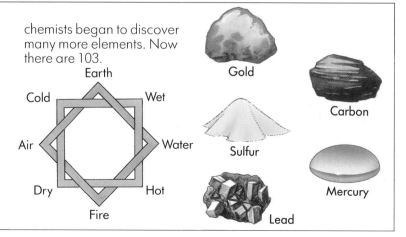

have claimed to have manufactured six more. Only 92 elements occur naturally on or in the EARTH, most of them found as compounds; the rest have been made artificially in controlled nuclear reactions, where high-speed SUBATOMIC PARTICLES have been used to change the makeup of atoms. All artificially made elements are radioactive, as are some of the naturally occurring ones.

Chemists use CHEMICAL SYMBOLS to denote elements in formulae and equations. If the list of all the known elements is arranged in the order of their ATOMIC NUMBERS, they form rows, or periods. In the 18 vertical columns of the PERIODIC TABLE, each element is related to the ones above it, having similar behavior and properties. These similarities result from similar arrangements of ELECTRONS in their atoms.

See also CHEMISTRY; ISOTOPE.

The human body contains many different chemicals. More than half the atoms in your body are hydrogen, the simplest element. Next in abundance is oxygen. Then comes carbon, making up one-tenth of the body's weight. That is enough, if it were in pure carbon form, to fill 3,000 "lead" pencils.

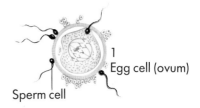

1 Egg cell (ovum)

Sperm cell

2

Elementary particles *See* Subatomic particles

Embryo

From the moment an EGG cell or ovum begins to develop after FERTILIZATION, it is known as an embryo. At first the embryo is a tiny bundle of CELLS, but these multiply rapidly and develop into the animal or plant. An embryo plant has a miniature root and shoot and one or more special leaves called COTYLEDONS. There is enough food in the SEED to feed the plant until it can grow up into the air and make its own food.

The embryos of birds and other egg-laying animals get the food and energy needed for their early growth and development from the yolk and other food stored in the egg. The mammalian embryo embeds itself in the mother's womb, or uterus, when it is still a bundle of cells, and is connected by the umbilical cord to the mother. From then on, the embryo gets its food and energy from the mother's bloodstream through the umbilical cord. The

3

▲ *The egg cell (ovum)* **1** *is fertilized by a single sperm that pierces the cell membrane.* **2** *Once fertilized the ovum divides into two cells, then* **3** *divides again and again until by the fourth day, the embryo consists of a ball containing 16 cells.*

▼ *By 8 weeks the human embryo is less than an inch (2 cm) in length, and has arms, legs, and eyes with eyelids.*

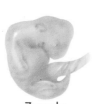

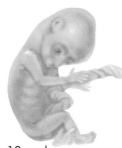

5 weeks　　6 weeks　　　7 weeks　　　　8 weeks　　　　12 weeks

▲ *Paint is one example of an emulsion. Because emulsions are not permanently stable, the liquids making up the paint separate from each other. Paint should, therefore, be stirred before use.*

embryo cells continue to divide rapidly and soon have special functions. Some will become the nervous system; others, the muscles, bones, or other organs. When the embryo has reached a later stage of development, it is usually called a *fetus*. The embryo continues to develop until birth.

Emulsion

An emulsion is a COLLOID of two LIQUIDS in which the particles of one are evenly scattered, or dispersed, throughout the other without being dissolved in it. Typical emulsions are foods, lotions, lubricants, medicines, and paints. Emulsions are not stable and the liquids forming them separate out after a time. An emulsifier helps to keep the liquids mixed. Milk is an emulsion of butterfat in water. The protein casein is the emulsifier that helps keep the butterfat dispersed in the water. Many commercially sold foods contain emulsifiers along with other preservatives. The coating on photographic film, called emulsion, is in fact a light-sensitive colloid.

SEE FOR YOURSELF
Shake half a cup of oil and a quarter of a cup of vinegar with a teaspoon of mustard together in a screw top jar. The resulting emulsion is a salad dressing. Tiny drops of the dispersed liquid remain suspended in the other liquid. After a while the mixture separates and has to be shaken again.

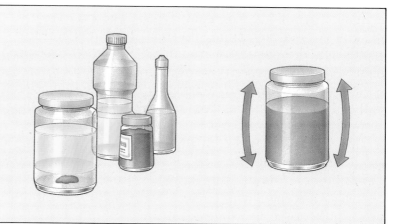

Endangered species

Hundreds of the world's animal and plant species are in danger of EXTINCTION in the near future. They are endangered species. Their populations have fallen to very low levels, or they live in just a few small areas, and any further interference could kill them off for ever. The main threat to these organisms is the destruction of their homes or habitats. All over the world people are cutting down forests and draining marshland to make way for farmland and the ever-increasing human population.

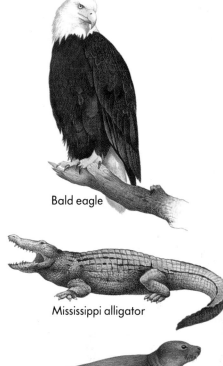

◄ The endangered giant rafflesia, which lives on the Malaysian rainforest floor, produces the largest flowers of any known plant.

Bald eagle

Mississippi alligator

Monk seal

Tiger

When these natural habitats disappear, the animals and plants that lived there disappear too. Hunting threatens the survival of some animals, while POLLUTION of rivers and the sea is threatening aquatic life.

According to the Worldwide Fund for Nature, the black rhinoceros is the most endangered of the large mammals. They have been hunted until there are only about 3,000 in the whole of Africa. The Philippines eagle is one of the most endangered birds, owing to the destruction of its rainforest home. The big-leaf palm of Madagascar is one of the rarest of all plants. It was not discovered by botanists until 1982 and part of its swampy habitat was recently cleared to make way for rice fields. Only about 50 specimens remain.

Endangered species	Where found	Numbers remaining
Plants		
Tarout cypress	Southeastern Algeria	About 140
Artemisia granaternsis	Sierra Nevada, Spain	Few remain
Bois de fer	Seychelles	About 150
Caoba	Ecuador	13
Hawaiian hau kuahiwi	Hawaii	10
Rafflesia	Malaysian forest	Few remain
Hedgehog cactus	Arizona	Few remain
Animals		
Asiatic buffalo	India, Nepal	2,200
Blue whale	World oceans	7,500
European bison	Poland	About 1,000
Giant panda	China	200
Polar bear	Arctic	8,000
Whooping crane	North America	About 50
Orangutan	Borneo, Sumatra	5,000

▲ Some of the animals whose population numbers are so low that there is a danger of them becoming extinct. These are among over 350 endangered species of amphibians, reptiles, birds, and mammals.

ENERGY ⚛

Energy is needed when a force is to be moved through some distance. Such a process involves doing work; energy is the ability to do work and it is measured in joules. Energy is conserved; the total amount of energy never changes, but it is converted from one form to another. If an object is moving, this gives it a form of energy known as *kinetic energy*. Heat is also a form of energy; kinetic energy is converted into heat by, for example, the action of the brakes in a car or train. Energy can be stored in the form called *potential energy*, for example, a diver standing on a board has potential energy, but when he dives the potential energy becomes kinetic energy. The theory of relativity tells us that mass is also a form of energy.

Most of the energy we use comes originally from the Sun, where it is produced by nuclear fusion. The energy arrives as sunlight. It heats the Earth's surface and atmosphere and is used by plants to photosynthesize, storing energy in chemical form. This is the source of the energy in our food. Geothermal power uses heat energy from the Earth, stored there since the Earth was formed, while nuclear power uses energy stored in heavy atoms formed millions of years ago.

Energy flow chart

Sun

Radiant light energy

Prehistoric forests grow

Chemical energy

Forests turn to coal beds

Coal mining

Burning coal

Power plant | **Heat energy**

Electrical energy

Heat energy | **Light energy**

▲ *The Sun is the source of most of the energy that is used on Earth. Every time it is used, energy is converted from one form to another. Energy resources include wood and large amounts of oil, gas, and coal. Nuclear energy is another important source of energy.*

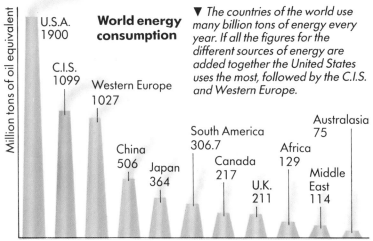

World energy consumption

Million tons of oil equivalent

U.S.A. 1900
C.I.S. 1099
Western Europe 1027
China 506
Japan 364
South America 306.7
Canada 217
U.K. 211
Africa 129
Middle East 114
Australasia 75

▼ *The countries of the world use many billion tons of energy every year. If all the figures for the different sources of energy are added together the United States uses the most, followed by the C.I.S. and Western Europe.*

SEE FOR YOURSELF
An object such as a jack-in-the-box has potential energy stored in it. In this case the lid of the box is opened and the jack-in-the-box, springs up. This is an example of kinetic energy.

Heat is the main kind of energy loss. Even the most efficient modern car engine wastes about three-fifths of the energy contained in the fuel it uses. Far more inefficient still, an electric light turns only about one-fifth of the electricity it uses into light. The rest is produced as heat which is not needed.

See also COAL; ELECTRICITY; FORCE; FOSSIL FUELS; JOULE; HEAT; LIGHT; NATURAL GAS; NUCLEAR ENERGY; OIL; RESOURCES; SOUND; SUN.

Engine

An engine is a machine used to convert ENERGY into mechanical WORK. The energy is supplied by a FUEL. Energy stored in the fuel is released by burning, or combustion. There are two types of engine: the INTERNAL-COMBUSTION ENGINE and the external-combustion engine. The steam engine is an example of an external-combustion engine. The fuel is burned outside the engine.

The engines used nowadays to power vehicles, boats, and aircraft are internal combustion engines. The oil or gasoline fuel is burned inside the engine. It is not a very efficient type of engine. Only about a quarter to a third of the energy stored in the fuel is converted into mechanical work. However, the energy can be released from the fuel quickly without having to wait for water to boil and build up PRESSURE as in a steam engine.

Aircraft were powered by the same piston engine as

Milestones in the Development of Engines
c. A.D. 62 Hero of Alexandria devised *Hero's engine*, a steam-powered engine.
1712 Thomas Newcomen invents the atmospheric steam engine.
1790 James Watt improves the piston engine.
1876 Nikolaus Otto devised the Otto cycle for the 4-stroke internal-combustion engine.
1890s Rudolf Diesel develops the diesel engine.
1940s Frank Whittle develops the turbojet engine.

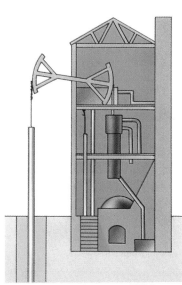

Newcomen's engine 1712

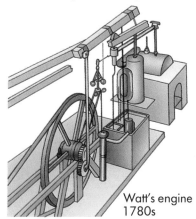

Watt's engine 1780s

▲ *Some examples of different types of engines. The modern car engine looks very different to its predecessors.*

Daimler's engine 1883

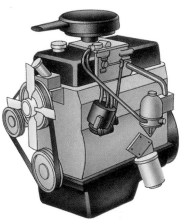

Modern car engine

cars until a new engine called a GAS TURBINE was invented in the 1940s by a British engineer, Frank Whittle. The hot combustion gases produced inside this engine are used to spin a TURBINE, or a shaft connected to the propeller, instead of pushing against pistons as in a car engine. A few experimental cars have been fitted with gas turbines but the piston engine still dominates. The gas turbine has been more successful as a power plant for ships, especially fast military vessels.

Entropy

Our universe appears to be running down or unwinding as its entropy increases. Every event in which energy is given off results in the waste of some energy and an increase in entropy. While it is easy to convert other forms of energy into heat, heat can only be converted into other forms of energy very inefficiently. The lowest grade of energy is heat energy when molecules are simply moving about at random.

Entropy is a measure of the amount of disorder in a system. The entropy of a system is very much more likely to increase than to decrease, because there are very many more disordered states than ordered ones. The disorder in a system increases because at every stage some of the energy is wasted; for example, the human body wastes about 80 percent of the energy it takes in as food. One consequence of entropy is that HEAT flows from a hotter object to a colder one rather than the other way around. No matter what anyone does, energy is always spreading out more and more evenly. The amount of entropy is always increasing. This law of increase of entropy is also called the Second Law of THERMODYNAMICS.

Environment

The surroundings in which you live form your environment. This includes your home, your school, your town or city and all the people and other animals and plants that live there with you. It also includes the AIR around you and the SOIL under your feet. Every plant and animal has its own environment. All environments have living and nonliving parts. Imagine a freshwater stream. The living parts of this environment include all the plants and animals that live in the stream, competing with each other for food or eating each other. The stones over which the water flows; the air and minerals dissolved in the water; the temperature; and the total amount of light

▼ Most city environments are dirty, noisy, and overcrowded. About 40 percent of the world's population live in cities.

► A coral outcrop is just one marine environment. Unlike land environments the sea is very stable and does not change dramatically throughout the day or the year. For example, its temperature remains fairly constant.

are all non-living parts of the stream's environment.

Some environments, such as the open sea, are very stable and remain more or less unchanged throughout the year. Others change dramatically from season to season. The stream environment, for example, is very different in winter and summer. Unusual weather can change local environments for a time, by bringing down trees for example, but nature can repair the damage and as long as humans do not interfere, our natural environments can remain much the same for long periods of time. Unfortunately, people do interfere and we are seriously damaging the environment of the whole world. Unless we learn to reverse these changes and to protect the environment, the world will not be a fit place for us or anything else to live in.

See also ECOSYSTEM; CONSERVATION, ENVIRONMENTAL.

Enzymes

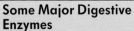

Enzymes are CATALYSTS produced by living CELLS. Like all catalysts, they greatly speed up chemical reactions. There are enzymes to help and to speed up all the processes that go on inside living organisms. A single cell may contain 100,000 different enzymes which are needed to take part in its 1,000 to 2,000 chemical reactions. For example, digestive enzymes convert food to simpler substances. Many enzymes work in the opposite way, linking simple substances together to form the more complex ones needed to build up tissues. The enzymes themselves are made of PROTEIN and each one has a differently-shaped MOLECULE. It is this shape which

Environmental pollution increases as industry expands, motor vehicles increase in numbers, and the human population explodes. In the United States alone, the waste from households amounts to more than 200 million tons every year. This solid waste includes about 9 million cars scrapped each year. It does not include the billions of tons of waste from mining, manufacturing, and agriculture.

Some Major Digestive Enzymes
Amylase Present in saliva and pancreatic juice. Converts starch to sugar.
Maltase Present in saliva and in the small intestine. Converts starch to sugar.
Pepsin Produced in the stomach. Breaks down protein.
Renin Present in the stomach. Helps to digest milk.
Trypsin Produced by the pancreas. Continues breakdown of protein.

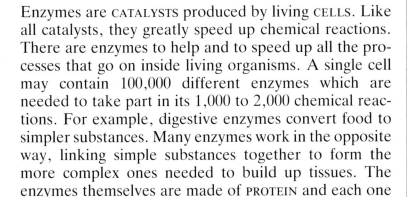

SEE FOR YOURSELF
Put some saliva into four tubes. Add acid (for example, lemon juice) to the first, alkali (baking soda) to the second. Place the third tube in very hot water and do nothing to the fourth. To each of the tubes, add a solution of boiled starch. Put a drop from each tube onto a slide and add iodine solution to each. The solutions which are not stained blue by the iodine show that starch is no longer present. The starch is changed by the action of the enzymes in the saliva.

Molecules

Product

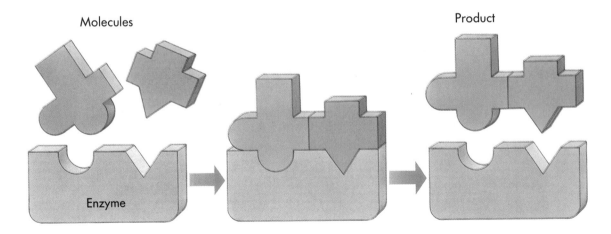

Enzyme

▲ *Enzymes have an active site, the "lock." It is shaped so that only a molecule of the correct shape and size, the "key," can produce a chemical reaction. After the reaction has taken place, the product separates from the enzyme.*

allows it to help in a particular chemical reaction.

Biochemists believe that other molecules lock onto the enzyme molecules, like a key fitting a lock, and themselves become linked together. The new COM- POUNDS then break away, leaving the enzymes to start again. Only substances that fit an enzyme's molecular pattern can lock onto it, so each enzyme can take part in only one particular reaction. Enzymes work best at a particular temperature, which is one of the reasons why our bodies are kept at constant temperatures.

Epoxy resin adhesives are sold for home use in two containers. One contains the epoxy resin, the other a catalyst hardening compound. The two are mixed together just before use to produce a strong adhesive which works on a large number of materials.

Epoxy resin

An epoxy resin is one of a class of synthetic (non-natural) resins that are used as ADHESIVES and in the pro-duction of PLASTIC objects. Unlike natural resins, which are obtained from trees and plants, epoxy resins are chemically manufactured, thermosetting plastic

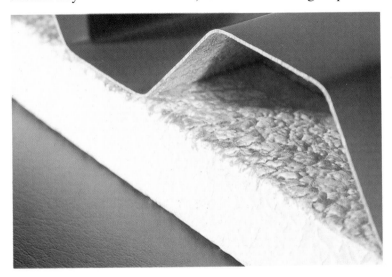

▶ *The pink layer between these two roofing materials is epoxy resin. It is used because it is both water- and weather-resistant.*

materials. This means that they are used in a hot melted form which makes them easy to spread or pour, but later they harden to produce an extremely resistant plastic material. Epoxy resins harden very rapidly, are both water- and weather-resistant, and provide a very strong adhesive bond. They are used in laminating (sticking together sheets of material suitable for the making of table tops and printed circuits), making castings and reinforced plastics, and making protective coatings.

Equilibrium

Something is in a state of equilibrium when it does not change over time. In CHEMISTRY, the term is used to describe systems in which the rate of forward and backward reactions is the same, so that the same number of MOLECULES of each type are formed as are broken up. In PHYSICS, a system is said to be in equilibrium if all the

$$N_2 + 3H_2$$
$$\mathrel{\substack{\textstyle\downarrow\\[-0.3em]\textstyle\uparrow}}$$
$$2NH_3$$

▲ The gases nitrogen, N_2, and hydrogen, H_2 react to form ammonia (NH_3). The reaction is in chemical equilibrium because the amounts of nitrogen and hydrogen reacting to give ammonia are the same as the amounts of N_2 and H_2 being produced by the ammonia breaking down.

Stable equilibrium

Center of gravity

▲ An object is in stable equilibrium when a vertical line from its center of gravity stays within its base when it is displaced.

Unstable equilibrium

Center of gravity

▲ An object is in unstable equilibrium when the vertical line from its center of gravity falls outside its base when it is displaced.

▼ An object is in neutral equilibrium when it moves to a new position, similar to the old position, after it has been displaced.

Neutral equilibrium

Center of gravity

SEE FOR YOURSELF
Try making some balancing toys. Put a thumbtack into the bottom of a cork. Make a modeling clay hat and draw a face on the cork. Poke 2 knitting needles, the ends weighted with modeling clay, into the side of the cork. Balance the whole thing on top of a plastic cup. You may need to alter the positions of the knitting needles to get the little man to balance.

Examples of Chemical Equilibrium in the Human Body
Blood Intake and release of oxygen in blood.
Ear The semicircular canals in the inner ear are concerned with the sense of equilibrium (balance). Damage to the inner ear causes disturbances of equilibrium.
The eyes and certain sensory cells in the skin also maintain equilibrium.

▼ *There are several forces of erosion. Rocks in mountainous areas are broken up by the process of weathering. Melting ice forms lakes in hollows blocked by falling rocks and deposits from glaciers. Water runs from springs, melting snowfields, and overflowing lakes, forming rivers. Rivers have an eroding action as they meander (make bends) across plains. Meandering rivers move very slowly and so have relatively little erosive effects. Rocks and soil are moved from higher levels and deposited along the route or out at sea. The action of wind and rain erodes top soil. This increases when land is cleared of trees and cultivated. The sea is also a powerful eroding force; softer layers of rock are eroded away by the action of the sea currents and rocks pushed against them. Pillars and arches are the result of many thousands of years of erosion.*

FORCES acting on each part of it cancel each other out, so that it can remain in the same state.

There are three sorts of equilibrium. If the system returns to the equilibrium position when it is slightly moved or displaced, the equilibrium is *stable*, while if a displacement causes the system to move away from equilibrium then that equilibrium is said to be *unstable*. If the displacement produces a new equilibrium position, the equilibrium is said to be *neutral*.
See also ENERGY.

Erosion and Weathering

Weathering leads to the disintegration of ROCKS and MINERALS at the surface of the EARTH. The weathered rocks are then worn down by erosion. Following erosion, the material may be carried away and deposited elsewhere.

There are two main kinds of weathering, physical and chemical. Physical weathering includes the breakdown of rock through its own expansion. In parts of the world, there is a large difference between daytime and night-time temperatures, and rocks may heat and cool quickly. Sometimes, water that fills cracks in rocks may freeze and expand, prying the crack open a little. This causes them to shatter in a way that resembles the peeling away of the skins of an onion. One form of chemical weathering takes place when atmospheric CARBON DIOXIDE dissolves in rainwater, forming a weak acid. The rain falls

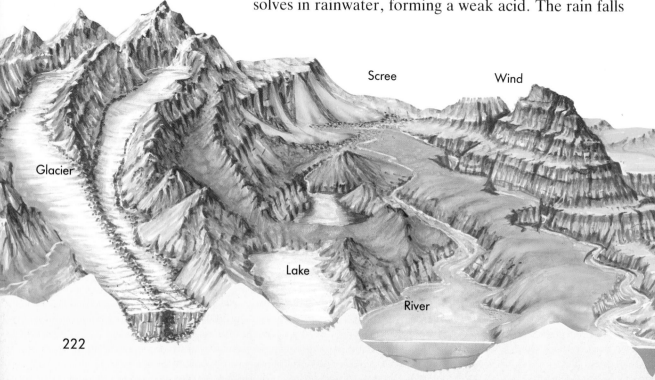

Glacier

Scree

Wind

Lake

River

◄ *This arch found in the Monument Valley, in Utah, has been formed over millions of years by the action of wind and rain which has eroded the rock.*

onto limestone, reacts with the calcium carbonate, and dissolves it away.

The main agents of erosion are GRAVITY, running water, ICE, and WIND. Debris from weathering may fall down a slope under the influence of gravity. A river may carry boulders, stones, gravel, and silt far from the places where they were formed. Ice in the form of GLA-CIERS has carved its way through valleys. And finally, strong winds may pick up debris and carry it away, and this may also cause further erosion as the windblown material literally sandblasts other rocks.

Different types of rock show great differences in their resistance to erosion. Rocks such as granite, lava, the harder sandstones and quartzites, limestones, and dolomites have relatively high resistance to erosion. Clays, sandstones, and tufas are easily eroded.

Escape velocity

Escape velocity is the speed an object must reach if it is to break free from the gravitational pull of a PLANET or other massive object. When a spacecraft is launched from EARTH, if it does not reach a high enough speed, GRAVITY will pull it back to Earth. If it reaches *orbital*

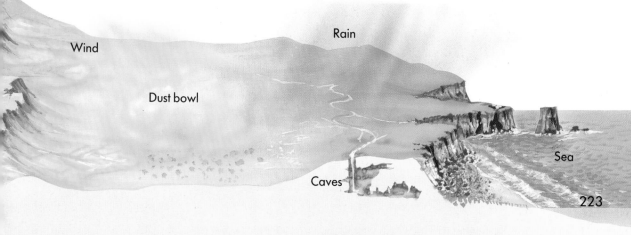

Wind

Rain

Dust bowl

Caves

Sea

► *In order to escape the pull of Earth's gravity a rocket must have an escape velocity of 7 miles per second (11.20 km/s). At about 1,000 miles (1,600 km) Earth's atmosphere is so thin that it is no different to space.*

Escape Velocities of Planets in the Solar System
Mercury 2.7 mps
Venus 6.4 mps
Earth 7.0 mps
Mars 3.2 mps
Jupiter 37.0 mps
Uranus 13.7 mps
Saturn 21.7 mps
Neptune 15.5 mps
Pluto Unknown

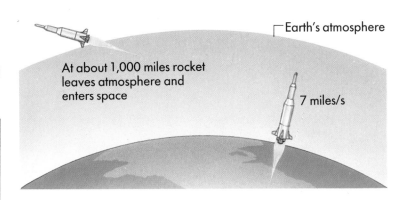

At about 1,000 miles rocket leaves atmosphere and enters space

Earth's atmosphere

7 miles/s

velocity, it loses height at the same rate as the Earth's surface curves away underneath it. It therefore remains at the same distance from Earth and orbits it. If it reaches escape velocity, it overcomes the pull of gravity altogether and flies out toward the Moon and planets.

Evaporation

Evaporation is the process by which a LIQUID turns into a GAS. Heat speeds up evaporation. Wet clothes hung out to dry on a warm, sunny day lose their moisture quickly by evaporation. Puddles that form on the ground during rain soon disappear when the Sun comes out because the Sun's heat evaporates the water. Evaporation occurs because the MOLECULES in all substances vibrate. Molecules at the surface of a liquid are freer to move than those in the middle of a liquid. If the TEMPERATURE of a liquid is increased, the molecules move faster and so

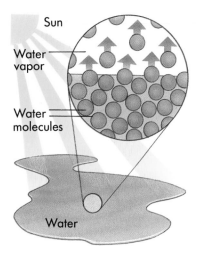

Sun

Water vapor

Water molecules

Water

▲ *Evaporation occurs when the heat of the Sun causes the water molecules in a puddle to gain enough energy to escape from the puddle.*

► *One traditional method of obtaining salt is to flood coastal hollows (salt pans) and allow the Sun's heat to evaporate the seawater, leaving behind the salt.*

SEE FOR YOURSELF
Put a tablespoon of salt into a cup full of water. Mix the salt well into the water. Pour some of the water into a saucer and put it on a windowsill. After two or three days the water will have evaporated. Salt crystals will be left behind in the saucer.

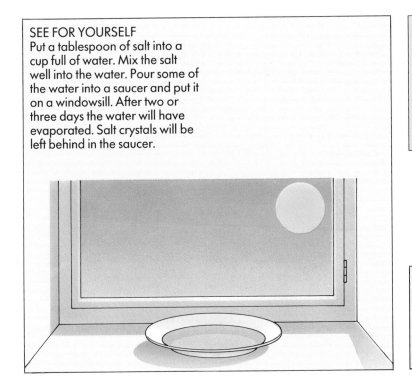

The Dead Sea is so salty that nothing can live in it. The dry heat of the Middle East has caused much of its water to evaporate over the centuries. As a result, the Dead Sea has both shrunk in size and become extremely salty.

Volatile A substance which is volatile is able to change easily from a solid or a liquid to a vapor. Volatile substances therefore evaporate quickly.

more of them escape from the liquid into the air. These molecules exert a VAPOR pressure on the surrounding air. When the vapor pressure reaches EQUILIBRIUM, evaporation stops. If the air is already full of vapor, for example when the HUMIDITY is high, then evaporation is slower.

When molecules escape from a liquid by evaporation they take heat energy away with them, and so the liquid cools down. Thus evaporation is used in REFRIGERATION and AIR CONDITIONING systems. In industry, evaporation through boiling is used in DISTILLATION.

Evaporation is a very important part of the water cycle. Moisture evaporates from the oceans, rivers, and lakes, cools and condenses in the air to form clouds, and eventually falls back to EARTH as rain or snow.

Evaporation is part of our daily lives. When we get hot we sweat. The sweat evaporates, taking heat away with it, so we cool down. Mammals try to keep their body temperatures steady. The camel, however, is adapted to desert life and so needs to retain as much moisture as it can. In order to do this, its body temperature can rise much higher than that of other mammals without harming it. Therefore the camel does not have to sweat to cool its body down.

Evolution

The gradual change of one type of animal or plant over a long time is called evolution. Biologists believe that all of today's plants and animals have descended from simple ancestors by a process of evolution. The changes from one generation to the next would have been very small, but over millions of years they could have added up to some very big changes. *See* pages 226 and 227.

EVOLUTION

The idea of evolution was suggested by the Greeks more than 2,500 years ago, but it was not until the 19th century that Charles Darwin provided a clear explanation of how the changes could have taken place. The individuals of a species always vary: some can run faster, some have better camouflage, and some are better at finding food than others. The individuals with the most useful features survive best and have the most offspring and, because offspring tend to resemble their parents, some of the useful features are passed on to the next generation. So the animals gradually get better suited to their surroundings and more efficient at catching food or escaping from their enemies. Conditions are not the same everywhere, so a variation that is useful in one place might not be useful in another. A species can therefore evolve differently in different places and give rise to two or more new species, each well suited to its own habitat. Those which are not well suited die out; Darwin called the process natural selection. We now believe that all plants and animals have evolved and become adapted to their surroundings in this way. Although Darwin generally gets all the credit for explaining evolution, another naturalist named Alfred Wallace worked on the same theory. There are several series of fossils from rocks of different ages that support this theory; for example, fossils show how today's elephants have descended from pig-sized animals.

Evolution of Cereals
It is likely that species such as wheat, barley, and corn have evolved from a common ancestor, grass. This type of species development is called speciation. Scientists believe that speciation occurs after a species has been separated into two or more isolated populations. They then develop different traits through natural selection and adapt to changes in the environment.

▼ *About 60 million years ago a mammal called* Hyracotherium *was living on the land. It was about as big as a fox, but its teeth proved that it was a grazing animal. It is thought this and other larger "horse-like" animals whose fossil remains have been found in rocks of about 30 million years old were the predecessors of the modern horse.*

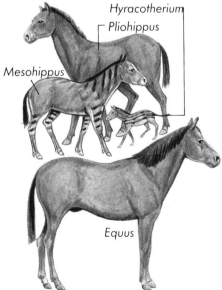

Hyracotherium

Pliohippus

Mesohippus

Equus

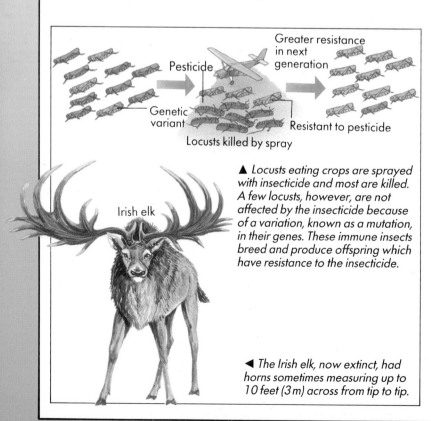

Greater resistance in next generation

Pesticide

Genetic variant

Resistant to pesticide

Locusts killed by spray

▲ *Locusts eating crops are sprayed with insecticide and most are killed. A few locusts, however, are not affected by the insecticide because of a variation, known as a mutation, in their genes. These immune insects breed and produce offspring which have resistance to the insecticide.*

Irish elk

◄ *The Irish elk, now extinct, had horns sometimes measuring up to 10 feet (3 m) across from tip to tip.*

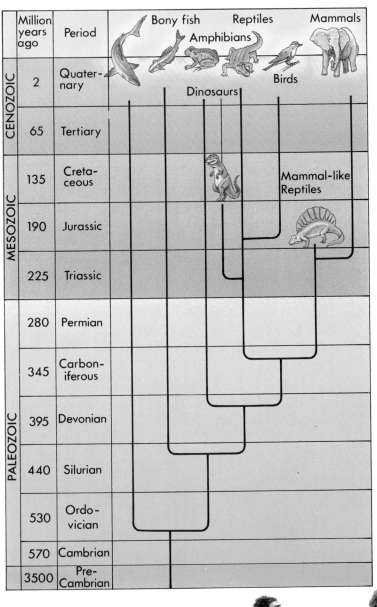

	Million years ago	Period					
CENOZOIC	2	Quater-nary					
	65	Tertiary					
MESOZOIC	135	Creta-ceous					
	190	Jurassic					
	225	Triassic					
PALEOZOIC	280	Permian					
	345	Carbon-iferous					
	395	Devonian					
	440	Silurian					
	530	Ordo-vician					
	570	Cambrian					
	3500	Pre-Cambrian					

Bony fish Reptiles Mammals Amphibians Birds Dinosaurs Mammal-like Reptiles

◄ The first vertebrates appeared about 500 million years ago. Mammals and birds, however, are much later additions to the evolutionary timetable.

▼ The forelimbs of a human, bird, and a whale are all much the same. Each has a different function but the basic similarity in the pattern of the bones gives us evidence of evolution from a common source.

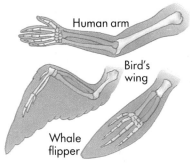

Human arm

Bird's wing

Whale flipper

▼ The evolution of modern humans has taken millions of years. It started with the appearance of the Australopithecus in Africa. This was followed by Homo habilis, and Homo erectus. It is thought that Neanderthals and modern humans came into being only about 100,000 years ago.

Australopithecus
1 – 4 million
years ago
Africa

Homo habilis
1.5 – 2 million
years ago
Africa

Homo erectus
0.1 – 1.5 million
years ago Asia,
Africa, Europe

Neanderthal man
35,000 – 100,000
years ago
Europe

Modern human
Since 100,000
years ago
Worldwide

See also BIOLOGY; DARWIN; ECOLOGY; ENVIRONMENT; FOSSIL; GENETICS; HEREDITY; LAMARCK; MUTATION; NATURAL SELECTION; SPECIES.

227

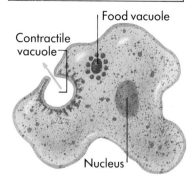

▲ In single-celled organisms, excess water is collected in tiny sacs which burst when full, shooting water out through the outer membrane.

▼ Freshwater fish would become waterlogged if their kidneys did not constantly remove water from their tissues. Sea fish have the opposite problem; they lose their body water to the salty water.

Freshwater fish

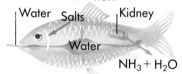

Sea fish

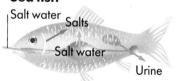

Excretion

When chemical reactions take place in any living organism, some unwanted waste products are produced. If these built up, they could harm the organism, so the waste materials are excreted. In very simple animals and plants, waste simply leaks out of the CELL, but in more complicated animals, a special excretory system has been developed. In animals, the most common waste products are water, CARBON DIOXIDE, and urea which is produced by the breakdown of PROTEIN. These materials pass into the BLOOD. Carbon dioxide is breathed out from the LUNGS, together with some water vapor. Most of human liquid waste is excreted by the KIDNEYS, in the form of urine. Water and urea are extracted from the blood through a web of tiny blood vessels and tubes. Some valuable substances also leak out, and these, together with 99 percent of the water, are reabsorbed before the urine leaves the kidneys. The urine travels to the bladder, from where it is passed out of the body. Desert animals such as gerbils pass hardly any urine because they need to save all their body water.

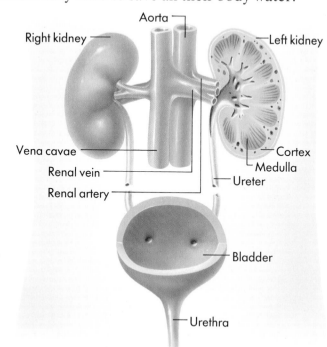

▲ The urinary system, which includes the kidneys, removes poisonous substances from the blood and eliminates excess water and salts. This keeps the concentration of the blood constant. The kidneys eliminate about 3 pints of urine per day. Water and salts are also excreted through the skin.

Expansion

Expansion is the increase in the volume or length of an object. Expansion often occurs when the TEMPERATURE changes; usually an increase in the temperature causes the object to expand. This is because the higher temperature causes the MOLECULES that make up the material to move around more and they tend to push each other apart. This property is used in THERMOMETERS; the mercury thermometer, for example, relies on the expansion of mercury as the temperature rises to indicate the temperature. Some materials, however, expand when they are cooled. For example, water, contracts as it is cooled, but when its temperature reaches 39°F (4°C) it begins to expand, becoming less dense as it freezes to form ice. This is why water can damage pipes when it freezes and why ice floats on water.

The expansion of iron when heated was used by wheel-makers for fixing iron tires onto the wheels of carts. The tire was made as a band just too small to fit around the rim of the wheel when cold. The tire was expanded by heating it over a ring-shaped fire and then forced onto the rim. As it cooled it contracted to grip the rim firmly.

SEE FOR YOURSELF
Find a small bottle, preferably with a narrow neck. Fill it carefully to the brim with water. Make a loose-fitting cap out of foil. Put the bottle in the freezer and leave it until the water has frozen. When you look at it again, you will see that the ice has pushed up the cap.

Expansion theory

The expansion theory of the UNIVERSE states that the GALAXIES found throughout space are flying away from each other, as if from an explosion, the BIG BANG.

Astronomers can measure the speed at which the galaxies are traveling by studying the RED SHIFT in their light. They have found that this speed increases by about 9 miles per second (15 km/s) for every extra million light years of distance.

This fact was discovered by the American astronomer Edwin Hubble (1889–1953), so the connection between speed and distance is known as Hubble's law. The idea of an "expanding universe" which began with Big Bang is the basic foundation of modern COSMOLOGY.

▶ The expansion theory says that galaxies are flying away from each other.

EXPERIMENT

Scientists set up experiments to discover new information and gather evidence about every aspect of the world around us. Experiments often begin with an idea that can be tested (the hypothesis). A hypothesis might be that beans need warmth and moisture to grow. Or a scientist may begin with a problem, for example, which of a number of balls will bounce the highest? When planning an experiment, all the different variables must be removed except for the one being tested. For example, if the bounciness of balls is being tested, they must all be dropped from the same height onto the same surface. The idea of a "fair test" is central to experiments.

Keeping accurate records is essential. Every detail concerning what is done and what is observed must be noted. Experiments often require careful measurement and the calculation of averages from a whole series of tests. The results can then be analyzed to determine what happened and why, and are then written up and communicated to others.

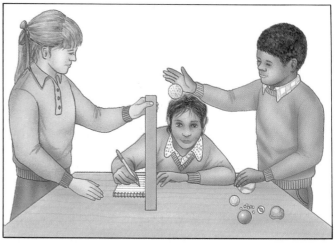

▲ Experiments are used to develop and test scientific theories. You can do experiments too. How high will these different balls bounce off the table? Will each one always bounce to the same height if dropped from the same point?

Question
↓
Plan test
↓
Observe and measure
↓
Record results
↓
Analyze
↓
Conclusion

◀ Most scientific research involves a number of steps: Scientists make hypotheses which try to explain events or things that have been observed in nature. They use experimentation to test the hypothesis. The results are often analyzed by using statistics.

SEE FOR YOURSELF

Consider how you would set up an experiment to discover the bounciest ball. Would it matter if the balls were different shapes or made from different materials? When testing the balls, should they be thrown or simply dropped and onto what type of surface? These are all called variables. To see if one ball bounces higher than another, all the other possible variables must be made the same. If you predict that a rubber ball will bounce higher than a steel ball and you discover the opposite, it may make you question how things bounce and lead to further important discoveries.

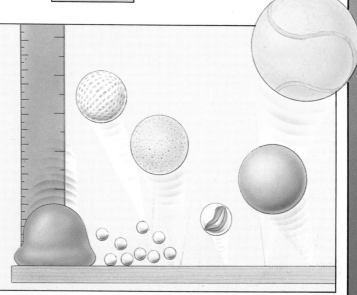

See also AVERAGE; BIOLOGY; CHEMISTRY; FEEDBACK; GRAPH; INVENTION; MATERIALS; MEASUREMENT; PHYSICS; PROBABILITY; STATISTICS.

Explosives

An explosive is a material that releases a large amount of ENERGY very rapidly and with violent FORCE, when acted upon by heat or struck by a blow. In most explosions, the explosive releases a large amount of gas at high PRESSURE. Explosives play a major role in military warfare, and in various industries such as building and CONSTRUCTION (for example, for clearing building land), mining and quarrying, and tunnel building.

Conventional (that is, non-nuclear) explosives include several types. Primary explosives, such as lead azide or mercury fulminate, are unstable and very sensitive to heat and can even be set off by a spark of static electricity. They are used in detonators (devices that set off other explosions). High explosives are more stable than primary explosives but are much more powerful. High explosives such as TNT and PETN are used for blasting and also in bombs and artillery shells. Plastic explosive is a puttylike mixture made from a high explosive and oil. Blasting agents, the most stable and cheapest explosives, are used for blasting rock in the mining and quarrying industries. Blasting agents include dynamite, invented by the Swedish chemist Alfred NOBEL in 1867. Low explosives burn rapidly instead of exploding, or detonating; an example would be the GUNPOWDER used in fireworks and as a propellant for firing shells.

▲ Blasting agents, such as dynamite, are the type of explosives used to move rock for construction.

◄ When flammable materials catch fire and begin to burn in a small space, the rapidly expanding gases cause an explosion.

231

During the last 200 years more than 50 species of birds and over 75 species of mammals have become extinct. Other species, such as Przewalski's horse, the Arabian oryx, and the European bison, have died out in the wild but have been preserved in game reserves or in captivity.

Extinction

The dying out of any plant or animal species is called extinction. Rocks contain the remains of thousands of plant and animal species that are not alive today, showing that extinctions have occurred all through Earth's history. Most of these ancient organisms probably became extinct because they could not cope with changing CLIMATE or because they could not compete with newer and more efficient forms of life that arose by EVOLUTION.

There have been certain periods of the Earth's history during which many animal species became extinct at more or less the same time. The biggest of these mass extinctions occurred at the end of the Paleozoic era about 225 million years ago. Geologists estimate that 90 percent of all species died out then. It took millions of

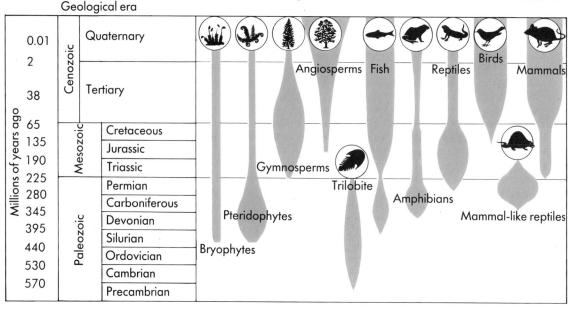

▲ This time chart compares the abundance of particular plant and animal groups during the Earth's history. The wider the colored band the more species of that particular group of animals and plants existed at that time. The trilobites and mammallike reptiles are now extinct.

years for life to recover and some groups, like the trilobites, failed to recover at all. Another mass extinction took place about 75 million years ago when the dinosaurs died out, along with the ammonites and many other groups of sea creatures. Changes in climate were probably the main reasons for the mass extinctions, but we do not really understand what happened. Some people think that a huge asteroid or comet collided with the Earth. This would certainly have upset the climate for a long time and would have made conditions difficult for all kinds of life.

Extrusion

Extrusion is a manufacturing process used to produce PLASTIC and METAL strips, threads, tubes, and rods by forcing material through a shaped nozzle. The raw material is loaded into a cylinder. A ram is fitted into one end of the cylinder. As the ram is pushed into the cylin-

▼ *In the hot extrusion of plastics, the solid pellet melts as a large screw pushes it through a heating chamber and then through an opening.*

▼ *In the cold extrusion of metal, the solid billet is forced through the opening in a die. Most other extrusion processes shape metal that has been heated because heat increases a metal's ability to be shaped.*

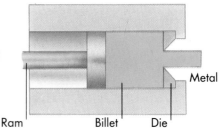

Hot extrusion

Plastic pellets

Plastic

Heating element

Extruded plastic tube

Cold extrusion

Metal

Ram

Billet

Die

der, the raw material is squeezed through a small hole, called a die, in the other end of the cylinder. The shape of the extruded material depends on the shape of the die. Plastic components such as pipes used for water systems are formed by squeezing molten plastic through a ring-shaped die. By changing the shape of the hole or nozzle, different extruded shapes are made. Many metals can be shaped by extrusion. Most of them must be softened by heating before they can be extruded, although lead is soft enough to be extruded without preheating.

Eye

The eye is the organ with which animals see what is going on in their surroundings. Human eyes are round and fit into bony sockets in the skull. Muscles turn them in the socket so they can look in any direction. The human eye, like that of other vertebrate animals, is a fluid-filled ball with a transparent window at the front. This is called the cornea and when light rays pass through it they are bent so that they pass through the pupil and into the LENS. The pupil is a hole in the center of the colored iris. The light rays are bent again as they pass through the lens and

SEE FOR YOURSELF
Look through a tube with your right eye and hold your left hand up next to the tube with the palm toward you. It looks as if there is a hole through the middle of your palm. Your right eye sees inside the tube and your left eye sees your open hand. The brain combines the images and you appear to see a hole in your hand.

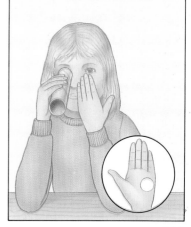

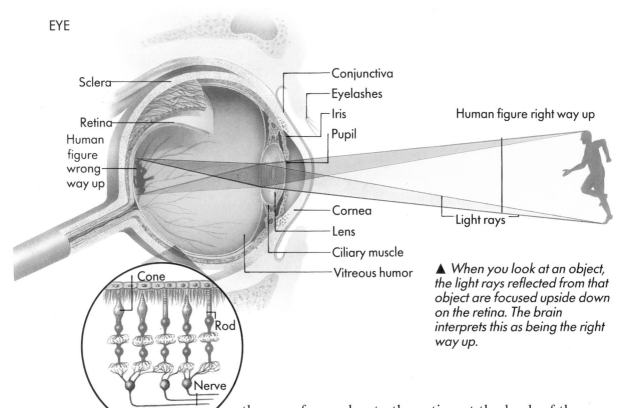

Sclera
Retina
Human figure wrong way up

Conjunctiva
Eyelashes
Iris
Pupil

Human figure right way up

Cornea
Lens
Ciliary muscle
Vitreous humor

Light rays

▲ *When you look at an object, the light rays reflected from that object are focused upside down on the retina. The brain interprets this as being the right way up.*

Cone
Rod
Nerve

▲ *Millions of receptor cells called rods and cones make up the retina. They send messages to the brain when they receive particular types of light. Rods are more sensitive to dim light and are used for black and white vision. Cones respond to bright light and can detect color.*

The Sphenodon or tuatara, a small lizardlike animal found only in New Zealand, has a primitive third eye. Its purpose is still unknown.

▶ *People who are nearsighted (myopic), cannot focus on distant objects. This can be corrected with a concave lens. People who are farsighted (hypermetropic), cannot focus on near objects. This can be corrected using a convex lens. The darker lines show how each lens corrects the point of focus.*

they are focused onto the retina at the back of the eye, where they form a picture. Small light-sensitive CELLS in the retina then respond to light and pass messages along the optic nerve to the BRAIN, where we "see" a picture. Too much light can damage the retina, so in bright light the pupils are very small. Other muscles in the eye can alter the shape of the lens so that the eye can focus on both near and distant objects, but sometimes these muscles do not work properly and the lens cannot form a sharp image on the retina. The focus point is either in front or behind the retina. Eyeglasses are used to change the focal length, so the image is formed on the retina. In older people, the lens becomes harder and cannot be focused properly, so glasses are often necessary.

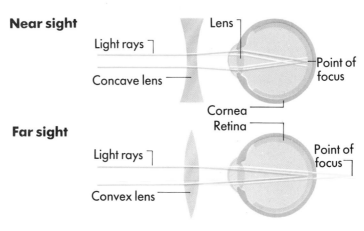

Near sight

Lens
Light rays
Concave lens
Point of focus

Cornea
Retina

Far sight

Light rays
Convex lens
Point of focus

234

Fahrenheit

Fahrenheit is one of the scales for measuring TEMPERA-TURE. It is named after the German scientist Gabriel David Fahrenheit (1686–1736) who was the first person to make an alcohol THERMOMETER (in 1709) and a mercury thermometer (in 1714). He took zero as the temperature of an equal mixture of ice and salt, and the normal temperature of the human body as 96°F (in fact, normal body temperature is 98.6°F). On this scale, the freezing point of pure water is at 32°F and the boiling point at 212°F. The Fahrenheit scale is still used in the United States, but in countries which use SI UNITS, temperature is usually measured on the CELSIUS scale.

Fallout, radioactive

Radioactive fallout is the cloud of radioactive particles that is thrown out by the explosion of a nuclear bomb or an accident at a nuclear power station. When a nuclear bomb explodes, it produces a fireball that rises at up to 300 mph (500 km/h). This causes a 180 mph (300 km/h) wind on the ground rushing toward the fireball. It sucks dust and soil into the air. Radioactive particles from the explosion settle on this material, which falls back to Earth as fallout. Particles larger than about a tenth of an inch across fall near where the bomb exploded. Smaller

Fahrenheit
To convert a temperature in Fahrenheit to Celsius first subtract 32, then divide by 9 and multiply by 5. To convert a temperature in Celsius to Fahrenheit, multiply by 9, divide by 5 and then add 32.

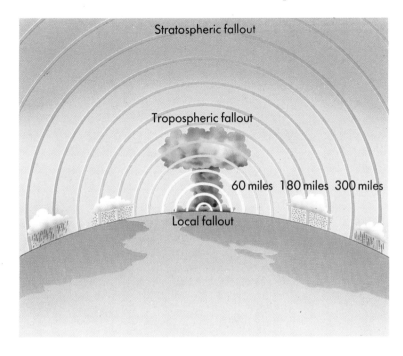

Stratospheric fallout

Tropospheric fallout

60 miles 180 miles 300 miles

Local fallout

◄ *Fallout can be local or it can travel in the wind before it is brought down in rain, snow, or fog, many hundreds of miles from its source. Fallout can be dangerous to plants and animals because it contains radioactive elements. Some of these radioactive elements go on giving off radiation for a long time. The radioactive elements enter plants and animals instead of the normal similar non-radioactive elements. Strontium-90 has many similarities to calcium and so can be absorbed into the bones and teeth of animals.*

235

When a Geiger counter is used to measure radioactivity in a substance, the results are often complicated by the fact that the Geiger counter picks up radiation from the surroundings as well as from the substance being measured. This background radiation may come from rocks, such as granite, as well as cosmic rays in the atmosphere.

particles are carried higher into the ATMOSPHERE. Depending on their size and the wind-strength, they may be blown hundreds of miles before landing.

The RADIOACTIVITY is given off in three forms: alpha particles, beta particles, and gamma rays. Alpha particles are four times as heavy as hydrogen ATOMS. They are stopped by a few inches of air and cannot travel through clothes or unbroken skin. Beta particles are very fast ELECTRONS. They are stopped by several yards of air and cannot get through thick clothing or more than surface skin layers, but can cause skin burns. Gamma radiation is a wave like LIGHT or HEAT. It can travel several hundred or thousand feet in air and can affect the whole body.

False-color photography

By adding colors, false-color photography is used to reveal information that is otherwise invisible. Photographs normally show images of the world as we see it, in the colors of the spectrum, but, for example, infrared FILM records images that we cannot see. It is sensitive to ELECTROMAGNETIC RADIATION beyond the red end of the visible light spectrum. False-color photography is also used to emphasize information in pictures by changing the colors. For example, photomicrographs taken with an ELECTRON MICROSCOPE are only one color and so false-color can be used to separate the details.

See also INFRARED PHOTOGRAPHY; PHOTOGRAPHY.

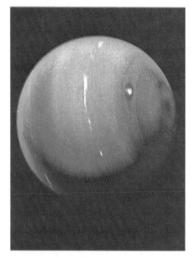

▲ *This image of Neptune was taken from Voyager 2 using false-color photography. It was photographed through three filters: blue, green, and a filter that passes light at a wavelength of the light which has been emitted by Neptune's methane-rich atmosphere.*

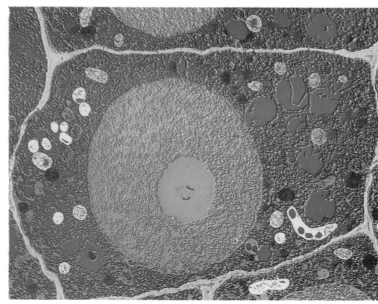

▶ *False-color has been used to highlight the photograph of the parts of a plant cell. The external plant cell wall is seen as a green boxlike line.*

Faraday, Michael

Michael Faraday (1791–1867) was a British physicist and chemist. His experiments are the basis for our understanding of the forces of ELECTRICITY and MAGNETISM. His father was a blacksmith, and Faraday had very little formal education, but he read science books in the store where he worked. He went to Humphry DAVY's lectures at the Royal Institution in London and persuaded Davy to let him work as his assistant. In 1821, he began to study the magnetic effects of an electric current which Oersted had discovered. He became the director of the Royal Institution in 1825. In 1831 he found that when he moved a magnet through a coil of wire, an electric current was produced in the wire. This enabled him to make the first electrical GENERATOR or dynamo. He also investigated ELECTROLYSIS.

▲ Faraday invented the electric generator and discovered elements by using electrolysis.

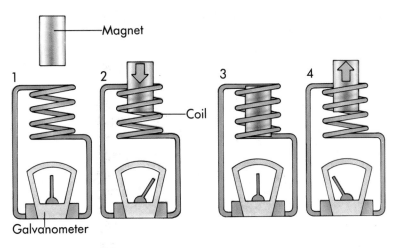

Magnet

Coil

Galvanometer

◄ In one of his experiments Faraday used a galvanometer, a device that detects electric current, to investigate the flow of current. He showed that current flows only while a magnet is put into (2) or taken out of (4) a coil. When the magnet is stationary outside (1) or inside (3) the coil, no current flows.

▼ About three-fourths of the world's production of fats and oils comes from vegetable oils.

Fats

A fat is one of a group of complex organic COMPOUNDS (consisting of carbon, hydrogen, and oxygen) existing in both animals and plants. A fat is an important, highly concentrated source of ENERGY for animals and plants. It provides an insulating layer under the SKIN to keep HEAT from escaping from an animal's body. It also forms the outer membrane of CELLS.

Fats can be solid and hard at room temperature, such as beef fat; solid and soft, such as butter, lard, or MARGARINE; or liquid, such as vegetable oil. Liquid fats are known as OILS. Fats belong to a class of natural compounds called *lipids*, which also includes waxes. Fats are insoluble in water but will dissolve in certain ALCOHOLS.

Sources of oils and fats

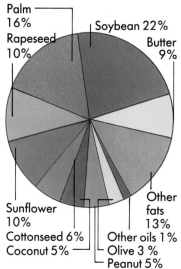

Palm 16%
Rapeseed 10%
Soybean 22%
Butter 9%
Sunflower 10%
Cottonseed 6%
Coconut 5%
Other fats 13%
Other oils 1%
Olive 3 %
Peanut 5%

▶ Cooking oil is made largely from vegetable oils but animal fats are also used. Products such as chemicals, soap, and candles can be made from cow's milk and palm oil. Whales were a popular source of fat for hundreds of years but they are now protected.

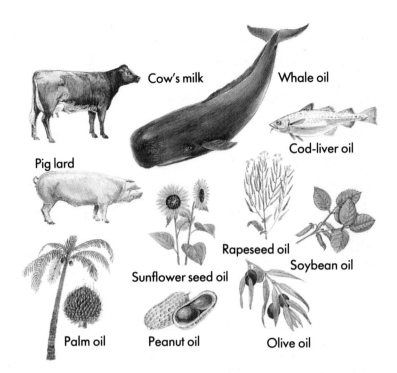

Cow's milk

Whale oil

Cod-liver oil

Pig lard

Rapeseed oil

Soybean oil

Sunflower seed oil

Palm oil

Peanut oil

Olive oil

▼ Fat molecules consist of three fatty acid chains joined to a molecule of glycerol. Saturated fats have chains in which the carbon atoms are linked to as many hydrogen atoms as possible. In unsaturated fat chains fewer hydrogen atoms are linked to the carbon atoms, resulting in at least one double bond.

Saturated fat

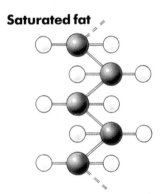

Unsaturated fat

Double bond

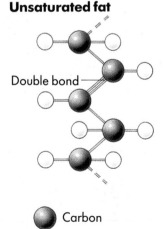

Carbon

Hydrogen

A fat consists of a fatty acid and GLYCEROL. Some fatty acids are essential for the healthy growth and development of the body, and need to be part of the diet. Fats that contain as many hydrogen atoms as they can are called saturated fats. Research has shown that saturated fats cause a build up of CHOLESTEROL in the blood, which can lead to heart disease. Unsaturated and polyunsaturated fats, in which there are fewer hydrogen atoms, do not produce high cholesterol levels.

Natural fats are the raw materials for many manufacturing processes and go into the making of such products as margarine, soap, and lipstick.

See also CARBOHYDRATES; NUTRITION; PROTEINS.

Fax

Facsimile transmission, or fax, is a system for sending information on paper by TELEPHONE lines. Fax is different from other COMMUNICATIONS systems such as telex and electronic mail. These transmit the information content of a document, but a fax machine transmits a copy of the document itself. It can, therefore, transmit drawings in addition to printed text. The first fax machines were ANALOG, but DIGITAL machines are becoming more common. Before a fax machine sends a document, it tests the telephone line it is going to use. If it detects a

◄ *A modern fax machine takes less than 30 seconds to transmit a one-page document.*

bad line, one with interference and noise, it automatically switches to a slower data transmission speed. This reduces the risk of data being lost during transmission. The document is scanned and the image is converted into electrical signals. At the other end of the telephone line, another fax machine receives the signals, decodes them, and prints out a copy of the original document. To make sure that every fax machine in the world can decode the data sent by other fax machines, they must all use the same coding and decoding system.

▼ *When the signals for a facsimile transmission arrive at the telephone receiver of the fax machine, the signals are separated from the carrier wave and fed into the printer. The printer recreates the document in horizontal chains of dots built up into lines.*

Feathers

Feathers are found only on birds. They keep the birds warm and they also enable them to fly. Feathers are made of a horny material called keratin, and they are extremely light. Each one consists of a hollow central shaft with lots of slender branches called barbs. The largest of the four main kinds of feathers are the *flight feathers* of the wings and tail. *Contour feathers* cover the body and the front edges of the wings, providing the smooth surface necessary for efficient flight. The contour feathers are like small flight feathers but they are more symmetrical. Underneath the contour feathers there is a layer of *down feathers* which keeps the bird warm. Scattered among the down feathers there are some tiny hairlike feathers, known as *filoplumes*. Connected to NERVES in the SKIN, they tell the bird when its feathers become

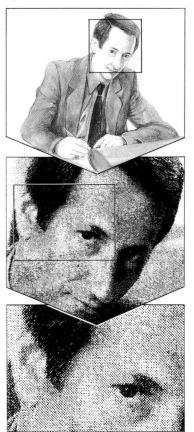

▶ Water runs off a duck's back because the oil on the feathers makes them waterproof.

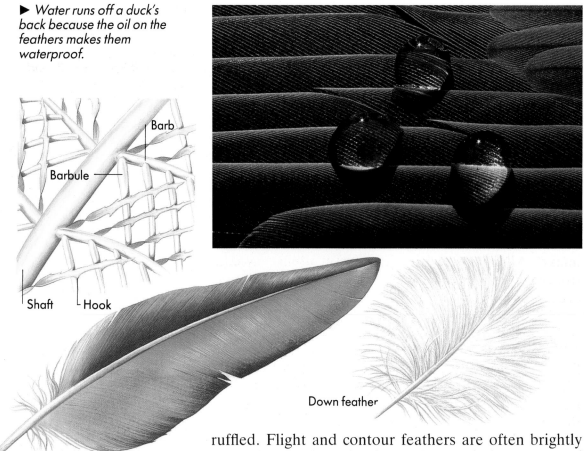

Barb

Barbule

Shaft Hook

Flight feather

▲ Each feather has a hollow shaft running down its middle. Barbs grow out on either side, which are locked together in a crisscross pattern with tiny, hooked barbules. Under the flight feathers are down feathers, each with a short shaft and a tuft of fluffy barbs. These feathers trap a lot of air around the bird's body and keep it warm.

Down feather

ruffled. Flight and contour feathers are often brightly colored, especially in the males, and they are used in DISPLAY to attract mates. Some of the colors are produced by PIGMENTS in the feathers, but others are produced by IRIDESCENCE.

See also AERODYNAMICS; HAIR; INSULATION, THERMAL.

Feedback

Feedback is a mechanism which allows an organism, or an electronic or mechanical system, to control its own processes. Feedback operates automatically, like the THERMOSTAT in a hot water system. In this case, the thermostat controls the heater, measuring the increasing temperature, and switching off the heat when it reaches the preset point. In a living organism, the same method switches CHEMICAL REACTIONS on and off. For example, a stimulus may cause an ENZYME to be produced. When the body detects that the enzyme has reached the proper level, the process of feedback switches off the production of the enzyme. This is called *negative feedback*. In our own bodies, carbon dioxide is produced as a waste

Negative feedback

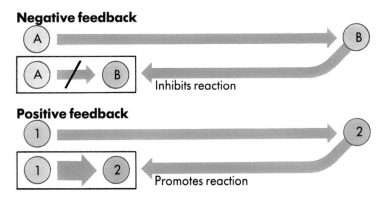

◀ *If **A** produces **B** , and the presence of more than a certain amount of **B** stops the reaction, it is negative feedback. If **1** produces **2** , and the presence of **2** keeps the reaction going, it is positive feedback.*

A → B Inhibits reaction

Positive feedback

1 → 2 Promotes reaction

product. As this increases in CONCENTRATION, a *positive feedback* mechanism causes us to breathe more deeply, flushing out the carbon dioxide and increasing oxygen intake. All of the body's chemistry is ultimately controlled by these feedback mechanisms.

See also AUTOMATION; COORDINATION; METABOLISM.

Feeding

Plants and animals all need food in order to stay alive. The food provides the materials needed for GROWTH and the ENERGY needed for all the processes that go on inside the body. Plants make their own food by PHOTO-SYNTHESIS, which uses the energy of sunlight to make SUGARS and other foods from water and carbon dioxide. Energy is locked up in these foods, and it passes to animals when they eat the plants.

Animals that eat plants are called *herbivores*. They include sheep, rabbits, and many other grazing mammals, all of which have large molar TEETH for grinding up the vegetation. Many herbivores carry huge numbers of MICROORGANISMS inside their digestive canals to help them digest the plant material. This relationship of two organisms contributing to each other's welfare is a good

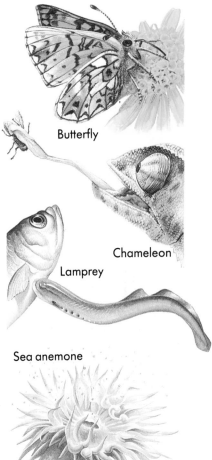

Butterfly

Chameleon

Lamprey

Sea anemone

▲ *These animals feed in very different ways; butterflies suck nectar; chameleons eat flies; lampreys feed on other fish; and sea anemones filter particles from passing water.*

◀ *Lions hunt large prey. This zebra will provide food for the whole pride of lions.*

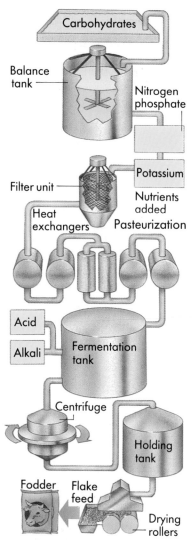

Production of fodder from carbohydrate waste

▲ *The waste products from a candy factory are made into animal feeds by using a specially developed fermentation process. Carbohydrates are collected. Nutrients are added, the liquid is pasteurized and then fermented. Temperature and acidity are controlled to enable the yeast to grow. The liquid is drained off and the yeast cream is dried to produce animal fodder.*

▶ *During fermentation the yeast used to make beer rises to the top of the tanks.*

example of SYMBIOSIS. Animals that eat other animals are called *carnivores* and employ many different methods for catching their prey. Some go out and hunt, whereas others lie in wait to ambush their prey. Carnivorous mammals have stabbing canine teeth for killing their prey, and sharp-edged cheek teeth for slicing meat.

Animals that eat both plant and animal matter are called *omnivores*. They include bears, badgers, and humans. Scavengers, such as vultures and dung beetles, feed mainly on dead animals or their droppings. Many water-living animals, including clams and other bivalves and many worms, feed by filtering tiny plants or animals or particles of dead matter from the water. These animals are called filter feeders.

See also DIGESTION; FOOD CHAIN; NUTRITION; PARASITE.

Fermentation

Fermentation is a biochemical process in which MICROORGANISMS such as bacteria, molds, fungi, and YEASTS break down an organic COMPOUND (consisting of carbon, hydrogen, and oxygen). Fermentation is the basic process used in the production of alcoholic beverages such as beer, wine, and cider. Yeast reacts with SUGAR to turn it into ALCOHOL and bubbles of CARBON DIOXIDE. During the 20th century, fermentation has also been used to make ANTIBIOTICS and other important DRUGS. For example, molds act on mixtures of inorganic salts and molasses to make penicillin, a vital medicine. Modern BIOTECHNOLOGY relies on a kind of fermentation to produce many of the materials used in GENETIC ENGINEERING. Fermentation is also important in

making many kinds of bread, cheese, and yogurt.

Not all fermentation is useful. If MILK is allowed to ferment, the bacteria it contains turn it sour. Though fermentation has been used for centuries in brewing and baking, the part played by microorganisms was first discovered by the 19th-century French scientist Louis Pasteur. *See also* PASTEURIZATION.

Fermi, Enrico *See* Neutron

Fertilization

Almost all plants and animals begin life when a male CELL, or sperm, joins with a female cell, or EGG, of the same species. This joining of cells is called fertilization. In most animals the male cells fertilize the eggs inside the female's body after mating, but fertilization of many water-living animals takes place outside the body; the males scatter their sperm over the eggs after the females have laid them. Fertilization in FLOWERS takes place when male cells from the POLLEN grains join with egg cells in the ovary after pollination. After fertilization each egg grows into an EMBRYO and then into a completely new plant or animal. The fertilized egg contains genetic "instructions" from both parents, so the new individual has some features from each.
See also CHROMOSOMES AND GENES; REPRODUCTION.

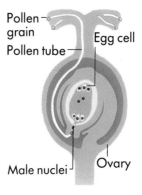

▼ *Fertilization in flowering plants starts when a grain of pollen lands on the stigma of a flower. The pollen grain makes a path to the ovary of the flower. The male gametes (sex cells) from the pollen travel down the path. One of the gametes fuses with the egg cell to form a fertilized egg.*

Pollen grain
Pollen tube
Egg cell
Male nuclei
Ovary

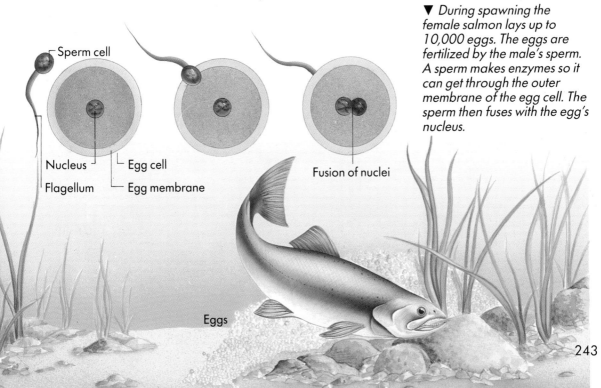

Sperm cell
Nucleus
Flagellum
Egg cell
Egg membrane
Fusion of nuclei
Eggs

▼ *During spawning the female salmon lays up to 10,000 eggs. The eggs are fertilized by the male's sperm. A sperm makes enzymes so it can get through the outer membrane of the egg cell. The sperm then fuses with the egg's nucleus.*

▲ *The fields on either side of this ditch have been treated with fertilizers. The excess nutrients have drained off into the ditch, where they have encouraged the growth of algae and surface plants, such as duckweed, which completely cover the surface of the water. The resulting shortage of oxygen prevents the growth of water lilies and other plants and animals that normally grow there.*

Fertilizers

Fertilizers are chemicals added to the SOIL in order to improve the size and quantity of food crops, flowers, and other plants. Plants make food for GROWTH by PHOTOSYNTHESIS. In addition to sunlight, this process needs large amounts of certain ELEMENTS and tiny "trace" amounts of others. These elements are required for NUTRITION, so they are called *nutrients*. Carbon, hydrogen, NITROGEN, and oxygen come from the air and water in the ENVIRONMENT. Plants must absorb the other elements, such as calcium, sulfur, PHOSPHORUS, and magnesium, from the soil. If the soil does not contain enough nutrients then farmers and gardeners can add fertilizers to provide the missing elements. Food production throughout the world is so important that fertilizer manufacture is a multimillion-dollar industry. Too much fertilizer, however, can cause pollution. The increased use of some elements can affect animal life as well.

Mineral fertilizers are the most widely used. They supply nitrogen, phosphorus, and POTASSIUM to the soil. Fertilizer packages indicate the concentration of these minerals. For example, a 4:4:4 fertilizer contains equal amounts (4 percent) of nitrogen, phosphorus, and potassium. Nitrogen fertilizers are produced mainly from AMMONIA. Naturally occurring potassium chloride is used to make potassium fertilizers. Natural fertilizers include decayed plant matter, animal waste (manure), and sewage. They have a lower concentration of nutrients than mineral fertilizers.

SEE FOR YOURSELF

Take three plant seedlings and water them every day. For the first use ordinary water. Water the second also with ordinary water, but once a week add a few drops of liquid fertilizer, carefully following the instructions on the bottle. Give water and fertilizer to the third plant every day. After a week or so you will see the effects of no fertilizer and too much fertilizer on seedlings 1 and 3.

Fiber optics *See* Optical fibers

Fibers, natural

Natural fibers are threads obtained from animals and plants. The fibers are spun into yarn which can then be woven on a loom to make cloth. The most commonly used animal fiber is sheep's wool. The breed of sheep the wool came from will determine the quality of the cloth. Other animals whose hair is used to make cloth include goats, alpacas, and rabbits. Silk is the only major natural fiber to be obtained from an insect. Silkworms spin a cocoon to prepare for their transformation into moths. The long fibers are obtained by unwinding the threads from the cocoon.

More fibers are obtained from plants than animals. Cotton fibers come from a hairy clump around the head of the cotton plant. Jute, sisal, and hemp are strong plant fibers that are used to make ropes and canvas. Linen is made from the stem fibers of flax. Fibers obtained from wood and grass are used to make paper and cardboard. Cellulose is extracted from plant CELL walls to make paper and synthetic materials.

See also CELLULOSE; SYNTHETIC FIBERS.

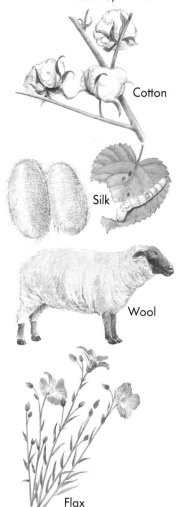

Cotton

Silk

Wool

Flax

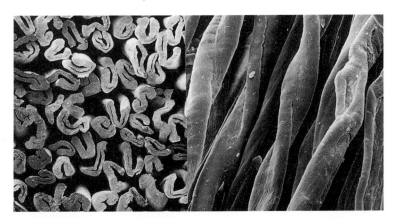

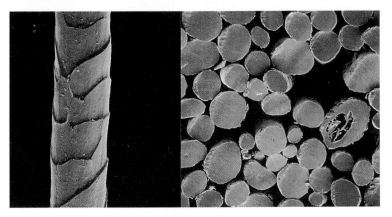

▲ Cotton is the most widely used natural fiber. The strongest natural fiber, however, is silk. It is used for clothing and decorative fabrics.

◄ The different highly magnified shapes are cotton fibers, seen from their ends and from the side. Cotton fibers do not have as many jagged edges as wool fibers, which is why cotton cloth feels smoother than wool.

◄ These wool fibers are shown magnified many times. The structure of wool fibers is similar to that of human hair.

245

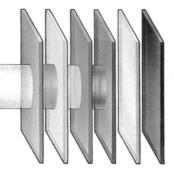

▲ *Color film is made up of six layers. One is an emulsion that records blue light, the second absorbs excess blue light, the third records green light, and the fourth records red light. The fifth, a plastic base, supports the emulsions. The last layer is a special backing that absorbs any remaining light.*

▶ *Developing and printing a black and white film: 1. the film is taken out of its case and wound around a special holder. This is done in a dark room. The film is placed inside a tank. 2. Chemicals known as developer, stop bath, and fixer are added in turn for carefully measured periods of time 3. The film is washed to remove the chemicals after they have done their job. 4. The film is removed from the tank and hung up to dry. When the film has been developed, the images are called negatives. The light areas of a subject appear dark and the dark areas appear light. 5. The negative is placed on a holder below the lens of an enlarger 6. Light is shone through the negative, which is enlarged onto the paper below it. Darker areas of the negative let through less light and light areas let through more. 7. The print is then developed and fixed in the same ways as the film. 8. The print is washed and dried on a heated metal flat bed or hung up.*

Film, photographic

Film is used in PHOTOGRAPHY for recording images. It consists of a strip of flexible plastic coated with a light-sensitive layer known as the emulsion. Holes punched along each edge of the film engage with toothed wheels called sprockets in the CAMERA. The first photographs were recorded on rigid plates. Flexible film made from CELLULOSE was introduced during the 19th century but cellulose-based film used to shoot the earliest movies is now breaking down. The PLASTIC base used in modern film is more stable. Film may be color or black and white, for making prints or slides. When print film is developed, the result is a negative image, which must then be turned into a positive image by printing it on photographic paper. When slide film is developed, it produces a positive image on the film itself.

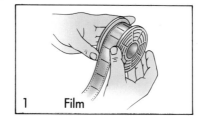

1   Film

Stop bath

Developer   Fixer

2

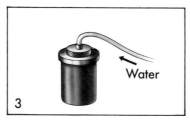

Water

3

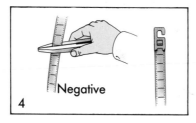

Negative

4

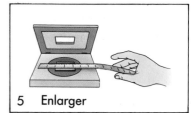

5   Enlarger

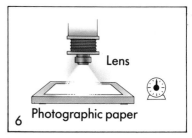

Lens

6   Photographic paper

Stop bath   Fixer

7   Developer

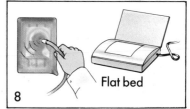

Flat bed

8

Filter, electronic

An electronic filter is a device used in a CIRCUIT to select which FREQUENCIES of an electromagnetic signal pass through to the rest of the circuit and which are blocked. Filters are used in RADIO transmission and reception. A low-pass filter allows all frequencies to pass through up to a certain cut-off frequency. All frequencies above the cut-off point are blocked. A high-pass filter allows all frequencies from a certain cut-off frequency (above zero) upward to pass through. These filters can be used in HI-FI systems to eliminate low pitched rumbles, high pitched whistles and other sorts of distortion when playing music. Linking a high-pass filter and a low-pass filter together and choosing their cut-off frequencies carefully can produce other types of filter. A band-pass filter blocks everything below a lower cut-off and above a higher cut-off frequency. A band-elimination filter blocks a certain band of frequencies and allows frequencies above and below to pass.
See also ELECTRONICS.

▼ *Electronic filters are used to filter certain frequencies out of a band width of radio waves. A high-pass filter allows high frequencies through but masks out low frequencies. A low-pass filter allows low frequencies through but blocks out high frequencies. Together the two filters enable a particular frequency band to be selected.*

Filtration

Filtration is the process of removing SOLID impurities from a GAS or LIQUID by passing the gas or liquid through a filter. For example, you can separate a mixture of sand and water by pouring the mixture through a filter paper. The filter paper acts like a sieve and traps the solid particles of sand while allowing the water through. The liquid that is allowed to pass through a filter is called the *filtrate*. The solid material trapped by the filter is called the *residue*. In vehicle engines, a filter is used to remove impurities from the air entering a carburetor. Filtration equipment at water treatment plants purifies drinking water from rivers and reservoirs before it is passed on to the WATER SUPPLY.

Different types of filtering materials are used in filtration processes. Filters made of sand or crushed

SEE FOR YOURSELF
Cut the top off a plastic bottle. Turn it upside down and place it in the bottom half of the bottle. Put in a coffee filter, layers of wet sand, and powdered charcoal. Pour some muddy water through the filter. The water becomes cleaner as it drips through.

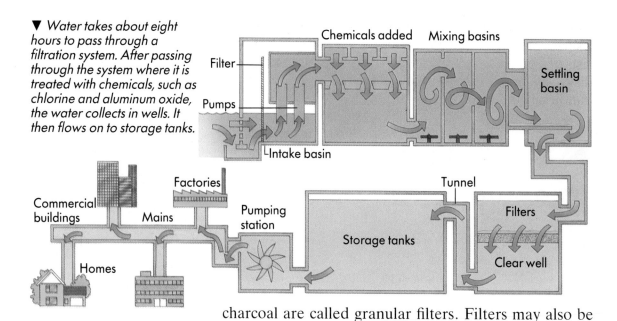

▼ Water takes about eight hours to pass through a filtration system. After passing through the system where it is treated with chemicals, such as chlorine and aluminum oxide, the water collects in wells. It then flows on to storage tanks.

charcoal are called granular filters. Filters may also be made of cloth or paper. Paper coffee filters have very tiny holes in them to allow water but not coffee grounds to pass through. Filters made of membranes are commonly used in KIDNEY dialysis machines.

Fireworks

A firework is any of several devices in which GUNPOWDER or other combustible material is set alight to produce colorful effects or explosions. Fireworks are extremely dangerous if used incorrectly and should always be handled with great care. In many countries, the law forbids the sale of fireworks to children below a certain age. Other laws limit the amount and power of EXPLOSIVE that firms that make fireworks can use.

The ancient Chinese developed fireworks along with gunpowder for military purposes and for celebration or entertainment. The fireworks used in displays today are of various types. Most are made by packing a hollow tube with gunpowder and other COMPOUNDS that color the flame or cause sparks. The powder is ignited by lighting a fuse. Firecrackers simply make a loud noise, colored fireworks contain CHEMICALS that burn to give distinctive colors. In a rocket, a lit fuse sets off a charge of coarsely ground gunpowder that releases gases behind the firework, propelling it into the air. Other fireworks in the rocket's nose are set off when the rocket reaches the top of its flight and produce colorful explosions. In a Roman candle, several gunpowder

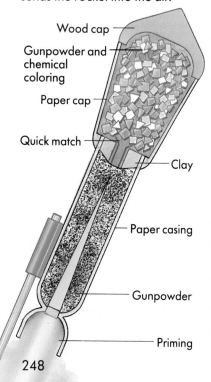

▼ A fuse is used to ignite the gunpowder in the body of the rocket. This produces a slow-burning explosion, which sends the rocket into the air.

Wood cap

Gunpowder and chemical coloring

Paper cap

Quick match

Clay

Paper casing

Gunpowder

Priming

charges are separated by nonexplosive material to cause a series of small explosions and sparks. A pinwheel consists of a gunpowder-filled tube bent around a cardboard disk. All fireworks are dangerous and should only be handled by adults

Each chemical used to produce color in fireworks gives off light of a characteristic color.
White is produced by magnesium.
Red is produced by strontium compounds.
Green is produced by barium compounds.
Yellow is produced by sodium compounds.
Blue is produced by copper compounds.
Charcoal is also sometimes added; it gives a rocket a sparkling tail.

◄ *Colorful fireworks produced by harnessing various chemical reactions are often used in dramatic displays for public celebration.*

Fission, nuclear *See* Nuclear physics

Flame *See* Combustion

Flame test *See* Analysis, chemical

Flash point

The flash point of certain LIQUIDS is the lowest TEMPERATURE at which the VAPOR above the liquid can be ignited in air. The vapor burns for a very short time, hence the term, flash point. Chemists apply the term mainly to liquid PETROLEUM products such as gasoline. The flash point is in effect the lowest temperature at which a liquid such as gasoline will burn, because below that temperature there is not enough vapor above the liquid's surface for COMBUSTION to take place. For safety reasons when storing or transporting flammable liquid such as gasoline or kerosene which form a vapor easily, it is important to know the flash point.

Fleming, Alexander *See* Antibiotic

FIREWORK SAFETY
All fireworks are dangerous. All fireworks burn vigorously, many explode, and most are made of poisonous chemicals.
• At a firework display, keep fireworks in a metal box with a tight-fitting lid.
• Keep the box well away from an open flame and the place where you set off the fireworks.
• Only open the box to take out fireworks. Keep it closed at all other times.
• Never carry fireworks in your pocket.
• Never try to light fireworks with a match or cigarette lighter. Use a special glowing rope fuse.
• Never hold lit fireworks in your hand.
• If a firework's fuse goes out before the firework goes off, leave it alone. Do not approach it and do not try to relight it.

FLIGHT ⚙

The earliest attempts to achieve human flight, which imitated birds by using flapping wings, were all unsuccessful.

The first successful human flights were made by balloon, using the principle that a bag full of warm air would float upward. In October 1783, two French brothers named Montgolfier sent up two friends in a hot-air balloon. In 1852, a Frenchman, Henri Giffard, made the first flight of a steerable balloon with a propeller driven by a steam engine.

This was the forerunner of the airship; a rigid container or envelope full of hydrogen gas, propelled by engines and carrying a passenger compartment or gondola. The gas-filled envelope, being lighter than air, floated upward. After a series of accidents in the 1920s and 1930s when the gas caught fire, destroying the craft, airships became unpopular. Modern airships use helium gas, which is not flammable.

In 1903, at Kitty Hawk, North Carolina, Orville Wright made the first powered flight in a heavier-than-air machine. When it was driven forward, the difference in airflow above and below its specially shaped wings created an upward force called lift. This is the same principle that enables birds to fly. Modern aircraft use this principle.

Today, there are many different types of aircraft, including vertical take-off aircraft, fighters, bombers, passenger airliners, small business jets, airships, flying boats, private planes, helicopters, and a range of different experimental aircraft.

◀ A bird has a specialized body for flight including feathers, wings, and strong, hollow bones.

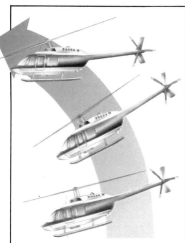

Helicopters do not need runways because they can take off vertically. They do this by spinning a set of thin wing-shaped rotor blades at high speed to create lift.

Lift · Drag · Gravity · Thrust

◀ To fly, aircraft need power from their engines. They need lift provided by the wings, to raise them from the ground and to keep them in the air. The forward thrust of the engines balances the resistance, or drag, set up by the air.

Milestones in the History of Flight
1492 Leonardo da Vinci draws concept of a flying machine.
1890 Adler's *Eole* becomes first full-sized aircraft to leave the ground under its own power.
1903 Orville Wright makes first sustained powered flight.
1908 Orville Wright makes first aircraft flight lasting 1 hour.
1909 Farman completes first aircraft flight of 100 miles (161 km).
1913 Sikorsky builds and flies a 4-engine aircraft.
1939 Sikorsky builds first modern helicopter.
1947 First aircraft flies at supersonic speed in U.S.A.
1970 First jumbo jet Boeing 747 brought into service.
1986 Rutan and Yeager pilot aircraft *Voyager* around the world without refueling in a 9-day flight.

George Cayley (1773–1857)
Cayley was an English engineer. He is known for the many ideas he contributed to the early history of aviation. He invented the biplane and built a glider that traveled 886 feet (270 m). He wrote about helicopters, parachutes, and streamlining the design of aircraft.

See also AERODYNAMICS; AIR; BALLOON; HYDROGEN; JET PROPULSION; TECHNOLOGY; WRIGHT, ORVILLE AND WILBUR.

Flotation

A body floats in a FLUID if the upward BUOYANCY force is great enough to overcome the downward force of its WEIGHT. The upward force occurs because the PRESSURE in the fluid increases the deeper one goes, so that the force of the pressure pushing up on the underside of the body is greater than the force of the pressure pushing down on the top. The principle of ARCHIMEDES states that the upward force is equal to the weight of the fluid that is displaced, or pushed out of the way, by the object. For an object to float, this upward force must balance the weight. This occurs if the object has a lower average DENSITY than the fluid, otherwise the fluid displaced will always be lighter than the object. Heavy ships float because they displace a large weight of water.

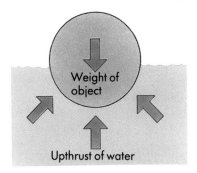

▲ This ball floats because its density is less than that of water. Only things that have a lower density than water can float in water.

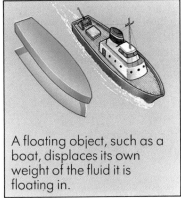

A floating object, such as a boat, displaces its own weight of the fluid it is floating in.

◀ An unladen ship rides high in the water.

SEE FOR YOURSELF
Put some raisins in the bottom of a glass. Fill the glass half full with any clear, carbonated drink such as tonic water. Watch what happens. The raisins will zoom up and down the glass as if by magic. But it's really science, not magic. Can you see what makes the raisins move up to the top? Look at all the air bubbles that stick to the raisins. The raisins rise to the surface when they have gathered enough air bubbles around them to make them rise. When they get to the top, they lose their bubbles and sink.

FLOWERS

Most of the plants around us have flowers at some time. The flowers contain the plants' reproductive organs which produce seeds. A typical flower has a number of sepals around the outside. They protect the flower bud and may fall off when the bud opens. The most obvious parts of the flower are the petals. These are often brightly colored, and they attract insects to the flowers for pollination. The petals of a flower may be all alike or of several different shapes, as in the sweet pea and the snapdragon. Inside the petals, there are a number of pinlike stamens. These are the male parts of the flower which produce pollen. In the center of the flower are one or more carpels, often joined together. These are the female parts containing the egg cells, or ovules, which eventually form the seeds. Everything is attached to the receptacle, which is the swollen top of the flower stalk.

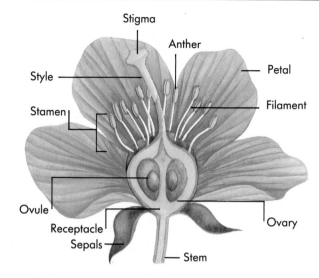

Stigma
Anther
Style
Petal
Stamen
Filament
Ovule
Ovary
Receptacle
Sepals
Stem

▲ This flower has been cut in half to reveal the main parts. Most flowers contain both stamens and carpels (male and female parts). The anther produces and stores the pollen. The stigma receives the pollen grains and it is here they germinate.

◄ There are about 50 species of the lady's slipper orchid, 12 of which are native to North America.

SEE FOR YOURSELF
Carefully pull a rose or other flower apart. See if you can identify the petals, stamens, sepals, and the carpel, which is found at the bottom of the stigma, the central piece of the flower.

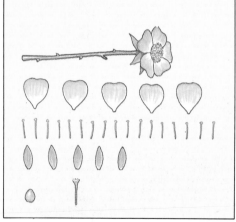

Bilaterally symmetrical flower

Composite flower

Flower with fused petals

▲ Bilaterally symmetrical flowers are not circular and have their structures arranged equally on both sides of a line. Composite flowers, like those of dahlias and daisies, are really many small flowers arranged in circles. The petals of some flowers are fused at their margins forming a tubular flower. Even prickly cactuses have flowers.

Cactus flower

See also BOTANY; COLOR; EGGS; ENDANGERED SPECIES; FERTILIZATION; FRUIT; POLLEN AND POLLINATION; REPRODUCTION; SEEDS.

Fluid

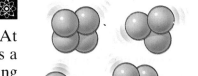

Together, LIQUIDS and GASES are known as fluids. At room temperature water is a fluid and a liquid, air is a fluid and a gas. Solids keep a definite shape by resisting forces that try to change their shape, or deform them. Fluids can flow to fill a container of any shape. This is because the MOLECULES which make up the fluid are able to move freely past each other, rather than being held rigidly to each other by the forces between them, as they are in a solid. Because they can change shape, or deform, to fill a different shaped space, fluids are useful in driving machinery. In a vehicle's braking system, for example, the braking force is transmitted from the brake pedal to the brake pads through the PRESSURE in a liquid (known as the brake fluid).

▲ Fluids flow easily. Any force or pressure will change the shape of a fluid. It will return to its former shape when the pressure is removed.

Fluorescence *See* Luminescence

Flywheel

A flywheel is a heavy wheel spinning on a shaft. It stores ENERGY which is released when needed. Once a flywheel is spinning, it slows down very slowly. Some ENGINES produce an uneven POWER output. This can be smoothed out by fitting a flywheel to the engine's output shaft. When the power output falls, the flywheel keeps spinning until the power level rises again. Vehicles, such as city buses, which have to start and stop frequently, are inefficient. Some experimental vehicles have been fitted with extra flywheels that spin up to high speeds when the vehicle brakes. The stored energy is used to get the vehicle going again, saving power and FUEL.

A fluid can be used like a flywheel (a fluid flywheel). The engine spins a propellerlike

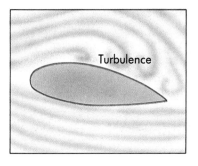

▲ Air is a fluid. When air flows around an object the airflow changes. The flow around an aircraft's wing is streamlined until the aircraft flies at a steep angle. Then the airflow becomes turbulent, increasing the drag.

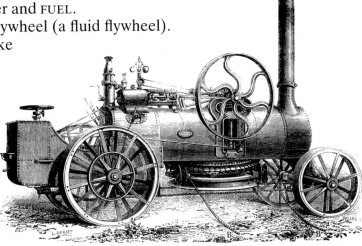

► This mid 18th-century steam locomotive plow had a flywheel fitted to the side of its boiler. The flywheel ensured that the plow had a constant amount of power passed to it by the engine.

▶ *The force of the water as the waves crash onto the shore traps air which forms foam full of millions of tiny bubbles. The foam looks like soap suds.*

device called an impeller sealed inside a fluid filled container. The fluid is forced to rotate with the impeller and its movement is transferred to a rotor on the vehicle's transmission system.

Foam

A foam is a COLLOID consisting of GAS bubbles scattered evenly throughout a LIQUID. Solid spongy materials are also called foams. A typical liquid foam is formed when air bubbles are forced into egg whites by whisking. A folding motion with a spoon or fork is used to keep the air in the liquid. Whipped cream is also a foam.

Foams are extremely useful. One consisting of bubbles of carbon dioxide in a nonflammable liquid is used in fighting gasoline or oil fires. Foams do not last long in nature because the gas bubbles eventually group together and separate from the liquid. Stabilizers are used to make the foam last longer. Typical stabilizers are PROTEINS (used in foods such as marshmallows and whipped cream) and SOAP.

Today foam-filled furniture must conform to strict government safety regulations. Toxic fumes should not be produced if the furniture catches fire. If older style furniture catches fire the smoke and fumes produced from the burning foam rubber can quickly suffocate and kill.

Foam rubber

Foam rubber is a spongy rubber which is full of air BUBBLES. Originally rubber was made from latex, the sap of some kinds of trees, but now it is usually made artificially. Foam rubber is made by blowing air through the liquid rubber to make it FOAM. It is then left to set. The end product is foam rubber which is used to make sponges and, in furniture manufacturing, to make the

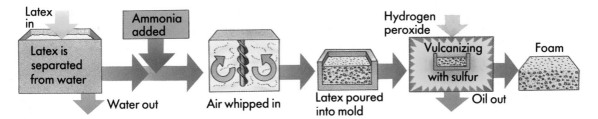

Latex in

Latex is separated from water

Water out

Ammonia added

Air whipped in

Latex poured into mold

Hydrogen peroxide

Vulcanizing with sulfur

Oil out

Foam

padding in chairs and cushions. A chemical called a blowing agent can be mixed with the liquid. It gives off a gas, forming tiny bubbles in the liquid. This type of foam rubber is not absorbent like a sponge. It is used as a layer of insulation between materials or spaces at different temperatures, for example, in refrigerators, and to line the frames of doors and windows to prevent cold drafts.

▲ *Foam rubber is made by whipping air into latex. Some foam rubber may be as much as 90 percent air. After being poured into a mold it is left to set, after which it is vulcanized. Rubber is vulcanized by having sulfur added to it while it is heated. This makes the rubber stronger and more elastic.*

Focus

A focus is a place where, for example, a beam of LIGHT is brought together to pass through a single point. This is often done by using a LENS; the light is bent when it passes from the air into the lens and bent again when it passes back from the lens to the air. The light is bent toward the focus of the lens. The *focal length* of a lens is the distance of the focus from the center of the lens. Lenses that bend light a lot (powerful lenses) have smaller focal lengths. Lenses are used to focus light in optical instruments such as MICROSCOPES and TELESCOPES. There is a lens in your EYE which focuses light so that you can see.

Mirrors can also focus light; a curved MIRROR will reflect light so that it passes through a focus.
See also REFLECTION; REFRACTION.

Focus can be used as a verb and a noun. *To focus* on something is to concentrate something, such as light or attention, on the object. *The focus* is the place where the light, or attention, is focused, and in the case of a lens, where an image is *in focus*. **Foci** is the plural of focus.

▼ *A converging lens brings an inverted image into focus in the image plane. In a camera, the film is in the image plane.*

◄ *The lens used to take this photograph was focused on the central bulb.*

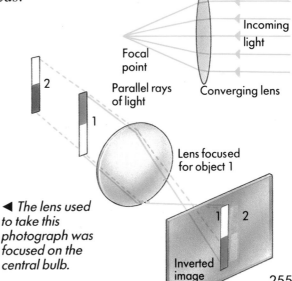

Incoming light

Focal point

Parallel rays of light

Converging lens

Lens focused for object 1

Inverted image

255

Fog

Fog consists of tiny droplets of water suspended in AIR close to the ground surface. Such a cloudlike blanket of fog may reduce the visibility dramatically, especially if the fog forms at night. When visibility has been reduced to less than 3,280 feet (1 km), it is called fog but if visibility is greater than this, it is referred to as "mist."

Fog usually occurs when the air near to ground level is almost saturated with water VAPOR. Fogs are caused when the air containing large amounts of water vapor is cooled suddenly, such as when it comes into contact with the cold ground. Fog is more likely to occur in areas where there is a high level of AIR POLLUTION, because the water vapor is more likely to condense around the particles in the ATMOSPHERE. Fog containing smoke is often called "smog."

▼ Advection fog forms when warm, moist air travels over a cool surface, or when cold air passes over warm water. Frontal fog forms where two air masses of different temperatures meet. Radiation fog forms at night in low places as the Earth's heat escapes upward, leaving cool air at ground level. As the temperature drops fog is formed. Upslope fog forms as moist air cools when it travels up a slope.

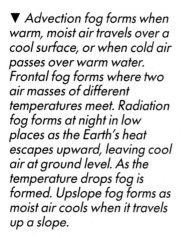

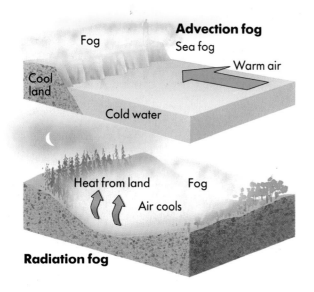

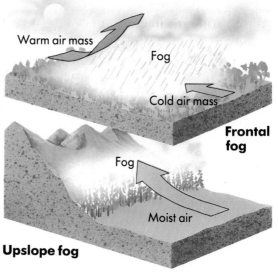

Food additives

Food additives are any of a group of substances that are added to processed foods by the manufacturers. They include colorings, preservatives, anti-oxidants (to stop food reacting with oxygen in the air), emulsifiers and stabilizers (to control the fat content of the food), sweeteners, solvents, flavor enhancers (to stimulate the taste buds), and added VITAMINS. Some food additives are natural materials such as salt and sugar which have been used for thousands of years. Modern CHEMISTRY has given rise to a large number of artificial food additives.

Some flavoring agents added to food add no flavor of their own, but improve a food's natural flavor. Monosodium glutamate is one of these agents. It is a white crystalline substance that improves the taste of meats, vegetables, soups, etc. and is often used in Chinese cooking.

FOOD ADDITIVES	Possible adverse effects
Tartrazine (artificial coloring)	Skin rashes, breathing problems, blurred vision, purple patches on skin, hyperactivity in children.
Potassium nitrate (preservative)	Severe stomach pain, vomiting, muscular weakness, irregular pulse.
Butylated hydroxytoluene (anti-oxidant)	Skin rashes, hyperactivity in children.
Monosodium glutamate (flavor enhancer)	Headaches, dizziness, neck pains, muscular weakness.

Some food additives have caused concern because of their apparent connection with health problems. Tartrazine, for example, is an artificial yellow coloring that has been linked with skin rashes and hyperactivity in children. Monosodium glutamate, a flavor enhancer made from sugar beets and wheat, has been linked to headaches and dizziness in some people. The vast majority of food additives are thought to be harmless. Some may cause problems in children or people with certain medical problems. The Food and Drug Administration ensures that manufacturers prove a food additive safe before using it.

See also FOOD PRESERVATION.

SEE FOR YOURSELF
Mix some powdered sugar and a little water in a bowl. Divide the mixture equally into three portions. To make brown icing add a teaspoon of cocoa to the first third of the icing mixture. To make pink icing, add some blackcurrant juice or a drop of red food coloring to the second third. To make yellow icing add a drop of yellow food coloring to the last third. Cocoa and blackcurrant juice are themselves natural food substances. But the red and yellow food colorings are probably vegetable dyes.

◀ *Artificial substances used in food must satisfy strict regulations regarding their effect on people. Many substances are no longer used as food colorings because their effects are known to be harmful.*

Food chain

Rabbits eat grass: foxes eat rabbits. This is a simple food chain or ENERGY chain. All animals belong to food chains because they depend on other ORGANISMS for their food and energy. If you upset one part of a food chain, you will unbalance it. *See* pages 258 and 259.

FOOD CHAIN

All animals depend ultimately on green plants. These plants are known as producers, because only they can produce energy-giving food by photosynthesis from nonliving matter. The next link in the chain must be a herbivore or plant eater. It gets all its energy from the plants that it eats and is known as a primary consumer. The rabbit is the primary consumer in the simple chain: rabbits eat grass, foxes eat rabbits. The next animal in the chain is a carnivore or flesh eater. It gets its energy by eating the primary consumer and is known as a secondary consumer. There may be one or even two more carnivores further up the chain, and the one at the top is called the top predator. The higher up food chains you go, the fewer animals you will find. On the African savanna, for example, there are about 100 gazelles for every lion, and those gazelles require millions of grass plants (over 600 acres of grassland) to keep them alive. There are rarely more than five links in a food chain, because energy is used up at each stage just to keep the animals alive. There would not be enough energy to go around if there were too many links in the chain.

Most animals eat more than one kind of food and belong to several different food chains. The chains in any particular habitat are thus linked together to form a food web. All the energy passing through the system comes originally from the Sun, trapped by the plants during photosynthesis.

The lanner falcon, the caracal, the lion, and the leopard are the top predators on the plains and they have no real enemies, but the food chains do not stop there. When these animals die a host of scavengers, including the vultures, will eat the dead bodies.

| Producer ➡ Primary consumer ➡ Secondary consumer |

▲ *In any food chain the producer is always a plant. This plant is fed upon by a herbivore or primary consumer which is eaten by a carnivore or secondary consumer.*

▶ *This is a small part of the food web on the African savanna. There are three main food chains, in which the primary consumers are the locust, the antelope, and the hare. You can see that the chains are linked by many cross-connections before they reach the top predators, but everything begins with the plants. The antelope produce dung, which is eaten by dung beetles and other insects. Each organism depends on the others. If the grass dies there will be nothing for the antelope to feed on so they will move away to try and find food. The lions and vultures will follow the antelope or eat a different animal.*

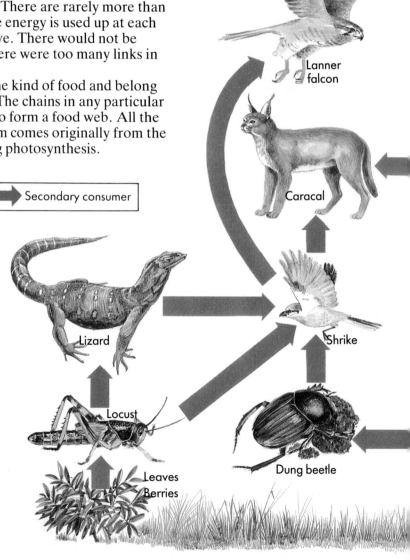

Lanner falcon

Caracal

Lizard

Shrike

Locust

Leaves
Berries

Dung beetle

258

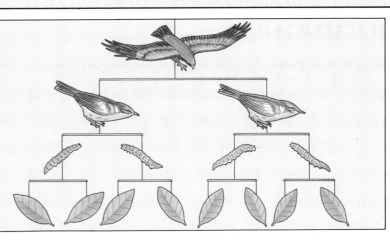

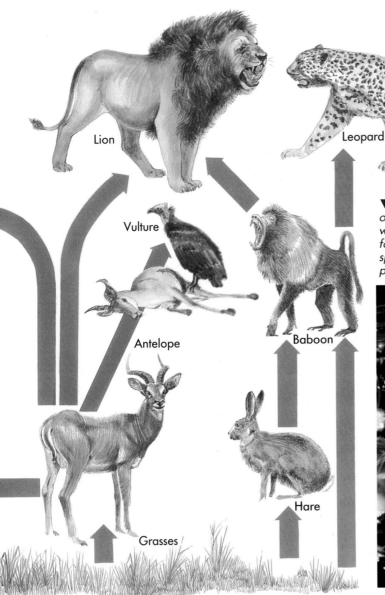

Lion

Leopard

Vulture

Antelope

Baboon

Hare

Grasses

▼ *Plankton is the name given to the variety of microscopic plants and animals that live in water. They serve as a primary food source for animals such as jellyfish, mollusks, sponges, and certain fish. These in turn provide food for larger fish.*

See also ECOLOGY; ECOSYSTEM; ENERGY; ENVIRONMENT; FEEDING; NUTRITION; MICROORGANISMS; ORGANISM; PHOTOSYNTHESIS; SUN.

The following seven precautions can help to prevent food poisoning:
1. Be sure food is fresh when you buy it.
2. Wash your hands before you handle food and be sure you don't have any open sores or skin infections.
3. Wash fruit and vegetables.
4. Refrigerate foods that spoil easily.
5. Boil home-canned foods before eating them.
6. Never eat raw or uncooked pork or chicken.

▶ *This photograph shows the bacterium* Salmonella enteritidis *greatly magnified by an electron microscope. This bacterium has been found to be a cause of food poisoning. It has been associated with infected hen's eggs and poultry.*

Irradiation is a method of preserving food. It involves bombarding food with gamma radiation, X-rays, or accelerated electrons to kill the microorganisms that make food decay.
Only some countries have allowed irradiation to be used for food preservation, others are not yet satisfied that it is entirely effective.

Food poisoning

Food poisoning can be caused by the presence of certain types of bacteria, or by substances (POISONS or toxins) that they produce, in our food. It may cause no more than temporary diarrhea or vomiting, but is sometimes very serious. Bacteria in food are difficult to detect, because they do not always cause a smell of decay. Food poisoning is usually caused by contamination during food processing or by incorrect storage methods.

Salmonella is a very common bacterium found in poultry. Chickens need to be cooked carefully to prevent the salmonella from increasing in number and caus-

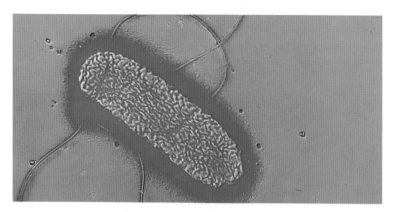

ing a health risk. The meat must be cooked properly, and no utensil that was used for the uncooked meat should be used for the cooked meat. Salmonella can even enter eggs. Listeria is another bacterium which is found in certain types of cheese. It can be dangerous to people who are not strong, the elderly, young children, and particularly to pregnant women. It can continue to grow at the low temperatures used for storing precooked foods. Staphyllococcus can be spread when a food handler has a skin infection like boils. Botulism is caused by a toxin released from the Clostridium bacteria and can cause paralysis and death. Fortunately it is rare and only occurs in poorly treated canned food. Food poisoning can be avoided by careful food storage and preparation.

Food preservation

Food preservation describes a range of methods used to prevent food from spoiling or decomposing. Without any form of preservation, MICROORGANISMS soon invade foods and make them inedible. People have been preserving food since prehistoric times. Traditional preservation methods include drying, smoking and salting, candying (sealing in a sugary coat), and pickling. Dried food is preserved because the microorganisms that spoil food cannot grow without moisture. Chemicals in the smoke used to smoke foods inhibit these organisms. Very salty and acid conditions have the same effect.

These methods are still used, but knowledge of the way that food-spoiling microorganisms grow and multiply has led to new methods including CANNING, FREEZING, and a combination of freezing and drying, called FREEZE-DRYING. Nuclear technology offers another method, called irradiation. If food is exposed to RADIOACTIVITY, microorganisms living in the food are killed, greatly extending the shelf life. Irradiation is still an experimental method and is not accepted by everyone.

▼ *It is important to keep food at a cool temperature to preserve the food between the time it is produced and the time it is eaten. The food may be kept in cold storage after production. It is then transported in a refrigerated truck to the supermarket where it is held in cold storage before being placed in the supermarket refrigerator. The consumer purchases the product and places it in his or her own refrigerator. Temperature change and repeated freezing and thawing can lead to deterioration of the food and cause the growth of microorganisms.*

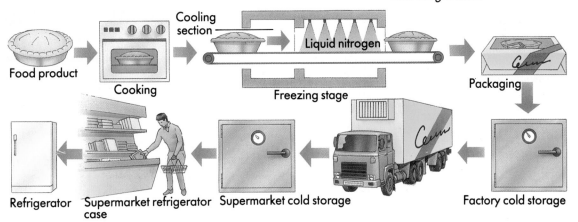

Food product | Cooking | Cooling section | Liquid nitrogen | Freezing stage | Packaging | Factory cold storage | Supermarket cold storage | Supermarket refrigerator case | Refrigerator

Force

A force is something that pushes or pulls an object in a particular direction. Isaac NEWTON realized that if one object produces a force on another, the first object experiences an equal and opposite reaction force. He also realized that forces cause objects to accelerate; to keep something moving in a straight line at a constant speed does not need a force, except to balance the force of FRICTION. When a force moves through some distance, for example, when you lift up a weight and put it on a table, the force does WORK and uses up ENERGY. When the object does not move, no work is done and it takes no energy for the table to continue supporting the weight once you have put it there. A lever can be used to convert a small force into a large force; in order that the amount of work done by both forces is the same, the

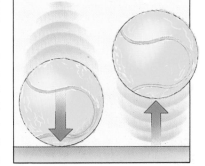

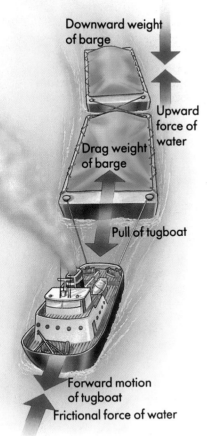

Downward weight of barge

Upward force of water

Drag weight of barge

Pull of tugboat

Forward motion of tugboat

Frictional force of water

▲ *Several forces act together on this tug and cargo. The frictional force of water acts against the direction of travel. The downward force of gravity on the barges acts against the upward force of the water. The pull of the tug acts against the drag weight of the cargo.*

▶ *Evidence collected at the scene of the crime is analyzed by forensic scientists in the laboratory. The results are used in the legal proceedings as part of the case brought against the accused.*

small force must be moved through a larger distance than the large force.

The force that pulls objects downward toward the Earth is called GRAVITY. The force of ELECTRICITY and MAGNETISM is called electromagnetic force.

Forensic science

Forensic science is used by police forces to provide technical information about a crime. It is the study of items associated with a crime, in order to deduce facts about them. For example, a forensic scientist will examine threads and fibers found at the scene of a crime, to see if they match up with fibers associated with a suspect. Forensic scientists may also examine a bullet to see if its markings can identify the gun from which it was fired.

Forensic medicine provides evidence about individuals. It can tell how long it is since a person died, from the body TEMPERATURE, or can prove that a particular weapon was used. Fingerprinting is used to identify a person, because no two people have identical fingerprints. Now there are techniques for the examination of blood and other body fluids that can identify a person.

Forging

Forging is a process for shaping METAL by hammering while it is still hot. When IRON or steel is heated to a high enough TEMPERATURE, it becomes soft and can be shaped. Until the 19th century, all forging was done by hand, usually by blacksmiths in forges. In 1839, the Scottish engineer James Nasmyth invented a steam powered hammer. A piece of metal formed by forging is less

◄ Blacksmiths forge small objects such as horseshoes by hand. The iron is heated in a forge (open furnace) until it glows red. The blacksmiths are then able to hammer the metal into shape.

Forging is probably the oldest method of shaping metal known. Metal was first forged over 6,000 years ago. The first iron worked by forging was found in meteorites and in many early languages the word "iron" meant "metal from the sky." By 1200 B.C. ironworkers could reheat, work, and cool iron to make wrought iron with properties similar to those of some carbon steels today.

brittle than one formed by CASTING. If a large number of identical metal parts are needed, they can be made by a process called drop forging. A piece of metal is positioned between an anvil and a drop hammer. The drop-hammer is a heavy metal block with a shaped "die" on the bottom. It drops with great force onto the piece of metal, forming the part instantly.
See also DUCTILITY; MALLEABILITY.

Formula, chemical

A chemical formula is a shorthand method of writing down the ingredients of a chemical COMPOUND. Each ELEMENT has its own CHEMICAL SYMBOL. A formula uses the symbols with figures to show the proportions in which the elements combine to form the compounds. The *empirical formula* of a compound indicates the ATOMS of each element in the compound in their simplest RATIO. The empirical formula for ethene is CH_2. The *molecular formula* of a compound gives the numbers of each atom making up a single MOLECULE of that compound. The molecular formula for ethene is C_2H_4. This shows that two atoms of carbon combine with four atoms of hydrogen in an ethene molecule. The *structural formula* of a compound is a way of indicating the chemical bonds that hold the atoms together in the molecule.

Fossil

A fossil is any remains or trace, such as a shell, bone, or a footprint, preserved in ROCK by gradually being changed into rock itself. These remains belonged to an animal or plant which lived a long time ago.

When an animal, for example, a clam, dies in the sea

▼ Chemical formulas are internationally agreed symbols that are used as a kind of shorthand for the names of chemical compounds. They show the different atoms of a molecule and sometimes how they are arranged.

Structural formula of ethene

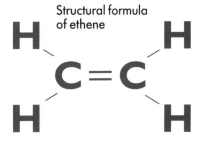

$$CH_2 = CH_2$$

Molecular formula of ethene

$$C_2H_4$$

▶ *Scientists carefully chip away rock to reveal the fossilized bones of a huge dinosaur.*

▼ *Fossils form when animal or plant remains get covered with sediments that later turn to rock.*

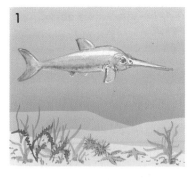
1

2

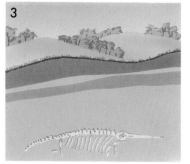
3

it sinks to the seafloor. There its soft parts will usually decay, but the clam's shell may soon become buried by sediment. More sediment is deposited and eventually the silt or mud hardens into rock and the MINERALS in the rock are replaced until the fossil turns to a kind of rock itself, different from the surrounding material.

Although millions of fossils have been found, they are very rare compared to the numbers of animals and plants that have lived since life on Earth first evolved 3 billion years ago. This is because the conditions in which fossilization can occur are rare. Most fossils are of sea organisms because fossilization is more likely to take place in the sea. If an animal dies on land, its flesh will be eaten and its SKELETON broken up before it could be covered with sediment that could harden into rock.

Fossil fuels

Fossil fuel is the name given to COAL, PETROLEUM, and NATURAL GAS which are extracted from the rocks of the Earth's crust and used to provide the FUEL for heating and the generation of power such as ELECTRICITY. Many chemicals are also derived from petroleum. These fuels are made from the animal and plant remains which have formed FOSSILS, hence their name. Peat is not strictly a fossil fuel because most peat has been formed since the last Ice Age and is continuing to be formed today. Fossil fuels are HYDROCARBONS.

Natural gas and oil are often found together, with the gas occupying pores in the rocks at a higher level than the oil. Petroleum also occupies pores in permeable rocks that allow liquids to pass through them. They are often capped by an impermeable layer such as clay.

▼ Coal can be extracted from seams that lie near the surface by removing the topsoil to make a strip mine. Deeper seams are reached by shafts and tunnels. Anthracite, the hardest and best coal, is usually the deepest.

Strip mine

Coal (lignite)
Sandstone
Shale
Coal (bituminous)

Coal (anthracite)

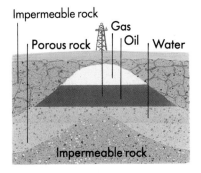

Impermeable rock
Porous rock
Gas
Oil
Water
Impermeable rock

▲ Oil-bearing rock holds drops of oil between its grains. It seeps up through porous rock, such as sandstone, until it is stopped by impermeable rock, such as granite.

Foucault pendulum

A Foucault pendulum is a PENDULUM that is free to swing in any direction. Once it has begun to swing in a particular direction, it will keep swinging back and forth in this direction unless it is disturbed by some outside FORCE. A pendulum like this can be used to detect the daily RO-TATION of the EARTH, since all the surrounding objects will rotate with the Earth, but the direction of the pendulum will not. It is named after Jean-Bernard Foucault (1819–1868), a French physicist who hung a brass ball weighing 300 pounds (137 kg) on a 230-foot (70 m)-long wire from the dome of the Panthéon in Paris in 1851 and demonstrated that the Earth rotates once a day.

▶ A strong piece of string, at least 20 feet (6 m) long, hung from the top of a stairwell, with a heavy weight (at least 10 pounds (5 kg)) attached to it, will show a change in its angle of swing during the day. The pendulum must be able to swing freely. The path of the pendulum can be marked at intervals to show the apparent changes of direction.

String (at least 20ft long)

Weight (at least 10lbs)

◀ A Foucault pendulum is designed to show the rotation of the Earth. It swings back and forth in the same plane, but the rotation of the Earth makes the pendulum appear to change its path gradually over a period of several hours.

265

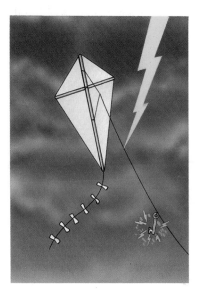

▲ Benjamin Franklin served the nation as a public leader, statesman, and scientist.

Franklin, Benjamin

Benjamin Franklin (1706–1790) was an American printer, scientist, publisher, and statesman who played an important part in the formation of the United States of America as a nation. Franklin was born in Boston, Massachusetts, the 15th of 17 children. At 12 years he went to work for his brother, a printer in Philadelphia, but gave it up in 1748 to study science. He proved that LIGHTNING is electrical and later invented the LIGHTNING ROD to protect buildings. His other inventions included the Franklin stove and bifocal eyeglasses. He was also the first scientist to study the movement of the Gulf Stream in the Atlantic Ocean.

Franklin helped draft the Declaration of Independence and was one of the signers of the Constitution.

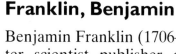

Lightning rod

Bifocal glasses

Franklin stove

▲ Franklin flew a kite during a thunderstorm—a very dangerous thing to do—and proved that lightning is electricity. The electricity passed from a metal spike on the kite down the string to a metal key, where it produced sparks. He also invented the lightning rod, bifocal glasses, and a smokeless stove.

Freeze-drying

Freeze-drying is a process used in FOOD PRESERVATION. One of the disadvantages of preserving food by drying it is that the flavor and appearance of the food can be impaired. The quality of the food can be improved if the drying time can be reduced as much as possible. One way is to freeze the food quickly in a VACUUM. Freeze-drying is particularly successful with meat products. When a piece of meat is frozen in a vacuum, water in the meat cells turns to ice and then, because of the vacuum, it turns into VAPOR. The ice formed in the meat cells has sublimed, gone from solid to vapor without becoming liquid in between.

 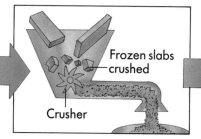 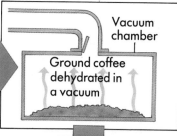

Freezing

Freezing describes the conversion of a material from its liquid or vapor state into its solid state by reducing its TEMPERATURE. Water, for example, normally exists as a liquid. If it is cooled, it eventually begins to change into a solid, ice. If ice is heated, it changes back to liquid. The temperature at which a material changes from a solid to a liquid is called its MELTING POINT.

Freezing is widely used in FOOD PRESERVATION. Frozen food does not decompose because the organisms responsible for spoiling food cannot grow in very low temperatures. A freezer uses a HEAT PUMP to transfer HEAT from the freezer compartment to its warmer surroundings. Food was preserved in ancient Rome by packing it in ice, but the widespread use of freezing as a method of food preservation was not possible until the invention of REFRIGERATION in 1858 and a quick freezing process developed in the 1920s. Domestic freezers can now store food safely for several months or up to a year, depending on the freezer's temperature and whether the food is fresh or already frozen.

▲ Freeze-dried instant coffee is made by freezing freshly made coffee extract into slabs. The slabs are ground and put into a vacuum chamber. Moisture in the form of ice is drawn off and dry crystals are left.

The freezing point of nearly all liquids is lowered by adding another substance. This is shown dramatically when an antifreeze containing ethanediol (ethylene glycol) is added to the water in a car's cooling system. The water freezes at 32°F (0°C), the ethanediol freezes at 9°F (−13°C), but a mixture of equal parts of water and ethanediol freezes at −35°F (−37°C)!

◀ Large woolly mammoths were common a million years ago. Dozens of deep-frozen mammoths have been dug up in almost perfect condition. This baby mammoth was found in Siberia in 1977. Dogs present at the dig tried to eat the mammoth flesh, which still smelled fresh.

FREEZING POINTS	
Carbon	6,422°F (3,550°C)
Copper	1,981°F (1,082.7°C)
Lead	621.4°F (327.4°C)
Tin	449.4°F (231.9°C)
Silver	1,761.4°F (960.8°C)
Mercury	−38.02°F (−38.9°C)

Heinrich Hertz (1857–1894)
Hertz was a German scientist. He was the first person to broadcast and receive radio waves. In 1883 he began working on electromagnetic radiation. He produced radio waves by using a rapidly oscillating electronic spark and was able to measure their velocity and their wavelength. This confirmed the theory developed by James Clerk Maxwell. The unit of frequency, the hertz, was named after him. One hertz (1 Hz), is equivalent to one cycle or oscillation per second.

Freezing point

The freezing point of a substance is the TEMPERATURE at which it changes from a LIQUID to a SOLID. For pure substances consisting of a single element or a simple compound, the freezing point is the same as the MELTING POINT. Different substances have widely differing freezing points. The element bromine, which is a volatile liquid at room temperature, freezes at 19°F (−7°C). Iron has a freezing point of 2,802°F (1,539°C). Pure water freezes at 32°F (0°C). But impure water freezes at a lower temperature. Water in a vehicle engine is stopped from FREEZING in winter by the addition of ANTIFREEZE, which lowers the freezing point to about −35°F (−37°C).

Frequency

Frequency is a measure of how often a process repeats itself. Frequency is used to describe the motion of waves, in which case it states how often a complete cycle of the WAVE MOTION is gone through in a certain time. The SI UNIT of frequency is the HERTZ (Hz) which corresponds to one wave cycle every second. Electromagnetic waves of a wide range of frequencies are used; RADIO waves have frequencies of a few hundred thousand hertz or a few million hertz; LIGHT waves have frequencies of a several hundred trillion hertz. Sound waves, which are waves of vibration in the air, have much lower frequencies than light; we can hear SOUND frequencies between about 50 Hz and 20,000 Hz. Musical notes correspond to different frequencies; "middle C" has a frequency of 256 Hz.

The frequency of a wave is related to its WAVELENGTH; the wavelength multiplied by the frequency gives the speed of the wave, so for a given speed higher frequency waves have shorter wavelengths.

▶ Frequency (pitch) of sound is determined by the number of air vibrations per second. The greater the number of complete wave cycles, the higher the frequency and the higher the pitch. The loudness of a sound depends on the amplitude, the height of the waves.

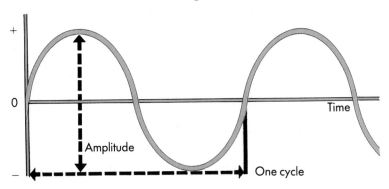

268

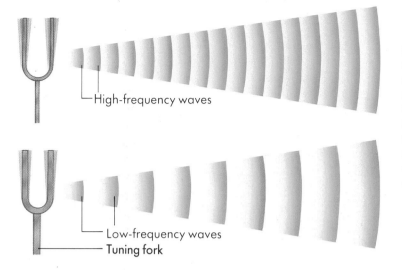

High-frequency waves

Low-frequency waves

Tuning fork

◀ *High notes have higher frequencies than low notes. The top tuning fork makes a note that is one octave (eight notes) higher than the note made by the bottom tuning fork. The note made by the top tuning fork has double the frequency of the bottom tuning fork. For example, C above middle C, is 512 Hz and middle C is 256 Hz.*

Frequency modulation *See* Radio

Freud, Sigmund

Sigmund Freud was born in Freiberg, then a part of the Austrian empire, in 1856. He was a neurologist who pioneered psychoanalysis, a technique for examining the motivations and hidden activities of the mind. Studying in Paris, Freud noted that, in patients suffering from hysteria, physical illness could also appear. This association of mind with body led him to study patients with mental disorders, and to develop psychoanalysis, in which patients were encouraged to tell him their dreams and deepest thoughts. Freud would prompt them to reconsider their dreams and earliest memories, in the belief that these had an effect on their current behavior. In the early 20th century, his theories became extremely popular, having a lasting effect on art, literature, education, and social attitudes. He died in London in 1939 after escaping from Nazi Germany.

▲ *Freud is famous for his much debated theory, in which he said that unconscious motives control much of our behavior.*

Friction

Friction is a FORCE which tends to stop objects sliding past each other. For example, if you try to push a heavy box of books across the floor, you have to push hard to overcome the friction between the box and the floor. Friction can be useful; for example, the friction between our shoes and the ground stops our feet sliding from under us when we push back with our feet to walk forward. Without friction, we could not walk or run. A car uses the friction between its tires and the road in a

Friction can be a problem in machines, which need bearings and lubrication to overcome it. But friction also has important uses.
• It makes a railroad locomotive's wheels grip the smooth steel rails.
• It makes car tires grip the road surface.
• It makes the soles of our shoes grip the ground when we walk.
• It allows a conveyor belt to run on pulley wheels without slipping.
• It makes nails stay in wood when they are hammered in.

▶ *A vehicle's brakes rely on friction. In a disc brake, hydraulic pressure forces friction pads to squeeze a metal disc that rotates on the same axle as the wheel. Here a disc brake is being tested. The force of the friction is so great that the disc brake had become hot and is glowing. Parts of machines that may have to be subjected to high temperatures are often made of special heat-resistant metals or other materials.*

similar way. Friction can also cause problems; if two moving parts of a machine rub each other, the friction can cause them to wear away and become damaged. Friction and wear can be reduced by LUBRICATION, coating the surface with a substance such as oil which enables sliding to take place more easily. Ball BEARINGS or roller bearings are used in machines so that surfaces do not rub against each other.

Friction causes ENERGY to be lost in the form of HEAT because as materials rub together the molecules they are made of vibrate, producing heat energy.

> Friction causes wasted energy in all machines. About one-fifth of the power used in the average car engine is wasted by friction of the moving parts.

SEE FOR YOURSELF
Arrange a selection of objects in a line along a piece of smooth wooden board. Among the objects include an ice cube, an eraser, and a toy car. Take hold of one end of the board and gradually lift it. Make a note of which objects move first. The objects that move more easily do so because there is less friction between their outer surface (which is smooth) and the surface of the board.

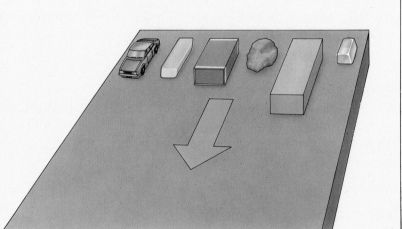

Front, weather

A weather front is the boundary between two masses of AIR at different TEMPERATURES and PRESSURES. One result of the difference in air pressure and temperature between two contrasting air masses is that the wind speed

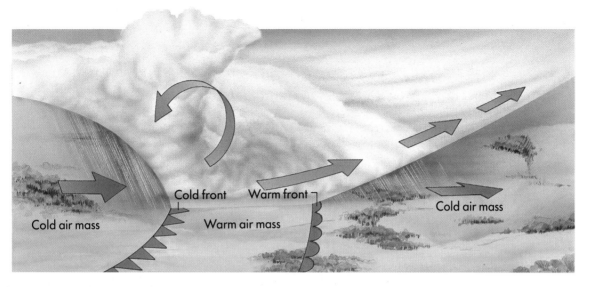

▲ A mass of warm air is enclosed between areas of cold air. At the warm air front (shown on a weather map by a curved line with solid semicircles on it), warm air rises over the cold air front (shown by a line with solid triangles), forming clouds.

◄ Thunderstorms occur when warm air, lying over a thin wedge of cold air, starts to rise quickly as the cold front advances.

may change markedly over a short distance.

There are three different kinds of front. In a warm front, the mass of warmer air moves over the mass of cooler air. As the warm front passes, the air temperature rises, rainfall decreases and, in the Northern Hemisphere, the wind veers southwest. In a cold front, cold air is moving under the mass of warm air. A cold front may bring with it a fall in air temperature and brighter weather with the wind, in the Northern Hemisphere, veering northwest. An occluded front forms when a warm front is overtaken by a cold one and the warm air is forced up.

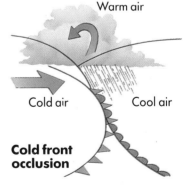

▲ Occluded fronts (shown by alternate solid semicircles and triangles) are a sandwich of cold air with warm air in the middle or cold air sandwiched by warm air.

Fruit

A fruit is the part of a plant which contains the SEEDS. Fruits develop from the carpels of FLOWERS, usually after FERTILIZATION. The fruits protect the seeds in the early stages, and when the seeds are ripe the fruits often help to scatter them. *See* pages 272 and 273.

FRUIT

The objects pictured below are all fruits. Ripe fruits are of two main kinds, dry and juicy. The poppy capsule and the pea pod are dry fruits with several or many seeds. They split open when they are ripe to allow the seeds to escape. The acorn is a single-seeded dry fruit and it does not split open: the germinating seeds simply force their way through the fruit walls. Tomatoes and summer squash are berries. Berries are juicy fruits containing several seeds. The cherry is a drupe, also called a stone fruit because the inner layer of the fruit forms a woody "stone." The blackberry is a cluster of very small drupes, each containing a tiny stone. The actual seeds, often called kernels, are inside the stones. Apples and pears belong to a fruit type called "pomes." These are fruits with a fleshy outer layer and a paperlike core that contains a number of seeds. Many of the juicy fruits that we eat are specially cultivated and much larger than their wild ancestors as a result of special breeding. Many of what we call vegetables are actually fruits, including green beans.

Most plants have developed ways of scattering their seeds so that they do not all fall under the parent plant. The hooked burs of some plants contain many small fruits, which gradually fall out as the burs are carried around by animals.

▲ *The seeds of the poppy develop in the poppy's dry fruits, or capsules.*

▼ *Some fruits, including pea pods, explode when they are ripe and throw out their seeds. The fruits of some waterside plants float away on the water, but most plants use animals or the wind to scatter their seeds. Maple fruits spiral to the ground and can be blown far from their parent tree. Other fruits rely on being eaten by animals and having their seeds deposited far from the parent plant.*

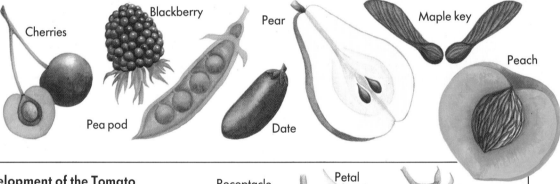

Development of the Tomato
Tomatoes are typical fruits of the type known as berries. This type also includes oranges, lemons, bananas, melons, and grapes, but only a very few of the fruits with "berry" in their names. Tomatoes develop from clusters of small yellow flowers. After the flowers are pollinated (usually by insects) the ovule begins to swell as the seeds develop inside the fleshy pericarp. The whole process takes 40 to 75 days.

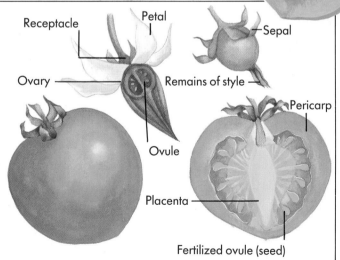

Ovary The hollow structure near the base of a flower where the seeds of the fruit are held.
Pericarp The three layers of the wall of an ovary of a mature fruit.
Simple fruit This type of fruit develops from a single ovary.
Compound fruit This type of fruit develops from two or more ovaries.
Receptacle The top of the stalk of a flower.

▼ *The acorn is a single-seeded dry fruit. The germinating seed forces its way through the fruit wall. The summer squash is a berry—a juicy fruit containing several seeds.*

Acorn

Squash

▲ *The coco de mer is a large kind of coconut. It is dropped from its parent palm onto the shore and is light enough to float to different islands.*

▼ *Fruits develop in the ovaries of the plant's flower. The apple, like the pear, is a type of fruit called a pome.*

SEE FOR YOURSELF
Cut an apple in half and look at its structure. Apples have a fleshy outer layer and a paper-like core which encloses two or more seeds. Compare the apple with other fruits, such as a peach, which is a fleshy fruit with a hard inner stone that encloses a single seed.

▼ *Bananas are odd-shaped berries. Wild bananas have seeds, but the cultivated ones we eat, which are hybrids, seldom have seeds because they are infertile.*

Banana

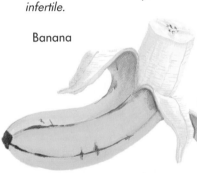

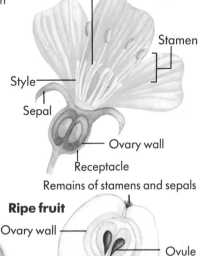

Stigma

Apple

Stamen

Style

Sepal

Ovary wall

Receptacle

Remains of stamens and sepals

Ripe fruit

Ovary wall

Ovule

Receptacle

See also BOTANY; BREEDING; CELL DIVISION; EGGS; FERTILIZATION; GROWTH; HYBRID; POLLEN AND POLLINATION; REPRODUCTION; SEEDS.

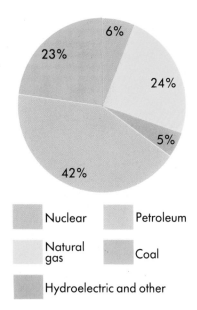

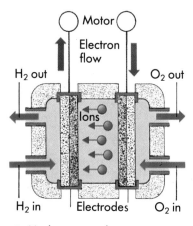

▲ *This chart shows that petroleum is now the leading source of energy in the United States. Coal was once the main source of energy.*

▶ *Since the 1970s, the shortage of some fuels has led to world exploitation of other sources of energy. Nuclear power is one such example.*

▲ *Hydrogen and oxygen are pumped into a cell where they are made to react by a catalyst in the electrodes. This reaction produces electricity, with water as a by-product.*

274

Fuel

A fuel is a material that has ENERGY stored inside it. When a fuel is burned, the energy is released as HEAT and it can be used to power MACHINES and ENGINES. The most widely used fuels are materials that were living organisms millions of years ago. These fuels are called FOSSIL FUELS. Coal, oil, and gas were all formed from layers of decomposing organisms which gradually became covered in layers of rocks and other deposits. The energy they absorbed from the Sun can be released by burning them. The most convenient form of energy is ELECTRICITY, but it is also a very inefficient use of fossil fuel because when electricity is made in power stations, over two-thirds of the energy in the coal or oil is lost as heat to the atmosphere. Nuclear reactors use a different

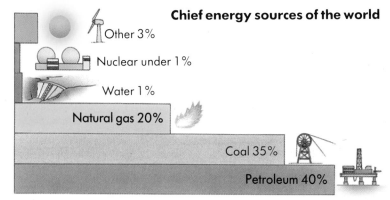

Chief energy sources of the world

Other 3%

Nuclear under 1%

Water 1%

Natural gas 20%

Coal 35%

Petroleum 40%

source of energy. They are fueled by unstable materials such as URANIUM and PLUTONIUM. These ATOMS continually split apart, releasing large amounts of energy. This is used to generate steam to drive steam turbine power generators to produce electricity.

Fuel cell

A fuel cell is a device that generates ELECTRICITY by converting the chemical ENERGY stored in a FUEL directly into electrical energy. This is a very efficient form of energy conversion. Fuel cells are used to generate electricity on board manned spacecraft. Hydrogen fuel and oxygen are combined chemically in the fuel cell to produce electricity and, as a by-product, water. The fuel cell provides all the water the crew needs during a mission for drinking, washing, and rehydrating dehydrated (dried) food.

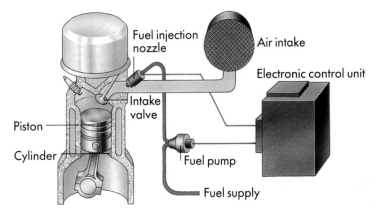

Fuel injection
nozzle

Air intake

Electronic control unit

Intake
valve

Piston

Cylinder

Fuel pump

Fuel supply

◄ *In a fuel injection system, fuel is sprayed into a chamber where it is mixed with air. A valve opens and admits the mixture to the cylinder. This process is computer controlled in new cars.*

Fuel injection

Fuel injection is a way of feeding FUEL to an INTERNAL-COMBUSTION ENGINE by pumping it into the ENGINE'S cylinders instead of sucking it in by the action of the pistons. In a gasoline engine without fuel injection, a valve is opened to a cylinder and the piston moves down inside the cylinder. A spray of fuel supplied by the carburetor is sucked into the cylinder. Fuel injection is more efficient than a carburetor because it distributes fuel more evenly to all the cylinders. In DIESEL ENGINES fuel injectors are also used to spray fuel into the cylinders. Engines with no pistons, such as gas turbines, cannot operate without a fuel injection system.

Fuse

A fuse is a device for protecting electric CIRCUITS and the people who use them. Every circuit needs an electric current to operate. If the circuit or its ELECTRICITY supply develop a fault, too much current may flow and damage the circuit or cause a fire. A fuse is placed in the electrical supply line to prevent this. The most commonly used type of fuse is a length of thin wire inside a glass tube between two metal end caps. When a circuit operates correctly, the fuse allows current to pass through. If the current rises, the fuse wire heats up and melts, or "blows," breaking the circuit. Thicker fuse wire allows a higher current to flow before it breaks. Fuses are available with different current "ratings." Some homes are fitted with CIRCUIT BREAKERS instead of fuses. These can be reset like a switch after a current overload.

Fusion, nuclear *See* Nuclear physics

SEE FOR YOURSELF
Make a circuit that includes a 4.5-volt battery, a 3.5-volt bulb and a switch. Using tape, attach a strand of fine steel wool to the circuit. Close the switch. After a few seconds the wire breaks and the bulb goes out. The steel wool does not conduct electricity as easily as the thicker wires in the circuit, so like a fuse it gets hot and breaks.

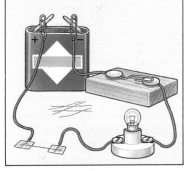

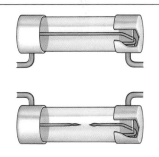

The wire in the bottom fuse has been melted by the heat of too large a current. Fuses are made in a variety of current ratings. Some can carry only a fraction of an amp, others can carry hundreds of amps. It is very important to fit the correct fuse to each appliance.

▶ *Spiral galaxies contain old stars but also large numbers of young stars, gas, and dust.*

▼ *Galaxies are different shapes. The Milky Way is a spiral galaxy, with arms wrapped around its nucleus or center. It takes about 225 million years to spin around once. Another type of spiral galaxy is known as a barred spiral galaxy. Elliptical galaxies are like spirals that have lost their arms, while some galaxies are irregular with no particular shape.*

Irregular galaxy

Elliptical galaxy

Spiral galaxy

Barred spiral galaxy

Galaxy

Stars occur in galaxies, independent "star cities" which formed soon after the UNIVERSE came into existence about 15 billion years ago. To begin with, the galaxies were just huge clouds of gas, mainly HYDROGEN. Then GRAVITY pulled the gas together into separate clouds that heated up and began to shine as STARS.

The stars that first formed have now cooled and dimmed, but new stars are still being born inside most galaxies. In our own galaxy, the Milky Way, there are huge clouds of hydrogen mixed with specks of solid matter, such as carbon, which may one day form stars.

Galaxies range from "dwarfs," with perhaps a million stars, to "supergiants," with perhaps a million million. The Milky Way has about 100 billion stars.

Galaxies occur in clusters. There are about 30 in the Milky Way's cluster, but some clusters contain hundreds. These clusters, in turn, may belong to "superclusters." The clusters of galaxies are flying apart from each other as the universe expands from the BIG BANG.

Galileo Galilei

Galileo (1564–1642), who lived in Italy, is remembered as the first person to turn a TELESCOPE to the sky and make important astronomical discoveries. He observed craters on the MOON, the bright satellites of JUPITER, SUNSPOTS, and other things.

He made himself unpopular because he lived at a time when belief about the world and the UNIVERSE was based on the Bible and on ARISTOTLE's teachings of 2,000 years earlier. For example, Aristotle had said that a heavy weight fell more quickly than a light one, but Galileo showed that they both fell at the same speed. The Bible said that everything moves around the Earth, but Galileo's observations showed that the Earth moves around the Sun. He was imprisoned and ended his life near Florence under "house arrest."

▲ In 1992, the Vatican admitted that the Roman Catholic Church had been wrong in condemning Galileo's ideas!

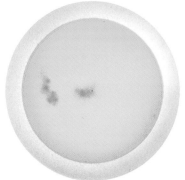

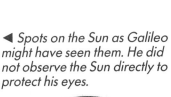

◀ Spots on the Sun as Galileo might have seen them. He did not observe the Sun directly to protect his eyes.

▶ Galileo observed objects circling Jupiter. The four largest moons of Jupiter are known as the Galilean Satellites.

▲ Galileo built several telescopes. He built the first in 1609. With his telescopes Galileo saw that the Moon was not smooth and perfect as generally believed, but that it was covered with mountains and craters. Galileo also discovered that a pendulum could be used to measure time. He found this out by watching a hanging lamp swinging in Pisa Cathedral. He realized that it took exactly the same time for each swing, whether the swings were large or small.

Galvani, Luigi *See* Galvanometer

Galvanizing

Galvanizing is an industrial process for rustproofing IRON AND STEEL by covering the metal with a thin layer of ZINC. It can be done in two ways: dipping and electrodeposition. In dipping, the metal is cleaned by dipping it in acid and then dipped into a bath of molten zinc. When it is taken out, it is covered by a thin layer of zinc. Alternatively, iron and steel can be galvanized by an electrical method. Two electrodes, a positive anode and a negative cathode, are dipped into a SOLUTION, or electrolyte, containing zinc, for example, zinc sulfate. The

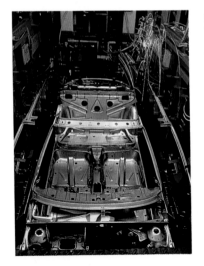

object to be galvanized is connected to the cathode. When the current flows, zinc ions from the solution are deposited over the cathode and the object connected to it. This is called ELECTROLYSIS. The thickness of the zinc coating depends on the time spent in the electrolyte.

Galvanometer

A galvanometer is a device for measuring the electric current flowing in a CIRCUIT. It uses Michael FARADAY's discovery that a wire carrying a current in a magnetic field experiences a FORCE. The current which is to be measured is passed through a coil of fine wire which is pivoted between the poles of a magnet. When the current passes through the coil, the coil becomes a magnet and tries to turn itself into line with the poles of the magnet. Springs attached to the coil hold it steady. A pointer or mirror is attached to the coil and enables the

▲ The steel shell of a car is galvanized, coated with a layer of zinc alloy, which protects it from corrosion.

Luigi Galvani (1737–1798)
Galvani was an Italian scientist. He is known for his experiments showing the effects of electricity on living tissue, particularly on muscles. He discovered that touching the nerves in a dead frog's leg with a pair of scissors during a thunderstorm caused the muscles to twitch. Galvani believed that he had discovered a new type of electricity, animal electricity, but Alessandro Volta showed that this was not the case. Galvani's name lives on in the "galvanometer" and in the word "galvanized."

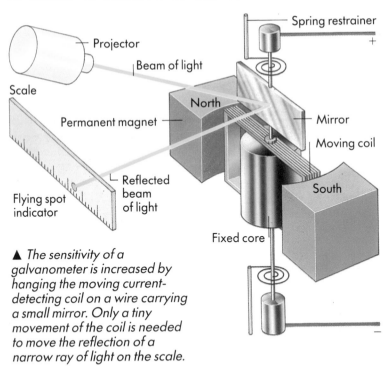

▲ The sensitivity of a galvanometer is increased by hanging the moving current-detecting coil on a wire carrying a small mirror. Only a tiny movement of the coil is needed to move the reflection of a narrow ray of light on the scale.

current flowing to be read from a scale. The electrical RESISTANCE of the galvanometer is very small so that it does not affect the current.

Galvanometers are now being replaced by more accurate DIGITAL instruments.

Gamma rays *See* Radioactivity

Gas

Gas is one of the three STATES OF MATTER, the others being SOLID and LIQUID. The tiny MOLECULES that make up matter are in constant motion. In a gas, the molecules are more loosely held together than they are in a solid or liquid. In a gas, they can move around freely. Thus, a gas will always expand to fill its container. It takes its shape from its container but does not take up a definite amount of space (that is, it has no fixed volume). Released from its container, it will go on expanding. The molecules in a gas move rapidly and randomly and bump into each other and into the inside of the container, exerting PRESSURE on it.

If the same amount of gas is put into a container half

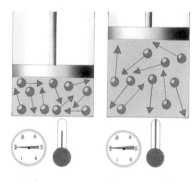

Pressure gauge   Temperature gauge

▲ Gas pressure doubles if its volume is halved and its temperature remains constant.

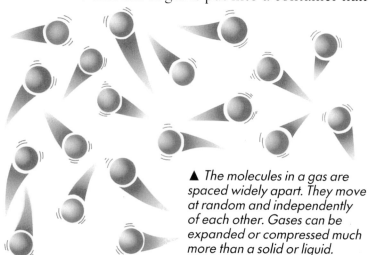

▲ The molecules in a gas are spaced widely apart. They move at random and independently of each other. Gases can be expanded or compressed much more than a solid or liquid.

▲ The pressure of gas stays the same if the temperature and the volume double. The rise in temperature makes the molecules move faster but in more space.

Gay-Lussac was a French chemist. In 1802, working independently, he repeated the discovery that another chemist, Jacques Charles, had already made about the constant expansion of gases with each degree rise in temperature. Gay-Lussac later showed that, when gaseous elements combine to form compounds, they do so in proportions by volume that can be expressed as simple whole numbers. For example, forming water, two parts by volume of hydrogen combine with one part by volume of oxygen.

Joseph Louis Gay-Lussac (1778–1850)

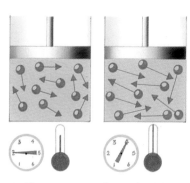

▲ The pressure of gas doubles if the volume remains the same and the temperature doubles. The rise in temperature causes the molecules to move faster in the same space.

**Jacques Charles
(1746–1823)**
Charles was a French chemist who was also a teacher and a minor government official. Charles is best known for stating the law that every gas expands by the same amount for a rise in temperature of one degree. This means that the volume of a fixed amount of gas is directly proportional to the temperature if the pressure remains constant. Charles did not publish his research, and it was later duplicated by Gay-Lussac. He was also interested in ballooning and suggested balloons could be filled with the very light hydrogen gas.

the size, the pressure of the gas doubles, as long as the TEMPERATURE remains unchanged. If, however, a gas is heated, the molecules will move faster and farther apart. If the gas is prevented from expanding by its container, its pressure on the container will increase. If a gas is cooled enough, it will become a liquid. If gases are squeezed during cooling, they become liquid at a temperature above their BOILING POINT.
See also NATURAL GAS.

Gas turbine

A gas turbine is a type of INTERNAL COMBUSTION ENGINE used by many aircraft, ships, and some tanks. It was invented in the 1940s during World War II (1939–1945) by the British engineer, Frank Whittle. It works by burning fuel in compressed air like a piston engine, but it has no pistons. Beyond a certain upper speed limit, piston engines risk shaking themselves apart. In a gas turbine, the expanding COMBUSTION gases are used to drive a TURBINE. This can power the compressor that sucks air into the engine and compresses it before it leaves the engine as a jet of hot gas. This gives the engine its popular name, the turbojet or jet engine. In the turboprop engine, the turbine drives a propeller. In a turboshaft

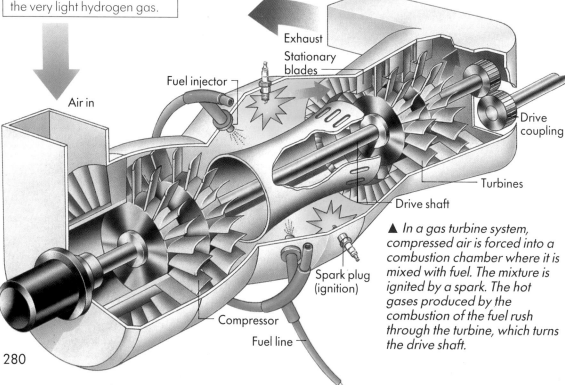

Air in

Exhaust
Stationary blades
Fuel injector
Drive coupling
Turbines
Drive shaft
Spark plug (ignition)
Compressor
Fuel line

▲ *In a gas turbine system, compressed air is forced into a combustion chamber where it is mixed with fuel. The mixture is ignited by a spark. The hot gases produced by the combustion of the fuel rush through the turbine, which turns the drive shaft.*

engine, the turbine drives a shaft that may power a tank's tracks or a helicopter's rotors.
See also JET PROPULSION.

Gasoline *See* Petroleum

Gay-Lussac, Joseph Louis *See* Gas

Gears

Gears are toothed wheels used in MACHINES to make one shaft turn another. The first wheel is called the driver and the second, the follower. Driver and follower rotate in opposite directions. If driver and follower are the same size, both shafts rotate at the same speed. Often one shaft is required to rotate more slowly or more quickly than the engine driving it. This can be achieved using gear wheels of different sizes. If a shaft fitted with a small driver drives a larger follower, the shaft from the follower rotates more slowly than the driver shaft. The opposite is also true. If the shafts need to rotate in the same direction, a third gear called an idler can be inserted between the driver and follower. In a car, gears are used to enable it to travel at a range of speeds. The engine is only connected directly to the road wheels in the highest gear.

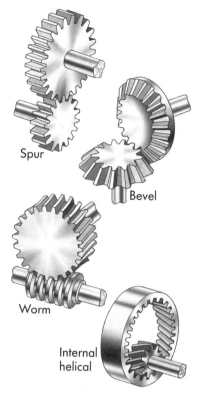

Spur
Bevel
Worm
Internal helical

▲ *These are some common types of gears. Gear teeth are specially constructed to fit smoothly, reducing wear and tear, vibration, and noise.*

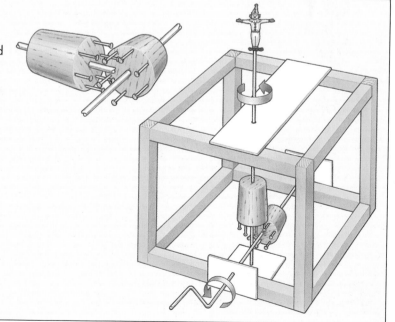

SEE FOR YOURSELF
Make a frame out of wood or use a cardboard box. Take two corks and stick six evenly spaced pins into each of them to make gears. Push fine knitting needles through each of the corks. Insert the ends of the knitting needles into pieces of stiff cardboard to hold them in place. Attach a handle to one end of the horizontal knitting needle and a small shape to the top of the vertical knitting needle. Make sure the pins on each of the gears overlap. By turning the handle on the horizontal shaft counterclockwise, the vertical shaft is caused to turn counterclockwise.

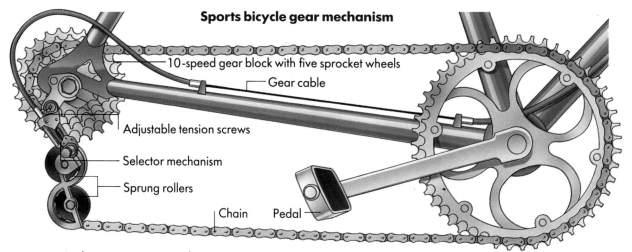

Sports bicycle gear mechanism

10-speed gear block with five sprocket wheels

Gear cable

Adjustable tension screws

Selector mechanism

Sprung rollers

Chain   Pedal

▲ In this gear system used on a racing bicycle, the selector moves the chain to a different sprocket wheel.

▼ Radiation entering a Geiger counter tube causes gas atoms inside it to ionize. This releases electrons which create electric pulses that are counted by a meter.

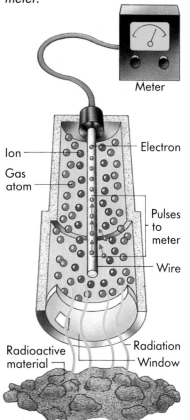

Meter

Ion

Gas atom

Electron

Pulses to meter

Wire

Radioactive material

Radiation

Window

Geiger counter

A Geiger counter is an instrument designed to detect and measure RADIOACTIVITY. It was invented in 1908 by the German scientist, Hans Geiger, for whom it is named. It consists of a sealed tube with one fine wire electrode running down the middle. The tube itself is the other electrode. The tube, filled with a GAS such as argon, is charged to a very high voltage, perhaps 1,000 volts. If an atomic particle enters the tube, it "ionizes" the gas, that is, it splits the electrically neutral gas into positively charged IONS and negatively charged ELECTRONS. The positive ions rush to one electrode and the electrons to the other electrode. This triggers a momentary electric current from one electrode to the other. The number of atomic particles detected by the counter can be displayed on a scale or as a series of audible clicks.

Gemstones *See* Minerals

Generator, electric

An electric generator is a machine that converts mechanical motion into an electrical current. Generators work by using the principle of electromagnetic INDUCTION discovered by FARADAY. Coils of wire are mounted so that they can be spun around in a magnetic field. This means that the magnetic field is pointing first one way through the coils, then the other; the changing magnetic field produces a current around the coil. This type of generator is called an *alternator* because the increase and

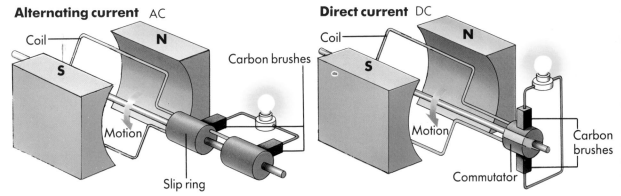

Alternating current AC

Coil

N

S

Carbon brushes

Motion

Slip ring

Direct current DC

Coil

N

S

Motion

Commutator

Carbon brushes

decrease of the magnetic field produces an alternating CURRENT. To generate a direct current (always in the same direction), the coil has to be connected to a *commutator*. The commutator makes the current flow continuously in one direction.

Mechanical ENERGY is needed to turn the coil to create electrical energy. The ELECTRICITY we use is generated by power plants; usually the energy from burning coal or from a nuclear reaction is used to make steam, which drives a TURBINE to produce the mechanical energy to turn the generator coils around. Large generators have efficiencies as high as 97 percent—97 percent of the mechanical energy used is turned into electrical energy.

▲ *These are two simple generators, an alternating current (AC) and a direct current (DC) generator. Inside each type of generator is a wire coil, which is held between the two poles of a magnet. When the wire coil turns in the magnetic field, electricity is produced in the wire. The magnetic force makes electrons in the wire coil move, generating an electric current. An AC generator is joined to the rest of the circuit by a slip ring and carbon brushes. The DC generator has a device, called a commutator, for reversing or altering the electric current. This insures that the current always flows the same way instead of alternating — flowing in one direction and then the other.*

Direct current (DC) generator

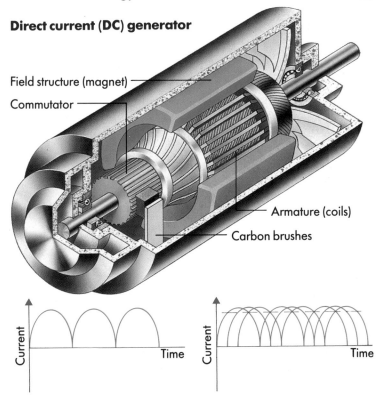

Field structure (magnet)

Commutator

Armature (coils)

Carbon brushes

Current

Time

Current

Time

◄ *The output values of a direct current generator, with a single coil, vary as the electromotive force changes direction. Because of this, commercial generators have several coils wound around the armature so that an almost constant amount of electricity can be produced. Each coil is connected to its own segment at the commutator.*

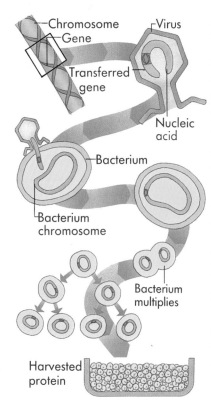

Genetic engineering

Genetic engineering is a form of BIOTECHNOLOGY in which the genes of an organism are deliberately altered in order to change its characteristics. A simple example is the development of genetically engineered grapefruit. The genes of an ordinary grapefruit were changed by exposing them to radiation, causing changes or MUTATIONS, which resulted in pink-fleshed grapefruit that taste sweeter than normal. In this case the results depended largely upon luck, but deliberate genetic engineering can make very dramatic changes. For example, genes controlling the production of insulin in humans or animals can be inserted into a bacterium which is easily grown and harvested, so the "human" insulin produced can be used to treat people with diabetes. Bacteria and yeasts are usually used for this type of genetic engineering because their genetic structure is well known and they can be easily grown in the laboratory by FERMENTATION.

Food crops are also produced by genetic engineering, and special types are being developed which resist DISEASE and grow faster than normal crops.

See also BREEDING; CHROMOSOMES AND GENES.

▲ *A protein-producing gene, such as that for insulin, is cut from human DNA. This is then spliced into the nucleic acid of a virus. The virus injects the nucleic acid into a bacterium. The gene becomes part of the bacterium's chromosome. This bacterium can now make insulin, which it couldn't make before. Many bacteria are grown together in a fermenter. The insulin they produce is separated and purified for use in treating diabetics.*

▶ *These false-colored molecules of bacterial DNA come from the bacterium Escherichia coli. "Foreign" DNA is joined to one of the molecules and the new molecule is then put into an Escherichia coli bacterium where it makes copies of the genetic information carried by the transplanted "foreign" DNA.*

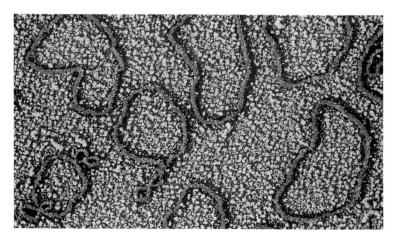

Geography

Geography was originally the study of the surface of the EARTH. Today, geography has been broadened to cover the study of the origins, formation, and landforms of the Earth, and the distribution of life upon it. Geography is sometimes divided into regional geography and systematic geography. *See pages 286 and 287.*

GENETICS

Genetics is based upon the scientific study of heredity. For centuries, farmers have carefully selected strains of livestock and crops and bred from them in order to improve their stock, to make them grow faster, or to develop some special characteristic. This was not done on a scientific basis, and it was often a matter of luck if the resulting animal or plant was better than its parents. The Austrian monk Gregor Mendel, experimenting with cross-breeding peas, was the first to deduce that some hereditary material came from both parents, and he laid down the simple rules that govern heredity in these plants. He published this information in 1866, but it was overlooked until 1900, when the science of genetics was just beginning. Since then, genetics has progressed very rapidly. Scientists are now able to understand much of the workings of the genetic material and to breed new strains of organisms with ease. This is the positive side of genetics, which has led to the development of crops yielding much more grain than was ever possible before, and sheep which routinely produce twins, and so double the farmers' output of lambs. Working at the microscopic level, the science of genetics is used to breed microorganisms which in turn will make useful substances such as protein and antibiotics. On the negative side, some people are worried that genetics could be misused, for example, to produce new diseases for biological warfare. Similarly, there are fears that new organisms produced by genetic engineering could escape into the environment and cause harm.

Barbara McClintock (1902–)
In 1983 McLintock was awarded the Nobel Prize for Physiology and Medicine for her discovery that some genes are able to change their position on the chromosomes. Earlier, she had shown that when eggs or sperm are produced the chromosomes can break apart and join up again in different ways, allowing different combinations of genes in the offspring.

▼ *Organisms have pairs of chromosomes that carry two genes for the same character. Often one is dominant and always shows its effects. Sometimes the two genes mix their effects as, for example, when a black female cat and a ginger male cat have kittens. Some will be tortoiseshell.*

▲ *This flower has a "jumping gene," which has changed the flower color to purple. The gene that controls the color of the flower is unstable and can move around. When this happens the color of the flower is changed.*

HEMOPHILIA

The hereditary disease hemophilia prevents blood from clotting normally. It is caused by a defective gene carried on the X chromosome, one of the two sex chromosomes. A male who inherits the defective gene suffers from the disease because he has only one X chromosome. A female who inherits the defective gene does not normally suffer from the disease because she has two X chromosomes and the hemophilia gene only shows effect when there is no normal blood clot gene present. But she may pass the disease to her children.

See also BIOTECHNOLOGY; BREEDING; CELL DIVISION; CHROMOSONES AND GENES; GENETIC ENGINEERING; HEREDITY; MICROORGANISMS.

GEOGRAPHY

Geography has its origins in the Greeks' attempts to describe the surface of the Earth on which they lived. Eratosthenes realized that the Earth was round in the 3rd century B.C. and 500 years later Ptolemy produced a map of the Earth which was used for centuries.

Modern geography is concerned with those aspects of the Earth's surface which could be described as the habitat occupied by the human species. Geography has many branches, some of which border other sciences very closely. As its name suggests, regional geography examines, on a regional basis, the ways in which the local people interact with the environment of the area in which they live. In its widest sense, systematic geography may include climatology (the study of weather and the climate), cartography (the study of maps and map projections), oceanography (the study of the seas and oceans), and even human geography and biogeography which deal with the distribution of people and their industries and systems of communications, as well as with the distribution of plants and animals.

Physical geography, which may also be called geomorphology, concentrates on the origins and formation of the landforms themselves, and often overlaps with aspects of geology, especially with regard to the processes of erosion and weathering or glaciation. The study of soils was also once lumped together with geography but, today, it is generally regarded as a separate discipline, called soil science. And human geography, of course, also overlaps the social sciences. Today, geographers are heavily involved with the actual planning of the cities, towns, and countryside in which we all live and work.

World population growth

- Asia
- Europe
- Africa
- South America
- C.I.S.
- North America
- Oceania
- World

▲ Since the 1800s, the world population has grown from one billion to over 5 billion. It is expected to double in the next 40 years.

SEE FOR YOURSELF

Go to the top of a small hill and look around you. If possible get a map of the area and see if you can identify the main features of the landscape on the map. Look for churches, the pattern of roads, railroads and rivers, woods, variations in land forms, and other dominant features.

EARTH FACTS

Highest mountain Mount Everest (summit 29,028 feet) on the borders of Tibet and Nepal in Asia.

Deepest ocean Marianas Trench in the Pacific Ocean (36,198 feet).

Longest river River Nile in Africa (4,145 miles).

Largest land mass If Europe and Asia are taken together their area is 20,732,818 square miles.

Largest island Greenland (839,768 square miles).

Largest lake Caspian Sea, C.I.S. (139,266 sq. miles).

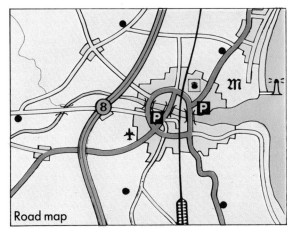

Road map

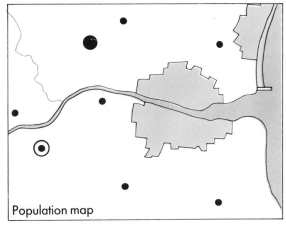

Population map

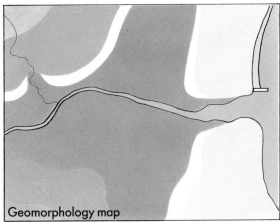

Geomorphology map

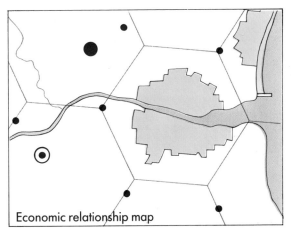

Economic relationship map

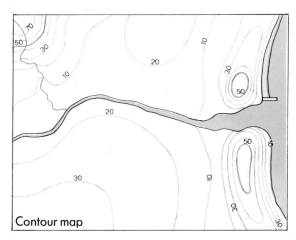

Contour map

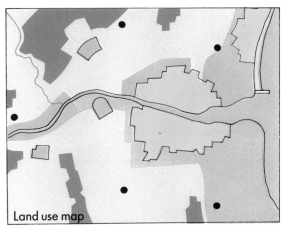

Land use map

▲ Different kinds of maps give us different kinds of information. They often present information in simplified form about an area. Symbols are used to represent features, such as railroad stations, airports, main roads and their junctions, bridges etc. Population maps show settlement sizes and distribution. Geomorphological maps show landforms and how they are made up. Economic maps show the environmental and human factors that affect the development and growth of a region. Contour maps are made up of lines (contours) that join points of equal height and show the physical features on the land. Today, contour maps are often produced from aerial photographs. Land use maps show the location of housing, farmland, woodland, and other vegetation.

See also CLIMATE; COMMUNICATIONS; EARTH; ENVIRONMENT; GEOLOGY; LANDFORMS; MAP; MAP PROJECTION; SOIL; STATISTICS; WEATHER.

GEOLOGY

Geology is the study of the Earth, its history as a planet, its composition, structure, and the changes it undergoes, especially as reflected in the rocks of which it is made. The study of the Moon in this way is called lunar geology.

   Like so many sciences today, geology is usually divided into separate branches and it overlaps with other disciplines, such as geography. Geologists study: fossils and ancient life forms (paleontology); the chemistry and physics of the Earth (geochemistry and geophysics); the composition and structure of rocks (petrology); the minerals that compose rocks (mineralogy); the layers or strata in which sedimentary rocks are deposited that reflect the geological history of the Earth (stratigraphy). Much of the pioneering work was carried out in the 19th century by workers such as Lyell, Murchison, Smith, Sedgewick and Geike, Buckland, and others. Some were amateurs, but they made important contributions by painstaking studies of cliff sections and quarries.

Era	Period	Epoch	Millions of years ago
CENOZOIC	Quaternary	Recent	
			0.01
		Pleistocene	
			2
	Tertiary	Pliocene	
			5
		Miocene	
			25
		Oligocene	
			35
		Eocene	
			60
		Paleocene	
			65
MESOZOIC	Cretaceous		
			145
	Jurassic		
			210
	Triassic		
			245
PALEOZOIC	Permian		
			285
	Carboniferous		
			360
	Devonian		
			410
	Silurian		
			440
	Ordovician		
			505
	Cambrian		
			570

Precambrian.
Time stretches back to the formation of the Earth 4.6 billion years ago

▲ Radioactive elements scattered through rocks have made it possible to determine their ages. Using this and the method of estimating the relative ages of rocks from the probable dates when they were formed, a general geological time scale has been worked out.

SEE FOR YOURSELF
Next time you visit a beach or an old quarry, see whether you can find different layers of rock in the cliffs. These may include sandstone, which is a streaky sandy color; clay, which is a dark reddish brown, and limestone, which is white.

Charles Lyell (1797–1875)
Lyell was a British scientist. He is often called the father of modern geology. In his book *Principles of Geology*, published between 1830 and 1833, he showed that the Earth has changed slowly and gradually through the ages by means of processes that are still going on. He was one of the first scientists to accept modern theories about the Ice Age and evolution.

See also FOSSILS; IGNEOUS ROCKS; METAMORPHIC ROCKS; MINERALS; PALEONTOLOGY; PLATE TECTONICS; ROCKS; SEDIMENTARY ROCKS.

Geomagnetism

Geomagnetism is the name given to the MAGNETISM of the EARTH. Like a planet-sized bar magnet, the Earth's magnetic field is oriented to give a magnetic North Pole and a magnetic South Pole. Magnetic North and South do not coincide exactly with the geographical poles and, because the Earth's magnetic field slowly changes (and even reverses over very long periods), the difference between magnetic and geographic north varies with time. A consequence of this is that MAPS must be adjusted to take account of such variations. It is thought that the Earth's magnetic field results from currents set up in the liquid outer core of the planet as it rotates.

Wilhelm Weber (1804–1891)
Weber was a German physicist known for his work on geomagnetism. He researched wave motion in 1824 and the mechanics of walking in 1833. The weber unit of magnetic flux (Wb) is named for him. A strong magnetic field may have a strength of two or more webers per square yard.

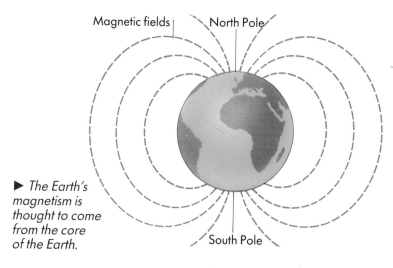

Magnetic fields | North Pole

South Pole

▶ *The Earth's magnetism is thought to come from the core of the Earth.*

Geometry

Geometry is the branch of MATHEMATICS that tells us about points, lines, curves, and surfaces, how they relate to each other, and how we measure them. It involves the study of plane (flat) figures, such as the square, triangle, and circle, and solid, three-dimensional figures, such as the cube, pyramid, and sphere. *Geometry* means "measurement of the Earth," and the first practical uses of it concerned the MEASUREMENT of land areas, such as fields. Today architects, builders, carpenters, civil engineers, navigators, artists, photographers, and jewelers rely on a knowledge of geometry to do their work.

Geometry accepts that certain definitions and statements (called axioms) are true and uses them to discover and prove or disprove other statements called theorems. *See also* ALGEBRA; ARITHMETIC; POLYGON; SYMMETRY.

Pythagoras (c. 560–480 B.C.)
Pythagoras was an ancient Greek philosopher and mathematician. He taught the importance of numbers, notably in music. His most famous work was in geometry. His famous Pythagorean Theorem states that in a right-angled triangle, the square on the hypotenuse (the side opposite the right angle) equals the sum of the squares on the other two sides.

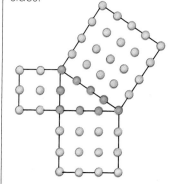

SEE FOR YOURSELF
Set a pair of compasses to a radius of 2 inches and draw a circle. Place the point of the compasses on the edge of the circle and draw another circle. Place the point of the compasses at the point where the second circle crosses the first circle and draw another circle. Continue until you have 7 circles. Connect up the points where the circles cross the edge of the first circle. You have a regular hexagon.

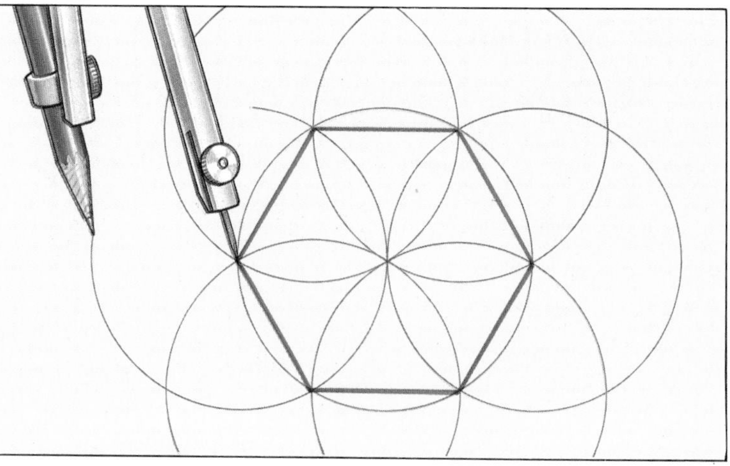

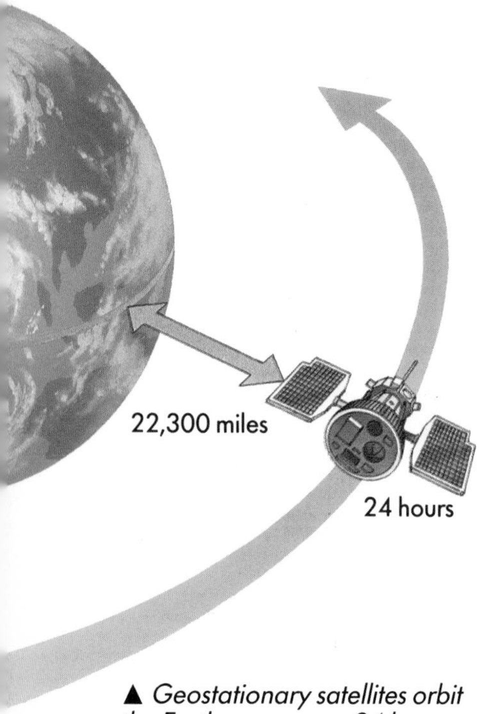

▲ *Geostationary satellites orbit the Earth once every 24 hours – the same time it takes the Earth to spin once on its axis, so that they remain in the same spot above the Earth's surface. They are used to receive telephone and television signals and retransmit them over long distances.*

Geostationary orbit

An artificial SATELLITE near the EARTH orbits faster than one far away. A satellite 22,300 miles (35,900 km) above the Earth's surface takes 24 hours to orbit once. Therefore it is always above the same point on the Earth's surface as our planet rotates. Geostationary orbit can also be called "geosynchronous" orbit.

Some kinds of radio waves are reflected around the Earth by the IONOSPHERE high in the ATMOSPHERE. But TELEVISION signals pass right through it and so geostationary satellites are used to transmit signals over long distances, for example, one over the Atlantic allows signals to pass between the United States and Europe.

Geothermal energy

Geothermal ENERGY is obtained by tapping the HEAT generated within the EARTH. It is noticeable descending into a deep mine that the temperature rises with depth. Heat generated beneath the Earth's crust is distributed through the crust by volcanic processes. If GROUNDWATER seeping deep within the crust should become trapped, it may be heated to form steam. By drilling a well, it is possible to harness this steam to drive electric GENERATORS.

Sometimes, water may not be hot enough to become steam but it is possible to use the hot water for domestic heating or in agriculture.

Geothermal energy is one of the kinds of "alternative energy." It is clean, but no one knows the effects on the Earth's system of tapping large amounts of energy.

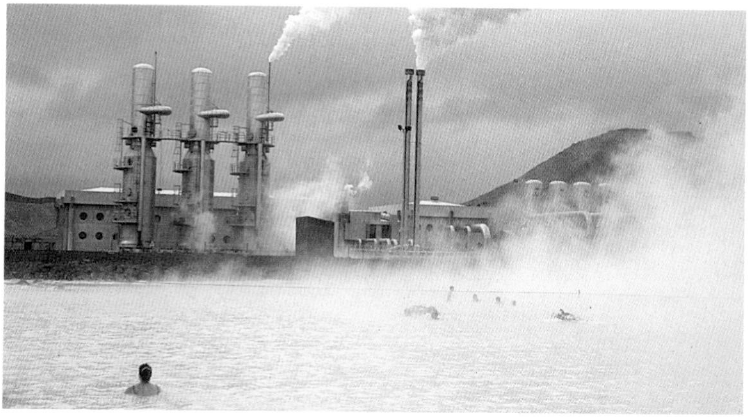

◀ *Geothermal power comes from water heated under the Earth's surface.*

▼ *Cold water seeps deep below ground until it reaches hot rocks. The water heats up, until some of it expands into steam, forcing out the rest in a rush of boiling water. This steam can be forced through a steam turbine to create power.*

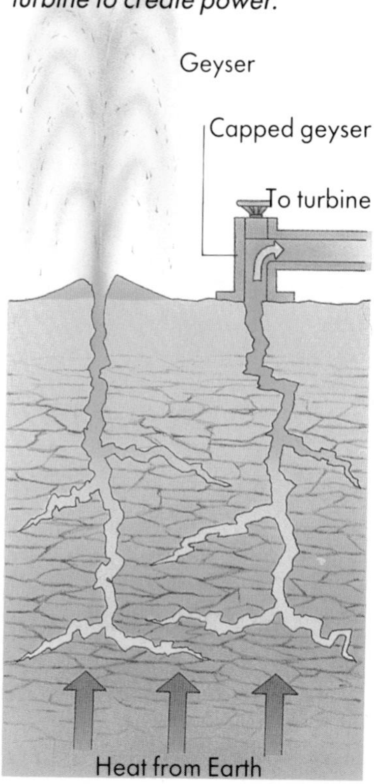
Geyser
Capped geyser
To turbine
Heat from Earth

Gestation

Gestation is the early development, from the time of FERTILIZATION to the moment of BIRTH. Before you were born, you spent about nine months growing inside your mother's body. Among mammals generally, the larger the animal the longer the gestation period, although there are some exceptions. Mammalian gestation periods range from about 18 days in some mice, to about 21 months in the Indian elephant. Domestic dogs and cats develop within the mother for about 2 months, and lions and tigers for about 3 months. Most other groups of animals lay EGGS, but some reptiles and amphibians, a number of fish, and some insects give birth to live young. The longest recorded gestation period is that of the Alpine salamander, which has been known to carry its babies for 38 months. Everything takes place very slowly in the cold mountain climate and the adults may only be active for three months in a year.

Gestation in Mammals
These vary, depending on the size of the mammal. The longer the gestation period the longer the offspring has to be taken care of by its parents.

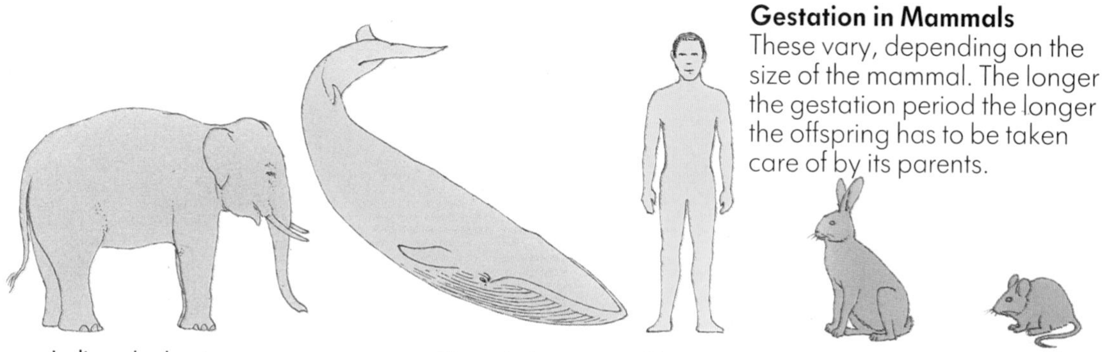
Indian elephant
18 – 23 months
Blue whale
12 months
Human
9 months
Hare
6 weeks
Mouse
18 days

▲ *This axolotl's external gills can be clearly seen. Oxygen from the water is transferred into the blood vessels of the gills and then into the body.*

Gilbert, William *See* Magnetism

Gills

All animals need to be able to obtain OXYGEN from the environment in which they live, and at the same time they must get rid of waste CARBON DIOXIDE. Land animals do this by extracting oxygen from the air with LUNGS or some similar organ. Animals which live in the water use gills. Gills have a mass of very fine BLOOD vessels exposed to water, allowing the transfer of oxygen and carbon dioxide. Simple gills are tufts of tissue containing blood vessels, such as are seen in young tadpoles. The tufts provide a large surface area for gas transfer. In fish, these gills are protected inside the head. Water is continuously pumped through the mouth past the gills, so they are always exposed to oxygen in the water.

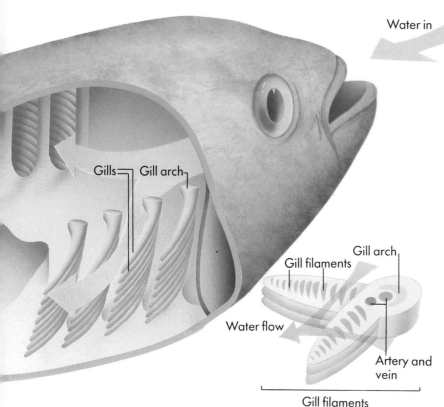

Water in

Gills Gill arch

Gill filaments

Gill arch

Water flow

Artery and vein

Gill filaments

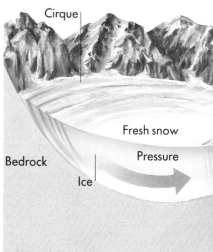

▼ *A glacier starts in a cirque, a bowl-shaped hollow near a mountain peak. The glacier picks up rocks and other debris and piles them up in ridges called moraines. The hilly ridge at the bottom of a glacier is called a terminal moraine. Glaciers move faster at the center than at the sides. This can create huge gaps or crevasses.*

Cirque

Fresh snow

Bedrock Pressure

Ice

▲ *Fish gills vary in form but all are designed to present the largest possible surface containing blood vessels to the water. Water enters through the*

mouth and flows over the gills and out through the gill slits. Gills are made of threadlike filaments attached to a gill arch. Most fish have four pairs of gills.

◄ *The Mendenhall glacier is a valley glacier. These are long, narrow bodies of ice that fill mountain valleys.*

▼ *When a glacier melts it leaves behind roches moutonnées, which are lumps of polished rock surfaces; rounded hills, called drumlins; and narrow ridges of rock debris, called eskers. Hollows in the loose rock trap water, forming meltwater and kettle lakes. A retreating glacier may leave great semicircular ridges in front of the outwash plain.*

Glacier

A glacier is a large body of ICE which may form in a MOUNTAIN valley or in an area where the volume of snow that falls in the cold season of the year is greater than the amount that melts during the warmer season. As the snow accumulates, the snow below is compressed and the spaces between the snowflakes are filled with ice. Ice is a solid material and, like most solids, it seems rigid. In fact, provided the temperature of the glacier is close to the MELTING POINT, the glacier is able to flow slowly downslope and to bend under its weight.

There are two main kinds of glaciers: the ice sheets of Antarctica which may reach thicknesses of 13,000 feet (4,000 m) and the ice which accumulates in snowy and mountainous areas, and flows slowly down the valley at speeds of between a foot and 50 feet per day.

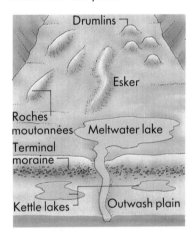

▼ *Rocks and other debris carried by the glacier are deposited as moraines. When glaciers meet they form a medial moraine.*

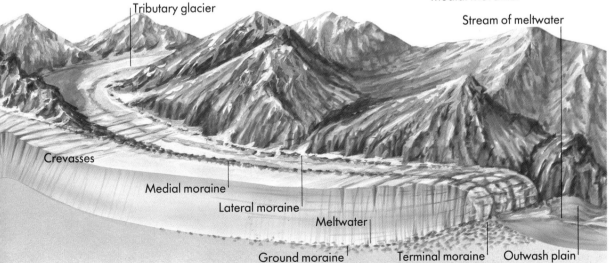

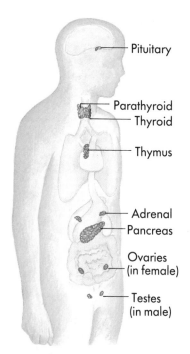

Pituitary

Parathyroid
Thyroid

Thymus

Adrenal
Pancreas

Ovaries
(in female)

Testes
(in male)

▲ *The positions of the major endocrine glands in the body.*

▼ *The sebaceous glands are the glands that lubricate the skin and hair.*

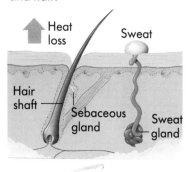

Heat loss

Sweat

Hair shaft

Sebaceous gland

Sweat gland

Glands

Glands are organs which produce secretions that are passed out of the gland to carry out their function elsewhere in the body. The secretions are made in special CELLS which are grouped into a gland. Sometimes these secretions are carried away through a duct. Other glands pass their secretions into the BLOOD, which circulates them around the body. These are called endocrine glands. Many glands pass their secretions into the gut, where they assist in DIGESTION. The stomach, duodenum, and small intestine are lined with glands which produce digestive ENZYMES. The pancreas is a large ducted gland which produces digestive enzymes but also secretes the HORMONE insulin directly into the blood. Many other glands in the body also produce hormones. These function as chemical messengers which stimulate other organs to begin working, or cut down their activity. The pituitary gland, situated at the base of the brain, produces hormones which control other glands. It produces growth hormones which are important during childhood and ADOLESCENCE. When a gland fails to work properly there can be serious physical effects or illness. There are many glands in the SKIN, producing an oily substance called sebum to lubricate and protect the skin surface, and sweat glands which produce a watery secretion to cool the skin and get rid of waste products.

Glass

Glass is a transparent material used to make windows, containers, and LENSES. It is also used in the manufacture of some electrical INSULATORS because it does not conduct ELECTRICITY. It is made mainly from silica, or sand. If lead oxide is added, the resulting sparkling glass, called lead crystal, is used to make fine drinking glasses.

▶ *The glass blower dips his blowpipe into molten glass. He then blows gently into the pipe while turning it. Turning the blowpipe prevents the glass from dropping off the end. As he blows, the glass bulges out and forms a hollow bulb, which can be squeezed, stretched, and cut.*

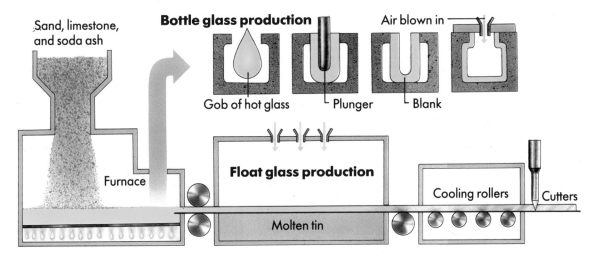

Glass can be colored by adding other metal OXIDES.

Glass is made by heating the raw materials in a furnace. They melt and combine to give a red-hot liquid which cools to form glass. While it is hot, it can be blown or cast into different shapes. Until the 1960s, window glass was made from plate glass which had to be ground flat and polished. It was replaced by float glass. Safety glass does not splinter when it breaks; toughened glass is made by rapidly cooling a sheet of glass in a jet of cold air; laminated glass consists of two sheets of glass with a layer of plastic in between. Glass fibers set in plastic resin are used to make strong lightweight structures including some vehicle bodies.

See also OPTICAL FIBERS; SILICON.

▲ *Silica, limestone, and coloring ingredients are the main materials used in making glass. These are loaded into a furnace where they melt at a temperature of 2190–2550°F (1200–1400°C). Molten glass from the furnace is molded and blown into hollow shapes or shaped into flat sheets by the float glass process. Float glass is made by letting a layer of molten glass set on top of a bath of molten tin until it is hard. The glass is then cooled and cut into lengths. This produces glass with a very smooth surface.*

Globular clusters

These are vast swarms of STARS, up to a hundred thousand or more, which were formed many billions of years ago. The stars in a globular cluster are RED GIANTS, much older than the SUN or SOLAR SYSTEM.

All stars are formed in clusters when a NEBULA starts to break up into separate clouds of material. But globular clusters are special, partly because they are so large, and also because the stars have not drifted apart. For example, there is now no trace of the cluster in which the Sun was born. About 100 globular clusters have been observed in our MILKY WAY galaxy. They are all very far away from us, grouped around the nucleus of the galaxy. They were probably formed soon after the galaxy, at least 10 billion years ago, so they are among the oldest objects in the UNIVERSE.

▲ *The Hercules star cluster is one example of a globular star cluster. These stars are much older than our Sun.*

The chemical formula of glycerol is $C_3 H_5 (OH)_3$. It is an alcohol but has a structure similar to a sugar. Glycerol draws water from its surroundings, which makes it a valuable moisturizing agent.

People have found many uses for gold. Gold coins have been used as money throughout history. Dentists use it for filling teeth. Pure gold is said to be 24-karat gold. Much jewelry is made of 14-karat gold, which contains 14 parts by weight of gold and 10 parts of another metal such as copper.

▶ Gold jewelry scrap. Gold was one of the first metals used by humans. Its chemical symbol, Au, comes from the Latin word for the metal, aurum. Apart from its use in making jewelry, coins, and in dentistry, the electrical contacts of microchips and other electronic devices are often plated with gold. This is because gold is a good electrical conductor.

Glycerol (Glycerin)

Glycerol is a thick, clear, odorless, colorless LIQUID with a very sweet taste. It is also known as glycerin (or glycerine). Glycerol occurs in nature as an ingredient of animal and vegetable FATS. It is very useful in industry and goes into making ice cream and candy, toothpaste, synthetic resins for paints, skin conditioners, and coatings for paper and cellophane to make them tough and flexible. It is also an ingredient of the EXPLOSIVE nitroglycerin, which is used to make dynamite. Glycerol for commercial use is obtained as a by-product in the making of soap or is synthesized from a HYDROCARBON called propylene.

Goddard, Robert Hutchings *See* Rockets

Gold

Gold is a metallic ELEMENT, bright yellow in color, whose great beauty and rarity have made it a highly prized treasure and a token of riches among humans for thousands of years. Gold is a soft but heavy METAL that can be freely shaped, drawn out into thin wires, and hammered into very thin gold leaf, but is resistant to the effects of many corrosive chemicals. It is very unreactive and forms few COMPOUNDS. It can be dissolved only by a mixture of nitric and hydrochloric acids. Gold is 19.3 times as dense as water.

Major deposits of gold are found in South Africa and Russia. The gold exists in lodes or veins (thin layers of ORE in rocks in the Earth's crust), in nuggets or grains in streams, and in seawater. Gold is extracted from its ores by various methods. It is alloyed with other metals to make jewelry.

Governor

A governor is used to control the speed of an ENGINE automatically. The first governors were used on STEAM ENGINES. They consist of two or three balls attached by hinged levers to a spindle driven by the engine. As the speed increases, the balls spinning around the spindle move outward because of the CENTRIFUGAL FORCE. A collar around the spindle attached to the balls is pushed along the spindle and operates a valve that reduces the flow of steam to the engine's cylinders. As the engine speed falls, the valve opens again.

Graft *See* Transplants

Graph

A graph is a drawing that shows the relative sizes of quantities or variables. Graphs show how values change with time or how one variable changes in relation to another. There are four main types of graph. In line graphs or curves, each value is plotted as a point on the graph. The position of each point is given by coordinates, which are the distances of the point from two lines called the x-axis (a horizontal line) and the y-axis (a vertical line that crosses the x-axis at right angles). Histograms or bar graphs show information as bars of different heights. Picture graphs use small pictures of different sizes or quantities instead of bars. Pie charts show the relation of the parts of something to the whole, for example, the percentages of a country's budget spent on health, education, defense, and so on.

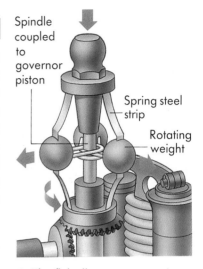

Spindle coupled to governor piston

Spring steel strip

Rotating weight

▲ The flyball governor works by the centrifugal force of rotating weights, which move outward against a spring. It keeps a machine running at a constant speed, normally by controlling the fuel supply.

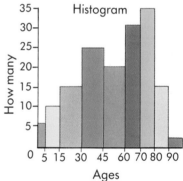

▲ The top graph is a histogram. It is a bar graph. The bottom graph shows distance (y-axis) covered in specific periods of time (x-axis).

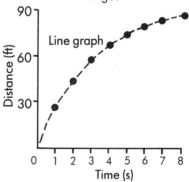

SEE FOR YOURSELF
Make a record of the heights of a friend and yourself over 6 months. Draw the axes of a graph. Make 6 divisions on the horizontal axis and label these months. Divide the vertical axis into quarter-inch units. Start at the height of the shorter person. Each month, mark on the graph your heights using different colors for your friend and yourself.

Gravity on the Planets	
compared to the Earth's gravity. On a planet with a greater gravity than that of the Earth an object will appear heavier.	
Mercury	0.38
Venus	0.9
Earth	1
Mars	0.38
Jupiter	2.87
Saturn	1.32
Uranus	0.93
Neptune	1.23
Pluto	0.03

Gravity

Gravity is the FORCE which pulls everything around us down toward the ground. Objects feel heavy because of the force of gravity on them. Isaac NEWTON realized that gravity is important not just for everyday objects around us, but also for the motion of PLANETS and stars. He was able to explain the orbits of all the planets known then by suggesting that gravity acts to pull together all pairs of objects with a force that depends on the amount of material or MASS in each object and on how far apart they are. The EARTH's mass is so much larger than the mass of other nearby objects that it is only the Earth's gravity that we usually notice. The gravity of more distant objects is also important; the gravitational force from the Moon moves water around in the oceans on the Earth's surface to create TIDES.

▶ In the absence of gravity, astronaut candidates experience weightlessness.

▼ Because the Moon is less massive than the Earth, the gravity it produces at its surface is only about one-sixth as strong as on Earth. Astronauts visiting the Moon are relatively only one-sixth as heavy as they would be on Earth, though their mass is the same. Therefore, they are able to jump around more easily.

Greenhouse effect

When FOSSIL FUELS, or other FUELS, such as wood or peat, which contain carbon are burned, CARBON DIOXIDE is released into the ATMOSPHERE. Vehicles are also major contributors to the increase in carbon dioxide in the atmosphere.

The Earth's atmosphere allows most of the Sun's rays to pass through it to heat the Earth's surface. The Earth reflects much of the heat energy back into the atmosphere, but much of this reflected radiation cannot escape because gases such as carbon dioxide absorb it. They grow warm and send heat radiation back to Earth. This

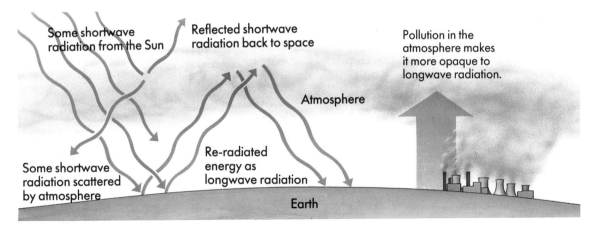

is the greenhouse effect. Many scientists think that the greenhouse effect may change the CLIMATE over the next hundred years or so. One consequence of so-called "global warming" resulting from the greenhouse effect could be melting of the polar ice. This, in turn, could lead to a rise in sea level which could flood areas of coastal land.

If carbon dioxide proves to be harmful as thought, we need to reduce carbon dioxide levels by reducing the amounts of carbon-rich fuels burned.

Groundwater

Groundwater is water which is distributed in the ROCKS beneath the surface of the EARTH. Water is continuously being circulated between the ATMOSPHERE, the land, and the oceans, seas, and rivers. Water may fall on the land as rain, snow, sleet, or hail. Some of this precipitation immediately evaporates back into the atmosphere, some runs off the surface, ultimately forming rivulets, streams, and then rivers, and some seeps through the soil and into the rocks beneath. Much of this groundwater is taken up by plants through their roots.

▲ *Pollution pumped into the atmosphere produces an increase in carbon dioxide, which makes it more opaque to radiation from the Earth's surface. This means that radiation is absorbed rather than passing through into space. Much of this absorbed radiation is reflected back to Earth. This may cause a gradual increase in temperature at the Earth's surface.*

▼ *Groundwater is water that comes from beneath the surface of the Earth. The level of groundwater is called the water table. The water is collected in a layer of porous material, called an aquifer, which usually lies between layers of impermeable rocks that do not hold water. Wells are drilled down into aquifers to bring the groundwater to the surface. Groundwater also provides water for many springs.*

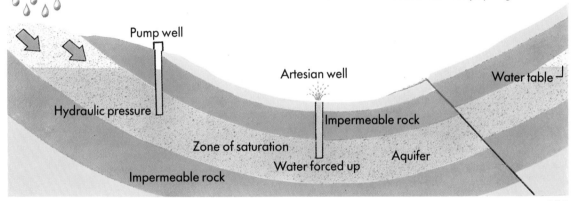

In order to reach maximum growth, an organism needs the proper nutrition at the right time. This is why adolescents usually have large appetites, to give them enough fuel to supply energy and body building materials for growth. Similarly, malnutrition, which often happens in times of famine, can have a serious effect on growth in children.

Humans grow fastest during the first six months of life. If this rate of growth was maintained, a 30-year-old man would weigh a billion tons!

Growth

Growth is an increase in size of a living organism. In simple animals and plants consisting of only one CELL, growth means simply that the organism gets larger and larger, until it must reproduce by dividing itself into two parts, each of which starts growing again. More complicated animals and plants made up of several cells increase in size and complexity. Usually, they begin by becoming more complex as they develop. For example, a frog starts out as a single cell, which becomes a ball of cells, then an EMBRYO, and eventually a tadpole. Through all these stages it becomes more complex. Once it has completed its change into a tiny frog it simply grows larger, and no further changes in its structure take place. The same thing happens in humans, where development takes place in the womb, but most of the growth takes place during the 18 years or so after BIRTH.

All organisms have a maximum size. Having reached this, their cells only divide to replace those which are damaged or worn out. Growth is controlled by HORMONES which govern the way cells divide. Growth hormones control the way in which a plant shoot develops and grows upward toward light, and the way the root grows down. Growth hormones also control the way we develop, the rapid growth during ADOLESCENCE, and the change to adulthood.

SEE FOR YOURSELF
Put some compost, or a mixture of soil and sand, in a flower pot. Make a hole about 2 inches deep and put a green bean seed in it. Cover it up with soil and water it. Place the flowerpot on a windowsill. After a few days a green shoot will appear. As the plant grows up you will need to support it with a stick. The plant starts to wind around the support once it has touched the support with one of its tendrils. It continues to climb in the same direction. Keep watering your plant and it should eventually produce some beans.

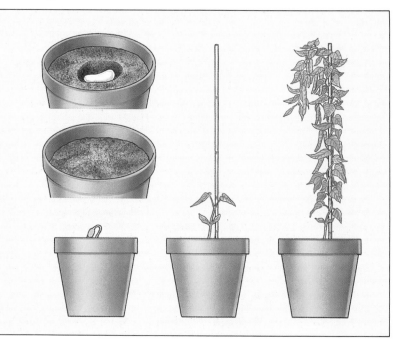

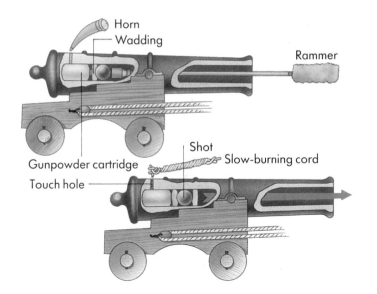

Horn
Wadding
Rammer
Gunpowder cartridge
Touch hole
Shot
Slow-burning cord

◄ *Gunpowder was needed to fire cannons on ships from the 1600s to the 1800s. A cartridge containing gunpowder was pushed into the barrel. This was followed by some wadding and a cannon ball. The cartridge was pricked and the touchhole at the breech was filled with powder. It was lit with a slow burning cord. The powder in the touch hole burned through to the gunpowder. When this happened the gunpowder exploded and the cannon ball shot out of the cannon.*

Gunpowder

Gunpowder is a fast-burning EXPLOSIVE material that releases rapidly expanding GAS when ignited. In the confined space of a gun barrel, this gas can give a bullet a very great ACCELERATION as it is shot out of the gun.

Gunpowder was traditionally made from saltpeter (potassium nitrate), a substance derived from plant and animal material that has decayed and oxidized, charcoal, and sulfur. Gunpowder was developed by the ancient Chinese. Since the 19th century, other forms of gunpowder have been developed, not only to fire ammunition but also for use in FIREWORKS and for quarry blasting. Sodium nitrate sometimes replaces saltpeter in gunpowder used for these particular purposes. Smokeless gunpowders such as cordite include the powerful liquid explosive NITROGLYCERIN.

Gyrocompass

A gyrocompass is a type of COMPASS, used for finding direction. The simplest type of compass uses a magnetized needle which swings to point at the North Pole. In fact, it points at the magnetic North Pole, which is not in the same place as the geographic or true North Pole. The gyrocompass, designed by Dr. Hermann Anschutz-Kaempfe in 1905, does not rely on MAGNETISM. A GYROSCOPE is pointed at the true North Pole and starts spinning. Then, wherever the gyroscope goes, the needle turns to point to the North Pole.

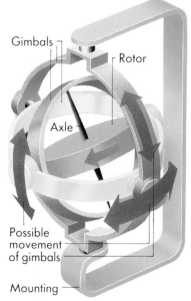

Gimbals
Rotor
Axle
Possible movement of gimbals
Mounting

▲ *A gyrocompass shows the direction of north like a magnetic compass but it does not use magnetism. Instead, it contains a spinning disk like a gyroscope. The disk is powered by an electric motor so that it spins nonstop. The axle of the disk always points in the same direction and can be set to point north. As the vessel changes direction, the mounting gimbals turn so that the rotor axle still points north.*

▶ *Gyroscopes consist of a wheel and an axle. This gyroscope is mounted in two rings, called gimbals, and so the axis of spin is free to point in the same direction no matter how the gyroscope is held.*

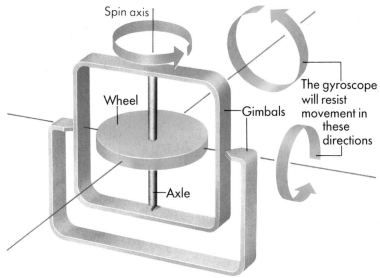

Spin axis

Wheel

Gimbals

Axle

The gyroscope will resist movement in these directions

▼ *When the wheel of a toy gyroscope is set spinning it can be balanced on a pencil point and will not fall as long as it spins fast enough.*

Gyroscope

A gyroscope is a wheel that can spin on its axle, mounted in a frame. When the wheel of a toy gyroscope is set spinning it can be balanced on a pencil point and will not fall as long as it spins fast enough. While the gyroscope wheel is spinning, the wheel's axle points continuously in the direction it was first set. The frame of the gyroscope can be turned in all directions, but the spinning wheel's axle always points in the same direction. Because of this, gyroscopes are used to steer ships and aircraft.

The gyroscope has another interesting property. If you push a toy gyroscope with your finger while it is rotating, the gyroscope does not move in the direction in which you push it. It moves at right angles to your push. This effect is called *precession*.

See also GYROCOMPASS; GYROSTABILIZER.

SEE FOR YOURSELF
You can demonstrate the effect of precession, the change in direction of the spin axis as displayed by a gyroscope, with a bicycle wheel. Spin the bicycle wheel fast. Try to twist the spinning wheel by pushing down with your left hand. The wheel will move at right angles to the source of the pressure (toward the left).

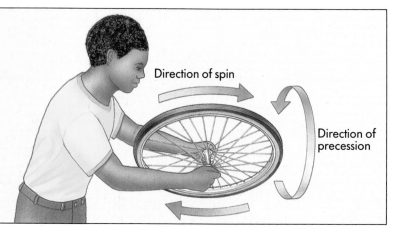

Direction of spin

Direction of precession

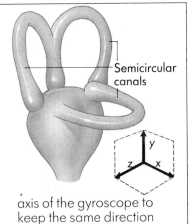

Semicircular
canals

axis of the gyroscope to
keep the same direction
even when the gyroscope's
support moves.

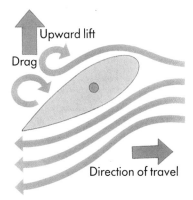

Upward lift

Drag

Direction of travel

Gyrostabilizer

A gyrostabilizer is a piece of equipment designed to
steady or stabilize whatever it is attached to. It relies on
the tendency of a GYROSCOPE to resist any FORCE that tries
to tilt it while it is spinning. Gyrostabilizers are often
used to counteract the rolling motion of a ship to make
the voyage more comfortable for passengers. A gyrostabilizer consists of a pair of swiveling fins, one mounted
on each side of the ship, linked to a motor-driven gyroscope. If the ship starts to roll, the fins try to swivel. The
gyroscope resists the motion of the fins and they in turn
resist the rolling of the ship.
See also SERVOMECHANISM.

▲ *The fins of a gyrostabilizer
are automatically angled to
make the ship float in a more
upright position.*

▼ *Gyrostabilizers are large
gyroscopes that are used to
stabilize a ship. A spinning
gyroscope resists forces that try
to change the direction of its
axis. This causes the
gyrostabilizer to resist the force
of the waves against the ship
and so reduce the rolling
motion.*

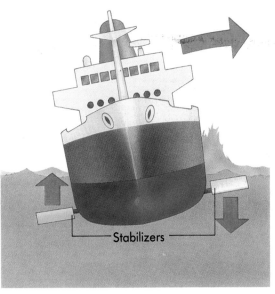

Stabilizers

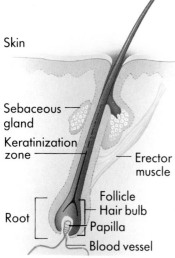

Skin

Sebaceous gland

Keratinization zone

Erector muscle

Follicle
Hair bulb

Root

Papilla

Blood vessel

▲ *Hair roots are enclosed in their own bulblike follicles, which have their own blood supply, a tiny erector muscle, and a nearby sebaceous gland which produces oil.*

▼ *Whether hair is straight or not depends partly on the shape of the hair follicles.*

Oval follicle — wavy hair

Round follicle — straight hair

Flat follicle — curly hair

Hahn, Otto *See* Nuclear physics

Hair

The presence of hair on the body is characteristic of mammals. Its most important function is to provide insulation to keep the body warm and to protect the SKIN. In humans, we have lost the need for insulating hair over much of our bodies, but we retain small sparse hairs over most of the body surface. Body hair in other mammals is very important. Hair can provide CAMOUFLAGE, by being colored or marked, as in tigers and zebras. In most mammals, large hairs around the muzzle and other parts of the face are a very important sense organ. A cat relies on these hairs when moving through bushes and undergrowth to tell if it can squeeze through a gap or avoid an obstruction.

Hair usually forms a dense coat which protects the skin from cold, and often, if it is oily, provides further protection against water. Each hair grows from a small pit in the skin, called a follicle. A papilla at the base carries arteries and nerves. The hair shaft is hollow and may be colored. Tiny muscles are attached to the side of the hair, so that when they contract, the hair is raised erect, increasing the thickness of the coat, keeping the mammal warmer. The same thing happens when we get "gooseflesh," and the hairs in our skin are erected.

▼ *The layers of dense hair or fur of the polar bear help to protect it from the cold.*

Hale, George Ellery *See* Sunspots

Half-life

The half-life of a radioactive ELEMENT is the time taken for half of it to decay, or change into a different element. It decays because it is unstable and particles from the nucleus at the center of each ATOM escape. Some materials have half-lives of a fraction of a second. Other materials have half-lives lasting millions of years. One kind of radium, for example, has a half-life of 1,600 years – it takes 1,600 years for half the atoms in a radium sample to break down. It also takes 1,600 years for half the remaining atoms in the sample to break down, and so on. The rate at which radioactive elements break down is used by scientists to find out the age of objects left behind by ancient peoples.

See also BARIUM; CARBON DATING; RADIOISOTOPE.

▼ *The element radon 222 takes approximately four days for half the original amount of atoms to decay. It has a half-life of four days. After a further four days, half of the remaining radon has decayed, and so on. As it decays the loss of an alpha particle from the radon 222 changes the radon into polonium 218.*

▶ *Some elements decay by losing an alpha particle, which is the same as the nucleus of a helium atom. Other elements decay by losing a beta particle, which is an electron. The table on the right shows the radioactive series that begins with uranium 238 and ends with lead. The half-life of each change is given.*

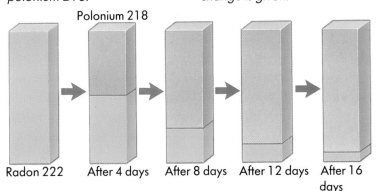

Polonium 218

Radon 222 | After 4 days | After 8 days | After 12 days | After 16 days

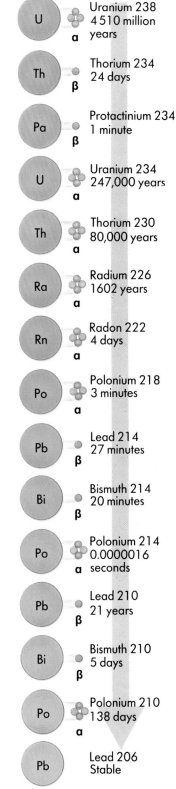

U	Uranium 238 — 4510 million years — α
Th	Thorium 234 — 24 days — β
Pa	Protactinium 234 — 1 minute — β
U	Uranium 234 — 247,000 years — α
Th	Thorium 230 — 80,000 years — α
Ra	Radium 226 — 1602 years — α
Rn	Radon 222 — 4 days — α
Po	Polonium 218 — 3 minutes — α
Pb	Lead 214 — 27 minutes — β
Bi	Bismuth 214 — 20 minutes — β
Po	Polonium 214 — 0.0000016 seconds — α
Pb	Lead 210 — 21 years — β
Bi	Bismuth 210 — 5 days — β
Po	Polonium 210 — 138 days — α
Pb	Lead 206 — Stable

Halley's Comet

Halley's is the most famous COMET of all, though it is not the largest or brightest. It takes about 76 years to orbit the SUN, and its first recorded sighting was 239 B.C. After the comet has passed close to the Sun, it travels nearly to

Edmund Halley (1656–1742)
Halley was an English astronomer and physicist. He is best known for his discoveries about the orbits of comets. He calculated that the orbits of comets seen in 1531, 1607, and 1682 were very similar and from this predicted that the comet he had observed in 1682 would return in 1758. The comet appeared on Christmas Day 1758 and was named Halley's Comet in his honor.

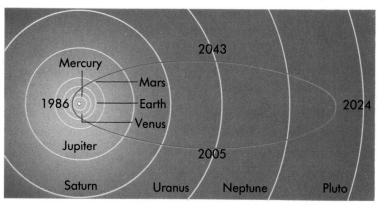

▲ *Halley's Comet last passed close to the Earth in 1986. By* *2024 it will have reached the farthest point on its orbit.*

Pluto before returning. In 1705, the astronomer Edmund Halley suggested that the comet would return in 1758. It reappeared as predicted, which was important proof that the law of GRAVITY, which explained the orbits of the Moon and planets, also worked for comets.

At its last return, in 1986, six spacecraft went close to Halley's Comet, three passing through its tail. Although its tail (of gas and dust from the rocky nucleus) could have stretched halfway from the Earth to the Sun, the nucleus itself was only about 7 by 4 miles (12 by 6 km)!

9	Fluorine
F	Atomic number 9
19.0	Atomic weight 19.0
17	Chlorine
Cl	Atomic number 17
35.5	Atomic weight 35.5
35	Bromine
Br	Atomic number 35
79.9	Atomic weight 79.9
53	Iodine
I	Atomic number 53
126.9	Atomic weight 126.9
85	Astatine
At	Atomic number 85
210.0	Atomic weight 210.0

▲ *The halogens are a group of five reactive elements. Fluorine (F), chlorine (Cl), bromine (Br), iodine (I), and astatine (At).*

Halogens

Halogens are a class of five nonmetallic ELEMENTS that have similar chemical characteristics and belong to Group VII of the PERIODIC TABLE. The halogen elements are fluorine, CHLORINE, bromine, IODINE, and astatine. They all react with metals and with hydrogen to form COMPOUNDS called halides. Many halides are found in seawater. In their pure form, all the halogens are poisonous and will burn the skin. Fluorine is a pale yellow gas. Calcium fluoride (fluorspar) is used in refining steel and in making aluminum. Very small amounts of fluorides are added to drinking water to prevent tooth decay. Bromine is a reddish brown, volatile liquid used mainly in making dyes, medicines, and chemicals for fighting fires. Light-sensitive silver bromide, like silver iodide, is used in the photographic industry. Astatine, the heaviest of the halogens, is a radioactive element with no stable ISOTOPES. It is used in medicine as a tracer. In a halogen lamp, adding a little iodine to the tungsten filament produces a whiter light than a conventional light bulb. The most important halogen is chlorine.

Hard water

Water that does not produce a good lather with soap is known as hard water. Consequently, water that does produce a good lather is called soft water. The hardness is caused by COMPOUNDS dissolved in the water.

When water passes through ROCKS and SOILS, some of the compounds are dissolved into the water. There are two kinds of hardness: temporary and permanent. Temporary hardness may be removed by boiling the water. It is caused by calcium bicarbonate dissolved in the water when the water has passed through limestones such as chalk. When boiled, the soluble bicarbonates change to insoluble calcium carbonates producing a scum which forms on glassware in hard water areas.

Permanent hardness can be removed by systems called "ion exchange" water softeners or by adding soda ash and lime to the water.

Elements causing hard water include the chlorides, carbonates, and sulfates of metals such as sodium, calcium, magnesium, and iron. Permanent hardness cannot be removed by boiling the water. It is caused by calcium sulfate and other salts dissolved in the water and, in areas where the water is permanently hard, it is still difficult to get a lather from soap even after the water has been boiled.

◀ This effect can be seen on the walls of caves in hard water areas. Water containing calcium carbonate seeps into the caves, and builds up into a solid mineral formation.

Hardness

The hardness of a SOLID, such as a METAL or MINERAL is measured by its ability to resist being scratched or indented. Hardness depends on the size of the ATOMS, the strength of their BONDS, and the way they are packed. The closely packed structure and small size of the atoms in DIAMOND contribute to its hardness; however, in soft graphite, the atoms are loosely bonded.

Hard materials wear away softer ones, so it is necessary to know the relative hardness of materials such as ABRASIVES. This is particularly important when making and using tools. The hardness of minerals is usually measured on a scale called the Mohs' scale.

SEE FOR YOURSELF
Make a chart of the hardness of different pencils. Soft pencils make thick black lines that are easily smudged. Hard pencils make a fine line. Very hard pencils may scratch the surface of the paper. You can estimate the hardness of other things by seeing if a pencil will scratch them.

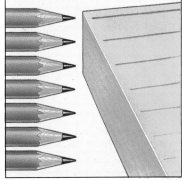

Mohs' Scale of Hardness

In 1822 the German mineralogist Friedrich Mohs made a list of 10 common minerals from which hardness could be measured. The mineral labeled 1 is the softest and the mineral labeled 10 the hardest. Because mineral 10 is hardest it can therefore scratch mineral 9, mineral 9 can scratch mineral 8, and so on down the scale. Talc, the softest mineral on Moh's scale, can be scratched with a fingernail. The minerals are:

10 diamond, **9** corundum, **8** topaz, **7** quartz, **6** orthoclase, **5** apatite, **4** fluorite, **3** calcite, **2** gypsum and **1** talc.

1. Talc

2. Gypsum

3. Calcite

4. Fluorite

5. Apatite

6. Orthoclase

7. Quartz

8. Topaz

9. Corundum

10. Diamond

A fingernail has a hardness of about 2½

A copper coin has a hardness of about 3½

Minerals of 6 or more can scratch glass

A penknife has a hardness of 5½ and can scratch apatite but not orthoclase

A special steel file can scratch quartz

The first electronic computer, built in 1945, weighed 30 tons and filled a large hall of 1,500 square feet. It contained more than 18,000 tubes. However, it was no more powerful than a small home computer of today. The development of the transistor and then the microchip mean that much less hardware is needed for today's computers. Modern computers are compact and powerful; most will fit on a desk top.

Hardware

Hardware is the physical part of an ELECTRONIC system, the electronic components and CIRCUITS that enable the system to function. "Hardware" is most frequently used to describe one of the two basic parts of a COMPUTER system, the other part being the computer programs, or SOFTWARE, that control the hardware. Each is useless without the other. The hardware of a computer system is its keyboard, screen, disk drives, and electronic circuits. Hardware and software are also commonly used terms in connection with TELEVISION and video. The hardware in

► A mainframe computer is a large powerful piece of hardware. This high-speed computer has a large storage capacity, to which one or more work stations have access.

the home consists of VIDEOCASSETTE RECORDERS and television sets. They are useless without the software, such as television programs and films. The magnetic disks and tapes for recording and storing computer programs are also described as software.

Harmonics

Harmonics are the different FREQUENCIES at which something can vibrate. For example, a string stretched between two supports can vibrate so that different numbers of WAVELENGTHS of the wave can fit along the string. The wave with the longest wavelength is called the fun-

> The quality of sound made by a musical instrument, the timbre, depends on a number of factors. The most important of these is the relative intensity of the harmonics, or overtones, produced. A note made by a violin has a full and vibrant sound because it is rich in overtones. A note made by a flute is almost a pure tone because it is produced by a vibration that has few overtones.

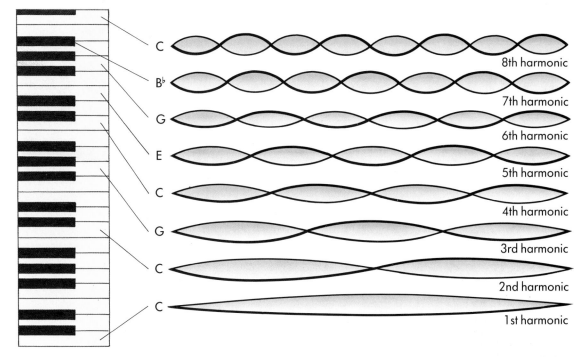

C — 8th harmonic

B♭ — 7th harmonic

G — 6th harmonic

E — 5th harmonic

C — 4th harmonic

G — 3rd harmonic

C — 2nd harmonic

C — 1st harmonic

damental; the other vibrations have wavelengths one half, one third, one quarter, and so on times the fundamental wavelength and frequencies two, three, four, and so on times the fundamental frequency. This series of frequencies is known as the harmonic series. There are similar series for the SOUND waves in pipes.

A musical note corresponds to a sound wave of a particular frequency; the different sounds of different-shaped MUSICAL INSTRUMENTS come from the different mixtures of harmonics of the fundamental notes.

▲ *A series of harmonics sound when a piano string vibrates. The position of the notes on the piano keyboard which give these harmonics are shown above. When these keys shown are pressed down without sounding them and the bottom key, C, is struck firmly, the harmonics will resonate.*

Harvey, William *See* Circulation

Hawking, Stephen *See* Black hole

Hearing *See* Ear

Heart

The heart is a muscular organ that pumps BLOOD around the body through arteries, capillaries, and veins as it contracts rhythmically. In mammals, birds, and crocodiles the blood is passed through a double CIRCULATION. The heart pumps blood from the right side of the heart to the LUNGS, then blood carrying OXYGEN returns to the left side of the heart to be pumped around the rest of the body. The heart is actually a pair of pumps, on each side of which the upper chamber or atrium collects incoming blood, then passes it through a one-way valve into the muscular ventricle beneath. This ventricle then contracts strongly and propels blood out of the heart and away to the lungs or the rest of the body. The human heart is mostly MUSCLE, and contracts or pumps about 70 times each minute. Contractions are controlled by a timing mechanism, which keeps the heart beating evenly. The speed of pumping can be increased by HORMONES and NERVE impulses when extra exertion means that more oxygen is needed in the tissues.

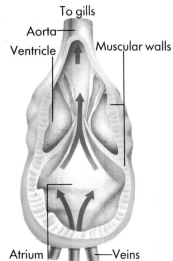

To gills
Aorta
Ventricle
Muscular walls
Atrium
Veins

▲ *In some vertebrate animals such as most reptiles, amphibians, and fish, the heart is not a double-pump structure.*

▶ *The human heart is really two pumps side by side. The right side (left side of diagram) pumps oxygen-poor blood to the lungs. The left side pumps oxygen-rich blood to the body's cells.*

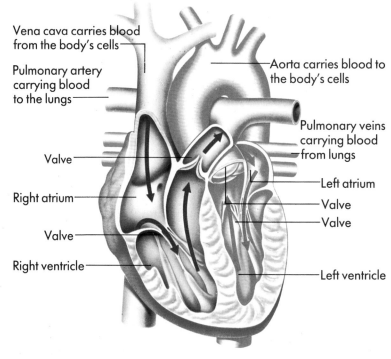

Vena cava carries blood from the body's cells
Pulmonary artery carrying blood to the lungs
Aorta carries blood to the body's cells
Pulmonary veins carrying blood from lungs
Valve
Left atrium
Right atrium
Valve
Valve
Valve
Right ventricle
Left ventricle

Heat

Heat is produced by the conversion of other forms of ENERGY. Heat is formed from kinetic energy by FRICTION. Electrical energy is converted into heat by an electric heater and during cooking. The food we eat is used to heat our bodies. *See* pages 312 and 313.

Heat exchanger

A heat exchanger is used to transfer HEAT from a hot object or space, to a cooler object or space. Heat exchangers are widely used for cooling MACHINES. Most vehicle ENGINES are cooled by circulating water around the engine. This is warmed by the hot engine and pumped to a radiator. Air rushing past the radiator cools the hot water inside. A hot liquid can be cooled by pumping it through a pipe surrounded by cold water. The heat transfers to the water. Spacecraft are cooled by emitting INFRARED RADIATION into space from radiators.

Heat pump

A heat pump is a device used to transfer HEAT from a cooler object or space, to a warmer object or space. Heat cannot flow in this direction without ENERGY because it normally flows from hot to cold. Refrigerators use heat pumps. A FLUID called a refrigerant is allowed to expand and change into a VAPOR in the refrigerator's freezing compartment. It takes the energy it needs for this from the freezer, cooling it in the process. The vapor is then compressed and passed through a condenser where it changes back to a liquid, giving out the energy from the freezer as heat.

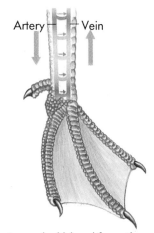

Artery — Vein

▲ As cooled blood from the foot of an Arctic bird travels up its leg it comes into close contact with warm blood in the artery. The bird's foot acts as a heat exchanger.

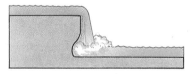

▲ Heat is like water flowing downhill. It flows from hotter to cooler places. Just as water can be dammed, heat loss can be slowed by insulation. If heat is to flow from a cool place to a warmer one, work must be done, just as it is when water is raised to a higher place (bottom).

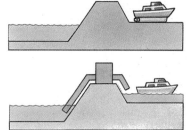

◀ A household refrigerator is a type of heat pump. It absorbs heat from the food inside it by the evaporator. The dry vapor is then compressed and as it cools it gives out heat energy as it becomes liquid. The heat is then passed into the outside air.

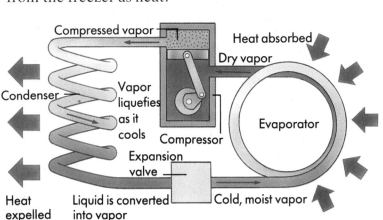

Compressed vapor

Heat absorbed

Dry vapor

Condenser

Vapor liquefies as it cools

Compressor

Evaporator

Expansion valve

Heat expelled

Liquid is converted into vapor

Cold, moist vapor

HEAT

Heat is a form of energy. Heat is stored in the form of motions and vibrations of the atoms which make up materials; the amount of vibration determines the temperature of the material. Larger objects contain more heat energy than smaller objects at the same temperature.

Heat travels from hotter bodies to colder ones, so it tends to even out differences in temperature. This is a consequence of the second law of thermodynamics which states that heat cannot be transferred from a colder to a hotter body without the addition of energy. There are three main ways in which heat can travel; by electromagnetic radiation; by conduction through a material of any sort; and by convection, which involves the circulation of a liquid or a gas which carries heat with it.

The molecules of an object are affected by heat energy. The most obvious effect of the loss or gain of heat energy is a change of state. A solid, for example, may melt, or a liquid may freeze, or it may boil and vaporize. Less obvious is the expansion or contraction of a material. Almost all substances expand when heated and contract when cooled because of the increased or decreased energy in the molecules.

Our bodies have to be maintained at a certain temperature which is high enough so that molecules are moving around quickly enough for chemical reactions to take place, but not so quickly that the molecules are changed.

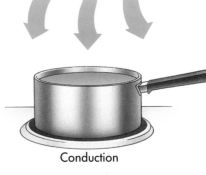

Sun

Radiation

Conduction

Convection

▲ Heat travels from the Sun by radiation in a stream of waves. When heat is conducted through the metal of a cooking pot, the metal molecules vibrate back and forth passing heat energy from one molecule to the next. When heat is carried through a fluid such as air, molecules in the air move, taking heat with them.

◀ Heat is generated in furnaces in which metals are produced. These two carbon electrodes are very hot because large amounts of electricity flow through them.

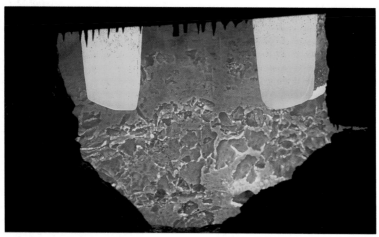

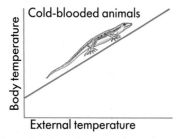

Cold-blooded animals

Body temperature

External temperature

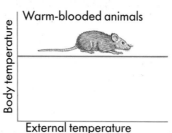

Warm-blooded animals

Body temperature

External temperature

◀ In many animals such as lizards, the body temperature fluctuates with the temperature of the surroundings. They are called cold-blooded animals though their temperature can rise much higher than that of warm-blooded animals, such as mammals. Warm-blooded animals maintain their body at a stable temperature despite changes in the external temperature.

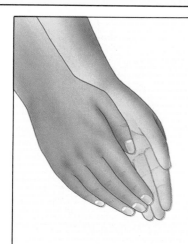

SEE FOR YOURSELF
Rub your hands together. You will find that they get warm. The heat energy comes from friction. The energy given off by a light bulb is 95 percent heat. You can feel this by holding your hands about 6 inches away from a naked light bulb. Do this for just a short time. Compare the intensity of the heat given off by a 25, 40, and 60 watt bulb. **Do not touch the bulbs because they could be very hot.**

Latent Heat
Heat makes liquids boil and solids melt. When heat is added to a solid, such as ice, its temperature is raised to the melting point. The temperature stops rising and remains constant until all the ice has melted, then it will rise again.

▶ *The human body generates energy and heat from carbohydrates in food. Heat is produced as a waste product by muscles when they have been doing strenuous work such as running.*

Joules are the main unit used to measure heat in the international SI units systems. The **calorie** has also been used as a unit. One calorie is equal to 4.1855 joules. One calorie is the amount of heat needed to raise the temperature of 1 gram of water through 1°C. Calories as well as joules are used to measure the energy content of foods, but because this energy can be quite large, the usual unit is the kilojoule (kJ) equal to 1,000 joules or kilocalories, which are often just referred to as calories.

SEE FOR YOURSELF
You need two large plastic beakers. Pour a cup of vinegar into each of the beakers. Heat the vinegar in one of the beakers by standing it in very hot water for a few minutes. Add a tablespoon of baking soda to each beaker. Both solutions start to foam as carbon dioxide gas is produced. The cold solution foams steadily, whereas the heated solution foams violently for a short while and then goes flat. This is because the heat speeds up the reaction between the vinegar and the baking soda.

See also CONDUCTION, HEAT; CONVECTION; ELECTROMAGNETIC RADIATION; ENERGY; INSULATION, THERMAL; RADIATION; TEMPERATURE.

▲ Parts of the Space Shuttle are exposed to temperatures of over 2,700°F (1,500°C) during reentry to the Earth's atmosphere. Heat resistant tiles made of carbon and silicon are used to insulate the shuttle.

▼ The nose of the Space Shuttle is being tested in a furnace.

▶ The Romans built underfloor heating systems, known as hypocausts, to heat their buildings. Air was heated by a furnace. It would then travel through a series of columns and archways under the floor and through hollow walls. The heat would then rise up to warm the rooms above it.

Heat shield

A heat shield is a layer of heat-resistant material applied to part of a rocket or spacecraft to protect it from high TEMPERATURES. In particular, it protects the spacecraft from the intense HEAT it experiences when it reenters the Earth's ATMOSPHERE from space. The heat is a result of FRICTION between the air and the vehicle. Originally, heat shields were made from materials that burned very slowly and could only be used once. The Space Shuttle uses a new type of heat shield that can be used over and over again like the spacecraft itself.

Heating systems

Heating systems are used to warm the spaces in which people live, work, and travel. They differ in detail but they all operate on the same principles. All heating systems generate the ENERGY needed to warm living spaces

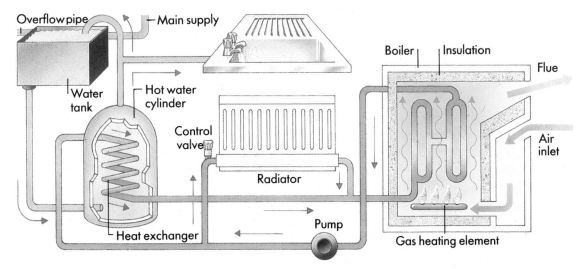

by BURNING a FUEL such as oil, gas, or coal. Electric systems obtain their energy from a power station which in turn generates energy by burning a fuel. Solar heating systems use energy collected from the SUN, where it was also generated by burning a fuel, hydrogen. Wherever the energy comes from, it is usually used to heat water and this is then pumped around coils of hollow metal pipes called radiators. Their large surface area allows the maximum heat exchange between the hot water and the surrounding air. The water in the radiators is returned to a boiler, where it is heated and pumped around the radiators again. This is commonly known as central heating. Stores and offices frequently use a system called AIR CONDITIONING, where the TEMPERATURE and HUMIDITY of the air circulating through them is controlled by HEAT EXCHANGERS and humidifiers.

▲ In a hot-water heating system, fuel is burned in a boiler, which heats the water in the central heating system. The same water is pumped around the system, called a closed system. Hot water is pumped along one set of pipes which supply hot water to faucets. Water pumped through another set of pipes heats the radiators.

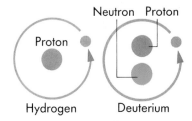

Heavy water

Heavy water is a form of water in which the HYDROGEN atoms are replaced by atoms of deuterium; it is also known as deuterium oxide. Deuterium is an ISOTOPE of hydrogen and has an ATOMIC WEIGHT double that of ordinary hydrogen. Ordinary natural water contains a minute amount of deuterium, one atom of deuterium to 6,760 atoms of hydrogen. Heavy water is usually obtained by fractional DISTILLATION. Its chief use is as the substance that limits the energy of the neutrons produced during a reaction in a NUCLEAR REACTOR.

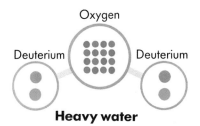

Heavy water

▲ A hydrogen atom has a single proton as its nucleus. Deuterium, or heavy hydrogen, has a proton and a neutron. Heavy water is a compound of deuterium and oxygen.

Helicopter *See* Flight

▲ *Multicolored helium-filled balloons rise to high altitudes because helium is lighter than air.*

▶ *The equator divides the Earth into the Northern (left) and the Southern (right) hemispheres. The word hemisphere comes from the Greek word* Hemisphairion *meaning half a sphere.*

Between two-thirds and three-fourths of the Earth's surface is covered with water and, of this, by far the greatest amount is to be found in the Southern Hemisphere. If you were to look from space at a point directly above the South Pole, you would see that, apart from the southern tips of the northern continents, the only significant land mass is the continent of Antarctica.

Helium

Helium is an unreactive NOBLE GAS with no color, taste, or smell. It is second only to hydrogen in lightness. Helium is formed in STARS such as the SUN as hydrogen nuclei are forced together by NUCLEAR FUSION. It is named after *helios*, the Greek for Sun. There is very little helium on Earth. The air contains five parts per million of it and it exists in certain rocks. Most of the world's helium comes from the United States, where it is found with NATURAL GAS. Helium becomes liquid at about –452°F (–268.9°C) (about 39°F/4°C) above absolute zero) and only becomes solid under pressure, so it is used as a refrigerant and in cold-temperature physics research. Liquid helium expands rather than contracts on cooling, and when it only partly fills a container, it will creep up the sides and spill over the rim.

Hemisphere

A hemisphere is one half of the EARTH's globe. The two halves of the globe most usually referred to are the Northern Hemisphere, covering the area north of the equator, and the Southern Hemisphere, the area south of the equator. It is also possible to divide the Earth from the North to the South Poles along 0° and 180° lines of LONGITUDE, giving Eastern and Western Hemispheres.

The Earth orbits the SUN and spins on its own axis at an angle to the plane of the Earth's orbit. Consequently, the Northern Hemisphere is tilted toward the Sun and experiences summer between March and September when it is winter in the Southern Hemisphere.

Hemophilia *See* Genetics

Herbicide *See* Pesticide

Heredity

Heredity is the transfer of characteristics from one generation to the next. You will have seen that some children have features, such as hair color, facial shape, or mannerisms, which make them look just like one of the parents. Each of these features comes about because the fertilized EGG from which a new human develops carries two sets of instructions, one from each parent, that tell the egg what sort of features the new individual will have. These instructions are called genes. Although we inherit genes from each parent, some genes can overrule others: they are said to be dominant. The effect of inherited genes depends on the interaction between genes from each parent.

Things like body weight, behavior, and fitness are not permanent features and are not inherited from your parents. They are the results of your lifestyle and environment. Things like the color of your EYES and your BLOOD group are inherited and are with you for life.

See also CHROMOSOMES AND GENES; GENETICS.

Gregor Mendel (1822–1884)
Mendel was an Austrian monk and amateur botanist who pioneered the study of heredity. Through his experiments on pea plants he noticed patterns from one generation to the next, now known as Mendel's laws of heredity. The importance of his work was not recognized until after his death.

▼ *The gene that produces brown eyes is dominant over the gene for blue eyes. If somebody has both genes, he or she has brown eyes, so the brown-eyed father may also have the blue-eye gene, but the blue-eyed mother cannot also carry the brown-eye gene. The children who received the blue-eye gene from both mother and father have blue eyes.*

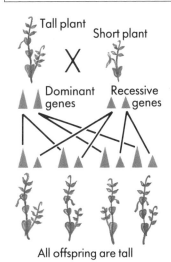

All offspring are tall

▲ *Gregor Mendel did his experiments on heredity using pea plants. By crossing tall plants with short ones, he showed that tallness is dominant over shortness, because all the offspring were tall. But these plants still carry the gene for shortness and if they are interbred, one in four of their offspring will be short.*

317

▲ The aeoliphile, also known as Hero's turbine, was the first steam-powered engine but the possibility of using it as a source of power does not seem to have occurred to Hero. Steam power remained undiscovered for another 1,700 years. As well as the aeoliphile, Hero invented devices to open doors automatically.

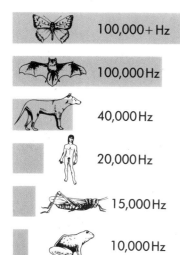

	100,000+ Hz
	100,000 Hz
	40,000 Hz
	20,000 Hz
	15,000 Hz
	10,000 Hz

▲ The range of sounds heard by different species varies greatly. Humans have relatively poor hearing, and cannot hear sound frequencies above about 20,000 Hz. A bat's hearing is far better.

318

Hero of Alexandria

Hero of Alexandria (1st century A.D.) was a Greek inventor and mathematician. He is famous for inventing the first steam-powered ENGINE and for his studies of GEOMETRY. His steam-powered engine, called an "aeoliphile," was the earliest predecessor of the modern JET engine, although Hero built it as a toy. It was a rotating hollow metal ball with two nozzles on opposite sides pointing in opposite directions. When STEAM was passed into the ball, steam escaping from the nozzles made the ball spin on its shaft. He produced many formulas for calculating areas of different shapes, and one still called Hero's formula, for calculating the area of a triangle. His inventions included the first automatic vending machine, which delivered a measured amount of holy water when a coin was put into a slot.

Herschel, William *See* Uranus

Hertz

The hertz (Hz) is the SI UNIT of FREQUENCY. One hertz corresponds to a vibration or wave that goes back and forth in one cycle every second, 10 Hz repeats 10 times a second, and so on. The kilohertz (kHz) corresponds to 1,000 cycles per second and the megahertz (MHz) 1,000,000 cycles per second. We can hear sound frequencies between about 20 Hz and 20 kHz. Radio waves have frequencies of 200 kHz to 100 MHz.

The hertz is named after Heinrich Hertz who was the first to demonstrate the existence of RADIO waves.

Hertz, Heinrich Rudolph *See* Frequency

Hibernation

Hibernation is the deep sleep in which many small mammals pass the winter. Hibernating mammals include bats, chipmunks, and many rodents. They go to sleep mainly because there is not enough food around for them in the winter, but hibernation is not an ordinary sleep. The heartbeat and breathing rate slow down and the body temperature falls almost to that of the surroundings. In this state the animals use hardly any energy and can survive on the food stored in their

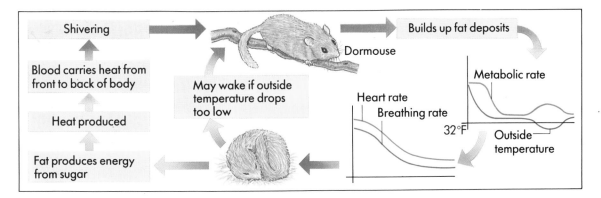

bodies. Some hibernators such as hamsters store food in their nests and wake up every now and then to eat it. Others, like bears, badgers, and squirrels, go to sleep for days on end during the winter, but do not really hibernate because their body temperatures do not fall more than a few degrees below normal.

Amphibians and reptiles sleep through the winter, and so do many land-living insects and other invertebrates, but their sleep is not true hibernation. Many of them wake up on mild days in the winter and then drift back to sleep when it gets cold again.

Hi-fi

Hi-fi is short for "high fidelity." It describes sound recording and playing equipment that satisfies a minimum standard for SOUND quality. Hi-fi equipment tries to reproduce sounds without distorting them. The sounds may include music and radio programs.

▲ *During hibernation, an animal's metabolism slowly consumes its body fat. The heat produced by the stored energy circulates in the blood and causes shivering. This keeps unused muscles toned-up. If the air temperature drops to dangerous levels, the animal may wake up but, during severe winters, many hibernating animals die.*

▼ *Most home hi-fi systems have the separate music sources stacked on top of each other and connected to the amplifier by internal wiring. CD decks and radio tuners often use illuminated numerical displays to indicate the CD track playing, or the frequency to which the radio is tuned.*

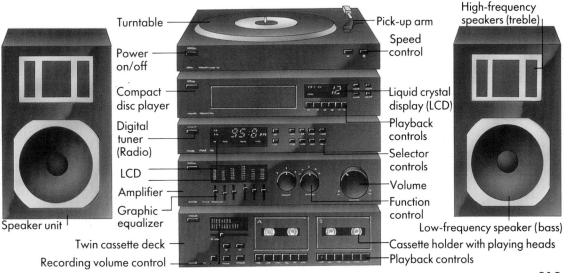

▲ The first record players had to be operated by hand. Turning the handle wound up a spring that worked the turntable. The trumpet-shaped metal speaker gave very lo-fi sound.

▲ Hippocrates, the father of medicine, lived during the "Golden Age" of ancient Greece (500–400 B.C.).

Holograms are used to record very small changes in the size of objects. This is because they can record an object at many angles with great accuracy. Holograms taken of the same object at different times are used to measure minute changes in size. Scientists use them to study the growth of crystals or the buildup of dirt on old oil paintings.

Whether the system is a single unit or a number of separate units connected together by wires, it has a number of music or program sources. Sources can include a tape CASSETTE RECORDER, a COMPACT DISC PLAYER, a RADIO tuner, and maybe a RECORD player. They are all plugged into the AMPLIFIER's input sockets. The amplifier boosts the small electrical signals from the sources, and LOUD-SPEAKERS turn the electrical signals into sounds. The amplifier also controls the volume and tone of the output. For STEREOPHONIC SOUND the original recording is made on two channels. They are amplified separately and fed to the two loudspeakers. Differences between the two channels make the sound more realistic than single-channel or mono sound reproduction.

Hippocrates

Hippocrates was an ancient Greek philosopher and physician who was born about 460 B.C. on the island of Kos. Little is known of his early life, but he traveled widely in Greece and the Middle East, teaching his theories of MEDICINE. He is often referred to as "the father of medicine." However, little is known about Hippocrates' own work, and most of the Hippocratic medicine we know about today was developed later by his followers. The most lasting influence of Hippocrates is the Hippocratic oath, which lays down a code of principles for the doctor, ensuring that the good of the patient is always the most important part of treatment.

History of Science

Ancient people knew the habits of animals and the powers of plants. But the Egyptians and Babylonians were the first to use science to explore nature and the universe. Our knowledge has increased greatly in the last hundred years; science has gone from the atom and out into space, and made greater strides than in all previous human history. *See* pages 322 to 325.

Hologram

A hologram is a three-dimensional (3-D) PHOTOGRAPH. A 3-D object has depth as well as length and breadth. To make a 3-D picture, a beam of LASER light is split into two separate beams. One part of the beam is aimed at the

Dennis Gabor (1906–1979)
Gabor was a Hungarian-born physicist who worked in Britain. He developed the theory behind holography during the 1940s, but actual holography became possible only after the laser was developed at the beginning of the 1960s. The powerful light of the laser allowed high quality holograms to be made. Gabor eventually received the Nobel Prize for Physics in 1971.

object being photographed. It is then reflected back from the object onto a photographic plate or FILM. The other part of the beam is aimed directly at the photographic plate. Interference between the two beams produces a pattern on the plate that is not recognizable as a photograph. This pattern is the hologram.

When the hologram is lit by a laser beam, it produces a three-dimensional image of the original object. A viewer would be able to get a different view of the object as he or she walked around. In the future, holograms may be used in COMPUTER MEMORY systems.

It is much more difficult to produce a hologram than a photograph; any kind of vibration will interfere with the taking of a hologram. However, they are becoming more widely used and appear in advertisements and all kinds of decorative objects. Holograms are increasingly used in industry for measurement and inspection. A television that shows 3-D images using the principles of holography may soon be possible.

▲ *The photographic technique of holography makes these images, produced on a flat screen, appear in three dimensions.*

▼ *Holograms are made possible by the highly organized light of lasers. Splitting the laser beam enables the photographic plate to record a three-dimensional image.*

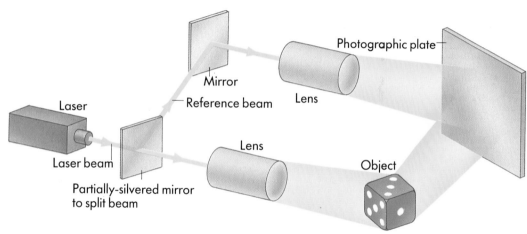

Photographic plate

Mirror

Reference beam

Lens

Laser

Laser beam

Partially-silvered mirror to split beam

Lens

Object

HISTORY OF SCIENCE

Last century, Mendel pioneered genetics, Darwin helped to develop the theory of evolution, and Babbage made the first mechanical computer. As the century closed, scientists studied the atom and motion at the speed of light in space. Here Newton's rules did not apply: Einstein's theories of relativity and Planck's laws of quantum mechanics were needed. This century, nuclear power was born and the transistor and modern computer. The space age began: men stood on the Moon in 1969.

1000 B.C.–A.D. 500

First Olympic Games 776 B.C.
Roman conquest of Britain A.D. 43
Vesuvius erupts, destroying Pompeii A.D. 79

Hippocrates establishes profession of physician and begins to free medicine from superstition.
Chinese develop acupuncture.

Democritus states all matter is made of atoms, solid particles that cannot be divided.
Aristotle develops theory of four basic elements.

A.D. 500–1499

Marco Polo visits Asia 1271–95
Black Death kills 1 in 4 in Europe 1334–51
Columbus lands in the Americas 1492

Avicenna writes *The Canon of Medicine* – most important medical book for centuries (▼).

Alchemy comes to Europe from Arabia where its practice has given rise to first known book on chemistry.

5000 B.C.–1000 B.C.

Tutankhamen Pharaoh of Egypt c.1358.
Israelites leave Egypt for Canaan c.1200.

Egyptians devise the first calendar and use it to predict the Nile floods.
Babylonians predict solar and lunar eclipses.

The wheel (▲)
Glass (▲)
Bricks fired in kilns
Potter's wheel

Archimedes discovers the principle of levers and pulleys.

Ptolemy states the Earth is round and is the motionless center of a revolving universe.

Hindus devise a system of numerals.
Euclid writes his *Elements*. It will be used as a textbook for next 2,000 years.

Water clocks c.650 B.C.
Abacus c.500 B.C.
Archimedes screw (▲) c.200 B.C.
Paper (for writing) c.100 B.C.

Roger Bacon experiments with lenses and discusses eyeglasses for the farsighted.
Leonardo da Vinci makes first observation of capillary action.

Chinese observe Crab supernovas.

| 0 | 1 | 2 | 3 | 4 | 5 |
| 6 | 7 | 8 | 9 | 10 |

Algebra developed by the Arabs.
Arabs introduce Hindu numerals to Europe (▲).

Gunpowder c.1000
Magnetic compass c.1100
Spectacles c.1280
First gun c.1288
Printing press c.1440

1500–1599	1600–1699	1700–1799
Luther begins Reformation 1517 Ferdinand Magellan voyage of circumnavigation 1519–21 England defeats Spanish Armada 1588	Pilgrims sail to America 1620 Louis XIV becomes King of France 1643 Plague kills 70,000 in England 1665	Cook discovers Australia 1770 American Declaration of Independence 1776 French revolution 1789
Vesalius's *On the Structure of the Human Body* – most accurate anatomy book (▼). John Gerard publishes his comprehensive *Herbal*.	Harvey discovers method of circulation of blood. Malpighi uses microscope to discover the structure of animals and plants.	Edward Jenner introduces smallpox vaccinations (▼). Linnaeus classifies 4,400 animals and nearly 8,000 plants.
	Boyle introduces modern idea of elements. 	 Lavoisier produces table of 31 chemical elements.
Galileo researches the laws governing falling bodies and pendulums. Stevinus conducts experiments for understanding gravity.	Newton makes discoveries about light and color and the laws of gravity and motion (▲). Bacon advocates experiments for proof of scientific laws.	Euler works out mathematics of refraction of light. Benjamin Franklin performs his kite experiment, proving that lightning is electricity. Herschel discovers Uranus.
Copernicus puts forward the theory that the whole universe circulates around the Sun (▼). Galileo first to use a telescope effectively and makes many new discoveries.	Kepler discovers planets do not orbit Sun in a circle but as ellipses – laws of planetary motion. Halley makes observations of comets. They later prove to be bodies with regular orbits (▶).	
	Calculus invented separately by Newton and Liebnitz. Napier develops logarithms. Pascal with Fermat develop the mathematics of probability.	
Leonardo da Vinci draws vertical takeoff flying machine c.1500 Compound microscope 1590 Thermometer 1592	Telescope c. 1608–09 Submarine c.1620 Calculating machine c.1643 Steam pump 1698	Steam engine c.1712 Iron smelting c.1750 Spinning Jenny c.1764 Power loom c.1785

1800–1840	1841–1880	1881–1920
Napoleon invades Russia 1812 Battle of Waterloo 1815 Introduction of Penny Post in England 1840	Marx and Engels publish *Communist Manifesto* 1848 Lincoln becomes president of U.S.A. 1860 Suez Canal opened 1869	Amundsen reaches South Pole 1911 World War I 1914–18 Russian Revolution 1917
Lyell publishes his theory of Earth's development.	Darwin's observations during the voyage of HMS *Beagle* confirm Lyell's theories.	Wegener introduces Continental drift theory.
Schleiden and Schwann show that all plants and animals are made up of cells.	Darwin publishes his *On the Origin of Species*. Lister begins antiseptic medicine and Pasteur shows microbes cause disease. Mendel's experiments reveal laws of inheritance of genes.	Freud's psychoanalysis experiments. Fleming discovers penicillin. Ehrlich begins treating disease with chemicals.
Dalton develops his atomic theory which is the basis of modern physics and chemistry. Davy isolates sodium and potassium using electrolysis.	Mendeleyev devises periodic table of elements. Bunsen and Kirchhoff design first spectroscope, discover caesium and rubidium with it.	Becquerel discovers radioactivity. Curies discover radioactivity of radium. Thomson discovers electrons.
Faraday conducts experiments with electricity and magnetism. Alessandro Volta invents first electric battery (▼).	Maxwell announces theory of electromagnetic waves. Joule measures amount of mechanical work required to produce an amount of heat.	Rutherford conducts nuclear physics experiments. Einstein presents his theory of relativity. Planck works on radiation.
		Ambrose Fleming produces first vacuum tube, which will be used in the development of radio and television.
Wallaston and Fraunhofer discover absorption lines in solar spectrum.	Adams and Leverrier pinpoint position of Neptune and Galle finds it with telescope (▲).	
Babbage develops program-mable analytical machine.	Möbius discovers a figure with only one side and one edge.	
Electric battery c.1800 Steam locomotive c.1804 Camera c.1822 Electromagnet c.1825 Telegraph c.1837	Safety pin c.1849 Passenger elevator c.1852 Refrigerator 1858 Telephone 1875 Light bulb c.1879	Gasoline engine car (▲) c.1885 Pneumatic tire c.1888 Radio c.1895 Airplane c.1903 Bakelite c.1908

1921–1960	1961–1992	
World War II 1939–1945 First atomic bomb explodes 1945 Edmund Hillary first to climb Everest 1953	Assassination of J.F. Kennedy 1963 Chernobyl explosion 1986 Germany reunited Collapse of USSR	◄ *Important world events that shaped the way people thought.* ▼ *Areas of scientific study.*
Discovery of paleomagnetism	First hole in ozone layer identified.	**EARTH SCIENCES** *See also* GEOLOGY; GEOGRAPHY.
Salk produces polio vaccine. Watson and Crick reveal the structure of DNA.	First human heart transplant 1967. Smallpox wiped out by vaccination. Developments in genetic engineering.	**LIFE SCIENCES** *See also* BIOLOGY; BOTANY; GENETICS; MEDICINE; MICROBIOLOGY; VETERINARY MEDICINE.
		CHEMISTRY *See also* INORGANIC CHEMISTRY; ORGANIC CHEMISTRY.
Chadwick discovers neutrons. Bohr discovers structure of atom (▲).	Gell-Mann suggests existence of quarks 1964. Quarks revealed 1971.	**PHYSICS** *See also* ELECTRICITY; HEAT; LIGHT; NUCLEAR PHYSICS; SOUND.
Transistor invented. First integrated circuit is made, start of microelectronics.	Development of microchips and microcomputers revolutionized production of all kinds of machines.	**ELECTRONICS** *See also* COMPUTER; ELECTRONICS.
Tombaugh discovers Pluto 1930. Hubble discovers universe is expanding.	Quasars observed. First Moon landings 1969. Hawking develops his theory of black holes 1970s. Soviet astronauts complete one year in space.	**ASTRONOMY** *See also* METEOROLOGY; STARS; SPACE EXPLORATION.
	A computer is used to solve a problem set by Archimedes.	**MATHEMATICS** *See also* NUMBERS; STATISTICS.
Electron microscope c.1939 Programmable electronic computer c.1943 Fiber optics c.1955 Artificial satellite (▲) c.1959	Laser c.1960 Silicon chip c.1961 Microprocessor (►) c.1971 Space shuttle c.1981 Superconductors c.1987	**TECHNOLOGY**

Homing

Homing is the ability of animals to find their way home. It is particularly important when animals have young waiting for food. Birds, bees, and wasps use landmarks when close to their nests, but many birds can find their way across the sea and across land which they have never seen before. People who keep racing pigeons send the birds hundreds of miles away and then release them to see which one gets home first. Pigeons' brains contain iron and some scientists believe that the birds use this iron like a compass to find their way. A pigeon taken from Britain to the U.S. in a closed box was back at its nest within 13 days of being released, having covered more than 2,800 miles (4,500 km) at an average speed of about 270 miles (440 km) per day! Homing pigeons have been known to fly 600 miles (970 km) in a day. Pigeons two or three years old make the best racers but older birds are better at finding their way in bad weather.

The homing mechanisms of guided MISSILES are different from those of animals. The missile is seeking the target. Detectors are linked to a COMPUTER which continuously adjusts the missile's flight path to keep it on course, even if the target is moving very rapidly. *See also* MIGRATION.

▲ *Pigeons' brains contain iron and this may act as a compass needle to help them find their way. They also have an excellent "internal clock" which tells them the time at home. The position of the Sun or stars tells them the time where they are, and from this information they can calculate the direction to home. Near home, they find their way using familiar landmarks.*

People have been using homing pigeons for thousands of years. In ancient Greece, homing pigeons were used to carry the results of the Olympic Games to the different cities. Homing pigeons can fly at an average speed of 45 mph (72 km/h) over distances of up to 500 miles (800 km).

▼ *Homing pigeons return.*

Homogenization

Homogenization is a way of mixing substances that usually will not mix. If water and oil are stirred together they immediately separate again. Sometimes droplets of one can be spread through, or suspended in, the other. Milk is a suspension of FAT droplets in water. The fatty cream will always come to the top. Milk is homogenized by forcing it, under high PRESSURE, through a nozzle with

tiny holes in it to break up the fat into very much smaller droplets and spread them evenly. These much smaller droplets will remain suspended throughout the liquid so the milk will not separate.
See also EMULSION; MILK.

Hooke, Robert *See* Elasticity

Hormone

Hormones occur in both plants and animals. They are substances produced within the organism in very small quantities, which have powerful effects on organs and systems. In animals, most hormones are produced in endocrine GLANDS. Hormones are often referred to as "chemical messengers," because of this controlling action in "switching on" or "switching off" the action of these other parts of the body, including other glands.

The rapid GROWTH of the growing tip of a shoot is controlled by plant growth hormones. In mammals, hormones control growth and development, and play a very important role in sexual development and REPRODUCTION. Hormones are produced in the sex organs, kidneys, intestine, thyroid gland in the neck, and the pituitary and hypothalamus glands within the BRAIN. The human body produces 30 hormones, many of which play an important part in the health and development of the body. There is also a group of hormones called stress hormones and these are secreted in the presence of fear, injury, or anger.

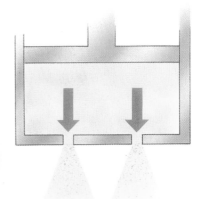

▲ *Forcing milk through tiny holes limits the size of individual fat droplets. Milk can then be stored without the fats separating out as a layer at the top of the milk.*

Homogeneous describes something that is the same throughout the whole of its volume. For instance a jelly is homogeneous but a chocolate chip cookie is not homogeneous because its composition varies.

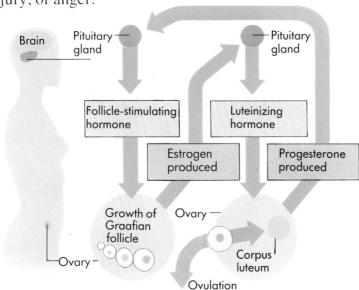

◀ *Several hormones from different sources may be involved during any single body process, such as the menstrual cycle. Two hormones produced by the pituitary gland – luteinizing hormone (LH) and follicle-stimulating hormone (FSH) – control the action of a woman's ovaries. FSH stimulates the growth of a Graafian follicle, producing an ovum. LH acts upon the corpus luteum releasing the ovum during ovulation. In turn the ovaries secrete two other hormones, estrogen and progesterone, which influence the activity of the pituitary gland and regulate the menstrual cycle.*

Hormones	Source	Function
Prolactin	Pituitary	Controls milk supply and production of female sex hormones
Growth hormone	Pituitary	Works directly on the tissues to cause growth
Cortisol and corticosterone	Adrenal glands	Helps the body cope with pain and shock, and increase the level of glucose in the blood when needed. Also helps control fat levels in the body
Adrenaline and noradrenaline	Adrenal glands	Prepares the body when sudden activity is needed
Oestradiol and progesterone	Ovaries	Controls development of female sexual characteristics and growth
Testosterone	Testes	Controls development of male sexual characteristics and growth
Thyroxine	Thyroid	Speeds up chemical reactions in the body
Insulin	Pancreas	Controls sugar levels in the blood

What Horsepower?

James Watt invented the term horsepower in the late 1700s. One horsepower is a rate of doing work equal to 550 foot-pounds per second. A foot-pound was the work needed to lift one pound one foot.

▼ Although brake horsepower is an old engineering term, it is still used to compare different engines and vehicles.

Horsepower

Horsepower is a unit invented by the British engineer James Watt to measure the POWER output of an ENGINE. One horsepower is equivalent to the rate of working of an average horse. The power of a car engine is usually given in *brake horsepower*. This is a measure of the power output of the engine measured by a machine called a dynamometer. Before car engines were tested on dynamometers, their power in horsepower was calculated from the size and number of cylinders in the engine, which usually underestimated its power. Horsepower has gradually been replaced by the WATT as a measure of power. One horsepower is equivalent to 746 watts.

Type of vehicle	hp	Type of vehicle	hp
	1		300–500 bhp
	4		4,500 bhp
	75–85 bhp		28,000 bhp
	80–105 bhp		

HORTICULTURE

Horticulture is the branch of crop-growing that deals with garden and greenhouse produce: flowers and vegetables and a certain amount of fruit. It is similar to agriculture in many ways, but is usually carried out on a smaller scale and unlike agriculture only covers plants. Gardens existed thousands of years ago, but horticulture did not become a science until the 20th century.

Horticulturalists produce many of the fruits and vegetables that we buy in the stores and they are also involved with the production of seeds and plants for sale to gardeners. A lot of this work involves finding out the best methods of harvesting seeds and storing them to make sure that they will grow properly. Much work is also done on breeding new and better varieties. Not all garden plants are grown from seeds. Horticulturalists propagate a lot of plants, especially trees and shrubs, from cuttings (small twigs cut from the plants and stuck in the ground or in pots of special soil). The twigs sprout roots after a few weeks and eventually grow into new plants. All are just like the parent plant, so the gardener knows exactly what variety he is buying at the nursery. Apples and roses are more often propagated by grafting. Horticulturalists take special cuttings, called scions, from a desired variety and bind them to cut surfaces of strongly growing young plants, called stocks, of another variety. The tissues unite and continue to grow, but everything springing from the scions is of the desired variety. It is possible to grow apple trees carrying several varieties of fruit by grafting several scions onto one sapling. Horticulture also involves recognizing the many pests that attack our garden plants and discovering ways to control them.

▲ *The same plant may grow better in some places than others, depending on the climate and type of soil. Such variation is shown by these ears of corn.*

> Grafting is often used to produce new or hardier plants. A piece of one plant, the "scion," is fitted into a cut made in the stem of another plant, the "stock." The two plants must be related: a piece of lemon tree can be grafted onto an orange tree, but not onto an elm tree. If a tomato plant is grafted to a potato stock the new plant will produce tomatoes, while the stock will still produce potatoes!

SEE FOR YOURSELF
Planting seeds is not the only way to grow a new plant. During spring you can take a cutting from a tree or shrub. Choose a twig with a bud at the tip, and cut it diagonally with a pair of strong scissors or pruning shears. Fill a small flower pot with a mixture of potting compost and soil, and plant your cutting (cut end down!) about 2 inches (5 cm) deep. Place the pot in a well-lighted spot and keep the soil moist. After about 10 days, your cutting should have sprouted roots and begun to grow.

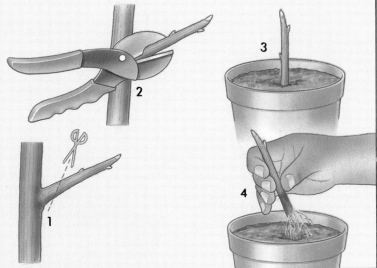

See also AGRICULTURE; BREEDING; CEREALS; FLOWERS; FRUIT; GENETICS; NATURAL SELECTION; SEEDS; SOIL; TRANSPLANTS.

▶ *The first diesel-powered hovercraft, the AP1-88, was launched in March 1983.*

Christopher Cockerell (1910–) Cockerell solved the problem of how to keep an air cushion underneath a hovercraft. Using part of a vacuum cleaner and old cans, he developed the principle of the air cushion. Cockerell put one can inside another and blew air into the space between them. He weighed the result on kitchen scales and found that the air jet when compressed like this had three times the pressure of air just blown onto the scales.

Hovercraft (Air cushion vehicle)

A hovercraft is a vehicle that floats on top of a cushion of AIR. Hovercraft can skim across land or water. The theory of hovercraft has been known since the 1870s, but the practical problems of building them were not solved until 1955. The main problem was how to stop the air cushion from simply blowing away from underneath the vehicle. The British engineer Christopher Cockerell solved this by blowing air, trapped in a ring or curtain, downward all around the vehicle. This has the effect of holding the air cushion inside it. He built the first modern hovercraft, the SRN1, in 1958. Later models improved on the SRN1 by attaching flexible skirts all around the vehicle to help keep the air cushion in.

Hovercraft are propelled by large pusher propellers driven by the same ENGINES that drive the air cushion fans. They can reach a speed of 60 knots and are often called air cushion vehicles.

The largest hovercraft now in use is over 180 feet (56 m) long and weighs 310 tons. It carries over 400 passengers and 60 cars.

▶ *On a hovercraft, most of the engine power maintains the cushion of air beneath the vehicle. A central fan draws in air from the atmosphere and forces it between the hull and the outer skirt. The air cushion reduces drag from the sea or land surface to a minimum, so relatively little power is needed for actual propulsion.*

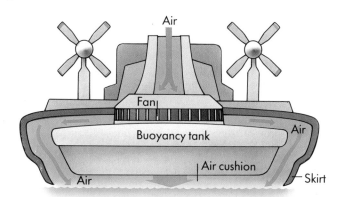

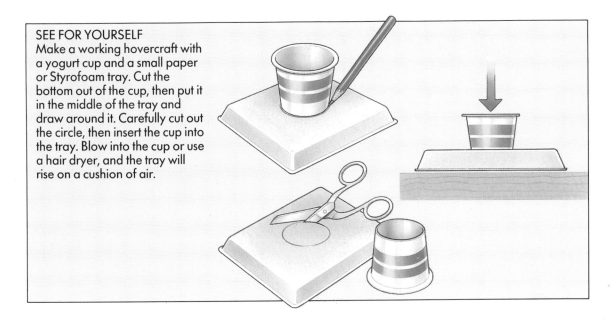

SEE FOR YOURSELF
Make a working hovercraft with a yogurt cup and a small paper or Styrofoam tray. Cut the bottom out of the cup, then put it in the middle of the tray and draw around it. Carefully cut out the circle, then insert the cup into the tray. Blow into the cup or use a hair dryer, and the tray will rise on a cushion of air.

Hoyle, Fred *See* Cosmology

Hubble, Edwin *See* Universe

Humidifier

A humidifier is a device that adds moisture to dry AIR. Air-conditioning systems used in offices and HEATING SYSTEMS can dry out the air too much to be comfortable for people. Breathing air that is too dry can irritate people's throats and noses. A humidifier works by trickling water over a material with a large surface area, enabling the maximum volume of water to come into contact with the dry air and evaporate into it. Alternatively, water may be sprayed directly into the air.
See also AIR CONDITIONING; EVAPORATION.

Home Humidifiers
People use humidifiers in the winter to help them feel more comfortable. Heated air from central heating systems is very dry and speeds up the evaporation of moisture from the skin. Humidifiers slow this process down and so reduce the cooling effect of evaporation, making people feel warmer at lower temperatures.

Humidity

Humidity is a measure of the water VAPOR content of the ATMOSPHERE. It is measured with an instrument called a HYGROMETER. Absolute humidity is defined as the actual amount of water vapor in the AIR. Relative humidity is the RATIO of water vapor in the air to the amount of water vapor needed to saturate the air at the same TEMPERATURE and PRESSURE. If the air contains only half the water it can hold, the relative humidity is 50 percent.

In clouds and fog the air is saturated and its relative humidity is 100 percent. In desert areas it may be as low

If we sweat when the humidity is high, the sweat does not evaporate quickly and we feel uncomfortable and sticky. In dry, desert conditions (where the humidity is low), sweat evaporates very quickly. An unwary traveler often does not realize how much liquid is lost as sweat, and so runs the risk of becoming dehydrated and losing too much vital salt.

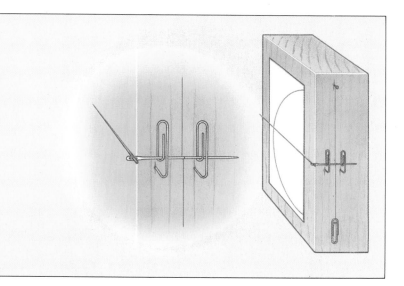

▶ *When a mass of air is warmed by the Sun, it can hold more water vapor. As surface water evaporates, the water vapor is absorbed by the air and its humidity increases. Eventually the air cannot absorb any more water vapor. It becomes saturated, and evaporation ceases.*

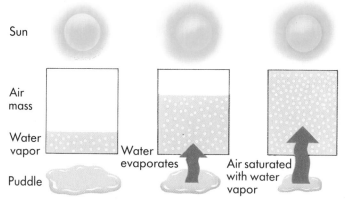

Sun

Air mass

Water vapor

Puddle

Water evaporates

Air saturated with water vapor

▼ *The winds in a hurricane spiral around the eye, a central calm area of low pressure and light winds about 20 miles (30 km) in diameter.*

as 10 percent. The relative humidity of air varies according to the temperature. Cold air can only hold a small amount of water, which is why dew forms in the early morning when the temperature is very low. As the air warms up it is able to hold more water.

Hurricane

A hurricane is a severe tropical storm in which the wind reaches a maximum speed of more than 150 mph (250 km/h) or Force 12 on the Beaufort scale (p.755). The average wind speed is greater than 73 mph (118 km/h).

A cyclonic tropical storm is usually called a hurricane when it occurs in the Caribbean area or around the northeastern coast of Australia. It can also be called a cyclone. The center of a hurricane is known as the "eye," and it usually stays out to sea but its high winds may cause destruction across nearby coastal lands.

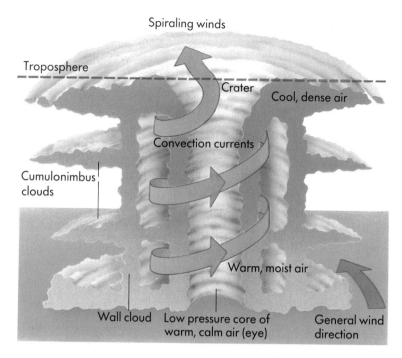

Spiraling winds

Troposphere

Crater

Cool, dense air

Convection currents

Cumulonimbus clouds

Warm, moist air

Wall cloud

Low pressure core of warm, calm air (eye)

General wind direction

◄ *In the Northern Hemisphere, hurricane winds blow in a counterclockwise direction, whereas in the Southern Hemisphere they blow clockwise. The winds reach their greatest speed (up to 150mph (250km/h)) within the wall of storm clouds surrounding the eye. As the winds spiral upward, they create tunnels of clear air inside the cloud wall. In a typical cyclone or hurricane, the winds rise as high as the top of the troposphere before losing their force in the thin air of the upper atmosphere.*

Huygens, Christiaan *See* Light

Hybrid

This word is most often used to describe an animal or a plant whose parents belong to two different SPECIES. One of the best known examples is the mule, which results from the mating of a male donkey and a female horse. Mules are usually tough animals but, like nearly all animal hybrids, they are sterile. This means that they cannot have offspring themselves.

Many plant hybrids are fully fertile and many of our cultivated plants, including most of our CEREAL crops, are hybrids. Plants resulting from crossing two different varieties of the same species are also called hybrids and, like those between different species, they are often bigger and stronger than their parents.

Producing plant hybrids can be a long process. Plants of the same species are inbred for several generations to give plants with pure heredity lines. These plants are then crossed with other inbred plants. Plant breeders work hard to produce hybrids of this kind in their search for bigger and better flowers and vegetables for the garden and the commercial market. Hybrids are also bred to have greater resistance to particular DISEASES.
See also BREEDING; HORTICULTURE.

Horse

Donkey

Mule

▲ *A horse is strong, but needs high quality food. A donkey is much weaker, but can live on a poor diet. The mule is a hybrid of the two that combines their advantages, but cannot breed.*

▶ *The wing flaps, under-carriage, and landing gear of this Russian Mig 29 fighter are hydraulically controlled.*

▼ *Using pistons of different diameters within connected cylinders, as in a hydraulic jack, gives a mechanical advantage. A large movement of the small piston causes a smaller movement of the large piston. But the large piston acts with much greater force than the smaller one.*

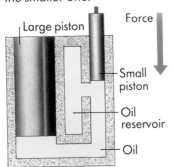

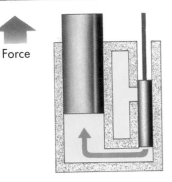

Hydraulics

Hydraulics describes the study of how FLUIDS behave. An understanding of hydraulics is very important in the design of harbors, docks, and dams in which water may be flowing through rivers or canals, or may be enclosed in narrow channels or pipes.

Hydraulic machinery can be operated and POWER transmitted by using the PRESSURE of a LIQUID. If a pipe is filled with oil and fitted with a piston at each end, pushing one piston into the pipe forces the piston at the other end outward. Power is transmitted from one end of the pipe to the other. Some excavators and cranes use this principle to lift heavy loads by the action of hydraulic rams. A hydraulic ram is a cylinder with a tight fitting piston, or ram. Oil pumped into one end of the cylinder forces the piston out of the other end. By attaching

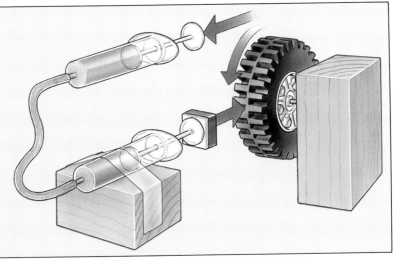

SEE FOR YOURSELF
To make a hydraulic brake system, you will need two plastic syringes, some thin plastic tubing, a toy wheel, and a piece of rubber brake pad from a bicycle. Attach the wheel to a wooden block, and tape one of the syringes to another block. Attach the brake pad to the end of this syringe. Then connect the syringes with the tubing, and fill them all with water. Spin the wheel with your finger, hold the other syringe in your hand, depress the plunger and the brake pad will stop the wheel.

several hydraulic rams to levers, loads can be raised and lowered very precisely. Some jacks used to raise cars for repairs, work on hydraulic principles. Dump trucks use hydraulic rams to tilt the back of the truck, cars have hydraulic brakes and many have hydraulic steering.

Hydrocarbons

Hydrocarbons are COMPOUNDS consisting of atoms of HYDROGEN and CARBON only. They form one of the most important classes of organic compounds. Hydrocarbons are found in PETROLEUM and NATURAL GAS and in coal tar, coal gas, kerosene, gasoline, and many other commercial petroleum products. The hydrocarbons in crude oil and natural gas provide the raw material from which plastics, solvents, and many synthetic fibers and materials are made.

Aliphatic hydrocarbons have their main carbon atoms arranged in chains. They include compounds called alkanes or paraffins (such as methane, ethane, and propane). *Aromatic hydrocarbons* are a small class in which the compounds are distinguished by a ring of six carbon atoms containing three double bonds. The best known aromatic is BENZENE, and the carbon rings are known as benzene rings. Hydrocarbons are different from CARBOHYDRATES, which are organic compounds consisting of atoms of carbon, hydrogen and oxygen, and PROTEINS, which contain nitrogen as well.

Hydrochloric acid

Hydrochloric ACID is a highly dangerous, colorless LIQUID that fumes when exposed to the air, has an irritating smell, is very corrosive, and can produce nasty burns. It is a solution of the gas hydrogen chloride dissolved in water. Concentrated hydrochloric acid con-

▲ Ethane, formula C_2H_6, is a typical member of the alkane group of hydrocarbons. Methylpropene is one of the alkene group, and has the formula C_4H_8 with a double bond between two of its carbon atoms.

▼ The formula for hydrochloric acid.

HCl

▼ Hydrochloric acid is used to etch copper plates for printing. Before etching, the design is engraved into an acid-resistant coating such as wax. The plate is then inked before being pressed against the printing paper in the rollers.

The etching process

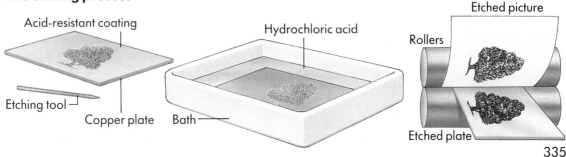

Acid-resistant coating

Etching tool

Copper plate

Hydrochloric acid

Bath

Etched picture

Rollers

Etched plate

tains three parts of hydrogen chloride to seven parts of water. The hydrogen chloride is produced when the two gases HYDROGEN and CHLORINE combine together or when sodium chloride (common salt) is treated with another acid, SULFURIC ACID.

Hydrochloric acid reacts with bases to form SALTS called chlorides. It is used in industry to make other chemicals and in the processing of certain foods. The human stomach produces weak hydrochloric acid to aid the breakdown of foods during DIGESTION.

Hydroelectricity

Hydroelectricity is ELECTRICITY produced from falling water. Rain falling on high ground flows as rivers down to sea level. If a dam is built to stop the water flowing, a large lake, or reservoir, builds up behind it. In a hydro-electric power station, valves allow some of the water to escape from the dam through TURBINES. The fast-flowing water spins the turbines which are connected to electricity GENERATORS. While the hydroelectric generator is working, water flows out, and the level of the reservoir falls. It is usually filled up by rain.

Some hydroelectric generators use a system called pumped storage to refill the reservoir. During the day,

▲ Hydroelectric plants generate about 20 percent of the world's electricity.

▼ Water to drive the turbines is taken from a point midway up the dam so that the generators operate even if the water level in the reservoir falls below normal. A spillway allows water to escape when the dam is full.

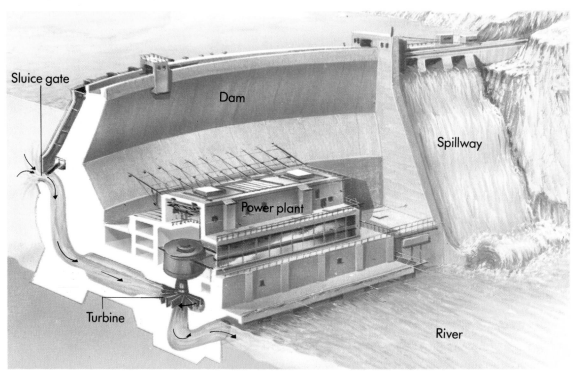

Sluice gate

Dam

Spillway

Power plant

Turbine

River

water flows from a high level reservoir through the turbines to a low level reservoir. At night, when electricity demand is low, the water is pumped from the low level to the high level reservoir. This ensures that POWER can be generated the next day. Hydroelectric plants cost less to operate than coal- or oil-driven plants, and they do not cause pollution. Unfortunately, they can only operate in places where high dams can be built.

Hydrofoil

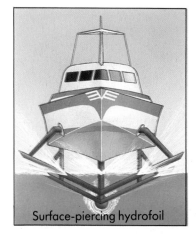
Surface-piercing hydrofoil

A hydrofoil is a type of boat named after the underwater wings attached to the front and rear of its hull. When the boat moves slowly, it behaves like any other boat. When it accelerates to higher speeds, the flow of water over and around the underwater wings produces an upward FORCE called lift and the boat rises up in the water. Eventually, most of the hull is out of the water. The force called drag that resists the movement of objects through FLUIDS is therefore reduced and the boat can travel much faster. Jetfoils are propelled by water jets instead of propellers and can reach speeds of 43 knots, or 50 mph (80 km/h). The first successful hydrofoil was developed by the Italian Enrico Forlanini in 1906. Alexander Graham BELL, the inventor of the TELEPHONE, developed the hydrofoil further.

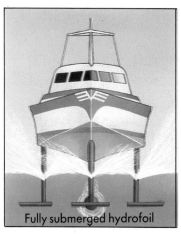
Fully submerged hydrofoil

▲ Hydrofoils can be classified according to the design of their underwater wings or foils. The more common surface-piercing types operate at an angle to the water, and gain some of their lift from the water surface. Fully submerged hydrofoils operate at much flatter angles, and gain lift in much the same way as an airplane wing in the air.

◄ This is a surface-piercing hydrofoil. When traveling at speed it uses the surface area of the foils for stability and control. This type of hydrofoil performs best on calm water such as lakes and rivers.

Hydrogen

Hydrogen is a colorless, odorless, tasteless, nonpoisonous GAS. It is the lightest, simplest, and most plentiful ELEMENT in the universe. The Sun's light and heat come from hydrogen atoms joining together in nuclear

**Henry Cavendish
(1731–1810)**
Cavendish was a British
scientist who was both a
chemist and a physicist. He is
most famous for his work on
the composition of air.
Cavendish discovered the
properties of hydrogen and
showed that air was a mixture
of more than one gas. He
was also the first to show that
water is in fact a compound
and not an element.

fusion. It is found in a whole range of compounds,
including ACIDS, HYDROXIDES, HYDROCARBONS, CARBO-
HYDRATES, and WATER. Hydrogen was used in ballooning, but because it readily bursts into flame, it caused
many accidents and now balloonists use hot air or
HELIUM. The ordinary hydrogen atom consists of a nucleus formed by one PROTON around which circles a single
ELECTRON. This form, or ISOTOPE, of hydrogen is called
protium. Two other isotopes exist, deuterium, a constituent of HEAVY WATER, and tritium. They are used to
make HYDROGEN BOMBS.

SEE FOR YOURSELF
Put some water in a dish and
add a spoonful of vinegar.
Connect wires to the terminals of
a large battery and put the bare
ends in the water. Bubbles will
start to form and these can be
collected as shown. Test the
gases by holding a lit splint to the
mouth of the tubes, the
hydrogen from the water will
make a "pop" and the oxygen
will burn with a strong flame.

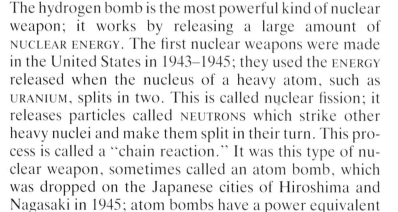

Hydrogen bomb

Nuclear fusion

Nuclear fission
Proton ————
Neutron ————

▲ *In nuclear fission, a
uranium-235 atom shoots out
a neutron from its center. This
neutron strikes another U-235
atom and breaks it apart,
releasing more neutrons. These
neutrons strike more U-235
atoms and so on. This chain
reaction, if not controlled, will
cause an atomic explosion.*

The hydrogen bomb is the most powerful kind of nuclear
weapon; it works by releasing a large amount of
NUCLEAR ENERGY. The first nuclear weapons were made
in the United States in 1943–1945; they used the ENERGY
released when the nucleus of a heavy atom, such as
URANIUM, splits in two. This is called nuclear fission; it
releases particles called NEUTRONS which strike other
heavy nuclei and make them split in their turn. This process is called a "chain reaction." It was this type of nuclear weapon, sometimes called an atom bomb, which
was dropped on the Japanese cities of Hiroshima and
Nagasaki in 1945; atom bombs have a power equivalent
to many thousands of tons of ordinary explosive.

   Later it was realized that more energy, equivalent to
hundreds of millions of tons of ordinary explosive, would
be released by the forcing together (or fusion) of two
light atomic nuclei at very high speeds. This is the source
of energy that is found in the Sun and other stars. The
first hydrogen bombs were tested by the United States
and the Soviet Union in 1953.

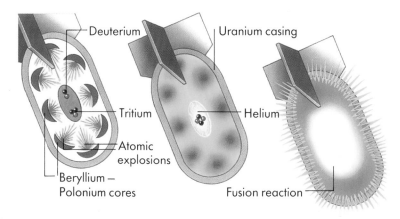

Deuterium — Uranium casing — Tritium — Helium — Atomic explosions — Beryllium — Polonium cores — Fusion reaction

◀ The hydrogen bomb needs an atom bomb just to trigger it off. The atomic explosion of beryllium-polonium cores creates the conditions under which heavy hydrogen (deuterium and tritium) fuse to form helium. Once the fusion reaction has started, it produces the energy which starts a second atomic explosion in the uranium casing. All three stages occur within a split second.

◀ A test hydrogen bomb explosion caused this huge fireball. This explosion took place on an island in Bikini Atoll, a group of islands in the Pacific Ocean, in 1956.

Andrei Sakharov (1921–1989)
Sakharov was a Soviet physicist who played a major role in the development of the Soviet hydrogen bomb. He later became a vocal campaigner for nuclear disarmament, and was labeled a dissident by the Soviet authorities and sent into internal exile. In 1975, Sakharov was awarded the Nobel Peace Prize. The more tolerant policies of the Soviet authorities allowed him to come out of exile in 1989. He died in Moscow shortly afterward.

Robert Oppenheimer (1904–1967)
Oppenheimer was a U.S. physicist, and is often described as the father of the atomic bomb. He was the senior scientist on the Manhattan Project which developed the atomic bombs dropped on Japan at the end of the World War II. After the war, Oppenheimer argued for the peaceful use of nuclear power. He continued working as a physicist and did important work on black holes.

Hydrogen bonds

Hydrogen bonds are fairly weak chemical BONDS that hold together ATOMS, MOLECULES, or IONS. An ice crystal is a giant network of water molecules held together by hydrogen bonds. They involve the interaction between certain chemical groups of atoms and other atoms that have a pair of nonbonding ELECTRONS.

When hydrogen combines with certain elements such as fluorine, nitrogen, or oxygen, the hydrogen atom bonds with two atoms of the other element at the same time. The group can then bond to yet another atom by means of a hydrogen bond. Hydrogen bonding plays a major part in the way in which large molecules such as deoxyribonucleic acid (DNA) are put together. The spiral structures of PROTEINS, essential for all animal and plant life, are held together by hydrogen bonds.

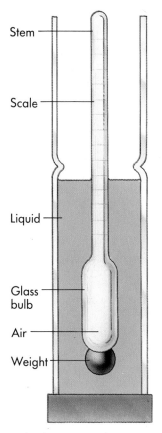

▲ A hydrometer uses the principle of flotation. The hydrometer has a constant mass, and the depth at which it floats in a liquid is directly related to the density of that liquid.

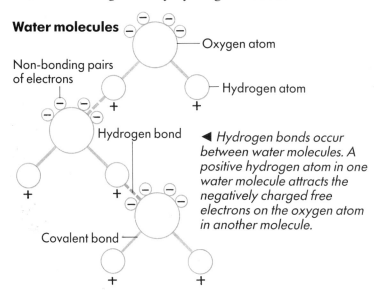

Water molecules

Oxygen atom

Non-bonding pairs of electrons

Hydrogen atom

Hydrogen bond

◄ Hydrogen bonds occur between water molecules. A positive hydrogen atom in one water molecule attracts the negatively charged free electrons on the oxygen atom in another molecule.

Covalent bond

Hydrometer

A hydrometer is an instrument used to measure the DENSITY of a LIQUID. It is used to measure the strength of acid in car batteries or ANTIFREEZE solutions and often in home brewing. The hydrometer floats upright in the liquid so that the lower the relative density of the liquid, the deeper the hydrometer sinks, and the farther up the graduated stem the liquid surface can be seen. Hydrometers are graduated so that the relative density of the liquid is measured compared to that of water, which has a density of one.

Stem

Scale

Liquid

Glass bulb

Air

Weight

Hydroponics

Hydroponics is a method of growing plants without SOIL. If you have ever grown radish seedlings on wet blotting paper you have done some hydroponics yourself. Water and air can supply all the carbon, hydrogen, and oxygen that plants need to make their food, but for healthy growth the plants need a number of other ELEMENTS, such as nitrogen, phosphorus, and potassium. These elements are normally taken from the soil by the plants' roots, but if we give the plants the correct amount of chemicals dissolved in water, perfectly healthy plants will grow without any soil at all. Tomatoes and other greenhouse vegetables and fruit are often grown in trays of gravel with the carefully calculated culture solution flowing through them.

See also PHOTOSYNTHESIS.

▲ The roots of hydroponically-grown plants are wrapped in polyethylene. The plants receive nourishment from water containing artificial fertilizers.

Hydroxides

A hydroxide is a COMPOUND of an ELEMENT (usually a metal or hydrogen) and a hydroxide group. Hydroxides are used to make detergents, drugs, paper, and textiles. Sodium hydroxide (CAUSTIC SODA) and potassium hydroxide (caustic potash) are dangerous compounds that are used to attack grease. Dilute ammonium hydroxide is the household AMMONIA you use for cleaning.

The hydroxide group (symbol –OH) is found in every alkali or base and in some organic compounds. Many alkalis, such as sodium hydroxide, form ionic solutions, which conduct ELECTRICITY. The solutions are bitter-tasting and soapy, and strong hydroxide solutions are corrosive and can burn the skin.

See also ACIDS AND BASES.

Hydroponics can be used to grow crops in places where there is no soil or the climate is unsuitable. It is used in the desert areas of Arizona, and in the Persian Gulf. Scientists have been experimenting growing plants in the Arctic, at sea, and in other places where plants could not normally grow.

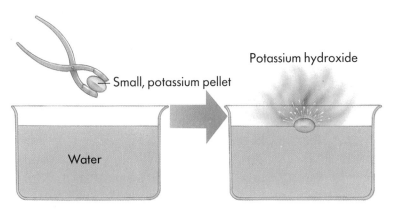

Potassium hydroxide

Small, potassium pellet

Water

◄ When a small piece of potassium is dropped into water it reacts to form potassium hydroxide, and hydrogen gas is given off. The heat of the chemical reaction ignites the hydrogen, which burns with a bright lilac flame.

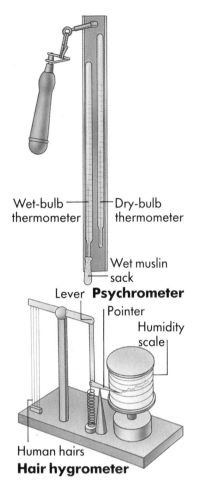

Wet-bulb thermometer — — Dry-bulb thermometer

Wet muslin sack

Lever **Psychrometer**

Pointer

Humidity scale

Human hairs
Hair hygrometer

▲ *A wet- and dry-bulb hygrometer, or psychrometer, makes use of two separate measurements. A hair hygrometer gives a single direct reading based on the effects of humidity on human hair.*

▶ *When the fluid within a cell becomes hypertonic to the surrounding fluid, water molecules move out of the cell until a balance is achieved.*

Hygrometer

A hygrometer is an instrument used for measuring the HUMIDITY of AIR. Some hygrometers, called wet-bulb/dry-bulb hygrometers, are more refined versions of a simple thermometer with its bulb covered with wet muslin (wet-bulb). This is also known as a psychrometer.

The electrical RESISTANCE of the atmosphere varies with the amount of water VAPOR in it. The more water there is in the air, the lower the air's resistance to ELECTRICITY. One type of hygrometer makes use of this property to measure humidity.

Hypertonic

A hypertonic SOLUTION is one in which the osmotic pressure is higher than that of another solution to which it is compared. Osmotic pressure is the PRESSURE that must by applied to a solution to stop the molecules of a liquid solvent from passing into the solution through a membrane by OSMOSIS. The more concentrated a solution is, the higher the osmotic pressure. A hypertonic solution is therefore more concentrated than the one to which it is compared if their temperatures are the same.
See also HYPOTONIC; ISOTONIC.

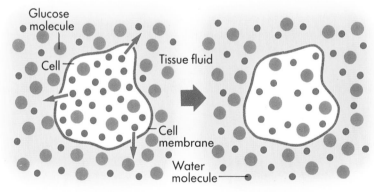

Glucose molecule

Cell

Tissue fluid

Cell membrane

Water molecule

Hypothermia

Hypothermia is a condition in which the body temperature of a warm-blooded animal drops so far below the normal level that it causes harm. If body HEAT is lost faster than it is generated, hypothermia results.

We shiver because the rapidly repeated muscular movements produce body heat. Cats and birds fluff themselves up when cold to increase the thickness of the

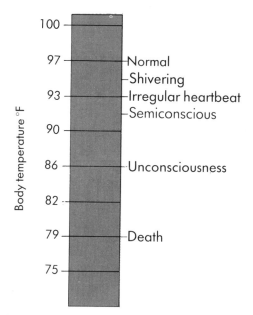

Body temperature °F

100

97 — Normal
— Shivering
93 — Irregular heartbeat
— Semiconscious
90

86 — Unconsciousness

82

79 — Death

75

◄ *The onset of hypothermia is quite slow, but once a person's body temperature has dropped by a few degrees the process speeds up.*

▲ *These marathon runners are wearing aluminum foil blankets to prevent them cooling down too fast. They have used up a lot of energy and need to conserve their body heat.*

insulating layer of air around them. Many elderly people cannot control their body temperature well, and when they get cold may not be aware of the signs of hypothermia, such as "gooseflesh" and shivering. If they are not warmed up quickly they become drowsy, lose consciousness, and die.

Hypotonic

One FLUID is said to be hypotonic in relation to a second fluid if its CONCENTRATION is lower than the concentration of the second fluid. This is the opposite of HYPERTONIC.

In a living organism, when a fluid is hypotonic to a particular CELL, water molecules pass into the cell until the concentrations of the fluids outside and inside of the cell are evened out. The fluid becomes ISOTONIC to the cell when the osmotic pressure of the fluid equals the osmotic pressure of the cell.

See also ISOTONIC; OSMOSIS.

There are a number of words that start with **hyper** and **hypo**. They have very different meanings.
Hyper means a greater than normal amount of something. In medicine hyperacidity means too much acid in the gastric juices.
Hypo means less than a normal amount of something. Hypothermia is a lower than normal body temperature.

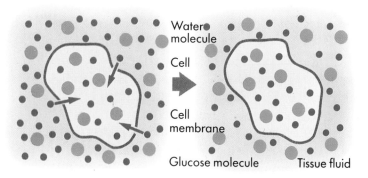

Water molecule

Cell

Cell membrane

Glucose molecule

Tissue fluid

◄ *When the fluid within a cell becomes hypotonic to the surroundings, water molecules are drawn into the cell until a balance is restored.*

343

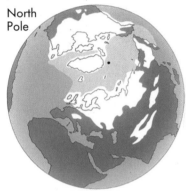

▶ Over 75 percent of an iceberg lies below the water. Icebergs are a hazard to shipping so special patrols track them and report their positions to ships.

North Pole

Farthest extent of ice sheet

Today

▲ During the last Ice Age, the Arctic ice cap was much larger than today. At the time of its greatest extent (about 100,000 years ago) it covered much of Europe and North America. The Antarctic ice sheet underwent an equally dramatic change.

Ice

Ice is WATER in its SOLID, frozen state. Pure water freezes to ice at a temperature of 32°F (0°C). Water containing salt or other compounds freezes at a lower temperature. This is why salt is used to treat icy patches on roads and sidewalks. Unlike other liquids, as water freezes into ice it expands rather than contracts, increasing in volume by about 9 percent. If water freezes in pipes, the pipes may burst. Because it expands as it freezes, ice is less

dense and therefore lighter than water. This gives an iceberg its BUOYANCY and allows ice cubes to float on top of a glass of water.

Ice is still used to chill and preserve meat, fish, fruit, and vegetables during storage or transit. It does this by lowering the temperature around the food and slowing down the action of destructive bacteria.

Ice Age

Ice Age is the name given to a period of the EARTH's geological history when the average temperature of the ATMOSPHERE over a large part of the globe fell to such an extent that ice sheets covered large areas of the Earth. Ice Ages are also known as glacial epochs. One important result of an Ice Age is a lowering of the sea level throughout the world as water turns to ice.

Within any Ice Age there are cold (glacial) periods and warmer (interglacial) periods. The Earth is passing through a warmer, interglacial period now, but 10,000 years ago, ice spread across wide areas of the northern hemisphere during what was a glacial period. There have been several Ice Ages during Eocene, Permian, Carboniferous, Cambrian, and Precambrian periods.

◄ *Granite rocks, formed underground but exposed by geological uplift and the forces of erosion. Granite is a very hard, weather-resistant rock.*

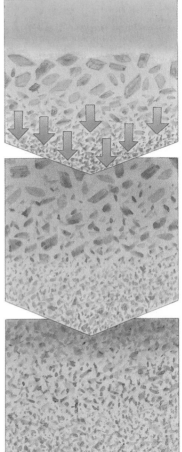

Igneous rocks

Igneous rocks are ROCKS, such as granite or basalt, which were originally molten magma or LAVA and which burst through the EARTH's crust. These rocks originate at fiery, white-hot temperatures.

As all igneous rocks cool, they tend to shrink and crack. Sometimes these cracks and joints take on particular shapes. If magma reaches the surface of the Earth still in a molten state, it may pour out as lava. Sometimes, lava may erupt under the sea and, as the sea water cools it, it takes on a characteristic form. Such lavas are usually called pillow lavas.

Granite is an example of an igneous rock that has cooled slowly. Its crystals have been able to grow to large size and so it is coarse grained. Basalt is an example of a fine-grained rock — it cooled quickly.

Diorite

Granite

Peridotite

Basalt

◄ *Liquid magma cools in a definite sequence (above), with rocks containing silicates of iron and magnesium (such as basalt and peridotite) sinking and solidifying first. Next to be formed are lighter rocks containing silicates of potassium, sodium, calcium, and aluminum (feldspar and hornblade). The remaining silica crystallizes partly as quartz (granite). The rate of cooling determines the size of the crystals; for example, slow cooling rocks are coarse-grained.*

345

▼ Antibody cells are sometimes called memory cells. Once they have encountered an antigen, they will always recognize it. When such a cell encounters the same antigens, it **1** joins onto them and **2** immobilizes them until they are consumed by macrophages. **3** The cell then rapidly makes copies of itself **4** called plasma cells. **5** These release antibodies into the bloodstream, where they attach to antigens and attract macrophages **6**.

Immune system

An organism's immune system protects it from INFECTIONS. The main task of the human immune system is the production of ANTIBODIES. These are produced by the white BLOOD cells in response to infection. Antibodies destroy the bacteria and VIRUSES, or poisons produced by them called antigens, in our bodies. Once our bodies have learned to produce a particular antibody in response to a DISEASE, the antibody can be produced quickly. We become immune to the disease because the antibody can prevent the disease from developing. This is how VACCINATION works. The body is given harmless or dead disease organisms, so it can "learn" to produce the antibody without risk of catching the disease. AIDS is dangerous because it damages the immune system, so the body cannot recognize invading viruses or bacteria.

"Rejection" occurs when the body attacks organs which have been transplanted or grafted from another person or animal. This is because the immune system does not recognize the new tissue, and attacks it as an invader. Strong drugs are needed to prevent rejection.

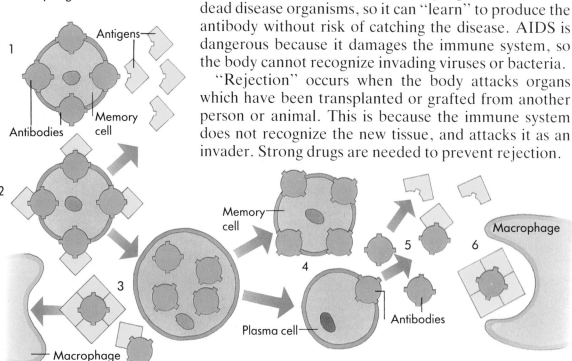

Most people carry the rhesus antigen. Those who have the rhesus antigen are designated RH+, those who do not are RH–. If an RH– woman is pregnant with an RH+ baby, leakage of the baby's blood to the mother causes the mother to produce antibodies. They do not develop fast enough to affect the baby she is carrying but may harm future children.

Implosion

An implosion is a sudden inrush of material. It is like an explosion except that the material is moving inward instead of outward. Implosions can happen because PRESSURE from outside pushes things into an empty space. Very large objects such as STARS can implode because the force of GRAVITY pulls everything toward the other parts. The implosion produces very dense material in the center of the star which can become a NEUTRON STAR or a BLACK HOLE.
See also EXPLOSIVES.

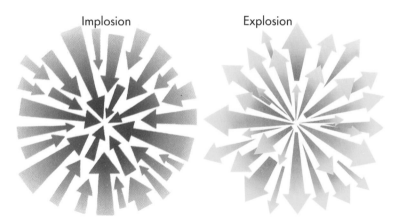

Implosion   Explosion

◄ *All the force of an implosion is directed inward toward the center. Certain types of military explosives use the implosion principle. A small explosion creates a vacuum and the resulting implosion is much more destructive than the initial explosion.*

Indicator, chemical

A chemical indicator is a substance that shows the level of acidity or alkalinity of a liquid. An indicator will be one color in an acidic solution and a different one in an alkaline solution. In some indicators, the intensity of the color indicates the strength of the acidity or alkalinity. Indicators play an important part in qualitative ANALYSIS. The best-known indicator is LITMUS, which is derived from lichen and algae. An ACID solution will turn blue litmus red but will not affect the color of red litmus. A solution containing a base, or alkali, will turn red litmus blue. Vinegar in water (an acid) will turn blue litmus paper red.
See also PH.

Universal indicator

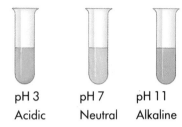

pH 3   pH 7   pH 11
Acidic   Neutral   Alkaline

Litmus paper

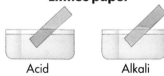

Acid   Alkali

Methyl Orange

Below pH 3   Above pH 4.5

▲ *Several different chemical indicators are used in laboratories. Litmus paper shows whether a liquid is acid or alkaline. A universal indicator enables the chemist to estimate the pH value of a solution fairly accurately. Methyl orange is useful only for acidic solutions. More sophisticated chemical indicators are used to measure other values, such as the amount of sugar in blood or urine.*

SEE FOR YOURSELF
Red cabbage juice makes a simple chemical indicator. Chop up some leaves, and simmer them for 10–15 minutes. When the water has cooled, pour it into some clear glasses. If you add an acid, such as vinegar, the purple juice will turn pink. If you add some weak alkali, such as baking soda, the cabbage juice will turn blue. Stronger alkalis, such as sodium carbonate, will turn it green.

Joseph Henry (1797–1878)
The U.S. physicist Joseph Henry was one of the earliest pioneers of electricity. He discovered electro-magnetic induction (the unit of inductance, the henry, is named after him) and invented an electric telegraph. Henry was appointed the the first director of the Smithsonian Institution in Washington D:C.

▼ *Moving a magnet through a coil of wire induces an electric current in the wire. The direction of the current flow depends on the direction of movement. Electrical generators use rotary movement and spin a coil within a magnetic field.*

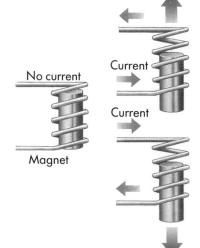

Inductance, self and magnetic

Inductance is a measure of the opposition to the change of current in a electrical CIRCUIT. Self-inductance occurs when the magnetic field in an electrical circuit changes. Magnetic induction is the process by which an electric current is made to flow in a circuit because a magnetic field has moved. If a wire carrying a current is wound into a coil, the inductance of the circuit is increased. The inductance is further increased by inserting an iron core into the coil.

Hans Oersted showed that there was a link between ELECTRICITY and MAGNETISM when he showed that an electric current can produce a magnetic field. Michael FARADAY in Britain and Joseph Henry in the United States developed this idea further when they showed that a magnetic field could produce an electric current. If a wire is made into a complete circuit and is moved through a magnetic field, or the circuit remains still and the magnetic field moves, then a voltage is induced in the circuit and electricity flows. When the magnetic field and

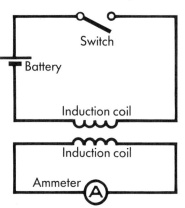

◄ *Because of inductance, a change in the electric current flowing in one circuit can cause a current to flow in a different circuit nearby. When the switch is closed in the upper circuit, current from the battery flows through the coil. This causes a changing magnetic field which links with the coil in the lower circuit. The ammeter shows that a current flows briefly.*

wire circuit are both stationary, no electricity flows in the wire circuit. This idea led to the development of the generator used in power stations to generate electricity. In a power station several coils of wire spin rapidly in a magnetic field and this induces an electric current in the moving coils. The electricity is then sent to our homes. When the coils stop spinning, the induced voltage ceases too. The generator that runs the lights on a bicycle is just a smaller version of a power station generator.

The SI UNIT of inductance is the henry (H). A potential difference of one volt will appear across a circuit with a self-inductance of one henry when the current changes by one AMPERE per second.

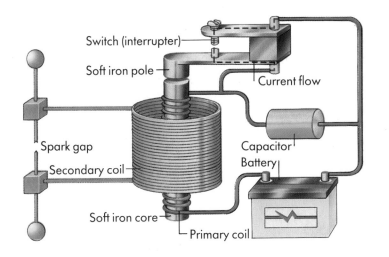

◀ In the ignition circuit of a car engine, the switch is initially operated by the capacitor which discharges at very brief intervals. Interrupting the low-voltage current through the primary coil induces a high-voltage current in the secondary coil. This causes sparks to arc across the spark gap, igniting the fuel/air mixture in the combustion chamber. When the engine is running normally, the timing of the interrupter switch is controlled by the speed of the engine.

Induction coil

An induction coil is a kind of TRANSFORMER that produces pulses of high-voltage electric current from lower voltage current. It consists of a primary coil of wire with several turns and a secondary coil of wire with a much larger number of turns in it. If an electric current in the primary coil is interrupted repeatedly, it creates a changing magnetic field around both coils. Induction causes a very large voltage in the secondary coil.

Induction coils are used to produce short bursts of high voltages, particularly in INTERNAL-COMBUSTION ENGINES in vehicles. Induction coils have a current driven through them by the relatively low voltage of the BATTERY and then produce a large voltage across the terminals of the spark plug. This voltage produces the spark which ignites the FUEL and air in the cylinder.

Cotton gin

Industrial Revolution

The Industrial Revolution was a period of great change in the 18th century. Before then most goods were made by hand and most people worked in the countryside. In the 18th century there were a number of inventions and developments that changed this. The STEAM ENGINE could operate machinery more quickly and reliably than the water wheels and mills that drove them before. Improvements in spinning and weaving MACHINES followed. The use of steam engines and more powerful machines made the COAL and iron industries the most important. Wood was replaced by IRON AND STEEL as a material for making things.

Spinning jenny

▲ Machines used in the cotton industry were among the first to be adapted to steam power. Removing seeds and impurities from the fibers could be done in hand-turned gins, but the externally powered spinning jenny enabled skilled workers to be many times more productive.

► *The spinning mule was introduced by Samuel Crompton in 1779. It produced very fine, uniform yarn.*

▼ *The weaving industry saw some of the first factory automation with the Jacquard loom. A series of cards containing a coded sequence of holes were used to control the weaving of elaborate patterns in cloth and carpets.*

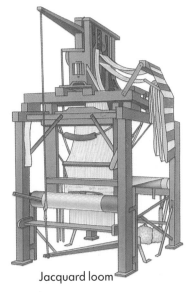

Jacquard loom

Factories were built for the new machines. They attracted workers who had lived in the countryside. This led to the growth of large industrial towns where living conditions were poor. Houses for the factory workers were packed close together and clean water supplies and proper drainage were rare. Sanitation did not improve until the middle of the 19th century.

The increasing quantities of goods being made in factories needed better transportation systems to carry them to stores and industries. The railroad network that spread across the country in the 19th century helped, as did the CONSTRUCTION of new roads. Steam engines propelled ships that no longer relied on the wind.

Inertia

Inertia is the name given to the tendency of an object to stay still or to move steadily in a straight line unless some FORCE pushes it and makes it behave in a different way. The greater an object's inertia, the larger is the force

SEE FOR YOURSELF
Balance a coin on top of a piece of cardboard on the end of one finger. Then flick the card away with the fingers of your other hand.

The card goes flying, but inertia makes the coin fall onto your fingertip.

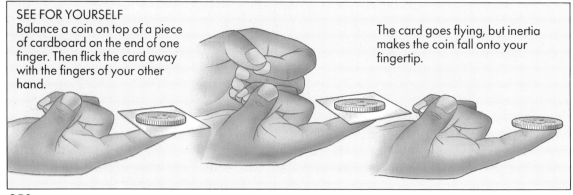

◀ *Inertia keeps these dummy passengers moving forward when the test car stops suddenly. It shows how important seat belts are in restraining these forces by stopping people from being thrown forward.*

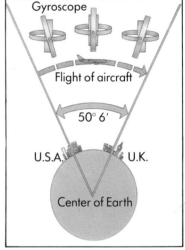

that is necessary to make it ACCELERATE (that is, move from rest or change the speed or direction of its motion). The amount of material (or MASS) which is present in an object determines how much inertia it has.

It was Isaac NEWTON who first realized that a force was needed to overcome inertia and make an object accelerate or decelerate.

Inertial guidance

Inertial guidance is a way of keeping a rocket, submarine, ship, or aircraft on course. In an inertial guidance system, a platform or table is kept stationary by three spinning, or LASER, GYROSCOPES, one for each of the three directions: up/down, forward/backward, and left/right. Whatever way the vehicle turns or changes speed, the gyroscopes resist these movements and keep the table steady. Devices called accelerometers measure the FORCES trying to move the table. Signals from the accelerometers are fed to a COMPUTER, which uses them to calculate how far the vehicle has moved and in which direction. If it has strayed off course, the computer calculates the correction and produces the electrical signals to operate the vehicle's steering gear to bring it back on course.

Infection

Infection takes place when an organism is invaded by harmful bacteria and VIRUSES which multiply in the organism and cause damage. These invaders can enter the organism through many routes. In humans, they may

▲ *An automatic pilot tracks an aircraft's progress by reference to the angle of the gyroscopes. An angular difference of 50° 6', equates to the 3,006 nautical miles between London and New York.*

▼ *Three gyroscopes provide the computer with information in three dimensions.*

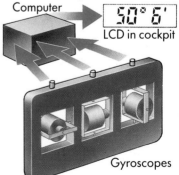

▶ *A cut tomato left exposed to the air soon goes moldy. This shows that germs and other infective organisms are in the air all the time, and attack anything they can live on. Most of the patches of mold are caused by varieties of fungus.*

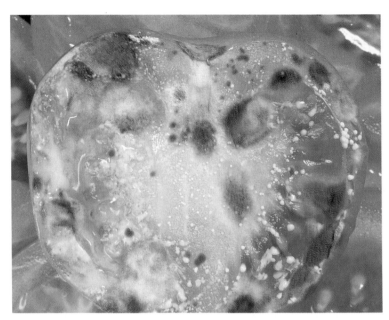

enter through the mouth when we eat contaminated food or drink dirty water, or they can be inhaled through the lungs. An important route of infection is through the skin, for example, an insect bite or a dirty cut. There are also some infections passed on during sexual activity with an infected person. Infection can be prevented by avoiding close contact with a sick person and by proper hygiene and the use of disinfectants to keep things clean.

Infinity

Infinity is a number, quantity, or distance that is so large it cannot be counted or measured. In GEOMETRY, infinity is an unreachable, distant point. The idea of infinity helps distinguish between two classes of sets. One type of set consists of a countable number of members. For example, the days of the week make up a finite set of seven members. All the positive whole numbers (1, 2, 3, 4, …) make up an infinite set because they go on for ever. Infinity is where the numbers finally run out, but this point can never be reached.

▲ *We are surrounded by possible sources of infection: household pests often carry dangerous microorganisms, some diseases are transmitted by close contact between people, and others arise from eating food that is not fresh.*

The Sun is not an infinite distance from the Earth (it is only 93 million miles (150 million km) away.

Even quasars, which can be more than 10 billion light-years from us, are still not an infinite distance away.

Sun

Information technology

Information technology describes the storage, processing, and transmission of information by computerized systems. In a world increasingly dependent on science and technology, fast and easy access to accurate information is very important. The development of inexpensive COMPUTERS and TELECOMMUNICATIONS made this possible in the 1980s. Information about all kinds of research and technology projects is stored in computers all over the world. The TELEPHONE network provides a global COMMUNICATIONS network capable of linking these computers together. Information stored in one computer can be sent to another computer anywhere in the world, provided that both are connected to a telephone line.

Information technology enables someone with a small home computer to look through a library of information, called a computer database, stored in a much bigger computer somewhere else in the world. Some stores, especially supermarkets, use information technology in monitoring their stock levels. The store's computer detects when stocks run low and automatically places a new order. Goods are paid for in some stores by wiping a plastic card through a slot in a card reader. It reads a magnetic stripe on the card, contacts the card owner's bank computer by telephone and automatically deducts the amount spent from the card owner's account.

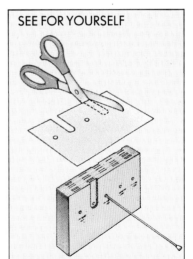

SEE FOR YOURSELF

Make a series of punch cards about your friends. Ask them each the same series of questions about themselves. The questions must have yes/no answers, e.g. are you more than 4 ft. 9 inches tall? Mark the answers in the same place on each card. Cut a hole for a yes, and a wide groove for a no. To find out how many of your friends are over 4 ft. 9 inches tall, push a knitting needle through the hole for that question. The cards with the answer "yes" will be threaded onto the needle. The "no" cards will fall away.

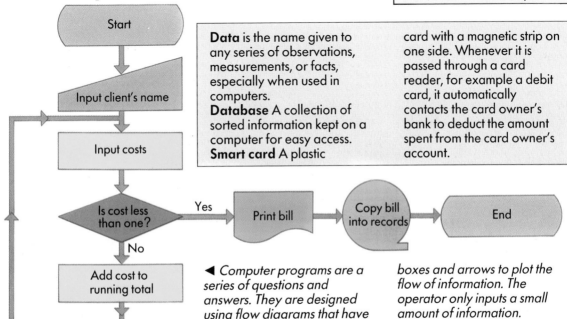

Data is the name given to any series of observations, measurements, or facts, especially when used in computers.
Database A collection of sorted information kept on a computer for easy access.
Smart card A plastic card with a magnetic strip on one side. Whenever it is passed through a card reader, for example a debit card, it automatically contacts the card owner's bank to deduct the amount spent from the card owner's account.

◄ Computer programs are a series of questions and answers. They are designed using flow diagrams that have boxes and arrows to plot the flow of information. The operator only inputs a small amount of information.

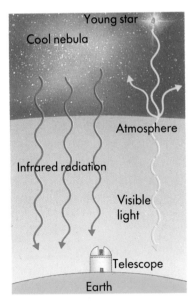

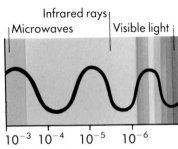

▲ Infrared radiation from distant objects in space can penetrate the Earth's atmosphere more easily than visible light, much of which is reflected. Astronomers use infrared photography to observe these objects because the human eye sees only visible light.

▶ Infrared photography shows one aircraft has already departed. The normally invisible heat imprint left behind, the thermal shadow, shows up on the runway.

Infrared rays
Microwaves | Visible light

10^{-3} 10^{-4} 10^{-5} 10^{-6}
Wavelength in meters

▲ Infrared radiation lies close to the visible band of the electromagnetic spectrum. The wavelength of infrared energy is greater than that of visible light, but shorter than that of microwaves.

Infrared astronomy

Infrared astronomy is a branch of ASTRONOMY which studies the INFRARED RADIATION from the STARS, PLANETS, and other bodies. Infrared wavelengths are longer than the WAVELENGTHS of visible light and shorter than radio wavelengths. Cooler objects send out less infrared radiation than hot ones do. Infrared radiation can also pass through "dusty" regions of the Galaxy, revealing otherwise invisible objects.

Infrared astronomers have detected very young stars that are not yet glowing brightly.

Infrared photography

Infrared PHOTOGRAPHY is used to obtain important information about crops, valuable MINERALS, forests, and POLLUTION by detecting the amount of heat they give out.

Hot materials send out ELECTROMAGNETIC RADIATION just beyond the red end of the range of colors that the human eye can see. It is therefore called INFRARED RADIATION. Chemicals polluting the sea soak up heat differently from the surrounding water and show up against the colder water in an infrared photograph, as do rocks containing valuable minerals.

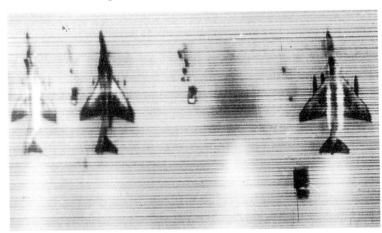

Infrared radiation

Infrared radiation, often called heat rays, is ELECTROMAGNETIC RADIATION which is similar to LIGHT but which lies beyond the red end of the visible SPECTRUM. The different colors of light look different from one another because the electromagnetic radiation which makes them up has different FREQUENCIES and WAVELENGTHS; infrared radiation has longer wavelengths and lower frequencies than visible light. Its wavelength can be between 800 nm (800 millionths of a millimeter) and a few tenths of a millimeter.

Infrared radiation allows us to "see" objects which do not transmit light and are therefore invisible. For example, people give out infrared radiation, so they can be detected at night or in a building that has been shattered by an earthquake.

See also INFRARED ASTRONOMY; INFRARED PHOTOGRAPHY.

Inheritance *See* Heredity

Injection molding

Injection molding is one way of making objects from PLASTIC. A mold is made in two halves which are clamped together. Plastic granules are heated to change them from a solid into a thick liquid. The hot molten plastic is then forced or injected into the mold.

▲ *Injection molding is often used in the manufacture of plastic pipes and pipe joints.*

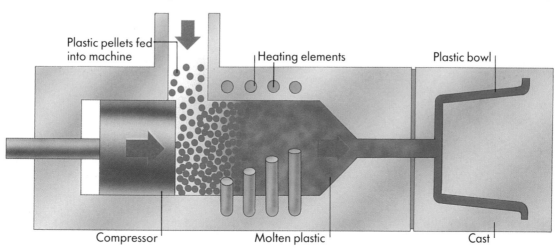

Plastic pellets fed into machine — Heating elements — Plastic bowl

Compressor — Molten plastic — Cast

Several objects can be molded at the same time by linking their separate molds by channels along which the molten plastic can flow. The plastic soon cools and sets. The mold is split apart and the plastic parts can be pulled out. On many plastic objects you can see the point where the plastic was injected into the mold as a small bump on the bottom of the object.

See also EXTRUSION.

▲ *Injection molding leaves distinctive traces on objects that have been produced by this method. A plastic bowl usually has a faint seam around its circumference, which shows the line where the two halves of the mold met. In the center of the underside, a circular bump indicates where the molten plastic was injected.*

Inoculation *See* Vaccination

INORGANIC CHEMISTRY

Inorganic chemistry is a major branch of chemistry that deals with the properties and reactions of substances that do not contain carbon atoms bonded to other carbon atoms. Inorganic chemistry covers the individual elements and all the simpler compounds such as oxides, mineral acids (nitric, sulfuric, or hydrochloric acid), bases and salts such as sodium chloride (common salt), copper sulfate, sodium nitrate, and so on. It also embraces the study of metals. Some elements are very similar and react strongly with particular compounds. Some carbon compounds, the carbonates and oxides, are treated as part of inorganic chemistry.

The physical properties of these various elements and compounds, such as their crystal structure, is studied separately as *physical chemistry*.

The history of chemistry prior to 1828 is really the story of inorganic chemistry. It concerns the discovery of certain elements such as mercury, sulfur, gold, silver, and copper in ancient times, the isolation of others, such as hydrogen, sodium, and potassium, and the preparation and identification of simple compounds such as carbon dioxide in the 1700s and 1800s. More recently inorganic chemistry has been distinguished from organic chemistry, which deals with the substances and reactions of living matter, such as carbohydrates, hydrocarbons, proteins, and amino acids, all of which contain carbon.

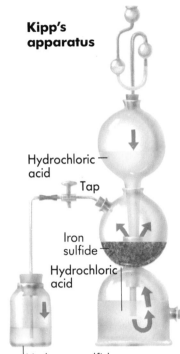

Kipp's apparatus

Hydrochloric acid

Tap

Iron sulfide

Hydrochloric acid

Hydrogen sulfide

▲ Kipp's apparatus was used to produce a gas by reacting a liquid with a solid. The action of hydrochloric acid on iron sulfide makes hydrogen sulfide. The apparatus incorporates a safety device. Closing the tap creates gas pressure in the middle flask, which prevents the acid from dripping down.

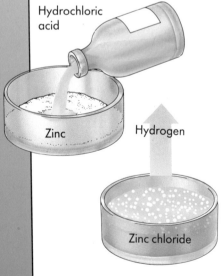

Hydrochloric acid

Zinc

Hydrogen

Zinc chloride

▲ Inorganic chemistry deals with basic chemical reactions such as the one that takes place between zinc and hydrochloric acid to produce zinc chloride and hydrogen gas.

Milestones in Inorganic Chemistry
1828 Friedrich Wöhler makes the first synthetic organic substance from inorganic compounds.
1856 The first synthetic dye made by William Perkin.
1895 August Kekulé's structure of benzene.
1910 Synthetic ammonia produced by Fritz Haber.
1950s Research into structure of DNA.

▶ The fountain experiment demonstrates the solubility of ammonia in water. As the ammonia dissolves, a partial vacuum is created in the upper flask, making a fountain. Adding red litmus to the water creates a fountain that changes color.

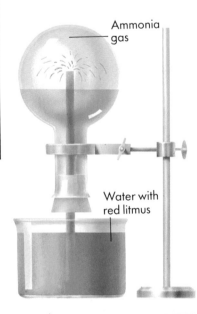

Ammonia gas

Water with red litmus

See also ATOM; BOND, CHEMICAL; CHEMISTRY; COMPOUND; ELEMENT, CHEMICAL; LABORATORY; ORGANIC CHEMISTRY; PERIODIC TABLE.

Insecticide *See* Pesticide

Instinct

A baby spider can spin a perfect web without having to learn how to do it. We call this kind of inborn behavior an instinct. Spiders of the same SPECIES all build in the same way because they are born with the same instinct, just as they are born the same shape and color.

Biologists once thought that all animal BEHAVIOR was instinctive, but as they studied the animals in more detail they discovered that this is not true. Although animals have a lot of instinctive ability, their reactions are almost always modified by experience or LEARNING. Most animal behavior is therefore a mixture of inborn (instinctive) and learned behavior. Young birds, for example, know how to sing, but they have to learn the right songs from their parents. Biologists and psychologists are generally interested in overall behavior not just instinctive patterns. In human beings, learning seems to be more important than instinct in determining final behavior patterns.

▲ *Gull chicks instinctively peck toward the red spot on a parent's beak, because "beak" means "food" for hungry chicks. A newly hatched chick will peck at any similar combination of colors.*

◄ *The female cuckoo lays her eggs in other birds' nests. When the egg hatches the cuckoo will instinctively knock all the other eggs out of the nest. The cuckoo never knows its parents but as it grows it will behave in the same way as its parents, not its foster-parent. This means the cuckoo must be born with its behavioral instincts since it has no one to learn them from.*

Instruments, musical

People have been making music for many years by hitting or blowing through shells, animal horns, and other materials. Modern musical instruments can be divided into four groups: woodwind, brass, percussion, and strings.

Woodwind instruments such as the recorder make a column of air vibrate inside a tube. The player can change the note produced by covering different holes to change the length of the vibrating air column. Brass

▼ *Human babies display a grasping instinct. Some scientists believe that this has been inherited from our tree dwelling ancestors.*

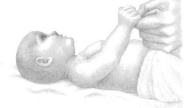

▶ All countries have developed different instruments using material that is available to them. Some of these instruments may make very different sounds from the music we normally hear.

Vibrating skin

▲ When a drum is struck, the vibrations inside the instrument are reflected back and forth. As they lose energy, the sound of the drumbeat gradually dies away.

▼ Some of the sound produced by the vibrating strings is trapped within the violin's delicately shaped body, where it resonates to create a rich tone.

Bow

String

instruments, including the trumpet and trombone, rely on the player blowing through lips tightly pressed against the mouthpiece. This makes a buzzing sound that is expanded and changed by the instrument. Percussion instruments are played by being struck like a drum. The piano is included in the percussion group because it is played by making hammers strike strings. Some stringed instruments such as the violin are played by drawing a bow across the strings to make them vibrate. Others such as the guitar are plucked. Different notes are produced by pressing the strings at different points.

Modern TECHNOLOGY has produced a new type of instrument called a synthesizer. This uses ELECTRONIC circuits to create electrical signals that, when amplified, make a loudspeaker vibrate. Computer controlled synthesizers can imitate other instruments and also make complicated new sounds.

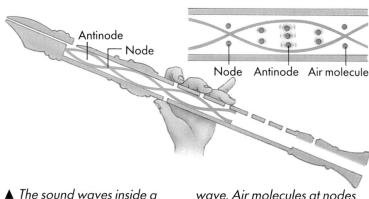

Antinode

Node

Node   Antinode   Air molecule

▲ The sound waves inside a wind instrument, such as a recorder, form a stationary pattern known as a standing wave. Air molecules at nodes do not vibrate, and the distance between nodes determines the pitch of the note.

INSTRUMENTS, SCIENTIFIC

Scientific instruments are devices, machines, and systems used by scientists and engineers for detection, observation, measurement, control, calculation, and analysis. Instruments extend the human senses. Some of them detect and measure radiations or particles that are invisible to the human eye. Microscopes and telescopes reveal objects that are too small or too far away to be seen by the unaided eye. Some instruments measure quantities that human senses are incapable of detecting or measuring, such as radio waves. All branches of experimental science depend on instruments.

Scientific instruments are limited by the science and technology of the day. Developments in science may suggest new instruments. For example, electrically powered instruments could not be made until the development of electric power. The electron microscope could not be designed until the structure of the atom and the properties of atomic particles were understood.

Instruments may measure the same property, for example length or distance, in different ways. A micrometer measures the thickness of small objects by clamping the object between two jaws, one of which has a measuring scale engraved on it so the thickness can be read. The distance between the Earth and the Moon was measured most accurately by bouncing a laser beam off a reflector placed on the Moon by the Apollo astronauts. The time taken for the beam to return allowed the distance to be calculated.

All scientific instruments disturb the thing they are measuring and this must be taken into account when instruments are designed. No instrument is absolutely accurate. There are always errors in detection, observation, and measurement. The instrument designer must minimize these errors.

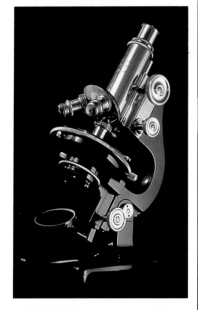

▲ Optical microscopes magnify objects so that they can be studied in detail. Magnifications of up to 1,500 times can be achieved.

▲ Samples of ice and snow brought from the Antarctic contain specks of dust. An instrument called a Coulter counter is used to detect the particles and count them.

◄ Laboratories are equipped with instruments for scientists to do experiments and carry out analysis. These biochemists are analyzing samples of tissues for a hospital.

See also ANALYSIS, CHEMICAL; COMPUTER; ELECTRON MICROSCOPE; EXPERIMENT; MEASUREMENT; MICROMETER; MICROSCOPE.

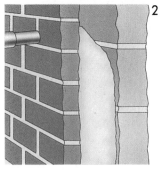

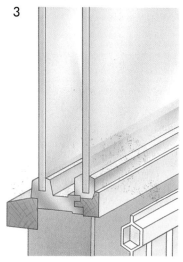

Insulation, thermal

Thermal insulation slows down the flow of HEAT from a hot object to a colder one. Heat can be carried by CONDUCTION, CONVECTION, and RADIATION, so thermal insulation must slow down all three. Thermal CONDUCTION can be reduced by using a material in which the electrons are not free to move and carry heat with them (such materials will also be electrical INSULATORS). Convection can be slowed down by limiting the circulation of FLUIDS

SEE FOR YOURSELF
Test the thermal insulating properties of different materials by wrapping them around empty soft drink cans. Then fill the cans with hot water and seal them with modeling clay. Place one unwrapped can of hot water in a sealed glass jar, thus wrapping it in air. Wrap one in newspaper, one in thin cotton, and one in a thick woolly material. Compare the water temperature in each can after 30 minutes.

that could carry the heat. Radiation can be reduced by using shiny surfaces. A VACUUM prevents conduction and convection, as in a vacuum bottle, which keeps hot things hot and cold things cold.

Many mammals and birds are insulated by a layer of fat beneath the SKIN or fur and by FEATHERS which trap a layer of air next to the skin.

▲ Many types of thermal insulation can be added to existing houses in order to reduce heat loss. Fiberglass is used to line roof spaces **1**, and insulating foam can be pumped into wall cavities **2**. Double-glazed windows also reduce heat loss **3**.

▶ The cockpits of spacecraft are covered with insulation blankets beneath the outer shell. This protects the interior of the craft from the extremes of temperature that may be experienced in outer space.

Insulators, electrical

Electrical insulators are materials which do not conduct ELECTRICITY well. In electrical CONDUCTORS, such as metals, charged particles called ELECTRONS are free to move through the material and carry the electric current; in insulators, however, the electrons are not free to move and cannot carry a current. Materials such as plastics, glass, CERAMICS, dry wood, and rubber are good insulators.

Insulators are important because they allow us to confine the flow of electric current to the places where it is wanted; for example, in an ordinary electrical cord, insulation is used to separate the wires which carry current in opposite directions. Dry air and some oils also act as insulators. A material that is a poor conductor of heat generally is also a poor conductor of electricity.

▲ High-voltage electric cables have to be well insulated. These are heavy duty porcelain insulators.

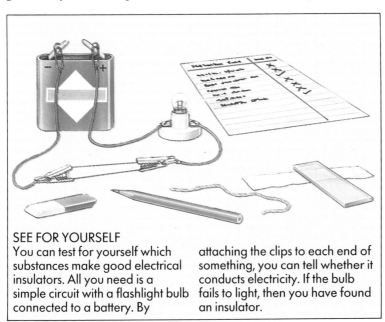

SEE FOR YOURSELF
You can test for yourself which substances make good electrical insulators. All you need is a simple circuit with a flashlight bulb connected to a battery. By attaching the clips to each end of something, you can tell whether it conducts electricity. If the bulb fails to light, then you have found an insulator.

Integrated circuit

An integrated circuit is an electronic CIRCUIT contained in a paper-thin chip of silicon roughly half an inch square. The circuit on the chip may contain up to several hundred thousand components. There are different types of circuits on chips. The most important is the MICROPROCESSOR. It forms the calculating and control center of a COMPUTER. Printed circuit boards may be fitted with sockets into which chips are plugged.

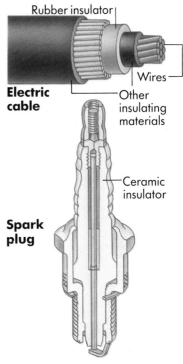

Rubber insulator

Electric cable

Wires

Other insulating materials

Ceramic insulator

Spark plug

▲ Rubber is the most effective natural electrical insulator, although in modern equipment it has largely been replaced by plastics. Ceramic insulators have many uses, from car spark plugs to power lines.

▶ *The first integrated circuits had fewer than 20 transistors but now, although the circuits are still very small, there may be more than 20,000.*

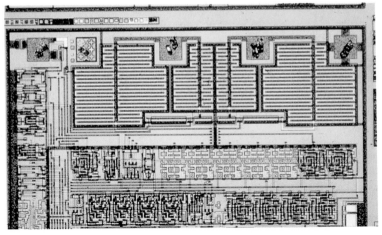

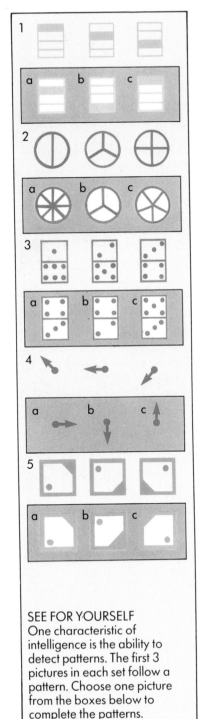

SEE FOR YOURSELF
One characteristic of intelligence is the ability to detect patterns. The first 3 pictures in each set follow a pattern. Choose one picture from the boxes below to complete the patterns. Answers on page 364.

Intelligence

Intelligence has been defined in many different ways, but perhaps the simplest definition is that intelligence is the ability to learn and, when we are talking about people, the ability to understand. All animals can learn to some extent, but some animals are better at it than others. Humans are the most intelligent of all animals.

Psychologists have always been interested in how much of our intelligence is inherited and how much learned. How clever someone is depends on both factors, but whether what you inherit through your CHROMOSOMES AND GENES is more important than what happens to you during your life, is hotly debated. However, there are some people who seem to be born with enormous mental abilities, both in what we call intelligence and in talents such as musical or artistic abilities.

Parents and teachers have an important role to play by encouraging children to develop their own mental abilities. If we are not encouraged to read and discuss, to solve problems, and to use our intelligence, it will not develop to its full power.

Internal-combustion engine

An internal-combustion engine is an ENGINE in which the FUEL is burned inside the engine. The engines in modern cars, ships, and aircraft are all internal-combustion engines. There are three types of internal-combustion engines: gasoline, DIESEL, and GAS TURBINE. In all three, the fuel is burned to heat air. As the air heats up, it expands and this can be made to do useful WORK. In

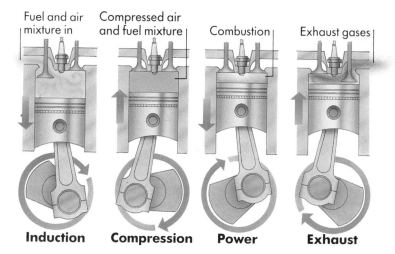

Fuel and air mixture in | Compressed air and fuel mixture | Combustion | Exhaust gases

Induction **Compression** **Power** **Exhaust**

◀ *In a four-stroke car engine, the combustion cycle begins with the induction stroke which pulls a fuel/air mixture into the cylinder. The next stroke compresses the mixture, which is then ignited to produce the power stroke. The exhaust stroke forces waste products out of the cylinder, ready for the next induction stroke.*

gasoline and diesel engines, the air expands inside a cylinder and pushes against a piston connected to the vehicle's wheels. The gasoline engine needs an electrical spark to ignite the fuel but the heavier diesel is ignited by pressure alone. A gas turbine, or jet, engine does not have any cylinders. Air flows through it from front to rear, being compressed by fans and heated on its way through. The engine's thrust is produced by the jet of escaping gases.

The first internal-combustion engines built in the 1860s used coal gas as a fuel. In 1885 Gottlieb Daimler built an internal-combustion engine that used a liquid fuel such as gasoline. In 1894 another German engineer, Rudolph Diesel, made the first diesel engine. The first practical gas turbines for aircraft were not built until World War II in Britain and Germany. Gas turbines are now often used to power fast boats and naval vessels. *See also* FLIGHT; JET PROPULSION.

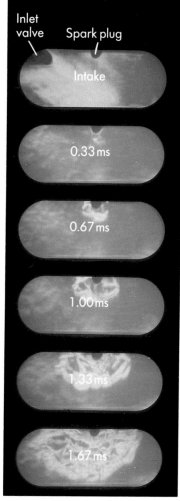

Inlet valve | Spark plug
Intake
0.33 ms
0.67 ms
1.00 ms
1.33 ms
1.67 ms

▲ *Filmed by a high-speed camera, the sequence shows the ignition of the fuel/air mixture inside an engine cylinder. Modern gasolines burn very smoothly, reducing engine vibration.*

Nikolaus Otto (1832–1891)
Otto was a German engineer who developed a four-stroke, coal gas-fueled internal-combustion engine which he patented in 1877. Otto did not invent the four-stroke cycle but was the first to incorporate it into a successful design. Otto's smooth running gas engines were widely used before World War I, after which they were superseded by gasoline engines.

▲ As well as the stars and planets in the universe there are huge clouds of interstellar dust. If you look up to the Milky Way on a clear night you will see a mass of shimmering starlight but also some black areas where there seem to be no stars. This is because great dust clouds are blocking out the starlight behind them.

Answers to Intelligence test on page 362:
1 b, 2 c, 3 a, 4 b, 5 c.

▶ The process of digestion begins in our mouths. By the time food reaches the small intestine (ileum) it has been broken down into its basic constituents by the action of digestive juices and enzymes. Nearly all the absorption of food takes place in the small intestine. Only water and waste matter pass along to the large intestine.

Interstellar matter

Interstellar means between the STARS, and in our GALAXY this space is occupied by scattered atoms of hydrogen and other ELEMENTS. In some regions these have collected together to form vast dark clouds or NEBULAE.

Some of this matter may be original leftover material from the galaxy's formation. But it is also added to by stars, particularly old RED GIANTS and SUPERNOVAS, pouring material out into space.
See also BIG CRUNCH; MILKY WAY.

Intestine

The intestine is the main part of the digestive system. In humans it consists of a 30-foot (9 m) tube stretching from the STOMACH to the anus. Most DIGESTION, the breaking down of food into simple substances which can be absorbed to nourish the body, occurs in the intestine. For its whole length, the intestine is covered with sheets of MUSCLE. These contract in waves to push the partly digested food along. This process is called *peristalsis*. The intestine is divided into distinct regions according to the ENZYMES produced and the food absorbed at that point. The final parts of the intestine are the wide colon, where the remaining food materials are solidified into feces, and the short rectum where feces are stored temporarily until they are discharged from the body.
See also LIVER; PANCREAS.

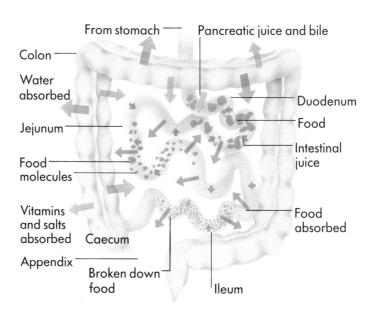

From stomach — Pancreatic juice and bile
Colon —
Water absorbed
Jejunum —
Food molecules
Vitamins and salts absorbed   Caecum
Appendix —
Broken down food
Duodenum
Food
Intestinal juice
Food absorbed
Ileum

Invention

An invention is a new machine, engine, tool, or other useful object or process that no one else has thought of before, or it can be a major improvement on something someone else has produced. Someone can protect what he or she has invented by applying for a patent. If the authority that grants patents in the inventor's country agrees that the inventor's work is indeed new, a patent is granted. As long as the inventor pays the required fees, the invention cannot be copied or made by anyone else for several years without the inventor's permission. This stops people from stealing an inventor's work. The first known patent for an invention was issued in Florence, Italy, in 1421. Many important inventions have come from the work of one person; others come from many people working as a team.

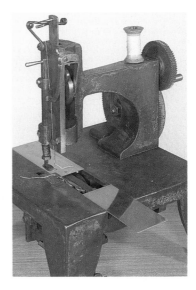

▲ In 1851 Isaac Singer made a considerable improvement to the sewing machine with his invention of the presser foot, which holds the fabric in place while it is being stitched.

Shaduf

◄ The shaduf is an early invention from ancient Egypt. It was used to move water from one place to another. This picture shows it being used in an irrigation system.

Iodine

Iodine is a nonmetallic ELEMENT that belongs to the HALOGEN group. At room temperature, iodine is a shiny bluish black solid with an irritating smell. When heated, it sublimes, that is, it turns directly from a solid into a vapor. Iodine vapor is purple and also possesses an irritating odor. Pure iodine is poisonous if swallowed, but minute amounts of iodine compounds are essential to plants and animals for healthy development. In the human body, the thyroid GLAND in the neck uses iodine to produce a HORMONE vital for healthy physical growth and mental development. Seaweed contains a great deal of iodine. Iodides (iodine SALTS) are used in the photographic industry and in medicine. The RADIOISOTOPE iodine-131 is used for diagnosing and treating diseases related to the thyroid gland.

▲ Iodine and its compounds are used as antiseptics and fungicides and in the manufacture of dyes.

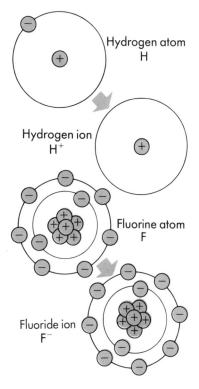

▲ Ions form when atoms and molecules lose or gain an electrical charge. A positive hydrogen ion is formed when a neutrally charged hydrogen atom loses its negatively charged electron, so that the atom is left with an overall positive charge. A negative fluorine ion is formed when the neutrally charged atom gains a negatively charged electron. The additional electron gives the whole atom an overall negative charge.

▶ In an ion motor a power source, such as a nuclear reactor, provides the energy to vaporize cesium. The cesium gas is absorbed by a platinum grid, which reemits positive ions. Negatively charged electrons are also given off by the platinum, and the two flows of charged particles are kept separate. Inside the thrust chamber the ions and electrons mix, driving the motor by a jet of neutral atoms.

Ion

An ion is an ATOM or group of atoms that possesses an electric charge through the gain or loss of one or more ELECTRONS. Usually, an atom is neutral (neither positively nor negatively charged) because the number of positively charged protons in its nucleus equals the number of its negatively charged electrons. In certain situations, however, atoms may lose some of their outer electrons to become positively charged ions. This is called ionization. A positive ion is known as a cation. A negatively charged ion is called an anion. Ions of opposite charges attract each other. Common salt (sodium chloride) is a solid crystalline COMPOUND in which positive sodium ions and negative chloride ions are held together by this attraction. During ELECTROLYSIS ions are attracted to electrodes of opposite charges.

Ion propulsion

Ion propulsion is a way of powering a spacecraft. The first ion engines were made at the Lewis Research Center in the United States in the 1960s. They relied on the behavior of electrically charged particles in an electric field. Negatively charged particles called ELECTRONS were stripped away from mercury or cesium ATOMS, leaving positively charged IONS. When the ions were acted on by an electric field, the forces between the ions and the field made them rush out of the engine through a nozzle, producing thrust.

Ion drives can only accelerate very slowly, but they can last a very long time. They are not used, therefore, for manned flight, but are ideal for long unmanned spaceflights needed for SPACE EXPLORATION.
See also ROCKETS; SPACE PROBES.

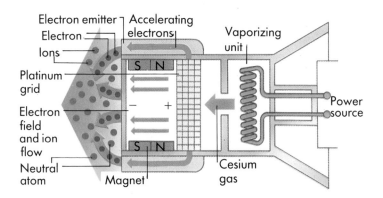

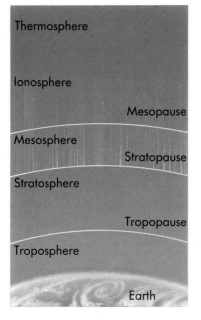

Thermosphere

Ionosphere

Mesopause

Mesosphere

Stratopause

Stratosphere

Tropopause

Troposphere

Earth

◀ *The ionosphere occurs at the upper edge of the atmosphere, about 50 miles (80 km) above the Earth's surface. At these altitudes the air is very thin, and atoms and molecules are easily ionized by radiation from space. Below the ionosphere, in the troposphere and stratosphere, the air is denser. Harmful radiation is absorbed, and virtually none reaches the surface of our planet.*

▶ *In terms of volume, the ionosphere is by far the largest portion of the atmosphere. But the air molecules are so far apart that, in terms of mass, the ionosphere is the smallest part.*

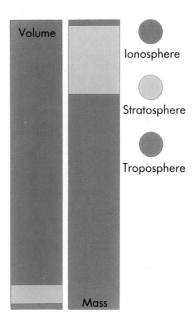

Volume

Ionosphere

Stratosphere

Troposphere

Mass

Ionosphere

The ionosphere is the outer region of the Earth's ATMOS-PHERE which lies above a height of 50 miles (80 km). The ionosphere gets its name because it contains the greatest concentration of IONS.

The ionosphere is vitally important to COMMUNI-CATIONS using RADIO waves. Because the Earth is a sphere and because radio waves can only travel in straight lines, you would expect radio signals would pass straight out into space. But some radio waves are reflected back toward the Earth by the charged particles in the ionosphere. Thus radio transmissions are possible over very long distances around the Earth. Short wave transmissions are reflected more strongly than longer waves, so all long-distance radio communication is carried on short wave bands. Very short radio waves however, such as those used for television and FM radio, pass right through the ionosphere into space. Only line of sight reception is possible with these very high frequency radio waves.

Iridescence

Iridescence is the name given to the multicolored rainbowlike reflections that can sometimes be seen from a layer of oil on water, from soap BUBBLES, or from certain MINERALS and gems. It happens because LIGHT can

Edward Appleton (1892–1965)
Appleton was the British physicist who discovered one of the layers of ionized particles that reflect radio waves in the ionosphere. This layer was often known as the Appleton layer, but is now understood to be two separate layers that are known as F1 and F2. Appleton's work in atmospheric physics was important to the development of radar, and in 1947 he was awarded the Nobel Prize for Physics.

▶ *The beautiful colors in the tail feathers of a peacock are produced by iridescence.*

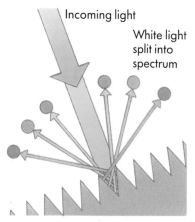

Incoming light

White light split into spectrum

▲ *Minerals sometimes appear iridescent because the light striking them is reflected back and forth between tiny irregularities on the surface. Iridescence on oily water is caused by light refracting through thin films of oil of differing thickness.*

bounce back and forth between the top and the bottom of the oil film or between the sides of tiny cracks in the mineral. It can also be caused by adjoining areas of minerals having differing optical properties. Iridescence should not be confused with the sparkling "fire" from gems such as diamonds. This is caused by the spreading out of colors in the diamond — a property named dispersion.

Henry Bessemer (1813–1898)
Bessemer was a British steel manufacturer who invented a cheap method for making large quantities of steel. At the heart of the process was the Bessemer converter, a large pear-shaped blast furnace. In the United States, Henry Kelly independently devised a similar process.

Iron and Steel

Iron is a metallic ELEMENT which in its pure form is silvery white in appearance. Our main sources of iron are ORES such as hematite and magnetite, in which the metal is combined with oxygen to form compounds. Iron is naturally magnetic and combines easily with nonmetals such as oxygen. Rust is iron oxide.

Pure iron can be cheaply extracted from ore in a BLAST FURNACE. The ore is heated with coke (carbon) and limestone to produce impure iron called pig iron. Pig iron is purified by being returned to a furnace along with scrap iron and more limestone to produce pure iron. Wrought iron is a type of iron which can be hammered into different shapes and drawn out into thin wires. Most iron goes into making different types of steel. The iron is mixed with carbon, and sometimes other elements to give it extra HARDNESS. Ordinary steel contains up to 1.7 percent carbon. It is used for building ships, bridges, and car bodies and rusts easily so needs to be coated with paint

◄ *Electric arc furnaces for making steel use graphite electrodes to conduct electricity to the contents and generate intense heat.*

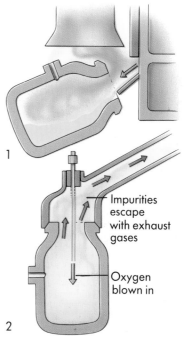

1

2

Impurities escape with exhaust gases

Oxygen blown in

or plastic, or with a protective coating such as zinc. The steel often used for cutlery and saucepans is a more expensive, nonrusting STAINLESS STEEL.

Iron is essential to CELLS in the human body, especially red BLOOD cells.

Irradiation

Irradiation is the exposing of something to RADIATION. This could be in the form of either ELECTROMAGNETIC RADIATION such as ultraviolet light, X rays or gamma rays, or particles from radioactive materials. Radiation above a certain level is harmful to organisms and it can be used to kill MICROORGANISMS. In FOOD PRESERVATION, irradiation is sometimes used to kill the microorganisms that could spoil or rot food. X rays and some radioactive particles are used in medicine and industry. The internal structure of a human being can be seen by irradiating the body from one side and placing a radiation detector on

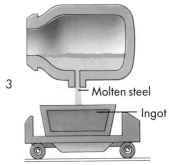

3

Molten steel

Ingot

▲ *The basic oxygen process produces steel in a pear-shaped vessel that rests on pivots. The vessel is tilted for loading with scrap iron **1**, but returns to the upright position while oxygen is blown in **2**. After refining, the vessel is tilted again to pour off the molten steel **3**.*

◄ *Fruit is lowered under water before being exposed to X rays. Irradiation prolongs the life of perishable foods.*

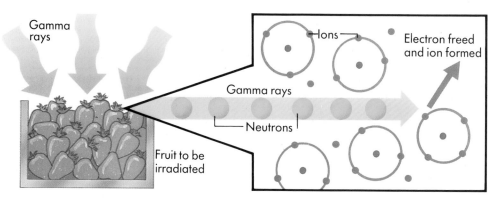

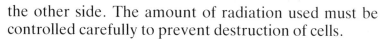

▲ *Gamma rays resemble very high-energy X rays. They can be used to irradiate food, such as fruit. This kills the germs and organisms that make food spoil. For this reason irradiated food keeps fresh for a long time.*

the other side. The amount of radiation used must be controlled carefully to prevent destruction of cells.

Irrigation

Irrigation describes the ways in which WATER is brought to land that is too dry for growing plants. Methods of irrigation have been used for over 5,000 years.

Irrigation plays an important part in AGRICULTURE today. In the United States, irrigation makes it possible to use about 40 million acres of land normally too dry for farming. The pumps of modern irrigation systems can move millions of gallons of water a day. Some systems take water from underground wells, but most systems get water from rivers that have been dammed. Pumps force water from the dam into canals or concrete channels. Pumping stations keep the water moving over long distances. These canals branch into smaller canals across the fields. Sometimes a whole field is flooded at regular intervals. Rows of sprinklers may be placed in a field. Irrigation has disadvantages too. Land can become so waterlogged that plant roots rot and die.

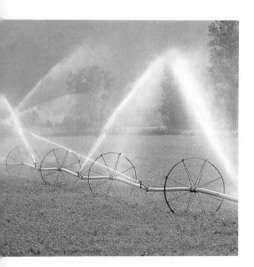

▲ *Movable sprinklers are a versatile method of irrigation. They can be moved to irrigate different areas and the amount of water can be controlled.*

▶ *Irrigation projects and hydroelectric power stations may both make use of water from a reservoir. Irrigation schemes often pump water into secondary canals for distribution at right angles to the flow of the main river.*

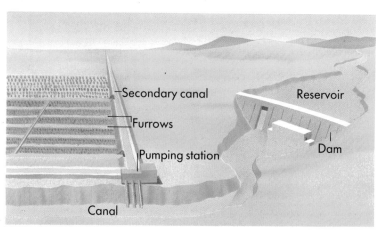

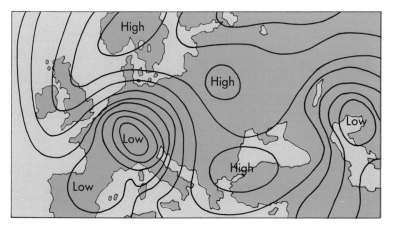

◄ *Weather maps use isobars to show atmospheric pressure. Because the different pressure systems cause different types of weather, such maps can be used to predict the weather. A high-pressure system, such as the one over central Europe, is also known as an anticyclone. Anticyclones usually bring clear skies and fine weather.*

Isobar

The word "isobar" comes from a Greek word, *isobares*, which means "equal weight." An isobar is a line drawn on a weather chart joining up points of equal atmospheric PRESSURE. Isobars are similar to contours on an ordinary map which join points of equal altitude.

The closer the isobars are together, the steeper the gradient of pressure difference over a given distance. Air moves from an area of high pressure to an area of low pressure, and the greater the pressure gradient, the faster the flow of air will be and the stronger the wind.

Isomer

An isomer is one of two or more COMPOUNDS in which the same atoms are present in the same proportions but in different arrangements. For example, butane and methylpropane are isomers. They both consist of carbon and hydrogen atoms and both have the formula C_4H_{10}.

Iso- at the beginning of a word means equal or identical.
Isobar is a line on a weather map joining two places of equal atmospheric pressure. An isotherm is a line joining places with equal temperature.
Isosceles triangles have two sides of equal length.
Isotonic fluids are fluids with equal pressure.
Isotopes are atoms with the same atomic number but a different number of neutrons.

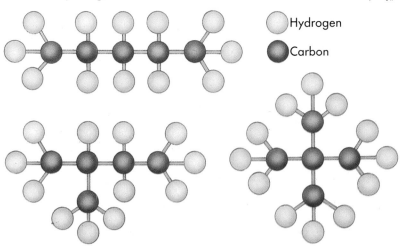

Hydrogen

Carbon

◄ *Pentane has three possible isomers based on different arrangements of the five carbon atoms and twelve hydrogen atoms — a straight chain, a branched chain, and a symmetrical cross. The different isomers have different chemical and physical properties.*

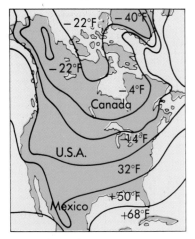

▲ Isotherms are lines drawn on a map joining places which have the same average temperature. The map shows January isotherms in North America. The cooling influence of the cold arctic seawater filling Canada's Hudson Bay is visible by the way the −22°F (−30°C) isotherm dips sharply southward. The long mountain chains down the western and eastern coasts of Mexico have a similar effect. These mountains isolate central Mexico from the effect of the much warmer oceans.

But in butane, the four carbon atoms are linked together in a straight chain, while in methylpropane, the carbon atoms form a branched chain with only three carbon atoms in the chain. Isomers may differ in their physical characteristics. The two forms of butane are colorless gases but methylpropane has a lower boiling point (10.4°F/−12°C) than butane (31°F/−0.5°C).

Isotherm

An isotherm is a line drawn on a CLIMATE chart joining points on the Earth that have the same TEMPERATURE at a particular time or where the temperature, averaged throughout the year, is the same.

Isotherms usually record the temperature as though it had been measured at sea level but, obviously, not all weather stations can be at zero height above sea level. To allow for the effects of PRESSURE resulting from the height of the station, the temperatures are adjusted by adding 1°C for each 165 m (541 feet) above sea level.

Isotonic

Two FLUIDS are said to be isotonic when they have the same osmotic pressure. Osmotic pressure is the PRESSURE which builds up in an enclosed space, such as a CELL, when a fluid enters the cell through the cell's semipermeable membrane. Fluid will pass through the membrane until the osmotic pressure is the same as on the other side. When this moment is reached, the fluids are said to be isotonic.

▶ Many of the fluids in the bodies of living organisms consist of a solution of sugar (glucose) in water. The membrane surrounding a cell permits small molecules such as water to pass through it, but not those of glucose. The cell remains isotonic by adjusting its internal osmotic pressure to that of the surrounding fluid, by gaining or losing water molecules.

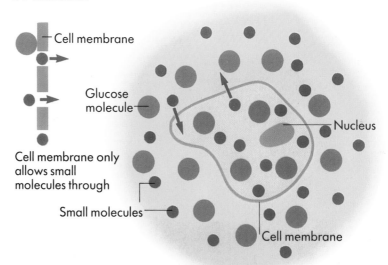

Cell membrane

Glucose molecule

Nucleus

Cell membrane only allows small molecules through

Small molecules

Cell membrane

The movement of fluids in and out of cells is essential to the life of an organism. Most solids and gases travel around in solutions and it is in this way that food matter is passed into cells and waste matter and harmful material pass out.

See also HYPERTONIC; HYPOTONIC; OSMOSIS.

Isotope

An isotope is one of two or more ATOMS of the same ELEMENT that differ from each other in ATOMIC WEIGHT. Isotopes of an element will all have the same number of protons in each of their nuclei but a different number of neutrons. A few elements have no isotopes, but most do. Different isotopes of an element are frequently found together in the same sample. For instance, in any sample of chlorine, 76 percent of the atoms have 18 neutrons and 24 percent have atoms with 20 neutrons. Many elements have a group of isotopes that are stable, but other elements have one or more radioactive isotopes, RADIOISOTOPES – they give off radiation or particles. Radioisotopes have a regular rate of decay (HALF-LIFE) that we can use as a kind of clock. For example, carbon-14 is used in this way. Radioisotopes of iodine and cobalt are used in medicine.

Frederick Soddy (1877–1956)
Soddy was a British chemist who worked with Ernest Rutherford and carried out pioneering research into radioactive decay. As a result, Soddy was able to formulate the theory of isotopes, and in 1921 he was awarded the Nobel Prize for Chemistry. Aware of the great potential of the energy contained in uranium, he became increasingly concerned about the use of atomic energy and the social responsibility of scientists.

◀ *This piece of equipment contains a radioisotope which is being used to test pipelines under the sea for faults.*

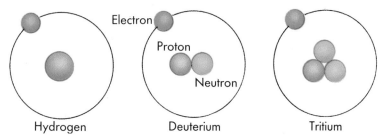

Hydrogen   Deuterium   Tritium

Electron   Proton   Neutron

◀ *Hydrogen has three isotopes. Protium, which has a nucleus of one proton, makes up nearly all naturally-occurring hydrogen. The isotope deuterium has a nucleus of one proton and one neutron. The third isotope, tritium, has a nucleus of one proton and two neutrons.*

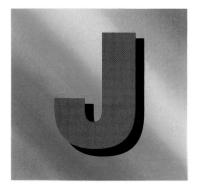

Frank Whittle (1907–1987)
Whittle, an officer in the British Royal Air Force, built the first successful jet engine. Whittle's turbojet design powered the world's first practical jet aircraft, the Gloster E.28/39, the prototype of which flew in 1941. The first jet-engined aircraft actually to fly was the German Heinkel He-178 in 1939. But this later proved impractical.

▶ *Jet propulsion is essential to attain high speeds, and at high altitudes a jet engine is more efficient than a propeller.*

▶ *Squid developed the principle of jet propulsion hundreds of millions of years ago, but can only travel backward. Squid draw water into their body cavity, then contract powerful muscles that force the water out through forward-pointing nozzles.*

Jenner, Edward *See* Vaccination

Jet propulsion

Jet propulsion is a way of powering something, usually an aircraft, by the force of a fast-moving stream of hot gas, using an ENGINE called a GAS TURBINE invented by Frank Whittle. Air is sucked into the front of the engine by a large spinning fan. Inside the engine, another fan compresses the air and pushes it into a COMBUSTION chamber, or burning chamber. Here, FUEL is sprayed into the air and burned. As the burning mixture of fuel and air heats up it expands and forces its way through the driven (rear) fan and out through the tail pipe. The rear fan is connected to and drives the compressor. This is the basic gas turbine or jet engine, also called a turbojet.

There are other types of gas turbine. In a turbofan engine, the jet of hot gas rotates a fan that pushes a large mass of air past the engine. In a turboprop engine, the jet spins a turbine connected to a propeller. A turboshaft engine uses the jet to rotate a turbine connected to a shaft which in turn rotates a helicopter's rotor blades. *See also* INTERNAL-COMBUSTION ENGINE.

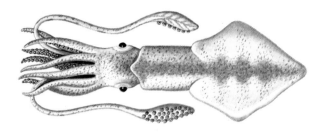

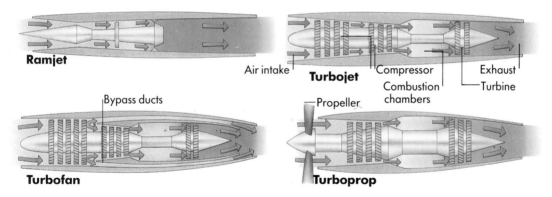

Ramjet

Air intake **Turbojet** Compressor Exhaust
Combustion Turbine
chambers

Bypass ducts Propeller

Turbofan **Turboprop**

Jet stream

In METEOROLOGY, a jet stream is a horizontal band of air which blows as an icy-cold and high-speed wind at heights of between about 6 and 10 miles (10 and 15 km). Sometimes jet stream winds may reach speeds of more than 200 mph (300 km/h).

The polar jet stream occurs in middle to high LATITUDES where polar and tropical air masses meet. The subtropical jet stream occurs in the regions between the tropics and temperate areas of the world. Unlike the polar and subtropical jet streams, the equatorial jet stream occurs only in the summer.

▲ *The ramjet is the simplest jet engine. It has neither compressor nor turbine, and is used in missiles. The turbojet is the most common type of engine on commercial airliners; the turbofan engine is a more fuel-efficient alternative. The turboprop gains most of its thrust from the propeller.*

▼ *The polar and subtropical jet streams weaken during the summer and move farther north.*

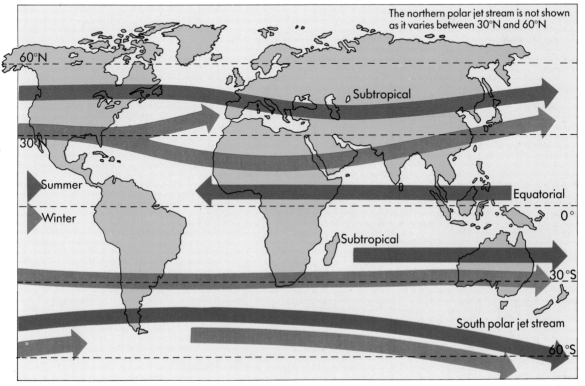

The northern polar jet stream is not shown as it varies between 30°N and 60°N

60°N

Subtropical

30°N

Summer

Equatorial

Winter

0°

Subtropical

30°S

South polar jet stream

60°S

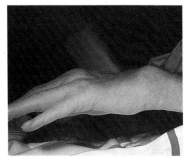

▲ *These are deformed hands of someone suffering from severe arthritis. Joints in the hands are among those most frequently affected by crippling arthritis.*

▼ *The most useful joint in the human body is the one that places our thumb opposite our fingers. The opposable thumb makes the human hand one of the most sophisticated natural devices, capable of a wide range of holding and turning movements. No other animal can match human dexterity.*

Joints

Joints are the points at which parts of something meet. In a human body, some joints, like those between most of the BONES of the skull, are rigidly fixed, but the most important joints have a complicated structure to allow them to move freely. The bones are joined by flexible strands of ligament, which stop the joint from popping apart. The ends of the bones are capped with rubbery cartilage, which cushions the shocks caused by walking and other movements, and also provides a slippery bearing surface. The most important joints have a flexible bag between the ends of the bones, containing synovial fluid. This acts like oil, to allow the joint to move without any FRICTION. In arthritis, this synovial joint becomes inflamed and damaged so the joint wears itself away, sometimes right down to the bone.

The structure of a joint also varies according to the type of movement it must make. For example, the knees and elbows work with a simple hingelike action, and their joints cannot move in any other way. The shoulder and hip, however, must allow limb movement in any direction, so they are ball and socket joints. The joints between vertebrae in the spine allow only a small amount of movement, while keeping the whole structure of the spine very strong.
See also SKELETON.

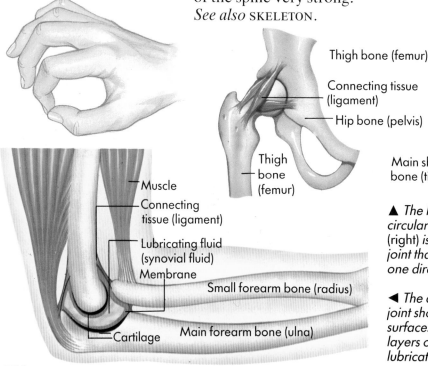

▲ *The hip joint* (left) *permits circular movement; the knee* (right) *is an example of a hinge joint that permits movement in one direction only.*

◄ *The diagram of the elbow joint shows that the moving surfaces are protected by layers of cartilage, and lubricated by synovial fluid.*

Joule

The joule (J) is the SI UNIT of ENERGY. The joule is named after a British scientist, James Prescott Joule who was born in Salford in 1818. Although there are many different types of energy, the joule is defined to be equal to the WORK which is done when a FORCE of one newton moves through a distance of one meter in the direction of the force. So, for example, if you need a force of one newton from your hand to lift up an apple and you move it up through a distance of one meter, you have used one joule of energy. The kilojoule (kJ) is equal to one thousand joules. One joule per second is called a WATT. To boil a pot containing a quart of water takes about 340,000 J; this amount of energy would also keep a 60-watt electric light bulb lit for an hour and a half. The kinetic energy of a one ton car traveling at 60 mph (100 km/h) is about 400,000 joules.

Energy used to be measured in calories (1 calorie equals 4.2 J). The energy values of different foods are given in joules, kilojoules and kilocalories.

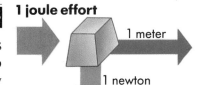

1 joule effort

▲ In SI units, one joule of work is done when a force of one newton moves through a distance of one meter.

James Joule (1818–1889)
James Prescott Joule was a British physicist who studied with Lord Kelvin and the chemist John Dalton. His experiments showed that the production of heat is always accompanied by a loss of another form of energy, so he deduced that heat is a form of energy. The joule, a unit of energy, is named after him.

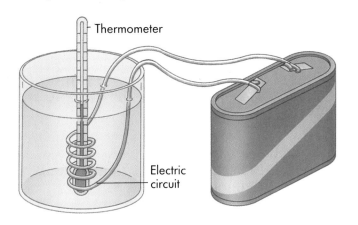

Thermometer

Electric circuit

◀ A simple experiment demonstrates Joule's law. Heat produced by the electric current causes the water temperature to rise steadily. The wire must be insulated.

Joule's law

Joule's law states the amount of HEAT generated when an electric current is passed through an electrical CONDUCTOR. Joule found that when mechanical ENERGY was converted to electrical energy, the amount of heat produced was always in proportion to the energy converted. So, the amount of heat that develops in a wire carrying a current is proportional to the resistance of the wire and the square of the current. If one wants to reduce the production of heat, for example in power lines, it is necessary to keep the flow of current as small as possible.

JUPITER FACTS
Diameter at the equator
88,700 miles (142,800 km)
Diameter at the poles
83,000 miles (133,570 km)
Average distance from Sun
483,000,000 miles
(778,000,000 km)
Length of year 11.9 years
Length of day 9h 50 minutes
Mass 318 Earths
Density 0.39 Earth
Surface Temperature −238°F

▶ *Turbulent winds and storms above the planet's surface create dramatic patterns in Jupiter's cloud layer.*

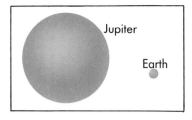

▲ *Jupiter has a mass 318 times that of Earth.*

▼ *The four largest moons orbiting Jupiter are called the Galilean satellites because they were first observed by the Italian astronomer.*

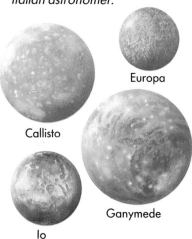

Europa

Callisto

Ganymede

Io

Jupiter

Jupiter is the largest PLANET in the SOLAR SYSTEM. It is so huge that a thousand Earths could fit inside it, but it spins so fast its "day" is less than 10 hours long. This rapid whirling has made its equator bulge outward.

Like the other giant planets (SATURN, URANUS, and NEPTUNE), Jupiter is made up mostly of hydrogen. Bands and whirls of other frozen chemicals, such as water and ammonia, swirl through the cloudy surface at hurricane force. The famous Great Red Spot is the top of a long lasting cyclone or whirlwind larger than the Earth. But although the temperature of these top layers is about −238°F (−150°C), the center of the planet is believed to be hotter than the surface of the Sun.

Jupiter and the other giant planets are made up of gas rather than rock and metal because they are so large. Molecules of gases fly about faster than molecules of solids and need stronger GRAVITY to hold them down. Small planets like Earth cannot hold onto hydrogen.

Jupiter has 16 satellites. Four of them are at least as large as our own MOON and they are visible with good binoculars. Voyagers 1 and 2 have shown that Callisto and Ganymede are covered with Moonlike craters, Europa is a smooth ball of ice, and Io, nearest to Jupiter, has a yellow sulfur-covered surface and volcanoes erupting material 60 miles (100 km) into space.

Kaleidoscope

A kaleidoscope is an instrument or toy containing MIRRORS which make multiple reflections and so create random regular patterns. It consists of a tube, usually about a foot (30 cm) long, with two or three long thin mirrors running the length of the tube. The mirrors are fixed in the tube at an angle to each other, usually 60 degrees.

The most common kaleidoscope has one end of the tube covered by a piece of ground glass or a similar semi-transparent plastic sheet. The other end of the tube has a small peephole in it. The tube also contains small pieces of colored glass or plastic. When the tube is held up to the eye and turned, the colored pieces tumble around the far end of the tube randomly. Several images of each piece are seen because they are reflected in the mirrors.

SEE FOR YOURSELF
To make your own kaleidoscope, tape three mirrors of the same size together as shown in the illustration. Tape a triangular piece of tracing paper to one end. Put some colored pieces of paper, cut into interesting shapes, inside the tube you have just made. Hold the kaleidoscope upright and look down inside to see the beautiful pattern made by the reflections. To change the pattern simply shake the kaleidoscope to move the pieces of paper.

Kelvin (K)

The kelvin is the unit used to measure the absolute TEMPERATURE of a system. Whereas the zero of the CELSIUS temperature scale happens to be chosen as the freezing point of a common substance (water), at zero kelvin an object is as cold as it can be. No further heat can be taken from it. Zero kelvin is –459.67°F (–273.15°C); apart from this, 1 K is equivalent to 1°C. It may be impossible to reach absolute zero, but scientists have cooled systems to a few millionths of a degree above absolute zero.

Kelvin, William Thomson

William Thomson (1824–1907), later Baron Kelvin of Largs, was a British physicist and engineer who was born in Belfast and died near Largs, Scotland. He entered the University of Glasgow when he was 10, published his first scientific article at 16 and went on to study at Cambridge. In 1846 he became a professor in Glasgow, where he worked for the rest of his life. He was one of the first people to state the Second Law of THERMODYNAMICS: that HEAT cannot be completely converted into WORK. He also estimated the age of the Earth from its

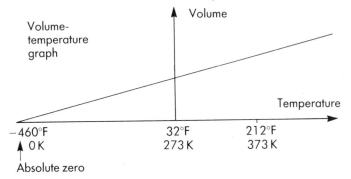

Volume-temperature graph

Volume

Temperature

–460°F   32°F   212°F
0 K   273 K   373 K

Absolute zero

temperature, although he was wrong because he did not know about the production of heat through RADIOACTIVITY in the Earth. He became rich because of his design for a GALVANOMETER to receive the signals sent through underwater TELEGRAPH cables.

Kepler, Johannes

Johannes Kepler (1571–1630) proved that the EARTH and the other PLANETS in the SOLAR SYSTEM orbit the SUN in elliptical paths. Kepler was born in what is now southwestern Germany. He was very frail, and often ill but

▼ *William Thomson, Lord Kelvin, was an energetic and enthusiastic scientist and worked with many leading scientists of his day. He worked with Joule on the relation between heat and work.*

▶ *On the absolute temperature scale, temperatures are given in kelvins (K). An object's temperature is a measure of its energy. At 0 K, called absolute zero, an object has no energy at all. The word "degree" and its symbol (°) are not used with the Kelvin scale.*

▲ *Kepler mainly studied the planets but also carried out important research into optics.*

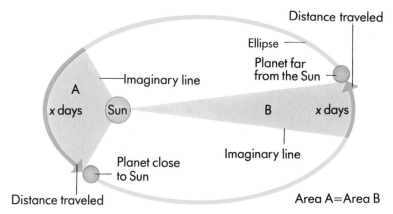

Distance traveled

Ellipse

Planet far
from the Sun

Imaginary line

A
x days

Sun

B

x days

Planet close
to Sun

Imaginary line

Distance traveled

Area A=Area B

◄ *Kepler's second law of
planetary motion states that an
imaginary line between the
Sun and a planet always
sweeps through the same area
during the same time. Planets
travel fastest when nearest the
Sun because they travel a
greater distance in the same
amount of time.*

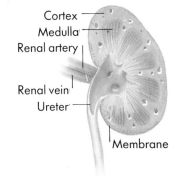

Cortex
Medulla
Renal artery

Renal vein
Ureter

Membrane

▲ *Cross-section of a kidney.*

▼ *Magnified detail of an
individual filtration tubule,
showing the area where urine
is separated from the blood.*

was a brilliant mathematician. He worked with Tycho
BRAHE in Prague and built on his theories and those of
COPERNICUS. Copernicus was the first to show that the
Earth revolved around the Sun. After years of painstaking observations and calculation Kepler discovered
planets do not move in circles as Copernicus believed,
but ellipses, which are like flattened circles.

Finally he published his laws of planetary motion to
explain the motion of the planets.

Kidneys

Kidneys, in humans, are paired organs at the back of the
abdomen, on either side of the spine. They remove
waste products from the BLOOD, passing them out of the
body as urine. They do this by filtering the blood. A kidney has two main parts, an outer cortex and an inner
medulla. Blood enters a kidney through an artery that
divides into branches within the medulla. These
branches go to the cortex, where they further divide into
tiny knots of capillaries called glomeruli. Surrounding
the glomeruli are small kidney tubules. Each tubule,
along with a single glomerulus, forms what is called a
nephron. Each kidney has thousands of nephrons. The
nephrons separate waste matter from plasma, the liquid
part of the blood. The waste, together with a small
amount of water in which it is dissolved, makes up urine.
The blood, cleaned of waste, goes out of the kidney
through a vein. Urine goes from a nephron to a collecting tubule. Urine from many collecting tubules flows
through a tube called a ureter, then into the bladder.

If the kidneys fail, a dialysis machine may be used to
clean the patient's blood, or the patient must have a kidney transplant.

Kidney tubule (Nephron)

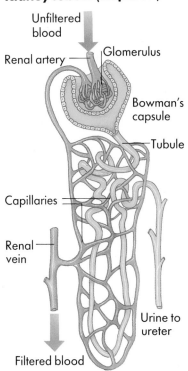

Unfiltered
blood

Renal artery

Glomerulus

Bowman's
capsule

Tubule

Capillaries

Renal
vein

Urine to
ureter

Filtered blood

▶ *This kiln in Bahrain is typical of those used there for firing pottery or for roasting limestone to make lime.*

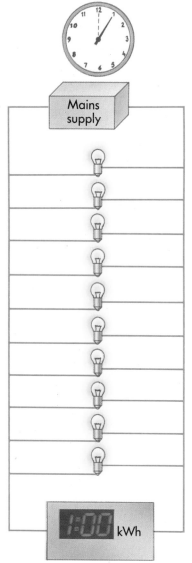

▲ *Ten 100-watt light bulbs (1,000 watts in total — a kilowatt) burning for one hour use one kilowatt-hour (or unit) of electrical energy.*

Kiln

A kiln is an oven or furnace used for drying and hardening objects made from clay such as bricks, plates, and cups. The process, called firing, was done in ancient times by placing the object in an open fire. The kiln allows things to be heated to very high temperatures. Fires burning underneath the kiln heat air which flows through the kiln, heating the objects inside. Kilns range in size from small tabletop models used to fire one or two pots to commercial kilns with space for thousands of bricks. Modern kilns are heated by gas or electricity.

Kilowatt-hour

The kilowatt-hour (kWh) is a measure of electrical ENERGY. It is the energy used when an electrical appliance with a POWER of one kilowatt is run for one hour. Since a power of one watt corresponds to using one JOULE of energy every second, a kilowatt-hour corresponds to 3,600,000 J. An electric toaster uses about 1 kW of electrical energy, so it uses one kilowatt-hour of energy every hour.

Kinetic energy *See* Energy

Koch, Robert *See* Medicine

Laboratory

When we think of a laboratory, we usually imagine a special room where scientific equipment is kept and EXPERIMENTS are carried out. Laboratory experiments are carried out under conditions where all the factors that might affect the outcome of the experiment are strictly controlled. There are different types of laboratories, their design and the things in them depend on the kinds of experiments that are to be done in them. All laboratories have some scientific INSTRUMENTS in them. The school laboratory has BUNSEN BURNERS and maybe a CENTRIFUGE. Laboratories often contain dangerous chemicals and equipment, even school laboratories. New products are developed and tested in laboratories. Many famous discoveries, such as the discovery of RADIUM, have been made in laboratories. New products and medicines have to go through many tests in laboratories before people can buy them.

People can also be studied in a laboratory. An experimenter may wish to find out, for example, how people perform in a memory test taken on their own or with a

Laboratory Safety
Scientists always observe safe practices to make sure accidents do not happen.
● Keep chemicals in safe containers.
● Wash your hands before and after using chemicals.
● Never put chemicals near your face or play with them to see what happens.

SEE FOR YOURSELF
Simple experiments can be done at home and you can make your own laboratory equipment using everyday objects. A filter funnel can be made from the top part of a plastic bottle and coffee filter papers can be placed inside it. A clothespin firmly attached to a wooden handle is good for holding hot test tubes. Things can be heated safely by placing them in very hot water in a heat-proof pitcher. You can heat substances more strongly with a short candle placed in sand in a metal tray. Rest a cooking rack on two bricks above the flame and things can be heated in heatproof dishes. A test tube rack can be made from a shoe box. An eye dropper will measure accurate amounts of liquid. Modeling clay can be used to seal all kinds of things.

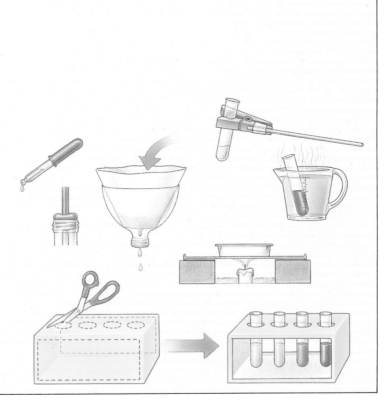

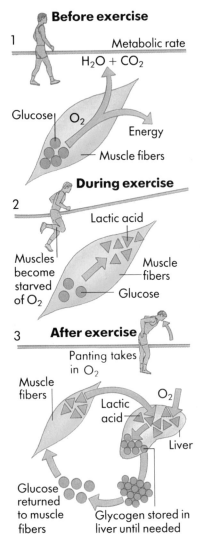

Before exercise

1

Metabolic rate

$H_2O + CO_2$

Glucose

O_2

Energy

Muscle fibers

During exercise

2

Lactic acid

Muscles become starved of O_2

Muscle fibers

Glucose

3 **After exercise**

Panting takes in O_2

Muscle fibers

Lactic acid

O_2

Liver

Glucose returned to muscle fibers

Glycogen stored in liver until needed

▶ *Laboratory instruments help in the search for oil.*

◀ *During gentle exercise, glucose in muscles is used to provide energy as well as producing carbon dioxide and water 1. In vigorous exercise there may not be enough oxygen to break down the glucose, so the glucose is converted into lactic acid 2. When there is plenty of oxygen in the blood again, the lactic acid is converted into glycogen and then glucose 3.*

group, at different times of day or in noise or quiet. These conditions can be controlled in a laboratory.

Lactic acid

Lactic acid is a colorless or yellowish liquid. It is commonly found in sour MILK or other dairy products that have curdled. It is also found in pickles and beer and is formed by the FERMENTATION of sugar. Lactic acid is produced commercially by fermentation and is used in the tanning and textile industries and to flavor food.

Lactic acid is often present in the BLOOD of people and animals. Normally when our MUSCLES need energy it is produced by the breakdown of CARBOHYDRATES by OXYGEN. However, in strenuous exercise the blood cannot deliver oxygen fast enough and so carbohydrate is broken down anaerobically (without oxygen). This produces lactic acid which can give a characteristic pain in muscle, called a "stitch."

Lamarck, Jean Baptiste

Jean Baptiste Lamarck (1744–1829) was a French biologist, best known for his attempts to explain EVOLUTION. He suggested that useful features acquired during the life of an individual could pass to the next generation, thus making each generation more efficient. Lamarck believed that giraffes stretched their necks as they reached for leaves, and then passed their longer necks on to their offspring. According to his theory, a person who trained to become an athlete would have athletic children. Neither Lamarck nor anyone else could

▲ *Lamarck was one of the first to propose a theory of evolution.*

First generation

Second generation

Third generation

provide any evidence for this kind of evolution and few people believed his theory. Body CELLS and reproductive cells are quite separate, and only the genes in the reproductive cells are passed on to the offspring.
See also CHROMOSOMES AND GENES; NATURAL SELECTION.

Laminates

Laminates are MATERIALS made by gluing thin layers of material together, usually under PRESSURE. The result is a strong yet thin sheet. Laminating materials can increase their strength. A thin sheet of wood resists bending along the grain of the wood, but it bends easily and breaks across the grain. If several sheets of wood are glued together so that the grain of each sheet lies in a different direction, the weakness of one sheet is offset by the strength of the next. The result, called plywood, is a very strong building material.

Plastics and new materials such as CARBON FIBER are also often laminated for the same reasons. Some materials are sealed inside a more attractive and hard-wearing laminate such as a thin layer of plastic material. Many kitchen surfaces are made of chipboard laminates.

Landforms

Landform is the form, or shape, of the surface of the EARTH's land masses. In other words, landforms are the relief (the hills and valleys) of the land. The science, a branch of GEOGRAPHY, which studies landforms is called geomorphology. *See* pages 386 and 387.

▲ Lamarck's idea that animals "improved" themselves through generations of effort, made for an attractive theory of evolution. But he was fundamentally mistaken; animals cannot rewrite their own genetic codes. Darwin's theory of evolution showed that animals do adapt to their environment, but that changes occur as a result of random mutation, modified by the process of natural selection.

▲ This wood has been laminated with a special metal surface.

LANDFORMS

Landforms are mostly shaped by the rocks that lie beneath the land, by their type and structure. For example, an old, hard, metamorphic rock is likely to be more resistant to the effects of erosion and weathering than a younger, soft clay is. Consequently, such hard rocks may give rise to upstanding hills or mountains while the clay may underlie a valley floor or a flat plain. A block of rock that has been "faulted" downward may produce a valley while rocks that have been "folded" may become a mountain chain.

Another important condition that affects landforms is climate which, together with the rocks, governs the soil type of the area and affects the plant life that grows there. These three linked conditions play a major part in forming the foundations of the land. For example, a landscape that is subjected to the dry heating and cooling of desert conditions where there is little or no soil and only sparse plant life will be quite different from that of a tropical rain forest or one that has been affected by glaciers.

The final condition determining landforms is the age of the landscape, the length of time to which the land has been subjected to weathering and erosion. For example, a mountain chain newly thrust up by the movements of the Earth's crust will have an appearance different from old mountain scenery where rivers and glaciers, freezing and thawing have shaped the rocks over millions of years.

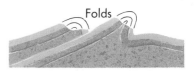

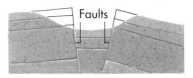

▲ The original folds and faults in the Earth's surface have undergone centuries of erosion to become the landforms that we see today.

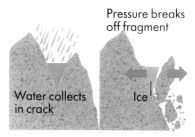

▲ Frost is one of the main causes of weathering in rocks. Rainwater seeps into cracks, then expands with great force when it freezes, breaking the rock into pieces.

◀ Two prominent buttes stick up above the surrounding desert in this region of northern Arizona and southern Utah.

▼ Simple folding produces hills and valleys (anticlines and synclines). When a fold collapses onto itself it forms a nappe. The complexity of the folding is hidden underground.

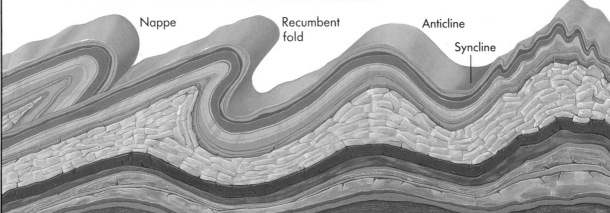

Nappe   Recumbent fold   Anticline   Syncline

SEE FOR YOURSELF

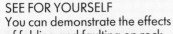

You can demonstrate the effects of folding and faulting on rock strata with a stack of different colored modeling clay layers. Pushing both sides of the stack produces a fold. If you cut the clay layers at a slight angle as shown, you can lift the outsides or push down inside forming a rift valley.

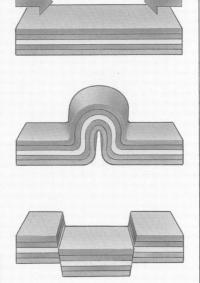

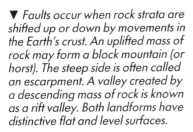

▲ Formed when the land shifted in prehistoric times, the Great Rift Valley runs through eastern Africa. It is mostly about 25 miles (40 km) wide and in some places is almost a mile (over 1 km) deep.

▶ The badlands in South Dakota have been made into a national park. Badlands are formed mainly by water erosion. Flashfloods cause the most erosion, wearing away great areas.

▼ Faults occur when rock strata are shifted up or down by movements in the Earth's crust. An uplifted mass of rock may form a block mountain (or horst). The steep side is often called an escarpment. A valley created by a descending mass of rock is known as a rift valley. Both landforms have distinctive flat and level surfaces.

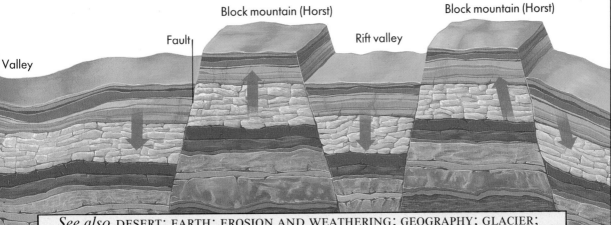

Block mountain (Horst)

Block mountain (Horst)

Fault

Rift valley

Valley

See also DESERT; EARTH; EROSION AND WEATHERING; GEOGRAPHY; GLACIER; MOUNTAINS; RIVERS AND LAKES; ROCKS; SOIL.

▲ *A tiny microcomputer is at the heart of this portable language translator. It is used by businessmen and travelers abroad.*

The principal purpose of larvae is to eat, and for many insects the larval diet is completely different from the insect's adult diet. It is thought that this is very advantageous because the larvae and the adults do not compete for the same food.

Language translation by computers

Language translation by computers is the conversion of one language into another by a COMPUTER. Words in one language and their equivalent words in another language can be stored in COMPUTER MEMORY. If the computer is given a word, it produces the equivalent word in the other language. To translate sentences is more complicated than translating a single word because the rules for putting words together are different in different languages. However, there are computer programs that include these rules and can translate sentences. Accurate translation by computer is not yet possible.

Larva

This name is given to the young form of an animal when it is distinctly different from the adult stage. The best known larvae are caterpillars, which eventually grow up into butterflies and moths. Other insects with larvae include flies, many of whose larvae are called maggots, and beetles. Not all insects have larvae. Young grasshoppers, for example, look like the adults and are called *nymphs*. Crab, starfish, and many other water-dwelling invertebrates pass through larval stages, but the only vertebrate (backboned) animals with larvae are the amphibians, the frogs, toads, newts, and their relatives. Their larvae live in water and are called tadpoles.

The change from larva to adult is called METAMORPHOSIS. Insect larvae first turn into pupae or chrysalises and while they are in this stage their bodies gradually change

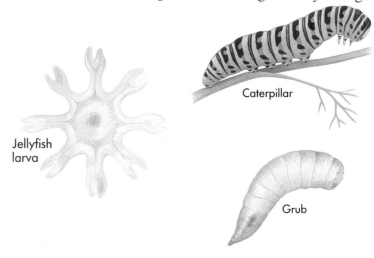

Caterpillar

Jellyfish larva

Grub

▶ *Caterpillars and other insect larvae (grubs) have the same basic design, but the adults are very different in appearance. Jellyfish larvae already have the characteristic shape of the adult.*

to the adult form. Other organisms change from larvae into a form very similar to a small adult which then grows into a full-sized adult.

Laser

A laser is a device that produces an intense beam of LIGHT. Laser light has only one WAVELENGTH and all the waves are in step with each other. The wavelength depends on the material used to make the laser. The word laser comes from Light Amplification by Stimulated Emission of Radiation, describing how a laser works. When an atom absorbs a unit of ENERGY called a PHOTON, it is said to be excited. If a second photon is fired at the excited atom, the extra energy is released as a burst of light (stimulated emission of radiation).

The first lasers used a ruby crystal excited by a powerful flash of light. Because ruby lasers produce brief flashes or pulses of laser light, they are described as *pulse*

Theodore Maiman (1927–) The United States physicist Theodore Maiman constructed the first working laser in 1960. After developing the maser (a device that generates or amplifies microwaves) in 1955 he began to work on an optical maser, or laser. His device consisted of a cylindrical artificial ruby crystal with parallel mirror-coated ends, one of which was semitransparent. Bursts of intense white light were provided by a flash lamp.

◄ A laser beam is being used to check the alignment of a tunnel under construction. This makes use of the fact that laser light does not spread out as ordinary light does.

◄ Lasers do not generate light, they amplify it. Inside a laser, light from an external source is trapped between semi-silvered mirrors. The light is reflected back and forth through an energized crystal or gas. The atoms in the crystal or gas absorb photons of light and become excited. When struck by other photons, the atoms release light energy. All the light produced is of exactly the same frequency, and is therefore known as coherent light.

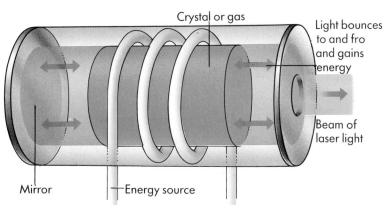

Crystal or gas

Light bounces to and fro and gains energy

Beam of laser light

Mirror — Energy source

▲ *Lasers are used in stores to read bar codes. Each item in the store will have a bar code. When an item is sold the laser at the checkout reads the bar code and registers the selling price at the register and on the bill. The information will also be passed on to a central data base so that levels of stock in the store can be monitored.*

▶ *The surface of a laser disc, magnified 100 times. Laser discs allow large amounts of information to be stored in a small area. A compact disc has a total track length of 35 miles (57 km). Thirty tracks are as wide as a human hair. A 4.7 inch (120 mm) compact disc will hold 74 minutes of programming.*

During the recording of a compact disc, each second of sound is broken up by a computer into 44,100 samples. The tiny samples are converted into a digital code. This code is cut by a laser into the master compact disc as millions of microscopic pits.

lasers. Gas lasers produce a continuous beam of light from a tube filled with gases such as argon, carbon dioxide, or a mixture of helium and neon. Lasers have many uses. Some are used to perform delicate surgical operations on a human eye. More powerful lasers can cut through concrete or steel.
See also HOLOGRAM; MASER.

Laser disc

A laser disc is a disc used to record SOUND or pictures or sometimes both as a pattern of dull spots on a shiny metallic background. The disc is played by shining a LASER beam on the disc as it spins at high speed. The beam reflects off the shiny metal surface back into a detector. It does not reflect into the detector from the dull spots which are tiny holes or pits burned into the disc when the recording was made. The flashing reflections picked up by the detector produce a series of DIGITAL electrical

pulses at the rate of over 44,000 per second. These are decoded by the player's ELECTRONICS and changed back into the original sound or pictures that were recorded on the disc. Laser discs can store sound only (compact discs), vision and sound (VIDEO discs), or data.

Latent heat

Latent heat is the amount of HEAT energy that is absorbed or given out without causing a change in TEMPERATURE when a substance undergoes a change of state, for example, from a SOLID to a LIQUID or from a liquid to a GAS. Latent heat changes the state of a substance with-

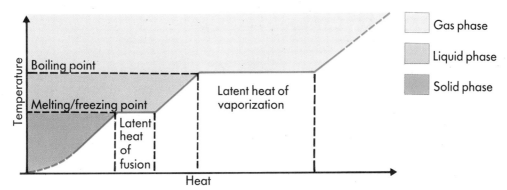

out altering the substance's temperature. For example, a kettle boils at 212°F (100°C), and this temperature remains constant until all the water has turned to water vapor. The extra heat or energy applied to the water in the kettle is used to change the water to water vapor.

In the change from solid to liquid and liquid to vapor, heat ENERGY is absorbed. In the reverse processes, when liquids freeze and become solids or gases condense into liquids, heat is given out.

▲ A change of physical state is also called a phase change. During a phase change, such as melting or freezing, a substance loses or absorbs heat without altering its temperature. Latent heat is the energy lost or gained during a phase change.

Lathe

A lathe is a MACHINE used to shape wood or metal in which the object to be shaped spins against a tool which does the shaping. The cutting tool is pushed against the spinning workpiece to shave away unwanted material. This is called turning. For wood turning, the tools may be held by hand and steadied against a toolrest. For metal turning, the cutting tools are clamped to a moving platform controlled by two handwheels.

A lathe can be used for drilling, polishing, and cutting screw threads into metal rods. On some lathes, the motor speed and tool position can be precisely controlled by computer.

▲ A modern lathe can create an artificial hip joint from information fed into it by a computer. Accurate drawings of the joint are first made on a computer and the information about the dimensions fed directly into the lathe.

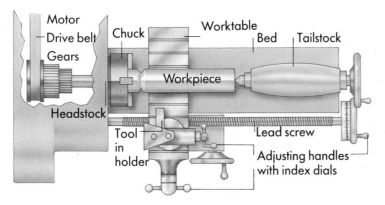

◄ Accurate machining on a lathe requires very precise adjustments to the angle of the cutting tool and the speed of rotation of the lathe.

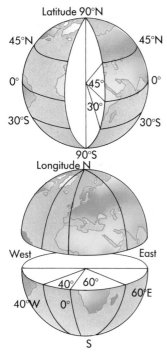

▲ Latitude is measured by degrees north or south of the equator; longitude, by degrees east or west of the Greenwich meridian. Each degree is divided into 60 minutes.

▼ Any point on the Earth's surface can be given a position by using latitude and longitude. For example, Rio de Janeiro is 23°S, 43°W; Dakar is 14°N, 17°W; and London is 51°N, 0°.

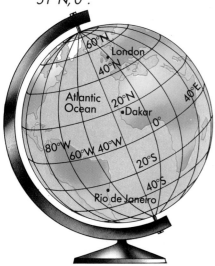

Latitude and Longitude

Latitude is the distance north or south of the equator, measured as an angle, of any point on the globe of the EARTH's surface. Thus, the equator is 0° while the North Pole is 90° north, and the South Pole is 90° south. For navigation and mapmaking, imaginary lines may be drawn on the globe parallel to each other and to the equator. These are known as lines of latitude.

A *meridian* is an imaginary circle drawn around the globe and passing through the North and South Poles. Longitude is the distance east or west of one particular meridian, the Greenwich Meridian, measured as an angle. In 1880 an international agreement was established that the meridian from which longitude is measured should be the one which passes through Greenwich Observatory in southeast London, England. Thus, this line of longitude is 0° while any point on this line of longitude on the opposite side of the globe is 180° and the longitude of all other points are given as an angle between 0° and 180° east or west of the Greenwich meridian.

SEE FOR YOURSELF
Wax behaves in the same way as magma and lava. Place a candle in sunlight for an hour or so, then handle it to see how it has softened. At higher temperatures, such as those produced by a candle flame, the wax flows like water, but quickly hardens.

Lava

Lava is the molten ROCK which spews out from a VOLCANO or some other kind of volcanic vent. If the lava contains a lot of dissolved gas, it may be frothy in character and may flow very rapidly. Pumice stone, which some people use to remove rough skin, is a kind of cooled lava which was so gassy that it is light enough to float on water. Some kinds of lavas are thick like molasses, and will only flow slowly. Some lavas are glassy, whereas others contain large CRYSTALS of MINERALS. Some IGNEOUS ROCKS are formed as lavas.

Sometimes, a lava flow may happen so suddenly and so quickly that large areas of land may be engulfed almost without warning. In 1961 the inhabitants of Tristan da Cunha, an island in the South Atlantic, were evacuated to escape from fast flowing lava.

Lavoisier, Antoine *See* Chemistry

Lead

Lead is a soft, heavy, bluish gray metallic ELEMENT which has many uses. It is used in the building and roofing trades, in the chemical industry, in building nuclear reactors, in making lead-acid storage batteries and high-quality glass, and in the oil industry. Lead can be easily hammered into flat sheets, cut with a knife, bent into different shapes, and drawn out into thin wires, but it cannot conduct ELECTRICITY well. Lead is very resistant to CORROSION by moisture or ACIDS and is often used as a protective covering. Lead cannot be expelled from the body and a buildup of too much of the metal leads to lead poisoning. Lead can also cause serious pollution, so people are increasingly converting their cars to run on lead-free gasoline, and replacing lead pipes with copper or plastic ones.

▲ Lava emerges from the earth at temperatures between 1,500 and 2,000°F (800 and 1,200°C). A lava flow may travel up to 6 miles (10 km) but as it flows it becomes cooler and slows down, until it finally solidifies.

Lead's chemical symbol Pb comes from *plumbum*, the Latin word for waterworks. This is because lead was used to make the ancient Roman water pipes. The Roman writer Plinius describes a disease among the slaves who extracted the lead that is clearly lead poisoning.

◀ Most of the world's lead comes from Australia and Russia, where it is mined as the ores galena and cerusite.

Ivan Pavlov (1849–1936)
Pavlov was a Russian biologist who was the first to make a scientific study of learning by association. He worked with dogs and noticed how their saliva began to run every time they were fed. This was a normal reflex action — the dogs did not have to think about it. Then Pavlov rang a bell every time the dogs were fed. After a while, he saw that the dogs' saliva began to run as soon as they heard the bell — even before the food arrived. The dogs had learned to associate the sound of the bell with food. Pavlov called this type of reaction a conditioned reflex.

▶ *Many animals can be trained to perform certain tasks or tricks. Offering rewards is an effective way of encouraging animals to learn.*

Between 10 and 15 percent of children between the ages of 5 and 17 have one or more learning disabilities. These children may have average or above average intelligence.

Learning

All animals are born with the ability to do certain things, but they soon begin to learn new things or to improve their inborn actions. Even earthworms can learn. If the worms are made to crawl along a forked tube and are given a mild electric shock in one arm of the fork they soon learn to take the other arm, and they can remember this for several days. This is an example of learning by trial and error. Many animals learn about food in this way. They instinctively peck at anything when they are young, but they soon discover which things are edible and which things are not. Birds and mammals learn a lot from their parents, by watching how they hunt or gather food and seeing just what kinds of food they bring home. Learning by association, which is also called *conditioning*, is another important learning method. If an

animal regularly finds food in a particular place or habitat it is likely to associate the two things and to visit the place when it is hungry. It will have a good chance of finding food there.

See also BEHAVIOR; INSTINCT; INTELLIGENCE.

Leaves

Leaves are often called food factories, for it is in the leaves that green plants make most of their food, by PHOTOSYNTHESIS. A typical leaf has a thin blade called the lamina on a slender stalk called the petiole. The leaf cells are packed with chloroplasts which contain CHLORO-

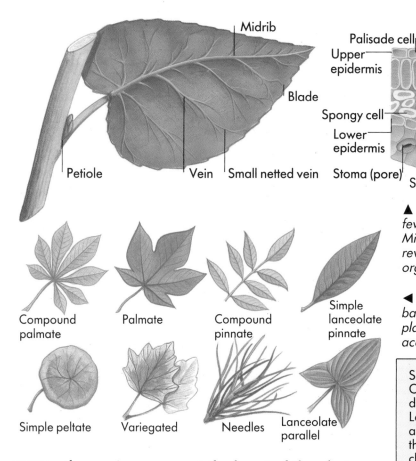

Midrib

Blade

Vein

Small netted vein

Petiole

Palisade cell

Upper epidermis

Chloroplasts

Spongy cell

Lower epidermis

Stoma (pore)

Supporting fibers

▲ To the naked eye, a leaf has few interesting features. Microscopic examination reveals the complex organization of leaf tissue.

Compound palmate

Palmate

Compound pinnate

Simple lanceolate pinnate

Simple peltate

Variegated

Needles

Lanceolate parallel

◀ There are fewer than ten basic designs for leaves, so plants are sometimes classified according to leaf shape.

PHYLL, the green PIGMENT at the heart of the photosynthetic process. Water needed for photosynthesis is carried to the veins, which also carry away the food produced. Microscopic holes called stomata are found mainly on the underside of the leaf. Excess water escapes through these holes and oxygen and carbon dioxide can pass through them too. Plants living in very dry places usually have small leaves with few stomata, so that they do not lose too much water and wilt.

A leaf does not live for more than a few years because the chlorophyll breaks down and the leaf can no longer make food. Even evergreen trees have to renew their leaves, although they do not replace them all at once. Deciduous trees drop their leaves every year, usually in the autumn. Before they fall, the leaves often take on brilliant colors.

See also TRANSPIRATION.

SEE FOR YOURSELF
Collect leaves from as many different plants as you can find. Look carefully at their shapes, are they a cluster of leaves, are they all one color. You can classify them according to the shapes shown above.

Leclanché cell *See* Battery

Leeuwenhoek, Anton van *See* Microscope

**Augustine Fresnel
(1788–1827)**
Fresnel was a French
physicist who developed the
wave theory of light, as a
result of his work on lenses
and optical interference.
Fresnel showed that normal
sunlight consisted of
vibrations that were at right
angles (transverse) to the
direction traveled by the light.
He also invented a type of
lens in which the surface is cut
into a series of concentric
steps rising toward the
center. These lenses are still
widely used in lighthouses.

Lens, optical

An optical lens is a device for changing the shape and
direction of a beam of LIGHT. It works by using the process of REFRACTION, which causes the direction of a wave
to change when it passes from one material to another.
The speed of light waves in ordinary glass is only about
three fourths of their speed in air, so light can be bent
when it passes from air into glass and out again. Glass
and transparent plastic lenses are made in two different
shapes, concave and convex; a concave lens bends the
light which passes through it outward away from the center, while a convex lens deflects the light inward. The
place at which the beam of light is brought together at a
single point is called the FOCUS of the lens; the distance of
the focus from the lens itself is called the focal length of
the lens.

Our EYES have lenses which focus all the light reaching them from a particular object onto a single point on
the retina at the back of the eye. The focal length of the
lens can be adjusted because the lens is flexible and its
shape can be changed by the surrounding MUSCLES; this
enables the eye to focus on objects at different distances.
The glass lens which does the same job in a camera is not
flexible and has to be moved in order to focus and so
allow photographs to be taken at different distances.
See also MICROSCOPE; TELESCOPE.

► *A convex lens produces a
real image (which can be
projected onto a screen), on
the opposite side of the lens.
The image is usually smaller
than the object and is upside
down. A concave lens
produces a virtual image
(which can be seen between
the object and the lens, but
which cannot be projected).
The image is the right way up,
but it is smaller. Most optical
instruments use a combination
of convex and concave lenses
to produce an image that is
bright and in focus.*

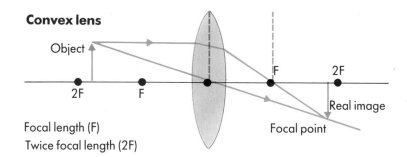

Convex lens

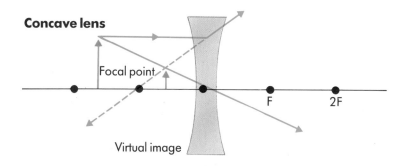

Concave lens

Leonardo da Vinci

Leonardo da Vinci (1452–1519) was a great Italian painter, sculptor, architect, and engineer who contributed an enormous amount to science, TECHNOLOGY, and art. Many of his ideas were hundreds of years ahead of their time. For example, his drawings included plans for a helicopter long before the MATERIALS and technology were available to build one. He was trained as an artist by the painter and sculptor Andrea del Verrocchio. While learning to draw things, he became interested in how they worked. His great paintings include *The Last Supper* and *Mona Lisa*. In 1513 Leonardo was invited to France by the French king, Francis I. He spent his last years living in a castle given to him by the king in Cloux, near Amboise. Many of Leonardo's sketch books are preserved in museums.

▲ *Leonardo da Vinci was an artist and an inventor. He also made important discoveries about the structure of the human body.*

Lever

A lever transmits a FORCE from one place to another. If you have used a nutcracker, punched a hole with a can opener, or pried up a rock with a stick, you have used a lever. The simplest lever is a rigid bar which is free to twist around a point called the fulcrum. To lift a heavy rock you place a small rock close to the heavy one and then push a bar over the small rock and under the heavy one. The small rock is the fulcrum. By pressing down on the lever (the effort), you will lift the heavy rock. But you have to push the lever down a long way to lift the

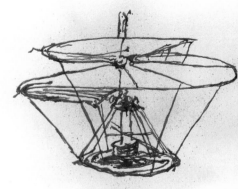

▲ *Leonardo sketched this helicopterlike flying machine in the early 1500s. There was no engine shown and this machine did not fly.*

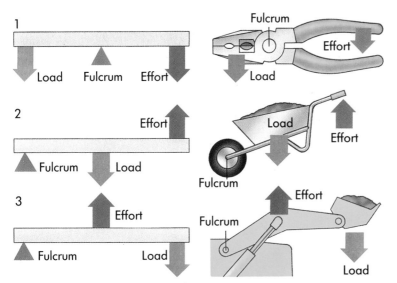
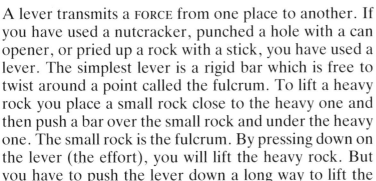

◄ *There are three different classes of levers. In a first-class lever, as used in a pair of pliers, the fulcrum is between the load and the effort. A wheelbarrow is an example of a second-class lever, with the load between the fulcrum and the effort. A third-class lever, which is used in a mechanical shovel, has the effort between the fulcrum and the load.*

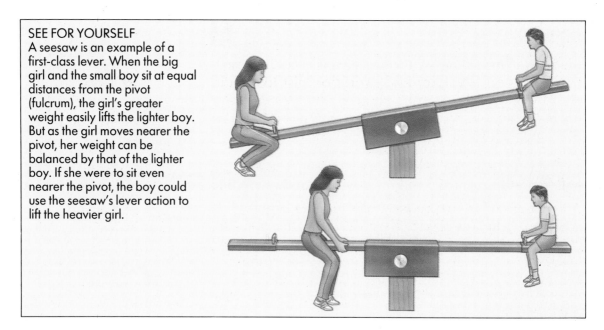

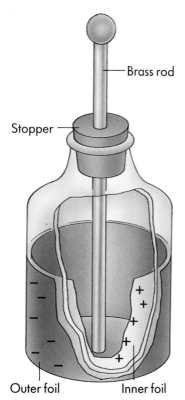

Brass rod

Stopper

Outer foil   Inner foil

▲ A Leyden jar is a type of
capacitor, one of the earliest
used to store electric charge.
Sheets of foil cover half the jar
inside and out. An electric
charge applied to the brass rod
is stored on the inner foil.

rock a short distance. Using a lever has reduced the
effort required but has not reduced the total WORK to be
done. By the principle of CONSERVATION of ENERGY, the
work done by the effort must equal the work done by the
load. The amount of work done is equal to the force multiplied by the distance through which the force moves.
For example, it would be possible to lift a car weighing
1,000 pounds with a force equivalent to the WEIGHT of
only 10 pounds, if the effort moved through a distance
100 times greater than the load.

Leyden jar

A Leyden jar is used to store ELECTRICITY. It is an early
sort of CAPACITOR. It was accidentally discovered by
Pieter van Musschenbroek in 1746 at the University of
Leiden in The Netherlands. Originally it consisted of a
GLASS jar of water with a needle or nail stuck into the
water through a cork in the neck of the jar. The glass is
an electrical INSULATOR which separates the positive and
negative charge. The jar can be charged up by bringing
the needle or nail into contact with a charged object; the
charge flows down through the needle and the water to
the inside edge of the glass.

A more efficient form of jar can be made by coating
the inside and the outside of the glass with conducting
metal foil and extending the nail or needle down so that
it touches the foil on the inside of the jar.

Light

Light is a form of ENERGY that travels freely through space. It is ELECTROMAGNETIC RADIATION just like radio waves, INFRARED RADIATION, and X-RAYS. We can see only part of the range of electromagnetic radiation. The part we can see is light. *See* pages 400 and 401.

Light bulb

A light bulb is used to produce LIGHT from ELECTRICITY. It consists of a hollow glass ball with a coil of thin wire (the filament) inside. When an electric current flows in the filament, it heats up until it is white hot. In air the filament would burn, so bulbs do not have air in them. They are filled with other gases, such as argon, at low pressure in which the filament does not burn.

In other types of bulbs, especially fluorescent lighting, the electric current excites gas molecules in the tube, which then emit light. The color of the light depends on the gas. A sodium vapor bulb, for example, shines yellow. *See also* CIRCUIT, ELECTRIC; LIGHTING, ARTIFICIAL; NEON.

Light meter

A light meter is an instrument for measuring the amount of LIGHT falling on it. Light on the meter's sensor changes the size of an electric current flowing through it. The change is detected and measured by the meter and shown as a reading of light level on a scale. Light meters are used in PHOTOGRAPHY to ensure that the CAMERA's shutter is open long enough for the correct amount of light to fall on the film. Modern cameras have built-in light meters. Light meters may also be used to regulate sun-shields in greenhouses.

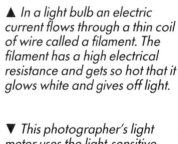

▲ In a light bulb an electric current flows through a thin coil of wire called a filament. The filament has a high electrical resistance and gets so hot that it glows white and gives off light.

▼ This photographer's light meter uses the light-sensitive metal selenium as the sensor in a photoelectric cell. When light shines on the selenium, its electrical resistance decreases because the electrons gain energy from the light and carry current from a battery through the cell more easily. This current registers on a galvanometer's scale.

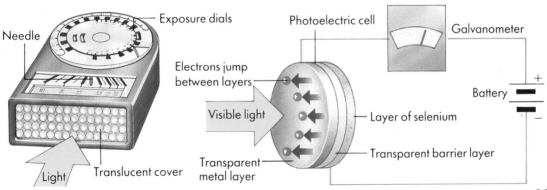

LIGHT

The waves of electromagnetic radiation that make up light do not involve the movement of any material such as air. This means that light can travel even in a vacuum where there is no material of any kind. (Sound waves are a different kind of wave which involve the movement of air and so cannot travel in a vacuum.) Light waves, like other electromagnetic waves, are made up of particles of energy called photons. This energy can be absorbed and reflected.

Most of the light we see comes originally from very hot objects. The hotter the object, the farther toward the blue end of the spectrum is the light that it gives out. (A piece of iron heated in a fire becomes red-hot, then yellow and finally it glows white-hot.) The surface of the Sun, which is heated by the nuclear fusion going on inside, is at a temperature of about 10,000°F (6,000°C) and it gives out the sunlight that we see.

In empty space, light travels at about 186,000 miles (300 million meters) per second! The light from the Sun takes 8 minutes to reach the Earth. In 1890 two American scientists, Michelson and Morley, found that even though the Earth is moving very quickly around the Sun, the speed of light does not change. This is quite different from what would happen in the case of sound or water waves if they were coming from the Sun. The theory of relativity explains this as well as why nothing can travel faster than light.

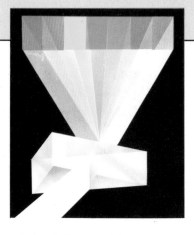

▲ White light passed through a prism bends at the boundary between the air and glass. Each color that makes up white light has a different wavelength, the red waves bend the least and the violet the most. The white light splits up into its component waves and shows the spectrum of colors known as the visible spectrum.

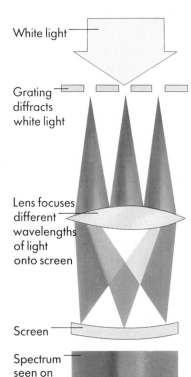

White light

Grating diffracts white light

Lens focuses different wavelengths of light onto screen

Screen

Spectrum seen on screen

▲ White light can also be split into a spectrum by the process of diffraction because the different wavelengths (colors) are diffracted different amounts. The light is passed through the very narrow slits of a diffraction grating.

▲ The colored lights at a disco are produced by shining white light through colored filters.

◄ Objects appear a certain color because they reflect part of the spectrum and absorb the rest. The leaves of plants appear green because they do not absorb the green part of the spectrum.

Glass   Plastic   Cardboard

▲ *Light travels through glass well, so objects can be clearly seen through it. Substances which allow light to pass well are called transparent. Some plastics absorb a small amount of light; they are translucent. Cardboard allows no light to pass through; it is opaque.*

▼ *Objects lit by a bright source of light cast shadows. These Indonesian shadow puppets cast shadows on a wall or a translucent screen and are used to illustrate stories.*

SEE FOR YOURSELF
You can test the translucency of various materials, such as sheets of paper, using a flashlight bulb in a cardboard box. Put sheets of paper onto the open top of the box one sheet at a time, and see how the layers become less translucent as the sheets are added.

Layers of paper

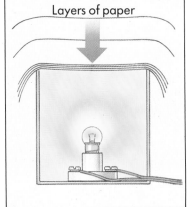

Christiaan Huygens (1629–1695)
Huygens was a Dutch physicist and mathematician who first suggested that light travels as waves. He explained reflection and refraction in terms of wave motion. He invented new ways of making glass lenses for telescopes. With his improved telescope, he was able to see the true shape of the rings around Saturn.

Light has the highest speed of anything known. It travels through the vacuum of empty space at a constant speed of about 186,000 miles (300,000 kilometers) per second. But light slows down when it travels through a material such as glass.

SEE FOR YOURSELF
To make a ray box, take a rectangular cardboard box with a lid and cut a narrow vertical slit in one end. Use strong sticky tape to attach a lamp holder wired to a battery inside the box. You can use the ray of light that comes out of the slit to see how an angled mirror reflects light around corners. You will be able to see the light ray more clearly in a darkened room.

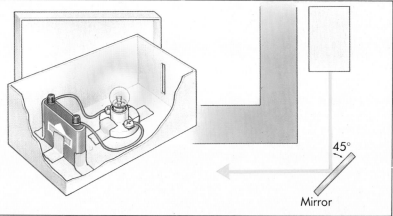

45°

Mirror

See also COLOR; DOPPLER EFECT; ELECTROMAGNETIC RADIATION; ENERGY; LENS; MIRROR; PRISM; SPECTRUM; SUN; VACUUM; WAVELENGTH; WAVES.

Thomas Edison not only invented the first successful electric light, he also invented the first efficient electric generators to supply his lights with current. In 1882 he began supplying current for more than a thousand of his lights in the Wall Street district of New York City. Edison's original light had a life of about 40 hours, compared to the modern lamp's 1,000 hours.

Lighting, artificial

Artificial lighting frees people from the natural cycle of day and night created by the SUN. Most artificial lights work by passing an electric current through a wire or a GAS to make it glow. Glass tubes filled with gases that produce colored light are used in decorative lighting for stores and advertising. Neon and other NOBLE GASES, such as argon and krypton, are used for this.

Colored lighting is not suitable for the home or work where white light is needed. Fluorescent lights are gas-filled tubes. A coating of phosphor inside the tube converts invisible ULTRAVIOLET energy produced by the gas into white light. Electric LIGHT BULBS are filled with inert gases at low pressure. These do not react with the hot wire, allowing it to reach a higher temperature and give out more light without burning.

► Fluorescent lights give out different colored lights, depending on the particular gas that the tube is filled with. The manufacturers test the tubes they produce and are always looking for ways to improve their efficiency and quality.

► Most fluorescent lamps contain mercury vapor at very low pressure. Electric current flowing through an electrode at one end of the tube produces a stream of electrons. These "excite" mercury atoms, making one of the mercury's electrons move into a higher orbit. When the excited electron jumps back to its normal orbit, the atom gives off invisible ultraviolet light. This hits a phosphor coating on the inside of the tube, making it glow and give off a bright light we can see.

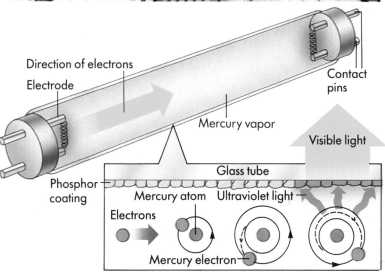

Direction of electrons

Electrode

Contact pins

Mercury vapor

Visible light

Phosphor coating

Glass tube

Mercury atom   Ultraviolet light

Electrons

Mercury electron

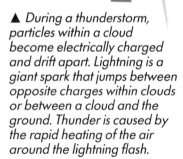

◀ *In a thunderstorm the sky may be filled with dramatic forked lightning.*

Positive charges rise

Negative charges sink

Positive charges rise from ground

▲ *During a thunderstorm, particles within a cloud become electrically charged and drift apart. Lightning is a giant spark that jumps between opposite charges within clouds or between a cloud and the ground. Thunder is caused by the rapid heating of the air around the lightning flash.*

▼ *An experimental lightning rod on top of a hill.*

Lightning

Lightning may be thought of as a huge spark of ELECTRICITY caused when there is a difference in electrical potential between some part of a thunder CLOUD and the ground, within the thunder cloud itself, or between two clouds. The spark, or electrical discharge, finds the line of least resistance so that it may take on a forked pattern (forked lightning). If the discharge takes place within the cloud, the cloud itself hides the forked pattern and a diffuse glow of LIGHT is seen (sheet lightning). When the lightning discharges its electricity to Earth, it tends to strike at a high point, such as a tree, or a tall building.

Lightning flashes produce about 100 million volts of electricity and heat the air to over 60,000°F (33,000°C). It is this rapid heating of the air that causes THUNDER. The buildup of an electrical charge in a thundercloud may last for more than an hour.

Lightning rod

A LIGHTNING rod consists of a METAL rod, often on the top of a building connected by a wire or cable to a ground rod buried in the Earth. Lightning tends to strike at high points. In areas where THUNDER storms are common, tall buildings could be damaged by lightning if they are struck. One way to protect such buildings is by means of a lightning rod. The lightning tends to be attracted to the lightning rod and is discharged safely to Earth.

The lightning rod was invented in the mid-18th century by the American statesman and scientist, Benjamin FRANKLIN.

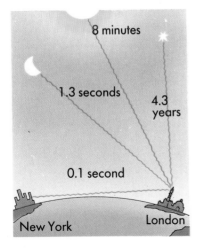

▲ *A light-year is the distance light travels in a year. Light takes 8 minutes to reach Earth from the Sun. Light from the next nearest star takes more than 4 years: the star is more than 4 light-years away.*

▼ *A linear motor train uses magnetic fields to provide it with forward movement. It also uses the repulsion between like magnetic poles to make the train hover over its single rail.*

Light-year

A light-year is the distance a beam of light travels in a year, 5.88 trillion miles (9.46 trillion km). Light travels at a speed of 186,287 miles per second (299,792 km/s). Light-years are a useful unit for measuring the huge distances between STARS. For example, the nearest star after our Sun, PROXIMA CENTAURI, is over four light-years away. Most astronomers prefer to measure distances with the PARSEC, which equals 3.2 light-years.

Linear motor

A linear motor, or linear induction motor, is a type of electric MOTOR. An electric motor is normally made from a series of ELECTROMAGNETS wrapped around a wire coil. When an electric current flows through the coil, magnetic and electric forces between the coil and the electromagnets make the coil spin. If the electromagnets are unrolled and laid flat, a metal bar can be made to skim along their length. This is a linear motor. The first linear motors were made during World War II to help launch aircraft from ships.

Linear motors are being used to propel high-speed trains that do not run on rails. They either float on a cushion of air or are supported by MAGNETS.

See also INDUCTANCE; MAGNETIC LEVITATION.

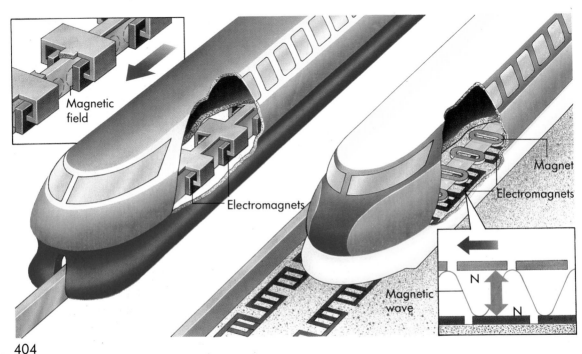

Magnetic field

Electromagnets

Magnet

Electromagnets

Magnetic wave

Daisy (*Bellis perennis* L.)

Dog rose(*Rosa canina* L.)

Common Juniper
(*Juniperus communis* L.)

▲ *Linnaeus used his two-word ("binomial") naming system to name many common plants. The first name is the plant's genus; the second, the species.*

Linnaeus, Carolus

Linnaeus (1707–1778) was a Swedish botanist who introduced a standard method of naming and classifying living things. Linnaeus spent much of his childhood collecting plants and animals before studying to become a doctor at the University of Uppsala. In 1741 he was appointed Professor of Medicine and Botany at Uppsala, and so spent more time studying the ECOLOGY and distribution of plants. He described nearly 8,000 plant SPECIES and about 4,400 animal species (almost everything known to Europeans at the time) and he gave each a scientific name in two parts. For example, he called the wolf *Canis lupus* and the jackal *Canis aureus*. *Canis* is the genus to which the animals belong, and so the scientific name shows that the animals are related.
See also CLASSIFICATION.

▲ *Linnaeus classified animals and plants scientifically.*

Lipids *See* Fats

Lippershey, Hans *See* Telescope

Liquid

A liquid is a STATE OF MATTER in which the ATOMS or MOLECULES are not fixed rigidly in position relative to each other, as they are in a SOLID, but do not move around quite as independently as they do in a GAS. This means that, unlike a solid, a liquid can flow freely and take up any shape but that, unlike a gas, the molecules tend to stick together in drops rather than simply spreading out to fill any container. A liquid is also unlike a gas in that it cannot easily be compressed, or squashed into a smaller

The most common, most useful, and in many ways most unusual liquid is water. It fills the world's lakes, rivers, and oceans, and falls as rain. It is essential for life — without it, plants and animals soon die. Water dissolves many substances, from salt and sugar to instant coffee. Like all liquids it changes to a solid if it is made cold enough. At below 32°F (0°C), water freezes to form ice. But unlike almost every other substance, frozen water expands as it cools.

405

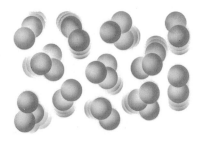

▲ *The molecules in a liquid are free to move around. Like a solid, a liquid has a definite volume but unlike a solid it has no shape of its own; it takes on the shape of the container that holds it.*

volume, by PRESSURE because the FORCES between the molecules prevent them from coming too close together.

Liquids can undergo changes of state to other forms of matter. If they are cooled down, the atoms move around less and FREEZE into fixed positions to form a solid; for example, water freezes to form ice. If liquids are heated, the molecules begin to move so quickly that they evaporate, escaping from the liquid to form a gas. Some substances, such as CARBON DIOXIDE, do not exist as liquids at ordinary pressures and sublime, that is change straight from a solid to a gas. A gas can be liquefied by being cooled. A VAPOR can be liquefied either by being cooled or by increasing pressure. Bottled gas is liquid butane under pressure. It vaporizes when it is released from the pressurized container.

See also EVAPORATION.

When we say liquid, we think of compounds that are liquid at room temperature. Of course many other things can be liquid too. Solid metals melt to become liquids at high temperatures and gases can be cooled to become liquids. Amazingly, there are many uses for liquid air. Air becomes liquid at about −310°F (−190°C) and it is used to produce liquid nitrogen and liquid oxygen. Liquid mercury becomes as hard as steel if liquid air is poured over it.

Liquid crystal display (LCD)

A liquid crystal display or LCD is a type of screen used in ELECTRONIC equipment such as digital watches and pocket calculators. It is a sandwich of two sheets of glass with a material called a LIQUID CRYSTAL between them. A thin clear layer of material that conducts ELECTRICITY is on the inside surfaces of the glass. When no current flows between the glass sheets, the liquid crystal is clear. When a current flows between them, crystals in the liquid turn and block the light, turning the display black. If the electrodes on the glass are divided into areas that are controlled separately, the display can show the time, a TELEVISION picture, or other shapes.

Liquid crystals were first observed by Friedrich Reinitzer in 1888, but no one could find a use for them. They remained a laboratory curiosity for about 70 years.

▶ *Calculators with liquid crystal displays are familiar objects. Special scientific calculators perform lots of different calculations and some even display graphs as well.*

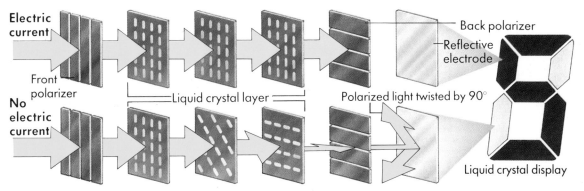

Electric current

Front polarizer

No electric current

Liquid crystal layer

Polarized light twisted by 90°

Back polarizer

Reflective electrode

Liquid crystal display

Liquid crystals

Liquid crystals are materials that flow like water but have a structure like a CRYSTAL. Small changes in electric current or TEMPERATURE can change the way that light passes through the liquid crystal. One type, used in LIQUID CRYSTAL DISPLAYS for calculators and watches, changes from transparent to opaque when an electric current flows through it. Another type, used to make paper-thin flexible thermometers, changes color when its temperature changes.

▲ *In a liquid crystal display the crystal is between two polarizing filters at right angles to each other, which together block polarized light. When there is no electric current, light is twisted through 90° by the crystals, so that it passes through the rear polarizer and is reflected back. Applying an electric current straightens the crystals so that the light cannot pass through the rear polarizer. This turns the segment black.*

Lister, Joseph *See* Antiseptics

Litmus

Litmus is a red or blue powder obtained from certain types of plants called lichens. It is a mixture of organic compounds that is prepared by treating the lichen with ammonia, potash, and lime. Litmus is SOLUBLE in water or alcohol and is used as a chemical INDICATOR to test whether SOLUTIONS are ACIDS or alkalis. Acids turn blue litmus red and alkalis turn red litmus blue. Litmus paper is absorbent paper impregnated with litmus solution. Most litmus is obtained from lichens that grow in the Netherlands. It was once used as a DYE.

▼ *A liquid crystal display consists of a clear front electrode, etched with a pattern of segments which form numbers. Behind this is a layer of liquid crystal, which is backed up by a reflecting electrode.*

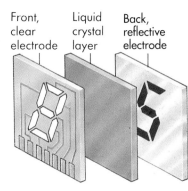

Front, clear electrode

Liquid crystal layer

Back, reflective electrode

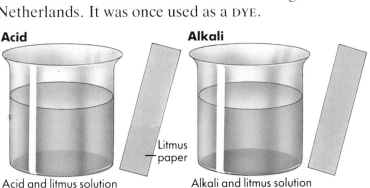

Acid

Acid and litmus solution

Alkali

Litmus paper

Alkali and litmus solution

◄ *Litmus is a vegetable dye that turns red in acids and blue in alkalis.*

The liver processes the digested food and drugs carried to it in the blood. Some of these can be poisonous in large amounts. The liver can only process some drugs fairly slowly, so if too much is in the bloodstream at one time the liver cannot cope. Liver disease means that the liver cannot purify the blood properly and so dangerous substances accumulate. A person who drinks too much alcohol over a long period of time may have permanent liver damage. One possible result is cirrhosis, in which useless scar tissue forms in the liver.

▼ *The liver acts as a chemical factory. One of its jobs is to store and process food materials coming from the digestive system. A blood vessel called the hepatic portal vein carries blood directly from the intestines to the liver. The hepatic artery brings blood directly from the heart to feed the liver itself. The liver also produces a digestive fluid called bile. This collects in the gall bladder and runs down the bile duct to the intestine, where it helps to breakdown fats. One of the liver's main tasks is to remove any poisons from the blood.*

Liver

The liver is the body's largest GLAND, weighing about 3 pounds (1.5 kg). It is positioned in the abdomen just below the ribs, and is a large, dark red, flattened organ. The liver is unusual in that it has two separate BLOOD supplies. One blood supply provides oxygen and removes waste, just like any other organ. The other blood supply comes directly from the intestine, carrying all the dissolved materials produced by the digestion of food. The liver is made up of thousands of lobules, which are small collections of cells surrounded by tiny blood vessels.

The liver processes food for the whole body. At least 500 CHEMICAL REACTIONS take place here. Among the most important is the processing of lipids, which are the result of digesting FAT. One of the products of this process is CHOLESTEROL which is needed by the nervous system and in the production of some HORMONES. The liver breaks down and rebuilds PROTEINS. It also produces urea as a waste product which is later removed by the KIDNEYS; and it converts SUGARS into glycogen, which is stored until needed to power MUSCLES.

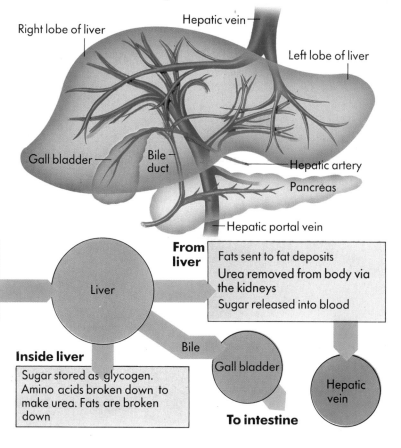

Right lobe of liver

Hepatic vein

Left lobe of liver

Gall bladder

Bile duct

Hepatic artery

Pancreas

Hepatic portal vein

Hepatic artery supplies oxygen

Hepatic portal vein carries digested food from intestine

Liver

From liver

Fats sent to fat deposits

Urea removed from body via the kidneys

Sugar released into blood

Inside liver

Sugar stored as glycogen. Amino acids broken down to make urea. Fats are broken down

Bile

Hepatic portal vein

Hepatic artery

Gall bladder

Hepatic vein

To intestine

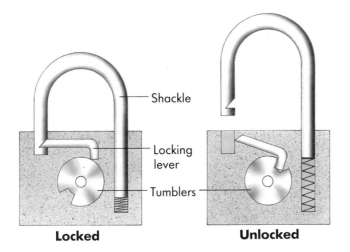

Shackle

Locking lever

Tumblers

Locked   **Unlocked**

◄ *A padlock stays locked because a locking lever engages with a notch in the shackle. Turning the key rotates the tumblers until a slot in the tumblers disengages the locking lever, and a spring pushes up the shackle.*

Locks and Keys

Locks are used to prevent doors, drawers, and containers from being opened. When a door is closed, a bolt slides out from the lock into a hole in the door frame, locking the two together. Pins inside the lock fall into place through the bolt and stop it from sliding back. The lock is opened by inserting the correct key in the keyhole to raise the pins and free the bolt. Ancient Egyptians first used locks like this 4,000 years ago.

In 1848, Linus Yale invented a modern version of the Egyptian pin lock. The jagged edge of its key raises metal pins or tumblers to the correct height to free the bolt. Most locks that protect outside doors are still Yale-type locks. Some locks are designed to be opened by magnetic keys. Magnets in the key repel the tumblers and free the bolt. Electronic locks work by operating the tumblers when the correct number or word is entered on a keypad. Some locks, especially in banks, are fitted with a timing device which allows the lock to be opened only at certain times. Combination locks are opened by turning a dial to a series of numbers which lines up slots in a series of rings. Electrical switch locks in vehicles need an ignition key. When the key is turned an electric current flows from the BATTERY to the starter motor.

Chemical Keys
The idea that there is a key to every lock has led to the word "key" being used to mean the answer to a problem. The word is also used when scientists are trying to explain the workings of complex biochemical processes. Catalysts, which help particular reactions but are not used up in them, can be likened to a "lock" that will only work when the right "key" molecules fit into them.

▼ *1 A cylinder lock, commonly known as a Yale lock, has a series of spring-loaded pins. The pins are in two parts of unequal lengths. 2 When the key is inserted into the lock, the springs push the pins down into notches in the key. 3 The divisions between the two parts of each pin line up, allowing the cylinder to turn and move the bolt across.*

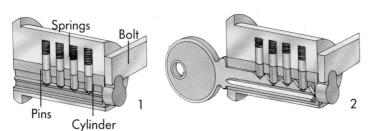

Springs   Bolt

Pins   Cylinder

1   2   3

Logic Gates

Sarah is invited to a party 20 miles away. Everyone has to wear orange and green and be under 15. Can she go? 1 = Yes, 0 = No.

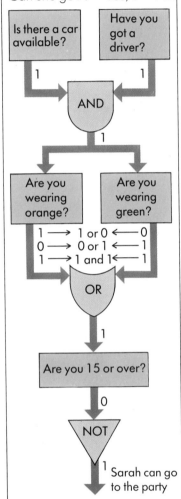

Electronic chips used in computers apply the rules of logic. The electrical switches, or logic gates, pass on, or change, the electrical 0s and 1s that go through them. An AND gate needs two 1s for a 1 to come out. An OR gate gives a 1 if either of the two input channels has a 1 going in and a NOT gate reverses the signal so a 0 going in becomes a 1.

Locomotion *See* Movement and Motion

Logic

Logic is a branch of philosophy that sets out the rules for correct reasoning. An argument (line of reasoning) consists of a series of statements called premises followed by another statement, called a conclusion. If the conclusion is supported by the premises, then the argument is sound or correct. If the conclusion does not follow from the premises, the argument is unsound. For example, the following argument is sound: all mammals are warm-blooded; all cats are mammals. Therefore all cats are warm-blooded. The following argument is unsound: No dogs are green; some parrots are green. Therefore, some parrots are not dogs. Both premises are true, but the conclusion is not.

The ancient Greek ARISTOTLE developed logic about 300 B.C. Today, logic is very important in MATHEMATICS and in COMPUTER programming where statements such as IF X = 1 THEN END are used to tell the computer to finish the program when X equals 1. Computers and other electronic devices contain logic circuits that perform logical operations on two or more input signals.

SEE FOR YOURSELF

Logic is a key tool in any kind of analysis, including that used by a detective. For instance, a detective was called to a hotel following the theft of a diamond ring. Only four people, the cleaner, the maid, the waiter, and the doorman, had a chance to steal it, and the detective questioned three of them. She then said she knew who the thief was. How could she have found the thief without talking to the fourth suspect? She had enough information to know who was guilty. Each of the three suspects had told one truth and one lie.
The cleaner said: "It wasn't me, it was the maid."
The maid said: "It wasn't the cleaner, it was the doorman."
The waiter said: "It wasn't the doorman, it was the maid."
Can you work out who the thief was?

First of all, you need to make an assumption and then test it. If your assumption produces two statements that contradict each other then your assumption is wrong and you need to make a different assumption. When all the statements agree with your assumption, then your assumption is correct and you too will know who is guilty. For example let's assume that the cleaner told a lie first and the truth second. This cannot be correct because the two statements contradict each other — if "it wasn't me" is a lie then it was the cleaner, but then "it was the maid" is true and it can't be, so the assumption that the cleaner told a lie followed by the truth is incorrect.
Answer on p. 412.

Longitude *See* Latitude and Longitude

Loudspeaker

A loudspeaker is a device for changing an electric current into SOUND. The output from a RADIO, TELEVISION, or HI-FI system is an electric current changing in step with the sounds that it represents. This is fed to a wire coil inside the loudspeaker. The changing electric current produces a magnetic field that changes in the same way. This changing field repeatedly pulls a MAGNET towards it and then pushes it away again, making the magnet vibrate. The magnet is attached to a paper or plastic cone which vibrates too. These vibrations pass through the air as a stream of pressure waves which our EARS hear as sounds. Most recorded music and many radio and television programs are now made in STEREO, requiring two loudspeakers.

See also MICROPHONE.

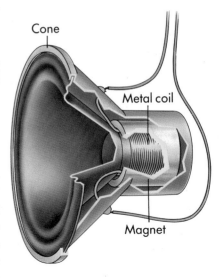

Cone

Metal coil

Magnet

▲ *A loudspeaker has a coil of wire attached to a diaphragm in the shape of a cone. A magnet surrounds the coil. When a sound signal from an amplifier passes through the coil, it moves in step with the signal and makes the cone vibrate, producing sound.*

Lubrication

Lubrication is the use of slippery MATERIALS to make surfaces slide over each other more easily and reduce FRICTION. Without lubrication, surfaces grind against each other and wear down very quickly, shortening the life of a MACHINE or ENGINE. Most lubricants (materials used for lubrication) are liquids made from crude oil, but some are solid. Graphite, also used in pencils, is a solid which can be used as a lubricant. There are also artificial or synthetic lubricants.

Most lubricants become thinner as their temperature

Lubrication is one of the most important techniques in modern industry and engineering. In the engine of a car or truck, oil is continuously pumped over all the moving parts to prevent them from wearing and getting hot. When a ship is launched, the slipway is greased so that the vessel slides easily down it into the water. In drilling a borehole to underground deposits of oil, engineers pour liquid mud down the hole to lubricate the drill.

Without lubrication

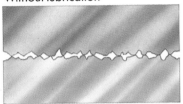

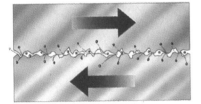

With lubrication

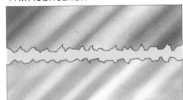

◄ *Seen under a microscope, no surface is perfectly smooth, not even polished metal. When two surfaces move past each other (left), their roughness causes friction. A lubricant holds the surfaces slightly apart (right) so that they slide easily over each other.*

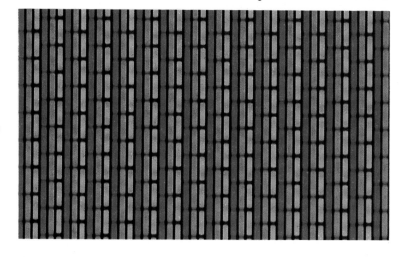

Answer to Logic problem:
If you assume that the three first statements were true, you get the following—
Cleaner: "It wasn't me" (true) "It was the maid" (false).
Maid: "It wasn't the cleaner" (true) "It was the doorman" (false).
Waiter: "It wasn't the doorman" (true) "It was the maid" (false). From this you can see that the thief was not the cleaner, the maid, or the doorman. It was the waiter.

rises and thinner lubricants provide less protection to moving parts. Some engines, race car engines for example, are fitted with oil coolers to keep the oil temperature down and give maximum protection to the engine. Although most vehicle engines have a separate cooling system that uses water and air, the lubrication system can also help to cool the engine.

There are natural lubricants too. Inside joints such as the knee a liquid called synovial fluid lubricates the cartilage caps on the ends of the bones and allows them to slide across each other.

Luminescence

Luminescence is the production of LIGHT by a material, usually a solid. It happens because ELECTRONS in the solid jump from a higher ENERGY to a lower energy; the total amount of energy is conserved, so the extra energy is given out as light. Energy has to be given to the electrons in the material in the first place to make the

▶ *The inside of a color television screen is covered with phosphor dots. When the beams of electrons strike these dots, they produce luminescence of three different colors. These red, blue, and green dots make up the color pictures we see.*

luminescence occur; this can be done in several ways. For example, when the energy comes from light shone onto the material, the luminescence is called *photoluminescence*, and when the energy comes from fast particles colliding with the material, it is called *fluorescence*. Often materials continue to give out light for some time after the input of energy has stopped; this is called *phosphorescence*.

The most common use for luminescence is on the screens of CATHODE-RAY TUBES in TELEVISIONS. The screen has phosphor dots on the inside which luminesce when hit by the beam of electrons in the tube, which scans the screen very quickly. Different phosphor dots, red, blue, and green, luminesce at different WAVELENGTHS in color television.

See also BIOLUMINESCENCE.

Fireflies produce a greenish light known as *bioluminescence*. This heatless light is caused by the effect which two or more chemicals have on each other, and is a much more efficient way of making light than we have yet produced. There is no waste of energy in the form of heat as in an electric light bulb.

Lungs

Lungs are large rubbery organs positioned in the chest, protected by the ribs. Their function is to take in oxygen needed for respiration, and to pass out waste carbon dioxide and water vapor from the body. Unlike many more primitive animals, all amphibians, reptiles, birds, and mammals have lungs to allow them to obtain OXYGEN from the air. Simpler animals, some larval amphib-

▼ The lungs remove carbon dioxide from the blood and replace it with oxygen. The oxygen comes from air breathed in through the trachea. The trachea divides into bronchi and these divide into bronchioles. The bronchioles end as tiny air sacs called alveoli. The pulmonary artery, a large blood vessel from the heart divides into two branches, each going to one of the lungs. Here they divide again and again until they become tiny blood vessels called capillaries. The oxygen breathed into the alveoli passes through the thin alveoli walls and enters the capillaries from the heart. Once this exchange of oxygen for carbon dioxide has taken place, the bright red oxygen-laden blood goes into the pulmonary veins and back to the heart to be pumped around the body.

Trachea
Vena cava
Pulmonary artery
Bronchiole
Aorta
Alveoli
Heart
Pulmonary veins
Bronchi

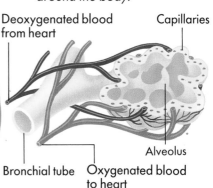

Deoxygenated blood from heart

Capillaries

Bronchial tube

Oxygenated blood to heart

Alveolus

▶ *During breathing we do not completely fill and empty our lungs. The lungs always contain about 100 cubic inches (1.5 liters) of air. Normal breathing involves breathing in and out about an extra 30 cubic inches (0.5 liters) of air. If we take a deep breath we can increase the air in our lungs by an extra 200 cubic inches (3 liters). If we breathe out hard, we can expel about an extra 60 cubic inches. During exercise, the volume of air involved in normal breathing can increase two or three times.*

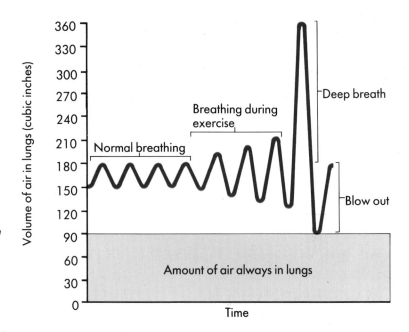

SEE FOR YOURSELF
Take a large plastic bottle and a dish. Put some water in the dish and fill the bottle completely. Then, with your hand over the end of the bottle so that no air gets in, turn it upside down and place it in the dish. (You may need someone to hold the bottle.) A couple of rubber bands and a ruler will make a scale. Place a tube in the end of the bottle. Take a deep breath and then blow into the tube. The air from your lungs will fill the bottle and give a measure of your lung capacity.

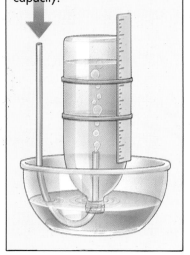

ians, and fish have GILLS or other organs for BREATHING.

In humans, air passes into the lungs along the trachea or windpipe, which splits into smaller bronchi, supplying the air to each lung. The bronchi divide again and again until very small air tubes open into groups of tiny bladders called alveoli. There are more than 300 million alveoli in the lungs. Oxygen can pass through the thin walls of the alveoli into BLOOD capillaries, while carbon dioxide passes out in the same way. The lungs fill when the muscular diaphragm beneath them contracts and the ribs are raised by the chest muscles. This makes the space inside the chest larger, and the lungs expand to fill the space, drawing in air.

Lyell, Charles *See* Geology

Lymph system

Lymph is a FLUID which leaks from the BLOOD capillaries, and resembles blood without the red cells. It contains many white cells which are used to fight INFECTION, and also contains fat droplets collected from the INTESTINES. Lymph travels through the body along the tubes of the lymph system, and eventually returns to the blood supply near the HEART.

At various points around this lymph system are the lymph glands, which are small swellings containing huge numbers of white blood cells. These white cells in the

The lymph system

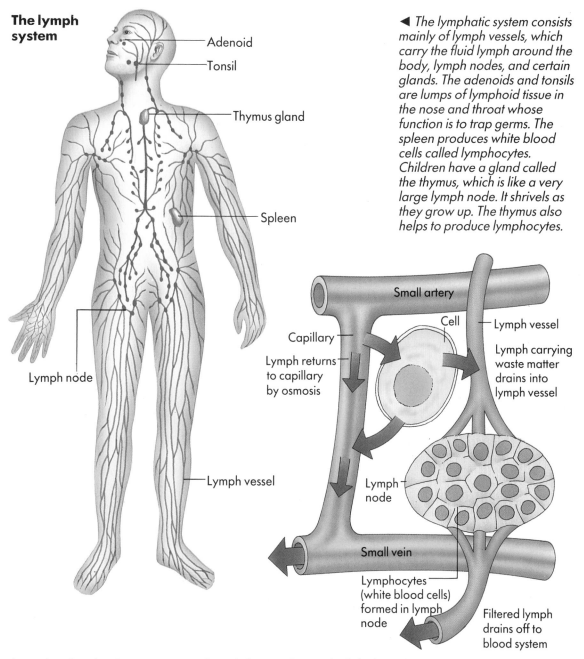

Adenoid

Tonsil

Thymus gland

Spleen

Lymph node

Lymph vessel

◄ *The lymphatic system consists mainly of lymph vessels, which carry the fluid lymph around the body, lymph nodes, and certain glands. The adenoids and tonsils are lumps of lymphoid tissue in the nose and throat whose function is to trap germs. The spleen produces white blood cells called lymphocytes. Children have a gland called the thymus, which is like a very large lymph node. It shrivels as they grow up. The thymus also helps to produce lymphocytes.*

Small artery

Cell

Lymph vessel

Capillary

Lymph returns to capillary by osmosis

Lymph carrying waste matter drains into lymph vessel

Lymph node

Small vein

Lymphocytes (white blood cells) formed in lymph node

Filtered lymph drains off to blood system

lymph glands destroy occasional bacteria and debris from dead cells. But when there is an infection, the white cells in the lymph glands multiply very rapidly to fight the infection. This extra activity causes the lymph glands to become swollen, and it is often a sign of infection when they can be felt in the side of the neck.

White blood cells are made in the lymph nodes of adults and the thymus in children. The thymus shrinks away in adults but does not disappear.
See also IMMUNE SYSTEM.

▲ *A lymph node is a lump of tissue along a lymph vessel. It forms lymphocytes, which are white blood cells that help to fight infection. It also filters the lymph, carrying waste matter from cells, before it passes into the blood system. Lymph nodes are concentrated in the armpits, groin, neck, and down the front of the chest.*

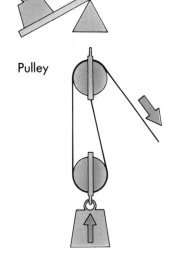

Lever

Pulley

Ramp

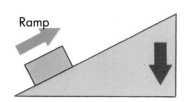

▲ *Simple machines include levers, pulleys, and an inclined plane or ramp, which give a mechanical advantage for lifting a load. An inclined plane may be used with a wheel and axle in the form of a winch (above right). A wedge (far right) is another simple machine which uses the force of a falling hammer, in this case to split a log.*

416

Mach, Ernst *See* Mach number

Machines, simple

Simple machines are used to help people do things that they could not otherwise do. There are six types of simple machines: the axle, LEVER, PULLEY, SCREW, wedge, and wheel. The wheel enables loads to be moved more easily by reducing the FRICTION between the load and the ground. An axle is a shaft that enables wheels to spin around the fixed axle.

A lever is simply a bar supported by a pivot or fulcrum. Pulling one end of the lever down raises the load at the other end. By choosing the position of the fulcrum carefully, a small FORCE on one end of the lever can raise a heavy load at the other end. The wedge, starting from a thin edge and gradually getting thicker, is very useful for separating things. An ax blade is a wedge. A pulley is a wheel with a grooved edge around which a rope or chain fits. Pulleys can change the direction of the force produced by pulling a rope. A number of pulleys can work like a lever by enabling a small force to move a heavy load. Screws are used to fasten things together or to move things.

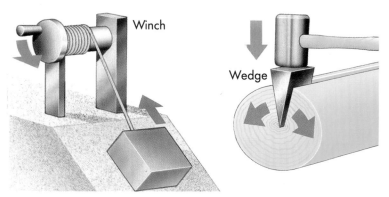

Winch

Wedge

Machine tools

Machine tools are powered tools designed to shape metal, wood, and other materials (called a workpiece) by shaving off unwanted material. There are several ways of doing this. The workpiece can be spun at high speed in a machine tool called a LATHE while cutting tools are pressed into it. Holes can be drilled in it by a drilling machine. Waste material can be cut away by a toothed wheel in a milling machine. It can also be planed in a

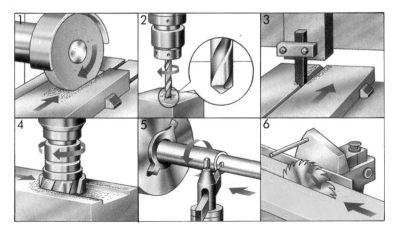

◀ Machine tools include **1** a grinding machine, **2** a drill, **3** a router, **4** a milling machine, **5** a lathe, and **6** a circular saw. In all but the drill, the workpiece moves past the cutting tool.

planing machine or worn down gradually by a roughened spinning wheel in a grinding machine.

The first machine tools were used during the INDUSTRIAL REVOLUTION when metal parts for STEAM ENGINES and other machines had to be exact so that they would fit any engine or machine. Before then, parts for machines were made by hand for one particular machine.

Mach number

The Mach number is a measurement of speed named after the man who suggested it, Ernst Mach. If the speed of an aircraft is divided by the speed of SOUND in air, the result is the Mach number. Speeds below Mach 1 are called *subsonic*. Speeds above Mach 1 are *supersonic* and speeds above Mach 5 are *hypersonic*. When an aircraft's speed increases beyond Mach 1, it is said to have broken the SOUND BARRIER. All passenger airliners are subsonic except the Concorde, which flies at speeds above Mach 2 (twice the speed of sound).

▼ At 1,340 miles per hour (about 2,150 km/h), the Concorde is approaching its top speed of about Mach 2.

▼ The top speeds of the world's fastest aircraft have increased by more than six times between 1940 and 1990.

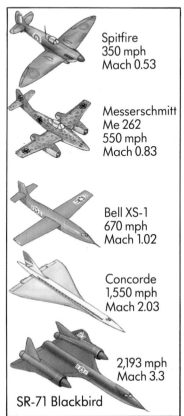

Spitfire
350 mph
Mach 0.53

Messerschmitt
Me 262
550 mph
Mach 0.83

Bell XS-1
670 mph
Mach 1.02

Concorde
1,550 mph
Mach 2.03

2,193 mph
Mach 3.3

SR-71 Blackbird

Ernst Mach (1838–1916)
Mach was an Austrian physicist who gave his name to the Mach number. This number is a method of relating an object's speed to the speed of sound in a particular medium, usually air. He also worked on shock waves and inertia, and taught that all knowlege of the physical world comes to us by our five senses.

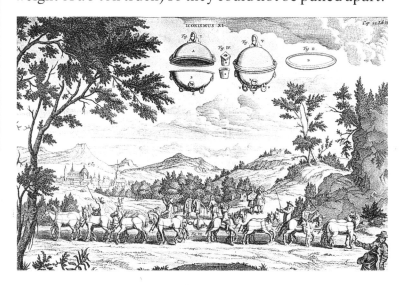

**Otto von Guericke
(1602–1686)**
Von Guericke was a
German physicist and
engineer who in 1650
invented the first air pump
(used in the Magdeburg
spheres) and later, the first
electric generator. With the
pump he was able to study
objects in a vacuum. For
instance, he showed that
sound needs air to travel in
and that air is essential for
burning.

▶ In his experiment von
Guericke joined together two
hollow hemispheres, pumped
out the air and then tried to get
two teams of horses to drag
them apart. They did not
succeed.

Macintosh, Charles *See* Rubber

Magdeburg spheres

The Magdeburg spheres were two hollow halves of a
copper sphere 14 inches (35.5 cm) in diameter, made by
Otto von Guericke who lived in the German city of Magdeburg. He used them to demonstrate how the atmosphere exerts a huge PRESSURE inward on any surface.
Normally there is also air, or some other FLUID, on the
inside of the surface pushing outward to balance the
inward force. However von Guericke, who had invented
the first air pump, was able to remove the air from inside
the sphere formed from the two halves. They only felt
the inward air pressure force (roughly equal to the
weight of a 3 ton truck) so they could not be pulled apart.

SEE FOR YOURSELF
Put a piece of aluminum foil at
the bottom of a plastic cup to
prevent the plastic from getting
scorched. Soak a piece of
blotting paper in water, light a
match and drop it onto the foil in
the cup. Quickly, put the blotting
paper on top of the cup and
place the other cup upside
down exactly on top of it. Pick
up the top cup when the match
has gone out. The bottom cup
should be attached to it because
as the match burned it used up
some of the air, creating a
partial vacuum.

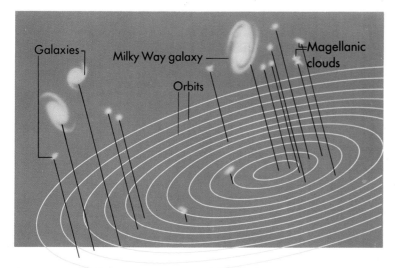

Galaxies

Milky Way galaxy

Orbits

Magellanic clouds

◀ The Magellanic clouds are part of the larger group to which our Milky Way galaxy belongs. All these galaxies are moving through space. The Magellanic clouds can be seen in the night sky in the southern hemisphere. Through a powerful telescope they can be seen to contain millions of stars (below).

Magellanic clouds

These two "satellites" of our MILKY WAY galaxy are the nearest galaxies in space. They were discovered around 1520 by the Portuguese adventurer Magellan when he sailed the southern seas. With the naked eye they look like hazy glowing patches. They can only be seen near the equator, or in the southern HEMISPHERE.

The Large Magellanic Cloud is about 180,000 LIGHT-YEARS away and contains about 10 billion STARS (about a tenth as many as our galaxy). The Small Magellanic Cloud is 230,000 light-years away and contains fewer stars. Both clouds contain bright NEBULAE where stars are being formed.

Magnesium

Magnesium is a chemically reactive, light, silvery white metallic ELEMENT. It exists in such crystalline minerals as dolomite and magnesite and is found in seawater. Magnesium is an ingredient of CHLOROPHYLL and helps in various biological processes in plants and animals. Magnesium burns in air with an intensely bright, white flame. Because of this it is used in FIREWORKS and flares and was once used in photographic lighting. Magnesium exposed to air forms a grayish oxide coating, which protects the metal from further CORROSION. Because of its lightness, it is used in ALLOYS with such metals as aluminum and zinc, for building aircraft and cars. Magnesium is refined by various means, including ELECTROLYSIS. Magnesium oxide is heat-resistant and is used to line furnaces.

▼ Magnesium burns with an intense white light, used in fireworks and flares.

▶ *A maglev train is used as a shuttle to carry passengers and their baggage between the terminals of large airports.*

▼ *Magnetic tape is used in audio and video tape recorders and in some types of computers. It consists of a plastic tape with a coating containing magnetic particles. Before recording, the particles have a random arrangement. After recording, they have a regular pattern, corresponding to the recorded signal. The recording head is an electromagnet energized by the signal to be recorded. It arranges the particles into patterns, which can be made random again by the erase head.*

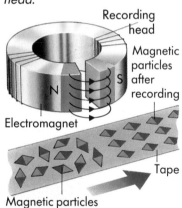

Recording head

Magnetic particles after recording

N S

Electromagnet

Tape

Magnetic particles before recording

Erase head

Record/ playback head

Magnetic levitation (Maglev)

Magnetic levitation is a way of lifting objects by using the FORCES that keep MAGNETS apart. Train designers use magnetic levitation to make trains that float above their tracks. The train carries powerful LINEAR MOTORS which push against magnets laid in the special track. The magnets in the track first attract the train, pulling it forward, and then, when it has passed, the direction of their magnetic fields is reversed, repelling the train and pushing it forward even faster. Since the train floats above the track, there is no contact between the two. There are no moving parts such as wheels to wear out and there is no FRICTION between the train and the track. Using magnetic levitation, a Japanese experimental train, the MLU-001, traveled at 249 mph (400.7 km/h) in 1987. It is used for studies of future passenger trains.

Magnetic tape

Magnetic tape is a strip of flexible PLASTIC with a magnetic coating used to record SOUND and pictures. To make a recording, the TAPE is wound past an ELECTROMAGNET (the *recording head*). The magnetic field it produces varies with the sounds or pictures that create the field. The changing field moves magnetic particles in the tape as it passes the head. To play the recording, the tape is wound past the same head again. This time, the pattern of magnetic particles in the tape makes electric currents flow in the head that match the currents that created them. The recording can be erased by destroying the pattern of magnetic particles on the tape.

MAGNETISM

Magnetism is the force that acts between certain objects at a distance or when they are touching. There are two types of magnets — *permanent magnets* and *electromagnets*. An ordinary bar magnet will pick up and support nails or other bits of iron and steel. Its magnetism is strongest at its ends — its poles. If a piece of iron or steel is stroked in one direction with the bar magnet, the piece becomes a magnet too. If we place two bar magnets on a table, the north poles if placed close together will push each other apart. So will the south poles. But north and south poles will attract each other.

An electromagnet can be made by winding a coil of wire around a bar of iron and passing an electric current through the wire. The strength of the magnet increases with the number of turns in the coil and with the strength of the electric current. Electromagnets can be made more powerful than ordinary magnets and are used around the home in TV sets, tape recorders, and telephones, as well as in huge industrial motors.

Two wires carrying electric currents in the same direction will attract each other magnetically.

▶ Magnets come in various shapes and sizes, including flat and round bars, rings, disks, and horseshoe magnets. Magnets can transfer their magnetism temporarily to other magnetic materials. When a magnet is held near a magnetic material, its magnetic force causes the particles in the material to line up, giving the material magnetic properties.

▼ Magnets exert invisible forces through their poles. The lines of force of the magnetic fields can be "seen" if iron filings are sprinkled onto some paper on top of the magnets. The iron filings follow the lines of force showing that these are concentrated at the magnets' poles and that like poles repel each other and unlike poles attract.

William Gilbert (1540–1603)
Gilbert was an English physician. He was physician to Elizabeth I and James I. He was the first to use the terms magnetic pole and electrical force, and suggested that the Earth's magnetism could be explained if the Earth was likened to a huge bar magnet. He thought (wrongly) that the planets held their orbits around the Sun by magnetic forces.

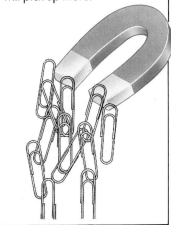

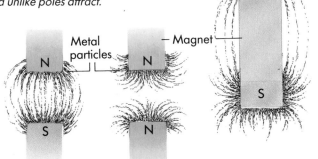

Metal particles — Magnet

N   N   N

N   N   S

See also COMPASS; ELECTRICITY; ELECTROMAGNET; FORCE; GENERATOR; GEOMAGNETISM; MATERIALS; METALS; PHYSICS; POLES.

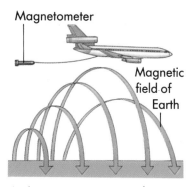

▲ A magnetometer can be towed behind an aircraft to detect the changes in the Earth's magnetic field that indicate the presence of minerals.

Magnetometer

A magnetometer is a device that is used to measure the strength of a magnetic field. The simplest type of magnetometer is a tiny coil of wire, which when moved through a magnetic field produces an electric voltage. Measuring this voltage indicates the strength of the field. More sensitive magnetometers, such as optically pumped magnetometers, can measure weaker magnetic fields. They can be towed behind aircraft to measure slight changes in the Earth's magnetic field. These changes help to locate deposits of iron, oil, and other RESOURCES.

Magnification

Magnification is the amount by which an image or picture of an object appears larger.

Optical instruments such as the MICROSCOPE and the TELESCOPE produce magnified images. The magnification that it is possible to obtain is limited by the quality of the LENSES or MIRRORS used, and by the DIFFRACTION of the LIGHT that passes into the instrument and affects the instrument's resolving power (its ability to separate closely spaced details). An ordinary optical microscope has a maximum useful magnifying power of about 1,500 times. Further magnification makes the specimen appear fuzzy because of the comparatively long wavelength of the light being used. Magnification can be increased by using waves of shorter WAVELENGTH than light. Since ELECTRONS behave like waves that have much smaller wavelengths than light, an electron microscope has much higher magnification than an optical microscope.

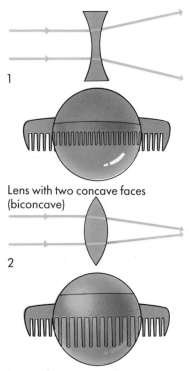

Lens with two concave faces (biconcave)

Lens with two convex faces (biconvex)

▲ The image produced by a concave lens 1 is smaller than life size. A convex lens 2 produces a magnified image. The difference is due to the different ways the two lenses bend light rays that pass through them.

▶ A magnified image of the threads in nylon stockings.

Malleability

Malleability is a characteristic of many METALS. Malleability indicates that a metal is capable of being pressed or hammered into thin sheets. The best-known malleable metals are copper, gold, and silver. Gold, for example, can be beaten into very thin sheets of gold foil or gold leaf just two microns (a micron is a 25 millionth of a inch) thick so that light shines through it.

Malleable metals are also ductile, that is, they can be stretched out into thin wires without breaking. Malleability and DUCTILITY are due to the molecular structure of the metal concerned. The framework or lattice of the solid structure can be changed a lot before the energies holding the atoms together are overcome and broken. When this happens, the metal breaks. Some metals are only malleable when heated.

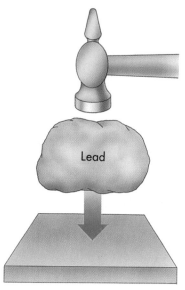

▲ Lead is a malleable metal. By hitting a lump of lead repeatedly with a hammer it can be beaten out into a thin sheet. Gold is the most malleable metal of all.

Malnutrition *See* Nutrition

Manganese

Manganese is a brittle, silvery gray metallic ELEMENT found naturally in many MINERALS including pyrolusite, manganite, braunite, and hausmannite, and in iron ore. The manganese is usually found as a COMPOUND with oxygen and so has to be extracted.

Small amounts of manganese are essential to plants and animals. At high temperatures, manganese reacts with carbon dioxide and carbon monoxide and even burns in nitrogen (which is very unreactive). About 95

Some areas of the ocean floor are covered with potato-sized manganese nodules. They occur at great depths and are most common in the Pacific Ocean. In addition to manganese, the nodules contain other metals such as copper and nickel.

◄ Manganese is added to iron to make alloy steels that are extremely hard. Manganese steel is used for making railroad rails and the rollers in machines for crushing rock.

The oldest map is a clay tablet that shows the line of the Euphrates River flowing through what was then known as Mesopotamia; the tablet is thought to be almost 6,000 years old.

percent of all manganese used in industry is used by the IRON AND STEEL industry. It is used in STAINLESS STEEL and in alloys of aluminum and copper. Manganese dioxide is used in dry cell batteries and in dyes. Manganese sulfate is used in paints and varnishes and in fertilizers. Potassium permanganate is an efficient disinfectant.

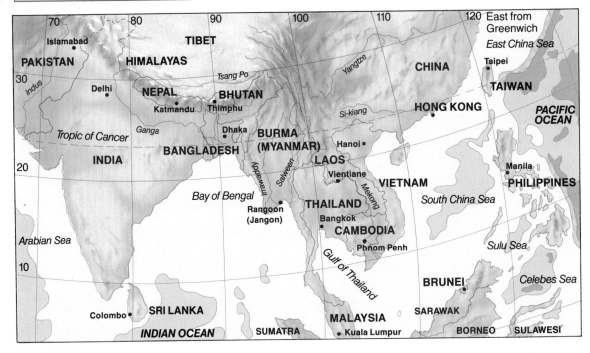

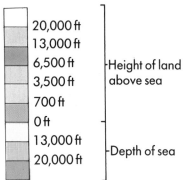

	Height of land above sea
20,000 ft	
13,000 ft	
6,500 ft	
3,500 ft	
700 ft	
0 ft	
13,000 ft	Depth of sea
20,000 ft	

▲ There are many different kinds of maps. A physical map, like the one above, shows the mountains, rivers, and types of vegetation in an area. A political map gives the names of the towns and countries and indicates their boundaries.

Map

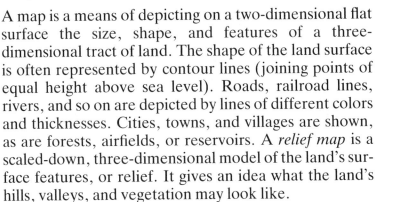

A map is a means of depicting on a two-dimensional flat surface the size, shape, and features of a three-dimensional tract of land. The shape of the land surface is often represented by contour lines (joining points of equal height above sea level). Roads, railroad lines, rivers, and so on are depicted by lines of different colors and thicknesses. Cities, towns, and villages are shown, as are forests, airfields, or reservoirs. A *relief map* is a scaled-down, three-dimensional model of the land's surface features, or relief. It gives an idea what the land's hills, valleys, and vegetation may look like.

To make a map, it is necessary to carry out an accurate survey of an area of land. Today, mapmaking is aided by aerial photography and surveys from SATELLITES. Maps may be drawn to different scales; that is, the length of line on the map which is used to depict a distance on the ground of, say, 1 mile, may vary and can be represented by half an inch on the map.

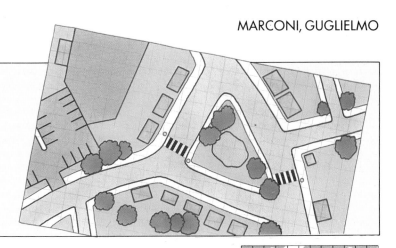

Map projections

Map projections are the way in which the curved surface of the EARTH is represented on a two-dimensional MAP. It is not possible to project a three-dimensional object such as the Earth onto a flat surface, just as the skin of an orange cannot be laid out flat.

The best that can be done produces a *projection* that is inaccurate in one direction, area, or distance. It is thought that the Greek geographer PTOLEMY was first to suggest a projection. His work was forgotten about until the 16th century, when the Flemish mapmaker and geographer, Gerhardus Mercator (1521–94), found Ptolemy's ideas and developed a map projection with a rectangular grid which is still called a Mercator projection. The Mercator projection is still used for navigation, but the shapes of large areas, such as Alaska, Greenland, and Antarctica, are distorted and the scale on the map varies with the LATITUDE. For example, Iceland looks seven times as big as it would if it were on the equator. Different projections are used depending on what shape, direction, distance, or area must be preserved accurately.

Marconi, Guglielmo

Guglielmo Marconi (1874–1937) was the Italian scientist who invented a system for sending messages (in Morse code) long distances without wires. He began experimenting with transmitting RADIO waves in 1894, having read about the work of Heinrich Hertz in producing electric waves. By inventing the ANTENNA and improving his receivers he succeeded in sending bursts of radio energy over about one and a half miles. He increased the range of his transmissions to 9 miles (across the Bristol Channel in England) and set up a land station in

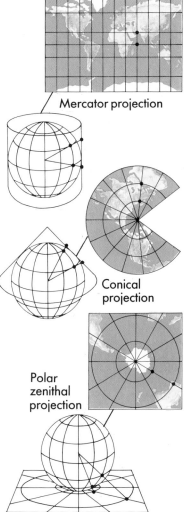

Mercator projection

Conical projection

Polar zenithal projection

▲ In a Mercator projection, Earth's features are projected onto a cylinder, which is then unrolled to form the map. A conical projection uses a cone, and a zenithal projection uses a flat sheet.

Italy to communicate with warships (12 miles) at sea. In 1899 British warships succeeded in communicating over 75 miles. In 1901, Marconi sent radio messages from Poldhu in Cornwall, England, to St. John's, Newfoundland — the beginning of worldwide radio COMMUNICATIONS.

▲ *Marconi developed radio communications.*

Margarine

Margarine is an artificial food used instead of butter. It is mainly a mixture of vegetable oils and milk products. It may also contain salt and FOOD ADDITIVES including flavoring, preservatives, and coloring. Some margarine contains less FAT than butter and, particularly, less CHOLESTEROL, which can cause heart disease.

Margarine was invented in the late 1860s by a Frenchman, Hippolyte Mège-Mouriès. Its flavor was improved in 1903 by replacing some of the milk and a hard animal fat called suet in its recipe by vegetable oils obtained from plants.

Margarine was, for a time, subjected to severe restrictions in the United States because of the opposition of the farmers and the dairy industry.

▼ *Margarine is made mainly from vegetable oil. First the oil is mixed with water and, after being purified, neutralized, and having natural colors removed, it is reacted with hydrogen. This reaction, carried out using a catalyst, converts the liquid oil into a solid fat. The fat is then deodorized, vitamins and coloring are added, and the resulting mixture is blended with milk products. The finished margarine is squeezed into containers. Low-fat margarines contain a higher proportion of water.*

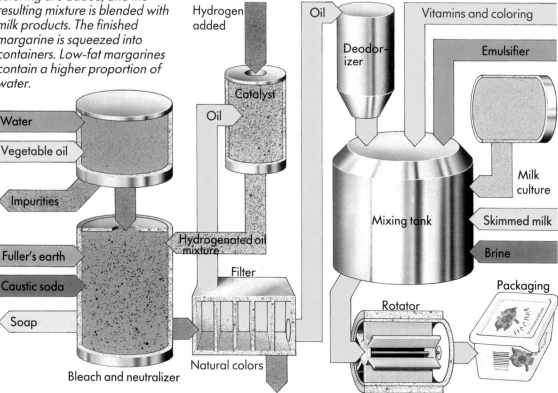

◀ Mars is the fourth planet out from the Sun, with its orbit between those of the Earth and Jupiter.

MARS FACTS
Diameter 4,220 miles (6,794 km)
Average distance from Sun 142,000,000 miles (228,000,000 km)
Year length 687 days
Day length 24 hours 37 min
Mass 0.11 of Earth
Density 0.71 of Earth
Surface temperature −22°F (−30°C) maximum

Mars

Mars is the PLANET nearest the EARTH. It is much smaller and far colder than Earth, and its atmosphere is very thin. Its mountains and valleys are higher and deeper than anything on Earth, evidence of violent surface up-heavals when it was younger. Its highest peak, Olympus Mons, rises 14 miles (23 km) above the desert, while its largest valley, Valles Marineris, is 2,500 miles (4,000 km) long (the width of the United States), 47 miles (75 km) wide, and in places 4 miles (7 km) deep!

The photographs taken by the two Viking landers in 1976 showed a stony, dusty landscape. Dust is blown up and carried for thousands of miles by storms. The ice deposits around the poles melt and form again as the seasons change.

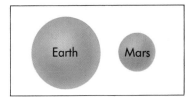

▲ Mars is half the size of the Earth but has a mass of only one tenth of Earth's.

▼ The surface of Mars is covered with craters, volcanoes, and gorges. Two of the largest are the volcano Olympus Mons and the gorge called Valles Marineris.

Giovanni Schiaparelli (1835–1910)
Schiaparelli was an Italian astronomer who believed he could see narrow lines on Mars. He called them "channels," meaning rivers or river beds. But his Italian word *canali* was mistranslated as "canals," meaning artificial waterways. American space probes have proved that there are no canals on Mars.

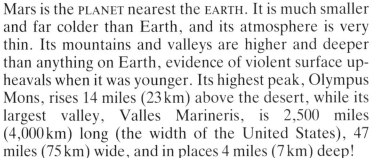

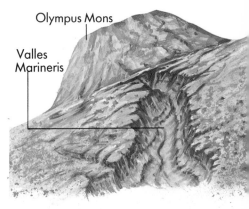

Olympus Mons

Valles Marineris

▶ *Much of the surface of Mars looks like a red, stony desert. This photograph was taken by a Viking Space probe in 1976.*

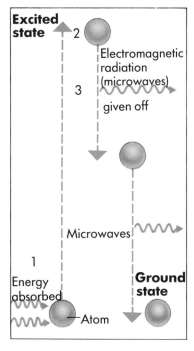

▲ *In a maser, **1** atoms are excited by firing bursts of energy at them. **2** Excited atoms lose this energy and **3** return to their original or ground state in two stages. Microwaves are released as the atom changes from one energy level to the lower one.*

There may be water permanently frozen below the surface. Some features which look like old water-channels have been photographed, and could mean that millions of years ago Mars was warmer, with liquid water. If this is true, there might have been life as well.

Mars has two tiny satellites: Phobos and Deimos. The larger, Phobos, measures only 17 miles (27 km) from end to end, and they are both irregular in shape. Phobos is only 4,000 miles (6,000 km) above the surface of Mars, and its "month" (the time it takes to go around Mars once) is 7 hours 39 minutes! It is gradually spiraling inward, and in about 40 million years it will crash.

Maser

A maser produces an intense beam of ENERGY. "Maser" stands for Microwave Amplification by Stimulated Emission of Radiation. (Microwaves have WAVE-LENGTHS of only a few centimeters.) In 1954, the American Charles H. Townes described how a maser might work: the ATOMS of a gas might be energized or "excited" by firing pulses of energy at them. They would release their excess energy as an amplified burst of microwaves. The first maser was made at the Bell Laboratories in the United States in 1956. Because a maser produces waves at a precise frequency, it can be used as a clock.

Masers are used as AMPLIFIERS in satellite communications and radio astronomy. As soon as the maser was successfully developed, scientists searched for its optical equivalent. The result was the LASER.

Mass

The mass of an object is the amount of material it contains. It determines two important things about a body: first its INERTIA, in other words how large a FORCE is needed to produce an ACCELERATION. (How much force do you need to push a stationary car?) If the mass of a body is doubled, so is its inertia. A bus has more inertia than a car. Second, the mass determines how strongly the force of GRAVITY attracts the body to other objects. The force of gravity toward the Earth is the WEIGHT of an object, so the mass also determines the weight. But mass and weight are different. Weight gets smaller the farther away from Earth you are. Mass remains the same. (Astronauts in space are weightless but their mass is always the same.)

Einstein discovered that mass is a form of ENERGY; an object traveling at 160,000 mps (257,500 km/s) has twice the mass that it had when it was standing still.

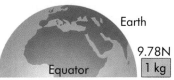

▲ Mass never changes, but weight depends on the force of gravity. The Earth is not perfectly round; it is wider at the equator than the poles. So while at the North Pole 1 kg (2.2 pounds) mass weighs 9.83 newtons (N), at the equator it weighs 9.78 N.

Mass number

The mass number is the total number of PROTONS and NEUTRONS in an ATOM. All atoms of a particular ELEMENT have the same number of protons at their center, but they may have different numbers of neutrons. These atoms with different numbers of neutrons are called ISOTOPES. For example, in one isotope of uranium called U-235, there are 92 protons and 143 neutrons (92 + 143 = 235). In U-238, there are 92 protons and 146 neutrons. Their mass numbers are 235 and 238 respectively.
See also ATOMIC WEIGHT.

Mass spectroscopy

Mass spectroscopy is used in chemical ANALYSIS to detect what ELEMENTS are present in a compound or mixture and to find out which ISOTOPES of an element are

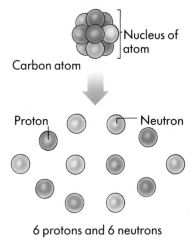

▲ The mass number of an element is the total of the protons and neutrons in its atomic nucleus. Carbon atoms have 6 protons and 6 neutrons, and a mass number of 12.

◀ In a mass spectrometer, the atoms in a gas mixture are converted to ions by electron bombardment. The stream of ions passes through a magnetic field, which separates them by curving the paths of some ions more than others, depending on their masses.

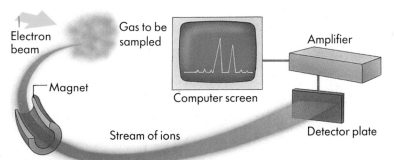

The importance of materials in the lives of people can be seen by the names given to major periods in history. More than 2 million years ago the Stone Age began, followed by the Bronze Age and then the Iron Age. By the mid-1700s, steel was the new material. Today, new materials appear every day. We could say that we are living in the Materials Age!

present in a sample. A machine called a mass spectrometer bombards a sample with ELECTRONS, thus producing IONS in the sample. The ions can be separated from each other by their MASS or electric charge. The ions are passed through an electric field, which separates them by the strength of their charges, and then through a magnetic field, which deflects the heavier ions more than the light ones. The ions are now spread out to give a pattern called a mass spectrum. Ions from each element produce unique patterns, so the elements in the sample can be identified.

Materials

Materials are substances used to make things. They may be natural or synthetic (man-made) or a mixture of the two. The first materials used by people were natural. Clothes were made from woven FIBERS from plants, and furs or skins from animals. Tools were carved from wood or animal bones, or by chipping away at a rock to make sharp-edged cutting tools. Homes were made from animal skins, leaves, or mud fixed to a wooden frame. All these materials were obtained easily and were given little or no processing. But often a suitable natural material was not available or not strong enough.

People learned how to produce new materials. From ORES found in the Earth's surface, METALS were extracted. New building materials were made from clay blocks fired in a furnace or KILN. Sand was used to make GLASS. During the 20th century, scientists began to make

▲ *Plastic is an artificial material with many uses. A special kind of light (polarized light) produces rainbow colors where there are strains in this molded plastic bottle.*

▶ *A modern racing yacht uses many different materials, from wood and metal to fiberglass and plastic for the hull and polymers for the sails and ropes. A strong material called kevlar is used in sails and ropes (and also in bullet-proof vests).*

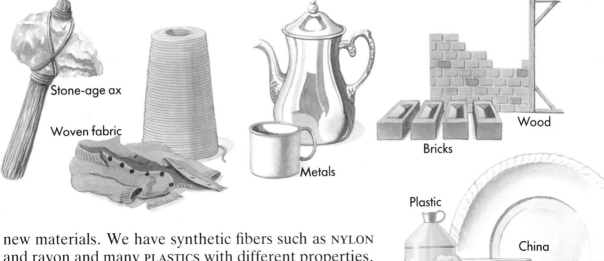

Stone-age ax

Woven fabric

Metals

Bricks

Wood

Plastic

Rubber

China

Glass

new materials. We have synthetic fibers such as NYLON and rayon and many PLASTICS with different properties. Some are transparent like glass but less brittle, others are good electrical INSULATORS or resistant to heat. Making anything, from a shirt or COMPUTER to a motor vehicle or house, requires an understanding of how materials behave in order to choose the best materials.

Mathematics $\sqrt{}$

Mathematics is the name of a group of sciences concerned with number, quantity, shape, and place, and their various relationships. Learning to count and work with amounts, shapes, and angles is one of humankind's major achievements. *See* pages 432 and 433.

▲ *Through the ages, people have had more and more materials from which to make things. At first, there were only stones and wood. Today there is a whole range of synthetic materials, such as plastics, in addition to all the natural ones.*

Matter

Matter is all the material in the UNIVERSE. There are several STATES OF MATTER; the matter around us on Earth is made up of ATOMS in the form of SOLIDS, LIQUIDS, and GASES. At very high temperatures, the electrons of an atom can become separated from its nucleus and a fourth state of matter called plasma is formed. The Sun and other stars are made of plasma.

Astronomers can only detect matter in the universe directly if it gives off LIGHT or some other form of ELECTROMAGNETIC RADIATION that can be detected. Matter that cannot be seen in this way is often referred to as "dark matter." Dark matter can still be detected because its GRAVITY produces forces on other objects. At present it seems that dark matter makes up as much as 90 percent of all matter in the universe.

> The three normal states of matter are solids, liquids, and gases. Most substances can exist in all three states, depending on the temperature. At low temperatures they are a solid. If the solid is heated, it eventually melts to form a liquid. At even higher temperatures, the liquid boils to form a gas or vapor. At extremely high temperatures, such as that in the Sun, there is a fourth state of matter called plasma.

MATHEMATICS

Ancient Egyptians used arithmetic and geometry more than 5,000 years ago to measure out plots of land and to build the pyramids with great accuracy. Arithmetic deals with numbers and calculating. Addition, subtraction, multiplication, and division are its four main operations. Geometry is concerned with lines, angles, figures, and solids. Greeks such as Euclid worked out most of the general principles of geometry, called theorems, about 2,500 years ago. Algebra is a kind of mathematical shorthand that uses symbols such as x and y to stand for unknown quantities. It was developed by the Arabs less than 1,200 years ago in the 9th century. Arithmetic, geometry, and algebra are the foundations of mathematics.

Mathematics is the language of science. Engineers, physicists, and other scientists all use mathematics. Other experts, who are interested in numbers, quantities, shapes, and space for their own sake, use pure mathematics. Number theory, the study of whole numbers and how they behave, is a typical branch of pure mathematics. In the modern world, mathematics is a key element in electronics and computing.

MILESTONES IN MATHEMATICS
3000 B.C. Ancient Egyptians use geometry for land surveys and for building.
300 B.C. The Greek mathematician Euclid uses logic to work out theorems in geometry.
800s Arab mathematicians invent algebra.
1100s Arabic numerals introduced into Europe.
1514 John Napier invents logarithms.
1680s Sir Isaac Newton and Gottfried von Leibnitz develop calculus.
1820s Charles Babbage begins building a mechanical computer.
1854 George Boole develops Boolean algebra for solving logic problems.
1960s Schools begin teaching new math, such as set theory.
1970s–1980s Themetical models are used on computers to study engineering problems, to predict changes in weather patterns, and so on.

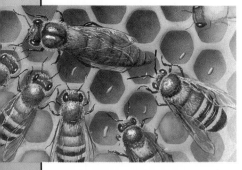

◀ *Only regular shapes with fewer than seven sides will fit together alone to make a pattern with no gaps. This is called tessellation. Squares, equilateral triangles (six of which make a hexagon), and hexagons (six-sided regular polygons, the shape of bees' cells) will all tessellate. Octagons (eight sides) will tessellate with squares.*

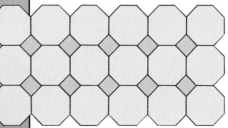

▶ *Before the electronic calculator was developed, people used a slide rule to make quick calculations. The numbers on a slide rule are arranged logarithmically. Napier invented logarithms in the 16th century and for hundreds of years the use of tables of logarithms enabled accurate multiplication and division of large numbers.*

Spider Paths
A spider wants to walk both ways along each edge of a cube without going along the same path twice. You can show the cube on a piece of paper as in the diagram on the right. The clever spider starts along the base of the cube (1), and so on.

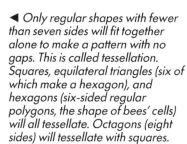

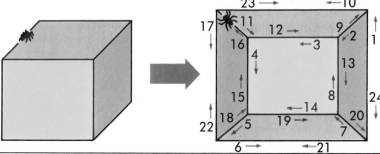

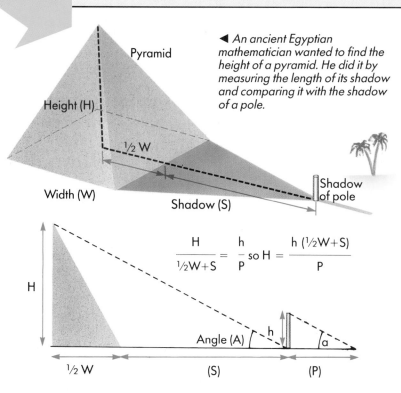

Pyramid

Height (H)

½ W

Width (W)

Shadow (S)

Shadow of pole

◄ *An ancient Egyptian mathematician wanted to find the height of a pyramid. He did it by measuring the length of its shadow and comparing it with the shadow of a pole.*

$$\frac{H}{\frac{1}{2}W+S} = \frac{h}{P} \text{ so } H = \frac{h\left(\frac{1}{2}W+S\right)}{P}$$

H

Angle (A)

h

a

½ W   (S)   (P)

▲ *Here is how the mathematician did the calculation. First he added half the width of the pyramid ($\frac{1}{2}$W) to the length of the pyramid's shadow on the ground (S) to give the total length of the shadow ($\frac{1}{2}$W + S). He then measured the length of the pole's shadow (P). He could measure the height of the pole directly (h). He then reasoned that the height of the pyramid (H) divided by the total length of the*

shadow must be the same as the height of the pole divided by the length of its shadow. Knowing three of these lengths, he was able to calculate the fourth. You can try this for yourself using a tall object such as a tree or a building and a pole that you have measured to find the length.

Powerful Mathematics

To square a number, you multiply it by itself. For example, 10^2 is $10 \times 10 = 100$. We have raised 10 to the power 2. To cube a number, you multiply it by itself twice. For example, 10^3 is $10 \times 10 \times 10 = 1,000$. We have raised 10 to the power 3. Similarly, $10^1 = 10$ and $10^0 = 1$ (any number to the power 1 equals the number; any number to the power 0 equals 1). You can also use negative powers. For example, $10^{-1} = 1 \div 10 = 0.1$ and $10^{-2} = 1 \div 100 = 0.01$.

Mathematicians call a power an index (plural indices). Indices are useful for expressing very large or very small numbers. For example, the speed of light is about 1,000,000,000 feet per second, written as 10^9 feet per second. The minute particle called an electron that makes up part of an atom is very small. It weighs about 9×10^{-28} gram or 9 divided by 1 followed by 28 zeros.

SEE FOR YOURSELF

Statistics are facts and figures about a particular subject, such as the type and number of vehicles that use a certain road. They can often best be presented in the form of a graph, such as a bar chart. Make a list of the kinds of different vehicles that use the road where you live, and count how may of each kind pass in a particular time. Then draw a bar chart like the one shown here.

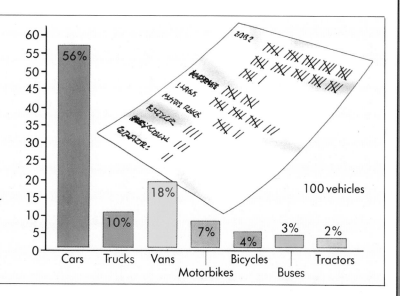

100 vehicles

56%						
		18%				
	10%		7%		3%	2%
				4%		

Cars   Trucks   Vans   Motorbikes   Bicycles   Buses   Tractors

See also ALGEBRA; ARITHMETIC; BABBAGE; CALCULATOR; COMPUTERS; ELECTRONICS; GEOMETRY; MEASUREMENT; NUMBERS; STATISTICS

People have been using the mechanics of pulleys for hundreds of years. It is said that Hieron II, King of Syracuse, challenged Archimedes to demonstrate the power of simple machines that the great scientist had been boasting about. Archimedes arranged a system of pulleys which allowed him single-handedly, to pull a fully-laden ship out of the water and on to dry land.

Maxwell, James Clerk *See* Electromagnet

McClintock, Barbara *See* Genetics

McMillan, Edwin *See* Uranium

Measurement

People need to know how big something is, how much it weighs, how much space it takes up, and so on. A farmer needs to know how much land he has for planting a certain amount of grain. These questions can be answered by measurement. *See* pages 436 and 437.

Mechanics

Mechanics is the part of PHYSICS which deals with the way objects move in response to the FORCES between them. The laws which govern the mechanics of everyday objects around us were discovered by Isaac NEWTON more than three hundred years ago; he showed how forces cause the MOMENTUM of an object to change. He also showed how the force of GRAVITY which is responsible for the WEIGHT of objects on the Earth also causes the planets to orbit the Sun. The laws of mechanics are important for the design of machines.

Although Newton's mechanics correctly predicts how planets and objects of everyday sizes behave, it cannot correctly explain the behavior of very small objects such as ATOMS. A new type of mechanics, QUANTUM MECHANICS, is needed to explain this.

▼ Mechanics involves the application of Newton's three laws of motion. These state that: *1* an object at rest remains at rest unless acted on by a force. Also an object moving in a straight line continues to do so unless acted on by force. *2* When a moving object is acted on by a force, its rate of change of momentum is proportional to the force and in the direction of that force. *3* When two objects interact, the force exerted by the first (the action) results in a corresponding force by the second (the reaction). Action and reaction are equal and opposite.

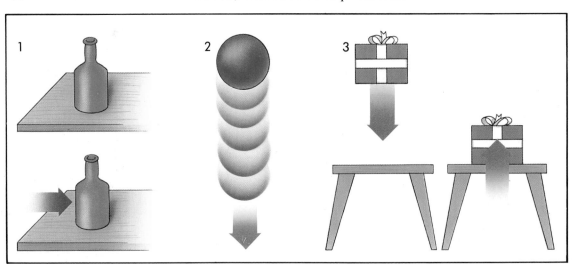

MEDICINE

Medicine is the science and art of healing. There are dozens of specialized branches of medicine such as cardiology (treatment of disorders of the heart), dermatology (treatment of diseases of the skin), orthopedics (treatment of disorders of the skeleton and muscles), and pediatrics (treatment of children's diseases).

Medicine has been practiced since the earliest recorded time. Clay tablets describing medical treatment were found in Babylon (3000 B.C.). In Europe and the Middle East, medicine was influenced by the ancient Greeks and later preserved by Arab and Jewish doctors, who continued to improve on the older knowledge. In fact, apart from some surgery, up to the end of the 18th century there was very little that a doctor could do for a patient, and many of the "cures" were worse than the disease. Now medicine is a true science, and every drug or technique that the doctor uses must be carefully tested and proved to work. The modern doctor makes a diagnosis on the basis of signs, which can be seen; symptoms, which the patient describes; and often, pathology reports on material from the patient that has been sent to a specialized laboratory to be tested. Most medicine is aimed at treating illness or damage with drugs or surgery. Many doctors now undertake preventive medicine, which is aimed at keeping the body healthy.

MILESTONES IN MEDICINE
2000 B.C. Medicine practiced in China.
1651 William Harvey describes the circulation of the blood.
1700s John Hunter perfects surgical techniques.
1846 William Morton uses ether as an anesthetic.
1895 Wilhelm Roentgen discovers X-rays.
1920s Frederick Banting and Charles Best use insulin to treat diabetes.
1960 Albert Sabin develops oral polio vaccine.
1967 Christiaan Barnard carries out the first human heart transplant.
1985 Lasers are used during surgery.

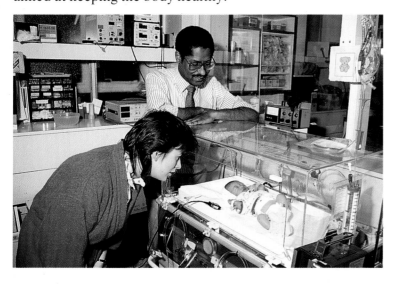

Robert Koch (1843–1910)
Koch was a German doctor who founded bacteriology, the study of bacteria. He identified the bacteria that cause such diseases as anthrax, cholera, and tuberculosis. He also studied malaria and concluded that it is caused by mosquito bites, at the same time as the British doctor Ronald Ross. Koch received the 1905 Nobel Prize in Medicine.

▲ *A baby that is born early or which has a very low birth weight may be cared for in an incubator. Inside the incubator, the temperature and the oxygen content of the air can be carefully controlled. The parents may not be allowed to touch their baby very often to reduce the risk of infection.*

Alternative Medicine
Some doctors use holistic (whole body) methods. These can be special diets or medical techniques such as acupuncture and osteopathy.

See also DISEASE; DRUGS; HIPPOCRATES; PAIN; PATHOLOGY; PSYCHOLOGY AND PSYCHIATRY; TRANSPLANTS; VETERINARY MEDICINE; X-RAYS.

MEASUREMENT

Measurement is the process of comparing something unknown with something known and generally accepted. The thing that is known becomes a standard from which we can derive units that are used for direct measurements.

In early history, parts of the body and other daily examples were taken as units. The yard, foot, and inch were based on parts of the body, the furlong (220 yards) was the length of furrow an ox could plow without a rest, and an acre (4,840 square yards) the area that the ox could plow in a day. Since these quantities were not standard they were not reliable measurements. In time, fixed standards were agreed on for the various measures. In the 1790s during the French Revolution, scientists in Paris developed the metric system, based on the centimeter, gram, and second (cgs system). It was adopted for scientific purposes in Britain in 1852, but this system was inconvenient when defining electrical and magnetic quantities, so in 1901 the Italian engineer Giovanni Giorgi suggested a system based on the meter, kilogram, and second (mks system). This became the basis of the Système International d'Unités (SI units), which was adopted by an international conference in 1960.

Scientists and instrument makers ensure that instruments give accurate readings by marking, or calibrating, the scale in appropriate units. A mercury thermometer can be calibrated in the following way. First, it is placed in water that is just boiling. A mark is made on the glass parallel with the top of the mercury: 212°F (100°C), the boiling point of water. Later the thermometer is placed in water in which ice is forming and a mark is made in line with the top of the mercury: 32°F (0°C), the freezing point of water.

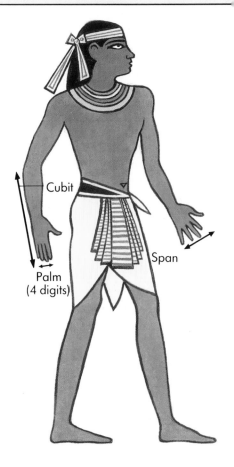

▲ Many measurements of dimensions (height, width, depth, and breadth) were originally based on parts of the body. The Egyptians used the palm (equal to 4 fingers), the span (a handspan) and the cubit (length of forearm).

▲ A micrometer is used to make very accurate measurements, such as the diameter of high precision metal tubes.

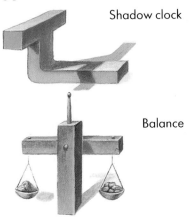

▲ Early methods of measuring included the shadow clock, which told the time by the position of a shadow along a bar, and a beam balance which weighed things against known weights.

Area and Volume
The length of a straight line is measured in feet or sometimes in smaller (inches) or larger (miles) parts of feet. Ordinary feet cannot be used to measure areas or volumes. A square with sides of one foot has an area of one foot times one foot or one square foot. A cube with sides of one foot has a volume of one foot times one foot times one foot or one cubic foot.

Anders Ångström (1814–1874)

Ångström was a Swedish physicist who studied light and the spectrum of the Sun. In 1868 he discovered hydrogen in the Sun's spectrum. He gave his name to a very small unit of length (the ångström), used for measuring the wavelengths of light and the distances between atoms. There are ten billion ångströms in a meter.

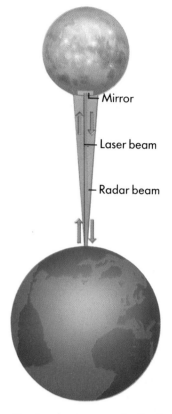

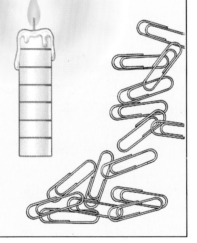

▲ The distance between the Earth and the Moon can be measured accurately by timing how long it takes a laser beam to reach the Moon and be reflected back again (astronauts left a mirror there). A radar beam spreads out as it travels, and so is not as accurate.

SEE FOR YOURSELF

You can measure length using a chain of paperclips, and mass using glass marbles. You could call your units "clips" and "marbles." A cup may be 3 clips tall and weigh 12 marbles. You can measure time by painting stripes around a candle and counting them as the candle burns down.

SEE FOR YOURSELF

A clinometer is used to measure angles in surveying. You can make your own by taping a drinking straw and a protractor to a piece of cardboard. Hang a small weight from a thread at the protractor's center. Look along the straw and read off the angle on the scale.

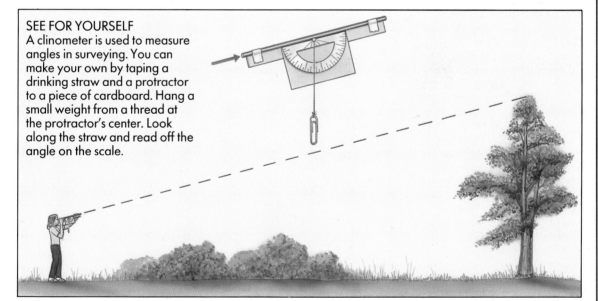

See also INSTRUMENTS, SCIENTIFIC; METRIC SYSTEM; MICROMETER; SCALES AND BALANCES; SI UNITS; THERMOMETER; WEIGHTS AND MEASURES.

Meiosis *See* Cell division

Meitner, Lise *See* Nuclear energy

Some solids do not melt to a liquid when heated; they change directly from a solid to a gas. This process is called *sublimation* and happens to such substances as camphor, iodine, and arsenic.

Melting point

Melting point is the TEMPERATURE at which a SOLID turns into a LIQUID. For pure elements such as copper or simple compounds such as water, the melting point is the same as the FREEZING POINT. When a solid is heated so that it melts, the molecules vibrate rapidly and partly overcome the forces that hold them together. They move around but cannot break away completely from each other. Pure elements or compounds melt at a precise and definite temperature. Mixtures melt over a wider range of temperatures. For example, zinc melts at 787.24°F (419.58°C), while copper melts at 1982.12°F (1083.4°C). Together they form brass with a melting point that ranges from 1650°F to 1800°F (900° to 1000°C).

▶ *The melting point of a solid is the same as the freezing point of its liquid; ice melts at 32°F (0°C) and water freezes at the same temperature. The chart shows the melting points of various substances. Helium turns to a gas at temperatures above −452°F (−269°C), and solid mercury melts at −38°F (−38.9°C).*

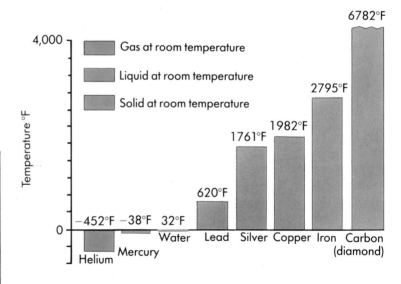

Nobody really knows how memories are stored in the brain or how we recall them when we want to. (Or why we cannot remember some things when we try hard to do so.) Memories probably involve chemical changes in groups of nerve cells in the brain. These changes affect the ways the cells connect together and how messages pass between them. When a group of nerve cells are used again and again, they develop more connections between each other, allowing them to pass messages better. When cells lose their connections because they are not used, memory fails and we forget things.

Memory

Memory is the ability to store information so that it can be recalled for use later. Computers are said to have a memory as well as animals.

Although some small areas in the BRAIN are known to play an important part in memory the function is spread around the brain, making it difficult to study how it works. There are several types of memory. One is called sensory storage, and lasts for a very short time. It allows us to take in what the eye sees, and then almost

Many people think they can improve their memory by practicing remembering things. This is not so; but we can help our ability to remember by using mental aids such as rhymes, mental pictures, clues, and other devices. How many of us would remember the days in each month without the rhyme "Thirty days has September..."?

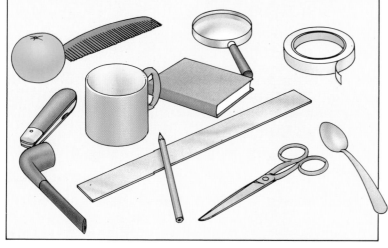

immediately fades away. If we think about the picture we have been looking at, or the sound we have heard, it becomes part of our *short term memory*. If you meet someone new only once their face or name will quickly disappear from the short term memory. But if you see them frequently, or repeat their name a number of times, it is transferred to the *long term memory*, and may be remembered for years. The more you refer to a stored memory, the more firmly established it becomes. Moving experiences into the long term memory is part of the LEARNING process which starts after birth.

Mendel, Gregor *See* Heredity

Mendeleyev, Dmitri *See* Periodic table

Meniscus

The meniscus of a LIQUID is the upper surface of the liquid contained in a partly filled narrow tube. The meniscus of a liquid is curved. This is caused by SURFACE TENSION. The meniscus may be upward-curving (convex) or downward-curving (concave). When measuring liquids against scales, the reading should be taken from

▼ *Mercury is a liquid metal with a very high surface tension. This can be seen by comparing the surface of mercury in a test tube with the surface of water. With water, the meniscus, the shape of the surface, curves upward at the edges where the liquid is in contact with the tube. With mercury, the meniscus curves downward.*

Water   **Mercury**

▶ *The meniscus on a liquid forms a sort of skin and is caused by surface tension. Many insects and other animals take advantage of this "skin," which enables them to walk on water, just as this raft spider is walking on a pool.*

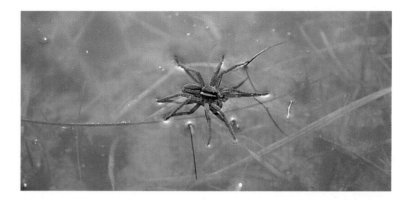

the middle of the meniscus. Meniscus (from the Greek for "crescent") is also the name for a LENS that is convex on one side and concave on the other.
See also CAPILLARY ACTION.

Mercury compounds are poisonous and can cause mental illness. At one time felt for making hats was manufactured from rabbit fur. Mercury salts were used to remove the hairs from rabbit skins, and people who did this job gradually became poisoned by mercury. This is the origin of the expression "as mad as a hatter."

Mercury

Mercury is the only metallic ELEMENT that is a LIQUID at ordinary room temperatures. People have known of mercury since ancient times. Its silvery color and the fact that it flows easily, have earned it the name quicksilver. It's more than 13 times heavier than water.

Mercury is obtained by heating a bright red ore called cinnabar, a COMPOUND of mercury and SULFUR. Mercury expands at a constant and even rate when heated and contracts evenly when cooled. It stays liquid from −37.97°F to +673.84°F (−38.87°C to +356.58°C) and so has been widely used in THERMOMETERS and BAROMETERS. It conducts electricity. A current passing through mercury VAPOR "excites" the atoms and makes them give out ultraviolet and visible light. The ultraviolet light is filtered out in street lights.

▶ *Droplets of mercury look like tiny polished metal domes because the liquid metal acts as a curved mirror and reflects light.*

MERCURY FACTS
Diameter 3,030 miles
(4,878 km)
Average distance from Sun
36,000,000 miles
(58,000,000 km)
Year length 88 days
Day length 59 days
Mass 0.055 of Earth
Density 0.98 of Earth
Surface temperature
840°F (450°C) maximum

◄ *Mercury is the planet nearest the Sun, which it orbits every 88 days. Daytime temperatures reach 842°F (450°C).*

Mercury (planet)

The innermost PLANET of the SOLAR SYSTEM, Mercury has been visited by one spacecraft, Mariner 10 in 1974. Its camera shows an atmosphereless, cratered world much like the MOON. This was expected, though Mercury is hard to study from the Earth; only Pluto is smaller, and Mercury's weak GRAVITY could not hold on to any gases to form an atmosphere.

The SUN beats down furiously on Mercury as it slowly rotates, taking two months to pass from sunrise to sunset. During the long night the temperature falls to about –274°F (–170°C), as cold as icy Saturn!

There are two main differences between the surfaces of Mercury and the Moon. Mercury has no dark, dusty plains, and the surface is wrinkled, as though the underlayers have shrunk, leaving the outer skin slightly too large. A huge body must have crashed into Mercury several billion years ago, causing a circular area 800 miles (1300 km) across, known as Caloris Basin.

Most of the planets have orbits that are almost circular, but Mercury's is an obvious ellipse. Its distance from the Sun changes from 43 million miles (70 million km) when farthest away to only 29 million miles (46 million km) when nearest, so that from Mercury the Sun sometimes appears to be one and a half times larger than at other times.

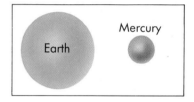

▲ *Mercury is not much larger than the Moon and is the smallest planet after Pluto, the outermost planet.*

▼ *The surface of Mercury is pitted with thousands of craters left after meteors crashed into the planet.*

441

▲ *Physical metallurgists may study the behavior of metals under great stress. This piece of metal has been greatly magnified to show a fracture. By studying the breaks in metals, metallurgists are able to understand more about their structure and how to reduce the chances of them breaking.*

▼ *Metals have many uses. Precious metals such as gold and silver are used for making jewelry. Base metals like iron and steel are important in construction and for making cars and ships. Tin and zinc give protective coatings. Useful alloys include brass, bronze, and aluminum alloys.*

Metallurgy

Metallurgy is the branch of CHEMISTRY that studies METALS. There are two types of metallurgy: *extractive metallurgy* and *physical metallurgy*. Extractive metallurgy deals with the various ways in which metals are separated from their ORES. Physical metallurgy is the study of the structure and properties of metals.

Metallurgists use microscopes to check for surface flaws in metals. From their analyses, they can find out how best to protect metals from the effects of RUST, other CORROSION, and METAL FATIGUE. The improvement and strengthening of metals for use in manufacturing includes such processes as making ALLOYS, heat treatment (such as the tempering or annealing of steel), ANODIZING, ELECTROPLATING, GALVANIZING, and carburizing (adding carbon to a metal). The formation of the metal into its final shape by hammering, casting, rolling, or extrusion (stretching) is also a part of physical metallurgy. Recent developments in the science include the study of materials called composites, in which metals are combined with fiberglass or plastic.

Metals

A metal is an ELEMENT, such as sodium, gold, or zinc, with certain properties. Most metals are shiny, all except mercury are solid at room temperature, and most have the qualities of MALLEABILITY and DUCTILITY.

About 80 metals are known. Most can be found in the EARTH'S crust. Few occur in a pure state. Most are

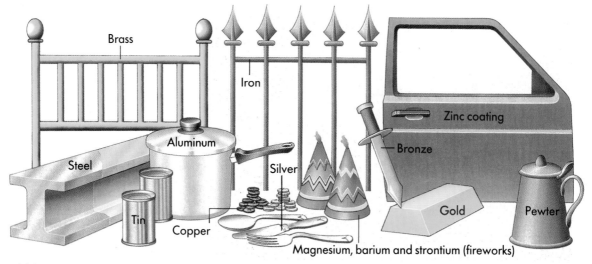

Brass

Iron

Zinc coating

Bronze

Steel

Aluminum

Silver

Gold

Pewter

Tin

Copper

Magnesium, barium and strontium (fireworks)

combined with other elements in rocklike deposits called MINERALS and ORES that are removed from the Earth by mining and other methods. They can be separated from their ores, but such REFINING often uses large amounts of ENERGY. The most common method of separating metals from their ores is smelting in a BLAST FURNACE.

Pure metals are rarely used, but in solid mixtures called ALLOYS (such as bronze or steel) they provide hard, strong, long-lasting materials for all kinds of building, construction, and manufactured goods. These alloys are often referred to as metals. Small amounts of certain metals are essential to plants and animals. Iron for animals' blood cells and calcium for teeth and bones are particularly important.

Metals are good conductors of heat and electricity because the electrons of a metal are able to move around more easily than those of a nonmetal. Metal atoms join together to make up larger units called CRYSTALS that have a regular structure.

Metamorphic rocks

Metamorphic ROCKS have been changed during their formation in terms of texture, chemical composition, or in the MINERALS from which they are made. The change may be brought about by a rock being subjected to heat, or pressure, or both. Metamorphic rocks may originally have been IGNEOUS ROCKS, SEDIMENTARY ROCKS, or even a different kind of metamorphic rock. The process which forms metamorphic rocks is known as *metamorphism*. For example, a large body of igneous rock may be

Slate

Marble

Gneiss

Cordierite hornfels

▲ Metamorphic rocks include slate, used for roofing, and marble, which can be carved and polished. In gneiss there are bands of light and dark minerals, and cordierite hornfels is a fine-grained silicate rock.

◄ Sometimes boulders of metamorphic rocks such as gneiss are embedded in an otherwise sandy area.

445

▶ *Metamorphic rocks are formed by the action of heat and pressure on sedimentary rocks within the Earth's crust. The sedimentary rock limestone, for example, can be changed into the metamorphic rock marble; both are forms of the mineral calcium carbonate. Soft clay minerals are changed into slate and shale. Large crustal movements that form mountains cause large scale regional metamorphism, whereas an intrusion of molten igneous rock may bring about thermal metamorphism.*

Fold mountains

Regional metamorphism

Slate

Shale

Fault

The metamorphosis of frogs is controlled by the thyroid gland, a small gland in the neck. If this gland is removed from the tadpole or if there is no iodine for the gland to function properly, then the frog just keeps growing in its tadpole state and never metamorphoses.

intruded into the surrounding rocks or the rocks may be subjected to heat and pressure as a result of major mountain-building events in the processes of PLATE TEC-TONICS. Marble is metamorphosed limestone while a hard, crystalline rock, called quartzite, is sandstone that has been metamorphosed.

Metamorphosis

A butterfly spends the early part of its life as a wingless caterpillar called a LARVA. The amazing change from the crawling, leaf-eating larva to the flying, nectar-sucking adult is called metamorphosis. Many other animals, including crabs and frogs, undergo metamorphosis, although the change is not always as striking as that shown by the butterfly. Larvae usually live in different habitats from the adults and commonly feed on different foods. This is a very useful arrangement because it means that more individuals of one SPECIES can live in one area than

▼ *A butterfly is an insect that undergoes complete metamorphosis. An egg hatches into a caterpillar, which changes its skin several times as it grows before becoming a pupa. After a few weeks the pupa splits open and the adult butterfly emerges. At first its wings are limp and shriveled, but they soon enlarge and harden in the sunlight.*

Egg   Caterpillar   Pupa   Adult emerging from pupa   Adult drying its wings

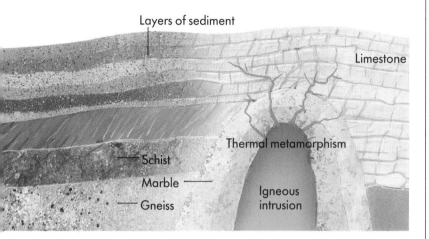

Layers of sediment

Limestone

Thermal metamorphism

Schist

Marble

Gneiss

Igneous
intrusion

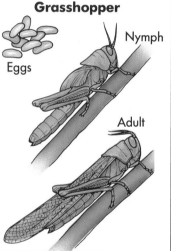

Grasshopper

Nymph

Eggs

Adult

would be possible if the adults and larvae all fed on the same foods.

Metamorphosis is controlled by HORMONES which circulate in the body. A caterpillar, for example, contains supplies of juvenile hormone which ensure that it stays a caterpillar for a while. But when it is time to change to a butterfly the supply of juvenile hormone stops, and when it next changes its skin the caterpillar becomes a *chrysalis* or pupa. Injecting juvenile hormone into caterpillars causes them to stay as caterpillars.

Meteor

A meteor is a particle sometimes as small as a sand grain hurtling at up to 25 mps (40 km/s) into the atmosphere. Most meteors burn up above an altitude of 60 miles (100 km). If you gaze at the stars for half an hour on a clear night, you will see an occasional meteor streak.

Meteor particles (known as meteoroids) are fragments of MATTER orbiting the SUN like minute planets. Some originated from the beginning of the SOLAR SYSTEM, others are thrown out by COMETS. Meteoroids from comets usually travel in swarms with many miles between each tiny particle. When the Earth passes through a swarm, a "meteor shower" is seen. Regular meteor showers are seen on the same date each year, when the Earth returns to the swarm. Some of the best occur around January 4, August 12, and December 13.

▲ A meteor is a small object that enters the Earth's atmosphere and burns up.

Composition of Meteorites

Meteorites reach the Earth from outer space and they vary in composition. The two main types are stony meteorites, which are made of rock, and iron meteorites, which consist mainly of iron or iron-nickel alloy. One rare type, called carbonaceous chondrites, contains particles of carbon. Meteorites were probably formed at the same time as the Solar System and have remained unchanged ever since.

▶ A meteorite is a traveler from outer space, a lump of stone or metal that has survived being burned up as it rushes through the Earth's atmosphere to crash to the ground.

Meteorite

Meteorites are bodies from space that are large enough to reach the ground without burning up in the atmosphere as METEORS do. The largest known meteorite weighs about 60 tons and landed in Namibia, southern Africa. About 25,000 years ago, an object about 330 feet (100 m) wide fell in Arizona, producing a crater 4,000 feet (1,200 m) across.

A falling meteorite will leave a brilliant trail in the sky known as a "fireball." Since they can look like ordinary dark stones, most meteorites have been discovered by special searches in areas where they stand out, such as the snowfields of Antarctica.

Some meteorites are mostly metal (iron and nickel), while others are made of stone. These may be fragments from ASTEROIDS that later broke up in collisions.

In 1908 a large meteorite weighing several hundred tons crashed into the forest near the town of Tunguske in Siberia, Russia. It flattened thousands of trees, scorched an area 20 miles across and caused a blast felt up to 50 miles away. People 500 miles away saw the meteorite in full daylight. The largest known crater (2½ miles wide) believed to be made by a meteorite is in Quebec, Canada.

Meteorology

Meteorology is the study of WEATHER over a relatively short period, by looking at temperature, rainfall, air pressure, hours of sunshine, and so on. Climatology, the study of CLIMATE as a whole, is concerned with long-term weather patterns. *See* pages 450 and 451.

Meters, electricity and gas

Electricity and gas meters are instruments used to measure how much ELECTRICITY or NATURAL GAS an appliance or household has used. An electricity meter consists of a rotating metal disk with ELECTROMAGNETS above and below it. The size of the magnetic fields produced by the electromagnets depends on the amount of electricity used. The fields interact with the metal disk and make it rotate. The number of turns it makes are counted automatically and appear as a number on the meter.

A gas meter works by pumping the gas alternately through two chambers. As each fills and empties in turn, levers attached to the valves of the containers drive a counter which shows the amount of gas used.

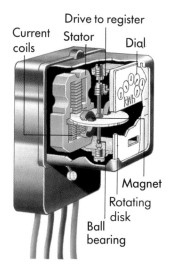

▲ An electricity meter measures electricity used in kilowatt-hours, also called units.

Methane

Methane, or marsh gas, is a colorless, odorless, nontoxic, highly flammable GAS. It is a HYDROCARBON that is made up one atom of CARBON to every four atoms of HYDROGEN. It is the simplest of the alkanes, a series of hydrocarbons that includes PROPANE.

Methane is a natural product of rotting vegetation in marshes and bogs and some mammals produce it during DIGESTION. It is used as a FUEL and is the main ingredient of the NATURAL GAS used in homes for heating and cooking. It is also the main gas in firedamp, which causes explosions in mines.

Methane is the starting point for the commercial production of several chemicals, including hydrogen, carbon monoxide, and hydrogen cyanide. Methane makes up a large part of the atmospheres of the giant planets Jupiter, Saturn, Uranus, and Neptune.

▼ A methane molecule is shaped like a triangular-based pyramid. It has a carbon atom in the middle, bonded to four hydrogen atoms located at the corners of the pyramid.

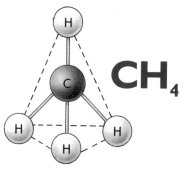

CH_4

◄ Methane is produced when dead plants rot. This process can be used to make the gas for use as a fuel. Here a submarine-shaped tank is filled with leaves and plant waste, and methane is tapped off through a pipe.

449

METEOROLOGY

The patterns of the weather have long been important to people, especially farmers, whose crops, animals and therefore livelihood depends upon them. In the days of sailing ships, being able to predict the weather could be the difference between a speedy voyage to a distant land or shipwreck in a storm. So, farmers and sailors were among the first to try to forecast the weather by observing its patterns.

Even though weather satellites now provide much of the information on which forecasts are based, weather stations still supply important data, especially at a local level. A typical weather station might include a barometer to measure air pressure, a maximum/minimum thermometer to record the highest and lowest temperatures, an anemometer and wind vane to measure wind speed and direction, a rain gauge to measure the amount of rainfall, and a hygrometer to measure the humidity of the atmosphere.

Satellites and computers are vital to modern weather forecasters. The computers use information from the satellites to predict the global weather patterns over various periods of time. There are two main kinds of satellite but both make their observations using ordinary visible light during the day and infrared radiation at night. One kind of satellite which is in a geostationary orbit, orbits directly above the Earth's equator at the same speed as the Earth rotates. This means that it is effectively stationary and can take pictures of the same place at intervals of, for example, thirty minutes. The other kind of weather satellite rotates the Earth from pole to pole so that, because the Earth is rotating, it takes observations of successive strips of the planet between the North and South Poles.

Cloud cover measured in eighths (oktas)

- ○ 0
- ◑ 6
- ◔ 1 or less
- ◗ 7
- ◔ 2
- ● 8
- ◕ 3
- ⊗ Sky obscured
- ◑ 4
- ⊗ Missing or doubtful data
- ◕ 5

Weather

= Mist	▽̇ Rain shower
≡ Fog	⁎̇ Rain and snow
❜ Drizzle	⁎̇ Snow shower
● Rain	△̇ Hail shower
✳ Snow	⎍ Thunderstorm

Wind speed (knots)

◎ Calm	⊸ 8 – 12
⌐ 1 – 2	⊸ 13 – 17
⌐ 3 – 7	◟ 48 – 52

▲ *Meteorologists use various symbols to indicate cloud cover, weather, and wind speed. For winds over 17 knots, each extra "feather" adds 5 knots.*

Weather Lore

There are many sayings about the weather and some have a basis in truth. For example, "Red sky at night, sailor's delight. Red sky in the morning, sailor's warning." In the Northern Hemisphere, when the sky in the west (after sunset) is red, the air is clear and dry. Most of the weather comes from the west and so the next day is likely to be fine and dry. A red sky in the morning occurs when the Sun lights up ice particles in the air, and rain clouds are likely to follow.

◄ *Scientists at the South Pole send up instruments suspended from a balloon to study weather conditions in the upper atmosphere.*

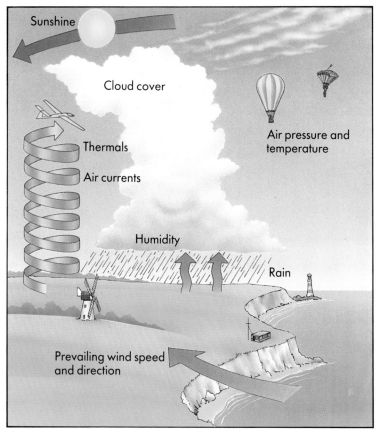

Sunshine

Cloud cover

Thermals

Air currents

Air pressure and temperature

Humidity

Rain

Prevailing wind speed and direction

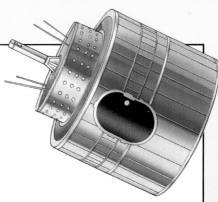

▲ Artificial satellites such as Meteostat orbit the Earth and send back photographs of cloud formations. Using these pictures meteorologists can watch the development of a weather system, such as a hurricane, track its direction, and warn people of its approach.

◄ The chief factors that affect the weather, and are therefore measured in order to prepare weather forecasts, are air pressure, air temperature, and the speed and direction of the wind.

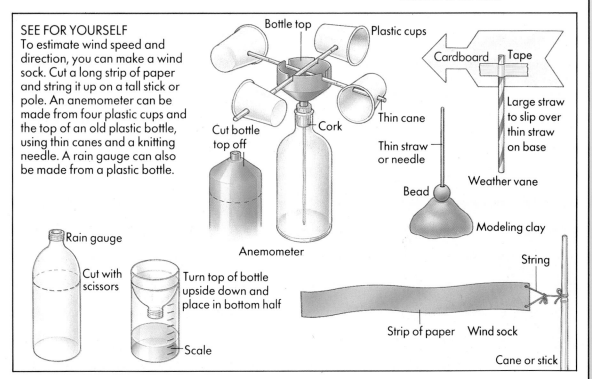

SEE FOR YOURSELF
To estimate wind speed and direction, you can make a wind sock. Cut a long strip of paper and string it up on a tall stick or pole. An anemometer can be made from four plastic cups and the top of an old plastic bottle, using thin canes and a knitting needle. A rain gauge can also be made from a plastic bottle.

Bottle top

Plastic cups

Cardboard   Tape

Cut bottle top off

Cork

Thin cane

Large straw to slip over thin straw on base

Thin straw or needle

Weather vane

Bead

Modeling clay

Anemometer

Rain gauge

Cut with scissors

Turn top of bottle upside down and place in bottom half

Scale

String

Strip of paper   Wind sock

Cane or stick

See also ANEMOMETER; BAROMETER; FRONT, WEATHER; HUMIDITY; HURRICANE; PRECIPITATION; SATELLITE, ARTIFICIAL; WEATHER; WIND.

The metric system, so-called because it began with the meter, is a decimal system of units. Multiplying or dividing numbers by 10 is easy because it only involves changing the position of the decimal point.
The United States is slowly changing over to the metric system. The Trade Act of 1988 called for the U.S. federal government to adopt metric specifications by December 31, 1992.

Metric Prefixes	Symbol	Multiplication		Power of 10	
tera-	(T)	×	1,000,000,000,000	=	10^{12}
giga-	(G)	×	1,000,000,000	=	10^{9}
mega-	(M)	×	1,000,000	=	10^{6}
kilo-	(k)	×	1000	=	10^{3}
hecto-	(h)	×	100	=	10^{2}
deca-	(da)	×	10	=	10^{1}
deci-	(d)	×	0.1	=	10^{-1}
centi-	(c)	×	0.01	=	10^{-2}
milli-	(m)	×	0.001	=	10^{-3}
micro-	(µ)	×	0.000001	=	10^{-6}
nano-	(n)	×	0.000000001	=	10^{-9}
pico-	(p)	×	0.000000000001	=	10^{-12}

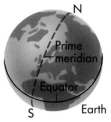

N
Prime meridian
Equator
S
Earth   Platinum-iridium

▲ *In the original metric system, the meter was defined as a ten-millionth of the distance between the North Pole and the equator, and a kilogram as the mass of a standard platinum-iridium cylinder.*

▼ *Mica is a mineral that consists of flaky layers that can easily be split apart to give very thin slices of rock.*

Metric system

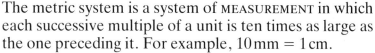

The metric system is a system of MEASUREMENT in which each successive multiple of a unit is ten times as large as the one preceding it. For example, 10 mm = 1 cm.

The system uses seven basic units of measurement whose values are fixed by reference to international standards. These units are the meter (length or distance), the kilogram (mass), the second (time), the kelvin (temperature), the ampere (electric current), the mole (amount of a substance), and the candela (intensity of light). Metric units have a prefix in front of them to indicate how they relate to the basic unit, whether they are multiples or fractions of the basic unit. French scientists devised this system in the 1790s. Since then it has been improved and the Système International d'Unités (SI UNITS) has been adopted in most countries.

Mica

Micas are a group of MINERALS that have a structure such that the atoms of SILICON and OXYGEN, of which micas are partly composed, are arranged in layers or sheets. Because the sheets of silicon and oxygen are held together only weakly, micas tend to have a flaky structure and split cleanly into sheets. The best-known micas are biotite, which is shiny black, and muscovite, which is silvery and almost transparent. Biotite and muscovite are found in IGNEOUS ROCKS, such as granite, and in certain kinds of METAMORPHIC ROCKS, especially the schists, where the micas give the rock a structure like the pages of a book.

MICROBIOLOGY

Microbiology is the study of microscopic organisms, such as bacteria, viruses, molds, and yeasts. It is concerned with their classification, structure, and function, and how they can be controlled and used. In 75B.C, Lucretius believed that plague was caused by "atoms," but it was not until the 18th century that Pasteur and Koch began to explore the part microorganisms play in causing disease. Pasteur noted the association of bacteria with fermentation and disease, and developed pasteurization to kill microorganisms. Koch demonstrated that particular bacteria could cause a particular disease, and developed ways of cultivating bacteria in the laboratory.

Microbiology progressed quickly, helped by the invention of better microscopes and laboratory techniques. Since the 1940s, microbiology has progressed enormously, helped by the development of electron microscopes which reveal the detail of even the smallest microorganisms. Molds, yeasts, and bacteria have all been cultivated and changed by genetic engineering or selection of useful characteristics. They now produce antibiotics, substances mimicking those in the body, vaccines, and antibodies.

▲ Microbiologists use chemical reagents and microscopes to study minute organisms such as molds and bacteria.

Euglena

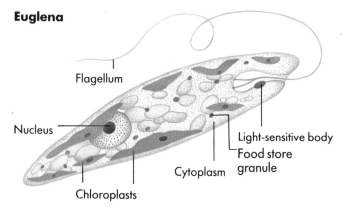

Flagellum

Nucleus

Chloroplasts

Cytoplasm

Light-sensitive body

Food store granule

Antibiotics are products of microbiology. Penicillin was first made in quantity during the 1940s, when it became possible to cultivate the mold which produces it. Many antibiotics are now made synthetically.

▲ Euglena is a single-celled aquatic organism. It makes its own food by photosynthesis but eats other food when there is no light. It moves around by lashing its whiplike flagellum.

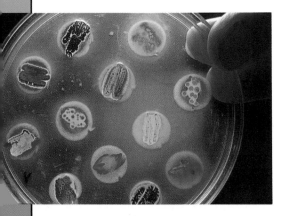

◄ Microorganisms can be grown or "cultured" in a jellylike substance in a glass dish. Scientists can then study the effects of drugs on the microorganisms.

See also DISEASE; DRUGS; FERMENTATION; GENETIC ENGINEERING; MICROORGANISM; MICROSCOPE; PASTEURIZATION; YEAST.

Microchips are able to perform at almost the speed of light — at more than a million operations per second. A microprocessor has the power of a large computer but is made up of only one integrated circuit held on a microchip. Early microprocessors could handle 50,000 to 100,000 operations per second — many fewer than they can today.

▶ *A microchip contains thousands of electronic components all mounted in a single block of plastic.*

▼ *A micrometer measures small dimensions very accurately. Turning the thimble along a screw thread moves the spindle and uncovers a scale. The micrometer may also have a vernier scale which allows for even more accuracy.*

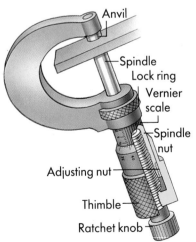

Microchip

A microchip is an INTEGRATED CIRCUIT constructed on a single piece of SILICON. The silicon chip is sealed inside a black plastic block with metal contacts along its sides for connecting it to a printed circuit board.

The personal COMPUTER or microcomputer would be impossible without the miniaturization of electronic components that resulted in the microchip. A microchip can contain hundreds of thousands of individual electronic components. In the early days of computing in the 1940s and 1950s, this number of components would have filled several rooms. There are different types of microchips for different jobs. Memory chips store computer data. A MICROPROCESSOR controls a computer connected to other equipment by an interface chip.

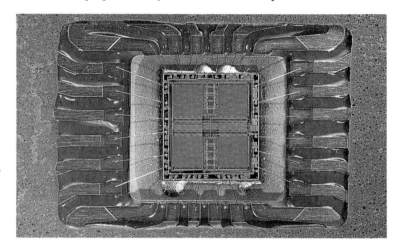

Micrometer

A micrometer is an instrument used to measure accurately the length, diameter, or thickness of small items. It works on the principle that a screw moves forward by a certain amount for every turn of the screw.

To measure the thickness of an object, the object is placed between the jaws of the micrometer and the handle which contains the spindle and screw is tightened on it. The thickness of the object is then read off a scale on the micrometer's handle. Sometimes the scale can be difficult to read. To make micrometers easier to use accurately, some of the latest micrometers register the number of turns of the handle, and therefore the thickness of objects, electronically. The measurement appears as a LIQUID CRYSTAL DISPLAY.

Microorganism

A microorganism is a living ORGANISM which cannot be seen properly with the naked eye. A MICROSCOPE must be used to study it. There are several different groups of microorganisms: microscopic animals and plants, bacteria, VIRUSES, and some small fungi.

Bacteria have a very simple structure, usually with a cell wall to protect them from drying out. Huge numbers live in the SOIL, where they break down dead material and help it to decay. Many animals, including humans, have millions of bacteria living harmlessly in the gut, as well as on the skin. Only a few bacteria cause disease, such as salmonella which causes one kind of food poisoning. Viruses are also microorganisms, but they cannot move, grow, or reproduce on their own. They enter a living cell and combine themselves with the cell con-

> The first person to see microorganisms was Anton van Leeuwenhoek, a Dutchman who ground lenses as a hobby. Leeuwenhoek spent hours peering through his simple lenses at flies, pieces of skin, and even scrapings from his teeth. Then, one day he examined a drop of dirty rainwater. In it he could see, as he wrote, "Wretched beasties swimming and playing, a thousand times smaller than one can see with the eye alone." This was the first sighting of bacteria made by humans.

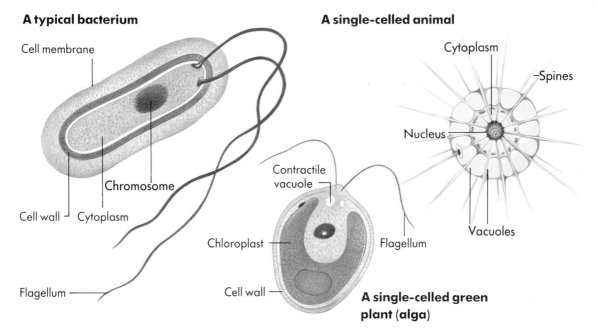

A typical bacterium

Cell membrane
Chromosome
Cell wall
Cytoplasm
Flagellum

A single-celled animal

Cytoplasm
Spines
Nucleus
Vacuoles

Contractile vacuole
Chloroplast
Flagellum
Cell wall

A single-celled green plant (alga)

tents so they can take over the cell's activities. Viruses cause many diseases in animals and plants.

Protozoa are a group of tiny animals, many of which live in water or in the soil, and a few of which cause serious diseases such as dysentery. A minute fungus called YEAST ferments sugar into alcohol and is used in wine and beer making, and also helps bread to rise. Other fungi are found in the soil and work like bacteria to break down dead material. Both bacteria and fungi are used to produce substances such as medicinal drugs.

▲ Microorganisms include bacteria and various single-celled animals and plants. All are too small to be seen by the naked eye and can be studied by using a microscope. Some microorganisms make their own food by photosynthesis in chloroplasts and others take in particles from around them. Some have flagella which they beat to move around.

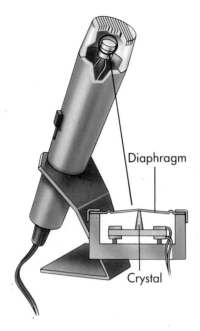

Diaphragm

Crystal

▲ *In a crystal microphone, sound waves vibrate a diaphragm whose movement squeezes a piezoelectric crystal. The pressure on the crystal makes it produce an electric current which varies in step with the vibrations.*

▶ *The heart of a microprocessor is a silicon chip integrated circuit, mounted on a base with two rows of pins or terminals. Microprocessors are used in automatic control systems for various machines, and may make up the chief components of a microcomputer.*

Glass globes filled with water were probably used as magnifying glasses at least 3,000 years ago. The Romans may have used clear crystals as magnifying glasses.

Microphone

A microphone changes SOUNDS into an electric current. Sound waves in the air strike a paper or plastic surface called a "diaphragm" and make it vibrate in step with the sound waves. These vibrations are used to change the electric current flowing through an electric CIRCUIT. This can be done in different ways. A dynamic microphone works like a LOUDSPEAKER in reverse. A coil of wire attached to the diaphragm vibrates in a magnetic field, causing an electric current to flow through the coil by electromagnetic INDUCTION. In a *carbon microphone*, the vibrating diaphragm varies the electrical resistance of a carbon contact. In a *condenser microphone*, it varies a property called CAPACITANCE in the circuit. A *crystal microphone* uses a PIEZOELECTRIC crystal to convert the vibrations directly to an electric current.

Microprocessor

A microprocessor is the control center and electronic calculator of a COMPUTER. It was introduced in the early 1970s by the U.S. Intel Corporation; it was the first time a computer's central processing unit could fit on a single

Chip in its package

Pins

chip. The tiny size of the microprocessor enabled computer manufacturers to produce smaller, more powerful computers that were also less expensive. The microprocessor made the microcomputer possible.

Microscope

A microscope is an instrument used to produce a larger image of an object. Light shining through the object is bent by a LENS before it enters the observer's eye, making the object appear larger than it really is. By adding a second lens to magnify the image produced by the first, the image can be made even larger. Microscopes with more than one lens are called compound microscopes. The microscopes used by scientists to look at plant and animal cells are compound microscopes. In the 1930s, a new type of microscope called an ELECTRON MICROSCOPE was developed. It uses streams of ELECTRONS instead of LIGHT to give a higher magnification. The most powerful microscopes are scanning tunneling microscopes. They also use electrons but in a different way and they can now magnify 100 million times.

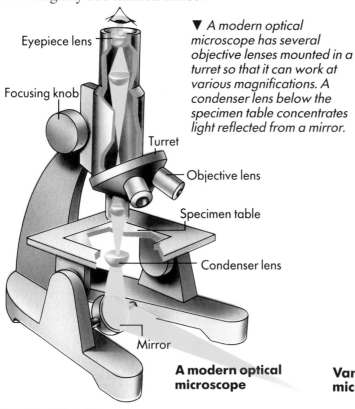

Eyepiece lens

Focusing knob

Turret

Objective lens

Specimen table

Condenser lens

Mirror

▼ *A modern optical microscope has several objective lenses mounted in a turret so that it can work at various magnifications. A condenser lens below the specimen table concentrates light reflected from a mirror.*

A modern optical microscope

SEE FOR YOURSELF

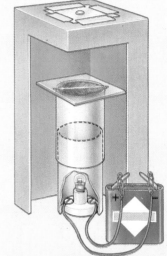

You can make a simple microscope. Cut a hole in a piece of cardboard and tape some clear film over it. A drop of water over the hole will act as a lens to magnify objects. Take 2 cardboard tubes, split one from top to bottom and fit it over the other one tightly. Place your object on top of the tubes and move them up or down until it is in focus through your lens. A light bulb will help you to see the object.

Anton van Leeuwenhoek (1632–1723)
Leeuwenhoek was a Dutch draper who also ground magnifying lenses and used them to study the things around him. He made his first microscope in the 1670s, and was later to become the first person to see bacteria, the cells that make up yeast and some blood cells. He lived to age 90 and during his life, he ground a total of 419 lenses.

Van Leeuwenhoek's microscope

Lens

Specimen holder

Adjusting screw

▶ *This microscope is very different from modern ones. It had a single hand-ground lens.*
The specimen was placed on the pointed rod and viewed from the other side through the minute lens. The long screw moved the specimen into the line of sight.

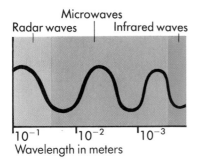

Microwaves
Radar waves | Microwaves | Infrared waves

10^{-1} 10^{-2} 10^{-3}
Wavelength in meters

▲ *Microwaves are a form of electromagnetic radiation with wavelengths between those of infrared and radar waves. They correspond to extremely high frequency radio waves.*

▶ *The heart of a microwave oven is a magnetron. This is a two-electrode tube that generates microwaves, which are usually reflected onto the food to be cooked. The waves agitate water molecules in the food. The molecules rub against each other and the friction produces heat, which cooks the food. Other parts of the oven consist of a timer and a switch to vary the output power of the magnetron.*

Microwaves

Microwaves are a form of ELECTROMAGNETIC RADIATION, typically with a WAVELENGTH of a few centimeters. They are used for communications, since their wavelength is a convenient size, easy to direct and control. Microwaves are usually produced from a metal cavity into which a whole number of wavelengths will fit exactly; this is much like the way in which SOUND is produced by an organ pipe. Very intense microwave beams can be produced using a MASER.

Microwaves can be used for cooking. In a microwave oven, the water molecules in the food absorb microwave ENERGY and so the food is heated through and cooks.

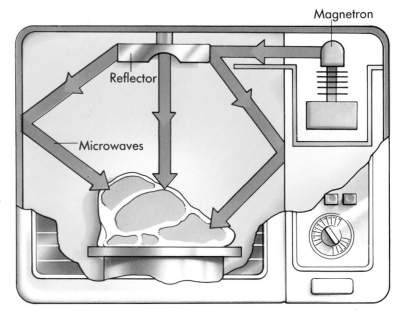

Magnetron

Reflector

Microwaves

Migration

Migration is the regular movement of animals to and from certain areas. It usually takes place at particular seasons. Swallows and many other birds, for example, spend the winter in tropical areas and then fly off to breed in cooler regions during the summer. By doing this they avoid the competition for food in the TROPICS and they have longer summer days in which to collect insects to feed their young. They return to the tropics for winter because there are not enough insects for them to eat in the cooler areas. Some birds fly thousands of miles between their summer and winter homes.

Many mammals also migrate. Humpback whales, for

In ancient times, people did not understand why some birds or other animals disappeared at certain times of the year. Some people thought that birds spent the winter in caves or in the mud of swamps and lakes. As recently as the 18th century, one writer tried to prove that birds flew to the Moon for the winter!

◄ *Monarch butterflies gather in their thousands before beginning their long flight down the west coast of North America.*

▼ *The map shows the distances traveled by some of the world's long-distance migratory animals. Most of them are birds, but also represented are an insect (the monarch butterfly) and two mammals, the caribou and the blue whale.*

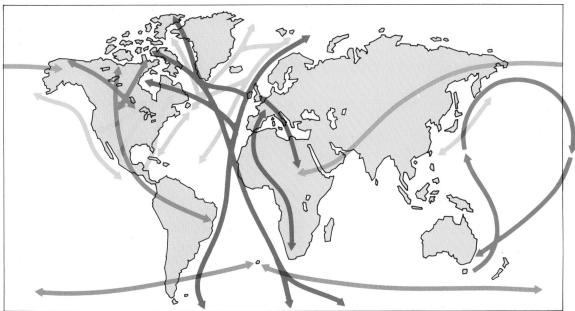

⇨ Short-tailed shearwater

⇨ Golden plover

⇨ Arctic tern

⇨ Blue whale

⇨ Monarch butterfly

⇨ Wandering albatross

⇨ Cuckoo

⇨ Wheatear

⇨ Caribou

example, feed in the polar OCEANS but when winter comes they move to the tropical oceans to breed. Mountain mammals move to lower levels to escape the winter snows, and reindeer living in the far north move farther south for the winter. European eels swim all the way to the Sargasso Sea in the western part of the Atlantic Ocean to lay their eggs. The baby eels then take three years to swim back to the European rivers.

Even insects migrate. Monarch butterflies fly all the way from Canada to Mexico to sleep through the winter. Immense swarms of locusts occasionally fly out from overcrowded areas to settle elsewhere, but since they do not return, we call these movements emigrations.

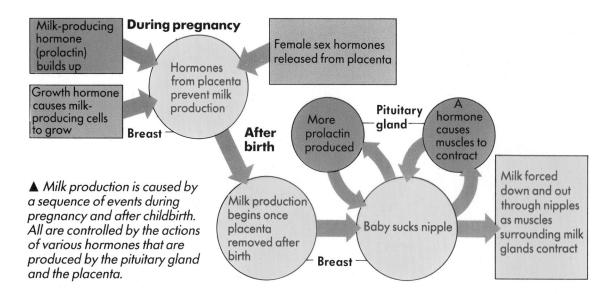

▲ Milk production is caused by a sequence of events during pregnancy and after childbirth. All are controlled by the actions of various hormones that are produced by the pituitary gland and the placenta.

Each Western dairy cow produces about 1,000 gallons of milk a year. About two-thirds of our milk is drunk fresh; the rest is made into butter and cheese. Some people cannot digest a substance called lactose (milk sugar) which makes up about 5 percent of cow's milk.

Milk

Milk is the liquid food produced by a female mammal to feed her babies. It is formed in the mother's mammary GLANDS and starts to flow as soon as the babies are born. It contains water, FAT, PROTEIN, SUGAR, VITAMINS, and MINERALS that the babies need for the first few days or months of their lives. The milk is different for each kind of mammal. Seal milk has a large amount of fat, so that baby seals can quickly build up a layer of fat or blubber under the skin to insulate them from the cold. Cows' milk is a valuable food for people, but not suitable for very young babies.

The milk we drink is heated for a short time to kill any dangerous bacteria. This is called PASTEURIZATION. It does not kill all the bacteria and after a few days the bacteria make the milk sour. People drink the milk of buffalo, goats, sheep, reindeer, cows, and other animals.

MILKY WAY FACTS
Diameter 100,000 light-years
Thickness at center 15,000 light-years
Speed of rotation once every 225 million years
Speed through space 1.4 million miles per hour
Age 15 billion years
Estimated mass about 1,000 billion Suns

Milky Way galaxy

We exist in space in the company of about 1,000 billion STARS and vast clouds of gas and dust called NEBULAE. This is our galaxy, and it measures about 100,000 light-years across. The SUN is about 30,000 light-years from the center, and the Milky Way effect seen crossing a dark starlit sky is caused by the faint light from millions of stars in the galaxy's spiral arms.

Our galaxy probably began soon after the UNIVERSE, about 15 billion years ago. To begin with it may have

been a cloud of hydrogen gas. At the center, where the gas was densest, stars began to form, these "first generation" stars have long ago died away. Some of these stars exploded as SUPERNOVAS, throwing out all the new elements such as carbon and iron.

The galaxy now has long spiral arms made up of these clouds of material and new stars. Our Sun and SOLAR SYSTEM were born in one of the arms. Every few hundred million years the Sun "orbits" the galaxy, moving from one arm to the next. There is enough material in the arms for many generations of stars.

Millikan, Robert *See* Electron

Minerals

Minerals are the compounds that make up the ROCKS of the Earth. Some minerals are composed of single ELEMENTS, such as gold, copper, and sulfur. Others are composed of two or more elements, such as quartz and MICA. Minerals are nonliving, they are inorganic. Coal, oil, and similar materials are composed of organic (once-living) matter and therefore are not minerals even though they are sometimes called minerals.

Scientists have named more than 2,000 minerals, but only about 30 are common in rocks. Minerals can be

1. Solar System
2. Ring nebula
3. Orion nebula
4. Lagoon nebula
5. Triffid nebula
6. Crab nebula
7. Eagle nebula
8. Eta carinae nebula
A. Centaurus arm
B. Sagittarius arm
C. Orion arm
D. Perseus arm

▲ *Four of the spiral arms of the Milky Way galaxy are named after major constellations.*

461

▼ *Minerals vary in color, hardness, and composition. They include single elements, such as copper, gold, silver, and sulfur, as well as simple and complex compounds. Some are mined for the metals they contain, such as hematite, which is an ore of iron. Malachite contains copper and is also used as an ornamental stone. Stibnite is a compound of sulfur and antimony which is found in quartz veins. Gypsum is also a sulfur compound but with calcium (calcium sulfate).*

identified by such features as color, HARDNESS, the amount of light that can pass through them, their DENSITY, and the CRYSTAL formation. The ELECTRON MICROSCOPE allows minerals to be studied in detail.

In the Earth's crust, 95 percent of the minerals are silicates, made up of different arrangements of atoms of SILICON and OXYGEN, held together by other atoms such as iron, magnesium, calcium, aluminum, and potassium. Glass, brick, and ceramics are mostly silicates, as are emeralds, aquamarine, topaz, agate, and jasper. Decorative minerals can be polished to make gemstones.

Salt (sodium chloride) is a mineral and it is compounds such as this that are essential for complete NUTRITION along with VITAMINS.

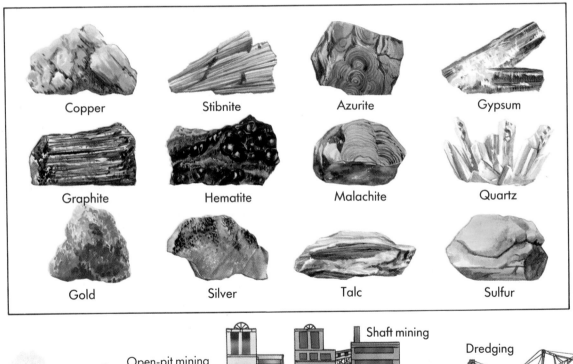

Copper   Stibnite   Azurite   Gypsum

Graphite   Hematite   Malachite   Quartz

Gold   Silver   Talc   Sulfur

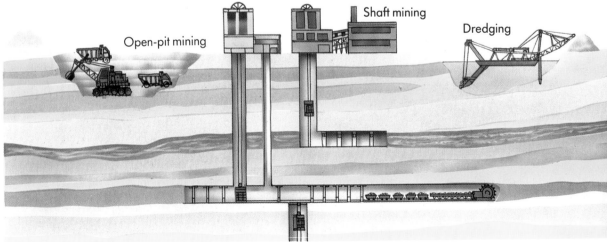

Open-pit mining   Shaft mining   Dredging

◄ *An aerial view of Kennecott's Bingham Canyon copper mine in Utah. This large open-pit mine produces much of Utah's copper.*

Mining is not a new industry. Ancient Egyptian records tell of an expedition to the Sinai peninsula around 2600 B.C. to mine for turquoise stones. While there, the Egyptians found a much more useful mineral: copper. The ancient Greeks mined silver at Laurion, south of Athens. Some of the shafts of these mines went to a depth of 400 feet.

Mining

Mining is the extraction of MATERIALS from the EARTH. Materials near the surface can be dug out by blasting with EXPLOSIVES or by dragging buckets across the ground to scrape away the soil and rock in an *open-pit mine*. If the material is cut out of the ground in long strips, the mine is called a *strip mine*. More commonly, mines are long shafts running deep underground following thin seams of valuable materials. Large deposits of ORES may be extracted through a network of horizontal tunnels spreading out from vertical shafts. The tunnels are extended by cutting with a large rotating drill head fitted with grinding wheels or by blasting with explosives. As material is taken out of the mine by underground conveyor belts, trains, and elevators, the tunnel roofs may need to be supported by wooden beams or HYDRAULIC pit props. Materials mined include coal, diamonds, and the ores of tin, iron, and aluminum.

▼ *There are many ways of mining, depending on the nature of the mineral deposit and its depth. Minerals that lie near the surface can be extracted by open-pit mining or by quarrying. Deposits on the bottom of a lake or river are removed by dredging. Drift mining and shaft mining are used to reach deeper deposits. Natural gas and oil are extracted by drilling, although some oil has to be pumped up to the surface.*

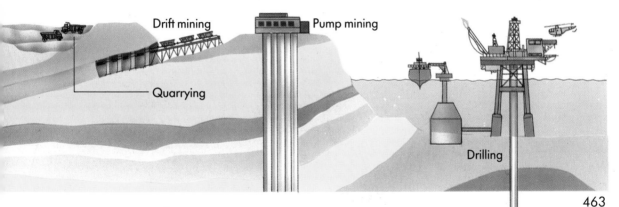

Drift mining
Pump mining
Quarrying
Drilling

▶ *A mirage is formed when rays of light are refracted, or bent, by a layer of warm air near the ground. This is why mirages are common in deserts and hot countries.*

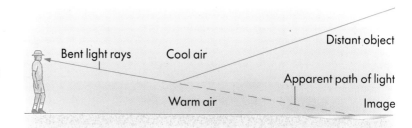

Bent light rays   Cool air   Distant object

Apparent path of light

Warm air   Image

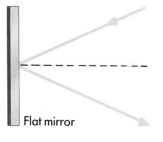

Flat mirror

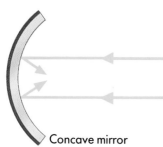

Concave mirror

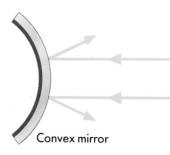

Convex mirror

▲ *A flat, or plane, mirror gives an undistorted image. A concave mirror, which is curved inward like a saucer, can produce a magnified image. A convex mirror, which is curved outward like the back of a spoon, gives a "wide-angle" image that is reduced in size.*

▶ *A mirror that is both concave and convex gives a distorted image that makes a person look very strange.*

Mirage

Mirages are seen when LIGHT traveling through AIR follows a curved, rather than a straight, line. This happens because the air near the ground is hotter than the air higher up and expands; light then travels through it more quickly. When the light from an object reaches the eye it is traveling upward and so appears to have come from beneath the ground. Light from the sky is also bent upward, so there seems to be a bright patch on the ground; it looks as though the sky and the object have been reflected by a pool of water. Similar effects occur at sea, when the air is colder at sea level and warmer higher up so the light is bent downward.

Mirror

A mirror is an object that reflects LIGHT. It is normally made from some sort of material with a smooth surface; ordinary mirrors are made from glass with a thin layer of silver on the back. A ray of light striking a flat mirror behaves like a ball striking a wall; it bounces back at the

same angle (called the *angle of reflection*) at which it made contact (the *angle of incidence*).

The surface of a *concave* mirror is curved inward, like the bowl of a spoon. Rays of light striking a concave mirror are reflected back to a point called the FOCUS. They then spread out and form an enlarged image of the object. *Convex* mirrors, curved outward, give a reduced image. Driving mirrors are like this. Concave mirrors are used instead of lenses to make reflecting telescopes because they produce clearer images.

Missiles

A missile is a weapon guided through the air to a target where it explodes. It is propelled through the sky by a ROCKET motor or JET ENGINE. Some missiles are directed to their targets automatically along a preprogrammed course. Others seek out a target and then lock onto it, and some are guided by the person who fires them.

In an automatically guided missile, an on-board INERTIAL GUIDANCE system compares the missile's position with its preprogrammed course. If it is off course, the guidance system moves the missile's fins to steer it back on course. Alternatively, the missile may home in on its target by locking on to the INFRARED RADIATION from the target's engines or radio energy from a RADAR antenna.

The target may be marked so that the missile recognizes it, such as by aiming an infrared beam at it. An infrared sensor in the missile steers it to the target. The person firing the missile may steer it, sending signals by

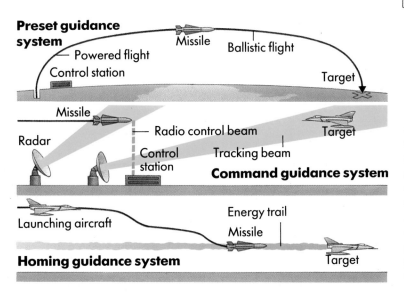

Preset guidance system
Missile
Powered flight
Ballistic flight
Control station
Target

Missile
Radar
Radio control beam
Target
Control station
Tracking beam
Command guidance system

Launching aircraft
Energy trail
Missile
Homing guidance system
Target

◀ *Guided missiles may be aimed in advance to fly to their target, using a preset guidance system. In a command guidance system, the missile obeys commands during flight which steer it to its target. Using a homing guidance system, a missile homes in on the target, perhaps by seeking the heat given out by the target's engines.*

465

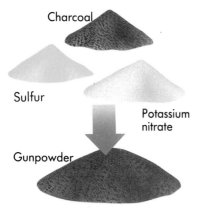

Charcoal

Sulfur

Potassium
nitrate

Gunpowder

▲ *Gunpowder is a mixture of chemicals, which can be separated. But when it burns, the chemicals combine to form new compounds.*

▼ *A mixture of iron filings and sulfur can be separated using a magnet. Heating them forms the compound iron sulfide, from which the iron cannot be removed by a magnet.*

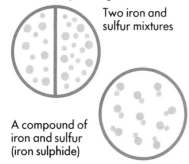

Two iron and
sulfur mixtures

A compound of
iron and sulfur
(iron sulphide)

radio to a receiver in the missile or along a trailing wire connecting the missile to the control unit.

The missile is becoming increasingly important in modern warfare because a single well-aimed unmanned missile can destroy a ship, aircraft, or tank.
See also BALLISTICS.

Mitosis *See* Cell division

Mixtures

A mixture consists of two or more substances which are not bound together chemically and so can be separated. A mixture is different from a COMPOUND, in which the substances are joined by chemical BONDS. In a mixture, the particles of each substance are distributed more or less evenly among the particles of the other substances. Powdered forms of solids put together can form mixtures. If iron filings are mixed with sand, for example, they can be separated again using a magnet.

Aerosols, COLLOIDS, EMULSIONS, foams, and SOLUTIONS are all types of mixtures in which particles of one substance are scattered throughout another. The particles may be solid specks, liquid droplets, or gas bubbles. The basic substances are usually liquids or gases. If the ingredients of such a mixture are evenly scattered among each other's particles, the substances are said to be *miscible*. If the particles of one stay completely separate from the particles of the other, the substances are *immiscible*. Alcohol and water are miscible. Oil and water

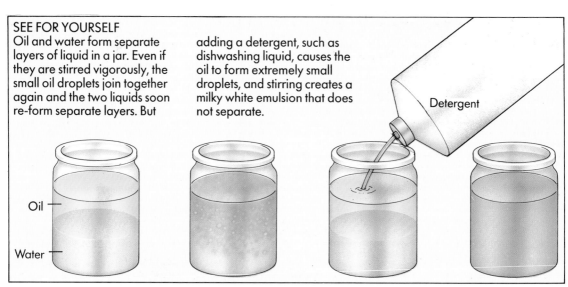

SEE FOR YOURSELF
Oil and water form separate layers of liquid in a jar. Even if they are stirred vigorously, the small oil droplets join together again and the two liquids soon re-form separate layers. But

adding a detergent, such as dishwashing liquid, causes the oil to form extremely small droplets, and stirring creates a milky white emulsion that does not separate.

Detergent

Oil

Water

are immiscible. In fact, oil floats on top of water. In most mixtures, the contents will eventually separate out naturally. The ingredients of mixtures can be separated by FILTRATION, precipitation, and other methods.

Modem

A modem connects a COMPUTER to other computers by TELEPHONE. The word comes from MOdulator–DEModulator. Computer data is a DIGITAL signal. Before it can be sent across a telephone line, it must be changed into an ANALOG form that a telephone can handle. Two notes, are used to represent a pulse and the absence of a pulse. This is called *modulation*. The notes are received by a modem at the other end and demodulated, or changed back into digital computer data.

Molecule

A molecule is the smallest particle of an ELEMENT or COMPOUND that can exist on its own. Molecules consist of from two to thousands of atoms held together by chemical BONDS. A molecule of the liquid water is made up of two atoms of the gas HYDROGEN and one of the gas OXYGEN. But molecules can be more complicated than that. The bonds holding a molecule together determine its shape. For example, a molecule of ammonia, made up of one nitrogen atom and three hydrogen atoms, is pyramid-shaped. All gases and organic compounds, most liquids, and many solids consist of molecules, but METALS and many compounds that form SOLUTIONS consist of IONS (atoms or groups of atoms with a positive or negative charge). Large molecules can be seen with an ELECTRON MICROSCOPE.

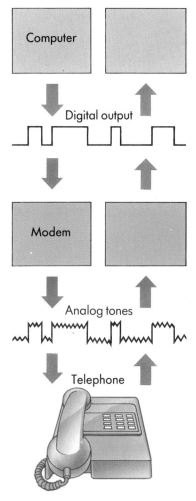

▲ A modem converts digital computer signals into analog ones for transmission over a telephone line. At the receiver it converts analog signals back to digital.

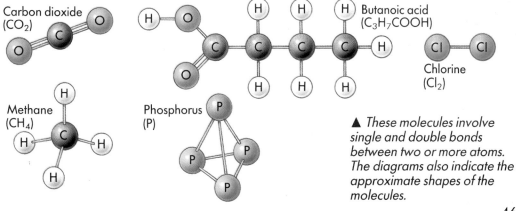

▲ These molecules involve single and double bonds between two or more atoms. The diagrams also indicate the approximate shapes of the molecules.

▶ *When the left-hand sphere collides with the one on its right, it passes on its momentum. This travels along the row of spheres to the one on the extreme right, which is forced to swing out.*

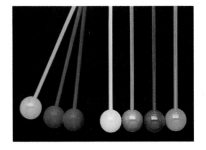
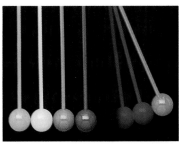

To find the **momentum** of a moving object we multiply its mass (its weight on Earth) by its velocity (its speed and direction). A car that weighs 2,000 pounds, driven south at a speed of 20 feet per second (about 14 mph) has a momentum of 2,000 x 20 = 40,000 pound feet per second toward the south.

Momentum

Momentum was the name given by NEWTON to an object's MASS multiplied by the VELOCITY with which it is moving. If someone taps you on the shoulder with a piece of wood, you hardly feel it. But if the person swings the wood and hits you with it, the blow really hurts. The wood is not heavier, but its momentum has increased because it is moving much faster.

Because the FORCE one object exerts on another is matched by an equal and opposite force from the second object on the first, the rates at which the momenta of the two objects are changing are equal and opposite. The total momentum of the two objects does not change but is *conserved*. You can see CONSERVATION of momentum when one pool ball strikes another so that the first ball stops dead. All its momentum has been transferred to the second ball; if the balls have the same mass, the second ball will move off with the same speed and direction as the first.

Monoclonal antibody

Antibodies are substances produced by the body in response to an antigen, which is usually the product of a harmful DISEASE. Antibodies destroy the antigen and so lessen the effect of the disease. Monoclonal antibodies

Production of monoclonal antibodies

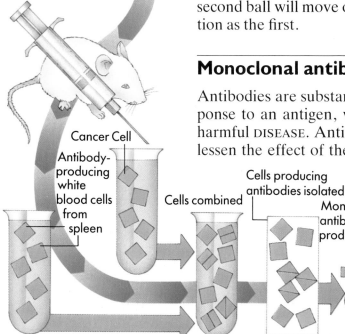

Antigen

Antigen injected into animal cancer cell

Cancer Cell

Antibody-producing white blood cells from spleen

Cells combined

Cells producing antibodies isolated

Monoclonal antibody produced

◀ *Monoclonal antibodies are produced using hybrids of white blood cells and types of cancer cells. These are cloned so that they produce pure strains of single antibodies.*

are ANTIBODIES that are produced artificially, usually by culturing, and so can be produced in large quantities and used in the treatment of many diseases. Formerly, antibodies could be given to people who were at risk of disease only by extracting them from the BLOOD of a person who had recovered from that disease. Sometimes this *serum* could be made by using the blood from animals that had been infected.

Monsoon

A monsoon describes any relatively constant WIND that tends to reverse its direction with the changing seasons. In the area around the Indian Ocean and southern Asia, as well as around the coasts of West Africa and northern Australia, the monsoon wind blows from the northeast in the winter and from the southwest in the summer. During the summer in India the wind brings with it the heavy rains which are known as the monsoon rains or "the rainy season." The changing direction of the wind is brought about by regional changes in air PRESSURE which take place with the seasons.

Although the idea of a rainy season may not seem pleasant, the summer monsoon is vital to the farmers of the area because most of the annual rainfall occurs at this time and, without it, crops could not be grown.

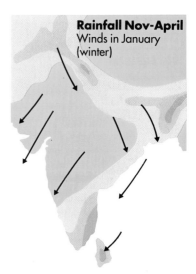

Rainfall Nov-April
Winds in January (winter)

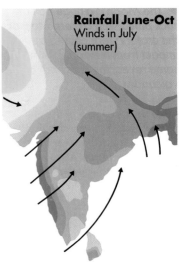

Rainfall June-Oct
Winds in July (summer)

Inches of rain

Over 70
40–70
20–40
10–20
5–10
1–5
Below 1

▲ *Monsoons are strong winds that blow in opposite directions at different times of the year. In Asia the summer monsoon, blowing off the Indian Ocean, brings a season of heavy rainfall (left). The rain falls so quickly that the ground is soon waterlogged.*

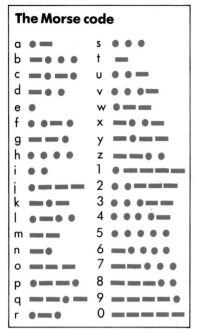

The Morse code

a	•—	s	•••
b	—•••	t	—
c	—•—•	u	••—
d	—••	v	•••—
e	•	w	•——
f	••—•	x	—••—
g	——•	y	—•——
h	••••	z	——••
i	••	1	•————
j	•———	2	••———
k	—•—	3	•••——
l	•—••	4	••••—
m	——	5	•••••
n	—•	6	—••••
o	———	7	——•••
p	•——•	8	———••
q	——•—	9	————•
r	•—•	0	—————

▲ The Morse code uses dots and dashes to stand for the letters and numbers.

▶ In a simple direct current electric motor, current from a battery flows through a coil of wire. The coil is pivoted in the magnetic field between the poles of a magnet, which make the wire move so that the coil rotates. Brushes keep the current flowing in the same direction.

caused a pencil to mark a moving strip of paper. The current was repeatedly turned on and off by a tapping key and information was sent in the form of on-off pulses. *See also* COMMUNICATIONS; DIGITAL.

Morton, William *See* Pain

Motion *See* Movement and Motion

Motor, electric

An electric motor is a MACHINE that converts electrical ENERGY into movement. It relies on the fact that a wire carrying an electric current moves in a magnetic field. There are electric motors in refrigerators, hair dryers, food processors, clocks, and many other objects.

In most motors the magnet stands still, while the coil of wire carrying the current moves inside it. When a current flows through the coil, the coil becomes a magnet, with a north and a south pole. Since unlike poles attract and like poles repel, the coil swings around between the

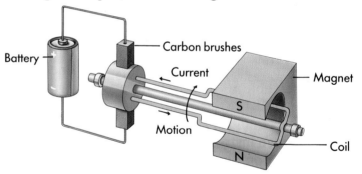

poles of the fixed magnet until its north pole is facing the south pole of the magnet and its south pole is facing the magnet's north pole. The direction of the current in the coil is therefore reversed so that the coil's poles are reversed. The coil swings around again half a turn to line up its poles once more. As the current keeps being reversed, the coil keeps turning. If the current supply to the coil is direct (D.C.), a commutator is needed to keep reversing the current.
See also GENERATOR; INDUCTANCE.

Mountains

A mountain is an area of high ground which usually rises steeply to a summit. Most mountains are formed by a

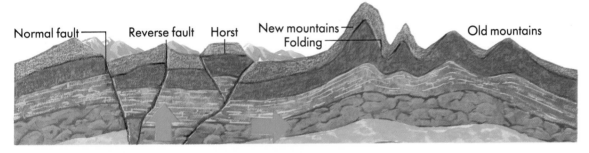

Normal fault — Reverse fault — Horst — New mountains — Folding — Old mountains

▲ Mountains are formed by faults and folding of the Earth's crust. New mountains are tall and jagged. Old mountains are more rounded because they have been worn down by weathering and erosion.

◄ The Andes form a chain of mountains that run down the western side of South America. Many of them are volcanoes.

process known as "mountain building" caused by the mechanisms of PLATE TECTONICS. The interior of the EARTH is constantly on the move, affecting the thin, solid crust on which we all live. Large amounts of sediment are deposited in a subsiding area of the sea. Later the processes of folding and faulting, associated with earthquake and volcanic activity at a plate margin, cause the sediments to be thrust upward as rugged mountains. Mountains' origins can be shown because the fossil remains of sea creatures have been found in the rocks hundreds of feet above sea level.

Consider three mountain ranges: the Caledonian mountains of Scotland; the Appalachians; and the Rockies. The mountains of Scotland are old and have undergone 500 million years of EROSION, while the Appalachians and Rockies are progressively younger and have had less time to be worn away and so are much higher. The Rockies are only 75 million years old.

1
2
3 Tree line
4
5

1 Snow cap
2 Alpine plants
3 Pasture
4 Coniferous trees
5 Deciduous trees

Movement and Motion

Motion occurs when something changes its position. Even plants move, though their ROOTS remain in the same place. Almost all animals can move, some farther than others. Humans can not only move but have invented objects that can move. *See* pages 474 and 475.

▲ The kinds of plants that grow on a mountain vary with the altitude. Below the tree line, the chief plants are trees. Above that line, the only plants are small ones that have adapted to growing in the low temperatures.

473

MOVEMENT AND MOTION

Everything in the universe is in motion. The Earth moves around the Sun and the Solar System is moving in relation to the galaxy. The rate of motion is called the speed and it is measured by calculating the distance moved in a certain time. Objects that are accelerating are increasing their speed. The velocity of an object describes its speed and its direction. A vehicle, or an animal, moving around a corner at a constant speed has a changing velocity. Machines can be made to move by a variety of means. They are supplied with energy which is converted into movement.

It is important for animals to be able to move around, to find food and mates, and to escape from their enemies, although some aquatic creatures remain in one place and sift their food from the passing water. These creatures are usually protected by shells. Most animals run, crawl, swim, or fly with the aid of limbs. The limbs are moved by muscles, which are attached to the skeleton. When the muscles contract they move the skeleton, and with it part or all of the body. The cheetah's powerful leg muscles allow the animal to reach speeds of over 60 mph for short distances. Animals without any hard skeleton, such as earthworms, rely on hydraulic mechanisms to produce movement. Their muscles act on the fluids in their bodies and, because fluids cannot be compressed, the body changes shape and moves. For example, when the circular muscles running around an earthworm's body contract and squeeze the body the worm becomes long and thin. When the muscles running along the body contract it becomes shorter, but the fluid has to go somewhere and so the worm becomes fat. The earthworm moves by alternately stretching and contracting its body.

▲ Every moving object has kinetic energy, which depends on the object's mass and how fast it is moving. A moving object can transfer kinetic energy to a stationary one.

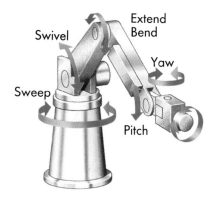

▲ Machines can carry out many different types of movements. The robot arm (top) can carry out combinations of movements that put the "hand" into any position that is required. The hydraulic shovel arm (bottom) can only move backward and forward.

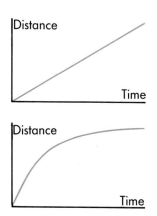

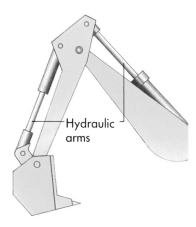

For a space rocket to escape from the Earth's gravity it has to reach the phenomenal speed of just over 7 miles per second (more than 25,000 mph).

▲ The speed of an object is the distance it travels in a certain time. On the graph a constant speed is a straight line. If the rate of change of distance with time changes, the object is accelerating.

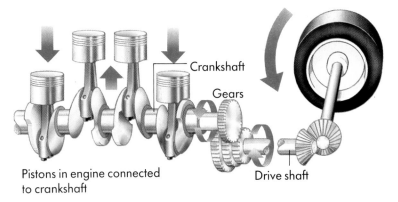

Crankshaft

Gears

Pistons in engine connected to crankshaft

Drive shaft

◄ Cranks and gears change the direction and speed of motion. In a car or other road vehicle, cranks convert the up-and-down motion of the pistons in the engine into the rotary motion of the drive shaft. A set of gears allows the shaft to turn at different speeds. A pair of bevel gears makes the drive shaft turn the axle and with it the vehicle's wheels.

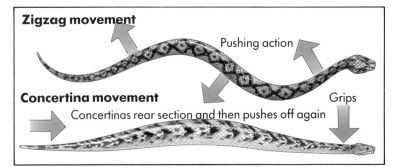

Zigzag movement

Pushing action

Concertina movement

Concertinas rear section and then pushes off again

Grips

◄ A snake moves by forming its body into a zigzag, gripping the ground with its underside and pushing itself forward.

▼ A fish swims by flexing its body and tail fins from side to side. It does this by alternately contracting muscles on each side of its body. As one set of muscles contract the muscles on the other side (sometimes known as the opposing muscles) are stretched to relax them and allow the body to retain its shape.

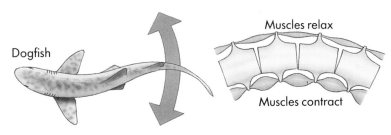

Dogfish

Muscles relax

Muscles contract

Muscles contract

Muscles relax

SEE FOR YOURSELF
Plants can move too. They move when they grow toward the light; also their stems grow upward and their roots grow down. You can see this by taking a potted plant and putting it on its side. Its horizontal stem will bend and gradually turn upward.

▲ A frog leaps powerfully out of the water to make a meal of an unsuspecting insect. Many predators rely on speed to catch their prey.

See also ACCELERATION; ENERGY; ENGINE; GEARS; HYDRAULICS; MASS; MECHANICS; MUSCLES; ORBIT; SKELETON; UNIVERSE; VELOCITY.

Muscle

All animal movements are controlled by muscles, which work by pulling against the SKELETON. Muscles are made of bundles of fibers, which shorten when they receive a signal from the NERVES. The power of a muscle depends on the number of fibers. These increase with exercise, which is why body builders develop big muscles.

There are three types of muscles. In humans, voluntary muscles produce most movements. As they shorten, they pull against the bone to which they are fastened, causing it to move. These muscles are usually found in

▶ Muscles consist of bundles of small fibers. Each fiber is in turn made up of many myofibrils, which lengthen or shorten as their filaments slide past each other. This movement makes the whole muscle contract. Tendons connect muscles to bones, and contraction of the muscles makes the bones move.

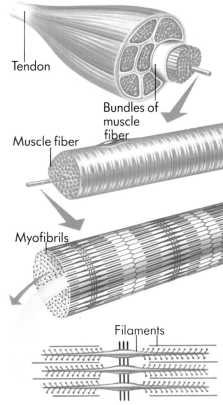

Tendon

Bundles of muscle fiber

Muscle fiber

Myofibrils

Filaments

◀ Movement of a limb, such as the forearm, requires the combined action of a pair of muscles. When the biceps muscle in the upper arm contracts, the arm bends at the elbow. To straighten the arm again, the triceps muscle at the back of the arm contracts causing the biceps to relax.

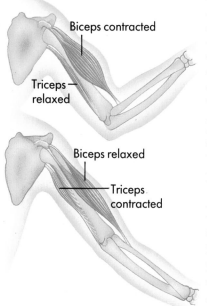

Biceps contracted

Triceps relaxed

Biceps relaxed

Triceps contracted

pairs, which can pull in opposite directions. They are said to be antagonistic. A few muscles are attached to the skin, and on the head and face these are responsible for facial expressions.

Smooth or involuntary muscles work automatically to keep the body systems operating properly; the intestines are a good example. The third type of muscle is cardiac muscle, which causes the heart to pump. This type of muscle works throughout life. It continues to pump even when it is disconnected from the nervous system, as happens in transplanted hearts.

Music

Music is a collection of sounds made up of combinations of SOUND waves. Musical sounds are called *tones* and all tones are made by something vibrating. For example, in a violin a bow is drawn across a tightly stretched string. The string vibrates, causing the violin's wooden body and the air inside it to vibrate. The air around the violin also vibrates and we hear a musical tone.

Tones have a definite *pitch* depending on how many vibrations take place each second. Slow vibrations create low tones; fast vibrations, high tones. The same tone sounds different on different INSTRUMENTS. The tone quality of a piano is different from that of a guitar. The main FREQUENCY of vibration, the fundamental frequency, is the same for each instrument, but other vibrations are produced at the same time. These other vibrations are called HARMONICS, and they differ from one musical instrument to another. They give a *timbre* to the sound produced by a particular instrument. In a stringed instrument, the fundamental frequency is produced when the whole string vibrates. But each half of the string also vibrates at the same time at a different frequency, giving a higher, weaker sound called the second harmonic. At the same time each third of the string vibrates, producing an even higher and weaker sound, and so on. The total of these and other harmonics gives the recognizable sound of a violin.

The kind of music we like depends a great deal on the music we heard in early life. Even today, Western people cannot easily appreciate the music of Eastern people, and they, in turn, find Western music strange. In Indian scales there is very little difference between one note and another — less than a quarter-tone — a difference that the Western ear finds difficult to separate. A scale in Western music has 12 steps to an octave; the Indian scale has 22 steps.

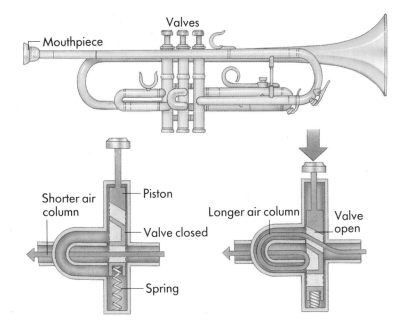

Mouthpiece

Valves

Shorter air column — Piston

— Valve closed

Longer air column

Valve open

— Spring

◄ *Valves on a trumpet change the length of the column of air in the instrument and alter the pitch of notes played on it — the longer the air column inside the trumpet, the lower the note. The valves act like taps to switch in extra loops of tubing.*

Mutation

A mutation is a sudden change in the structure of a gene or in the arrangement of genes on a CHROMOSOME. It may result in a change in the appearance or behavior of the plant or animal concerned. Such a change can occur in any CELL in the body, but the most important changes are those that take place in the reproductive cells, because the new characteristics then pass to the next generation. Most mutations are harmful and plants or animals with them usually die at an early stage, but some are useful and are handed down from generation to generation. This is one way in which EVOLUTION can occur. Mutations are quite rare in nature, but they can be encouraged by exposing plants and animals to radiation or to certain chemicals. Plants and animals showing the effects of mutations are called *mutants*.

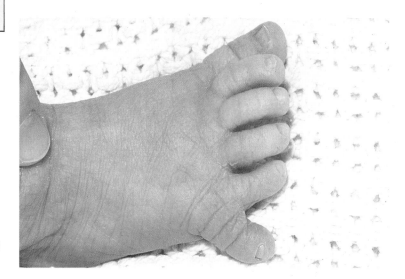

▶ A fairly common mutation causes a baby to be born with an extra toe or finger. It can easily be removed by a surgical operation.

▶ Mutations occur when the order of genes on a chromosome changes. In inversion mutation the gene sequence CD becomes detached, turned around, and restored as the new sequence DC. In deletion mutation a piece of the chromosome is lost, or deleted. From the sequence PQRSTU the RS has been lost leaving only PQTU.

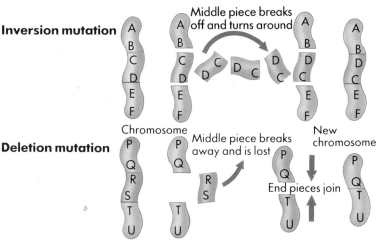

478

Natural fibers *See* Fibers, natural

Natural gas

Gas is an important source of ENERGY used for heating and cooking at home and to provide the power for many industrial processes. Natural gas is one of two types of FUEL gas, the other being manufactured or coal gas. Natural gas was formed millions of years ago by the same processes that produced other PETROLEUM products such as OIL. Geologists drilling for oil often find gas as well. Natural gas consists mainly of METHANE, the lightest HYDROCARBON, mixed with small amounts of other gase-

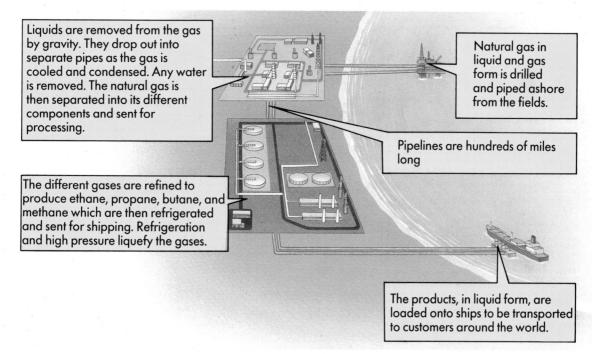

Liquids are removed from the gas by gravity. They drop out into separate pipes as the gas is cooled and condensed. Any water is removed. The natural gas is then separated into its different components and sent for processing.

Natural gas in liquid and gas form is drilled and piped ashore from the fields.

Pipelines are hundreds of miles long

The different gases are refined to produce ethane, propane, butane, and methane which are then refrigerated and sent for shipping. Refrigeration and high pressure liquefy the gases.

The products, in liquid form, are loaded onto ships to be transported to customers around the world.

ous hydrocarbons such as ethane, PROPANE, and butane. Russia, the United States, and Canada produce most of the world's natural gas. Gas provides about 25 percent of the fuel energy used in the United States.

▲ *Natural gas is sometimes drilled for and piped onshore from off-shore fields. Then it is separated into its components and refined.*

Natural selection

Natural selection is the process by which weak or poorly suited animals or plants are eliminated from a population, leaving the strongest and fittest to breed and carry on the SPECIES. It is the main process by which EVOLUTION works and was first described by Charles DARWIN in his book *On the Origin of Species.*

▲ Natural selection favored the dark form of the peppered moth, which was once rare but became common in industrial areas. At one time nearly all peppered moths were light. Only a few were dark and these could easily be seen by birds against the tree trunk. During the 1800s smoke from factories began to blacken the tree trunks with soot. Then the light moths became easier to spot. The number of light moths in industrial areas declined and the dark moths flourished because of natural selection.

Imagine a population of insects whose main protection is CAMOUFLAGE. The colors of the insects will vary slightly and some will be better camouflaged than others. Birds and other enemies will find and eat those that are not so well camouflaged, but they will not find the insects most suited to their ENVIRONMENT. The well-camouflaged insects will produce more insects, which will probably inherit the good camouflage even though they will not be identical. Because natural selection favors the insects that are well camouflaged in each generation, the camouflage gradually gets better. But, birds have to eat, and natural selection works for them as well. Those that find the most food will survive best, so while the insects are evolving better camouflage the birds are evolving better eyesight to find them.

Nebula

A nebula marks the beginning or the end of a STAR's life. It is a cloud of gas and solid particles or "dust" finer than powder. Stars are born inside nebulae, and when they die they pour gas and dust back into space.

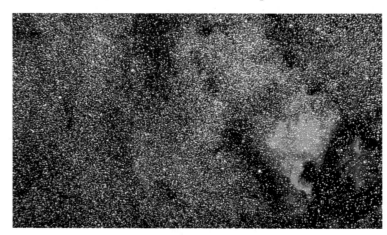

▶ The red region in this photograph of stars in our own Milky Way galaxy shows a nebula which is known as the North American Nebula because of its shape.

480

Our MILKY WAY GALAXY contains nebulae in its spiral arms. If you look at the Milky Way in a dark sky, it appears broken and ragged because of the dark nebulae blotting out the stars beyond.

Other nebulae shine brightly because nearby stars make them glow. The most famous, the Orion Nebula, is about 15 LIGHT-YEARS across and 1,300 light-years away. A cluster of stars is being formed inside it. Nebulae thrown out by dying stars are called *planetary nebulae*. One is forming around the SUPERNOVA whose explosion in the Large MAGELLANIC CLOUD was observed in 1987.

> If you look at the constellation Orion through a pair of binoculars you can see a nebula. You will notice a cloudy patch above the bottom star in Orion's sword — that is the Great Nebula in Orion.

◀ Neon and other noble gases are used inside the glass tubes of electric advertising signs. Neon tubes give a red or orange light.

▼ In a neon sign, a very high voltage turns neon gas at low pressure into ions that carry the electric current along the tube and give off a red-orange light.

Neon

Neon is an ELEMENT discovered in 1898 by the British chemists William Ramsay and Morris Travers. It is a GAS with no color, taste, or smell, and is one of the NOBLE GASES. Neon is obtained from AIR, but there is very little of it in air. Almost 45 tons of air must be processed to produce only a pound of neon. Neon normally exists as a gas but it will change to a liquid and a solid at very low temperatures. It turns to liquid at –410°F (–246°C) and it freezes at –415°F (–248.5°C). Neon is very stable. It does not form COMPOUNDS with other materials. No compounds such as neon oxide or neon nitrate have ever been found. When an electric current is passed through a tube of neon, the gas glows with a red-orange light. This effect is used to make colorful signs. Other colors are produced by using tubes containing different gases.

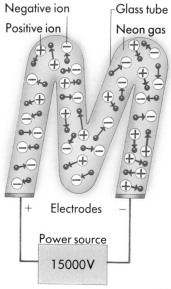

Negative ion — Glass tube
Positive ion — Neon gas

+ Electrodes —

Power source

15000V

NEPTUNE FACTS
Diameter at the equator
30,800 miles (49,560 km)
Diameter at the poles
30,262 miles (48,700 km)
Average distance from Sun
2,794,000,000 miles
(4,496,000,000 km)
Year length 164.8 years
Day length 18 hours
Mass 17 Earths
Density 0.03 of Earth
Surface temperature
−346°F (−210°C)

▶ *Neptune has a faint ring system and eight moons: six small ones and the larger Triton and Nereid.*

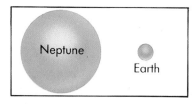

▲ *Neptune has a mass 17 times as large as the Earth and takes nearly 165 years to go once around the Sun.*

▼ *Triton is Neptune's largest moon, 2,300 miles in diameter and covered in icy mountains. It orbits the planet in the opposite direction to the other moons.*

Triton

Neptune

Neptune is usually the eighth of the nine SOLAR SYSTEM planets, PLUTO being the outermost. However, once every 248 years, for about 20 years, Pluto's ORBIT swings it closer than Neptune to the Sun. The two planets are now in such a period; Neptune will be the outermost planet until 1999. Neptune was discovered in 1846 from calculations made by both John Couch Adams in Britain and Urbain Leverrier in France. The planet URANUS was not keeping to its expected orbit, and they calculated that the GRAVITY of a new planet was pulling Uranus from its path.

Neptune is four times the diameter of the Earth, but it is so far away that it appears tiny even through the

John Couch Adams (1819–1892)
Adams was a British astronomer who in 1844, by studying the motion of Uranus, calculated the position of Neptune before it was discovered, as did the French scientist Urbain Leverrier in 1846. The planet was actually discovered in that year by German astronomers.

largest TELESCOPES. It is made up mainly of liquid and frozen gases. Much of our knowledge of Neptune comes from the SPACE PROBE Voyager II, which passed Neptune in August 1989. Its 9,000 photographs revealed the Great Dark Spot (a long-lived oval cloud feature which rotates and is as large as the Earth), a smaller dark cloud, and rapidly changing feathery white methane clouds scattered over a sky blue background. Winds blowing through this bitter atmosphere were measured at up to 1,240 mph (2,000 km/h).

Neptune was found to have two narrow rings and other fainter ones, as well as six new satellites.

Nerves

Nerves are made up of bundles of tiny nerve fibers or neurons. The nerves carry messages rapidly around the body. These messages are signals produced by sensory CELLS and passed to nerve fibers in the BRAIN or spinal column, or messages from the brain to the organs.

Hermann Ludwig Helmholtz (1821–1894) Helmholtz was a German scientist who worked in medicine and physics. He studied how the eye works, how the ear sorts out sounds of different pitch, and in 1850 he calculated how fast nerve impulses travel. In physics he was one of the first to propose the principle of conservation of energy.

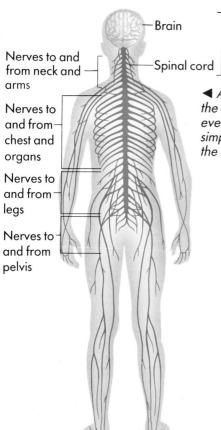

Brain

Spinal cord

Central nervous system

◄ *A network of nerves connects the brain and spinal cord to every part of the body. This simplified diagram shows only the main nerves.*

Nerves to and from neck and arms

Nerves to and from chest and organs

Nerves to and from legs

Nerves to and from pelvis

▼ *A typical nerve cell or neuron has a star-shaped cell body that is the nerve's control center. The axon is a tubelike extension that carries messages. It is covered by a sheath of fatty myelin. The dendrites are specialized to receive messages. Places where one neuron communicates with another are called synapses.*

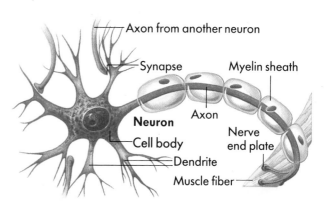

Axon from another neuron

Synapse

Myelin sheath

Neuron

Axon

Cell body

Nerve end plate

Dendrite

Muscle fiber

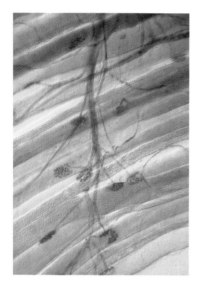

The network of nerves in the body controls the systems which keep us alive, such as BREATHING, a regular HEART beat, and the working of DIGESTION. These important functions operate automatically, whether or not we think about them. The system of nerves which maintains life is called the *autonomic nervous system*. Other nerves cause actions such as MUSCLES to react when we want to walk and write. These nerves are called the *voluntary nervous system*. Some nerves coordinate movement, and also protect us from injury. They operate by means of REFLEXES. This means that when we touch something hot with a finger, the receptors flash a message along a series of nerves and cause the muscles to snatch the finger away, without waiting for instructions from the brain.

▲ *A motor neuron is a nerve cell that carries messages to muscles.*

Neutrino *See* Subatomic particles

Neutron

The neutron is one of the kinds of particle which make up the nucleus of an ATOM. The neutron is very similar in mass to the PROTON, but carries no electric charge. This makes it harder to detect since it does not react to or produce electric forces. Atoms with different numbers of neutrons but the same number of protons in their nucleus are known as ISOTOPES. They behave in the same way chemically although their nuclei have different masses. The neutron was discovered in 1932 by James Chadwick. Neutrons are important in NUCLEAR ENERGY, since they can be absorbed by the nuclei of some atoms causing the nuclei to split in two.

James Chadwick (1891–1974)
Chadwick was a British physicist who in 1932 discovered the neutron, the uncharged subatomic particle that is found in the nuclei of all atoms except hydrogen. He produced neutrons by using the radiation from radioactive isotopes to bombard other atoms. For this work he was awarded the 1935 Nobel Prize for Physics.

Enrico Fermi (1901–1954)
Fermi was an Italian-born physicist who after 1939 came to live and work in the United States. He is best known for using neutrons as particles to bombard atoms to produce new radioactive isotopes.
The key to his success was using a block of wax to slow down the neutrons and make them more effective. He was awarded the 1938 Nobel Prize for Physics.

Neutron star

A neutron star is the smallest and densest kind of STAR. An ATOM is mostly space; the ELECTRONS, and the solid PROTONS and NEUTRONS that form the center or nucleus of all atoms take up very little room. As long as a star keeps shining, the power of its radiation (which is like an exploding bomb) holds all the parts of the atoms apart. But when some stars die, the GRAVITY in the star makes the outer layers collapse inward with such force that the center is crushed to solid neutrons because the electrons and protons are forced violently together to make neutrons. On Earth, a marble-sized piece of a neutron star would weigh about 100,000 tons. Some neutron stars are seen as flashing stars or PULSARS.

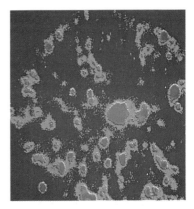

▲ Geninga is a neutron star only 10 to 20 miles across yet it weighs more than our Sun.

Newton, Isaac

Sir Isaac Newton (1643–1727) was born in Lincolnshire, England, and died in London. His father died before he was born and he had an unhappy childhood. He went to study in Cambridge in 1661 but had to return home in 1665 because of the plague. It seems to have been then that he discovered the laws of MECHANICS and the law of GRAVITY, as well as the beginnings of mathematical calculus. He was able to return to Cambridge in 1667 and in 1669 Newton took over as professor of mathematics. In 1686 he published a book, *The Mathematical Principles of Natural Philosophy*, in which he showed how his theories explained the orbits of the PLANETS and the MOON. He was also interested in ALCHEMY. Isaac Newton was one of the greatest scientists ever to have lived.

See also FORCE; GRAVITY; HISTORY OF SCIENCE; MECHANICS; PHYSICS.

▲ Sir Isaac Newton was a mathematician and physicist and much of modern science is based on his laws.

▼ A rocket is a type of reaction motor, demonstrating one of Newton's laws of motion: that action and reaction are equal and opposite.

SEE FOR YOURSELF
Newton's third law of motion states that action and reaction are equal and opposite. This is the principle of the rocket motor. You can demonstrate this by blowing up a balloon and letting it go. As the gas is forced out of the neck of the balloon (the action), the reaction makes it fly off in the opposite direction.

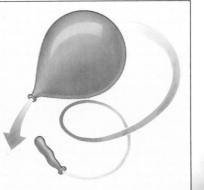

Nickel

Nickel is a hard, silver colored metal ELEMENT discovered in 1751 by a Swedish chemist, Axel Fredrik Cronstedt. It is found in the Earth's crust, most commonly in ORES called pentlandite and pyrrhotite in Canada and Australia. Although hard, nickel can be formed by hammering and molding without breaking. It is also very resistant to CORROSION from ACIDS and alkalis. It melts at 2,647°F (1,453°C) and boils at 4,950°F (2,732°C). Its name comes from the German word *Kupfernickel* which means "copper demon." It was given this name by miners who mistook its ore for a similar copper-bearing ore. In fact, nickel and COPPER are similar, particularly in their resistance to corrosion. Nickel is often combined with other metals to make ALLOYS including STAINLESS STEEL.

▲ *Nickel (Ni) is a silvery metal used for electroplating objects and for making alloys used in "silver" coins and stainless steel.*

▶ *The nicotine content of tobacco is measured by a machine that smokes 30 cigarettes at once.*

A cigarette smoker takes in many poisonous chemicals. Cigarette smoke contains hydrogen cyanide, nitrogen oxide, and carbon monoxide, all of which are poisonous. A cigarette smoker takes in between 1 and 2 milligrams of nicotine per cigarette. It takes only a thimbleful of nicotine to kill an adult.

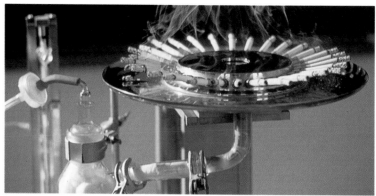

Nicotine

Nicotine is a powerful DRUG found in tobacco. When people smoke (or chew) tobacco, nicotine is absorbed into the BLOOD, reaching the BRAIN only seven seconds after inhaling tobacco smoke. Nicotine narrows the blood vessels, reducing the amount of blood reaching the HEART. It also increases the body's need for oxygen, so the heart speeds up and the blood pressure is raised. These effects, combined with other substances in tobacco smoke, can cause illness or shorten life. It is hard to stop smoking, because nicotine is addictive.

Niépce, Joseph Nicéphore *See* Photography

Night *See* Daylength

Nitrates

Nitrates are COMPOUNDS containing OXYGEN and NITRO-GEN combined with a metal. They are often made by reacting NITRIC ACID with a metal. Some bacteria that live in the SOIL can make nitrates by using nitrogen directly from the ATMOSPHERE.

Some nitrates are used as FERTILIZERS to provide plants with food for growth. Rain washes any extra nitrates that are not taken up by plants out of the soil into rivers where simple plants called algae, living in the water, feed on them and grow very quickly. They use up more and more oxygen in the water. The sudden shortage of oxygen can kill fish and other aquatic animals. Increasing nitrate levels in the WATER SUPPLIES in farming areas where large amounts of nitrates are used has become a problem in some places.

NO_3^-

▲ A nitrate (NO_3^-) is a salt of nitric acid, and should not be confused with a nitrite (NO_2^-), a salt of nitrous acid. Nitrates have more oxygen in them than nitrites.

◀ Nitrates are important fertilizers, either in natural compost and manure or in artificial fertilizers.

From the early 19th century, caves in the southern United States were important sources of potassium nitrate which was also known as saltpeter. This was especially important during the Civil War as saltpeter is an essential ingredient of gunpowder.

Nitric acid

Nitric acid is a fuming, colorless, and very corrosive LIQUID. A corrosive liquid can eat into materials by reacting with them. Nitric acid is a COMPOUND of hydrogen, NITROGEN, and oxygen. It is used to make FERTILIZERS and EXPLOSIVES such as NITROGLYCERINE. Nitric acid has been known since the 9th century. Until the beginning of the 20th century it was made by heating SULFURIC ACID and sodium nitrate, a natural material found in South America. When World War I began, lots of nitric acid was needed to make explosives. Germany was

HNO_3

▲ Nitric acid (HNO_3) is important in the manufacture of fertilizers and explosives.

487

Root Nodules

Some plants have small lumps, or nodules, on their roots which contain bacteria that are able to "fix" nitrogen from the air. They convert the nitrogen gas into nitrogen compounds that the plants can use as food. Nitrogen-fixing plants include clover and some peas and beans. Farmers cultivate such plants to increase the amount of nitrogen compounds in the soil.

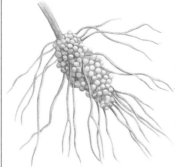

cut off from its supplies of sodium nitrate so Fritz Haber, a German chemist, developed a way of making nitric acid by heating AMMONIA and AIR. Hydrogen and nitrogen in the ammonia, and oxygen from the air combined to form nitric acid.

Nitrogen

Nitrogen is a colorless, gaseous ELEMENT with no taste or smell. More than three-fourths of the Earth's ATMOSPHERE is nitrogen. All living plants and animals need nitrogen but they cannot use it directly from the atmosphere. Plants obtain it from NITRATES made by bacteria in the soil or spread on the land by farmers and gardeners. Plants convert nitrates into PROTEINS that make new plant cells. Animals obtain nitrogen by eating plants, or by eating other animals that have eaten plants. When plants die, they rot and return their nitrogen to the soil. When animals die, their bodies decay and form nitrogen compounds. Animal waste also returns nitrogen to the soil in the form of nitrogen COMPOUNDS. These are changed to AMMONIA by bacteria. Other bacteria convert ammonia into nitrogen gas again.

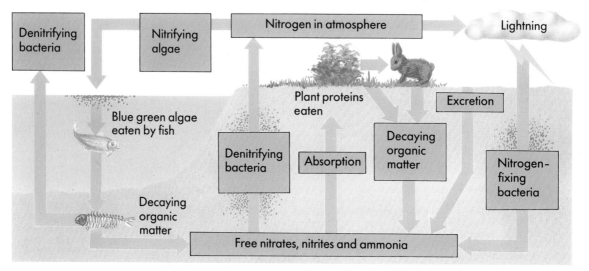

▲ *Nitrogen circulates between the air and living things. Nitrogen-fixing bacteria and lightning turn nitrogen in the air into a form living things can use. Denitrifying bacteria control the amount of nitrogen in circulation by changing some fixed nitrogen back into a gas.*

Nitroglycerin

Nitroglycerin is a very unstable liquid which explodes if it receives even a slight shock. It freezes at 55°F (13°C). Solid nitroglycerin is even more likely to explode when it is bumped! It begins to break down at about 130°F (55°C) and it explodes spontaneously at 424°F (218°C).

◄ *A man controls the temperature of an old process for making nitroglycerin by letting cold water through pipes in the reaction vessel. It was essential that the temperature wasn't allowed to get too high. He cannot doze while working because he would fall off his one-legged stool.*

Nitroglycerin is used as a medicine to treat the heart condition angina pectoris. People with angina get out of breath and have pain in the chest if they exert themselves. If they suck a nitroglycerin tablet before strenuous exercise, their heart beats more strongly and they do not have pain or get out of breath.

It is made from an ALCOHOL called GLYCEROL, a by-product of soap-making, and NITRIC ACID. Nitroglycerin was first made in 1846 by an Italian chemist Ascanio Soberro, and has been used as a powerful EXPLOSIVE itself, but is more commonly used to make other safer explosives such as dynamite, which was invented by Alfred NOBEL. It has also been used to make some rocket fuels.

Nobel, Alfred

Alfred Bernhard Nobel (1833–1896) was a Swedish chemist who invented some powerful EXPLOSIVES, including dynamite. Nobel's family moved to Russia in 1842. He worked in his father's factory until 1859. Then he returned to Sweden and began making an explosive called NITROGLYCERIN. His factory blew up, killing several people including his brother Emil. The Swedish

▲ *The Swedish chemist Alfred Nobel invented dynamite and other explosives.*

NOBEL PRIZEWINNERS 1987–1991		
Physics	**Chemistry**	**Physiology or Medicine**
1987 Bednorz, super-conductivity in ceramics	**1987** Lehn, Cram, and Pederson, work with artificial molecules	**1987** Tonegawa, genes and antibodies
1988 Lederman, Schwartz and Steinberger, work with neutrinos	**1988** Deisendorfer, Huber, and Michel, photosynthesis	**1988** Black, Elion, and Hitchings, drug treatment
1989 Ramsey, atomic clock; Dehmelt and Paul, atoms and subatomic particles	**1989** Altman and Cech, work on the genetic material RNA	**1989** Bishop and Varmus, cancer research
1990 Friedman, Kendall, and Taylor, quark model	**1990** Coray, theory and method of organic synthesis	**1990** Murray and Donnall-Thomas, organ rejection
1991 de Gennes, ordering of molecules in substances	**1991** Ernst, refinements in nuclear magnetic resonance spectroscopy	**1991** Neher and Sakmann, discoveries in basic cell function

▶ *The winners of the 1989 Nobel Prizes pose for the cameras with the Nobel Committee at the end of the prizegiving ceremony in Sweden.*

Nobel felt guilty at having made nitroglycerin, a substance that was used in war when he had invented it for peace. He decided to leave his fortune as a fund to give annual awards for outstanding work in physics; chemistry; physiology or medicine; literature, and, most important of all, peace. A sixth prize, for economics, was set up in 1969.

2 **He** **4.0**	Atomic number 2 Helium Atomic weight 4.0
10 **Ne** **20.2**	Atomic number 10 Neon Atomic weight 20.2
18 **Ar** **39.9**	Atomic number 18 Argon Atomic weight 39.9
36 **Kr** **83.8**	Atomic number 36 Krypton Atomic weight 83.8
54 **Xe** **131.3**	Atomic number 54 Xenon Atomic weight 131.3
86 **Rn** **222**	Atomic number 86 Radon Atomic weight 222

▲ *A part of the periodic table showing Group 0, the noble gases. Radon, the heaviest of the noble gases, is radioactive and can cause lung cancer if inhaled in large enough quantities.*

government refused to let him rebuild the factory so he continued his work on a barge. He discovered that nitroglycerin could be handled safely when it had soaked into a powdery rock. Nobel called this dynamite. He went on to develop more powerful explosives and became very wealthy. When he died he left most of his money to pay for a series of international awards that are still made every year. They are known as the Nobel Prizes.

Noble gases

The noble GASES are the ELEMENTS that form group 0 of the PERIODIC TABLE. The six noble gases are so inert, or stable, that they rarely react with other materials. In chemistry, "noble" means unreactive. None of them have any smell, color, or taste and they do not burn. The noble gases are, in order of lightest to heaviest: HELIUM, NEON, argon, krypton, xenon, and radon. Helium is the

William Ramsay (1852–1916)
Ramsay was a British chemist who in the 1890s discovered five of the noble gases. He extracted samples of most of the gases from air. He named them argon (from the Greek word for inactive), neon (new), xenon (stranger), and krypton (hidden). Helium (Sun) had been detected in the Sun's spectrum.

second most common element in the universe after HY-DROGEN and only hydrogen is lighter than helium. Because it is lighter than air, helium is used to fill BAL-LOONS. It is also used to replace NITROGEN in the gas breathed by deep-sea divers because of nitrogen's dangerous effects on the body when breathed at high pressures. Argon and neon give out brightly colored light when an electric current is passed through them and are used in artificial LIGHTING. Helium, neon, and argon are also used to produce the light beams of gas LASERS. The only compounds of noble gases found so far are fluorine combined with krypton, xenon, or radon.

Noise

Noise is a name given in science to background disturbance caused by signals that are random and unpredictable. The signals can be in the form of SOUND, which is what we refer to as noise in everyday life, or they can be electrical or of some other sort.

Often noise is a nuisance because it interferes with a MEASUREMENT that it is being made or with some signal that is being transmitted. For example, in a RADIO receiver there is electrical noise because ELECTRONS are moving around randomly and this noise competes with the received signal. The amount of signal, divided by the amount of noise that is also present, is often called the "signal-to-noise ratio." Techniques such as electronic FILTERING are often used to improve the signal-to-noise ratio. This is useful if the signal that is being looked for is at a particular FREQUENCY; the filter allows that frequency to pass through, but not the other frequencies which are present in the noise. The study of noise is important, because by understanding the processes that cause it we can try to reduce it.

SEE FOR YOURSELF
Noise will travel along a tube. Push the stems of two funnels into each end of a length of hose, and get a friend to put one funnel near a source of noise — such as a carbonated drink. Put the other funnel to your ear and you will hear the noise.

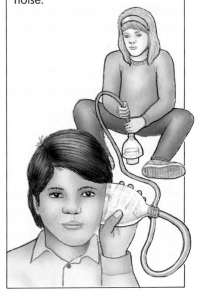

All electrical circuits possess some level of noise. Radiation and atmospheric disturbances interfere with the reception of radio and TV signals. Lightning, sunspots, electric motors, car ignition systems, all contribute to electrical noise. One way of judging the efficiency of electronic communications systems is to rate their signal-to-noise ratio.

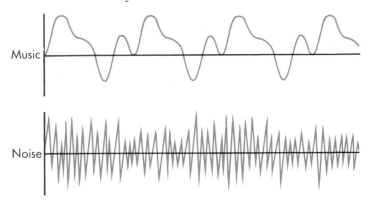

Music

Noise

◄ A pleasant sound, such as music, is generated by regular, gently curving waves (top). Noise consists of irregular, spiky waves (bottom).

The nose in addition to its other tasks, has an effect on the tone of the voice. This is one of the reasons why the voice becomes deeper when someone has a cold. Try saying a vowel sound and then holding your nostrils closed. You should notice the difference in tone.

► Receptors consisting of nerve fibers in the top of the nasal cavity, connected by nerves to the brain, give us our sense of smell. The same receptors are also important for the sense of taste.

▼ Nova Persei exploded in 1901. This photograph shows the gas cloud that is left.

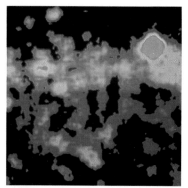

Non-biodegradable *See* Pollution

Nose

The nose and the SENSE organs in it produce our sense of smell, but they have other important functions too. The nasal cavity is a space behind the nose, connecting with the back of the mouth. When we breathe in through the nostrils, the air swirls around in the nasal cavity and is warmed so it is at body TEMPERATURE when it reaches the LUNGS. Hairs in the nostrils filter out any large objects we might breathe in, while smaller debris is trapped on damp sticky membranes lining the nasal cavity. The film of moisture, complete with its trapped material, is steadily pushed to the back of the throat by tiny beating hairs, where it is swallowed to make it harmless. If you have breathed dusty air, you will have seen the amount of trapped dirt when you blow your nose. The membrane in the top of the nasal cavity contains groups of sensory CELLS. There are up to 10 million of these cells, and they react with substances in the air. These cells can sense different types of smell. They pass messages to the brain which can then identify the individual cell and so the substance it has reacted with.

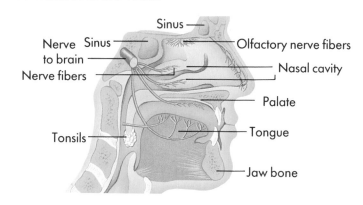

Nova

Nova is Latin for "new," and several "new" STARS appear every year in the sky. Some may be visible with the naked eye. They are faint stars that have increased their brightness perhaps 10,000 times, almost overnight.

All the novas that have been investigated are BINARY STARS, or twins. Each smaller one is much hotter than the SUN, while its companion is a RED GIANT, a huge globe of red-hot mist. If cool gas from the giant reaches the hot star, an explosion can result, with the outer layers of the hot star flying off into space. The last bright nova was discovered by naked-eye observers in the constellation of Cygnus, in 1975.

Nuclear energy

Nuclear energy is the name given to energy that is produced from changes in nuclei, the small, heavy centers of ATOMS. There are two ways of producing nuclear energy. The first method is nuclear *fission*; a heavy nucleus of a radioactive element such as URANIUM or PLUTONIUM splits in two. As it splits, it releases NEUTRONS which strike other nuclei and cause them to divide as well. This is known as a chain reaction. The neutrons are slowed down by their collisions with a substance called a moderator; this makes the neutrons more effective at producing fission in other nuclei and also heats up the moderator. This HEAT is used to heat water to form steam, which drives TURBINES to generate ELECTRICITY. The second type of nuclear energy is nuclear *fusion*, in which light nuclei are joined together. However, this has not yet proved to be an efficient source of energy.

The advantages of nuclear energy are that it produces a large amount of useful energy from a very small amount of fuel and does not produce gases contributing to the GREENHOUSE EFFECT. The disadvantages are that the NUCLEAR WASTE that is produced is very difficult to store safely. It is very difficult and expensive to make an old nuclear reactor safe and there is always a small chance of a serious accident if something goes wrong.

Lise Meitner (1878–1968)
Meitner was an Austrian-born chemist who in 1939 went to live and work in Sweden. She retired to Britain in 1960. In the late 1930s she did experiments to prove that heavy atoms can be split into lighter ones with the release of energy. She invented the term nuclear fission to describe the process.

About 1.8 billion tons of coal would have to be consumed annually by coal-powered plants to take care of the world's electricity demands. Just 135 tons of deuterium, one of the hydrogenlike fuels used in nuclear fusion, would give the same amount of energy. Each cubic yard of seawater contains an ounce of deuterium, so large supplies are available.

A chain reaction

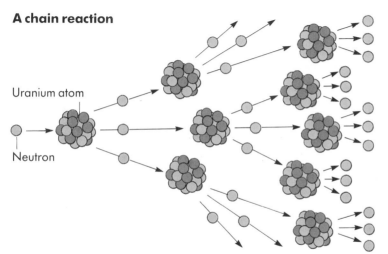

Uranium atom

Neutron

◀ *Nuclear fission releases large amounts of energy when a uranium atom is split by a neutron. Each uranium atom that splits releases three more neutrons, which go on to split more uranium and so on in a chain reaction.*

NUCLEAR PHYSICS

Nuclear physics is the study of what goes on inside the nucleus that lies at the center of an atom. A nucleus is roughly forty thousand million millionth of an inch across. Because the nucleus is much too small to see, physicists get information about it and the particles inside it by smashing nuclei and studying what happens.

A nucleus is made up of protons and neutrons, which are very similar to each other except that the proton carries a positive electric charge while the neutron carries no charge. Although the positive charges on the protons try to push each other apart, the protons and neutrons are held together by a very strong force. If the Earth were squeezed until it was as dense as an atomic nucleus, its diameter would be about a third of a mile (0.5 km).

Physicists believe that the proton and the neutron are themselves made up of other things called quarks. The quarks are also held together by the strong force, so tightly that they believe it is not possible to see a quark by itself.

Nuclei can change and decay into other nuclei. Nuclei decay by giving off subatomic particles or radiation. Medium-sized nuclei are more stable than very light or very heavy nuclei. This means that a lot of energy can be released if a very heavy nucleus splits into two (this is called *fission*) or if two light nuclei join together (this is called *fusion*).

Otto Hahn (1879–1968)
Hahn was a German chemist who worked with Lise Meitner and her nephew Fritz Strassman on experiments to split the atom. In 1917 Hahn and Meitner discovered the heavy radioactive element protactinium. But it was their experiments on nuclear fission in the 1930s that were so important to nuclear physics. Hahn was awarded the 1944 Nobel Prize for Chemistry for splitting the atom.

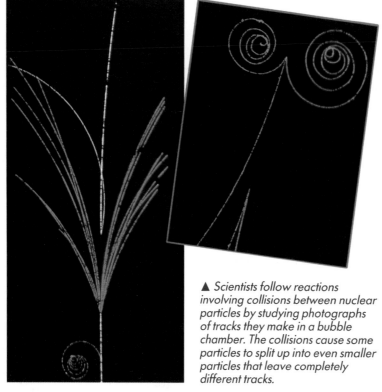

▲ *Scientists follow reactions involving collisions between nuclear particles by studying photographs of tracks they make in a bubble chamber. The collisions cause some particles to split up into even smaller particles that leave completely different tracks.*

▼ *The two principal ways of producing nuclear energy are fission (top), in which heavy atoms are split, and fusion (bottom) in which light atoms such as hydrogen combine to form heavier ones.*

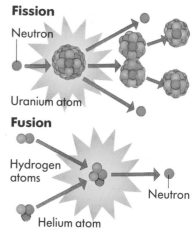

Fission

Neutron

Uranium atom

Fusion

Hydrogen atoms

Neutron

Helium atom

See also ATOM; ENERGY; HELIUM; HYDROGEN; METRIC SYSTEM; NEUTRON; PHYSICS; PROTON; RADIOACTIVITY; SUBATOMIC PARTICLES.

Nuclear reactor

A nuclear reactor is a power plant used to produce ENERGY from nuclear reactions. There are three types of reactor: thermal, fast-breeder, and fusion (or thermonuclear). In a thermal reactor, URANIUM atoms split, sending out NEUTRONS. A moderator such as graphite surrounds the fuel rods and slows the neutrons down so that they have more chance of hitting other uranium atoms and releasing more neutrons and HEAT energy.

In a fast-breeder reactor, the core of fuel is surrounded by low-grade natural uranium. Some neutrons escaping from the core strike the uranium, changing some of it into another ISOTOPE of uranium called U-239. This isotope changes into PLUTONIUM which can be used as a reactor fuel. The reactor "breeds" more plutonium than it needs as fuel, hence the name. Fusion reactors are not yet in commercial production. Instead of splitting heavy atoms, they force very light atoms together. In all reactors, the heat produced is used to change water into steam to drive generators that make ELECTRICITY.

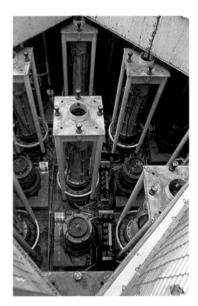

▲ Encased control rods stick up above the ends of fuel rods in the reactor at a nuclear power station.

◄ The core, the heart of a thermal nuclear reactor, is enclosed in a pressure vessel. Heat from the fission of uranium fuel converts water into steam for driving turbine generators, to produce electricity.

▼ A reactor's fuel rods are surrounded by a moderator such as graphite, which slows down neutrons produced so that they can split other uranium atoms. This chain reaction is controlled by rods that mop up the excess neutrons.

Thermal nuclear reactor

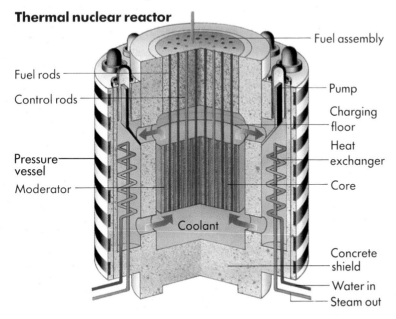

Fuel assembly
Fuel rods
Control rods
Pump
Charging floor
Heat exchanger
Pressure vessel
Moderator
Core
Coolant
Concrete shield
Water in
Steam out

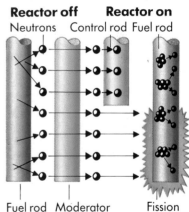

Reactor off   **Reactor on**

Neutrons   Control rod   Fuel rod

Fuel rod   Moderator   Fission

Nuclear waste

Nuclear waste is the radioactive waste material that is produced during ELECTRICITY generation at a nuclear power station. Fast-breeder NUCLEAR REACTORS particularly produce a lot of radioactive waste products which have a long HALF-LIFE. The waste may take hundreds of

▶ *Used fuel rods from some nuclear reactors can be made safe at a reprocessing plant. Here the spent fuel rods are being lowered into a pool for storage until the unused plutonium and uranium can be extracted for reuse.*

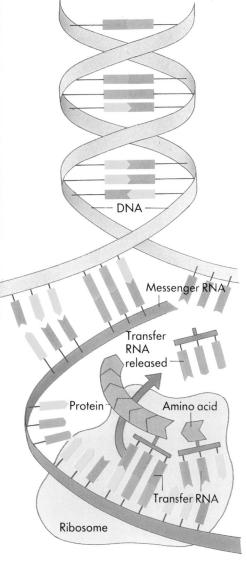

DNA

Messenger RNA

Transfer RNA released

Protein

Amino acid

Transfer RNA

Ribosome

▲ *The strands that form the double helix of DNA are assembled in the ribosomes of a cell. Messenger RNA carries the code for the correct sequence of amino acids and bases, and transfer RNA joins them in the right order to make a long chain protein molecule.*

years to decay into nonradioactive substances. During this time, particles and waves continue to be released from the waste, and this RADIOACTIVITY must be prevented from coming into contact with any living thing or with the surrounding ENVIRONMENT. It could cause widespread and probably life-threatening damage to plants and animals including, of course, people.

Nuclear waste must be handled with great care. It can be stored in drums made of material that will contain the radioactivity, and then must be constantly monitored, possibly for 1,000 years or more. Similar drums have also been dumped at sea or buried deep within the EARTH's crust, such as in very deep, worked out mines, though there is concern that an EARTHQUAKE, for example, could allow the radioactivity to be released.

Nucleic acid

There are two types of nucleic acid found in the NUCLEUS of a CELL. These are DNA (deoxyribonucleic acid) and RNA (ribonucleic acid), which control HEREDITY and life itself. The main function of DNA is to provide the plan or map from which a whole new organism is made, after the process of REPRODUCTION. RNA carries instructions from genes on the strand of DNA, so that new PROTEINS needed for life processes can be built by the cell. RNA is produced when COMPOUNDS in the cell attach themselves to part of the DNA, creating a strand of matching RNA like a key fitting a lock. This messenger-RNA contains the instructions for making one of the thousands of proteins needed by the body. It builds the proteins from amino acids which are brought to it by another kind of RNA, transfer RNA.

Nucleus, atomic *See* Atom

Nucleus, cell

Nearly all animal and plant CELLS have a nucleus (plural *nuclei*, pronounced "nucleai"). It is a small area inside the cell which can usually be seen under the MICROSCOPE as a darker patch in the cloudy cytoplasm. It contains the GENETIC material of the cell. Usually, this is in the form of unravelled threads of DNA, which are hard to see under the MICROSCOPE. When the cell is ready to divide, however, the contents of the nucleus condense into CHROMOSOMES, which are short objects containing long coiled up threads of DNA, carrying the genes. As the cell divides, the nucleus splits into two parts. When the two halves of the cell separate, each will have its own nucleus to control all its functions.

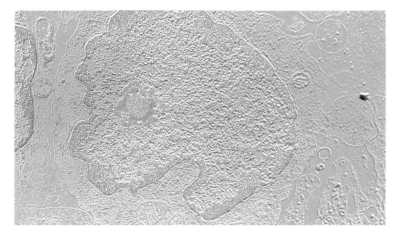

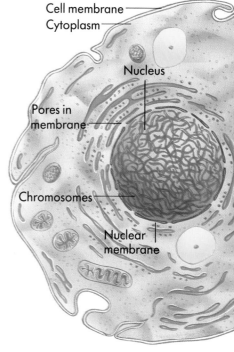

▼ *A typical animal cell has a central nucleus and various other organelles suspended in jellylike cytoplasm. The nucleus is the cell's control center, and holds the chromosomes and genes.*

Cell membrane
Cytoplasm
Nucleus
Pores in membrane
Chromosomes
Nuclear membrane

◄ *The irregular red area in this electron micrograph is the large nucleus of a white blood cell. It has been colored artificially.*

Numbers

It is easy to tell the difference between a few and many but how do we write the exact amount? Early people used a tallying system based on fingers or notches on wood but this method soon became unwieldy when the amounts got too large. *See* pages 498 and 499.

The nucleus is the heart of a cell. A typical human cell contains 85 percent water and 10 percent protein. Fats take up 2 percent and the rest is made up of DNA, RNA, and other organic and inorganic substances.

Nutrition

Nutrition is the general term used for the whole process of FEEDING, DIGESTION, and the supply of food materials to the CELLS. Good nutrition involves the intake of several classes of substances which are needed to sustain healthy life. *See* pages 500 and 501.

NUMBERS

Numbers are a convenient way of representing a quantity or amount. The numbers 1, 2, 3, 4, 5, 6, 7, 8…, which we use so often in everyday life, are called the natural numbers because they were thought to be natural in existence, and correspond to something in reality such as two eyes, four legs etc.

Our modern numbers are derived from Arabic numerals, which in turn were based on a Hindu system. Unlike many of the ancient systems, we, today, have a zero to represent nothing. The zero was introduced in its modern role in about 600 B.C. by Hindu mathematicians. By using the digits 0 to 9 we can construct any number we can think of.

Large numbers are awkward to write and can be confusing. Scientists and mathematicians use powers of ten to express large numbers because this makes them much clearer. For example, a million million or a trillion can be written as 10^{12} (1 followed by 12 zeros). The Greeks found that some numbers can be divided evenly only by themselves and 1. These are called prime numbers. The first prime numbers are 2, 3, 5, and 7.

▶ *Over the centuries, different people have devised various ways of writing numbers. Our modern Arabic numbers were originally developed in India.*

▼ *Numbers can be thought of as places along a line. Zero (0) is in the middle, with positive numbers stretching away to infinity on the right and negative numbers extending to minus infinity on the left. Negative numbers can be used, for example, when referring to a temperature such as −10°F. The diagram shows whole numbers or integers. Fractions and decimal fractions occupy spaces between the whole numbers.*

Chinese

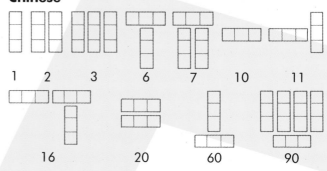

Roman

I	II	III	IV	V	VI	VII	VIII	IX	X
1	2	3	4	5	6	7	8	9	10

XI	XV	XX	L	XC	C	CX	CL	D	M
11	15	20	50	90	100	110	150	500	1000

Mayan

1	2	3	4	5	6	7	10

The Largest Number
What is the largest number you can think of? A billion? A trillion? A zillion? Whatever it is, there is always a number that is one bigger. This means that there is really no largest number. Mathematicians use the term infinity (symbol ∞) to stand for the largest number (infinitely large) in equations and calculations.

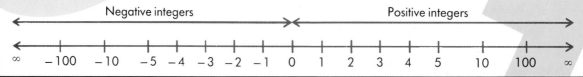

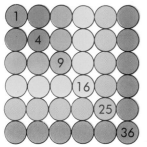

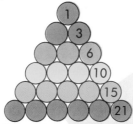

Square number progression

Triangular number progression

▶ *Some sequences of numbers can be shown as patterns. A number multiplied by itself is called a square, and a sequence of squares (far left) gives the progression 4, 9, 16, 25, 36, and so on (equal to the squares of 2, 3, 4, 5, 6, and so on). A triangular arrangement (left) gives the progression 1, 3, 6, 10, 15, 21 and so on. In Pascal's triangle (below), each number is the sum of the two numbers above it.*

Base Numbers

Our system of writing numbers today is based upon powers of 10. It is known as the base ten or decimal system and was introduced into Europe in about A.D. 1100 by Adelard of Bath.

The base is the number of digits involved in the number system. In base 10 the digits involved are 0 to 9. The value of the digit depends on its position in the number. For example, in the number 1234: 4 stands for 4 ones; 3 stands for 3 tens (3 x 10 = 30); 2 stands for 2 hundreds (2 x 100 = 200); and 1 stands for 1 thousand (1,000). The whole number is one thousand two hundred and thirty-four.

It is possible to use any base for a number system. Computers use base two, or binary, for their operations. For example, in the binary number 10101: there is 1 unit, no 2s, 1 four, no eights and 1 sixteen. The whole number is 21. Binary uses the digits 1 and 0 because they can be represented by a switch being on or off. Computer programmers often use base 16, or hexadecimal. This needs digits to represent every number from 0 to 15 so when 9 has been reached the remaining 6 digits are represented by the letters A to F, so A is the 10th digit and F, the 15th. In hexadecimal, 27 is written as 1B: B stands for 11 and 1 for 16 (11 + 16 = 27). Likewise 79 is written as 4F: F stands for 15 and 4 for 4 sixteens or 64 (15 + 64 = 79).

Pascal's triangle

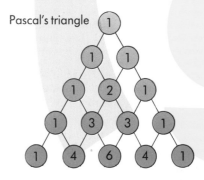

▼ *Each term in an arithmetic progression is equal to the previous one plus a common difference (equal to 1 in this example). In a geometric progression the terms increase by a common factor (in this case each is the previous one multiplied by 2). In the Fibonacci series, each term is the sum of the previous two.*

Arithmetic

1 2 3 4 5 6 7 8 9 . . . .

Geometric

2 4 8 16 32 64 128 . . . .

Fibonacci series

0 1 1 2 3 5 8 13 21 34

▼ *Sometimes we do not need an accurate answer and so we round a figure up or down. This is particularly useful for fractions of amounts such as 4.34 which can be rounded down to 4. If a grocer was selling three tomatoes for 35 cents and you only wanted one, you could not buy it for 11.7 cents, you would have to round up the price to 12 cents.*

SEE FOR YOURSELF

You can get a rough answer to a question such as how many blades of grass are there in a field, by estimating the number. If you count the number of blades of grass in a small area, you can then multiply that number by the larger area to get an estimate.

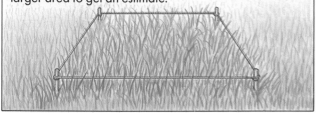

See also ALGEBRA; ARITHMETIC; BINARY NUMBERS; COMPUTER; DECIMAL; GEOMETRY; INFINITY; MATHEMATICS; METRIC SYSTEM; SI UNITS.

NUTRITION

A healthy diet contains a balanced mixture of all nutrients: proteins, carbohydrates, fats, vitamins, and some minerals, together with an undigestible form of carbohydrate called fiber (or roughage) which is needed to keep the bowel healthy. In many poor countries it is not possible to eat a well-balanced diet, so malnutrition is common, especially among children. Even though they may eat plenty of carbohydrates like rice, their diet usually lacks protein, which is needed in large amounts for healthy growth.

Although meat is a good source of protein, it is not essential for a healthy diet. Many vegetarians obtain adequate protein from cheese and eggs, and do not eat meat. Strict vegetarians eat nothing but vegetables and other plant products, and obtain most of their protein from cereals, peas and beans, and nuts. Some types of fat can be harmful if eaten in large amounts, but most vegetable fats contain less of these harmful substances. People with certain medical problems may need special diets. Diabetics need to control their intake of sugar and other carbohydrates, and children whose digestive systems cannot cope with sticky gluten, which is found in flour, need to have gluten eliminated from their diet. To be healthy, you need to eat a variety of foods which will provide the right amounts of nutrients. Eating large amounts of one type of food is not healthy, for example eating too many carbohydrates can make you overweight or cause tooth decay.

WHAT DIFFERENT PEOPLE EAT
Strict vegetarian diet A strict vegetarian is someone who eats no foods derived from animals, including meat and fish, eggs, milk, butter, and cheese, and even gelatin and yogurt.
Vegetarian diet A vegetarian does not eat meat or fish, but a vegetarian diet is not as strict as the one above and usually eggs and dairy products are eaten.
Macrobiotic diet This diet is based on the Chinese principles of Yin and Yang whereby everything is divided into two categories, one positive and one negative, and a happy existence relies on balancing the different components. The diet concentrates on whole grain cereals and vegetables grown without the use of artificial fertilizers or pesticides.
Gluten-free diet Gluten is a protein found in cereal grains and so in wheat flour and in bread and other foods made from it. People with celiac disease cannot tolerate gluten and have to eat a gluten-free diet.
Diabetic diet People with diabetes cannot control sugar (glucose) in their blood properly and have to avoid sugar and too much starchy food in their diet.
Allergic reactions Some people suffer allergic reactions from certain food products, such as milk, strawberries, chocolate, and food additives. The reaction may cause skin problems such as eczema. People with these allergies have to avoid such foods.

Calories
Food energy is measured in calories. A calorie is the amount of heat energy needed to raise the temperature of one gram of water by one degree Celsius. A gram of water is about $1/28$ ounce — only a few drops — so one calorie is a very small amount of heat. A breakfast of eggs, buttered toast, and milk produces about 500,000 calories. Numbers like this are unwieldly, so food energy is given in kilocalories — one thousand calories equal one kilocalorie. To make this more confusing, kilocalories are usually written as Calories with a capital C. So our breakfast produces 500 Calories of food energy.

▼ Fats are found in meat, vegetable oil, and dairy products such as cream, butter, and cheese. Too much animal fat is not good for health.

Carbohydrates

◄ The main carbohydrates in food are sugar (which is in all sweet foods) and starch, found in cereals and foods made from flour.

Fats

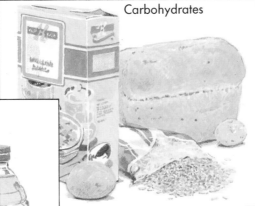

Vitamins and minerals

The Four Main Food Groups

Proteins

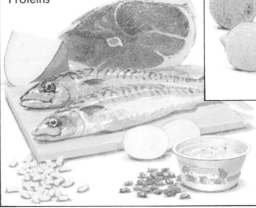

► Proteins are found mainly in meat and fish, as well as in eggs, cheese, legumes (such as peas and beans), and nuts.

▲ Other important substances in food include vitamins and minerals, found in fresh fruit and vegetables and in meat such as liver.

▲ A balanced diet contains all the foods you need to keep healthy: proteins to build tissues; fats and carbohydrates to provide energy and heat; and minerals and vitamins for growth, to maintain tissues, and regulate body functions.

◄ Malnutrition is a disorder that results from not having enough to eat. This South American child is in a hospital. She is being treated for malnutrition.

The amount of energy that can be produced from different foods is measured in Calories. A glass of milk contains about 150 Calories while a boiled egg has 80. The number of Calories a person needs each day depends on several things — age, height and weight, sex, and how active the person is. In the metric system, the energy produced from food is measured in Kilojoules (kJ).

See also CARBOHYDRATES; CEREALS; DIGESTION; FATS; FEEDING; JOULE; MILK; MINERALS; PROTEINS; STOMACH; SUGARS; TEETH; VITAMINS.

Nylon is a very strong fiber, much more so than wool or cotton. However it does not absorb water very well, which can cause problems by preventing sweat from evaporating. Yarn made from mixing wool and nylon fiber is best: it is long-wearing and gives good ventilation, ideal for such things as socks.

Nylon

Nylon was the first SYNTHETIC FIBER. It was developed in the 1930s by the U.S. chemist Wallace H. Carothers as a cheaper alternative to the natural silk spun by silk worms. Nylon is made from long chains of MOLECULES called POLYMERS. It is made in two forms: solid blocks and fibers. The solid form of nylon can be made hard or soft and rubbery. The hard form is suitable for making small GEAR wheels and BEARINGS for machines. It is also resistant to heat and chemicals.

▶ Nylon is a type of plastic. It is a polymer that can be molded into things like combs and gear wheels, or extruded into fibers that are stretched and crimped before being woven into cloth. Nylon fibers with different qualities are produced by using different raw materials. The raw materials are heated under pressure to make long polymer filaments which are cut into chips, washed, and dried. They are then melted and pumped through tiny holes. The threads harden in the air. Then they are stretched and crimped and either baled as filaments or chopped into fibers.

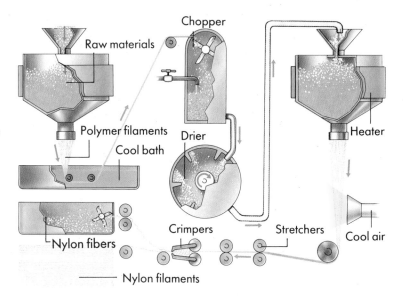

Raw materials — Chopper — Polymer filaments — Cool bath — Drier — Heater — Nylon fibers — Crimpers — Stretchers — Cool air — Nylon filaments

Nylon yarn is measured in deniers. A denier is the weight of 9,000 m (about 30,000 feet) of the yarn, in grams. For example, if 9,000 meters of yarn weigh 15 grams, the yarn is 15-denier.

Nylon fibers can be woven to make fabric for clothing. To make nylon fibers, chips of nylon are heated until they melt. The molten nylon is then forced through tiny holes called spinnerets to form the fibers. They dry and set hard almost as soon as they are formed. Fabric made from nylon fibers is also called nylon.

▶ A Velcro fastener, used to fasten clothing and luggage, is made of nylon. This highly magnified photograph shows the two halves. The hooks at the top catch in the looped whiskers at the bottom.

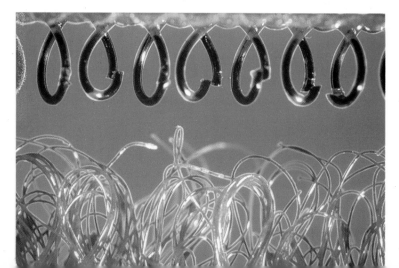

Ocean

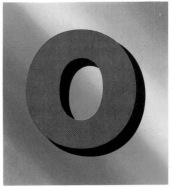

An ocean is one of the areas of SALT water that occur on the EARTH's surface. The oceans and seas of the world cover more than two-thirds of the total surface of the Earth. There are five oceans: the Atlantic, the Pacific, the Indian, the Arctic, and the Antarctic Oceans.

The Earth's crust beneath the oceans is thinner than beneath the continents, with an average thickness of about 3 miles (5 km). The positions and areas of the

◄ Coral reefs form in shallow tropical seas on the fringes of the Indian and Pacific Oceans. The coral, in turn, attracts many kinds of colorful fish.

▼ Most of the water on Earth is in the oceans, from which it evaporates to form rain and to which it returns via rivers. In some areas, the ocean bottom lies more than 6 miles (10 km) below the surface.

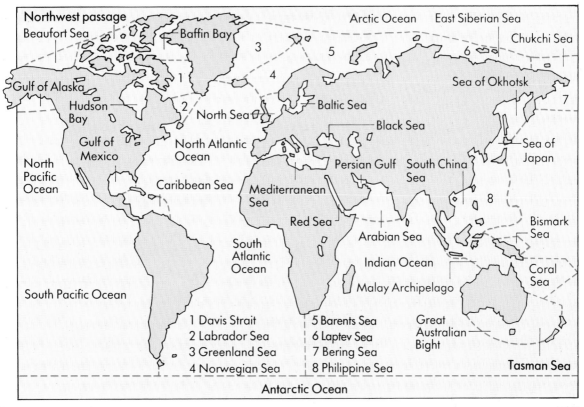

Northwest passage
Beaufort Sea
Baffin Bay
Arctic Ocean
East Siberian Sea
Chukchi Sea
3
5
6
Gulf of Alaska
1
4
Sea of Okhotsk
7
Hudson Bay
2
North Sea
Baltic Sea
Sea of Japan
Gulf of Mexico
North Atlantic Ocean
Black Sea
North Pacific Ocean
Caribbean Sea
Persian Gulf
South China Sea
8
Mediterranean Sea
Bismark Sea
Red Sea
Arabian Sea
Coral Sea
South Atlantic Ocean
Indian Ocean
South Pacific Ocean
Malay Archipelago
Great Australian Bight

1 Davis Strait
2 Labrador Sea
3 Greenland Sea
4 Norwegian Sea
5 Barents Sea
6 Laptev Sea
7 Bering Sea
8 Philippine Sea

Tasman Sea

Antarctic Ocean

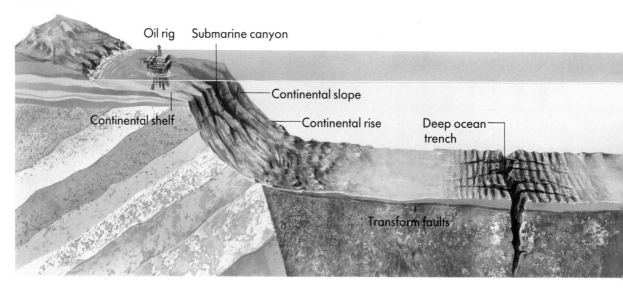

Oil rig Submarine canyon

Continental slope

Continental rise

Deep ocean trench

Continental shelf

Transform faults

▲ *A cross section through one of the world's oceans shows that the seabed is not flat and level, but more like a continental landscape. It is cut through by deep valleys called trenches, and forced up by underwater mountains and volcanoes. The continental shelf slopes gradually down from the edges of the continents to a depth of about 650 feet (200 m). It is on this shallow shelf that fish are caught and oil exploration takes place. A guyot is a flat-topped undersea mountain. Some guyots can be huge, with tops more than 6 miles (10 km) across.*

oceans change over the millions of years of geological time because of the processes of PLATE TECTONICS.

Seawater is salty because minerals from the land are washed into it. The water is warmed by the Sun and continually evaporates leaving the salt behind and gradually concentrating the salt. The pure water that evaporates will return to Earth as PRECIPITATION.

The oceans, because of their size, their stable temperatures, and their wetness, have a major effect on the world's CLIMATES. Areas surrounded by sea, such as Britain, have a much more moist and temperate climate than Siberia, which is landlocked.

Octane

Octane is a HYDROCARBON belonging to the same group, called the alkanes, as METHANE and PROPANE. Octane has 8 carbon atoms and 18 hydrogen atoms (C_8H_{18}).

The word octane is also a measure of the performance of gasoline. Gasoline comes in a range of qualities. The higher the octane number, the better the quality of the gasoline. The octane number is calculated by comparing gasoline to two standard FUELS whose performance is known. They are heptane (seven carbon atoms), a poor

▶ *Octane is the chief hydrocarbon in gasoline. The eight carbon atoms in its molecules may be arranged as a straight chain (right) or form branched chains to give a more compact molecule.*

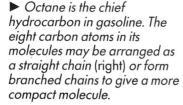

● Carbon

○ Hydrogen

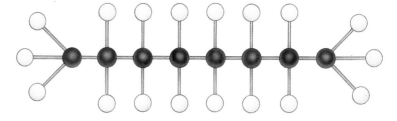

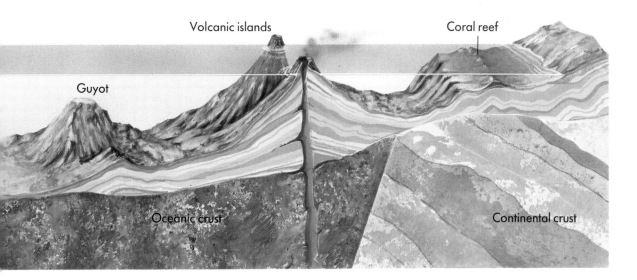

Volcanic islands

Coral reef

Guyot

Oceanic crust

Continental crust

quality fuel with an octane number of zero, and iso-octane, a high quality fuel with an octane number of 100. Most car ENGINES need fuel with an octane number of at least 90. This means that it performs as if it were a mixture of 90 parts iso-octane and 10 parts heptane. If the wrong quality fuel is put into an engine, the fuel will not burn efficiently, causing a banging noise called knocking which can damage the engine. Higher octane gasolines formerly had a LEAD compound as an antiknock additive. However, lead is poisonous and car engines are being converted to run on unleaded fuel.

Ohm, Georg Simon *See* Resistance, electrical

Oils

An oil is one of a group of complex organic COMPOUNDS consisting of carbon, hydrogen, and oxygen. Oils can be obtained from animals, plants, and mineral sources as well as being produced artificially. Together with FATS, animal and plant oils belong to a group of compounds called *lipids*. Most oils are liquid at room temperature, though some fats are solid at this temperature. Oils do not dissolve in water and are often lighter than the water. They are generally greasy and viscous.

Animal oils are chiefly formed by heating animal fats. Common plant oils include the vegetable oils extracted from corn, soy beans, olives, and some nuts. These are the oils used in cooking. Linseed oil from flax is used in making paints and varnishes. There are other plant oils, known as essential oils, which evaporate

> The prefix "oct-" comes from the Latin word for eight and is used in many words:
> **Octagon** an eight-sided figure.
> **Octahedron** an eight-faced solid.
> **Octane** a gas with eight carbon atoms.
> **Octave** eight notes forming a scale in music.
> **October** originally the eighth month of the year in the Roman calendar.
> **Octopus** a sea creature with eight legs.

▼ *One of the most common oils used in cooking is extracted from olives.*

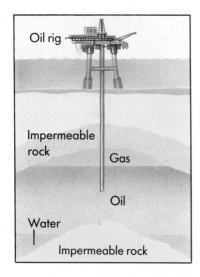

▲ Undersea oil deposits can be reached from a platform perched on long legs. Engineers bore a hole down through the rock to reach the oil.

▶ Unwanted petroleum gases are burned off at an oil refinery in the Middle East.

It is estimated that more than 500,000 different materials can be made from crude oil. During the refining process, 20 percent of each barrel of crude oil can be made into gasoline.

▼ Crude oil is refined to produce a wide range of petrochemicals, for making many substances from fuels to plastics.

quickly. These are used in making perfumes and as flavorings, for example, peppermint oil and rose oil.

Mineral oil is a FOSSIL FUEL. The general term, PETROLEUM, is usually used to describe all the HYDROCARBON materials (whether solid, waxy, or liquid) that occur naturally in rocks.

Oil refining

Oil refining converts PETROLEUM, or crude oil, into a range of FUELS, compounds, and other materials. There are two stages: fractional DISTILLATION and CRACKING.

Fractional distillation is carried out in a tall tower up to 250 feet (75 m) high, called a fractionating column. It separates the crude oil into its various constituents, called fractions. The crude oil is pumped into the bottom of the column at about 650°F (350°C). Some of the oil

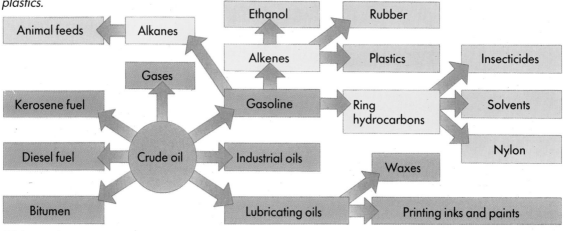

evaporates and rises through holes in a tray above it where some condenses back into a liquid that collects in the tray. The rest of the oil evaporates and rises up through further trays which become cooler the higher up the tower they are. The various constituents of the oil evaporate at different temperatures. The heaviest materials such as BITUMEN and heavy fuel oil stay at the bottom of the column, while lighter materials such as kerosene collect in trays higher up in the column. The heavier oils undergo a second process, cracking, to extract more of the valuable products. Cracking involves either heating the oil to about 900°F (500°C) and refining the resulting lighter oil, or treating the oil with a CATALYST to obtain lighter oils for further refinement.

> Crude oil doesn't always look the same. Sometimes it is thick and black, like molasses, sometimes it is a greenish brown; it can also be a light, clear oil. Experts believe that there are between 1 1/2 and 2 trillion barrels of oil that can be recovered from under the ground. (A barrel of oil is 42 gallons/159 liters.) In the United States, each person needs about 1,200 gallons of oil per year. Most is used by industry and transportation.

Oppenheimer, Robert *See* Hydrogen bomb

Optical character recognition

Optical character recognition is a process that allows a COMPUTER to read printed text. This can be letters, numbers, or other characters. These are optically scanned using an optical character reader. The initials OCR stand for both optical character recognition and optical character reader.

The process works by shining a beam of LIGHT onto the printed text and using a light-sensitive sensor to detect the reflections. The changing pattern of light that strikes the sensor produces a similarly changing electric current. This changing electrical current can be stored on magnetic tape or on a disk, and input into a computer. The computer can then produce a copy of the original text in the computer's memory.

▼ *Optical character recognition can be used to sort letters by their zip codes. A conveyor belt carries the letters past powerful lights, and a sensor picks up the characters of the code and controls a mechanism that sorts the letters into different piles, depending on their destination.*

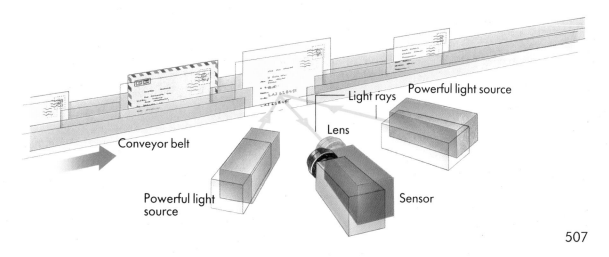

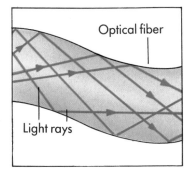

▲ *Optical fibers act like pipes that carry light instead of water. Any light that tries to escape from the pipe is reflected back into it. Using optical fibers, it is possible to channel light around corners.*

▶ *An optical fiber cable containing 2,000 tiny strands of glass is used to provide decorative lighting.*

▼ *Artificial satellites launched at a high enough speed go into orbit around the Earth. If their speed is increased even more they move into a higher orbit or escape from Earth altogether and drift off into space.*

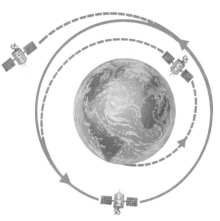

Optical fibers

Optical fibers are fine strands of GLASS. The fibers have a core of pure glass surrounded by a different kind of glass called cladding. The cladding bends any light rays that strike it back into the center of the fiber.

In TELECOMMUNICATIONS, optical fibres are replacing metal cables for transmitting TELEPHONE calls. Each caller's voice is changed into a DIGITAL signal and used to make the beam of LIGHT from a LASER switch on and off thousands of times every second. In medicine, optical fibers enable doctors to look inside the human body without having to use surgery. Optical fibers are very thin and so can be inserted into the body to transmit a picture of the stomach for example back out to the eye-piece at the other end of the instrument.

Orbit

An orbit is the path traced out by an object as it revolves around another body. The orbit is produced by the FORCE of attraction of GRAVITY between two bodies which causes the lighter body to move around the heavier one (though the heavier body moves around too).

The smallest known orbit in the SOLAR SYSTEM belongs to Mars' satellite Phobos; it is 11,650 miles (18,750 km) across. The largest orbits cannot be measured; some comets travel more than a trillion miles into space before turning back again toward the Sun.

The speed at which a planet or satellite travels

depends upon the size of its orbit. If the Earth were twice as far away from the Sun, so that its orbit was twice as long, it would take almost three years to go around the Sun once. If its distance from the Sun were halved, the "year" would be about four months long.

Ore

An ore is rock that contains deposits of metal, or that contains MINERALS that yield particular metals when processed. Such deposits are usually only referred to as an ore if they contain enough metal to be extracted profitably. Sometimes the ore is used to describe a deposit of any natural product which can be extracted usefully, such as a source of sulfur.

Ore deposits may be formed in a number of ways. Layers or seams are formed when IGNEOUS ROCKS are intruded into the surrounding rocks, and ore minerals crystallize out. Minerals, such as SALT or gypsum (calcium sulfate) may be formed when a body of water, such as an inland sea, dries up.

The ore's extraction depends upon what kind it is and where it occurs. Sometimes the surface soil and rock can be scraped away to reveal deposits of IRON which can then be extracted in open-pit mines. Some minerals require shafts hundreds of feet down into the rock to reach the seams of ore, whereas others can be dug out and loaded straight onto huge trucks.

▲ Tin ore looks like an ordinary lump of rock, but the extraction process turns it into one of the most useful metals.

▼ The extraction of tin is typical of the way ores are treated to remove the valuable metals they contain. The chief stages are separating the ore from rock, converting it to oxide by roasting, and smelting the oxide with carbon in a furnace. The waste slag is reprocessed to remove any remaining tin.

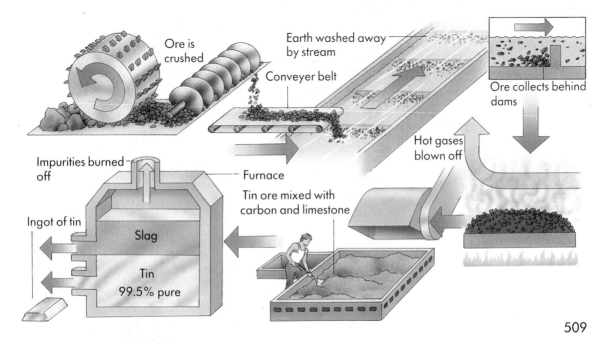

Ore is crushed

Earth washed away by stream

Conveyer belt

Ore collects behind dams

Hot gases blown off

Impurities burned off

Furnace

Tin ore mixed with carbon and limestone

Ingot of tin

Slag

Tin 99.5% pure

ORGANIC CHEMISTRY

Organic chemistry is the branch of chemistry that studies substances containing the element carbon. Carbon has a branch of chemistry all to itself for two reasons. First, carbon atoms can join together to make particularly complicated structures of rings and chains. This means that there are a very large number of compounds containing carbon. Second, molecules containing carbon are particularly important because they are responsible for many of the chemical processes that go on in living organisms.

Organic chemists have developed many techniques of synthesis (the name given to building up one molecule out of others). Using synthesis, many millions of different carbon-containing compounds can be created, some on a small scale in the laboratory and others on a very large scale in factories. For example, plastics, pesticides, and drugs are all organic chemicals.

Many of today's organic chemists are concerned with making new organic substances which will be useful to industry. Others study the ways in which organic chemicals work in living organisms; for example, they study enzymes by making several different but similar molecules and seeing how the enzyme affects each one.

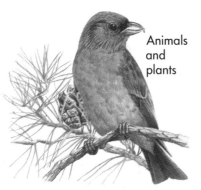

Animals and plants

Plastics and oil products

◄ All living things — animals, plants, and even molds and bacteria — are made up of complex organic chemicals. These chemicals also occur in oil and other fuels, and can be made into plastics, drugs, and other useful substances.

▼ Proteins are natural organic polymers that make up body tissues such as hair, nails, and muscle. The photograph shows a model of a protein molecule.

MILESTONES IN ORGANIC CHEMISTRY
1800s Chemists discover most organic compounds consist of carbon combined with hydrogen, nitrogen, and oxygen.
1828 Wöhler makes first synthetic organic substance.
1897 Adolf Spittler discovers casein plastics. Casein is the chief protein in milk.
1953 Watson and Crick determine structure of the genetic material DNA.

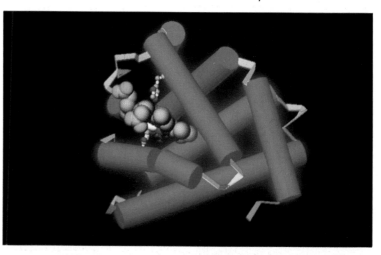

See also CARBON; CHEMISTRY; DRUGS; ENZYMES; HYDROGEN; INORGANIC CHEMISTRY; MOLECULE; ORGANISM; OXYGEN; PESTICIDES; PLASTICS.

Organism

Every living thing, whether it is a plant or an animal, is an organism. There are more than 1,500,000 known kinds or SPECIES of organisms. The largest are the giant redwood and wellingtonia trees of California, some of which weigh more than 1,500 tons, ten times as much as the Blue whale, which is the world's biggest animal. At the other end of the scale are minute organisms that cannot be seen without a MICROSCOPE. These microscopic particles of life, which include bacteria and VIRUSES, are called MICROORGANISMS.

Animals

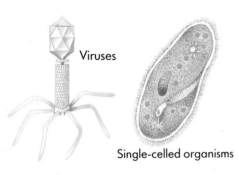

Viruses

Fungi

Single-celled organisms

Plants

Orrery

An orrery is a moving model of the SOLAR SYSTEM which was popular in the 18th and 19th centuries. By turning a handle, the positions of the PLANETS in their ORBITS could be turned to show the positions at a time in the future (or the past). Orreries were beautifully crafted of wood and brass, with hidden gear wheels that moved the planets accurately. Today, COMPUTER programs allow the positions of the planets to be displayed far more accurately.

▲ *Organisms include single-celled creatures, molds, and fungi, green plants, and all animals. They all need food and can reproduce, and are therefore alive. Some microorganisms, such as viruses, cannot exist on their own and are halfway between living and nonliving.*

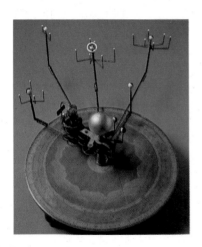

◄ *This beautifully engineered orrery was made nearly 200 years ago to demonstrate the movements of the planets around the Sun. An orrery is really a simple form of planetarium. The first orrery was built in 1700 for the Earl of Orrery, an Irish nobleman. Although orreries look quite simple, they do in fact give a fairly accurate demonstration of the movements of the planets in the Solar System.*

Oscillator

An oscillator is an ELECTRONIC device that turns direct current into an alternating current. Oscillators can produce a wide range of FREQUENCIES and wave shapes though some oscillators produce one frequency only. If an oscillator with a frequency of between 20 and 20,000 oscillations per second is connected to a LOUDSPEAKER, the vibrating loudspeaker produces a musical note. The oscillator can also be used to make electronic musical instruments. Oscillators are used to produce high frequency carrier waves for television and radio.

▼ *This oscilloscope voice print is an electronic graph of a person saying "Where are you?" It took one second to record.*

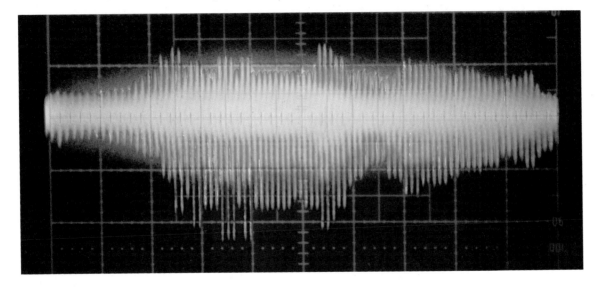

Oscilloscope

An oscilloscope is an instrument designed to convert electrical signals into wavelike patterns on a CATHODE-RAY TUBE. A beam of ELECTRONS produced by an electron gun is focused on the instrument's screen by a series of magnets and electrically charged metal plates. It appears as a bright dot on the screen. By varying the size of the charge on the metal plates controlling the beam's horizontal movement, the dot can be made to sweep from left to right across the screen, then return quickly to the beginning and sweep across again. The electrical signal to be studied, such as an electric current in wiring or the electrical activity of the heart (in an ECG), is used to vary the charge on the plates controlling the dot's vertical movement. As the signal changes, the dot moves up or down with it, making the signal visible.

▼ *An oscilloscope has a TV-type cathode-ray tube which shows a graph of how a voltage varies with time.*

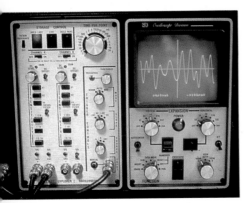

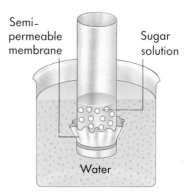

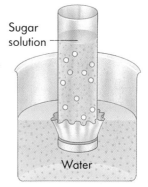

Osmosis

Osmosis is the movement of a LIQUID from one side to the other of a SEMIPERMEABLE MEMBRANE when, on one side of the membrane, there is a SOLUTION of both large and small MOLECULES, but on the other side there are fewer or no large molecules. The semipermeable membrane allows the small molecules to pass through it, but not the large ones. There is a DIFFUSION of small molecules from the side where they are in high CONCENTRATION to the side where they are in low concentration. Osmosis is important for living organisms in the movement of small food and water molecules across the semipermeable membranes of the CELLS. Without osmosis your body cells could not get the oxygen they need for life. Osmosis is one of the important processes by which water and MINERALS are taken into plant roots.

Otto, Nikolaus *See* Internal combustion engine

Oxidation and Reduction

Oxidation and reduction are processes which take place during CHEMICAL REACTIONS. All chemical reactions involve the ELECTRONS of the atoms taking part; atoms stick together in different ways because they share electrons or because electrons move from one atom to another. If an atom or a molecule gives up electrons during a reaction, we say that it has been oxidized; if it gains electrons, we say it has been reduced.

The name oxidation comes from the name of the element OXYGEN. Oxygen atoms are very effective at taking electrons from other atoms. For example, when a metal such as iron is heated in oxygen, the oxygen atoms react

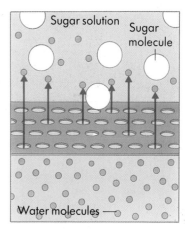

▲ In osmosis, the tiny holes in a semipermeable membrane are large enough to let through water molecules but too small for molecules of a dissolved sugar. The level of the sugar solution rises because more water molecules move into the solution than out.

◀ The rusting of steel is one of the most common types of oxidation. Here parts of old car bodies rust away in a scrap yard.

513

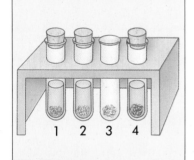

▲ An oxyacetylene torch cuts through a piece of steel. The torch can also be used for welding and, unlike other types of welding, does not cause oxidation of the metal.

514

with the metal atoms, taking electrons from them (oxidizing them) and forming a COMPOUND called iron oxide. Substances like oxygen which are good at oxidizing are often called oxidizing agents. When the iron oxide is itself heated in a gas such as HYDROGEN, the hydrogen gives up electrons to the iron and combines with the oxygen to form water vapor. Only the iron is left and its MASS is less than the mass of the iron oxide. The mass of the solid has been reduced in the reaction; this is the origin of the word reduction. Substances such as hydrogen which are good at reducing other things are known as reducing agents.

See also PERIODIC TABLE.

Oxides

An oxide is a COMPOUND of OXYGEN and another ELEMENT. Burning is rapid oxidation. Burning the oxygen in coal or wood gives carbon dioxide (CO_2) and carbon monoxide (CO). Rusting is slow oxidation. When sulfur and nitrogen combine with oxygen they can form the important sulfuric and nitric acids. Some oxides protect the metal underneath them. For example, the layer of aluminum oxide that forms on the surface of aluminum in air protects the rest of the metal from further CORROSION. Other oxides such as iron oxide (rust) are very destructive and eat into the metal. Different oxides of the same element can have very different properties. Carbon monoxide is a poisonous gas that will burn. Carbon dioxide is not poisonous and will not burn.

▼ These are the formulas for some common oxides.

CO_2 Carbon dioxide		Fe_2O_3 Iron oxide (rust)
PbO Lead oxide		CuO Copper oxide

Oxyacetylene welding

Oxyacetylene WELDING is one way of joining METAL parts. Two gases, oxygen and acetylene, are supplied to a welding tip from high pressure cylinders. Acetylene burns in oxygen with a very high flame temperature, around 6,000°F (3,300°C). To weld two pieces of metal

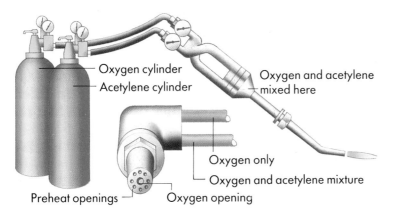

Oxygen cylinder
Acetylene cylinder
Oxygen and acetylene mixed here
Oxygen only
Oxygen and acetylene mixture
Preheat openings
Oxygen opening

◀ *An oxyacetylene torch produces an extremely hot flame, used for welding and cutting materials. It will even burn under water, and is used on underwater pipelines and oil rigs. Using preheat openings the metal can be heated so that it can be cut rather than welded by a jet of pure oxygen.*

H — C ≡ C — H

▲ *Acetylene, also called ethyne, is a highly energetic fuel gas. It can be liquefied and stored in strong steel containers.*

together, they are held next to one another and the flame from the welding torch is moved over them until they begin to melt. A rod of metal filler is melted along the joint. The molten metal runs together and when the torch is taken away, the joint cools and solidifies.

Oxygen

Oxygen is the GAS that nearly all organisms need to survive. They take it in and use it to release energy in a series of chemical reactions called RESPIRATION. Oxygen circulates between organisms and the atmosphere. It is an ELEMENT with no color, taste, or smell. It was named by the French chemist Antoine Lavoisier.

About one-fifth of the ATMOSPHERE around us is oxy-

SEE FOR YOURSELF
To show that plants make oxygen during photosynthesis put some pond weed in the bottom of a glass bowl full of water. Cover the weed with a plastic funnel and cover the funnel with a small plastic bottle.

You will see the plant gives off lots of little oxygen bubbles. When you have collected a quantity of bubbles test to see if the gas is oxygen using a smoldering stick. The stick should begin to burn strongly.

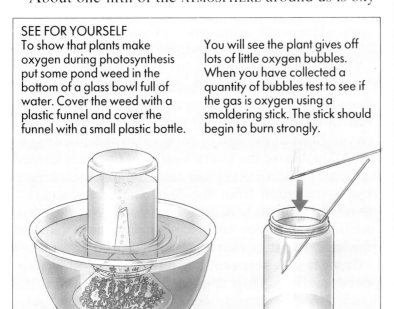

Joseph Priestley (1733–1804)
Priestley was a British chemist who in 1794 came to live in the United States. In 1774 he discovered oxygen, the gas that makes up about one-fifth of the gases in air. Priestley made oxygen by heating an oxide of mercury. The Swedish chemist Karl Scheele had found oxygen two years earlier, but did not tell anybody until 1777. Other gases that Priestley made for the first time include ammonia and sulfur dioxide.

▶ *The color of a paint is fixed when the pigment is added to the base of oil and resin. Here a chromium compound is being used to give a yellow color.*

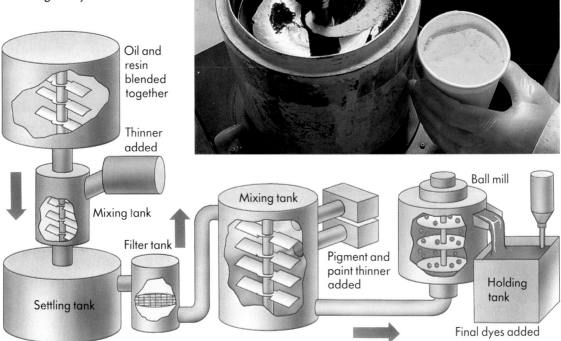

Oil and resin blended together

Thinner added

Mixing tank

Filter tank

Settling tank

Mixing tank

Pigment and paint thinner added

Ball mill

Holding tank

Final dyes added

▲ *The first stages in making paint involve blending together oils, resins, and solvents (thinners). Only later is the colored pigment added and the mixture ground in a ball mill until the paint is thoroughly mixed.*

THE FOUR ERAS OF PALEONTOLOGY ARE:
Precambrian, the very beginning of life about 4 billion years ago.
Paleozoic, from the earliest sea creatures to the development of reptiles.
Mesozoic, the era of the dinosaurs, their emergence and extinction.
Cenozoic, the era of the mammal, from the first mammals to the present day.

binding medium may contain drying oils and resins to help it to dry quickly and form a tough skin. The pigment may contain chalky extenders to increase the bulk and make the paint go farther.

Paints have been used for over 20,000 years. The earliest examples are the natural colors obtained from the earth and used by Stone Age people to paint pictures on the walls of their caves. Today, in addition to decorative paints and artists' paints, there are special paints for particular problems. Paint for marine use contains chemicals that help stop algae and barnacles from growing on a ship's hull. Paints can be applied by being brushed on, rolled on with a roller, or blown on in a jet of air from a spraygun.

Paleontology

The study of fossils is called paleontology and, as well as telling us what the organisms looked like, it can tell us about their EVOLUTION. No one has ever seen living dinosaurs, but we know a lot about them because their remains have been preserved in the ROCKS as FOSSILS. All

Baron Georges Cuvier (1769–1832)
Cuvier was a French naturalist who established the science of paleontology. He reconstructed fossil skeletons of previously unknown animals. He showed that rock layers of different ages contained different fossils. This was important when biologists began to study evolution.

▲ *A geologist's hammer gives an idea of the size of a fossil. This fossil is part of the skull of a dog-sized mammal, although judging by the teeth it probably lived on plants.*

kinds of animals and plants have been fossilized during the Earth's long history, and by studying the fossils we can learn a lot about these organisms and the environments in which they lived. Each rock layer can be dated fairly accurately using modern techniques, so paleontologists can tell when a particular SPECIES first appeared on earth. By looking at the fossils of each layer in turn, the paleontologists can also discover how one species gradually evolved into another.
See also CARBON DATING; GEOLOGY.

The oldest fossils found by paleontologists are one-celled organisms that lived about 3.3 billion years ago, when the Earth was 1.3 billion years old. From the fossils of dinosaurs we know that they lived 225 million years ago, but died out 160 million years later. Modern human beings first appeared only two million years ago.

Pancreas

The pancreas is a GLAND associated with DIGESTION. It is roughly carrot-shaped, and produces a complicated mixture of digestive ENZYMES, which pass through a short duct into the duodenum, just below the stomach. The pancreatic juices have to be strongly alkaline to neutralize the stomach acid. The pancreas is stimulated into producing pancreatic juice by the action of a HORMONE called secretin. The pancreas has another function, not

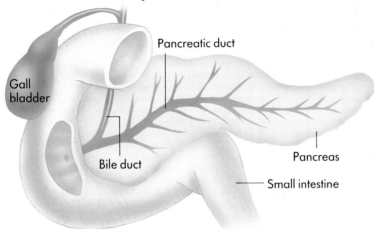

◀ *The pancreas is a dual-purpose gland located under the liver. It produces digestive juices and the hormone insulin, which controls the levels of the sugar glucose in the bloodstream.*

Pancreatic duct
Gall bladder
Bile duct
Pancreas
Small intestine

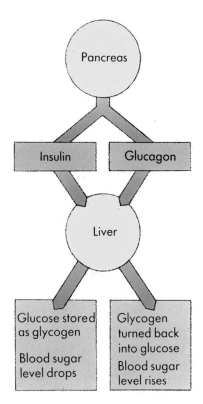

▲ The blood sugar glucose is stored in the liver in the form of glycogen. When energy is needed, the hormone glucagon from the pancreas acts on the liver to make it release glucose. But if glucose levels rise too high, the pancreas releases insulin to bring them down again.

▶ In Japan and Korea, people traditionally make windows and internal doors of paper in wooden frames. These women are drying sheets of paper made from mulberry leaves.

directly related to digestion. In clumps of cells called the islets of Langerhans, it produces the hormones insulin and glucagon, which control the levels of energy-giving glucose (sugar) in the blood. Insulin causes glucose from digestion to be stored in the liver ready for use. Glucagon has an opposite effect, causing the release of glucose when energy is required.

Paper

Paper, a sheet MATERIAL used for writing, printing, and packaging, was invented by the Chinese about the 2nd century B.C. Paper making reached Arabia in A.D.768 when the Arabs learned the secret from Chinese prisoners. From there, it spread slowly through Europe. Until the end of the 18th century, all paper was made by hand, sheet by sheet. A wooden frame with a wire mesh base was dipped into a watery pulp of FIBERS from wood, grass, or cotton. When the frame was lifted out of the pulp, the water drained through the mesh leaving a sheet of matted fibers. This was turned out of the frame and left to dry. In 1798, a machine for making a roll or web of

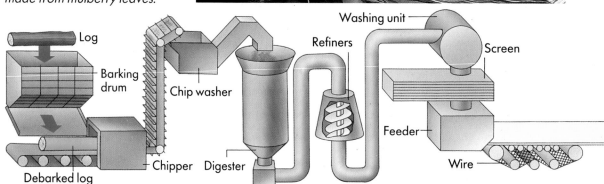

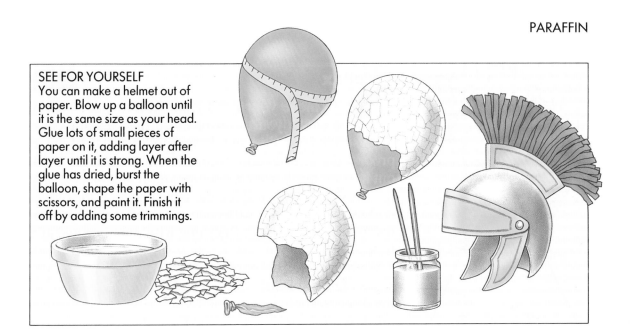

SEE FOR YOURSELF
You can make a helmet out of paper. Blow up a balloon until it is the same size as your head. Glue lots of small pieces of paper on it, adding layer after layer until it is strong. When the glue has dried, burst the balloon, shape the paper with scissors, and paint it. Finish it off by adding some trimmings.

paper was invented in France. It worked by feeding a continuous flow of pulp onto a traveling mesh belt. The pulp was drained and dried as it passed through rollers. Modern paper making is very similar. Most paper is made from wood pulp. Some high-quality paper is still made from cotton and linen fibers.

Paraffin

Paraffin is a white, waxlike, odorless, and tasteless by-product of oil refining. It forms a moisture-proof film and is used in the making of waterproof cardboard containers such as milk cartons. Paraffin is also used in making drugs, cosmetics, electrical insulation, and for sealing preserves. It is blended with other waxes to make candles and polishes. Paraffin is made from a mixture of products separated from petroleum. The petroleum products are chilled and pressed through filters to remove heavy oil. The result is paraffin wax. Paraffin was first produced commercially in 1867, soon after the first oil well was drilled.

The name paraffins was once used for the group of hydrocarbons now called alkanes. As the molecules in this group get longer there is a gradual change in their state. The shortest members, such as methane and propane are gases; longer members are named after the number of carbon atoms in the molecule, for example pentane (C_5H_{12}) is a liquid. Above heptadecane ($C_{17}H_{36}$) they are waxy solids. They are all obtained from natural gas or petroleum.

◀ Paper is manufactured by crushing or chemically treating logs to make wood pulp, which is made into a thin slurry with water. The slurry passes onto an endless loop of wire mesh, and as the water is sucked out the wood fibers form a web of paper. The web is squeezed between rollers, dried and usually coated with substances to make it smooth and white.

Press rollers   Steam heated cylinders

Paper reel

▶ *The two main types of particle accelerators are linear accelerators, which speed up particles moving in a straight line, and circular accelerators such as a cyclotron. In a cyclotron, the particles can go around many times getting faster and faster before being deflected onto a target.*

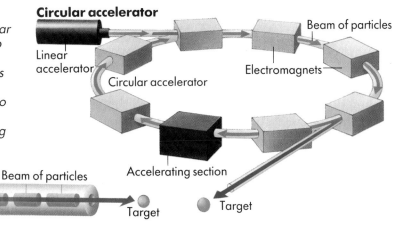

Circular accelerator

Linear accelerator

Circular accelerator

Beam of particles

Electromagnets

Accelerating section

Target

Target

Linear accelerator   Beam of particles

Target

Many particle accelerators have been built since the first one was made by Cockroft and Walton in 1932. The energies of modern machines are measured in millions of electron-volts (megaelectron-volts or MeV) or billions of electron-volts (gigaelectron-volts or GeV). The most powerful accelerator is the giant synchrotron at the Fermi National Accelerator Laboratory in Illinois. It has achieved 800 GeV.

Particle accelerator

A particle accelerator is a large machine that boosts tiny particles to very high speeds for scientific research. Physicists who study ATOMS and the SUBATOMIC PARTICLES they are made from can investigate the structure of MATTER by splitting atoms apart and studying the particles that stream away from them. To split an atom, electrically charged particles such as PROTONS, HELIUM nuclei, and ELECTRONS are placed in the electric field of a particle accelerator. The ELECTROMAGNETS produce a field that pushes against the particles and they begin to move. As they move, the field continues to increase their speed. When they are traveling at close to the speed of light, they are aimed at the atoms that are to be smashed open. The collision and the particles that result from it are monitored by detectors.

There are two types of particle accelerator, linear and circular. Linear accelerators, or linacs, accelerate particles in a straight line. Circular, or cyclic, accelerators

John Cockroft (1897–1967) and Ernest Walton (1903–)
In 1932, the British physicist Cockroft *(right)* and the Irish physicist Walton built a particle accelerator, which they used to split the atom for the first time (by firing accelerated protons at lithium atoms). For this achievement they were awarded the 1951 Nobel Prize for Physics.

accelerate particles around a circular path. Linacs have to be very long to accelerate particles to high enough speeds. Cyclic accelerators use a magnetic field to bend the path of a charged particle into a circle. They can therefore accelerate particles to much higher speeds in a smaller space.

The world's most powerful accelerators are at the Fermi National Accelerator Laboratory, near Batavia, Illinois, and at CERN, near Geneva in Switzerland. *See also* NUCLEAR PHYSICS.

Particles, elementary *See* Subatomic particles

Pascal, Blaise *See* Pressure

Pasteurizaton

Pasteurization is the process of killing disease-producing MICROORGANISMS in food and drink by heat. One common use of pasteurization is the heat treatment of MILK. Special equipment heats the milk to 143°F (62°C) for 30 minutes (or 162°F/72°C for 15 seconds). The milk is then immediately cooled to 50°F (10°C) or less to preserve the flavor. This kills dangerous bacteria which could cause tuberculosis, and damages or kills other bacteria which cause milk to become sour. Pasteurization does not affect the nutritive value of the milk. Pasteurization of milk is now very widely used, and has reduced the level of DISEASES causing diarrhea and sickness. Cream used in making butter is pasteurized before churning. Pasteurization is also used to extend the storage life of beer and wine.

Louis Pasteur (1822–95) Pasteur was a French chemist and biologist who invented pasteurization, the process for killing germs in liquids such as milk and wine. Pasteur also showed, using a swan-necked flask *(below)*, that food went bad because of airborne germs. In 1881 he developed a vaccine against the disease anthrax in sheep, and later made a vaccine that was effective against rabies in humans.

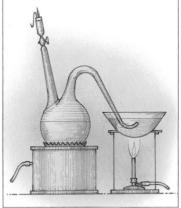

◀ Milk is pasteurized before being put into sterilized bottles. Cream and skimmed milk may be stored separately before being pasteurized and put through a homogenizer which forces the milk through narrow openings, breaking up the fat globules. The milk no longer separates into cream and skimmed liquid.

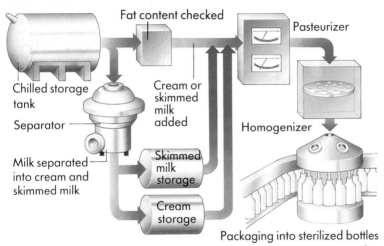

Fat content checked

Pasteurizer

Chilled storage tank

Separator

Milk separated into cream and skimmed milk

Cream or skimmed milk added

Skimmed milk storage

Cream storage

Homogenizer

Packaging into sterilized bottles

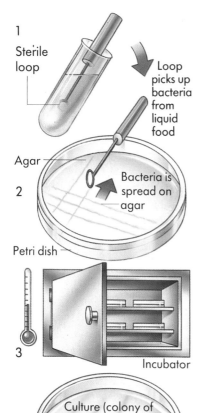

1 Sterile loop

Loop picks up bacteria from liquid food

Agar

2

Bacteria is spread on agar

Petri dish

3

Incubator

Culture (colony of bacteria)

View under microscope

4

▲ Pathologists identify bacteria by growing them on a culture. They use a sterile loop of wire to collect a sample 1, which they smear in lines on agar (a nutritious jelly) in a petri dish 2. After incubation at a controlled, warm temperature 3 the bacteria colonies grow and show up in the dish 4.

▶ At the extreme ends of its swing, the energy of a pendulum weight is potential energy due to its position. As it swings, the energy is converted to kinetic energy or the energy of movement, which is at a maximum at the bottom of the swing when the weight is moving fastest.

Pathology

Pathology is an important medical science which studies the causes of DISEASE and the resulting changes in the body. Pathology was first studied in the Middle Ages, when religious objections to dissecting dead bodies were overcome. The first book about pathology was published by Giovanni Morgagni in 1761, and showed some changes he had found in the organs of dead bodies.

However, it was not until the 19th century that doctors were able to relate the damage to the body to the symptoms experienced by their patients. In 1858, Rudolph Virchow predicted that microscopic examination could identify the type of disease produced, but it was not until late in the 19th century that Louis Pasteur and Robert Koch showed the association of disease with particular types of bacteria. Modern pathology is now a LABORATORY science, using specialized techniques and INSTRUMENTS such as ELECTRON MICROSCOPES and fiber optic probes to examine diseased tissues.

Pauling, Linus See Bond, chemical

Pavlov, Ivan Petrovitch See Learning

Pendulum

A pendulum consists of a weight, hanging from a fixed point. Its position of stable EQUILIBRIUM is when the center of MASS of the weight is directly below the fixed point; if it is pushed slightly away to one side, the FORCE of GRAVITY pulls it back toward the equilibrium position and it moves over to the other side. Then it is slowed

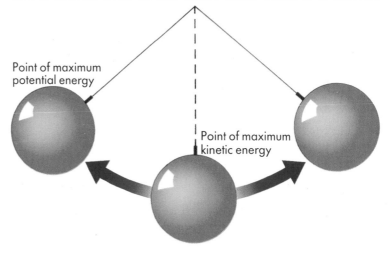

Point of maximum potential energy

Point of maximum kinetic energy

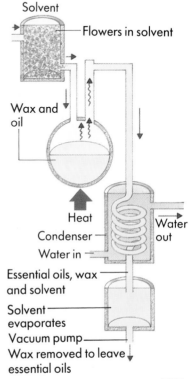

down by gravity, stops, and is pulled back once more toward the equilibrium position. The pendulum will swing for a while before FRICTION causes it to stop.

The period of a pendulum, the time that it takes to swing backward and forward once, is the same regardless of the weight of the weight. The period depends on the pendulum's length. This was discovered by GALILEO in the 16th century and is used in clocks to keep time; the clock mechanism gives the pendulum a nudge on each swing so it does not stop.

Perfume

Perfume is a pleasant-smelling mixture of alcohol and oils. It has been used for thousands of years. The earliest perfumes were probably the sweet-smelling smoke given off by certain woods when they were burned. Later, perfumes were made by extracting fragrant oils from some flowers, leaves, fruits, seeds, and woods, and also from some animals. A strong perfume called musk, for example, was obtained from a gland in the male musk deer that lives in the forests of central Asia.

Although perfumes are still made from natural compounds, chemists have analyzed them, identifying their active (smell-producing) ingredients and many perfumes can now be made artificially. Most perfumes are a mixture of natural and artificial ingredients.
See also COSMETICS.

Periodic table

The periodic table is a table of all the chemical ELEMENTS in order of their ATOMIC NUMBERS so that elements with similar properties are close to each other. Each element is made up of its own kind of ATOMS. *See* pages 528 and 529.

▼ *Perfume is traditionally made by dissolving essential oils out of flowers using solvents and distilling the solution in a vacuum.*

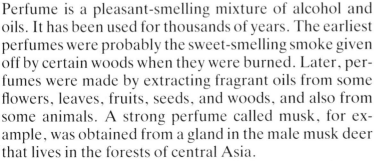

Solvent
Flowers in solvent
Wax and oil
Heat
Water out
Condenser
Water in
Essential oils, wax and solvent
Solvent evaporates
Vacuum pump
Wax removed to leave essential oils

PERIODIC TABLE

There are many different chemical elements; 92 are known to occur naturally and others can be made artificially in laboratories. The elements are organized so that the atomic number (the number of protons and also of electrons in an atom of that element) increases from left to right.

The periodic table is useful because there is regularity in the chemical properties of the elements. This happens because the electrons in atoms are arranged in shells and each shell holds a certain number of electrons. All the elements with the same number of electrons in the outermost shell behave in similar ways. So from the periodic table scientists can predict the properties of elements, or compounds of two or more elements, from what they know about neighboring elements in the table.

▼ *The periodic table contains all the known elements in order of increasing atomic number. Elements of atoms with similar structures have similar properties and so are positioned close to each other. Elements can be divided into metals and nonmetals but these groupings are very large. Therefore the metals are divided up into the three groups: alkali metals such as magnesium, the transition metals such as iron, and the inner transition series such as uranium.*

1		Atomic number
Hydrogen		Name of element
H		Chemical symbol

▶ *From the periodic table we can discover a lot of information about elements, including most simply their names and symbols. The table shows trends in the way the elements behave because of the increasing size of their atoms.*

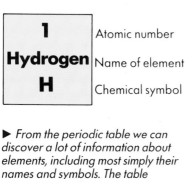

Across

Going across: the size of the atoms increases; the elements change from metals through metallike elements to nonmetals.

Down

Going down: the size of the atoms increases; all the elements in the same group behave very similarly because they all have the same number of electrons on the outside of their atoms.

| 1 Hydrogen H |

□ Alkali metals   □ Inner transition metals

□ Transition metals   □ Non-metals

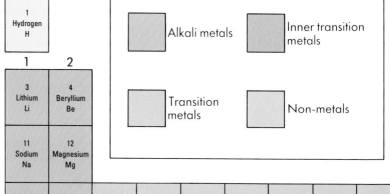

1	2							
3 Lithium Li	4 Beryllium Be							
11 Sodium Na	12 Magnesium Mg							
19 Potassium K	20 Calcium Ca	21 Scandium Sc	22 Titanium Ti	23 Vanadium V	24 Chromium Cr	25 Manganese Mn	26 Iron Fe	27 Cobalt Co
37 Rubidium Rb	38 Strontium Sr	39 Yttrium Y	40 Zirconium Zr	41 Niobium Nb	42 Molybdenum Mo	43 Technetium Tc	44 Ruthenium Ru	45 Rhodium Rh
55 Cesium Cs	56 Barium Ba	57–71 Lanthanide series	72 Hafnium Hf	73 Tantalum Ta	74 Tungsten W	75 Rhenium Re	76 Osmium Os	77 Iridium Ir
87 Francium Fr	88 Radium Ra	89–103 Actinide series	104 Rutherfordium Rf	105 Hanium Ha	106 Element 106	107 Element 107	108 Element 108	109 Element 109

57 Lanthanum La	58 Cerium Ce	59 Praseodymium Pr	60 Neodymium Nd	61 Prometheum Pm	62 Samarium Sm	63 Europium Eu	64 Gadolinium Gd	65 Terbium Tb
89 Actinium Ac	90 Thorium Th	91 Protactinium Pa	92 Uranium U	93 Neptunium Np	94 Plutonium Pu	95 Americium Am	96 Curium Cm	97 Berkelium Bk

Dmitri Mendeleyev (1834–1907)

Mendeleyev was a Russian chemist who drew up the first periodic table. He did this by charting the known chemical elements in order of increasing atomic weight, although we now know that it is the order of atomic numbers that is significant. From gaps in the table, he was able to predict the existence of elements that had yet to be discovered.

▲ *Hydrogen is the most abundant element in the universe. It is because it is the basic substance from which all stars are made.*

Both the United States and the former Soviet Union claim to have created elements 104 to 109. But these elements have not been accepted officially. They all have half-lives measured in seconds.

▼ *The usual fuel in nuclear power stations is uranium, a metallic element that was the last one in Mendeleyev's original periodic table.*

			3	4	5	6	7	8
								2 Helium He
			5 Boron B	6 Carbon C	7 Nitrogen N	8 Oxygen O	9 Fluorine F	10 Neon Ne
			13 Aluminum Al	14 Silicon Si	15 Phosphorus P	16 Sulfur S	17 Chlorine Cl	18 Argon Ar
28 Nickel Ni	29 Copper Cu	30 Zinc Zn	31 Gallium Ga	32 Germanium Ge	33 Arsenic As	34 Selenium Se	35 Bromine Br	36 Krypton Kr
46 Palladium Pd	47 Silver Ag	48 Cadmium Cd	49 Indium In	50 Tin Sn	51 Antimony Sb	52 Tellurium Te	53 Iodine I	54 Xenon Xe
78 Platinum Pt	79 Gold Au	80 Mercury Hg	81 Thallium Tl	82 Lead Pb	83 Bismuth Bi	84 Polonium Po	85 Astatine At	86 Radon Rn

66 Dysprosium Dy	67 Holmium Ho	68 Erbium Er	69 Thulium Tm	70 Ytterbium Yb	71 Lutetium Lu
98 Californium Cf	99 Einsteinium Es	100 Fermium Fm	101 Mendelev- ium Md	102 Nobelium No	103 Lawrencium Lr

◀ *Elements higher than element 92, uranium, are called transuranic elements and are all highly unstable and radioactive.*

See also ATOM; ATOMIC NUMBER; ATOMIC WEIGHT; CHEMICAL SYMBOLS; CHEMISTRY; ELECTRON; ELEMENT, CHEMICAL; HYDROGEN; METALS.

▲ *In this design, the metal ball is attracted up the slope by a magnet at the top. When it reaches the top, the ball is supposed to drop through the hole and return to the bottom of the slope repeatedly. It does not work because if the magnet is strong enough to pull the ball up it will not let it fall down again!*

▼ *Pesticides can cause harm when they get into the food chain. Humans may eat contaminated crops or animals that have been fed on them. Fish may be affected by pesticides that are washed off the land into rivers and seas.*

Perkin, William *See* Dye

Perpetual motion

Perpetual motion is movement that carries on forever without any ENERGY being supplied. If perpetual motion could be produced, it would be extremely useful; however it is against the laws of PHYSICS. This is because all movement produces FRICTION which slows movement down unless extra energy is supplied.

Despite this, people tried for many years to construct perpetual motion machines. Many of these people were genuine scientists, including famous people such as James Clerk Maxwell. Others were tricksters who cheated by using hidden sources of energy. So many people wanted to take out patents for perpetual motion machines that patent offices long ago ceased to accept applications for these inventions.

Pesticides

Pesticides are POISONS used to kill pests. The two main groups are *insecticides*, which are used to kill insect pests, and *herbicides* or weed killers. Each group includes many different types of chemicals. Most are made artificially, but some insecticides are obtained from plants. Pyrethrum, for example, is obtained from the daisylike flowers of the pyrethrum plant. Natural insecticides are generally less harmful to other forms of life than man-made insecticides. DDT was one of the earliest artificial insecticides. It was first used in the 1940s, and thought to be the perfect insecticide because it killed almost all insects and yet seemed harmless to people and other animals. But insect populations gradually became resistant to it. Higher doses were needed

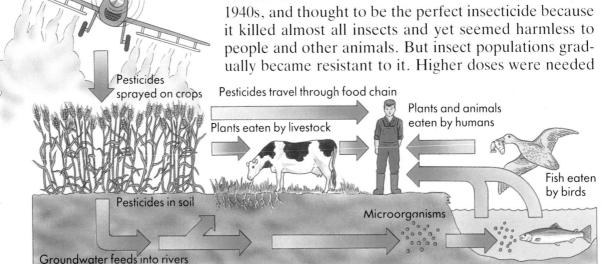

Pesticides sprayed on crops

Pesticides travel through food chain

Plants eaten by livestock

Plants and animals eaten by humans

Fish eaten by birds

Pesticides in soil

Microorganisms

Groundwater feeds into rivers

◄ *The sickly-looking cotton crop on the far left has been attacked by various pests. The plants on the right were treated with pesticides, and bear a good crop. Properly used, pesticides can also increase the yields of food plants, although some of the chemicals may be a danger to wildlife.*

▼ *Plastics are the chief products of petrochemicals, ranging from artificial rubber for tires to synthetic fibers for textiles, and resins for paint. Detergents, drugs, and fertilizers are also important petrochemical products.*

to kill them, and then scientists found that DDT accumulates in the ENVIRONMENT and damages other animals. DDT has now been largely replaced by other insecticides which do not build up in the environment, but because the insects eventually become resistant to each insecticide, new ones are always needed.

Herbicides are of two main types: total herbicides, which kill every plant that they touch, and selective herbicides. Selective herbicides kill only certain types of plants. Farmers and gardeners use them to kill weeds without harming their crops or flowers.

Petrochemicals

Petrochemicals are valuable chemicals obtained from crude oil (PETROLEUM) or NATURAL GAS and used to manufacture a wide range of useful materials, including plastics, detergents, drugs, and fertilizers. Petrochemicals include propanone (acetone) and ethene (ethylene). Propanone, a powerful solvent, is used in the manufacture of SYNTHETIC FIBERS including rayon. Ethene is used to make ethanol and polyethylene. Ethanol (ethyl alcohol) is the ALCOHOL in alcoholic drinks. It is

Nylon

Polyester

Vinyl

Synthetic rubber

Various petrochemicals

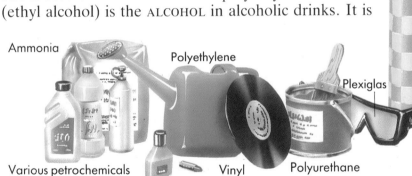

Ammonia

Polyethylene

Plexiglas

Various petrochemicals

Vinyl

Polyurethane

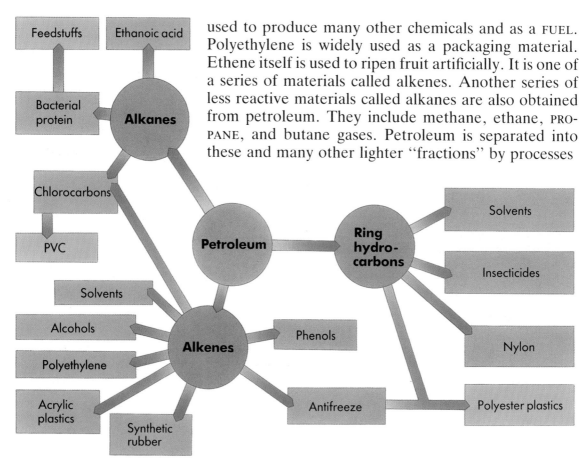

used to produce many other chemicals and as a FUEL. Polyethylene is widely used as a packaging material. Ethene itself is used to ripen fruit artificially. It is one of a series of materials called alkenes. Another series of less reactive materials called alkanes are also obtained from petroleum. They include methane, ethane, PRO-PANE, and butane gases. Petroleum is separated into these and many other lighter "fractions" by processes

▲ Petroleum, or crude oil, is used to make a huge range of chemicals. The two primary types of chemicals from the first stage of oil refining are straight chain hydrocarbons called alkanes and alkenes (such as ethane and ethene) and ring hydrocarbons such as benzene. These are in turn used to manufacture solvents, plastics, drugs, and even synthetic protein for animal food.

called CRACKING and fractional DISTILLATION which are carried out during OIL REFINING.
See also HYDROCARBONS; OCTANE; POLYMERS.

Petroleum

Petroleum is another name for crude or mineral oil, a thick dark liquid used to make a wide range of liquid and gas FUELS. Petroleum is a FOSSIL FUEL, made millions of years ago from tiny, decaying, dead plants and animals that lived in the sea. Geologists search for oil by looking for the types of ROCKS where oil is often found. When a promising site is found, test wells are drilled to discover how big the oil field is. Finally, the well itself is drilled to allow the oil to be pumped out.

Crude oil must be processed, or refined. The world's richest oil reserves are in the United States, the Middle East, and the CIS. Petroleum is described as a non-renewable RESOURCE because no new supplies are being made. When existing reserves are used up, there is no more to replace them.

World production of petroleum is about 19 billion barrels a year. Experts believe that there are between 1.5 and 2 trillion barrels of oil that can fairly easily be recovered from under the ground. A barrel of petroleum is 42 gallons.

pH

pH is a way of measuring how ACID a SOLUTION of a particular substance in water is. When certain COMPOUNDS are dissolved in water, they produce HYDROGEN ions. The pH scale measures the number of hydrogen ions which are present in a given volume of the solution. Chemicals which are alkaline lower the number of hydrogen ions below the level in pure water. Pure water has a pH value of 7; it is neutral, being neither acid nor alkali. Acids have a pH of less than 7, alkalis more than 7. The pH is often measured using substances called INDICATORS, which change color, depending on whether the solution is acidic or alkaline. For example, it can be important to test the pH of SOIL because some plants grow better in alkaline than acid soils. The hydrangea's colored flowers are different shades — blue in acid soils and red in alkaline soils.

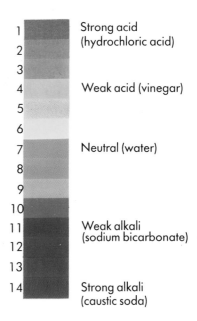

▲ The pH of a solution can be measured using a universal indicator, which changes color throughout the whole range of pH from 1 (strongly acid) to 14 (strongly alkaline).

Pharmacology

Pharmacology is a medical science which examines the effects of DRUGS on living organisms or tissues. It is particularly concerned with finding out how drugs work, so newer and better drugs can be developed. The Greek physician Dioscorides produced a book of herbal medicines in the 1st century AD. Herbal treatments were the only drugs available to doctors until the 19th century. Then German and French pharmacologists succeeded in extracting important drugs from plants such as belladonna or deadly nightshade to relax eye muscles. The drugs morphine and quinine were refined from plants.

In the early part of the 20th century, it was realized that certain "families" of substances would produce similar effects on the body. This allowed pharmacologists to develop more types of drugs, and to steadily improve

Pharmacologists know that because drugs usually cannot distinguish between healthy and diseased cells, no drug is completely safe. Useful drugs sometimes produce unwanted side effects. This is why it is important to use drugs exactly as they are prescribed. You should tell your doctor if a drug you are taking produces effects you cannot understand.

◄ Ever since the beginnings of pharmacology, the pharmacy has been an important place. Drugs are kept there to fill doctors' prescriptions. This print shows a pharmacy of 100 years ago.

$$PO_4^{3-}$$

▲ *Phosphates are salts of phosphoric acid. They are important chemicals in plant and animal tissues, in rocks, and in manufactured chemicals.*

Phosphates have been used extensively in detergents because they keep the dirt from settling back on the cleaned material. But phosphates are not removed by bacteria and are therefore not eliminated during the treatment of sewage. When sewage rich in phosphates reaches rivers and lakes it acts like a powerful fertilizer. Tiny plants multiply very quickly and choke out other forms of water life. Eventually, lakes are filled with rotting vegetation. Scientists have produced detergents without phosphates.

▲ *A type of phosphorus and its compounds are used in making matches.*

▶ *Phosphorus occurs as phosphates in many minerals, along with various metals. Those shown here include phosphates of aluminum, iron, yttrium, cerium, and thorium.*

534

their effects in treating disease. Antibiotics were discovered completely by accident, but pharmacologists were soon able to produce a stream of drugs which were more effective than the original penicillin. Modern techniques use computers to "build" a new drug with the required action on the body.

Phosphates

Phosphates are COMPOUNDS of PHOSPHORUS, used mainly as FERTILIZERS to provide food for plants. The most common is superphosphate (calcium hydrogenphosphate). Phosphates are also used in detergents and water softeners. Phosphates are obtained from granite rocks, bird droppings, and fish waste, which are processed to obtain the phosphates. Phosphate fertilizer and natural phosphates both dissolve in rainwater, which washes any phosphates not used by the plants out of the SOIL and into rivers. In the sea, phosphates are taken up by fish and plants. In some places phosphate levels in rivers running through farm land are very high. Increased plant growth caused by the phosphates uses, and so reduces, the OXYGEN dissolved in the water, killing fish. *See also* NITRATES.

Phosphorescence *See* Luminescence

Phosphorus

Phosphorus is a nonmetallic solid ELEMENT. It is essential for nearly all living CELLS. Teeth and bones contain a compound of calcium and phosphorus called calcium phosphate. Phosphorus was discovered in 1669 by a German alchemist, Hennig Brand.

Phosphorus is obtained mainly from an ore called phosphorite or phosphate rock, one form of a natural mineral called apatite. It is also found in wavellite and vivianite. There are several forms of phosphorus classified according to color: white, red, and black. White phosphorus is poisonous and it bursts into flames when it is exposed to air. It must be stored under water and is used to make incendiary devices and grenades. The strip on the side of a matchbox contains red phosphorus.

Photochemistry

Photochemistry is the study of CHEMICAL REACTIONS which take place when LIGHT is absorbed by a substance. Different reactions can take place when light is present because of the extra ENERGY from the light. For example, a MOLECULE that absorbs light can break apart or its ATOMS can rearrange themselves into a form that reacts more easily with other molecules. One very important example of photochemistry is PHOTOSYNTHESIS in which plants use the energy from sunlight in a reaction that makes CARBOHYDRATE molecules from CARBON DIOXIDE and water. Another is the process in the atmosphere that combines CHLOROFLUOROCARBONS (CFCs) with OZONE, thus damaging the OZONE LAYER.

▲ Photography uses photochemistry because it makes pictures by means of the action of light. Light reflected from an object forms a picture on a material sensitive to light. This picture is then chemically processed into a photograph.

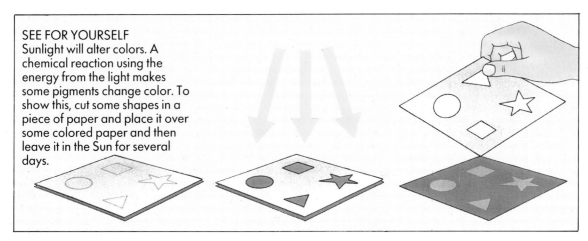

SEE FOR YOURSELF
Sunlight will alter colors. A chemical reaction using the energy from the light makes some pigments change color. To show this, cut some shapes in a piece of paper and place it over some colored paper and then leave it in the Sun for several days.

Photocopier

A photocopier is a machine used to produce copies of documents. Most photocopiers use a process called *xerography*, invented by Chester Carlson in the United States in 1937. Inside a photocopier, a drum-shaped metal plate is given a charge of STATIC ELECTRICITY

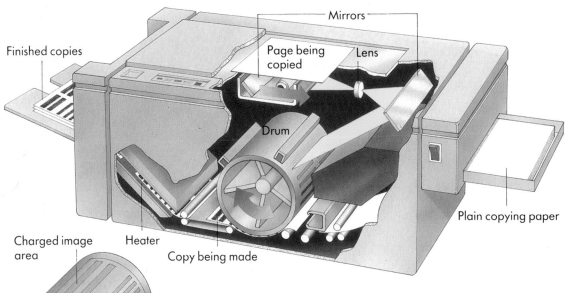

Finished copies

Mirrors

Page being copied

Lens

Drum

Plain copying paper

Charged image area

Heater

Copy being made

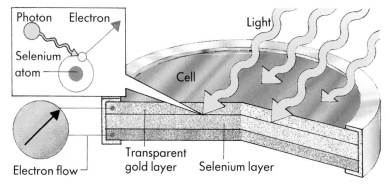

Toner dust attracted to charged image area

▲ *The key to a photocopier is the method of making powdered pigment, called toner, stick to paper in a pattern that corresponds to electrical charges on a rotating drum. This is done by giving the image area a charge of static electricity so that the toner will stick to it.*

The plate is coated so that it only conducts ELECTRICITY when a LIGHT shines on it. The document to be copied is placed on a sheet of glass. A bright image of the document is focused onto the charged plate. Where light strikes the plate, the electric charge flows away. The plate therefore carries an image of the original document in the form of a pattern of static electricity. Black "toning" powder is sprayed all over the plate. It sticks to the charged areas only. A sheet of paper is pressed against the charged plate. The toning powder sticks to the paper and the image is made permanent by heat.

Photoelectric cell

A photoelectric cell is a device that causes an electric current to flow when light falls on it. This is normally done by allowing the light to fall on a material called the cathode. The light causes ELECTRONS to leave the cathode. This produces an electric current when light falls on the cathode. Different choices of cathode material

▶ *One type of photocell is made of the semimetallic element selenium. It releases electrons when light (photons) shines on it, and the flow of electrons constitutes an electric current.*

Photon   Electron

Selenium atom

Light

Cell

Electron flow

Transparent gold layer

Selenium layer

536

are sensitive to light of different WAVELENGTHS.

Photoelectric cells are used in scientific research to measure the light given off by MATERIALS and MOLECULES. They are also used in control systems such as to count objects moving on a conveyor belt, and even in burglar alarm systems. They do this by detecting whether an object is present between a light source and the cell.

Photography

Photography is the process of recording images on light-sensitive FILM using a CAMERA. The earliest cameras recorded images on metal or glass plates. More convenient PLASTIC roll film was available in 1889. Several chemical processes for developing photographic images were invented in the mid-19th century, including the DAGUERREOTYPE and the calotype negative-positive process. A negative-positive process is still used today.

All cameras work by focusing LIGHT through a LENS onto a piece of film. When this is developed in a chemical solution, an image appears on the film. Instant picture POLAROID CAMERAS use film that develops by itself. Photographic film sensitive to X-RAYS reveals images from inside the human body.

Toward the end of the 19th century, people began looking for a way of recording moving images on film. An Englishman, W. K. L. Dickson, working with the U.S. inventor Thomas EDISON, made the first movie film. The world's first movie studio was set up at Edison's laboratories in 1893. These early films could only be seen by one person at a time. The first practical movie projector was made by the French Lumière brothers, Auguste and Louis. It projected films onto a screen,

William Fox-Talbot (1800–77)
Fox-Talbot was a British scientist who in 1841 invented the first practical photographic process that used a negative to make a positive print. His calotype process used wet glass plates sensitized with silver iodide. Later he developed a paper sensitized with silver iodide for making photographic prints.

▼ *High-speed photography, with the camera shutter opening and closing hundreds of times a second, can "freeze" the action as a pole vaulter makes his jump.*

George Eastman (1854–1932)
Eastman was a United States inventor who developed flexible roll films for cameras (previously glass plates had been used) and in 1892 founded the Kodak company. He introduced cheap and simple-to-use box cameras, and made photography available to everyone.

You can make a photomontage after taking overlapping photographs of a scene by pointing the camera in slightly different directions for each shot. Carefully match pairs of prints together where they overlap and tape them together. Then cut through both prints and retape them on the back at the seam, or paste them onto a large sheet of paper. In this way you can build up a large, poster-sized photograph of the scene.

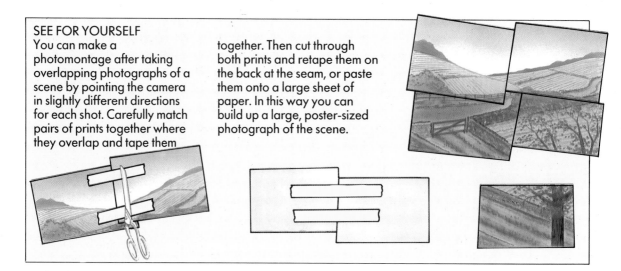

Photography really started in 1727 when a German doctor, Johann Schulze, discovered that sunlight blackened chalk that had been treated with a solution of silver nitrate. All photography is based on Schulze's discovery that light affects certain silver compounds.

Joseph Nicéphore Niepce (1765–1833)
Niepce was a French pioneer of photography, usually credited with taking the first photograph, using a pewter plate sensitized with bitumen and an 8-hour exposure. He also worked with Louis Daguerre in the development of the daguerreotype process.

Louis Daguerre took the first photograph of a living person in 1839. He photographed people in the street in Paris, but because the exposure time was several minutes long, moving objects made no impression and the only visible person is a man pausing for a shoeshine.

enabling many people to see a film at the same time.

Photography enables us to keep images of people and places from the past. We also receive information in the form of photographs in books, magazines, and newspapers. Infrared photography is widely used in MEDICINE. In these and many other ways, photography provides an important contribution to our lives.
See also COMMUNICATIONS; VIDEO CAMERA.

Photon

A photon is a particle of ELECTROMAGNETIC RADIATION. Although electromagnetic radiation behaves like a WAVE, we now know that the waves can only occur in packets or particles with a certain definite ENERGY. The energy of the packet is proportional to the FREQUENCY of the radiation. The German physicist Max PLANCK was the first to realize this.
See also QUANTUM MECHANICS; WAVE MOTION.

Photosynthesis

Photosynthesis, which means building with LIGHT, is the remarkable process by which green plants make their food. It is a very complex process with several stages, but the end result is that the plants combine water from the soil with carbon dioxide from the air to make glucose SUGAR. The process takes place only in the light and in the presence of CHLOROPHYLL (the green coloring matter in plants). Chlorophyll absorbs some of the light falling on it and uses this ENERGY to drive the food-making process. The energy passes from stage to stage and finally ends up as glucose, the starting point for CELLULOSE

▼ *In the presence of chlorophyll, the green pigment in the leaves of plants, photosynthesis makes water and carbon dioxide combine to form the sugar glucose. The water gets to leaves from the roots of a plant, which absorb it from the soil. Carbon dioxide enters leaves from the air. The energy to drive the process comes from sunlight. Respiration (below right) is almost the reverse process: carbon dioxide and water vapor are released from the leaves into the air.*

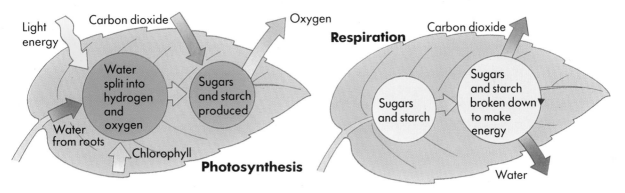

AND STARCH. Oxygen is given off during the process. The chlorophyll is unchanged and goes on absorbing light to keep the process running.

Photosynthesis is important for all life on Earth. Only green plants can convert sunlight into chemical energy and store it in their bodies. All animals depend on this energy, which they get through the FOOD CHAIN by eating the plants or by eating other animals that have already eaten plants. Animals (and plants) release the energy from food by the process of RESPIRATION, during which oxygen reacts with the glucose. Water and carbon dioxide are given out in this process, which is almost the exact reverse of photosynthesis, except that no chlorophyll is involved.

Physics

Physics is the study of the most basic things about the world we live in, particularly the study of ENERGY and MATTER. Physicists ask questions like: What are things made of? How did they come into existence in the first place? *See* pages 540 and 541.

Photosynthesis taking place in all the world's green plants makes and moves vast quantities of chemicals every day. Using the energy of sunlight, millions of tons of carbon dioxide are removed from the atmosphere and replaced with oxygen. Plants produce sugars for their energy needs, as well as cellulose and starch to build their tissues. And because all animals either eat plants or eat other animals that live on plants, photosynthesis is the ultimate source of all the food on Earth.

PHYSICS

The first writings we have which show that people were thinking about physics come from the civilization of ancient Greece, about 2,500 years ago. The most influential of these was written by Aristotle, who was so greatly respected that for about 1,800 years after his death there was very little advance made on his work. Then, in the 16th century, people began to start approaching physical problems, not just by thinking about them as the ancient Greeks had done but by carrying out experiments to see what the world was like. At the end of the 17th century a great step forward was taken when Isaac Newton discovered the laws of motion and of gravity. Through the 18th and 19th centuries, the forces of electricity and magnetism were investigated; finally electromagnetic radiation was discovered and the nature of light was explained.

The beginning of the 20th century was marked by the development of the theory of relativity, which tells us how very large objects behave, and of the ideas of quantum mechanics, which concern the behavior of very small objects such as the electrons that are parts of atoms.

Physics today is concerned with questions such as: How did the universe begin? How can we dispose of nuclear waste and combat pollution? How can we improve communication systems and medical technology.

MILESTONES IN PHYSICS:
c. 200 b.c. Archimedes discovers laws of levers and pulleys.
c.1270 Roger Bacon conducts studies in optics.
1687 Isaac Newton publishes laws of motion.
1803 John Dalton first proposes his atomic theory of atoms.
1830s Faraday and Henry independently link electricity with magnetism.
1932 Cockcroft and Walton build first particle accelerator.
1947 Bardeen and Brattain invent the transistor.
1960 Maiman builds first laser.
1980s Development of ceramic superconductors.

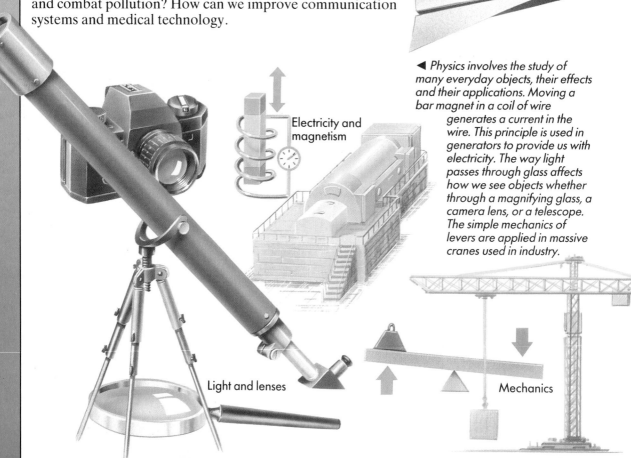

◀ Physics involves the study of many everyday objects, their effects and their applications. Moving a bar magnet in a coil of wire generates a current in the wire. This principle is used in generators to provide us with electricity. The way light passes through glass affects how we see objects whether through a magnifying glass, a camera lens, or a telescope. The simple mechanics of levers are applied in massive cranes used in industry.

Electricity and magnetism

Light and lenses

Mechanics

BRANCHES OF PHYSICS:
Mechanics the study of forces and the properties of matter.
Heat and thermodynamics the study of heat and how it travels.
Optics the study of light, including the effects of mirrors and lenses.
Electricity and magnetism the study of static and current electricity, permanent magnetism, and electromagnetism.
Acoustics the study of sound and its effects.

The first people to record their discoveries in physics were the ancient Sumerians and Babylonians around 3000 B.C. But even before this, people must have had some knowledge of mechanics. Stonehenge could not have been built if its builders did not know how to transport and raise the great stones.

▼ *Daggerlike noses and swept back wings help planes fly better at high speeds because they reduce drag. The Concorde has swept back wings and can change the position of its nose to allow both high speed flight and safe low speed landings.*

▲ *Aerodynamics studies how objects behave when they move through air. The reason a paper airplane flies, because its "wings" give it lift, is basically the same for a supersonic aircraft such as the Concorde.*

▶ *As with all science teaching, experiments are used to study physical effects. These students are making simple circuits to investigate the conduction of an electric current.*

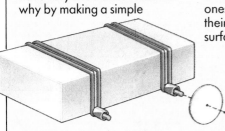

See also ACOUSTICS; AERODYNAMICS; ELECTRICITY; GRAVITY; HEAT; LIGHT; MAGNETISM; MECHANICS; NEWTON; SOUND; THERMODYNAMICS.

▶ *Through a microscope, muscle can be seen to consist of parallel strands of fibers. Physiologists use microscopes to study tissues and find out how they work.*

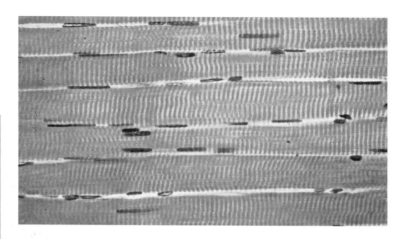

Claude Bernard (1813–78)
Bernard was a French physiologist who discovered how the pancreas makes many of the enzyme-containing juices that cause digestion of food in the stomach. He showed how glucose, the main source of energy in the body, is stored in the liver in the form of glycogen, to be broken down and released into the bloodstream as required. He also studied the workings of the nervous system and how it is affected by certain drugs.

Together with anatomy, physiology is the foundation for medical practice and research. Medical students first learn **anatomy**, how the body is put together. Next they study **physiology**, how the various parts of the body, the cells, tissues, and organs work. Only then do the students begin to learn how the body can change and behave in conditions of disease.

Physiology

Physiology is the scientific study of the life processes of plants and animals, including study of organs and individual living CELLS. It involves studying how living things function and what reactions are occurring in the organism. Physiology has been revolutionized by the introduction of the ELECTRON MICROSCOPE and other LABORATORY techniques which can show the smallest details and structures. For example, some electron microscopes can even reveal the structure of a single molecule of the red BLOOD pigment hemoglobin.

Physiology also studies the complicated relationships between all the chemical processes of the body, discovering how all these varying activities can produce constant body conditions. A lot of physiology is based on study of the way in which living organisms or parts of organisms react when their environment is changed.

Study of the cells is particularly valuable. It has led to a better understanding of DISEASES, like cancer, that upset normal cell division processes, and has revealed how the nucleic acid DNA governs the REPRODUCTION of new living creatures. Physiology serves as a link between several other sciences, such as PHYSICS, CHEMISTRY, GENETICS, PHARMACOLOGY, and many others.

Pickup

A pickup is a device that converts the information stored in the grooves of a vinyl RECORD into an electrical signal. A stereo pickup cartridge consists of two parts: a stylus and two transducers. The grooves in a stereo record make the stylus vibrate in two directions.

Two transducers convert these vibrations into electrical signals. The two main types of pickup transducers are PIEZOELECTRIC and magnetic. A piezoelectric transducer is made from a CRYSTAL that produces a voltage when it is twisted or vibrated. A magnetic pickup cartridge works by making either a coil or a magnet move with the stylus so that an electric current is induced in the coil. *See also* HI-FI; INDUCTION COIL; STEREOPHONIC SOUND.

▼ *A crystal pickup on a record player works by converting the rapid vibrations of the stylus into tiny electric currents. The currents are amplified and fed to loudspeakers.*

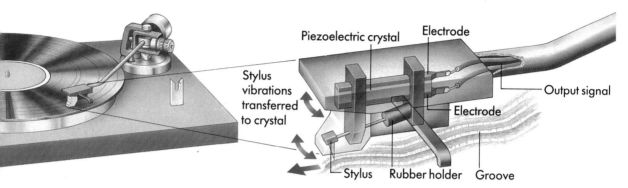

Piezoelectric crystal · Electrode · Stylus vibrations transferred to crystal · Output signal · Electrode · Stylus · Rubber holder · Groove

Piezoelectricity

When certain CRYSTALS are squashed or stretched slightly, they develop an electrical potential or voltage. This is called the piezoelectric effect. It happens because the ATOMS in the crystal each carry a small electrical charge and as the crystal is squashed or stretched the atoms move relative to each other. The effect also works the other way around; an electrical signal makes the crystal distort slightly.

The most common piezoelectric crystal is quartz; a quartz watch contains a quartz crystal which is made to vibrate very fast. The regular piezoelectric signal that it produces as it vibrates is used to keep TIME.

Piezoelectricity is a key element of quartz and digital watches. Scientists have developed ways of growing pure quartz crystals in the laboratory. These crystals are cut to vibrate at only one frequency when a voltage is applied to them. The vibrations can then be turned into seconds, minutes, and hours.

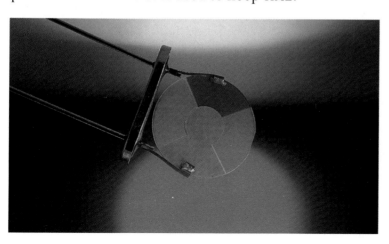

◄ *A shaped quartz crystal out of an electronic watch. In an electric field, the piezoelectric effect causes the crystal to vibrate at a definite frequency, which is used to make the watch keep almost perfect time.*

Many pigments occur naturally in plants. Try grinding up some leaves and an orange or yellow flower in a few drops of water. To separate the mixture of pigments, put a drop of the greenish liquid at the center of a circle of filter paper or blotting paper. The colors will separate as the drop spreads outward.

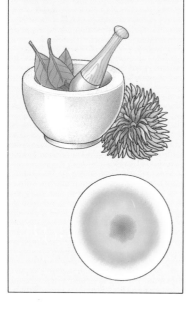

▼ The dark skin color of African people is produced by the pigment melanin. An albino, like this African boy, has no melanin and his skin and hair are white.

Pigments

Pigments are responsible for most of the COLORS in plants and animals. Pigments are complex substances and there are many different kinds. Plants contain green CHLOROPHYLL, which is essential for the plants' food-making process, PHOTOSYNTHESIS. Most animals contain pigments called melanins, which give a brown or black color to HAIR, FEATHERS, and SKIN. In insects, yellow, orange, and red are generally produced by pigments called pteridines. Carotenoids produce the same colors in other animals and in plants. Hemoglobin is the red pigment found in the red blood cells and which makes our BLOOD red. It can combine with OXYGEN to make oxyhemoglobin and is the means by which oxygen is transported in the blood system around our bodies. Many animals use hemoglobin but others use different pigments, such as the chlorocruorin in some kinds of worms which makes their blood green.

Many pigments are now produced artificially for making PAINTS and other materials. Pigments produce their colors by absorbing certain WAVELENGTHS OF LIGHT and reflecting others. The color which is reflected is the color that you see, for example most plants are green because chlorophyll reflects green light. The three most important pigment colors are yellow, blue, and red, because when they are mixed in the correct way they can reflect light of any color.

See also DYES.

Name	Color	Use
Melanin	Dark brown	Found in the skin. Absorbs the Sun's harmful radiations.
Rhodopsin	Purple	Found in the eyes. Makes eyes more sensitive in dim light.
Carotene	Yellow/orange	Found in plants and converted into vitamin A by animals. Also used by some plants for photosynthesis
Chlorophyll	Green	Found in plants. Used by green plants to make food by photosynthesis
Safrole (saffron)	Yellow	Found in plants. Used as food and clothing dye
Indigo	Blue	Found in plants. Used as a dye.
Phthalo-cyanine	Blue/green	Chemical used in paint, printing ink, plastics, and enamels

Pile, atomic *See* Nuclear reactor

Pitchblende

Pitchblende is the name commonly given to a form of the MINERAL uraninite (URANIUM oxide) which is one of the main ORES for uranium. Uraninite is called pitchblende because it rarely occurs in crystal form but is more usually found as black, RADIOACTIVE, pitchlike masses. Pitchblende also contains a highly radioactive ELEMENT called RADIUM which was first discovered by the CURIES in the late 19th century.

The Black Mineral
No one suspected the existence of uranium until 1789, when the German chemist Martin Klaproth was investigating the pitch black ore called pitchblende. Klaproth found a new element in the ore and named it uranium after the planet Uranus.

◄ *In order to separate a few grams of radium from pitchblende, the Curies had to process tons of the mineral in their Paris laboratory. Here a helper is stoking up the furnace.*

Planck, Max

Max Planck (1858–1947) was a German physicist who was born in Kiel and died in Gottingen. He was the first person to realize that the ordinary laws of MECHANICS, which describe large objects, cannot work for very small objects such as ATOMS. He studied at the University of Munich and nearly became a professional musician, but instead went on to study at Berlin with Kirchhoff and Helmholtz. His great discovery followed measurements of the amount of ENERGY that is present in the form of ELECTROMAGNETIC RADIATION at a given temperature. Planck showed that the results could be explained if the energy in electromagnetic radiation such as light could exist only in tiny bits of energy called quanta. These tiny bits are today called PHOTONS. He was awarded the Nobel Prize for Physics in 1918. His work led to the development of QUANTUM MECHANICS.

▲ *Max Planck put forward the idea that atoms emit or absorb energy in separate packets. This led to quantum theory, one of the most important theories in modern physics.*

► Planets go around the Sun in elliptical orbits and reflect its light. All the planets except Mercury and Venus have at least one orbiting moon, or satellite. The moons orbit the planets, also in elliptical orbits.

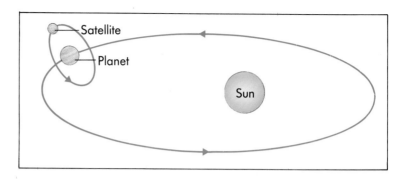

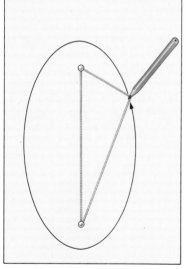

Planet

A planet is a solid body orbiting a STAR and illuminated by it; for example, the EARTH orbits and is lit by the SUN. A star is hot enough on the surface to shine brightly. The planets in the SOLAR SYSTEM, the only ones we can observe, form two groups: smaller ones including the Earth, made of rock and metal with shallow atmospheres or none at all, and giant planets, which are mostly liquid hydrogen, helium, and other gases.

Planetarium

A planetarium projects images of the STARS and PLANETS on the inside of a dome. It can show the appearance of the sky for many years into the past and future, as well as the view from different parts of the world.

A planetarium can be used for teaching, research, or entertainment. It is a good way of learning the CONSTEL-LATIONS. Nowadays the use of COMPUTER GRAPHICS makes it possible to leave the Earth behind and take the

► The audience inside a planetarium can watch how the positions of the stars appear to change during the course of a year. The planetarium's projector can also show the tracks of the planets across the heavens.

audience on spectacular journeys through space. Research studies using birds in a planetarium have shown that some do use stars, or star patterns, to navigate at night and also during their annual MIGRATION.

Plastics

Plastics are synthetic MATERIALS which have changed the appearance of our world. The first plastic was celluloid, made in 1869 by U.S. printer John W. Hyatt from cotton and camphor. This plastic was used in the manufacture of photographic FILM. *See* pages 548 and 549.

Plastic surgery

Plastic surgery is a means of reshaping parts of the body. It is sometimes used for cosmetic reasons to improve the appearance of features such as a hooked nose, or protruding ears. Injuries such as burns can be very disfiguring, and a plastic surgeon may carry out a SKIN graft,

taking a patch of healthy skin from another area, and attaching it to the damaged part so it grows together. If the wound is very large, it may not be possible to graft the new skin without leaving another scar where it was removed so new techniques have been developed to remove all the sensitizing substances from animal skin, leaving only the fibrous collagen layer. This fibrous patch can then be used to seal the wound, and soon new skin CELLS migrate into it and build up normal skin. *See also* MEDICINE; TRANSPLANTS.

Planetarium Facts
The ancestor of the planetarium is the orrery, a model of the planets in orbit around the Sun, first made in the 1700s. The first modern planetarium was opened by the Zeiss Company in Germany in 1923. The world's largest planetarium is in Japan and has a dome 90 feet high.

◀ *A plastic surgeon separates layers of skin cells before "sowing" them on small samples of skin to grow large pieces for use in skin grafts. These skin grafts are used as permanent grafts for victims of extensive burns. The skin is grown from tiny patches of healthy skin taken from the patient's body.*

Plastic surgery has been practiced for hundreds of years. Chinese and Indian doctors were reshaping noses and lips long ago. During the 15th century, surgeons were using practices that are still employed by today's plastic surgeons.

PLASTICS

All plastics consist of long chain molecules called polymers. There are two main types of plastics: thermosetting materials and thermoplastics. When thermoplastics are heated, the links between the chains break, allowing the chains to move across each other. The plastic becomes soft and it can be shaped and molded. It sets hard when cooled and the links between the chains re-form, but it softens again when heated. Plexiglas, polyethylene, and polyvinyl chloride (PVC) are examples of thermoplastics. Thermosetting plastics are composed of a network of interlinked chains which sets hard after it has been heated. Further heating will not soften the plastic again. Urethane foam, silicones, and epoxy resins are examples of thermosetting plastics.

Since celluloid was made from naturally occurring polymers, scientists have invented an enormous range of synthetic plastics with different properties. The main source of raw materials for plastics is petroleum. The first synthetic plastic was Bakelite, invented in 1908 by Leo Baekeland. It was a hard plastic and a good electrical insulator. Since then the plastics industry has grown into one of the world's biggest. The plastics industry in the United States includes over 25,000 companies. They produce about 20 million tons of plastics a year. Plastics are formed by injection molding, vacuum extrusion, and machining.

SEE FOR YOURSELF
Warm some whole milk in a saucepan. When it is simmering, slowly stir in a few teaspoons of vinegar. Keep stirring until it becomes rubbery. Just before it turns rubbery, add some red food coloring if you want colored plastic. Let it cool and wash it under running water. You now have your own "plastic."

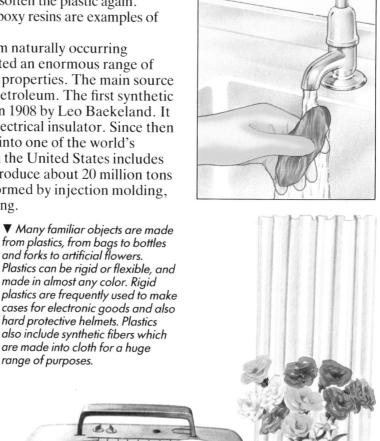

▼ Many familiar objects are made from plastics, from bags to bottles and forks to artificial flowers. Plastics can be rigid or flexible, and made in almost any color. Rigid plastics are frequently used to make cases for electronic goods and also hard protective helmets. Plastics also include synthetic fibers which are made into cloth for a huge range of purposes.

▲ Wire and cables with plastic insulation are produced in a wide range of colors, which helps to identify which wire is which in a complicated circuit. The plastic coating protects the wires, but is also flexible enough to allow the wires to be bent into any shape.

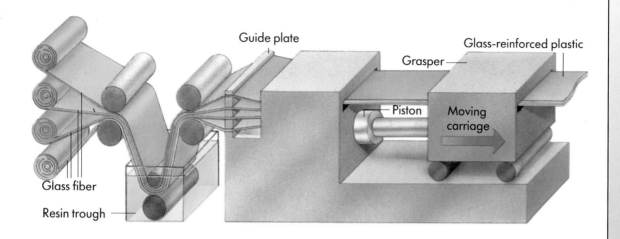

Guide plate

Glass-reinforced plastic

Grasper

Piston

Moving carriage

Glass fiber

Resin trough

▲ Thin layers of fiberglass can be bonded together with plastic to form a very strong, hard-wearing laminate. Laminating involves coating sheets of fiberglass with melted plastic resin, then stacking and squeezing these sheets together in a press. When the sticky resin hardens it holds the layers tightly together.

◄ Perspex or Plexiglas is a plastic that is see-through like glass but much stronger — ideal for making see-through squash courts that allow many more spectators.

▼ Hollow plastic shapes can be made by vacuum forming (for example egg boxes) or blow molding (for example bottles). Calendering coats a flexible material with a layer of plastic.

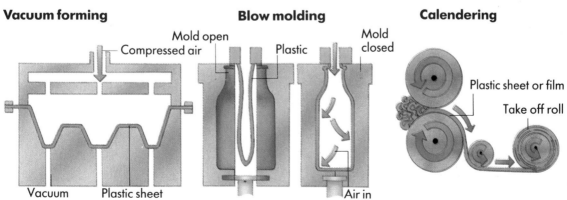

Vacuum forming

Compressed air

Vacuum

Plastic sheet

Blow molding

Mold open

Plastic

Mold closed

Air in

Calendering

Plastic sheet or film

Take off roll

See also EPOXY RESIN; EXTRUSION; INJECTION MOLDING; LAMINATES; MOLECULE; PETROLEUM; POLYMER; SYNTHETIC FIBERS; WIRE.

200 million years ago

135 million years ago

Today

←Direction of drift

▲ The map of the world has changed greatly over the last 200 million years as the continental plates have drifted apart.

▶ This diagram shows the main continental plates with their boundaries and the direction of movement.

Plate tectonics

Plate tectonics is the name given to the theory, developed in the late 1960s, for the mechanism of *continental drift*. The theory says that the EARTH's crust is made up of several giant plates of solid ROCK. These plates "float" on the moving molten rock of the Earth's mantle beneath. The plates fit together like a three-dimensional, spherical jigsaw. Continental drifting results from the movement of the crustal plates in relation to one another. It is usually believed that the movement is caused by what are termed "convection currents" which occur in the "plasticlike" material of the upper mantle. New crust is formed at the edges of plates where rising convection currents brings up new material from the mantle. Some plates may be "sliding" in relation to one another along margins where there are huge fault

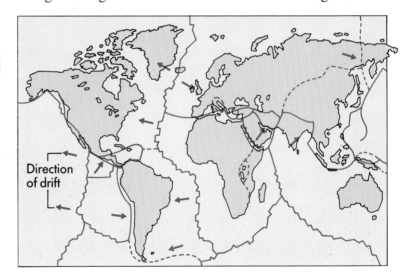

Direction of drift

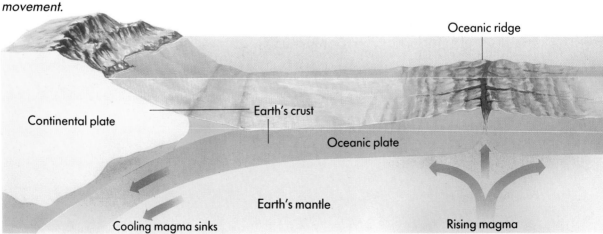

Oceanic ridge

Continental plate

Earth's crust

Oceanic plate

Earth's mantle

Cooling magma sinks

Rising magma

systems, such as that of the San Andreas fault system off the Californian coast. It is believed that MOUNTAIN building results from one crustal plate pushing into another, forcing the land upward under huge pressure.
See also EARTHQUAKES; VOLCANOES.

Platinum

Platinum is a heavy metallic ELEMENT which does not react with air, water, or strong ACIDS except a mixture of hydrochloric acid and nitric acid. Platinum is found in small quantities in NICKEL ore. It is a good electrical CONDUCTOR. This and its resistance to CORROSION make it suitable for use in electronic printed circuits and as high quality electrical contacts in switches and connectors. It can withstand high temperatures; it melts at 3,222°F (1,772°C). An ALLOY of platinum and iridium is even more resistant to heat and is used in instruments for measuring very high temperatures. Platinum is also used to make jewelry. Platinum black, a black form of platinum, is used as a CATALYST in chemical reactions. Platinum can absorb hydrogen and is used in CATALYTIC CONVERTERS for vehicles to help "clean" exhaust gases.

Pluto

Remote Pluto is the only PLANET in the SOLAR SYSTEM that has not been visited by a spacecraft. We still know very little about it. With a diameter of about 1,400 miles (2,280 km) it is even smaller than our Moon, and its one known satellite, Charon, is about half of Pluto's diameter. The two bodies are like a tiny "double planet".

▲ *Platinum is a valuable metal that does not corrode. It is used for making electrical contacts, laboratory apparatus, and jewelry.*

Platinum as a Catalyst
Platinum is an excellent catalyst — a substance that speeds up chemical reactions. This is why it is used in catalytic converters that clean up the exhaust emissions of cars. The platinum, often mixed with similar metals such as palladium and rhodium, causes pollutants such as carbon monoxide to change to substances such as water, oxygen, and carbon dioxide.

◀ *In the middle of the oceans, the seafloor spreads at ridges as molten magma wells up from the Earth's mantle. At the edges of oceans new mountain ranges can be pushed up as the oceanic plate collides with a continental plate. The continental plate is pushed down and melts as it heats up, turning to magma. Where there is a lot of magma, some of it pushes to the surface and triggers a volcanic eruption.*

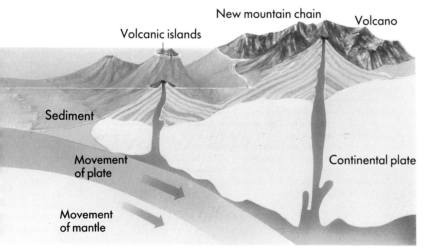

New mountain chain

Volcano

Volcanic islands

Sediment

Movement of plate

Movement of mantle

Continental plate

551

PLUTO

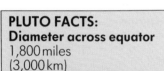

► *Pluto's frozen satellite Charon is about half as big as its parent planet. But Pluto itself is smaller than our Moon with a day that is more than six Earth days long.*

Pluto is named after the Greek god of the underworld. Its satellite Charon is named after the ferryman who took people across the river Styx, which was the only way into the underworld.

PLUTO FACTS:
Diameter across equator
1,800 miles
(3,000 km)
Average distance from Sun
3,660,000,000 miles
(5,900,000,000 km
Year length 248 years
Day length 6 days 9 hours
Mass 0.002 of Earth
Density 0.64 of Earth
Surface temperature
−382°F (−230°C)

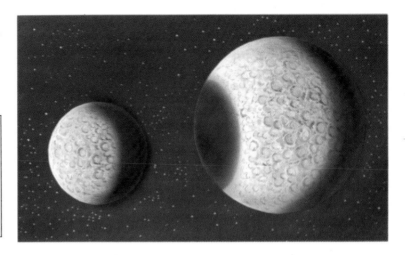

The orbit of Pluto is the most elliptical of all the planets, and in 1989 it was at its "perihelion," the moment when it was closest to the Sun. This last happened in 1741! Astronomers have recently detected a very thin atmosphere of METHANE gas, but it is possible that this only forms near perihelion. When Pluto is at the far reaches of its orbit the Sun's heating effect is less than half as strong, and the gas may freeze back on the surface again during the 21st century.

Pluto is so tiny that no one has ever seen any details on it, although it is likely to be a rocky body with a coating of methane ice. However, astronomers know that there are lighter and darker areas on its surface which suggests that it may have brighter ice caps at the poles and darker material near its equator. A study of its nightly changes in brightness shows that Pluto and Charon always present the same faces to each other, spinning on their axes in the 6 days 9 hours it takes Charon to complete one whole orbit.

▼ *Pluto is tiny, about one-sixth the diameter of the Earth and weighs only one five-hundredth as much as Earth.*

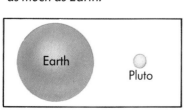

Percival Lowell (1855–1916)
Lowell was a United States astronomer who predicted the existence of Pluto by studying the orbits of Neptune and Uranus, its neighboring planets. The planet was finally discovered in 1930, 14 years after Lowell's death. Lowell also studied Mars, wrongly concluding that it was covered with canals and vegetation.

Plutonium

Plutonium is a RADIOACTIVE element and one of the most dangerous known. Small quantities of plutonium are found in URANIUM ore, but most of it is made inside NU-CLEAR REACTORS. Plutonium was first detected when it was made in a laboratory in the United States in 1940 by bombarding uranium with heavy particles called deuterons. They changed the uranium into the new element, plutonium. One form or ISOTOPE of plutonium, known as plutonium-239, is fissionable, that is, its ATOMS split apart releasing huge amounts of ENERGY. This makes it suitable for use as a nuclear FUEL for reactors and weapons. Plutonium is also used in small nuclear power generators carried by SPACE PROBES such as the Voyager and Pioneer probes that flew past the outer planets.

▲ A scientist removes a single plutonium fuel rod from a bundle of rods for an experimental nuclear reactor. The scientist is protected from the harmful effects of the radiation by the rod's coating of stainless steel.

Pneumatics

Pneumatics describes the TECHNOLOGY of machines and tools that make or use compressed AIR. Air-powered equipment has several advantages over electrically powered equipment. There is no possibility of air-powered equipment causing an electric shock or producing a spark that might start a fire in a flammable atmosphere, or detonate an explosive atmosphere.

Pneumatic machines and tools are driven by two main types of pneumatic motors. One consists of a shaft fitted with vanes, like a propeller. The vaned shaft is housed inside an airtight chamber. Air from a compressor is supplied to the chamber, where it blows against the vanes and spins the shaft. A grinding wheel or a drill may be fixed to the shaft. The second type of pneumatic

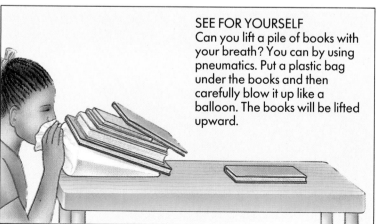

SEE FOR YOURSELF
Can you lift a pile of books with your breath? You can by using pneumatics. Put a plastic bag under the books and then carefully blow it up like a balloon. The books will be lifted upward.

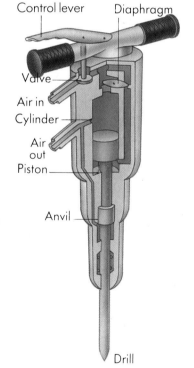

Control lever   Diaphragm
Valve
Air in
Cylinder
Air out
Piston
Anvil
Drill

▲ A jackhammer makes use of the power of compressed air to cut into hard materials such as rock and concrete.

Poison Any substance that can injure the body.
Toxin Any poisonous substance from plants or animals.
Venom A poisonous substance made by some snakes and scorpions.

The most deadly poison produced by any animal comes from the skin of the Kokoi arrow-poison frog that lives in Colombia, South America. About 0.0000003 ounce of the substance is enough to kill a human being. About an ounce of the poison could kill over two million people.

▼ There are poisonous members of both the plant and animal kingdoms, such as deadly nightshade and the Amanita pantherina toadstool known as the panther. The largest group of poisonous animals are snakes (although not all snakes are poisonous), and there are also poisonous frogs and spiders.

motor uses a piston in a cylinder. Compressed air forces the piston to move in one direction. A spring or the PRESSURE of air on the other side of the piston makes it return again. The rapid back and forth "reciprocating" action can power hammer drills used in MINING. Many trucks and trains use air-operated brakes.

Poisons

Any substance that damages or destroys living tissue is a poison. It is difficult to define a poison very accurately because almost any substance is poisonous if we take in enough, even salt or water. In large amounts, commonly used DRUGS, even aspirin, are also poisonous. Many dangerous poisons are produced by plants as a protection against being eaten, while snakes and spiders use poison to subdue their prey, as well as for defense. Poisons are recorded from the earliest known times, and they were used by the ancient Chinese, Greeks, and Egyptians for medical purposes and for murder.

Poisons may enter the body through the mouth, or can be inhaled, or pass through the SKIN. Some poisons like ACIDS and CAUSTIC SODA destroy tissue directly, but others work by interfering with the CHEMICAL REACTIONS that support life. Some of the most powerful poisons affect the NERVES, and similar but less dangerous poisons are used in fly sprays. Some poisons are difficult for the body to get rid of, so they build up until they begin to damage the body.

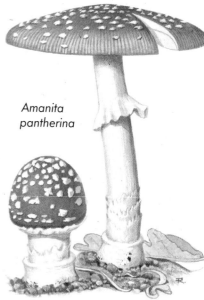

Amanita pantherina

Arrow poison frog

Coral snake

Deadly nightshade

Polarized light

Polarized light is LIGHT in which the direction of its vibrating waves is limited in some way. Normally, the light we see is made up of waves vibrating in a mixture of directions. Light is a form of ELECTROMAGNETIC RADIATION and so is made up of an electric field and a magnetic field vibrating at right angles to each other. If all the electric fields in a light ray vibrate in one direction only, this is described as polarized light. Polarization occurs when light passes through some CRYSTALS or when it is reflected by a surface. Light waves vibrating in one direction pass through or are reflected, while waves vibrating in all other directions are absorbed. A material that polarizes light is known as a polarizer. Polarizers are used in sunglasses; sunlight that is reflected upward from the ground is partly polarized, so the sunglasses can be used to cut out a higher proportion of this glare from the Sun than they do of other light. The light from a LASER is also polarized.

All forms of electromagnetic radiation, including RADIO waves, can be polarized.

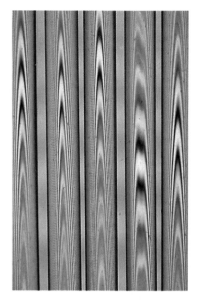

▲ Polarized light reveals stresses in plastics as bands of rainbow colors. This photograph is a close-up of toothbrush bristles.

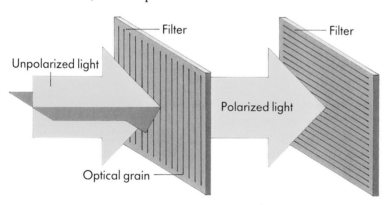

Unpolarized light

Filter

Polarized light

Filter

Optical grain

◄ Polarized light vibrates in one direction only, unlike ordinary (unpolarized) light which vibrates in two directions at right angles. A Polaroid filter lets through only polarized light, which can be blocked by a second Polaroid filter if its grain is at right angles to the first one.

Polaroid camera

A Polaroid camera produces photographs that are already developed. Most CAMERAS use FILM that has to be removed from the camera to be developed and printed. In 1948, the U.S. inventor Edwin Land developed the Polaroid Land camera. Early versions used a film pack in which each segment of film came with its own pod of chemicals. When a photograph was taken, the film was ejected from the camera through a pair of rollers. These burst the pod and spread the chemicals across the film. The film was made in two parts. The exposed film had to

▲ Even the first Polaroid Land cameras were lightweight and designed for everyday use.

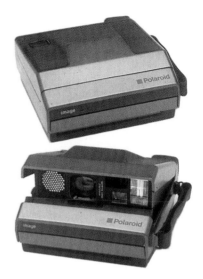

◀ In this type of polaroid camera, the film passes through rollers which burst a pod of chemicals spread between the two layers of film. After 60 seconds the two layers are peeled apart, revealing the photograph underneath.

▶ This polaroid camera is more modern. The film develops in daylight without any need to time the development or peel a layer off.

be timed for 60 seconds or so and then the two halves were peeled apart revealing the photograph underneath. A later version produced a film that would develop by itself in daylight without any need to time the development or peel off a layer.

Poles

The EARTH has two sets of poles, the geographic and the magnetic poles. The geographic poles are the points that represent the ends of the axis about which the PLANET spins or rotates. The two poles are referred to as the North Pole and the South Pole and are at LATITUDES of 90° North and 90° South.

The Earth also behaves like a huge bar magnet and the end of a magnet that is attracted toward the magnetic North Pole is known as the north pole of the magnet. Unfortunately, magnetic north and magnetic south do not correspond exactly with geographic north and south because the axis of the Earth's magnetism does not precisely coincide with the Earth's axis of ROTATION. Magnetic compasses have to be adjusted to compensate for the difference in position.

▼ A bar magnet has two poles, called north and south poles, where its magnetism is concentrated. The Earth also has a pair of magnetic poles, and behaves as if there were a giant magnet through the middle of the planet between the North Pole and the South Pole.

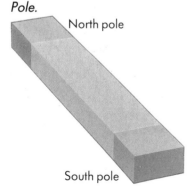

North pole

South pole

▶ The Earth's North Pole is covered by an ocean on which floats a thick layer of ice. The South Pole is on land — the continent of Antarctica. It too is covered with a thick layer of ice.

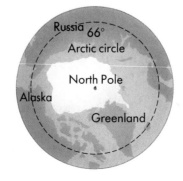

Russia 66°
Arctic circle
North Pole
Alaska
Greenland

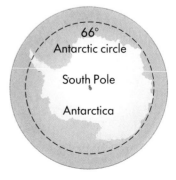

66°
Antarctic circle
South Pole
Antarctica

Pollen and Pollination

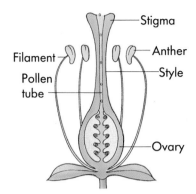

Pollination is the first stage in the REPRODUCTION of flowering plants. It is the process by which the pollen is transferred from the stamens to the stigmas of FLOWERS. The dustlike pollen itself is produced by the stamens and it contains the male gametes or sex CELLS. The stigma is on the female part of the flower, and when it receives the right kind of pollen, the flower begins to make SEEDS. The pollen grows down the stigma into the ovary, where FERTILIZATION takes place when the male sex cells join with the female ones.

▲ *Pollination occurs when pollen is transferred from the male stamens (made up of an anther and a filament) to the female stigma of a flower.*

Some flowers can be *self-pollinated* with their own pollen, but most flowers prevent this, often by having the stamens and stigmas ripening at different times. These flowers need to be *cross-pollinated* with pollen from another flower of the same kind, usually one from another plant. Most flowers employ insects to carry their pollen. The insects are attracted by the flowers' scent and bright COLORS and by their sweet nectar. While drinking a flower's nectar an insect picks up pollen on its body, and when it visits another flower it brushes some of this pollen on to the stigmas. Grasses and many trees use the wind to carry their pollen. Their flowers are small and dull but scatter large amounts of pollen from their hanging stamens. Their stigmas are usually large and feathery to trap the pollen.

SEE FOR YOURSELF
You can help the pollination of a self-pollinating plant by shaking the anthers of one flower so that the pollen falls on the stigma of another flower. Gardeners pollinate flowers using a brush to transfer pollen from one plant to another.

Pollution

Pollution is the term used to describe all the ways in which the natural ENVIRONMENT is contaminated by harmful or unpleasant substances, such as industrial waste, in the form of liquids or gases. *See* pages 558 and 559.

▲ *Pollen may be spread by the wind, as it is from these birch tree catkins (top), or on the legs and hairs of insects such as bees (bottom).*

POLLUTION

Air or water which contains substances at levels harmful to wildlife or humans is described as polluted. Air pollution occurs when harmful gases, such as carbon monoxide, are released into the atmosphere. Cars are a major source of carbon monoxide. Similarly, water pollution results from harmful materials, such as aluminum or industrial waste, being released into rivers, lakes, and seas accidentally or even deliberately. Pollution can include thermal (heat) pollution when, for example, industries release hot but otherwise clean water which has been used for cooling into a river; raising the water temperature may be harmful to the river's wildlife.

Modern farming methods can cause water pollution. When large numbers of farm animals are kept in small areas, the liquid dung, or slurry, they produce may find its way into rivers, ponds, and streams. It is very rich in nitrates, which cause some of the water plants to grow very rapidly. The plants choke the water and use up all the oxygen so that the other wildlife may die.

Some of the worst air pollution caused by sulfur dioxide from old factories has been almost completely eliminated by clean air controls. However, the gases produced by burning fossil fuels, in particular from vehicle exhausts, are still causing concern. Nitrogen oxide and sulfur dioxide combine with moisture in the atmosphere and fall to Earth as acid rain, which damages buildings, poisons lakes, and destroys forests. Some governments require industries to clean up waste before releasing it.

▲ The dumping of garbage spoils the landscape and causes pollution. If more packaging was biodegradable (able to be broken down by bacteria) this type of pollution would be reduced.

▼ Exhaust fumes from road vehicles, smoke from factory chimneys, and burning refuse are all causes of air pollution. Our rivers are polluted by the dumping of industrial waste and chemical fertilizers being washed into them. The sea is being contaminated by sewage, oil spills, and the dumping of highly toxic materials.

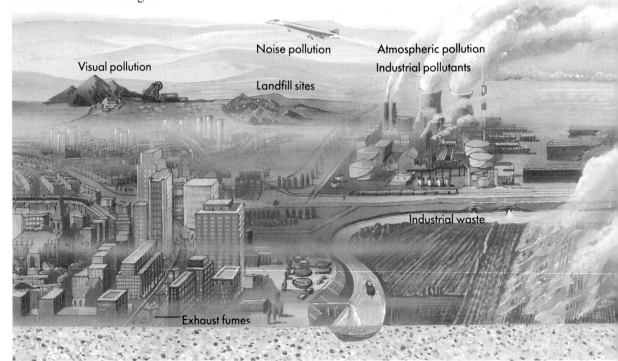

Noise pollution

Visual pollution

Landfill sites

Atmospheric pollution

Industrial pollutants

Industrial waste

Exhaust fumes

◄ The Exxon Valdez *oil tanker released 35,000 tons of toxic oil off the coast of Alaska. Although attempts were made to clean up the oil, thousands of seabirds and many other animals were killed by this environmental disaster.*

Reduction in energy use and pollution by reusing resources

Paper — Energy use 40%, Pollution 47%
Aluminum — Energy use 95%, Pollution 97%
Glass — Energy use 40%, Pollution 55%

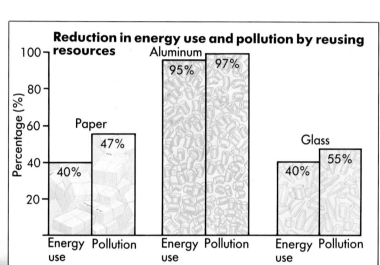

▲ *Centuries of air pollution have blackened the stonework of this church, which is white where it has been cleaned.*

◄ *Recycling waste materials helps to reduce pollution and saves energy. This graph shows the reductions in the use of energy and of pollution if paper, glass, and aluminum cans are made from recycled material rather than new raw materials.*

Exhaust fumes

Fertilizers

Pesticides

Nuclear pollution

Marine pollution

Oil slick

Incinerating

Dumping

See also AIR POLLUTION; CONSERVATION, ENVIRONMENTAL; FOSSIL FUELS; HEAT; NOISE; RECYCLING; WASTE DISPOSAL; WATER POLLUTION.

Except for a **square** (a regular four-sided polygon) and a **triangle** (which takes its name from its three angles), polygons are named after their number of sides: **pentagon** (five-sided), **hexagon** (six), **heptagon** (seven), **octagon** (eight), **nonagon** (nine), **decagon** (ten), and so on.

▶ *The illustration shows five regular polygons, with all their sides and internal angles equal, and three irregular ones. The last shape, an example of an irregular four-sided polygon, is called a quadrilateral.*

Polygon

Polygon is a term used in GEOMETRY to describe a plane shape bounded by straight lines. The word polygon comes originally from the Greek words *poly* (meaning many) and *gonia* (meaning angles). Polygons are named according to the number of sides or angles that they have; for example, a hexagon has six sides.

Polygons are all around us. The honeycomb made by bees is hexagonal, as are metal nuts. Certain foreign coins and ceramic tiles are also regular polygons. A poly-

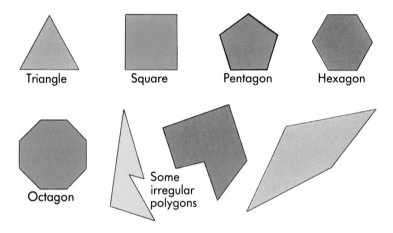

Triangle   Square   Pentagon   Hexagon

Octagon   Some irregular polygons

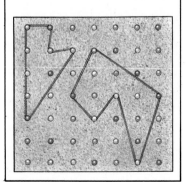

gon is regular when all its angles are the same and all its sides are the same length. For example, all triangles are polygons but only equilateral triangles with three equal sides and angles are regular polygons. Isosceles triangles with two equal sides and angles and right-angled triangles with no equal sides or angles are irregular.

Some regular polygons will fit together without overlapping so that they can completely cover an area. They are said to tessellate. Some polygons will not tessellate on their own but will with another polygon. *See also* MATHEMATICS.

Polymer

A polymer is a chemical COMPOUND that has very large MOLECULES made up of thousands of smaller molecules joined together. Rubber, wool, and CELLULOSE are polymers that occur naturally in plants and animals. Artificial polymers include all PLASTICS, such as NYLON and polystyrene. In many polymers, the smaller molecules (*monomers*) join end-to-end and form chains.

The chemical names of polymers are formed by adding the prefix *poly-* to the name of the monomer of which it is made. Many polymers are known by their old chemical names and some are also known by their initials or trade names.

Monomer	Polymer	Other name
amide	polyamide	nylon
ester	polyester	Dacron
ethene (ethylene)	polyethene (polyethylene)	polythene
phenylethene (styrene)	polyphenylethene (polystyrene)	Styrofoam
tetrafluoroethene	polytetrafluoroethene	PTFE, Teflon
chloroethene (vinyl chloride)	polychloroethene (polyvinyl chloride)	PVC

Large Molecules
Not all large molecules are polymers. Large molecules can be known as macromolecules, for example, proteins are macromolecules because, although they consist of lots of amino acids, the amino acids are all different. Polymers are also large but are made up of lots of the same units (the monomer).

Many natural FIBERS, such as silk, contain long-chain polymers. In some polymers the chains are kinked, as in rubber. When rubber is stretched the chains straighten out, but they snap back when the force is removed. This is what makes rubber and some plastics elastic. In other polymers, the monomers link together in all directions to form a strong network, as in rigid plastics such as Plexiglas and melamine.

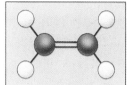

Ethene (monomer)

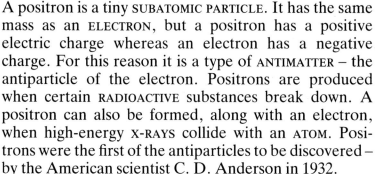

Polyethylene (polymer)

▲ Many polymers are formed when monomer molecules join together end-to-end to form long chains. Cross-links between chains make the polymer harder and less flexible.

Positron

A positron is a tiny SUBATOMIC PARTICLE. It has the same mass as an ELECTRON, but a positron has a positive electric charge whereas an electron has a negative charge. For this reason it is a type of ANTIMATTER – the antiparticle of the electron. Positrons are produced when certain RADIOACTIVE substances break down. A positron can also be formed, along with an electron, when high-energy X-RAYS collide with an ATOM. Positrons were the first of the antiparticles to be discovered – by the American scientist C. D. Anderson in 1932.

Potassium

Potassium is a silvery white ELEMENT. It is a METAL so soft that it can be cut with a knife. Potassium is very reactive, and occurs in nature only in COMPOUNDS. Chief of these is potassium chloride, which is found dissolved in seawater and as solid deposits that can be dug out of the ground. Potassium is an essential element for plants and animals, which obtain it from their food. Farmers add FERTILIZERS containing potassium compounds, such as potash, to the SOIL. Potassium reacts violently with water to form hydrogen and

Scientists have developed many uses for potassium and its compounds:
potassium carbonate, also called potash, is used in making glass and soap,
potassium nitrate, also called saltpeter, is used in explosives and matches,
potassium bromide is used in medicine as a sedative,
potassium chloride is widely used as a fertilizer.

▶ *Potassium dichromate forms bright orange crystals. The substance is a powerful oxidizing agent (a substance that combines easily with oxygen) and is used in making glass, printed circuits, and fireworks.*

▼ *Cups, saucers, and even figures made out of clay are fired (roasted) in a kiln to convert them into pottery. Later they are glazed to make them waterproof.*

▼ *Bone china is a type of fine porcelain made from kaolin (China clay), the mineral petuntse (China stone), and bones that have been roasted and ground to a powder. They are mixed with water to make clay, which is molded to make an object. The object is fired in a kiln to harden it, painted with a glaze, and fired again.*

alkaline potassium hydroxide, which is also known as caustic potash. Potassium hydroxide is a useful chemical, employed in some BATTERIES and in making SOAP and special kinds of GLASS.
See also CAUSTIC SODA; PERIODIC TABLE; SODIUM.

Potential energy *See* Energy

Pottery and Porcelain

Pottery and porcelain are materials made from clay that has been heated to high TEMPERATURES. They are used to make containers and decorative objects. A clay object made by an artist or molded in a machine, dries and becomes dull and porous. To make it waterproof, it is first fired in a KILN to dry and harden it and then covered with a glaze. When fired again at a higher temperature, the glaze melts and forms a glassy layer over the clay. Colored glazes are used to decorate objects. The style and decoration of pottery gives archeologists clues to who made it and when.

Porcelain is very fine pottery made from white china clay or kaolin instead of red or brown clay. Imitation porcelain can be made from kaolin and sand or lime.
See also CERAMICS; GLASS.

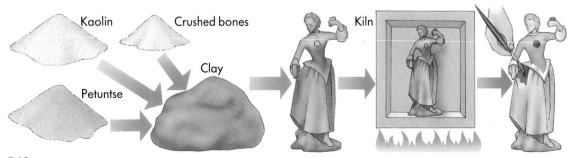

Kaolin   Crushed bones   Kiln

Petuntse   Clay

Power

Power is the rate at which ENERGY is turned from one form into another. The SI UNIT of power is the WATT (W). Power is important because almost all the processes in our everyday lives involve using energy to do WORK. For example, the power of the ENGINE in a vehicle is the rate at which it can turn the chemical energy stored in the FUEL into mechanical energy to drive the vehicle; the power of a LIGHT BULB is the rate at which it can turn electrical energy into HEAT and LIGHT. Our bodies too produce power; for example, they can convert the energy present in food into heat energy and mechanical energy. Usually a part of the energy that is put into any device is not turned into the useful form of energy that is needed but is wasted; for example, a vehicle engine converts much of the chemical energy in its fuel into heat and vibrational energy.

Since energy cannot be created, all the power which is used must come from a source of stored energy such as FOSSIL FUELS or NUCLEAR ENERGY.

See also CONSERVATION; EFFICIENCY; NUTRITION.

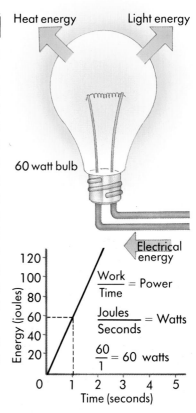

$$\frac{\text{Work}}{\text{Time}} = \text{Power}$$

$$\frac{\text{Joules}}{\text{Seconds}} = \text{Watts}$$

$$\frac{60}{1} = 60 \text{ watts}$$

▲ *Power is the rate of doing work — that is, the rate at which one form of energy is converted into another form of energy. The graph shows how an electric light converts electrical energy into light and heat at a rate of 60 joules per second. A watt is the power needed to perform one joule of work per second. The power of the lamp is therefore 60 watts.*

James Watt (1736–1819)

Watt was a British engineer and inventor whose improvements to the steam engine made it into a useful source of power. In 1764 he invented an outside condenser (which turned waste steam back into water). He then designed engines in which the steam acted on both sides of the piston. The watt (unit of power) was named after him.

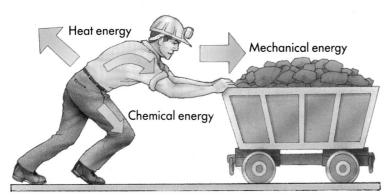

◀ *Various kinds of energy conversions are involved when a man pushes a heavy truck. Chemical energy, used up in his muscles, is converted partly into heat (which is why hard work makes you hot) and partly into mechanical energy to move the truck. Formerly measured in horsepower, power is now measured in watts.*

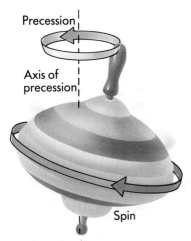

▲ *The axis of a spinning top gradually moves in a circle because of precession. As the top slows down, the circle of precession gets larger and larger until the top wobbles and finally falls over.*

▶ *The Earth's axis undergoes precession caused by the gravitational pull of the Moon, Sun, and planets on the Earth. The two points in the sky that are in line with the axis (north and south) are called the celestial poles. Because of precession, these are also moving. At present, the north celestial pole points toward the North Star, Polaris. But in 11,000 years time the axis will have moved to point toward the bright star Vega, which will become the new "north star."*

Precipitation is a meteorologist's word for rain, snow, hail, and so on. But to a chemist, precipitation is what happens when a solid substance is formed in a solution. The solid is called a precipitate. Chemists often make precipitates during chemical analysis because the way they are formed and their color helps to identify substances.

Precession

Precession is the gradual change in direction of the axis of a spinning body such as the EARTH. The spinning Earth is like a huge top, but its axis is not fixed. This is because the gravitational forces of the Sun and Moon are pulling on the slight bulge around the equator. If the Earth did not spin, these forces would have pulled our planet "upright" so that the Sun was exactly in line with the equator. Instead, there is a struggle between these gravitational pulls and the Earth's gyroscopic inertia, making the Earth's axis slowly revolve in space. The axis will have moved in a complete circle in 26,000 years. (A spinning object such as a top has "gyroscopic inertia" which means that it stays spinning on its axis at the same angle and can be hard to push over.)

See also GRAVITY; GYROSCOPE; TIDES.

Circle of precession
Earth's axis
Equatorial bulge
Gravitational pull
Equator
Gravitational pull of Sun, Moon, and other planets on Earth's equatorial bulge
Ecliptic axis

Precipitation

Precipitation is the word meteorologists use to describe all of the solid (snow, hail, frost) and liquid (rain, drizzle, mist, dew) WATER released by the ATMOSPHERE. Usually, precipitation includes that water which falls to the ground and which can be measured using a carefully made rain gauge. Sometimes, however, the precipitation released by clouds evaporates before reaching the Earth's surface. This is because some types of clouds are quite thin and hold relatively small amounts of water VAPOR.

Usually, when the temperature falls to 32°F (0°C), liquid water freezes and becomes solid ICE. Ice, like other solids, has a regular arrangement of its ATOMS. Before water can freeze to ice, there must be some kind of nucleus, such as a speck of dust, in the water. This nucleus enables the regular atomic structure of the ice to form around it. If the water is pure and contains no dust, the temperature of water can fall below 32° (0°C) without turning to ice. This water is supercooled.

Precipitation falls from a cloud when the tiny droplets of water join the supercooled drops and fall as rain. Sometimes CRYSTALS of ice form high in the clouds and join with the supercooled drops to grow and become snowflakes. In some cases where the precipitation might have fallen as snow, it changes to a mixture of snowflakes and drizzle which is sometimes known as sleet. Hail (pellets of hard, stonelike ice) forms in the great cumulonimbus clouds where drops of supercooled water are blown about and freeze instantly among the ice crystals at the top of the cloud. The hailstones become larger until they are big enough to fall.

SEE FOR YOURSELF
Make a rain gauge using a jar, a plastic funnel with the same diameter as the jar and a piece of stiff plastic. Bury the jar in the ground, make a small hole in the piece of plastic and put the spout of the funnel through it, put them over the jar.

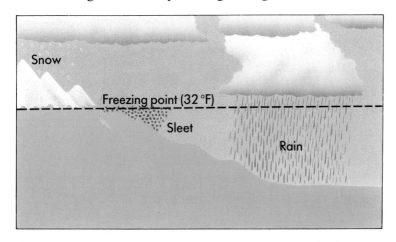

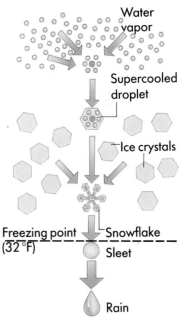

▲ Precipitation takes the form of snow or rain depending on the air temperature. Below the freezing point of water, it falls as sleet or rain.

▼ Snow consists of tiny crystals of ice. Every snow crystal is different but they are all hexagonal, based on a six-pointed star.

▲ Water vapor in clouds condenses to form supercooled droplets that will crystallize to snow flakes if the air is cold enough. As these fall they may meet warmer air and change into sleet and finally into raindrops.

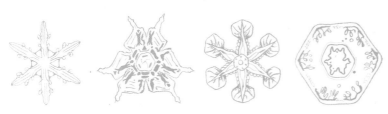

Blaise Pascal (1623–1662)
Pascal was a French mathematician and physicist. When he was only 20 he made the first mechanical calculator. He used mercury barometers to study pressure, and discovered that pressure is transmitted equally through a fluid in all directions (Pascal's principle). Using this principle he invented the hydraulic press. After 1654 he devoted himself solely to religious philosophy.

Excited gas molecule under pressure

▲ *A gas exerts a pressure because its molecules move rapidly and bounce off the sides of its container. If the gas is compressed, to get more of it into the container, it exerts a higher pressure.*

566

Pressure

The pressure exerted by a FORCE on a surface is the strength of the force divided by the area of the surface to which it is applied (pounds per square inch). The SI UNIT of pressure is the pascal (Pa). One pascal corresponds to a force of one newton for every square meter of surface. The smaller the area of the surface on which the force acts, the larger the pressure. For example, if the weight of a person whose mass is 110 pounds (50 kg) is supported by the soles of ordinary shoes whose area is 15 square inches (100 cm^2), the pressure on the floor is about 50,000 Pa. If the same person is supported by high heels whose area is $^1/_8$ square inch (1 cm^2), the pressure on the floor is about 5,000,000 Pa. This is the same as the pressure from a truck with a mass of 5 tons supported by tires of area 15 square inches (100 cm^2)!

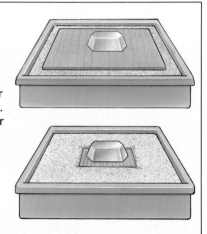

SEE FOR YOURSELF
Pressure is the force acting per unit surface area. You can demonstrate this with a tray of fine dry sand, a heavy weight, and two pieces of cardboard or thin wood, one small, one large. First put the weight on the larger piece of cardboard placed on the sand. See how far it sinks into the sand. Then put the weight on the small piece of cardboard. The pressure is now much greater and it sinks deeper.

A FLUID (a LIQUID or a GAS) exerts a pressure on any surface with which it comes into contact, for example, its container. This pressure comes from the collisions of the ATOMS or MOLECULES of the fluid with the container. The pressure depends on the DENSITY of the fluid, in other words on how many molecules are in a given volume, and on the TEMPERATURE. As the temperature is raised, the molecules hit the surface more often and more quickly, so the pressure goes up.

The air in the ATMOSPHERE exerts a pressure of about 100 kPa (a kPa is one thousand pascals) at sea level (14.7 pounds per square inch).

Priestley, Joseph *See* Oxygen

Printing

Printing is a process for producing copies of text and pictures, usually on PAPER. The oldest printing method was invented in China about the 6th century A.D. and 500 years later the Chinese invented movable type. Characters were carved which could be put together to make different words. Movable type was reinvented in Europe by a German, Johannes Gutenberg, in the 15th century. William Caxton set up the first printing press in Britain in 1476. Printing enabled books and leaflets to be printed in large numbers, rapidly spreading knowledge.

The platen press, which printed one sheet at a time, was replaced by the rotary press, which prints continuously on a roll of paper. Printing using movable type is called letterpress. In lithography, the printing plate is smooth. The image, whether text or illustration, is transferred onto the plate as a greasy layer. The rest of the

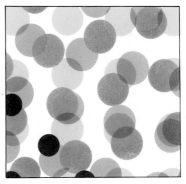

▲ *Printed photographs appear to have various colors and depths of color, or tones. This effect is achieved using dots of three colors and black, and varying the sizes of the dots to create tones. This is how they look when greatly enlarged.*

SEE FOR YOURSELF
You can print letters or designs by cutting them onto the surface of a sliced potato. Dip your block into paint or ink and press it onto a sheet of paper. You will need to cut away all the parts you do not want to print, leaving a raised design. Letters have to be cut backward to print the right way around.

▼ *A press for printing colored pictures uses four different inks on four cylindrical printing plates, one each for yellow, magenta (red), cyan (blue), and black. Each color is printed in turn, one after the other. Mixed together, these four give the effect of all other colors. Use a magnifying glass to look at one of the color photographs in this book, and you will see that the image is made up of tiny printed dots of yellow, magenta, cyan, and black ink.*

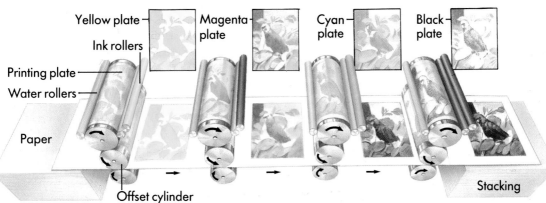

Yellow plate — Magenta plate — Cyan plate — Black plate

Ink rollers

Printing plate —
Water rollers —

Paper

Offset cylinder

Stacking

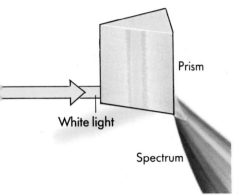

Prism

White light

Spectrum

▲ *A prism splits a beam of white light into the colors of the spectrum. This is because white light is really a mixture of all the colors. A prism bends light rays, but it bends each color by a slightly different amount, and so separates them.*

plate is covered with grease-repelling material such as water. When greasy ink is applied to the plate, it sticks to the greasy areas only. In gravure printing, the image is etched in the plate by acid. Ink applied to the plate is trapped by holes etched by the acid. The rest of the plate is polished clean and the inky image transferred onto paper. Color images are produced by using a mixture of colored inks. Today, text can be edited and pages designed and printed using a COMPUTER system.

Prism

A prism is a solid figure. The most common kind is a triangular prism, which resembles a wedge. Optical prisms of GLASS or clear PLASTIC can bend LIGHT that enters them, and are used instead of MIRRORS in optical instruments and some kinds of cameras. A prism can also split white light into its colored SPECTRUM.
See also COLOR; RAINBOW; REFRACTION.

SEE FOR YOURSELF
You can split sunlight into the colors of the spectrum by using water as a prism. Put a bowl of water near a sunny window and arrange a sloping mirror and a piece of cardboard (for a screen) as shown in the diagram. When the Sun comes out, adjust the angle of the mirror until it projects a spectrum onto the cardboard screen.

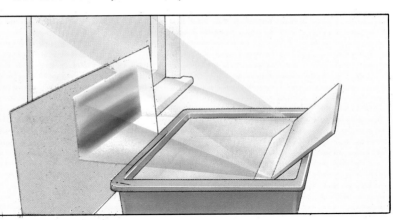

First flip

$\frac{1}{2}$ $\frac{1}{2}$

Second flip

$\frac{1}{4}$ $\frac{1}{4}$ $\frac{1}{4}$ $\frac{1}{4}$

▲ *Toss a coin twice. The first toss gives, a head, or a tail, so does the second toss. The probability of two heads is $^1/_4$.*

568

Probability

Probability is the measure of the chance of an event occurring. In MATHEMATICS we use a scale from 0 to 1 to define the probability of a given event with 0 as impossible and 1 as absolutely certain. For example, if it is Thursday the probability of tomorrow being Friday is 1 while the probability of it being Monday is 0.

All probabilities lie within these extremes and are expressed as a RATIO of the number of times a possible event could occur to the total number of possible outcomes. For example, a coin tossed once has a $^1/_2$ chance of coming down heads. There is one chance of it being heads but there are two possible outcomes.

Probability of throwing a number greater than two

Possible outcomes

Successful outcomes

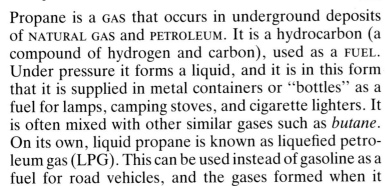

Probability of throwing greater than two is therefore four out of six or $\frac{4}{6} = \frac{2}{3}$

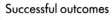

How to Work it Out
If you roll a die, what is the probability of rolling a number higher than 2? Four of the six possible numbers are greater than 2, so the probability of rolling one of them is $^4/_6 = ^2/_3$. Put another way, if you roll the die a great number of times, two out of every three rolls will give a number greater than 2.

Probability theory cannot predict the outcome of a single random event, but over many occurrences a pattern can be built up. For example, we cannot predict what number will turn up when we throw a die, but over thousands of throws we would expect to get the same occurrence of each number because the probability of each number is $^1/_6$. If we threw the die 6,000 times, we would expect to get almost exactly 1,000 twos, for example.

Propane

Propane is a GAS that occurs in underground deposits of NATURAL GAS and PETROLEUM. It is a hydrocarbon (a compound of hydrogen and carbon), used as a FUEL. Under pressure it forms a liquid, and it is in this form that it is supplied in metal containers or "bottles" as a fuel for lamps, camping stoves, and cigarette lighters. It is often mixed with other similar gases such as *butane*. On its own, liquid propane is known as liquefied petroleum gas (LPG). This can be used instead of gasoline as a fuel for road vehicles, and the gases formed when it

SEE FOR YOURSELF
If you toss 2 coins together, what is the probability of getting a head and a tail? These are the possibilities:
First coin Second coin
Head Head
Head Tail
Tail Tail
Tail Head
Since each possibility is equally likely, the probability of two heads is $^1/_4$, once out of 4 times (the same as two tails). But a head and a tail has a probability of $^2/_4 = ^1/_2$.

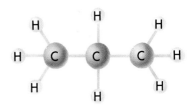

Alkane Name	Number of Carbon Atoms	Formula	State at 32°F (0°C)
Methane	1	CH_4	Gas
Ethane	2	C_2H_6	Gas
Propane	3	C_3H_8	Gas
Butane	4	C_4H_{10}	Gas
Pentane	5	C_5H_{12}	Liquid
Hexane	6	C_6H_{14}	Liquid
Hexadecane	16	$C_{16}H_{34}$	Solid

▲ Propane, formula C_3H_8, is a gas. It is the third member of the series of hydrocarbons called alkanes.

burns do not cause POLLUTION of the ATMOSPHERE. Propane belongs to a series of organic chemicals called alkanes, all of which burn in air to form carbon dioxide and water. The simplest is the gas METHANE. Other alkanes are liquids, including gasoline and kerosene.

Protein

Proteins are large MOLECULES made from amino acids that all organisms need. Humans cannot absorb protein from food, so it is broken down by DIGESTION, releasing the smaller amino acids which can be absorbed. These amino acids are used to build new proteins.

Amino acids

▲ Propane used as a fuel for engines causes less pollution than gasoline.

▶ Proteins are made up of amino acids; different combinations of amino acids give different kinds of proteins.

In the CELLS of the human body, proteins are built up from combinations of 20 different amino acids. These are joined together in strings which become folded to give the new protein molecule. There are thousands of different types, but they are all constructed to form a similar pattern. The order in which the amino acids are strung together governs the property of the protein. This buildup of protein from amino acids takes place in all organisms. A large part of the solid material of animals is made of protein, for example, the MUSCLES. Enzymes and other important compounds are also proteins. Protein can be broken down and used as a source of energy by the body in extreme circumstances. This is why people who are starved become very thin. Their fat breaks down first, followed by protein in their muscles.

▲ Foods rich in protein are meat, fish, cheese, and eggs. High-protein vegetable foods include legumes, such as peas and beans, and nuts.

Proton

A proton is a positively charged SUBATOMIC PARTICLE. They are found inside the nucleus at the center of an ATOM, along with other particles, the NEUTRONS. Protons are slightly lighter than neutrons but about 2,000 times heavier than ELECTRONS. The simplest atomic nucleus, that of HYDROGEN, contains just one proton. The positive electrical charge of protons attracts the negatively charged electrons in the atom to the atom's nucleus.

Johannes Hans Jensen (1907–1973)
Jensen was a German physicist who in 1949 developed the theory that the protons and neutrons within the nucleus of an atom are arranged in layers or "shells". A nucleus with filled shells is particularly stable. He shared the 1963 Nobel Prize in Physics for this work.

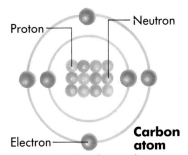

Proton — Neutron

Electron — **Carbon atom**

▲ An un-ionized atom has as many protons and neutrons in its nucleus as there are electrons orbiting around it. In carbon this is six.

The number of protons in the nucleus is known as the ATOMIC NUMBER. The chemical properties of an atom can be predicted from its atomic number.

Proxima Centauri

Proxima Centauri is a faint red dwarf STAR about 10,000 times dimmer than the SUN and is the closest known star to our SOLAR SYSTEM. It is about 4.3 LIGHT-YEARS away, and is visible with binoculars in the CONSTELLATION of Centaurus. Proxima is the faintest member of a triple star system called Alpha Centauri. The two others form a brilliant double star when viewed through a small astronomical telescope. They are each about as bright as the Sun, and take 80 years to orbit each other.

Tiny Proxima, which flares up every now and then and appears brighter than normal for just a few minutes, takes about a million years to orbit the bright stars.

Maria Goeppert Mayer (1906–1972)
Mayer was a German physicist who, from 1931, lived and worked in the United States. In 1949, independently of J. Hans Jensen in Germany, she proposed that protons and neutrons are arranged in shells inside the nuclei of atoms. For this theory she shared the 1963 Nobel Prize in Physics.

◀ Proxima Centauri is the closest star to the Sun. With two other stars it makes up Alpha Centauri, which is the bright light near the top of this photograph. The bright light near the bottom is Beta Centauri.

PSYCHOLOGY AND PSYCHIATRY

Psychology and psychiatry are related sciences, and both are concerned with the way we think and behave. Psychology is the study of normal minds, and involves careful analysis of how we, and animals, behave in response to our environment. For example, it might be used to plan a color scheme for a public building or factory, by using a study of people's behavior that shows they react favorably to particular colors. Like other sciences, psychology involves experimental work which allows the psychologist to predict how people or animals will react. Medical psychology is used to help people suffering from emotional problems. Disturbed children with difficulty at school may be put under the care of an educational psychologist. The psychologist may work with a psychiatrist.

Psychiatry is a medical science, which examines and treats abnormal mental states. Most psychiatric disorders do not involve any disease, but are thought to be due to some fault in the workings of the brain. Sometimes the psychiatrist helps by talking with the patient, or by prescribing a drug. Depression is a common mental illness. It is natural to feel depressed for a while but sometimes the depression lasts for months. Schizophrenia is an illness in which people lose their grasp of reality. In all these problems, there seem to be faults in the way that nerve cells in the brain communicate with each other by means of chemicals. Drug treatment is used to try and restore the normal balance.

PHOBIAS

A phobia is an irrational fear of something. The fear is so strong that it prevents the person from behaving normally. Here are some common and not so common phobias:

Acrophobia fear of heights
Agoraphobia fear of going out of the home or into wide open spaces
Arachnaphobia fear of spiders
Claustrophobia fear of being shut in confined spaces
Hemophobia fear of blood
Hippophobia fear of horses
Microbiophobia fear of germs
Ophidiophobia fear of snakes
Ornithophobia fear of birds
Phasmophobia fear of ghosts
Triskaidekaphobia fear of the number 13
Xenophobia fear of foreigners
Perhaps the strangest phobia is **phobophobia**, which is the fear of being afraid!

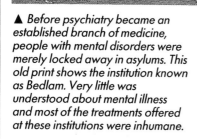

▲ Before psychiatry became an established branch of medicine, people with mental disorders were merely locked away in asylums. This old print shows the institution known as Bedlam. Very little was understood about mental illness and most of the treatments offered at these institutions were inhumane.

▼ A modern form of treatment for psychological problems is group therapy. Patients meet, together with a psychiatrist or psychologist, and discuss their problems, learning from each other's experiences.

See also BEHAVIOR; BRAIN; DISEASE; DRUGS; ENVIRONMENT; FREUD; MEDICINE; NERVES; TRANQUILIZERS AND STIMULANTS.

Ptolemy

Ptolemy (A.D. 100–c.165), who lived in Alexandria, Egypt, was a mathematician, geographer, and astronomer. He believed the "inhabited" EARTH measured about 4,000 miles (7,000 km) from north to south and 7,000 miles (12,000 km) from east to west. Beyond these limits lay "unknown land" or sea. In those days the Earth was believed to be at the center of the UNIVERSE. The planets' movements around the sky, with their loops and changes of brightness, had puzzled astronomers for centuries. Ptolemy suggested that as each PLANET moves around the Earth, it also moves in a much smaller circle called an "epicycle." Even though completely wrong, this more or less matched the planets' observed motion around the sky. Ptolemy also produced a star catalog containing 48 constellations, still recognized today.

▲ Ptolemy's (incorrect) theory of the universe, with the Earth at the center, went unchallenged for 1,500 years.

◄ The Ptolemaic system of the universe had the Earth at the center with the Sun and planets orbiting around it.

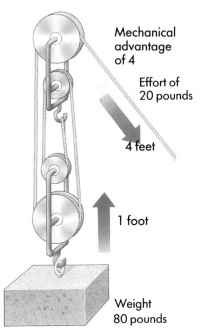

Mechanical advantage of 4

Effort of 20 pounds

4 feet

1 foot

Weight 80 pounds

▲ Using four pulleys, giving a mechanical advantage of 4, an effort of 20 pounds has to move a distance of 4 feet to raise a weight of 80 pounds through 1 foot.

Pulley

A pulley is a wheel with a grooved rim. A rope or chain is passed around the groove. The wheel rotates around an axle. If the pulley on its axle is positioned above the ground, pulling one end of the rope will raise a load tied to the other end. Several pulleys can be used together to make it easier to raise a heavy load. This is called a block and tackle. A number of pulleys called a block are

▶ *Dockside cranes make great use of the mechanical advantage provided by pulleys.*

attached to a fixed point and the same number of pulleys called a tackle are suspended on ropes passing through the block. The load is attached to the tackle. Pulling the rope a long way raises the load a shorter distance. The RATIO of the load to the effort put into raising it is called the mechanical advantage and it is a measure of the EFFICIENCY of the system.

See also MACHINES, SIMPLE.

Pulsar

A pulsar is the tiny but brilliant NEUTRON STAR that may be left after a SUPERNOVA explosion. Its fierce magnetic field squirts LIGHT and RADIO waves into beams that sweep around as the pulsar spins. If the Earth lies in the track of one of these beams the object is detected by its pulsing effects. The first pulsar to be discovered was at first thought to be radio messages from space! Then the pulses were found to come from the Crab Nebula in Taurus, the remains of a supernova seen in A.D. 1054. The pulsar rotates once in about 0.03 seconds.

▶ *As a pulsar, or neutron star, spins, its signal sweeps through space like a lighthouse beam. The signal will reach Earth once in every rotation and will seem to pulse rapidly on and off as the beam sweeps around.*

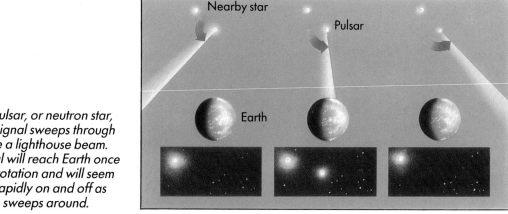

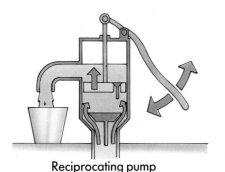

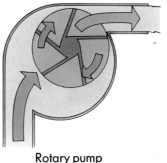

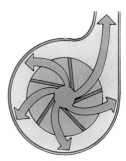

Reciprocating pump   Rotary pump   Centrifugal pump

Pump

A pump is a machine used to move a FLUID. There are two main types of pumps: reciprocating and rotary. A reciprocating pump consists of a piston in a cylinder. Fluid is pulled into the cylinder when the piston moves in one direction and forced out through a valve when it moves in the opposite direction. Reciprocating pumps are used to raise water from underground. They can raise water from a depth of more than 23 feet (7m). A bicycle pump is a reciprocating pump.

A rotary pump uses GEAR wheels or a spinning wheel with blades, called an impeller, to accelerate a fluid. The gear pumps used to supply oil to ENGINES are an example of such a pump. Centrifugal pumps are rotary pumps that use a spinning wheel to throw the fluid outward and through an exit hole.

▲ A reciprocating pump has a piston that moves up and down to lift water, perhaps from a well. In a rotary pump, a set of vanes called an impeller acts like a waterwheel to force a liquid along a pipe. In a centrifugal pump, the liquid enters at the center of the impeller and is flung outward as it rapidly spins around.

Pyrex

Pyrex is a type of GLASS designed to resist HEAT. It was developed by the Corning Glass Works' laboratories in New York in 1915. It is made by replacing some of the silica (SILICON dioxide) in normal glass with boron trioxide. It is also known as a borosilicate glass. Pyrex expands very little when it is heated and this prevents it from cracking. It has a higher MELTING POINT than normal glass, and it is resistant to many chemicals. This makes Pyrex containers suitable for use in LABORATORIES and for ovenware in the home. Because of its resistance to EXPANSION or CONTRACTION, Pyrex is also used to make astronomical telescopes.

▲ A Pyrex measuring cup will not crack or deform no matter how hot the liquid poured into it.

Pythagoras See Geometry

Quantum mechanics

Quantum mechanics tells us about the structure of the atom and how atoms give off ENERGY in small packets called quanta. To understand quantum mechanics it is necessary to examine how atoms behave. In each atom, tiny negatively charged particles called ELECTRONS move in orbits around the positive nucleus. The electrons move only in certain orbits unless they are disturbed. Each orbit has a fixed energy level. But if the atom is heated or if light shines on it, an electron can jump to a higher orbit around the nucleus; as it does this it absorbs some energy. When the electron falls back to its original orbit it shoots out the tiny bundle of light energy it has absorbed. This light energy is called a quantum or photon.

Before quantum mechanics, scientists assumed that light was sent out in a continuous wave flow. But quantum mechanics explains that LIGHT is really a stream

Erwin Schrödinger (1887–1961)
Schrödinger was an Austrian physicist who lived and worked in Ireland from 1939 to 1956. In 1926, while working in Switzerland, he devised the Schrödinger equation, which established wave mechanics as an alternative to the quantum theory as formulated by Heisenberg. The equation was a mathematical way of describing the electrons in an atom or molecule in terms of waves. For this work he shared the 1933 Nobel Prize in Physics with the British physicist Paul Dirac.

Werner Heisenberg (1901–1976)

Heisenberg was a German physicist who put forward the theory of quantum mechanics to explain the structure of the atom and the behavior of subatomic particles such as electrons. In 1927 he formulated his uncertainty principle, which states that it is not possible to know exactly both the position of an electron and its momentum. For this work he was awarded the 1932 Nobel Prize in Physics.

of tiny PHOTONS which act both as WAVES and particles. Quantum mechanics also explains how the nucleus of an atom is formed, how nuclei can split in two (nuclear fission) and join together (nuclear fusion) or decay to produce RADIOACTIVITY.

Another important idea that stems from quantum mechanics is the *uncertainty principle*, developed by Werner Heisenberg. This principle states that it is impossible to know exactly at the same time both where a SUBATOMIC PARTICLE is and how fast it is moving. This means that there is always a limit to the amount of information that we can have about the state of any particle. No matter what we do to measure the particle's position and speed, we will always disturb the particle in some way. Quantum mechanics tells us only what the chances are of getting our measurements right.

Quantum theory

Quantum theory was developed early this century as an attempt to explain certain phenomena that could not be explained by the classical principles of physics. In 1900, Max PLANCK, the German scientist, suggested the idea of quanta to explain the way LIGHT was emitted by hot objects. Albert EINSTEIN built on Planck's theory and established that light consists of tiny particles of ENERGY that behave like WAVES. In 1913, Niels Bohr, the Danish scientist, showed how ATOMS radiate light. Much of this original quantum theory has been replaced by further developments in QUANTUM MECHANICS.

Quasar

Quasars, or quasi-stellar radio sources, have been one of the greatest astronomical puzzles of the past 25 years. They were first observed by RADIO ASTRONOMERS, who measured such powerful signals that they thought the objects must be in the MILKY WAY. To everyone's amazement, once their RED SHIFT was measured, they

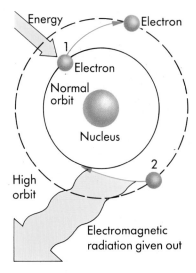

▲ Quantum theory states that electromagnetic radiation, such as light, is emitted in separate packets of energy called quanta or photons. Electrons move in fixed orbits around the atom's nucleus. When an atom of a substance absorbs energy, perhaps by being heated, one of its electrons is given a "kick" of energy and moves into a higher orbit **1**. When it returns to its original orbit, it emits the same packet of energy as a photon of radiation **2**.

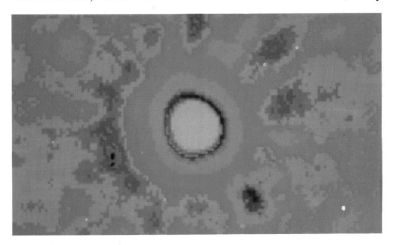

◄ The quasar called 3C 273 is a powerful emitter of X-rays. This X-ray photograph shows the quasar with a jet of matter emerging at the bottom right-hand side.

turned out to be superbright GALAXIES much farther away than any normal galaxy could be detected. The most distant quasar is moving away at about 174,000 miles per second (280,000 km/s), over 90 percent of the speed of light. The light we see now left it a few billion years after the formation of the UNIVERSE.

Radar

Radar is a system used to locate distant objects such as aircraft and ships. The word radar comes from RAdio Direction And Ranging. A German physicist, Christian Helsmeyer, suggested using RADIO reflections from ships to prevent collisions at sea in 1904, but the first practical radar system was developed in the 1930s in Britain by a team led by Robert Watson-Watt. By 1937 a chain of radar stations was being built. Radar was used during

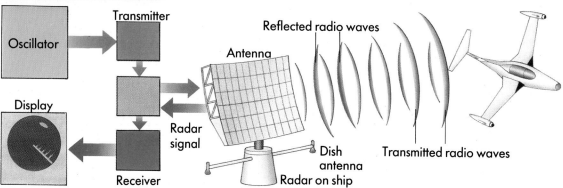

▲ *Radar detects the distance and direction of something by sending out high-frequency radio waves and picking up the signals reflected by the object. The signals that bounce back are displayed on a TV-type cathode-ray tube.*

World War II to warn of the approach of enemy aircraft and to guide aircraft onto their targets.

Radar works by transmitting short pulses of high FREQUENCY radio waves from a rotating antenna. The pulses are reflected back by anything they strike. The REFLECTIONS, or echoes, are received and used to produce a trace on a CATHODE-RAY TUBE. Metal objects reflect radio waves strongly and show up clearly but nonmetals show up too, so radar is used in weather forecasting to show the progress of storms. Some spacecraft also carry radar to detect the surface of planets hidden by thick clouds so they can be mapped.

▼ *Radar screens show air traffic controllers the positions of aircraft approaching a large airport.*

Radiation

Radiation is a form of ENERGY. High-energy particles such as RADIOACTIVITY from rocks, and ELECTROMAGNETIC RADIATION such as LIGHT and RADIO waves are known as radiation. Radioactive particles and high-FREQUENCY electromagnetic radiation such as X-RAYS are known as "ionizing radiation" because they can knock ELECTRONS out of an ATOM to form an ION. Ionizing radiation can produce changes in living tissues, the CELLS in the body. Very large doses of radiation cause radiation sickness. The other main natural source of radiation is COSMIC

RAYS, which are atomic particles produced by the Sun.

Radiation also refers to the transfer of HEAT energy. In CONVECTION and CONDUCTION, moving particles carry heat, but radiated heat can pass through a VACUUM where there are no particles. Hot objects give off INFRARED waves which transfer heat to cooler objects.

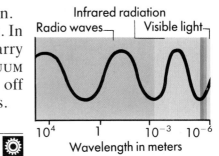

Radio

Radio describes the use of radio waves to transmit and receive information. Radio waves are similar to visible LIGHT waves except that their longer WAVELENGTH, makes them invisible. Radio waves with very short wavelengths pass through the ATMOSPHERE into space and are used to communicate with spacecraft. Radio waves with longer wavelengths are reflected back to EARTH by a layer in the atmosphere called the IONOSPHERE. Radio waves can be sent around the world by bouncing them off the ionosphere. The first person to develop practical radio equipment was Guglielmo MARCONI. Radio is used to transmit television and radio

▲ Radio waves form part of the electromagnetic spectrum. They have longer wavelengths (and lower frequencies) than infrared radiation or visible light.

▼ A simple radio is shown below with its circuit diagram. In the coil the radio signals are passed on from the antenna to the tuning circuit — the coil and the capacitor can be tuned to the radio station required. The diode produces audio frequency current that is turned into sound in the earpiece.

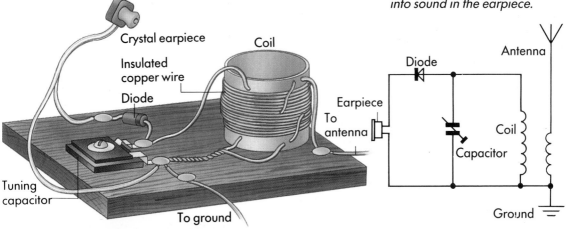

◀ The Italian inventor Guglielmo Marconi was a pioneer of long-distance radio transmission between ships at sea and between continents. Here he is seen by the radio equipment on board his yacht.

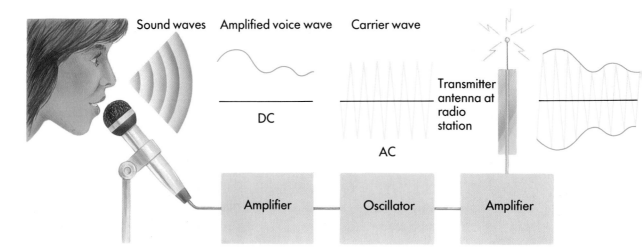

Sound waves   Amplified voice wave   Carrier wave

DC

AC

Transmitter antenna at radio station

Amplifier   Oscillator   Amplifier

▲ The diagram shows how a voice signal is transmitted and received by radio using amplitude modulation (AM). Amplitude describes the height of the peaks and troughs of any wave. In AM, the amplified signal from a microphone is made to modulate, or vary, the amplitude of a carrier wave which is continuously transmitted at the radio station. The combined signal is picked up by the receiver's antenna, amplified and demodulated to reproduce the original voice signal. An amplified version of this works the loudspeaker. In an alternative technique, called frequency modulation (FM), the voice signal is made to modulate the frequency of the carrier wave.

programs, voice communications, COMPUTER data, spacecraft control, and data from automatic beacons.

Information is transmitted by superimposing it on a radio wave called a carrier wave. This is called modulation. The signal, which might be a TELEVISION program, modulates the carrier. Two types of modulation are commonly used: amplitude modulation (AM) and frequency modulation (FM).

Radio astronomy

Light waves and radio waves are forms of ELECTROMAGNETIC RADIATION, and both are sent out by astronomical objects. Ordinary stars emit light much more powerfully than radio waves, while NEBULAE may appear quite dark but send out strong radio emissions.

Radio astronomy began in 1933 when an American amateur radio enthusiast heard a "hiss" coming from space. Later, in the 1950s, a few pioneers such as Bernard

▶ Radio astronomy uses large dish antennas called radio telescopes to pick up the weak radio signals that arrive at Earth from distant stars and galaxies.

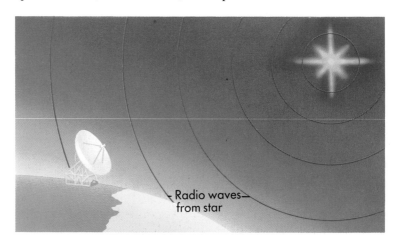

Radio waves from star

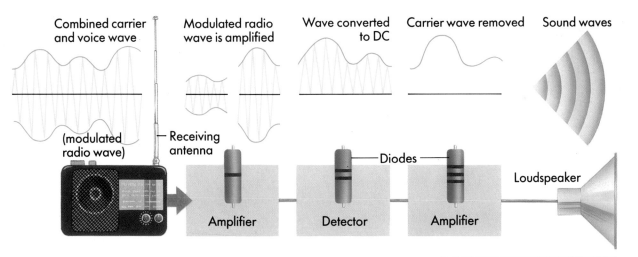

Combined carrier and voice wave | Modulated radio wave is amplified | Wave converted to DC | Carrier wave removed | Sound waves

(modulated radio wave) | Receiving antenna | Diodes | Loudspeaker

Amplifier | Detector | Amplifier

Lovell at Manchester, England, discovered that RADIO TELESCOPES can "see" objects that are too dim or far away to be made out with ordinary telescopes. The most common WAVELENGTH for astronomical "broadcasts" is 210 mm (about 8 inches). This radiation is sent out by hydrogen atoms, which make up most of the UNIVERSE, and it is used to "map" hydrogen clouds in the MILKY WAY.

Our own galaxy is only a weak radio transmitter, but some galaxies, such as Centaurus A, are very powerful and were discovered early. The hydrogen in their vast gas clouds sends out radio waves. Radio astronomers also discovered QUASARS and PULSARS.

Radio telescope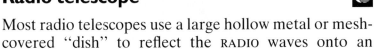

Most radio telescopes use a large hollow metal or mesh-covered "dish" to reflect the RADIO waves onto an ANTENNA in the center of the dish, which sends the signal to an AMPLIFIER. Usually the dish can be pointed in any

Martin Ryle (1918–1984)
Ryle was a British radio astronomer who became interested in radio astronomy after having worked on radar during World War II. He devised a method of using several small radio telescopes to give the effect of one very large one. He and his colleagues discovered many quasars and radio galaxies. Ryle shared the 1974 Nobel Prize in Physics.

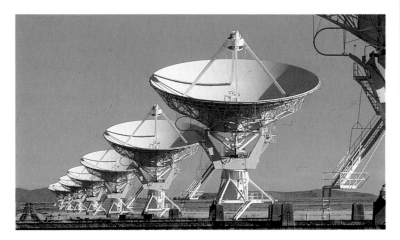

◄ *This row of radio telescopes, called an array, is located in the desert of New Mexico. The telescopes are mounted on rails so that they can be moved.*

direction. The largest "steerable" radio telescope is at Effelsberg in Germany, and measures 330 feet (100 m) across. However, the largest radio telescope in the world has a dish 1,000 feet (305 m) across, formed by hanging a wire-mesh reflector over a natural hollow in Arecibo, Puerto Rico.

Radioactivity

Radioactivity describes the tiny SUBATOMIC PARTICLES and high-energy rays that are given out by the nuclei at the center of certain kinds of ATOM. There are at least three types of radioactivity, called alpha, beta, and gamma radiation. Alpha radiation consists of two PROTONS and two NEUTRONS bound together, identical to the nucleus of a HELIUM atom. Beta radiation consists of ELECTRONS or POSITRONS, and is produced when a neutron inside the nucleus turns into a proton or a proton into a neutron. Both alpha and beta radioactivity change the ATOMIC NUMBER of the atom left behind. Gamma radiation consists of ELECTROMAGNETIC RADIATION of very high FREQUENCY. Gamma radiation does not change the type of nucleus that is left behind and penetrates farther than alpha and beta particles.

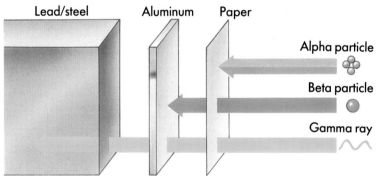

Radioactivity is a random process; it is not possible to say when a particular atom will give out radioactivity. It is possible, however, given a large number of atoms, to say how long it will be before half of them have decayed; this time is called the HALF-LIFE.

Radioisotope

The nucleus of an ATOM of a chemical ELEMENT has a certain number of protons and neutrons. If the element has two or more forms with different numbers of neutrons in

Antoine Henri Becquerel (1852–1908)
Becquerel was a French physicist who in 1896 discovered radioactivity. He found that radiation given off by uranium salts fogged photographic plates. He went on to investigate the radiation, and three years later proved that some of it consisted of charged particles. For this work he shared the 1903 Nobel Prize in Physics with Pierre and Marie Curie, the discoverers of radium.

▶ *The three forms of radiation that make up radioactivity are alpha particles, beta particles, and gamma rays. Low energy alpha particles can be stopped by a sheet of paper. Beta particles will penetrate paper but not aluminum. But gamma rays can be stopped only by a thick layer of steel or lead.*

Radioactivity is measured in units called **becquerels**, named after the French scientist who discovered radioactivity. The SI unit for radiation dosage or exposure is the **sievert**, named after the Swedish physicist Rolf Sievert.

their nuclei, they are known as ISOTOPES. A radioisotope is an isotope that gives off RADIOACTIVITY. Its nucleus is unstable, and it becomes stable by giving off heat and RADIATION, often in the form of alpha particles or beta particles. The rate at which a radioisotope breaks down, or decays, is indicated by its HALF-LIFE, which is the time taken for half of its nuclei to decay. For example, the radioisotope strontium 90 has a half-life of 28 years. The radiation from radioisotopes is used in MEDICINE, for example, to treat disorders such as certain types of CANCER.

Radium

Radium is a chemical ELEMENT. It is a white RADIOACTIVE metal found in URANIUM ores, from which it is extracted. It also occurs in the water from some mineral springs and in seawater. Radium was used to treat CANCER and in luminous paints. All its medical and industrial uses have now been taken over by more easily obtained radioactive materials. Radium was discovered in 1898 by the Polish born French scientist Marie CURIE and her husband Pierre.

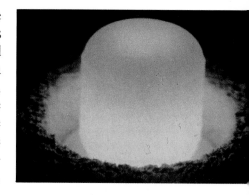

▲ Radioactivity causes the radioisotope plutonium 238 to glow in the dark. It is used as a long-life power source in spacecraft and satellites.

Rain *See* Precipitation

Rainbow

A rainbow is a bow or arc-shaped band of COLORS in the sky. A rainbow may be a nearly complete circle, the more bow, the lower the Sun in the sky. If the Sun is higher than 42°, no bow will appear. To see a rainbow the Sun must be behind you. The Sun's LIGHT is reflected and refracted by raindrops. Although not all of the colors are always clearly visible, the white light is split into the same colors that are produced using a PRISM: red, orange, yellow, green, blue, indigo, and violet.

Rainbows may also be produced at night from light reflected by the Moon but the colors are much weaker. *See also* REFLECTION; REFRACTION.

▶ A rainbow forms when sunlight is bent, or refracted, by raindrops. The light is bent as it enters the drop, and is reflected from the back before being bent again as it leaves the drop. Each color in white light is bent to a slightly different extent, and so the drops split the light into the colors of the spectrum.

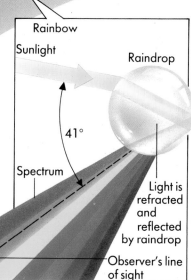

Rainbow

Sunlight

Raindrop

41°

Spectrum

Light is refracted and reflected by raindrop

Observer's line of sight

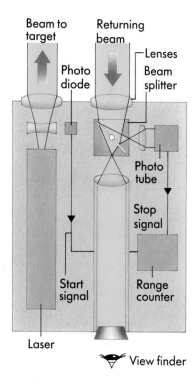

Beam to target

Returning beam

Lenses

Photo diode

Beam splitter

Photo tube

Stop signal

Start signal

Range counter

Laser

View finder

▲ *A modern laser rangefinder works by timing how long it takes for a pulse of laser light to travel to and from a target. When the trigger button is pressed a pulse of high intensity laser light is directed at the target. A small part of the light pulse is fed to the receiver, which starts the electronic timer. The light returning from the target stops the timer and the range is calculated electronically.*

The golden ratio, or golden section, is thought by artists and architects to be an ideal proportion. It is found by cutting a line unequally in such a way that the ratio of the shorter length to the longer length is the same as the ratio of the longer length to the length of the whole uncut line. It is equal to 1:1.618, or very roughly 2:3.

Ramsay, William *See* Noble gases

Rangefinder

A rangefinder is a device used to measure how far away an object is. Most rely on an effect called PARALLAX. Parallax describes the way things seem to move when viewed from a different place. Light enters the rangefinder through two LENSES a few inches apart. The two images are superimposed in the viewfinder. Adjusting the rangefinder swivels a mirror inside. When the two images lie on top of each other, the range can be read off a scale. Another type of highly accurate rangefinder uses LASER light.

Ratio

Ratios are the comparison of one amount to another. For example, if you had four red balls and two blue balls the ratio of red to blue would be 4:2. Like fractions, ratios are written in their lowest terms, so 4:2 becomes 2:1. You have twice as many red balls as blue balls.

Ratios can be easily expressed as fractions. For example, if there are twelve fish on a slab and the ratio of mackerel to herring is 2:1 it means that two out of every three fish are mackerel. So two-thirds ($^2/_3$) of the 12 fish are mackerel. One out of every three fish is a herring so one-third ($^1/_3$) of the 12 fish are herring. Therefore there are 8 mackerel and 4 herring.

SEE FOR YOURSELF
You can alter the proportions of a design using ratios. Draw a square grid over a simple drawing. Now make another grid with the vertical lines 1 $^1/_2$ times as far apart as the horizontal lines. Copy the drawing onto the new grid and see how its proportions change.

Y

X

$1\frac{1}{2}$X

Rayon *See* Synthetic fibers

Reactions, chemical *See* Chemical reactions

Records

Records are plastic discs that store SOUND recordings. The sound is stored in the form of a spiral groove cut into the disc. The sounds were originally vibrations in the air. Two MICROPHONES, one on either side of the performers, convert the sounds into electric currents. They are fed to two ELECTROMAGNETS attached to two cutters which cut the sides of a V-shaped groove so that the shape of one side represents the sound from the left and the shape of the other, the sound from the right. The first disc cut is called a lacquer. The lacquer is coated with SILVER and

SEE FOR YOURSELF
Make your own record-player by pushing a pin through the base of a polystyrene cup (from the inside). Ask somebody for an old record that they no longer want. Put it on a rotating turntable and carefully rest the pin in the groove. The base of the cup will vibrate and generate sound.

◀ *LP records are mass-produced by pressing them from discs of black vinyl plastic.*

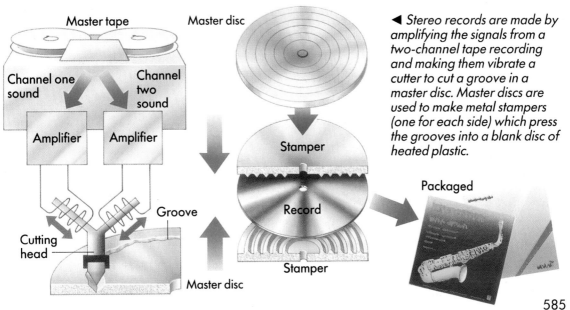

◀ *Stereo records are made by amplifying the signals from a two-channel tape recording and making them vibrate a cutter to cut a groove in a master disc. Master discs are used to make metal stampers (one for each side) which press the grooves into a blank disc of heated plastic.*

Master tape

Channel one sound

Channel two sound

Amplifier

Amplifier

Cutting head

Groove

Master disc

Master disc

Stamper

Record

Stamper

Packaged

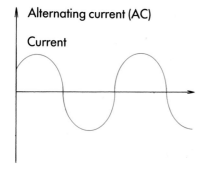

Alternating current (AC)

Current

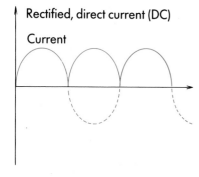

Rectified, direct current (DC)

Current

▲ *Rectifiers only allow current to flow one way. They can be used to turn an alternating current (A.C.) which continually changes direction into a direct current (D.C.) which flows smoothly in one direction.*

NICKEL to form a metal master disc with bumps instead of grooves. More metal is laid on the back of this to form a positive disc. A stamper disc is then made to make all the records sold by stores.

When a record is played, a stylus with a specially shaped tip is inserted in the groove as the record revolves. The shape of the groove makes it vibrate and the vibrations are turned into electric currents by two electromagnets. The left and right channels are amplified and fed to two LOUDSPEAKERS to give the sounds.

Rectifier

A rectifier is an ELECTRONIC device used to change an alternating current (A.C.) into an electric current that flows in only one direction, called direct current (D.C.). There are two types of rectifier: half-wave and full-wave. In a half-wave rectifier, a DIODE allows electric current to flow in one direction only and eliminates any current flowing the other way. In a full-wave rectifier, four diodes change A.C. to D.C. by reversing the direction of any electric current that flows in the wrong direction.
See also ELECTRICITY.

Recycling

Recycling is the name given to the ways in which MATERIALS can be saved after they have been used so they can be used again. Recycling enables us to use smaller amounts of those RESOURCES which do not renew themselves naturally.

People today make use of vast quantities of materials such as paper, glass, steel, and aluminum to make books, packaging, newspapers, bottles and jars, vehicles,

▼ *Recycling takes scrap metals, glass, paper, and organic materials and processes them so that they can be used again.*

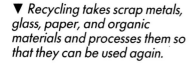

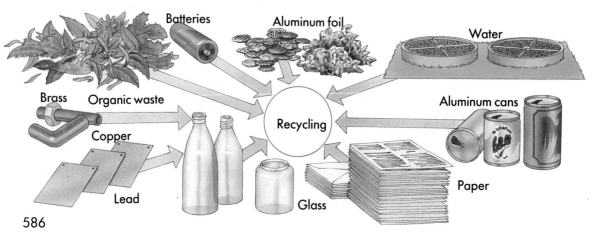

Batteries

Aluminum foil

Water

Brass   Organic waste

Copper

Recycling

Aluminum cans

Lead

Glass

Paper

cans, and much more. As soon as the product comes to the end of its useful life, it is often thrown away, creating two main problems. First, large amounts of long-lasting trash need to be disposed of safely. Second, there is a continuous and growing demand for the raw materials from which these products were made. The EARTH does not have an everlasting supply of materials and if a change in use does not take place, many resources will be quickly used up.

Today, some governments and organizations arrange the collection of waste paper so that it can be treated and made into more paper products. Many people can now recycle their glass and cans. In future, it seems likely that more products, including materials such as plastics, will be recycled.

Red giant

A red giant is an old STAR. Many stars, including the SUN, will eventually become red giants.

As a star ages it grows hotter, and the RADIATION from the core tries to blow it apart. Eventually the outer layers puff outward, becoming cooler and therefore redder. Betelgeuse, in the constellation Orion, is larger than the orbit of MARS, but the gas in the outer parts is so thin it is nearly a VACUUM. In about 5 billion years the Sun will become a red giant, swallowing Mercury and Venus. Some red giants become WHITE DWARFS.

Red shift

A beam of LIGHT moves as a wave, and the light's color depends upon the WAVELENGTH of its waves. About 2,500 wavelengths of blue light would fit into a millimeter (four-hundredths of an inch), compared with only 1,500 wavelengths of red light because red light has a

Many newspapers use between 25 percent and 50 percent recycled paper. In the packaging industry, nearly 80 percent of all cardboard boxes are recycled. The metal with the best record is aluminum from soft drink cans and beer cans, nearly half of which are recycled.

▼ *Aldebaran is a red giant star more than 35 times as big as the Sun.*

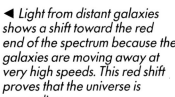

Our Sun
865,000 miles
in diameter

Red giant Aldebaran
31,130,000 miles
in diameter

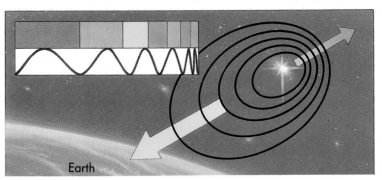

Earth

◄ *Light from distant galaxies shows a shift toward the red end of the spectrum because the galaxies are moving away at very high speeds. This red shift proves that the universe is expanding.*

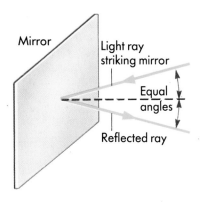

▲ *Light is reflected from a flat mirror at the same angle as it strikes it. Reflection actually takes place at the thin layer of metal on the back of the mirror.*

Hendrik Antoon Lorentz (1853–1928)
Lorentz was a Dutch theoretical physicist who first explained reflection and refraction in terms of the electromagnetic theory of light. This theory, put forward by James Clerk Maxwell, says that light consists of electric and magnetic waves at right-angles to each other. Lorentz also predicted the existence of electrons and shared the 1902 Nobel Prize in Physics for his work on spectra and magnetic fields.

longer wavelength. If a moving object is sending out light, the waves reaching the observer are stretched apart (made redder) when the object is going away, or pushed together (made bluer) when it is approaching. This effect, called the DOPPLER EFFECT, becomes measurable at speeds of several miles per second, but the red shift of distant QUASARS can show speeds of more than 124,000 miles per second (200,000 km/s). The U.S. astronomer Edwin Hubble was the first person to show that the UNIVERSE is expanding.

Reflection

When rays of LIGHT, SOUND or HEAT, or RADIO waves bounce off a surface they are reflected. We see objects that don't themselves give off light because they reflect or bend back any light that falls on them. We see the Sun and stars because they are so hot they send out light. We see the Moon and planets because they reflect the Sun's light to us. Generally speaking, smooth surfaces are the best reflectors, such as polished metal or, of course, MIRRORS. Rough surfaces are bad reflectors because their surface particles are all facing in different directions and the light is reflected in all directions.

If a ray of light shines squarely at right angles to a plane (flat) mirror, the light is reflected straight back in the opposite direction. A ray that hits the mirror at an angle will bounce off at the same angle as that at which it met the mirror. When we look at ourselves in a mirror, our image appears to be as far behind the mirror as we are in front of it. Also, our left eye is opposite the right eye of the image.
See also OPTICAL FIBERS.

SEE FOR YOURSELF
Prop up a mirror at the edge of a cork tile and stick in a row of pins at an angle to the mirror. Looking from the right at the reflection of the row of pins, stick in another row that lines up with it. A flashlight beam shone along the first row will be reflected along the second.

Angle of incidence

Angle of reflection

Equal angles

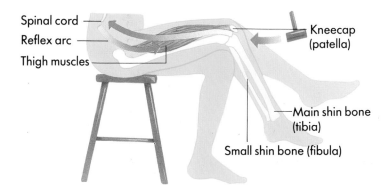

Spinal cord

Reflex arc

Thigh muscles

Kneecap (patella)

Main shin bone (tibia)

Small shin bone (fibula)

◀ *If someone sits with their legs crossed, a sharp tap at the base of the kneecap makes the foot jerk forward. This is a reflex action. A nerve message travels from the knee to the spinal cord, and then to the muscles in the thigh. These contract to move the lower leg. Doctors often use this to test a person's reflex actions.*

Reflex

A reflex is an automatic response of the body, which does not involve the BRAIN. For example, if you touch a hot object, a reflex causes you to snatch your hand away. The PAIN comes a few moments later. This is because pain receptors in your SKIN react instantly to the heat, and pass a message to the spinal cord. A message is sent back to the arm MUSCLES, and they pull your hand away. A few moments later, the first message, continuing up the spinal cord reaches the brain so you are aware of the pain. A *conditioned reflex* is one learned by associating two stimuli. For example, if a dog is always fed just after a bell sounds, after a while it will salivate when it hears the bell, even if it is not feeding time.

See also LEARNING; NERVES.

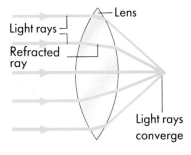

Lens

Light rays

Refracted ray

Light rays converge

▲ *A convex, or converging, lens brings light rays to a focus because of refraction. The rays are bent as they enter the glass of the lens and again when they leave it.*

SEE FOR YOURSELF
Put 2 drinking straws in a glass of water. If you look down into the glass, refraction makes the straws appear bent. If you look through the side of the glass, you can see they are not bent.

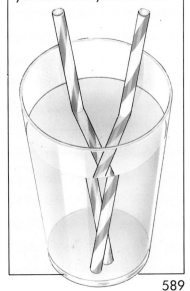

Refraction

Refraction is the bending of the direction of a WAVE that happens when the wave's speed changes. For example, LIGHT is bent when it passes from air into water or glass, in which it travels more slowly than in air. Refraction occurs because the WAVELENGTH of the wave is smaller in the region where it travels more slowly. The amount of bending depends on the material and on the direction of the incoming rays. Different materials refract light by different amounts. These amounts can be measured very accurately and are useful in testing various materials, from butter to diamonds. The different colors in white light are not refracted to the same degree and can be broken up into the colors of the SPECTRUM — this is how a PRISM works.

The most important use of refraction is connected with lenses used in telescopes, microscopes, cameras,

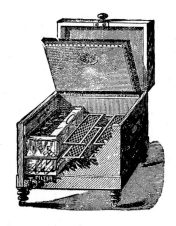

▲ *An early refrigerator made in about 1900 was an ice box, with a container for ice and shelves for food.*

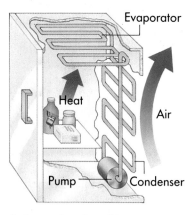

▲ *In an electric refrigerator, a liquid refrigerant takes heat from the inside of the refrigerator as it evaporates into a gas inside coils in the freezing compartment. A pump compresses the gas and turns it back to a liquid. This produces heat which is dispelled as the liquid circulates in coils outside the refrigerator.*

▶ *Time appears to pass more slowly on an object that is moving very fast, at speeds approaching that of light. This is one effect of relativity. Another is that the object's length appears to decrease with speed: the faster it goes, the shorter it appears.*

590

and many other instruments. Refraction allows LENSES to focus at a single point. Lenses are curved so that all the light rays passing through them are refracted so that they form a clear image, or picture.
See also MIRAGE; REFLECTION.

Refrigeration

Refrigeration is the process of lowering the TEMPERATURE inside a container. It is used in the home to cool food and slow down the growth of organisms that would spoil it. It is also used in AIR CONDITIONING systems.

Refrigerators rely on the fact that a LIQUID absorbs HEAT when it evaporates to become a gas and gives off heat when it condenses back to a liquid. In most domestic refrigerators, a fluid called a refrigerant evaporates inside pipes that pass through the freezer compartment, absorbing heat from the freezer and lowering the temperature. The gas flows to an electrically driven compressor which compresses the gas, turning it back to a liquid. It releases the heat absorbed from the freezer compartment to the room outside the refrigerator. The most common refrigerant is freon, a CFC. If CFCs are allowed to escape from discarded refrigerators, they rise in the ATMOSPHERE and damage the OZONE LAYER.

Relative density *See* Specific gravity

Relativity

Relativity is the name of two theories, developed by Albert EINSTEIN, which describe very large or fast-moving objects. The simpler theory, called special relativity, assumes that it is impossible to tell how fast a steadily moving aircraft is going just by performing experiments inside. This theory states that if

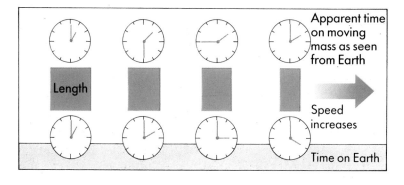

someone passes you at immense speed, time will seem to be passing much more slowly for you than for them; this effect can be seen in certain SUBATOMIC PARTICLES, which last longer when they move very quickly. The shapes of things seen by the quickly moving person will be distorted. These effects would not be noticeable unless you were traveling at more than 100,000 miles per second (160,000 km/s)! The second theory, of general relativity, tells us that GRAVITY should be thought of as a bending of space and time.

Reproduction

Reproduction is the process by which plants and animals produce more organisms of the same kind. It is the most important function of a SPECIES, because a species that fails to reproduce will die out.

Most forms of reproduction involve the joining together of special CELLS, called gametes, from male and female individuals. The gametes are brought together when animals mate and when flowers are pollinated. The joining of the gametes is called FERTILIZATION and

▲ A puffball is a type of fungus which reproduces by means of spores. When the ball is ripe, it fires thousands of microscopic spores into the air like a puff of smoke.

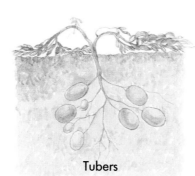

Young potato plant Tubers New shoots

the whole process is called *sexual reproduction. Asexual reproduction* does not involve gametes. Many MICRO-ORGANISMS that consist of a single cell merely split in half and each new half then goes on growing as a new individual. Strawberry plants send out lots of slender STEMS called runners, each of which forms a new plant at its tip. The runners then wither and the new plants grow on their own. Plant reproduction of this kind is called *vegetative reproduction*. Each new plant is just like the

▲ Potatoes grow from tubers, the swollen parts of the roots that we normally eat. When the parent plant dies down, the tubers stay in the soil over the winter. Then in the spring they sprout new stems from the "eyes" on the potatoes. This is an example of vegetative reproduction.

591

▶ *A deer licks the fur of her new born fawn. The fawn is only 11 minutes old. It is the result of sexual reproduction in which the parents' genes mix to produce a unique offspring.*

Georg Simon Ohm (1789–1854)
Ohm was a German physicist who in 1827 developed Ohm's law. This states that the ratio of the voltage across a conductor to the current flowing through it is a constant, the resistance. Ohm also found that the resistance of a conductor depends on its thickness, its length, and the material it is made from. The unit of resistance, the ohm, is named after him.

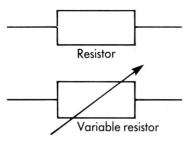

Resistor

Variable resistor

▲ *In electronics, a circuit component that has resistance is called a resistor, shown by the top symbol. A variable resistor, whose resistance can be altered, has the bottom symbol. Variable resistors are used as volume controls on radios and record players.*

592

parent. Sexual reproduction is important because the CHROMOSOMES AND GENES are mixed up when the gametes join together and this leads to variety among the offspring. Because they are not all alike, they are more able to cope with different conditions.
See also EVOLUTION; GENETICS; POLLEN AND POLLINATION.

Resistance, electrical

Electrical resistance measures how difficult it is for an electric current to flow through a MATERIAL. We can think of current being carried by ELECTRONS; if they were completely free to flow, there would be no electrical resistance. However, the electrons collide with each other and with the ATOMS in the material and lose ENERGY. So more energy has to be supplied to keep the current flowing to push the electrons through the material. This extra energy is called the voltage or potential difference. The energy that is lost in the material causes it to HEAT up; this is why the filament of an electric light bulb or heater gets hot. The SI UNIT of resistance is the ohm; one ohm of resistance means that a voltage of one volt is required to keep a current of one AMPERE flowing.

Resonance

Resonance occurs when an object has a natural FRE-QUENCY at which it vibrates. A large vibration can be set up if a FORCE is applied which vibrates at the same natural frequency. For example, a swing does not move very far if you try to push it quickly, but the vibration soon builds up if you let it swing and give it one push on each cycle, so that your pushing is in time with the swing. Electrical resonance is used in RADIO and TELEVISION receivers so that only signals of a particular frequency are received. Resonance can be dangerous; soldiers do not march in step across a bridge because this might set up a resonance and make the bridge vibrate violently.

Resources

Resources are all those raw MATERIALS and sources of ENERGY that the EARTH provides and that humans and other kinds of life depend upon to supply the everyday products (including the air we breathe) which we need to survive. *See* pages 594 and 595.

Respiration

Respiration has two meanings. It means BREATHING, in which AIR is pumped in and out of the LUNGS. It also means the CHEMISTRY of producing ENERGY, from food, in the cells themselves. All living things respire. Most living organisms use OXYGEN to break down stored food substances and provide energy for the body. Water and CARBON DIOXIDE are waste products from this process, which because it depends on oxygen, is called *aerobic respiration*. Some organisms like bacteria use a different chemical reaction which does not need oxygen. This is called *anaerobic respiration*. We can release energy without oxygen, but only for a short time. Waste products such as LACTIC ACID are produced, and these can lead to painful muscle cramps or a "stitch." Plants also respire aerobically, but in daytime they also absorb carbon dioxide for PHOTOSYNTHESIS.

▲ *A frog calls by vibrating a sac of air in its throat. The column of air in the sac resonates to produce sound in the same way that a column of air in a musical instrument does.*

▼ *In an animal that breathes air, external respiration takes place in the lungs. There oxygen from the air is exchanged for carbon dioxide, which is a waste product of internal respiration. This takes place inside body cells which generate energy, using oxygen carried there in the blood from the lungs. The blood also carries carbon dioxide back to the lungs.*

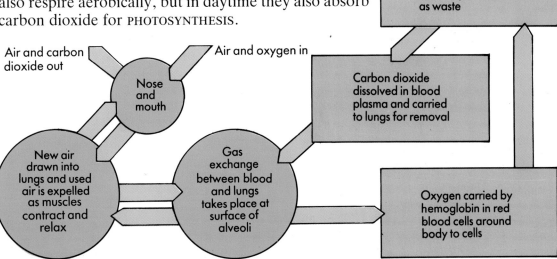

Air and carbon dioxide out

Air and oxygen in

Nose and mouth

New air drawn into lungs and used air is expelled as muscles contract and relax

Gas exchange between blood and lungs takes place at surface of alveoli

Oxygen used in cells to produce energy from sugars. Carbon dioxide produced as waste

Carbon dioxide dissolved in blood plasma and carried to lungs for removal

Oxygen carried by hemoglobin in red blood cells around body to cells

RESOURCES

Our planet has been described as "spaceship Earth." If you imagine you are in a spaceship, you soon realize that it can hold only a limited amount of air, fuel, and food. Eventually, unless the spaceship is given new supplies or unless the air and other resources can be recycled, the resources will be used up and the passengers will die. The Earth's resources will not last forever so ways must be found to recycle the resources or to reduce the demand for them.

One of the most important resources is energy. We need energy to warm our houses, to run factories and vehicles, to light streets, and even to recycle materials. Today, much energy is supplied as electricity, often generated by burning fossil fuels such as coal, oil, and gas. Although the amounts of these fuels present in the Earth are greater than was once thought, they will eventually run out. Therefore, these fossil fuels are often described as *nonrenewable resources*. Once they have been used up, they cannot be replaced. Burning these fuels also causes pollution.

Some sources of energy are described as *renewable resources* because there is no foreseeable way that they can run out. For example, the wind blows more or less strongly and continuously, so it can be used to turn a windmill and create electricity. Using the tides or sunlight to generate electricity is also described as renewable.

Animals and plants make use of renewable resources by recycling. For example, an antelope feeds on grass and its droppings are used as a source of food by various insects. Their bodies and by-products eventually find their way back into the soil. This increases the soil's fertility so that more grass can grow which is then eaten by the antelope.

▲ Resources can be preserved by recycling materials instead of throwing them away. Here paper is being sorted before going to a mill to be made into new paper or cardboard. Not all paper can be recycled. Paper that contains a large amount of dye or has a special finish cannot easily be recycled.

▼ Among the world's most important resources are fossil fuels (oil, coal, and natural gas), and uranium. This map shows where the main deposits are found. As they are used up, people will have to find other sources of power and energy.

- Uranium
- Oil
- Coal
- Natural gas

◀ Renewable resources include plants such as trees which are a source of timber. As long as we do not use them up faster than they grow again, we can go on using them for ever. The wind (which can turn windmills) and flowing water (which can turn turbines) are also renewable sources of energy.

◀ Once fossil fuels such as coal and oil are burned, they are gone forever. They are nonrenewable resources. So too are minerals from which we extract metals, although we can slow down the rate at which they are used up by recycling scrap metal and using it again and again.

SEE FOR YOURSELF

Everybody can help to conserve resources by not wasting energy and materials. Do not waste water or electricity, and do your own recycling of things such as envelopes which can be used more than once. Doing this will also save money!

Only use as much water as you really need

Write on both sides of paper and reuse envelopes

Switch off lights when not in use

Alternative Energy

One way of helping to conserve resources such as fossil fuels is to find and use other forms of energy. Not using fossil fuels also has the advantage of not adding carbon dioxide to the atmosphere which is thought to increase "global warming" and the greenhouse effect. Wind power can be used to generate electricity without causing pollution. We also use fast flowing water to drive turbines in hydroelectric power plants, and we can harness the power of the tides. Solar power, using sunlight to generate electricity, is a possibility but it is fairly expensive and is only possible where there is a reliable amount of sunshine.

See also CONSERVATION; ENERGY; FUEL; FOSSIL FUELS; MATERIALS; MINING; NUCLEAR POWER; RECYCLING; TIDAL POWER; WIND POWER.

In astronomy, **revolution** describes the circular motion of one body around another. For example, the Earth takes about 365 days to make one revolution of the Sun. This type of revolution is also called an orbit. The word **rotation** describes the spinning of a planet or moon on its axis. For example, the Earth makes one rotation every 24 hours. Our Moon makes one rotation in relation to the Sun every 28 days.

Revolution

Revolution describes a circular motion. Circular motion is an important way of transmitting POWER from an ENGINE or machine. As the wheels of a vehicle revolve around their axles, they transmit the vehicle's engine power to the ground. As a ship's propeller spins, it transmits the engine power to the water around it. A spinning TURBINE transmits power to FLUIDS.

In astronomy, revolution means the motion of one body around another, such as that of the Moon around the Earth or the Earth around the Sun. The spinning motion of the PLANETS is described as ROTATION.

Revolution can also mean a sudden change in a system, often brought about by force, as in the INDUSTRIAL REVOLUTION or the American Revolution.
See also MACHINES, SIMPLE; ORBIT.

▶ *Most kinds of machinery have shafts, gears, and pulleys that go around – they rotate or revolve. In many kinds of engines, such as steam engines, gasoline engines, and diesel engines, the principal movement is up and down or from side to side. Such engines need a mechanism to convert sideways movement to rotation or revolution. This is usually achieved using a crank of some kind. This diagram shows how this is done in a two-stroke gasoline engine of the kind common in small motorcycles.*

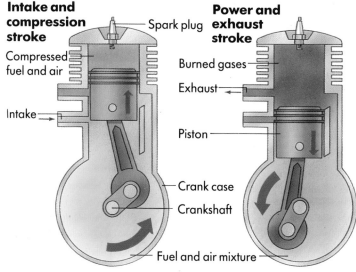

Intake and compression stroke — Spark plug — **Power and exhaust stroke**
Compressed fuel and air
Burned gases
Exhaust
Intake
Piston
Crank case
Crankshaft
Fuel and air mixture

In history, the term **revolution** describes a total change in a system or government. Some famous revolutions include:
Industrial Revolution from 1750
French Revolution 1789
American Revolution 1775-1783
Russian Revolution 1917
Hungarian Revolution 1956

SEE FOR YOURSELF
The pitch of the music from a record — whether it sounds high or low — depends on its speed of revolution. For instance if a record is meant to be played at 33 revolutions per minute (rpm), the music sounds right only if it is played at this speed. Using an old 45 rpm record, try playing it at different speeds. If it is played fast, at 78 rpm, the pitch is too high. If it is played slowly, at 33 rpm, the pitch is too low.

Richter scale

The Richter scale, sometimes also called the Gutenberg–Richter scale, is a series of numbers from 1 to 12 used to express the severity of an EARTHQUAKE. The scale was named after the U.S. seismologists Charles Robert Richter and Beno Gutenberg. Each number refers to the magnitude of the earthquake as a logarithmic expression of the amount of ENERGY released during the tremor. The logarithmic scale means that an earth tremor of magnitude two is ten times as strong as a tremor of magnitude one, while an earth tremor of magnitude three is one hundred times as strong as magnitude one and so on.

▼ *Two scales are commonly used to measure earthquakes, the Richter scale and the Mercalli scale. Earthquakes which rate less than 4 on both scales are usually too small to be felt by humans and can only be detected by sensitive instruments. In the diagram below the number on the Mercalli scale is shown first, with the number on the Richter scale shown in brackets.*

1. **Felt only by** seismographs (less than 3)

2. **Feeble** Just noticeable by some people (3–3.4)
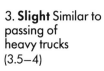

3. **Slight** Similar to passing of heavy trucks (3.5–4)
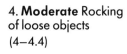

4. **Moderate** Rocking of loose objects (4–4.4)

5. **Quite strong** Felt by most people even when sleeping (4.5–4.8)

6. **Strong** Trees rock and some structural damage caused (4.9–5.4)
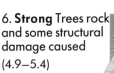
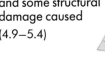

7. **Very strong** Walls crack (5.5–6)
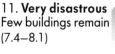

8. **Destructive** Weak buildings collapse (6.1–6.5)

9. **Ruinous** Houses collapse and ground pipes crack (6.6–7)
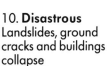
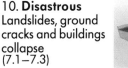

10. **Disastrous** Landslides, ground cracks and buildings collapse (7.1–7.3)
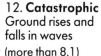

11. **Very disastrous** Few buildings remain (7.4–8.1)

12. **Catastrophic** Ground rises and falls in waves (more than 8.1)

Rivers and Lakes

The EARTH and its ATMOSPHERE are continuously circulating WATER. Water, from the OCEANS and other large bodies of water such as rivers and lakes, passes into the atmosphere by EVAPORATION. It returns to Earth by PRECIPITATION (rain and snow), much of it soaking through the soil to become GROUNDWATER. The water that runs off the surface or emerges from the ground as springs returns to the oceans via rivers and lakes.

When rain falls on high ground, some of it soaks into the ground until the soil is saturated. When the soil is waterlogged, water will run downhill as very small

The longest river in the world is the Nile, which is 4,145 miles (6,670 km) long and flows through five countries of northeast Africa to the Mediterranean Sea. The world's largest lake is the Caspian Sea on the border of the Commonwealth of Independent States and Iran.

▶ *This aerial photograph clearly shows a mature river meandering across its flood plain and forming curved oxbow lakes as it changes course and leaves them behind.*

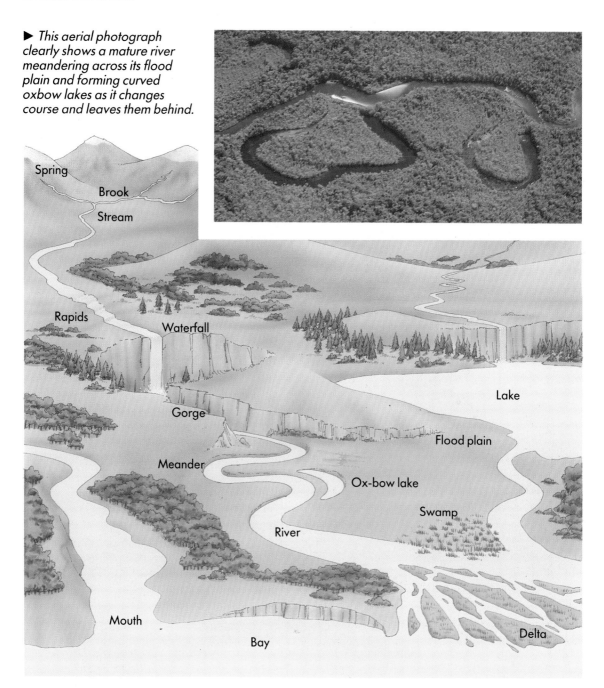

Spring

Brook

Stream

Rapids

Waterfall

Gorge

Meander

River

Mouth

Bay

Lake

Flood plain

Ox-bow lake

Swamp

Delta

▲ *The shape of a river, from its beginnings as a stream to its end as a broad estuary or delta, depends on the type of land it flows through and the amount of water it carries.*

streams. Several small streams will join and a larger stream is formed. The larger stream tends to cut out a valley by EROSION, and smaller streams run into it as it flows farther down the slope. Eventually a larger river is formed which makes its way to the sea, growing slower and wider as the land flattens out near the coast.

A lake is a large body of fresh water which may form in ice-cut hollows or, for example, where river valleys have been blocked by debris from a GLACIER.

Robots

Robots are machines programmed to carry out actions in a way similar to humans. The word robot, from the Czech word for work, comes from the play *Rossum's Universal Robots* written in 1920 by Karel Capek. Developments in ELECTRONICS in the 1960s made programmable machines a possibility. They were not walking and talking metal people, but mechanical hands and arms. The first robot hand capable of imitating the gripping action of the human hand was used in a U.S. nuclear plant in 1960. The first industrial robot, sold in the U.S. in 1962, could pick things up and move them around. Although industrial robots were invented in the U.S., Japan took them up and used them for WELDING, painting, and controlling other machines. Robots are popular with automobile and other manufacturers because they don't get tired and almost never make mistakes. They perform tasks that are too difficult or dangerous for human workers. Advances in computer programming have produced robots that can see and avoid obstacles as they move around.

▲ Sparks fly as a robot arm welds machinery parts in a fully automated factory. Most industrial robots are mechanical hands and arms.

◀ This firefighting robot helps save lives by getting close to the fire and allowing human firefighters to keep well back in case of an explosion.

Rockets

A rocket is a device containing FUEL and OXYGEN, which, when burned together, create a jet of gas that propels the rocket. Because rockets do not need oxygen from the AIR, they can propel vehicles in space.

A fuel and an oxidizer, a chemical that contains oxygen, are mixed and burned in a COMBUSTION chamber. The burning fuel expands, forcing its way out of the

▲ Robby was a fictitious robot in the film *Forbidden Planet*. Few modern robots resemble human beings.

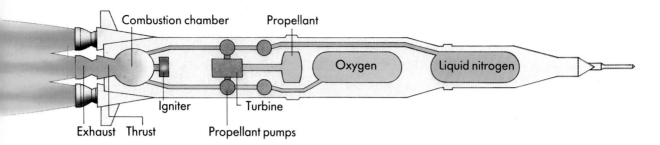

Combustion chamber　　Propellant

Oxygen　　Liquid nitrogen

Igniter　　Turbine

Exhaust　Thrust　　Propellant pumps

▲ *A typical liquid fuel rocket has separate tanks containing liquid oxygen and a propellant, such as kerosene or liquid hydrogen. Another tank holds nitrogen, which is used to drive pumps for the oxygen and propellant. The two mix and burn in the combustion chamber, producing a high-speed exhaust of very hot gases that gives the rocket its thrust.*

Robert H. Goddard (1882–1945)
Goddard was a United States physicist who designed, and in 1926 launched, the first successful liquid-fueled rocket. By 1935 his gyroscopically controlled rockets flew at supersonic speeds. He got financial help from private investors, but it was many years before the American government took an interest in his work.

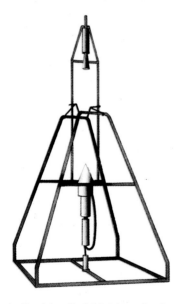

▲ *Goddard's 1926 liquid-fueled rocket on its launch frame. It used gasoline as fuel and liquid oxygen as oxidizer. The rocket flew for only 2 seconds, and reached a height of 40 feet (12 m) but it was an important start.*

engine as a jet of gas through a bell-shaped nozzle and propelling the rocket in the opposite direction. Rockets using solid fuel, GUNPOWDER, were invented in China in the 11th century and used in Europe 200 years later to bombard enemies. In the 19th century, William Congreve developed military rockets capable of flying over 6,000 feet (1,800 m). The first liquid fuel rocket was launched in 1926 by the American, Robert H. Goddard. In World War II long-range liquid fuel rockets were developed. Since then rockets have been used mostly for SPACE EXPLORATION and launching SATELLITES.

Rocks

Rocks are any of the masses of solid MINERAL materials which make up the crust of the EARTH. About 99 percent of all rocks are composed of the so-called "rock-forming minerals." *See* pages 602 and 603.

Roots

Plant roots anchor the plants in the ground and soak up the WATER and MINERALS needed for making food. Roots are soft at the tip, but they force their way down into the SOIL with surprising force. They branch in all directions

Taproot (dandelion)

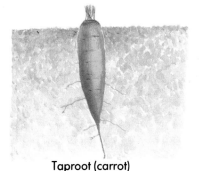

Taproot (carrot)

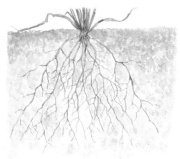

Fibrous root (grass)

to hold the plant firmly. The root system of a plant is often extensive. Water gets into the roots from the soil by OSMOSIS. It passes into minute hairs on the younger parts of the roots, and then moves to the center where tough-walled tubes carry it up to the STEM and LEAVES. The tubes and their tough walls give the roots their strength. Some roots also store food. Carrots and parsnips are full of SUGARS and other foods that the plants had stored up to survive the winter and produce new leaves in spring.

Rotation

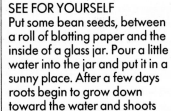

Rotation is a spinning motion around a central point or axis. The EARTH rotates on its axis once every 24 hours, while it also revolves around the SUN. In physics and chemistry, if a MOLECULE or a CRYSTAL looks and behaves identically when it has been rotated, it is said to exhibit rotational SYMMETRY. For example, a simple crystal shaped like a square with an identical ATOM at each corner looks the same if it is rotated a quarter turn in either direction. In LIQUID CRYSTAL DISPLAYS, on the other hand, when the crystals are rotated by electrical activity, the way they transmit light alters dramatically, changing from transparent to opaque.

▲ *Many plants have swollen taproots which store starch or sugar as food. Some of these are grown as crops. Other plants have an extensive system of fibrous roots.*

SEE FOR YOURSELF
Put some bean seeds, between a roll of blotting paper and the inside of a glass jar. Pour a little water into the jar and put it in a sunny place. After a few days roots begin to grow down toward the water and shoots grow toward the light.

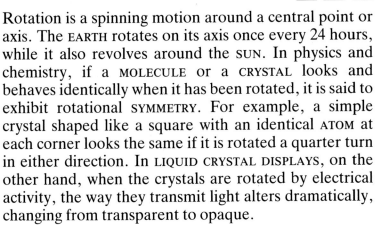

SEE FOR YOURSELF
The illustration shows the letter F turned or rotated through three 90° angles. What will it look like if turned once more? Try doing this with other letters, for example the letter H. Does it always look different or does it sometimes look the same? If it always looks the same the letter has rotational symmetry.

ROCKS

Almost all of the minerals that make up rocks are made up of compounds of only about eight elements: oxygen, silicon, aluminum, iron, calcium, sodium, potassium, and magnesium. Rocks are the foundations from which soil is made and on which all life on Earth is supported.

There are three main groups of rocks: igneous rocks, sedimentary rocks, and metamorphic rocks. Igneous rocks, pushed up from within the Earth as lava or forced upward as massive intrusions, provide the source for the other two classes of rocks. Sedimentary rocks are formed when rocks are attacked by the processes of erosion and weathering, breaking them down into boulders, pebbles, sands, and fine-grained silts or muds. The different sized particles are carried by water or by the wind and deposited elsewhere, such as on the seabed, where they build up and eventually harden into rocks. Metamorphic rocks occur when rocks are affected by heat or pressure, or both, from the intrusion of certain igneous rocks, or by movements deep within the Earth's crust and mantle. For example, the metamorphic rock, hornfels, is formed by the action of heat on clays.

The crystals or fragments of a rock may be different sizes so the grain of the rock is fine (small particles), medium (average size), or coarse (large or very large).

▲ Individual crystals can be seen in a rock that is cut into a thin slice, polished and viewed under a microscope.

▼ Most metamorphic rocks were formerly sedimentary rocks that have been altered by tremendous heat and pressure underground.

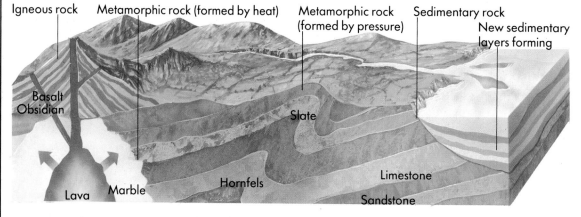

Igneous rock   Metamorphic rock (formed by heat)   Metamorphic rock (formed by pressure)   Sedimentary rock   New sedimentary layers forming

Basalt
Obsidian

Slate

Lava   Marble   Hornfels   Limestone   Sandstone

▲ Igneous rocks such as granite have welled up from the Earth's mantle, and sedimentary rocks like chalk and limestone were originally formed from layers of deposits at the bottom of ancient seas and lakes.

◄ Columns of basalt look like a bundle of giant pencils. Basalt is an igneous rock, the most common form of lava produced by volcanoes.

Igneous rocks

Granite

Pumice

Obsidian

Peridotite

Metamorphic rocks

Marble

Slate

Quartzite

Gneiss

Sedimentary rocks

Limestone

Sandstone

Coal

Ironstone

▲ *Each vertical row contains examples of the three major types of rock. The igneous rock granite is one of the hardest. The metamorphic rocks marble and slate were formed out of the sedimentary rocks limestone and clay. Obsidian is a natural glass. Pumice is thrown out during volcanic eruptions*

◄ *This "pavement" of limestone is called karst. It was probably formed by an underground stream whose waters opened up the cracks between the slabs.*

SEE FOR YOURSELF
You can make your own rock collection. Collect samples of rocks by breaking off pieces with a hammer (wear goggles to protect your eyes) or pick up small pieces. Make a note of where you find the rocks and what the landscape is like. Find a book that will help you identify them and then label the samples.

See also CRYSTALS; EARTH; EROSION AND WEATHERING; GEOLOGY; IGNEOUS ROCKS; METAMORPHIC ROCKS; MINERALS; SEDIMENTARY ROCKS.

Royal Society

The equivalent organization to the Royal Society in the United States is the American Association for the Advancement of Science. It was founded in 1848 in Boston at a meeting of geologists and naturalists, and is now the world's largest federation of scientific organizations. Membership in the society is open to anyone interested in furthering the progress of science and in promoting human welfare. It publishes a weekly journal called *Science*. The association's headquarters are in Washington, D.C. The American Academy of Arts and Sciences was founded in 1780 to advance research. The Rumford Medal in physics is one of its best-known prizes.

The Royal Society is an organization based in London, England, that encourages new ideas in science. It does this by holding lectures, running a large library, giving grants of money for scientific research, and publishing articles on the latest advances in science. Its members include chemists, physicists, mathematicians, and engineers. One of the highest honors for a scientist is to be made a Fellow of the Royal Society (FRS) or to be awarded one of its medals. Many famous scientists have been members of the Royal Society. It was founded

► In the 1700s, meetings of the Royal Society were held in rooms off Fleet Street in London. The chairman in this old picture is Sir Isaac Newton.

more than 300 years ago in 1660 and is the world's oldest scientific organization. It shares scientific information with many other similar societies throughout the world, encouraging scientists from all countries to work together.

▼ A Brazilian worker "taps" a rubber tree so that the milky latex will drip into the collecting cup.

Rubber

Natural rubber is a substance made from the sap of a tree grown on plantations in tropical countries, particularly in southeastern Asia. The world's leading producer is Malaysia. The liquid sap is called latex. Other kinds of rubber are made artificially from chemicals by the PLASTICS industry. The United States and Russia lead the world in the production of artificial rubber. All kinds of rubber are POLYMERS. Crude rubber is soft and used for making the soles of shoes and sandals. It is called crepe rubber. It can be hardened by VULCANIZING (adding

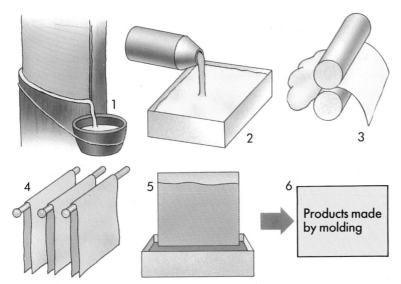

◄ The production of natural rubber involves several stages: **1** collecting latex, **2** coagulating it by adding acid, **3** rolling it into sheets, **4** hanging it up to dry, and **5** dyeing it. Most products **6** are then made by molding.

Products made by molding

sulfur and heating) and then made into a wide variety of products from rubber bands and rubber gloves to tires and inner tubes for road vehicles and aircraft. It can also be foamed for making sponges, cushions, and pillows. Rubber is the chief component of golf balls and tennis balls, which bounce because rubber is elastic.
See also ELASTICITY; FOAM RUBBER.

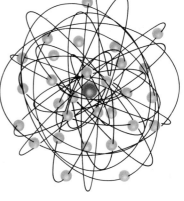

▲ Following Rutherford's discovery of the atomic nucleus, scientists pictured the atom with its mass concentrated at the central nucleus, with electrons orbiting around it. This is a model of a copper atom.

Rust *See* Oxidation and Reduction

Rutherford, Ernest

Ernest Rutherford (1871–1937) was a physicist who discovered the atomic nucleus and many of its properties. He was born in New Zealand and after studying there he won a scholarship to Cambridge, Britain, in 1894. There he began research on ELECTROMAGNETIC RADIATION, but then turned his attention to X-RAYS and RADIOACTIVITY. He showed that there were different types of radioactivity, which he called alpha, beta, and gamma radiation. In 1898 he moved to Montreal, Canada, as a professor and while there he and Frederick Soddy, a chemist, discovered that ATOMS are turned into atoms of a different type by radioactive decay. He was awarded the Nobel Prize for Chemistry in 1908. In 1907 he returned to Britain to become a professor at the University of Manchester; there, in 1911, he discovered the tiny nucleus, which contains most of the atom's mass, at the center of an atom. In 1919 he moved to Cambridge, where he succeeded in splitting an atom.

▲ Ernest Rutherford was awarded the 1908 Nobel Prize for Chemistry for his work on radioactive elements. He was the first scientist to change one element into another.

Safety glass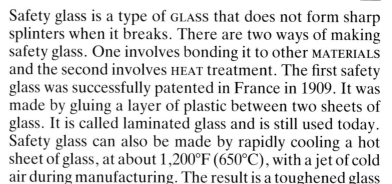

Safety glass is a type of GLASS that does not form sharp splinters when it breaks. There are two ways of making safety glass. One involves bonding it to other MATERIALS and the second involves HEAT treatment. The first safety glass was successfully patented in France in 1909. It was made by gluing a layer of plastic between two sheets of glass. It is called laminated glass and is still used today. Safety glass can also be made by rapidly cooling a hot sheet of glass, at about 1,200°F (650°C), with a jet of cold air during manufacturing. The result is a toughened glass sheet which is six times stronger than untreated glass. *See also* LAMINATES; PLASTICS; PYREX.

▶ *A sheet of safety glass is tested by firing at it with a shotgun. Even though there is a central hole, the rest of the sheet is breaking into angular pieces, not dangerously sharp splinters.*

▼ *Saint Elmo's fire is visible only in complete darkness. Sailors once thought that the eerie glow of St. Elmo's fire around the masts of ships indicated saintly protection. This phenomenon can sometimes be seen around the propellers of aircraft flying through electrified clouds.*

Saint Elmo's fire

Saint Elmo's fire is a glow which can sometimes be seen around pointed buildings in stormy weather, or around aircraft flying in stormy air or dry snow. It occurs because large electric forces arise around the pointed ends of objects. These forces tend to pull ELECTRONS from the MOLECULES in the air until they collide with other molecules. Light is given off in the collision. The name was given to the phenomenon by sailors who thought that the glow around the masts of their ships was a sign Saint Elmo (St. Erasmus) was taking care of them. *See also* ELECTRICITY; STATIC ELECTRICITY.

Sakharov, Andrei *See* Hydrogen bomb

Salmonella *See* Food poisoning

Salt

Salt is a COMPOUND we use in cooking and put on food to improve its flavor. It is also called table salt or common salt. Its chemical name is sodium chloride. Salt is found in seawater, in which it makes up four-fifths of the substances dissolved in the sea, and in deposits that can be dug out of the ground. In hot countries, people get salt from seawater by letting the water flow into ponds, called salt pans, and leaving them to dry up in the Sun. The salt crystallizes out and can be collected. Where fresh water is scarce, engineers remove the salt from sea water by DESALINATION to produce water that is pure enough to drink. Salt is needed in our diet to keep us healthy, and forms part of BLOOD, tears, and sweat. It is used for preserving foods such as ham, and is an important starting material for making CHLORINE, SODIUM, and sodium hydroxide (CAUSTIC SODA).

See also DEHYDRATION; DISTILLATION; EVAPORATION.

▲ *The salt which is dug out of underground mines was laid down millions of years ago as ancient seas dried up.*

NaCl

▲ *The chemical formula of sodium chloride, the chemical name for common salt.*

Salts, chemical

Salts are COMPOUNDS formed when an ACID reacts with a base. For instance, the reaction between hydrochloric acid and sodium hydroxide forms sodium chloride, which is also known as common salt or simply SALT. Salts may also be made in various other ways. They form when a METAL or metal oxide dissolves in an acid; when two salts react together (to form two new salts); and also when a metallic ELEMENT combines directly with a nonmetallic one.

▼ *Copper sulfate is a salt that can be made by dissolving a base (copper oxide) in an acid (sulfuric acid) and evaporating the solution formed until it crystallizes.*

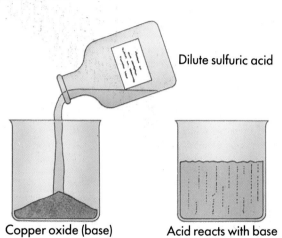

Dilute sulfuric acid

Copper oxide (base)

Acid reacts with base

Water evaporates

Copper sulfate crystals remain in dish

Heat

607

HISTORIC SATELLITES
Sputnik 1 (U.S.S.R., 1957)
First artificial satellite
Explorer I (U.S.A., 1958)
First U.S. satellite, discovered
Van Allen radiation belts
Tiros I (U.S.A., 1960) First
weather satellite
Transit IB (U.S.A., 1960)
First navigational satellite
Telstar I (U.S.A., 1962) First
TV communications satellite
Syncom II (U.S.A., 1963)
First geostationary satellite
Early Bird (U.S.A., 1965)
First commercial
communications satellite

Salts are named after the metal and the nonmetal, or acid, involved in their formation. For example, the metal POTASSIUM combines vigorously with the nonmetal fluorine to form the salt potassium fluoride. Calcium dissolves in nitric acid to form calcium nitrate. The molecules of all salts contain ATOMS of a metal and atoms of one or more nonmetals. When a salt dissolves in water, the atoms split apart into electrically charged IONS. For example, sodium chloride forms positively charged sodium ions and negatively charged chloride ions. The ions supplied by the breakdown of sodium and potassium chloride are needed by NERVE cells to keep them healthy.

See also CHEMICAL REACTIONS; SOLUTION.

Satellite, artificial

An artificial satellite is a spacecraft placed in ORBIT around a PLANET. The first artificial satellite was Sputnik 1, launched by the Soviet Union on October 4, 1957. Since then, hundreds of artificial satellites have been launched. Satellites are used for a wide range of applications. Some are COMMUNICATIONS satellites, relaying telephone conversations and television broadcasts

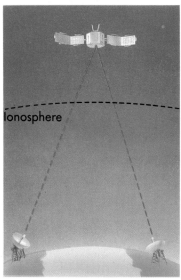

Ionosphere

▲ *A geostationary communications satellite can pass telephone messages, TV programs, and computer data between relay stations on different continents.*

▶ *Tiros I was the first satellite to take detailed pictures of the patterns of weather across the Earth.*

around the world. They occupy a special orbit called a GEOSTATIONARY ORBIT. A satellite placed about 22,300 miles (36,000 km) above the Earth takes the same time to orbit the Earth as the Earth takes to spin once. Therefore the satellite appears to be stationary in the sky. This has the advantage that transmitters and receivers on Earth do not need to move and track the satellite.

Other types of satellite include meteorological satellites used in weather forecasting, Earth RESOURCES satellites designed to send back images and MEASUREMENTS of the Earth, and astronomy satellites designed to monitor the stars and planets. The equipment carried on-board satellites requires electrical power and this is usually provided by SOLAR CELLS. The panels of solar cells convert sunlight into ELECTRICITY. Spacecraft traveling so far from the Sun that there is not enough sunlight to make electricity carry small NUCLEAR REACTORS to generate power. Satellites are kept in the correct position with their dish antennas pointing to Earth by small ROCKET motors called thrusters. When the thrusters run out of fuel, the satellite eventually drifts out of position and becomes unusable.

Satellite, astronomical

All the PLANETS in the SOLAR SYSTEM, except Mercury and Venus, seem to have a moon, or satellite. The Earth and Pluto have just one each, while 24 have been discovered around Saturn.

PLANET	SATELLITES
Mercury	none
Venus	none
Earth	1 The Moon
Mars	2 Phobos and Deimos
Jupiter	16 Four largest are known as "Galilean" moons.
Saturn	24 The largest, Titan has an atmosphere.
Uranus	15 All named after characters in Shakespeare's plays. Ariel, Umbriel, Titania and Miranda are the largest.
Neptune	8 Triton, Nereid, and six smaller moons.
Pluto	1 Charon

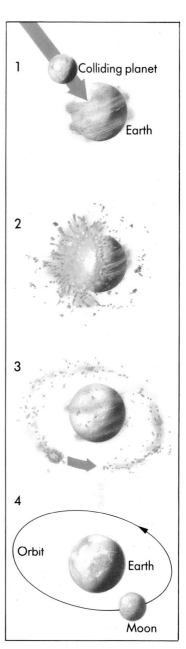

▲ One theory about the formation of the Moon supposes that another small planet approached on a collision course with Earth 1, causing a huge explosion and scattering debris into space 2. The debris went into orbit around Earth and began to collect together 3, until the Moon was formed 4. There are several other theories about the origin of the Moon.

The ones up to a few hundred miles across are mostly bare ROCK and irregular in shape. But the larger ones may be dead and cratered like the MOON, smooth and icy (Jupiter's Europa), have active volcanoes (Jupiter's Io), or even have an ATMOSPHERE (Saturn's Titan). The smallest satellite is Mars's Deimos (about 7 miles (12 km) across), and the largest is Jupiter's Ganymede, with a diameter of 3,270 miles (5,262 km). *See also* individual planet entries.

Saturated solution

A SOLUTION is formed when a solid substance, called the SOLUTE, dissolves in a liquid, called the SOLVENT. When the solvent has dissolved all the solute it can, and it will dissolve no more, the solution has become a saturated solution.

If a saturated solution is heated, it will dissolve more solute. If a saturated solution is cooled, some of the solute has to come out of solution, which it does in the form of CRYSTALS. A similar thing happens when a saturated solution is left and some of the solvent evaporates. The smaller volume of solvent that remains cannot hold as much solute, and some of it crystallizes out. This gives chemists a way of purifying substances. An impure substance is dissolved to make a saturated solution, which is cooled or evaporated until pure crystals of the desired COMPOUND form.

▲ *The rings around the planet Saturn, like those around Uranus, consist of thousands of tiny moons. These rocky particles are kept in place in separate bands by slightly larger "shepherd moons" 60 to 120 miles (100 to 200 km) across.*

▼ *Saturn has at least 18 major satellites, which orbit in three separate groups. The innermost, Group A, are within 300,000 miles (500,000 km) of Saturn; Group B orbit between 600,000 and 3 million miles (1 and 5 million km) out; and group C are nearly 15 million miles away.*

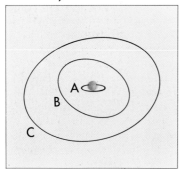

SEE FOR YOURSELF
If you put a teaspoonful of sugar into a jar of water it will soon dissolve, you will not be able to see it. If you go on adding sugar, eventually the water will not be able to hold any more sugar crystals and they will sink to the bottom. The solution has become saturated.

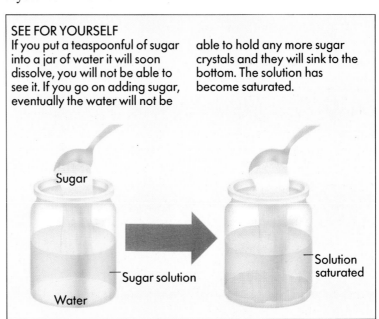

SATURN FACTS:
Diameter at equator
75,000 miles (120,000 km)
Diameter at poles
67,000 miles (108,000 km)
Distance from Sun
936,000,000 miles
(1,507,000,000 km) max.
837,000,000 miles
(1,347,000,000 km) min.
Year length 29.5 years
Day length 10 hours 14 m.
Mass 95 Earths
Density 0.13 of Earth
Surface temperature
−274°F (−170°C)

◄ *The most obvious feature of Saturn is the system of rings that surrounds it.*

Saturn

Saturn used to be known as "the planet with the rings." Ring systems have now been discovered around its three neighboring, giant PLANETS, but of these four, Saturn's rings are by far the brightest. Saturn rotates faster than any other planet except JUPITER and this rapid rotation causes it to bulge at its equator and flatten at its poles.

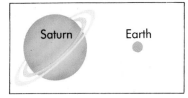

▲ *Saturn is 10 times the diameter of the Earth but is only one-eighth of its density.*

Saturn itself is a chilly world of GAS and ICE. The markings on its globe are clouds of frozen water, METHANE, and other compounds of hydrogen. Unlike Earth, Saturn has no solid surface. In fact a sample of Saturn would weigh less than the same volume of water. This can be compared with an average sample of our own rocky planet, which would be five and a half times heavier than water.

Saturn's ring system is vast; 21 times the diameter of the Earth, but only a few miles thick. To realize how thin this is, imagine a flat ring of newspaper about 15 feet across! This sounds too fragile to survive, but the rings have grown like this because the fine particles of ROCK and ice continuously collide with each other, spreading out into a thin sheet of numerous narrow rings. The wider gaps are caused by the GRAVITY of a few tiny satellites pulling the particles out of particular ORBITS.

Saturn has 24 satellites, of which Titan, the largest and most important, is the only moon in the SOLAR SYSTEM with a noticeable ATMOSPHERE.

▼ *Two of Saturn's moons are Mimas and Titan. Mimas orbits closest to the planet, making a complete revolution in less than a day. Titan is the largest (3,180 miles/5,120 km across) and is the only moon in the Solar System with an atmosphere.*

Titan

Mimas

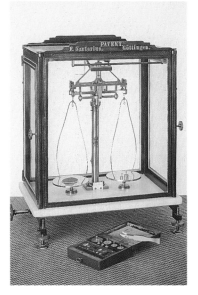

▲ *An analytical balance, used in chemistry laboratories, can weigh objects as light as a ten-thousandth of a gram.*

Scales and Balances

Scales and balances are devices for weighing things. They can be strong enough to weigh a truck or sensitive enough to weigh minute quantities.

There are two basic types. One type works on the principle of a LEVER (like a seesaw) and the other on the principle of stretching or compressing a spring. Using pan scales we can directly compare objects and find out simply which is heaviest, or we can use standard weights on one side to determine the WEIGHT of an object on the other side. This type of balance was used in places such as stores, but in general they have been replaced by more accurate ELECTRONIC balances.

Spring balances have a spring attached to an indicator which points to readings on a calibrated scale. One version works by compressing the spring, as in bathroom and kitchen scales. Other spring balances rely on stretching a spring. These often have a hook on the end and are used by, for example, butchers and fishermen.

Modern electronic balances work in the same way as compression spring balances but are far more accurate.

Scanner, body *See* Body scanner

Screws

The screw is one of the six simple MACHINES. It is very useful. Instruments using a screw gauge, such as a MICROMETER, can make very accurate measurements of the size and thickness of objects. Screws and bolts can fasten things together. Jackscrews are used to raise heavy loads such as cars. The worm GEAR uses screw threads to transmit the rotary motion of one shaft to another shaft at right angles to it. It consists of a shaft with a screw thread, the worm, that engages with a gear wheel.

Clamps use a screw thread to move the jaws of the clamp together. Camera LENSES are focused by a screw mechanism. Many of the fine adjustments necessary to

▶ *A wood screw acts like a long thin wedge that has been wrapped around a cylinder. When you turn the screw, the action of the wedge forces the two pieces of wood together.*

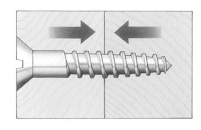

make machines work efficiently use screw mechanisms to open or close valves or to change the value of variable components in an electrical CIRCUIT.

Seasons *See* Daylength

Sedimentary rocks

Sedimentary rocks are made from particles of other ROCKS or hard animal and plant remains which become compressed. Rocks and MINERALS are worn away by EROSION AND WEATHERING. These sediments are carried along by water, wind, or ice. They are then deposited, usually in the sea, and eventually harden into rocks as more layers are piled on top. The particles in sedimentary rocks vary in size from fine-grained muds (clays and mudstones), through medium-grained sands (sandstones), to pebbles and boulders (conglomerates).

Limestones are formed from animal and plant remains. For example, CHALK is made from the microscopically small shells of billions of tiny animals which once lived in the sea. When they died, their shells fell to the seabed and built up into thick, chalky sediments.

Devonian sandstone

Limestone

Chalk

▲ *Sandstone, limestone, and chalk are all types of sedimentary rock. Sandstone is formed when grains of sand become cemented together. Chalk is made from the shells and skeletons of millions of tiny sea creatures. Limestone is usually formed when chalk is subjected to pressure.*

◄ *Pinnacles of limestone tower above the desert in Utah. The softer sedimentary rocks that once surrounded them have been completely eroded away.*

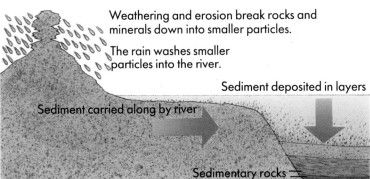

Weathering and erosion break rocks and minerals down into smaller particles.

The rain washes smaller particles into the river.

Sediment deposited in layers

Sediment carried along by river

Sedimentary rocks

◄ *Some sedimentary rocks are formed when particles from the weathering of other rocks are washed into lakes and seas, to form layers on the bottom. Over millions of years, the layers of deposit become hardened into solid rock.*

613

SEEDS

Seeds are the reproductive structures of flowering plants and cone-bearing trees. They are formed after the fertilization of egg cells by male cells from the pollen grains. Each seed has a tough coat, and if you look at this coat you will see a scar showing where the seed was attached inside its fruit or cone. Inside each seed there is a tiny plant, called the embryo, and a store of food provided by the parent. This food is usually packed around the embryo, but in beans and peas and some other seeds it is actually stored inside the embryo.

As long as a seed has moisture, warmth, and oxygen it can begin to grow into a new plant. The process is called germination, and it begins with the seed taking in water. The embryo begins to grow and its root pushes its way through the seed coat. The seed-leaves or cotyledons and the shoot soon follow, although the food-filled cotyledons of peas and beans usually stay inside the seed coat and do not appear above ground. The energy for the early stages of germination comes from the food stored in the seed. Some seeds can remain dormant, in a resting state, for hundreds of years if the conditions are not right for them to germinate.

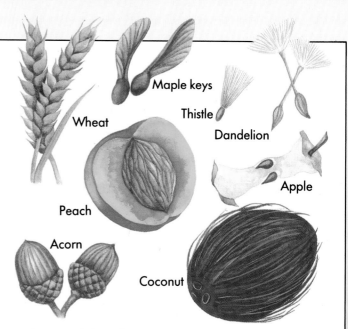

▲ Some seeds have feathery parachutes that carry them on the wind, others are distributed by animals who eat the fruit.

SEE FOR YOURSELF
Some tree seeds, such as those of ash and maple, act like propellers and spin through the air to travel away from the parent tree. You can copy the principle with a piece of cardboard cut and bent as shown, weighted with a paper clip. Throw it in the air and watch it spin.

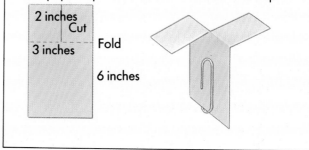

2 inches
Cut
3 inches
Fold
6 inches

Once the seed of the tree *Calvaria major* could only be cracked by the Dodo's stone-filled gullet, but the Dodo has been extinct since 1680. Today the seeds can be cracked by turkeys and machines used to polish gems.

▶ These seeds need to be dispersed by the wind and by animals, so that new plants can grow. Many fruit seeds are eaten by animals and passed out with the animal's droppings. The poppy relies on the "pepper-pot" effect. When the ovary is ripe it swells into a dry hollow container with holes around the rim, and when it is shaken by the wind the tiny seeds inside are sprinkled on the ground.

See also BOTANY; CELLS; COTYLEDON; EMBRYO; FLOWER; FRUIT; GERMINATION; GROWTH; POLLEN AND POLLINATION; REPRODUCTION.

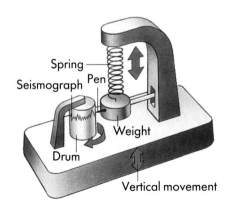

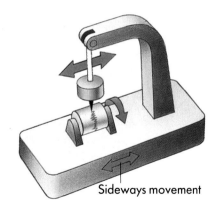

Spring

Seismograph Pen

Weight

Drum

Vertical movement

Sideways movement

Seismograph

A seismograph, or seismometer, is a very sensitive instrument which is used to record the magnitude of an EARTHQUAKE in terms of the shock waves it produces. All seismographs work similarly. Earthquakes produce shock waves from the focus (center) in all directions, so usually three seismographs are used. One records the horizontal movements in a north-south direction, one those in an east-west direction, and another, the vertical movements.

One part of the seismograph remains stationary while the rest shakes with the earthquake waves. A weighted boom with a mirror reflects a beam of light onto a sheet of photographic paper on which it traces a record of the earthquake waves. Some smaller instruments use a sprung horizontal bar, with a damping mechanism, connected to a pen which records the waves as a trace. *See also* INSTRUMENTS, SCIENTIFIC; RICHTER SCALE.

▲ *Seismographs measure two types of movement, vertical and horizontal. Both types make use of the inertia of a heavy weight, which tends not to move when the stand it is mounted on vibrates in an earthquake. The weight is suspended on a spring or on a pendulum and connected to a pen that traces lines on a rotating drum.*

Semiconductor

A semiconductor is a material that can behave either as a CONDUCTOR of ELECTRICITY or an INSULATOR depending on what is done to it. We can control the amount of current that can pass through a semiconductor. For example, heating will allow more current to flow. The most commonly used semiconductor is SILICON. Others are germanium and gallium arsenide. The properties of a semiconductor can be changed by adding small impurities. This is called doping. Some impurities increase the number of ELECTRONS available for carrying a current to give an n-type semiconductor. Other impurities soak up electrons, creating "holes" in the semiconductor

▲ *The first known seismographs were made in about A.D. 100 in China. These early seismographs were about 6 feet across and consisted of a pot bearing a ring of dragon's heads. Each dragon's mouth held a small ball balanced behind its lower teeth. In the event of an earthquake, a ball was shaken out of one of the dragons' mouths and caught by the frog below. The position of the frog indicated the direction of the earthquake.*

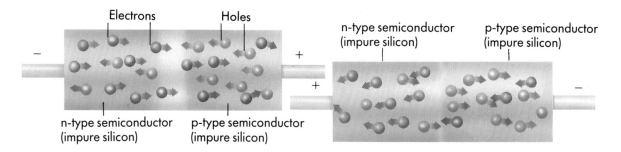

Electrons　　Holes

n-type semiconductor
(impure silicon)　　p-type semiconductor
(impure silicon)

n-type semiconductor
(impure silicon)　　p-type semiconductor
(impure silicon)

▲ *Two pieces of semiconductor material, one n-type and one p-type, may be joined together to make a diode — a circuit device that allows current to pass through it in one direction only. In the left-hand diagram electrons move from the n-type silicon which is connected to a negative terminal to the p-type silicon and so current flows. In the right-hand diagram (where the electricity is connected the other way around) the current does not flow, because the holes and electrons are held back in their own areas.*

(p-type) that behave like positive charges and enable a current to flow. Different parts of the same piece of silicon can be doped as p-type and n-type. Many components in ELECTRONIC circuits rely on what happens at the junctions between p-type and n-type semiconductors.

Semiconductors are important because of their use as the silicon chips in tiny electrical CIRCUITS used in COMPUTERS and MICROPROCESSORS, for example.

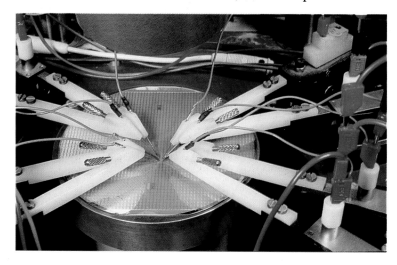

▶ *Hundreds of semiconductor microprocessors etched on a single slice of silicon are tested before the slice is cut into individual components.*

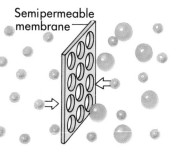

Semipermeable membrane

▲ *The holes in a semipermeable membrane are large enough to let through small molecules, such as those of water, but too small for larger molecules, such as those of proteins.*

Semipermeable membrane

A semipermeable, or selectively permeable, membrane allows only small MOLECULES to pass through it. The membrane surrounds CELLS in animals and plants and allows them to take in food materials and release waste. It protects the watery cell material and often gives the cell its shape. This membrane is an extremely thin and flexible layer. Very large molecules like PROTEINS cannot pass into the cell through the membrane. The smaller molecules in the BLOOD find their way through tiny holes in the semipermeable membrane, while the larger types are unable to pass through. Molecules pass through the membrane by DIFFUSION and OSMOSIS.

Senses

Animals use their senses to obtain information about their ENVIRONMENT. There are five main senses: sight, smell, touch, hearing, and TASTE. The combination of all these senses provides information so the animal can function efficiently. You can demonstrate how important these senses are by trying to do without them. For example, try eating something with your nostrils pinched shut so your sense of smell does not add to the sense of taste. The food will seem tasteless, which is why people cannot taste their food when suffering from a cold.

▲ *A shark has an extremely good sense of smell and can detect blood in the water from an injured animal several miles away. Sensors on its skin also detect the vibrations in the water made by a struggling animal.*

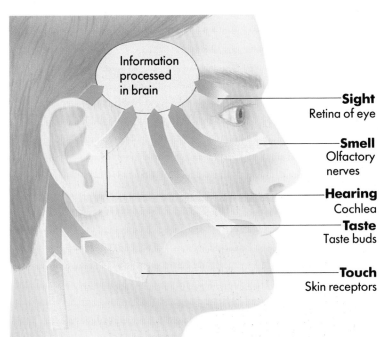

Information processed in brain

Sight
Retina of eye

Smell
Olfactory nerves

Hearing
Cochlea

Taste
Taste buds

Touch
Skin receptors

◄ *Four of our senses rely on organs in the head. Our eyes provide the sense of sight, ears give us our hearing, olfactory bulbs in the nose provide the sense of smell, and taste buds on the tongue are responsible for the sense of taste. Receptors in the skin on the face and over all the rest of the body provide our sense of touch. There are different receptors for pain, temperature, and pressure.*

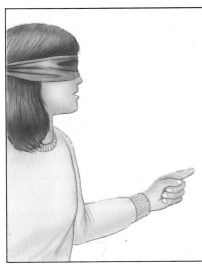

SEE FOR YOURSELF
Blindfold yourself, turn around several times, and then try to find the direction of a certain sound. It helps if you move your head from side to side because your brain can detect the difference in the sounds reaching each ear. This tiny difference gives you a "fix" on the direction of the sound. You are facing the source of the sound when it can be heard equally strongly in each ear. Blind people become very good at this, and it helps them to find their way around.

Fish have an unusual sense organ called the lateral line that runs along each side of their bodies. It detects vibrations in the water and is therefore similar to an ear, which detects vibrations in the air (sounds).

Eyeglasses or contact lenses can improve sight in people with eye defects, and a TELESCOPE and binoculars improve normal sight. Similarly, AMPLIFIERS magnify SOUNDS which are normally too quiet to be heard.
See also EAR; EYE; NOSE; SKIN.

Servomechanism

A servomechanism is an automatic device used to control machinery. An error in the operation of the machine produces a small mechanical FORCE, a change in speed, or an electrical signal. The servomechanism converts this to a force or signal to correct the error. Originally, servomechanisms such as GOVERNORS were mechanical.

▼ *One type of servomechanism is used to keep a ship on course. If it goes slightly off course, signals from its gyrocompass are made to operate a servomotor, which drives gears that adjust the angle of the ship's rudder until it is back on course.*

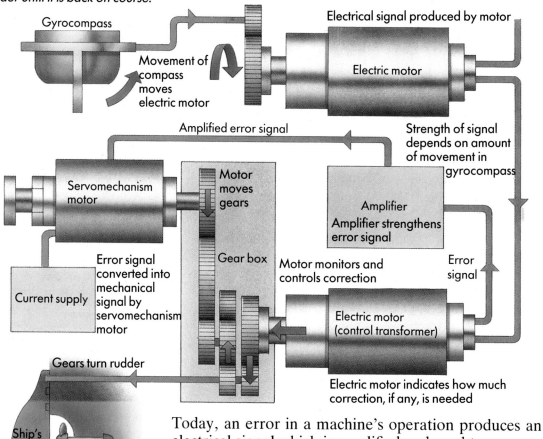

Gyrocompass

Movement of compass moves electric motor

Electrical signal produced by motor

Electric motor

Amplified error signal

Strength of signal depends on amount of movement in gyrocompass

Servomechanism motor

Motor moves gears

Amplifier
Amplifier strengthens error signal

Current supply

Error signal converted into mechanical signal by servomechanism motor

Gear box

Motor monitors and controls correction

Error signal

Electric motor (control transformer)

Gears turn rudder

Electric motor indicates how much correction, if any, is needed

Ship's rudder

Today, an error in a machine's operation produces an electrical signal which is amplified and used to power a servomotor. This corrects the error until the error signal falls to zero. Servomechanisms are used to keep dish antennas on Earth pointing at SATELLITES and to keep telescopes pointing at the same position in the sky.

Shooting star *See* Meteor

SI UNITS

SI units are the units of measurement used all over the world for scientific work. They were adopted by an international conference in 1960 to put an end to the confusion caused by different people using different units. There are seven base SI units, and many other derived units to measure different things.

The base units are the meter, the kilogram, the second, the ampere, the kelvin, the candela, and the mole. For each of these units there is a standard definition. The units used to be defined in terms of a particular example, or prototype; for example, the meter used to be the length of a standard rule kept in Paris. Now the base units are defined in terms of measurements of physical phenomena, for example, the meter is defined as the distance light can travel in a vacuum in a very small fraction of a second. A second is defined as the time taken for a certain number of cycles of a certain frequency of light given out by an atom of the element cesium. The kilogram is the only unit still defined as being equal to a prototype. The kelvin, defined as the temperature at which ice, water, and water vapor can all exist together (that is 0°C) is 273.16 K above absolute zero.

Unit name and symbol	Physical quantity
Meter (m)	Length
Kilogram (kg)	Mass
Second (s)	Time
Ampere (A)	Electric current
Kelvin (K)	Thermodynamic temperature
Candela (cd)	Luminous intensity
Mole (mol)	Amount of substance

▲ The base units of the SI system measure the seven fundamental quantities that are used throughout the world in science and technology.

▲ The original standard kilogram, used in the MKS (meter-kilogram-second) system of units, was a weight made of brass. The modern prototype kilogram is a cylinder of platinum-iridium alloy.

Unit (Symbol)	What It Measures	In Other Units
Newton (N)	Force	kg m/s^2
Joule (J)	Work, energy, heat	N m
Watt (W)	Power	J/s
Coulomb (C)	Electric charge	A s
Hertz (Hz)	Frequency	1/s
Pascal (Pa)	Pressure and stress	N/m^2
Volt (V)	Voltage (also known as potential difference)	J/C
Ohm (Ω)	Electrical resistance	V/A

◄ The SI system has various derived units, used for measuring force, energy, and so on. They can be expressed in terms of the base units.

See also AMPERE; FREQUENCY; KELVIN; MASS; MEASUREMENT; METRIC SYSTEM; TEMPERATURE; TIME; VACUUM; WEIGHTS AND MEASURES.

▲ *Silicon is produced in the form of very pure crystals for making semiconductors.*

Silicon atom

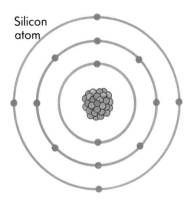

Silicon crystal

▲ *An atom of silicon has 14 electrons orbiting the central nucleus. Its crystals contain groups of four atoms arranged as a triangular pyramid.*

▶ *Silver often occurs along with other metals such as copper, gold, lead, and zinc. Most of the world's silver is extracted from copper and lead ores. But some pure silver metal can be dug up as lumps of feathery crystals shown in this photograph.*

620

Sight *See* Eye

Silicon

Silicon is the second most common ELEMENT in the Earth's crust (after oxygen) but it only occurs naturally combined with other elements. It occurs in many ROCKS as silicates. Silicon dioxide, called silica, is found as sand and other minerals. Silica also occurs in the skeletons of some microscopic animals and in the stems of some plants. Silicon is a nonmetal, and normally does not conduct ELECTRICITY but when tiny amounts of other elements are added to extremely pure silicon, it becomes a SEMICONDUCTOR. Thus the chief use of silicon is in making TRANSISTORS and silicon chips containing microcircuits for COMPUTERS and other types of ELECTRONIC equipment. It is also used to make PHOTOELECTRIC CELLS for cameras and exposure meters. Silica is important in making GLASS and CERAMICS.

Silicon chip *See* Integrated circuit

Silver

Silver is a shiny, precious, metallic ELEMENT. It can be found as lumps of METAL in the ground in some parts of the world. It also occurs combined with sulfur or chlorine in various MINERALS, often mixed with lead or copper, from which it is extracted. People have used silver since ancient times to make ornaments, coins, and jewelry, and it is still used for these purposes and for making MIRRORS and ELECTROPLATING tableware. Its chief use, usually in the form of silver chloride or silver

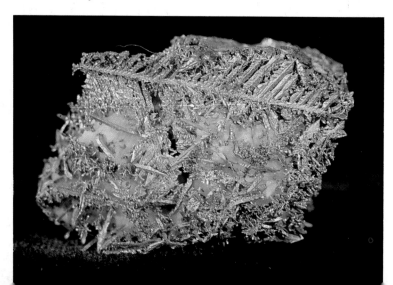

bromide, is in making the light-sensitive coating on photographic films and papers. In a black and white negative or photograph, the black areas are actually made up of tiny grains of silver. Another silver salt, silver nitrate, is used in medicine.
See also PHOTOGRAPHY.

Siphon

A siphon is a tube used to make a LIQUID flow from a higher level to a lower level. The tube is positioned with one end in the container of liquid at the higher level. The other end of the tube is placed in another container lower down. When the siphon is "primed" by sucking liquid through it or filling it some other way, the liquid continues to flow through the tube even when the initial suction is removed. The liquid flows because of the PRESSURE difference between the two ends of the tube. The liquid continues to flow until either the higher container is drained or the liquids at the ends of the siphon reach the same level.

Sirius

Sirius is the brightest STAR in the sky, mainly because it is so close, 9.5 LIGHT-YEARS away. It is sometimes called the Dog Star because it lies in the constellation of Canis Major, the Greater Dog. Sirius is a BINARY STAR, with a faint WHITE DWARF companion. Ages ago, this white

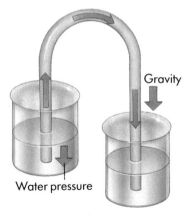

▲ A siphon can be used for emptying liquid out of a vessel without the need for a pump. The receiving vessel must be at a lower level.

SEE FOR YOURSELF
You can make a siphon using a piece of plastic or rubber tube. First put a jar of water on a shelf or table and arrange another container at a lower level. Put one end of the tube in the upper jar, suck at the other end until the tube is full of water, and then quickly put that end in the lower container.

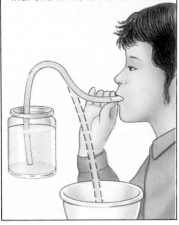

◀ Sirius, the Dog Star, is actually two stars that orbit around each other. Only the brighter of the pair can be seen with the naked eye.

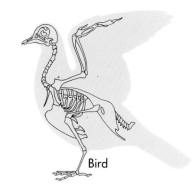

Bird

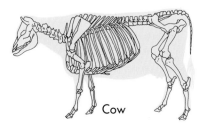

Cow

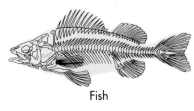

Fish

▲ *Birds, mammals, and some fish have internal skeletons made of bones. Each is adapted to suit the way of life of the animal. A bird's bones are light, because it has to fly. A large mammal, like a cow, has to have strong bones to carry its weight. And a fish has a very flexible backbone (for swimming) and spiny bones to support its fins.*

▶ *The human skeleton is adapted for us to stand and walk upright. At the hips the strong leg bones join the pelvis, which also carries the weight of the upper body by supporting the backbone, or spine.*

dwarf must have been a RED GIANT, shining down on prehistoric animals on Earth.

Sirius was important in ancient Egypt before modern CALENDARS were developed, because its appearance coincided with the annual flooding of the Nile.

Skeleton

The skeleton is the framework of a body, providing support and protection. Our skeletons are jointed to allow the MUSCLES to move the arms, legs, and other parts of the body. Like humans, many animals are vertebrates (they have a backbone), but invertebrates or animals without backbones often have a different type of skeleton. Insects, spiders, and crustaceans such as crabs and lobsters have their skeleton on the outside of their bodies. This is very strong, but has the disadvantage of having to be shed frequently as the animal grows.

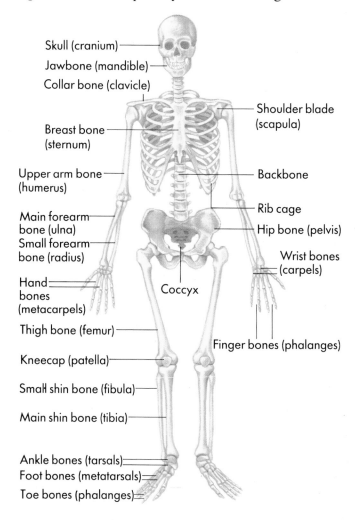

Skull (cranium)
Jawbone (mandible)
Collar bone (clavicle)
Shoulder blade (scapula)
Breast bone (sternum)
Upper arm bone (humerus)
Backbone
Main forearm bone (ulna)
Small forearm bone (radius)
Rib cage
Hip bone (pelvis)
Wrist bones (carpels)
Hand bones (metacarpels)
Coccyx
Thigh bone (femur)
Finger bones (phalanges)
Kneecap (patella)
Small shin bone (fibula)
Main shin bone (tibia)
Ankle bones (tarsals)
Foot bones (metatarsals)
Toe bones (phalanges)

Spiny lobster   External skeleton

Shell — **Limpet**

Backbone — Shell — **Tortoise**

Our skeleton grows with us. In babies the skeleton is rubbery and flexible, but it gradually hardens to BONE as we grow. The bones are strong but light and are particularly strong in the areas under greatest stress, such as the thigh and hip, while in other areas of less stress, the bones are hollow or spongy to save weight. The bones of our arms and legs are tubular and contain marrow; a soft material which produces red BLOOD cells. Efficient JOINTS are needed to allow the bones of the skeleton to move freely. Many of these joints are lined with lubricating substances to reduce FRICTION. The spine serves as the main support for the body. It consists of many small bones called vertebrae, which are jointed together in such a way that the spine is very strong, but can move enough to allow us to twist and turn.

▲ Insects, spiders, and crustaceans, such as a lobster, have an external skeleton made of chitin. The shells of mollusks, such as a limpet, are made of hard calcium carbonate (chalk). A tortoise also has a shell, with ordinary bones inside.

Skin

Skin covers all the human body except for the EYES and has several functions. It provides a barrier against infection by organisms, and protects against minor injuries. It is also waterproof. Skin helps to maintain the correct body TEMPERATURE. When we exercise and feel hot, the skin changes color because tiny capillary BLOOD vessels in the skin have widened to increase the

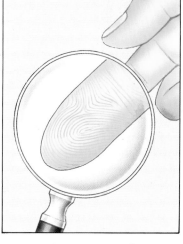

SEE FOR YOURSELF
The skin on your fingertips has patterns of minute ridges arranged in loops and whorls. These fingerprints are unique, and no two persons' are the same — not even those of identical twins. Use a magnifying glass to compare your fingerprints with those of some friends.

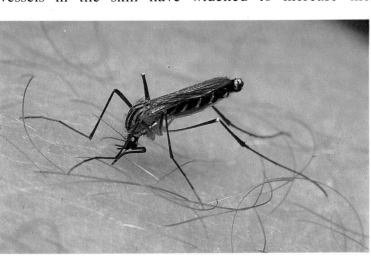

◄ The skin serves as a barrier to prevent germs from entering the body. But this barrier can be broken. When a mosquito punctures the skin to suck blood it can also pass on the germs of malaria.

▶ *Seen in microscopic section, the skin is a marvelous layered structure containing glands, nerves, blood vessels, and hair follicles. The cells in the outermost layer, the epidermis, are dead and continually worn away to be replaced from below. Hair grows all the time, lubricated by a greasy liquid called sebum produced in the sebaceous glands.*

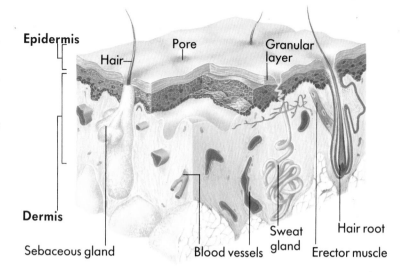

Epidermis
Hair
Pore
Granular layer
Dermis
Sebaceous gland
Blood vessels
Sweat gland
Hair root
Erector muscle

In an adult the skin covers an area of about 18 square feet (1.7 square meters) and weighs over 6 pounds (3 kilograms). Except for the lips, palms of the hands, and soles of the feet, every square inch grows hair.

blood flow, so the excess heat can be radiated out through the skin surface. It also helps to retain heat when the body is cold by narrowing the blood vessels to the skin to reduce the amount of heat the body gives off. Sweat is produced in special GLANDS in the skin. It is a salty, watery liquid that cools the body by EVAPORATION. The skin contains many tiny NERVE endings and receptors. These provide our sense of touch, temperature, pressure, and PAIN, generating signals which pass back along the nerves to the BRAIN. Hair is rooted in the dermis layer of the skin within a deep follicle.

Sleep

Sleep is a period when the body shuts down many of its systems. Although the body is resting, the BRAIN is still active, and can be monitored by taking measurements of its tiny electrical currents. These currents vary rhythmically. When we first go to sleep, the brain rhythms are

If human beings are deprived of sleep they will first lose energy and become bad tempered. After two days without sleep a person finds concentrating difficult — many mistakes are made in routine tasks. People who go without sleep for more than three days have great difficulty thinking, seeing, and hearing clearly and some will have hallucinations.

▶ *A grizzly bear takes a nap in the afternoon sunshine. All animals sleep, although some sleep far longer than others. Humans seem to need more sleep than other animals, up to eight hours a day for an adult.*

slow, showing that not much is happening in the brain. After a while, the rhythms become erratic, similar to those produced while awake, and as the body relaxes more, the eyes move about beneath the eyelids. This is called REM (Rapid Eye Movement) sleep, and it is when DREAMS apparently take place. If you are awakened during REM sleep, you remember your dreams clearly; otherwise you will dream several times during each night but you will not be able to remember them. The function of sleep is not fully understood. All animals sleep, but the length of time they sleep varies widely: Cattle sleep for only a few minutes at a time, while cats sleep for much of the day. Few animals sleep as much as humans. If we are prevented from sleeping for a long time, we show signs of mental disturbance.

Smell *See* Nose

Soaps and Detergents

Soaps and detergents are used in washing. They work in much the same way, chiefly by making grease dissolve in WATER, because it is usually grease that holds dirt on clothes and SKIN. But chemically soaps and detergents are different. Soap is a COMPOUND of a metal, such as sodium or potassium, and an organic acid called a fatty acid. It is made by heating FAT or vegetable oil with a strong alkali such as sodium hydroxide (CAUSTIC SODA). Salt is then added to the mixture to make the soap come out of SOLUTION, and GLYCEROL (also called glycerin) is left as a useful by-product. The soap is shaped into

SEE FOR YOURSELF
Soaps and detergents act by making grease mix with water. Put some water in a dish and add a little cooking oil. The oil floats on the water and does not mix, even if you stir it. Now add a little dishwashing liquid (a detergent) and stir again. This time the oil and water mix, forming a milky emulsion.

▼ *Soap is made by treating fat or vegetable oil with hot caustic soda solution. The crude soap is precipitated by adding salt solution, and further purified using more caustic soda and brine. The "neat soap" is run off and made into bars or soap flakes.*

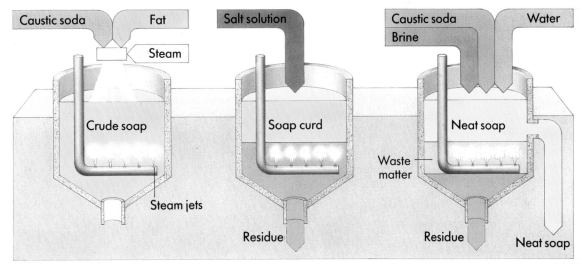

▶ *This manufactured neat soap will be mixed with additives such as colors, perfumes, and bactericides (substances that kill bacteria) before it is shaped into bars.*

▼ *The diagrams show detergent molecules removing a blob of grease from cloth 1. They have a water-soluble end and a fat-soluble end. They surround the blob of grease with their fat-soluble ends 2 and lift it off the cloth, with their water-soluble ends facing outward 3.*

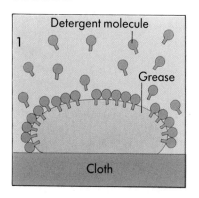

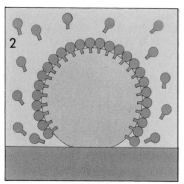

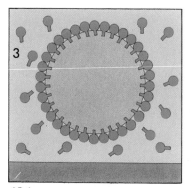

bars or made into flakes, and may have PERFUME added.

If soap is used with HARD WATER, it reacts with SALTS in the water to produce an insoluble scum. This does not happen with detergents. They are usually sodium salts of sulfur-containing acids, produced by the PETROCHEMICAL industry. They can be liquids, such as shampoos and dishwashing liquids, or powdered solids. Detergents for washing clothes may contain ENZYMES, for breaking down biological dirt, and whitening agents, called optical brighteners. Detergents are also used for making EMULSIONS and FOAMS. Any that drain into rivers and streams create foams that are a type of POLLUTION.

Soddy, Frederick *See* Isotope

Sodium

Sodium is a silvery white metallic ELEMENT. It is a soft METAL that reacts vigorously with water to produce hydrogen gas and the alkali sodium hydroxide (also known as CAUSTIC SODA). Because sodium is so reactive, it occurs only as its COMPOUNDS. Chief of these is sodium chloride or common SALT, which is found in seawater and in underground deposits.

Sodium is extracted from salt using ELECTROLYSIS. The process also produces CHLORINE gas as a useful by-product. Sodium itself has only a few uses: in sodium street lamps that give off a bright yellow light, and as a cooling fluid in some types of NUCLEAR REACTOR. But many of sodium's compounds are widely used such as

◄ *Sodium metal is so reactive that it has to be kept under a layer of oil, which keeps out air and moisture. This piece has been cut with a knife, showing how soft sodium is.*

sodium hydrogencarbonate (baking soda) and sodium carbonate (soda) used in making glass and paper.

Software

Software is another word for COMPUTER programs. A computer system has two parts: HARDWARE and software. The hardware is the machinery and the ELECTRONICS. It can only follow a list of instructions called a program. Built-in software stored on chips tells a computer what to do when it receives information from the keyboard and how to form letters, numbers, and symbols on the VISUAL DISPLAY UNIT. It also handles COMMUNICATIONS between the computer and the outside world via a number of ports. These are sockets used to connect the computer to other equipment such as a printer. This software is sometimes called firmware to distinguish it from programs stored outside the computer on magnetic disks or tapes. There are different types of software. For example, WORD PROCESSING software enables a computer to process and store text.

▼ *Software consists of programs that tell a computer what to do and how to do it. Some of the most advanced software programs the computer has to deal with are graphic images which enable engineers to test designs without having to build expensive prototypes. Using computer software means that you can look at the design from a different angle or enlarge it. These three screens show one of the original designs for the Space Shuttle from different angles and at different sizes.*

SOIL

Soil is a mixture of differently sized fragments of rocks and minerals, together with plant and animal debris, water, air, soil animals, and plants. The soil is the surface layer of the Earth, beneath which is broken rock, the subsoil, and then bedrock. Soils may also form directly on sands and gravels. Soils contain organic material which makes them different from rock waste. Soils may form on roofs, in walls, or in cracks in sidewalks. It is usually microscopic bacteria and mosses and lichens which begin the formation of soil from rock debris.

The dark organic material, called humus, builds up from dead plants. It retains moisture and provides the nutrients essential for the growth of new plants. The roots of plants push through the soil, creating air spaces, enabling air-breathing animals and bacteria to live in the soil. A healthy soil contains a rich balance of minerals, humus, bacteria, soil animals, air, and water. This balance depends on the bedrock, the climate, the shape of the land, as well as on the length of time over which the soil has developed.

Plants
Decaying organic matter (humus)
Topsoil
Subsoil
Fragmented rock
Bedrock

▲ Topsoil, which holds the roots of most small plants, is the uppermost layer. Below it is the subsoil, which overlies fragmented rock on top of bedrock. The upper layers contain humus, used by plants for food, which is formed by the decay of organic matter.

SEE FOR YOURSELF
You can find out the components of soil by filling a jar half full of soil and filling it with water. Put the lid on the jar and shake it vigorously. Then leave the jar to stand. After several hours the soil will separate into layers, with the finest particles at the top and the coarsest at the bottom.

Floating humus
Clay
Silt
Fine sand
Coarse sand

Sandy soil   Clay soil   Loamy soil

▲ Soils differ in the sizes of the tiny particles that make them up. In sandy soil, the particles are comparatively large (up to a tenth of an inch (2 mm) in size) and the soil contains a lot of air; it allows water to drain through it rapidly. A clay soil has very small particles holding little air and having poor drainage. Loamy soil, with a mixture of large and small particles, is best for crops.

See also AIR; CLIMATE; EROSION AND WEATHERING; ECOSYSTEM; FOOD CHAIN; MICROORGANISMS; MINERALS; ROCKS; ROOTS; WATER.

◀ *Solar cells can be mounted in panels for generating electricity. Solar panels like these are made into huge "paddles" or "wings" that extend from orbiting spacecraft and provide them with power. Obviously they do not work in the dark, and so the spacecraft have to carry batteries to provide electricity when they are in the Earth's shadow.*

Solar cells are used to power satellites. They require almost no maintenance and so are suitable for use in space. Early solar cells had an efficiency of only 8–11 percent; this had increased to 20 percent by the mid-1980s. However, they are still an expensive and inefficient source of power.

Solar cell

A solar cell converts sunlight directly into ELECTRICITY. It relies on the effect that LIGHT has on the meeting point between two types of SEMICONDUCTOR called p-type and n-type. N-type has an excess of electrons and p-type has a shortage of electrons. When a bright light shines on a cell, ENERGY from the light enables electrons to break free from the junction between them. This is called the photoelectric effect. The free electrons flow through the semiconductor as an electric current. The cell can be used like a small BATTERY. The strength of the current depends on the brightness of the light and the EFFIC-IENCY of the solar cell. Satellites orbiting the Earth are powered by hundreds of solar cells attached to the satellite body itself or to large flat panels called solar panels.

▼ *A solar cell is usually made from silicon. It consists of a sandwich of n-type semiconductor and p-type semiconductor. When light strikes the junction between the two types, electrons move from the silicon atoms in the n-type to fill holes in the p-type, creating a flow of electrons or an electric current across the junction.*

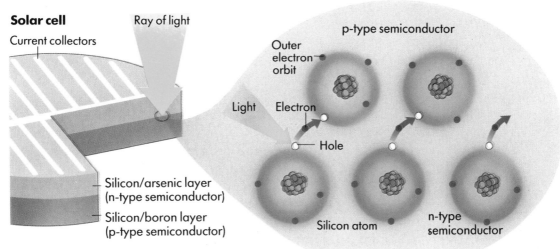

Solar cell

Current collectors

Ray of light

Silicon/arsenic layer (n-type semiconductor)

Silicon/boron layer (p-type semiconductor)

p-type semiconductor

Outer electron orbit

Light

Electron

Hole

Silicon atom

n-type semiconductor

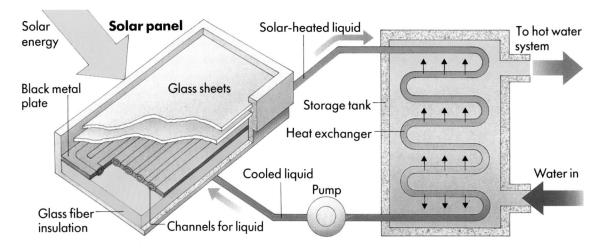

Solar energy

Solar panel

Black metal plate

Glass sheets

Solar-heated liquid

To hot water system

Storage tank

Heat exchanger

Cooled liquid

Pump

Water in

Glass fiber insulation

Channels for liquid

▲ Solar energy in the form of heat from the Sun can be used directly to heat water for a home's hot water system.

▶ A solar furnace uses a huge curved mirror to focus the Sun's rays. It provides a very clean form of heat with no fumes or ash.

▼ The energy of the Sun comes from nuclear fusion, in which hydrogen atoms join to form atoms of helium.

Hydrogen atoms

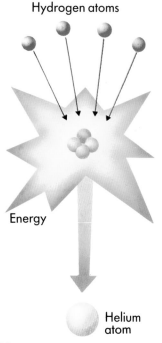

Energy

Helium atom

Solar energy

All the HEAT that warms the Earth and makes life possible comes from NUCLEAR ENERGY at the center of the Sun. At a temperature of about 25 million degrees, HYDROGEN atoms break up and reform into HELIUM atoms, which can survive even this temperature.

This "nuclear fusion" gives out ENERGY, which keeps the center of the Sun hot and also very slowly works its way up to the surface. It is calculated that the energy which makes the Sun's surface shine today was created about a million years ago, and has taken all that time to pass through the "insulation" surrounding the core.

The Earth receives about one two-thousand-millionth of the energy sent out by the Sun, and a minute fraction of this amount, if it could be collected by SOLAR CELLS and used for making ELECTRICITY, or by solar panels for heating water, would solve our energy problems for ever. The FOSSIL FUELS (coal and oil) from which much of our energy supplies come, are the remains of decayed plant cells that grew by the Sun's energy acting on leaves through PHOTOSYNTHESIS.

Solar System

The Solar System is the group of PLANETS which orbit the STAR we call the SUN. There are nine planets in the Solar System and the EARTH is the third from the Sun. *See* pages 632 and 633.

Solar wind

The Sun pours atomic particles into space, as well as giving out heat and light (ELECTROMAGNETIC RADIATION). Most of the particles in this "wind" are ELECTRONS. Near the Sun's surface they form the bright halo or CORONA. At the distance of the planets this invisible wind, "blowing" at about 400 miles per second (700 km/s), forces COMET tails to point away from the Sun. Since the wind is electrically charged, it affects the Earth's magnetic field. Extra activity on the Sun's surface, particularly a flare over a SUNSPOT, pours a burst of extra particles into the solar wind and can upset the Earth's magnetic field so much that radio communications are interrupted.

▲ When the solar wind carries particularly strong bursts of particles sprayed out from sunspots they make the Earth's upper atmosphere glow. This produces auroras at the North and South Poles.

▼ The solar wind makes the Earth's magnetic field lopsided, so that it extends much farther into space on the side of the Earth farthest from the Sun.

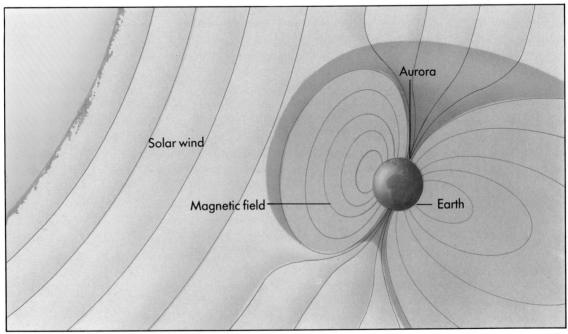

Aurora

Solar wind

Magnetic field — Earth

SOLAR SYSTEM

The Sun and the planets are the result of an event that occurred about 4.6 billion years ago, when a dark cloud of gas and solid grains many light-years across condensed into a cluster of young stars. One of these was the Sun, and the nine major planets formed inside a flat disk of material revolving around it. Now they are separate worlds moving along their orbits through space, one half lit by the Sun, the other half in starlit darkness.

Five of the nine major planets can be seen with the naked eye, although Mercury can only be made out on a few occasions each year, at twilight.

In addition to the major planets, there are countless millions of other much smaller bodies orbiting the Sun. Thousands of minor planets, or asteroids, have been discovered in the wide zone between the orbits of Mars and Jupiter, while comets in their long narrow orbits sweep near the Sun and back into the realm of the outer planets and beyond. Particles the size of sand grains, thrown out from old comets, orbit the Sun in loose clouds and become meteors when they flash down through the Earth's atmosphere.

▶ *The planets of our Solar System are drawn here to the same scale, so that you can compare their sizes. They are 1 Mercury, 2 Venus, 3 Earth, 4 Mars, 5 Jupiter, 6 Saturn, 7 Uranus, 8 Neptune, and 9 Pluto. They are arranged here in their order from the Sun, Mercury is closest to the Sun and Pluto is normally farthest away.*

▼ *The four innermost planets, which include Earth, are all comparatively small. Then come the four giant planets, of which Jupiter is the largest. Finally there is tiny Pluto, which some astronomers think may be a moon that escaped from Neptune.*

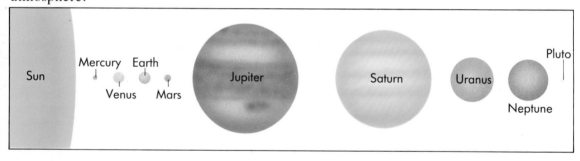

Planet Name	Diameter (miles)	Distance from Sun (millions miles)	Year Length	Day Length	Maximum Temperature	Satellites
Mercury	3,030	36	88 days	59 days	840°F	no
Venus	7,545	67	225 days	117 days	900°F	no
Earth	7,927	93	365¼ days	23 hours 56 min.	140°F	yes
Mars	4,220	142	687 days	24 hours 37 min.	−22°F	yes
Jupiter	88,700	483	11.9 years	9 hours 50 min.	−240°F	yes
Saturn	75,000	887	29.5 years	10 hours 14 min.	−270°F	yes
Uranus	32,300	1,783	84 years	17 hours 18 min.	−330°F	yes
Neptune	30,800	2,794	164.8 years	18 hours	−350°F	yes
Pluto	1,800	3,660	248 years	6 days 9 hours	−380°F	yes

▲ The star Beta Pictoris is surrounded by a disk of rocky materials which may one day condense to form the planets of another solar system.

See also ASTEROIDS; COMET; METEOR; METEORITE; PLANET; STARS; SUN; UNIVERSE.

▲ *The atoms in a solid are in a regular arrangement called a lattice. This makes solids hard materials that hold their shape.*

Nearly all solids melt if they are heated to a sufficiently high temperature. Even a metal such as tungsten, one of the hardest known, melts at 6,100°F (3,370°C). But a few solids do not melt. On heating they turn directly into a gas, without ever becoming a liquid. This is called sublimation. Examples of solids that sublime are solid carbon dioxide (dry ice) and iodine.

▼ *One way of picturing how a solid solute dissolves in a liquid solvent is to imagine the small solvent molecules getting between the larger solute molecules and forcing them apart. The solute mixes with the solvent to form a solution.*

Solid

A solid is a material in which the ATOMS are held in definite positions relative to each other. This means that the material is rigid; it resists if it is pushed into a different shape and does not flow like a FLUID to fill a container. In many solids the atoms are arranged in a regular pattern that repeats itself over and over again; these solids are called CRYSTALS. Even in crystals, however, there are always "defects," places where atoms are in the wrong place, or atoms of a different kind are present. These defects can have a very important effect on the properties of the material; for example, the materials used in the ELECTRONICS industry have defects, or impurities, deliberately introduced into them to modify their electrical properties. Not all solids are crystals, however. There are also disordered solids, in which the arrangement of the atoms is more like the arrangement in a LIQUID, but the atoms are not free to move around. Glass is an example of a disordered solid.

Even though the atoms in a solid are usually held close to their neighbors and cannot move away, they vibrate back and forth. As the TEMPERATURE rises, these vibrations get larger and when they become so large that each atom moves away from its neighbors, the rigid structure breaks apart and the solid becomes a liquid.
See also SUPERCONDUCTOR; X-RAY DIFFRACTION.

Solute

A solute is the substance that dissolves in a liquid to form a SOLUTION (the liquid is called a SOLVENT). For example, in a solution of salt in water, salt is the solute. Often, as in this example, the solute is a solid. But a solute can be a liquid, as in vinegar, which is a solution of ethanoic acid

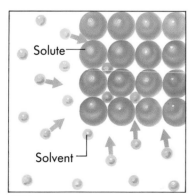

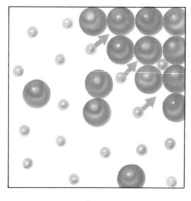

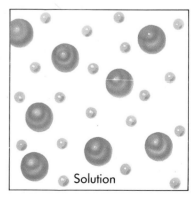

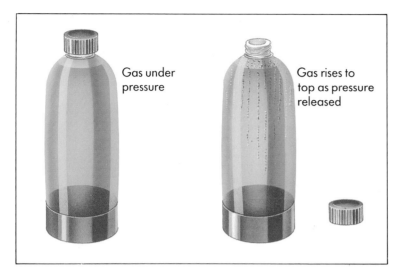

Gas under pressure

Gas rises to top as pressure released

◀ *A gas is a solute when it dissolves in a liquid. For example, carbon dioxide dissolves in water. More carbon dioxide can be made to dissolve by increasing the pressure on the liquid. This is how a carbonated drink such as ginger ale is made. When the pressure is released (by opening the bottle), the extra gas quickly bubbles out of solution.*

(acetic acid), a liquid, in water. In ammonia solution, used as a household cleaner, the solute is a gas (ammonia). When a solution of a solid solute evaporates, a process that can be speeded up by heating the solution, it eventually becomes a SATURATED SOLUTION and the solute crystallizes out.
See also CRYSTALS; EVAPORATION.

Solution

A solution is a liquid MIXTURE. It forms when a substance, called a SOLUTE, dissolves in a liquid, called a SOLVENT. For example, salt and sugar both dissolve in water to form solutions; they are said to be *soluble*. Substances that do not dissolve in a solvent are said to be *insoluble*. When a solution forms, the ATOMS or MOLECULES that make up the solute spread throughout the solvent. When the solvent has dissolved all the solute it can, it cannot dissolve any more, it is a SATURATED SOLUTION. The components of a solution, like those of any other mixture, can be separated. If a solution is heated, the solvent evaporates and the solute is left behind. Seawater is a solution of salt. People extract the salt by letting shallow ponds of seawater evaporate in the heat of the Sun. Many other familiar liquids are solutions, including syrup, vinegar, lemonade, and colored inks. If you make a mixture of colored inks and put a drop of the mixture onto a piece of blotting paper, the colors gradually separate as the ink blot spreads outward. This is another way of separating substances in solution and is used in CHROMATOGRAPHY.

▼ *Some solutions are formed as a result of a chemical reaction. For example, iron oxide dissolves in dilute hydrochloric acid to form a solution of iron chloride.*

Iron oxide

Hydrochloric acid added

Iron chloride solution formed

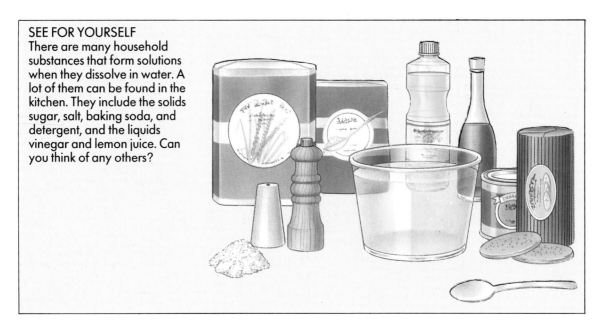

Solvent

A solvent is a LIQUID in which a substance will dissolve to form a SOLUTION. The dissolved substance is called the SOLUTE. The most common solvent is water, which dissolves many different substances. Other solvents, often made from PETROCHEMICALS, are used to dissolve oil and grease (as in the dry cleaning of clothes) and to dissolve PLASTICS to make glue and paint. The smell of such products is usually due to the solvent in them partly evaporating. This VAPOR is nearly always very poisonous. Some substances may dissolve in some solvents and not others, for example, the alcohol ethanol will dissolve in water but oil will not.
See also EVAPORATION.

▼ A paint brush can be cleaned using a solvent such as paint thinner. The solvent dissolves the paint off the brush, leaving the bristles clean.

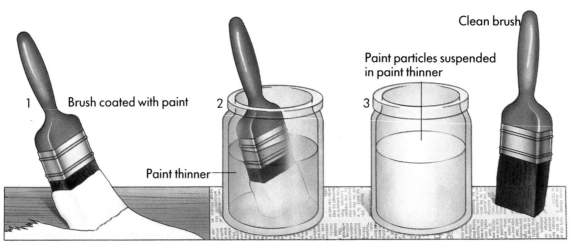

1 Brush coated with paint

Paint thinner

2

3 Paint particles suspended in paint thinner

Clean brush

Sonar

Sonar is a system used to locate things underwater such as shipwrecks. It is also used to measure the depth of the sea underneath a vessel and to locate schools of fish. It was invented in 1915 by Professor Langevin in France to detect icebergs following the sinking of the passenger ship *Titanic* by an iceberg in 1912.

Sonar works by transmitting short bursts of SOUND and picking up reflections or ECHOES bouncing back from obstacles in their path. The distance or range of the obstacle is calculated from the time interval between the transmitted and reflected pulses. The FREQUENCY of sound used is so high that it is beyond the highest frequency that can be heard by the human EAR. For this reason it is called ULTRASOUND. Sonar itself takes its name from Sound Navigation And Ranging.

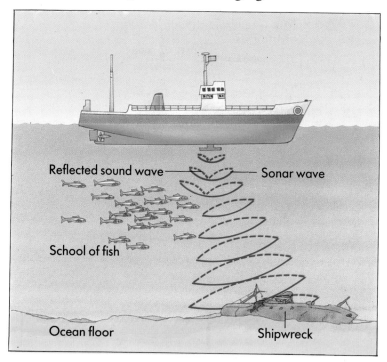

Reflected sound wave — Sonar wave

School of fish

Ocean floor

Shipwreck

▲ Modern naval vessels use a side-scan shadow sonar to detect submarines (top). Reflected ultrasound waves are used to build up a picture of submerged objects, such as this submarine lying on the ocean floor.

◄ A ship's sonar under the keel gives out high frequency sound waves into the water. Objects in their path, such as a school of fish or a shipwreck, reflect the sound back. The time it takes the sound waves to come back indicates the object's depth.

▼ Sonar screens use sound waves to build up pictures like this one.

Sound

Sound is a form of WAVE MOTION. Sound is produced whenever things move or vibrate. For example, when the skin of a drum is struck with a drumstick, it moves back and forth. This movement causes a similar movement in the air nearby as the air vibrates and sets up a sound wave. *See* pages 638 and 639.

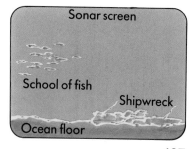

Sonar screen

School of fish

Shipwreck

Ocean floor

SOUND

We are most familiar with sound waves that travel in the air. However sound can also travel through water, metal, or any other material. Unlike electromagnetic radiation, such as light, it cannot travel through a vacuum.

Different sound waves have different frequencies (sometimes called pitches) and therefore different wavelengths. Two sound waves can also be different because one produces a larger amount of movement in the material than the other. In this case we say that the waves have different amplitudes. How loud a sound is depends on the amplitude of the sound waves.

Scientists are not certain exactly how our ears work to enable us to hear sound, but it seems that the tiny hairs in our inner ear may each resonate at a particular frequency, so that it responds to sound at that frequency. Young people can hear sounds with frequencies between about 20 hertz (cycles per second) and 20,000 Hz (20 kHz). As people get older, the range of frequencies they can hear gets smaller.

Sound travels at different speeds in different media, the denser the medium, the faster it travels. For example, sound travels faster through water than through air. The speed of sound does *not* depend on how loud the sound is, nor its pitch—how high or low it is. Sound waves travel much more slowly than light waves. This is why we see a flash of lightning long before we hear the thunder. Sound in air travels at about 740 mph (1,200 km/h).

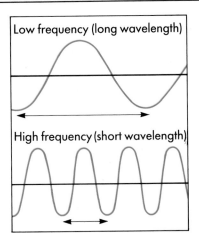

▲ *The pitch of a sound—whether it is high or low—depends on its frequency or wavelength. Long waves have a lower frequency and pitch than short waves.*

▼ *The loudness of a sound depends on the height of its waves, called the amplitude. Quiet sounds have a small amplitude; loud sounds have a large amplitude.*

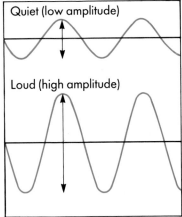

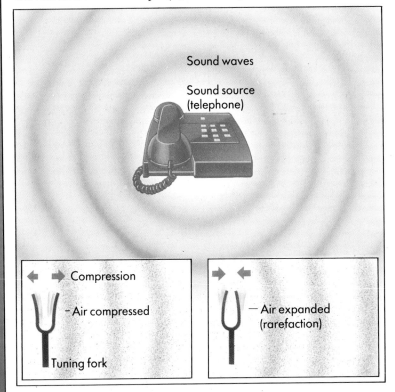

◄ *When the prongs of a tuning fork vibrate outward, they compress the air near them creating high pressure. When they vibrate the other way, the air expands leaving an area of low pressure. Waves of high and low pressure in the air form sound waves that radiate outward from everything that vibrates.*

► *Sound is a form of energy. When converting energy from fuel into movement, some energy is wasted as sound. Stock cars make a lot of noise, which is a mixture of irregular sounds covering a wide range of frequencies.*

▲ *Thunder is the cracking sound made by rapidly expanding air heated up by a lightning flash. We hear the noise some time after the flash because sound travels much more slowly than light.*

Sound travels faster in a dense medium than in a less dense one.
Speed in air
(at sea level) 1,100 feet per second
Speed in water 4,920 feet per second
Speed in glass 16,400 feet per second

▼ *Sound travels faster through water than through air so it can travel farther before it fades. High frequency sounds with short wavelengths also travel farther before fading. Whales communicate using high-pitched sounds which they can hear hundreds of miles away.*

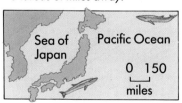

Sea of Japan   Pacific Ocean

0   150
miles

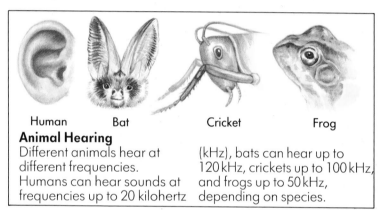

Human   Bat   Cricket   Frog

Animal Hearing
Different animals hear at different frequencies. Humans can hear sounds at frequencies up to 20 kilohertz (kHz), bats can hear up to 120 kHz, crickets up to 100 kHz, and frogs up to 50 kHz, depending on species.

SEE FOR YOURSELF
You can make a musical instrument like a zither from a box and some rubber bands. Cut an oval hole in the top of the box and use two pieces of wood as bridges. Stretch the rubber bands around the box as shown and twang them. The thinner the band, or the tighter it is, the higher the note.

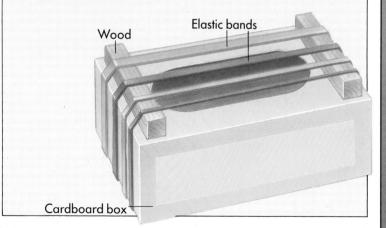

Wood

Elastic bands

Cardboard box

See also ACOUSTICS; COMMUNICATIONS; DECIBEL; DOPPLER EFFECT; EAR; ECHO; FREQUENCY; HEARING; HERTZ; MACH NUMBER; NOISE.

Sound barrier

The sound barrier is a real obstacle to any aircraft that tries to fly faster than the speed of SOUND. As an aircraft's speed increases to the speed of sound, the aircraft produces a wave of compressed air, called a shock wave. The shock wave increases drag, the FORCE that resists the aircraft's motion, and destroys lift, the force that supports it. These two effects make the aircraft difficult to control. At subsonic speeds (lower than the speed of sound), air piles up in front of the aircraft, forming pressure waves. As the aircraft passes through the sound barrier, it begins to travel faster than the pressure waves. This produces a shock wave or sonic boom.
See also AERODYNAMICS; MACH NUMBER; SUPERSONIC FLIGHT.

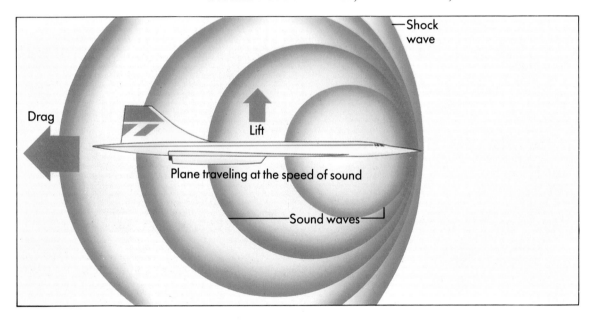

▲ With aircraft flying at the speed of sound, pressure waves build up in front of the aircraft and form a shock wave. The waves also exert a drag force, which tends to hold the aircraft back. But as the aircraft accelerates through the sound barrier and flies faster than sound, the shock wave breaks away and can be heard, after the aircraft has passed, as a sonic boom. You cannot hear an approaching aircraft traveling at supersonic speeds.

Sound recording

Sound recording is the storage of SOUNDS so that they can be replayed later. There are three methods: mechanical, magnetic, and optical. The first practical mechanical sound recording machine, the phonograph, was invented by Thomas EDISON in 1877. Sounds made a needle vibrate against a rotating wax cylinder, cutting a groove in the wax. When the cylinder was replayed, the needle vibrating in the groove recreated the sounds. Cylinders were later replaced by discs or RECORDS which store a greater amount of sound.

Magnetic recording was invented in 1898 but was not

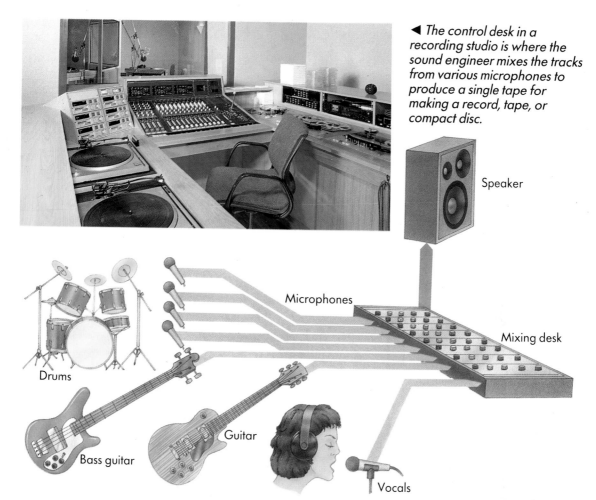

◀ The control desk in a recording studio is where the sound engineer mixes the tracks from various microphones to produce a single tape for making a record, tape, or compact disc.

Speaker

Microphones

Mixing desk

Drums

Bass guitar

Guitar

Vocals

widespread until the 1950s when plastic recording TAPE became available. Sounds are converted into electrical signals and used to magnetize particles in the tape. In Digital Audio Tape (DAT) the sounds are changed into a DIGITAL code before being recorded.

Optical sound recording has been used in the movies since the 1920s. A transparent track on one edge of the film varies the amount of light that passes through to a PHOTOELECTRIC CELL on the other side. Optical recording is also used in COMPACT DISCS where sound is recorded as pits etched in a reflective layer and played by bouncing a LASER beam off the disc onto a detector.

▲ Each singer and each instrument in a pop group has a separate microphone. The signals from these are mixed to give one composite signal for playback or recording.

Space exploration

Space exploration began in 1957 with the launch of Sputnik 1, the first artificial SATELLITE. Since then, hundreds of spacecraft have been launched from the Earth's surface by ROCKETS. See pages 642 and 643.

Loudspeakers in record and CD playing equipment have to produce sounds that are good copies of the original sounds. They must cover a wide range of frequencies. A "high-fidelity" loudspeaker system will have several separate speakers. Some will handle low frequencies, others handle high-pitched sounds up to the top range of human hearing.

SPACE EXPLORATION

Most of the spacecraft that have gone into orbit around the Earth are artificial satellites. These are used to examine the Earth's surface (for example, to forecast the weather or to study natural resources), or to observe objects in the sky without the atmosphere dimming and blurring them.

Many space probes have also been launched, traveling around the solar system, and will never return. Probes have landed on Venus and Mars, and sent back photographs and measurements. All the planets except Pluto have been studied.

Men and women have traveled in space. The Soviet manned space station Mir, launched in 1986, may be used for many years. Between 1969 and 1972 there were six successful flights by American astronauts to the Moon, while unmanned Soviet spacecraft brought back samples of the Moon's surface rocks.

Future space plans include the American eight-man orbiting space station Freedom in the late 1990s, and possible flights to Mars by astronauts early next century.

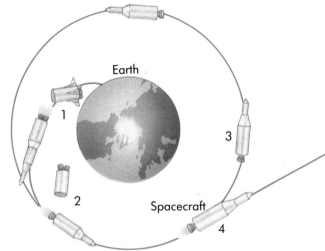

▲ The Apollo mission, which put astronauts from the United States on the Moon, was an ambitious project. The three-man crew was fired into space on top of a three-stage, 360-foot Saturn launch rocket **1**. Stages one and two fell away after launching the rocket into orbit **2**. After orbiting the Earth once **3**, the third stage carried the Command and Service Modules at nearly 25,000 mph toward the Moon **4**. During the flight the Command Module turned around **5**, and docked with the Lunar Module **6**. The third stage then separated and fell away **7**. The spacecraft's course was then corrected so that it went into orbit around the Moon **8**. Two of the astronauts transferred to the Lunar Module, which separated **9**, made the descent to the Moon's surface **10** and landed **11**. One astronaut remained in the Command Module, orbiting the Moon **12**. After completing their tasks on the Moon, the two astronauts were launched in the Lunar Module **13** to dock with the Command Module **14** and make their return to Earth **15**.

Milestones in Space Exploration

1957 Sputnik 1 (USSR) launched.
1961 First manned satellite (USSR).
1965 First close-up photographs of a planet, Mars from Mariner 4 (USA).
1969 The first men land on the Moon from Apollo 11 (USA).
1970 Venera 7 (USSR), first space probe to land on a planet, Venus.
1971 The first orbiting space station, Salyut 1, launched (USSR).
1975 The Viking probes I and II (USA) land on Mars.
1977 Voyager 2 (USA) launched. By 1989 it had passed four planets.
1981 Space Shuttle *Columbia* (USA) first launched.
1986 Launch of the Mir space station (USSR).
1990 Hubble Space Telescope (USA) launched.

▲ Venera 4 was a Soviet space probe that sent back to Earth the first pictures of the atmosphere of Venus. Later Venera probes landed on the planet's surface. Unmanned space probes have now visited all the planets of the solar system except Pluto, either to fly past or land on them. The Voyager probes, sent by the United States, have made a "grand tour" of the outer planets and their moons. Recently Ulysses was sent to fly over the poles of the Sun.

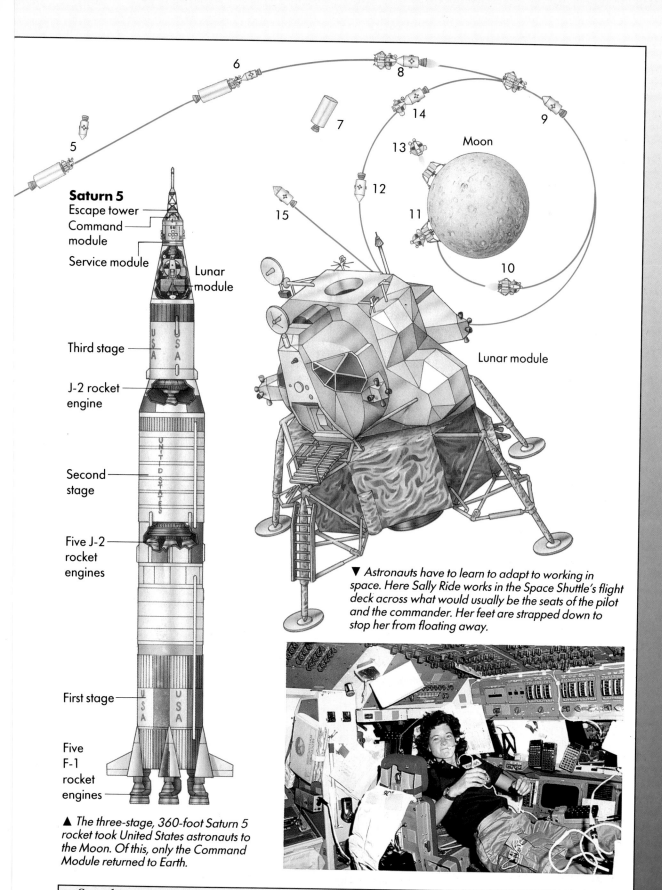

Saturn 5
Escape tower
Command module
Service module

Lunar module

Third stage

J-2 rocket engine

Second stage

Five J-2 rocket engines

First stage

Five F-1 rocket engines

▲ The three-stage, 360-foot Saturn 5 rocket took United States astronauts to the Moon. Of this, only the Command Module returned to Earth.

Moon

Lunar module

▼ Astronauts have to learn to adapt to working in space. Here Sally Ride works in the Space Shuttle's flight deck across what would usually be the seats of the pilot and the commander. Her feet are strapped down to stop her from floating away.

See also ASTRONAUT; MOON; PLANET; ROCKET; SATELLITE, ARTIFICIAL; SOLAR SYSTEM; SPACE PROBE; SPACE SHUTTLE; SPACE STATION.

▲ The Space Shuttle roars into the sky strapped to its launch vehicle. Its own rocket motors steer it in orbit, but it returns without power and glides to a landing.

Space Shuttle

The Shuttle is a type of spacecraft. Launched like an ordinary ROCKET into Earth ORBIT (taking about 15 minutes to reach its orbital altitude), it can stay in orbit for a few days. It lands like a glider on a special runway at either Kennedy Space Center, where it is launched, or at Vandenberg Air Force Base in California. After landing, new fuel tanks are fitted for the next launch.

When fully fueled, the Shuttle weighs 2,000 tons. It can carry up to seven crew members and passengers, and has a cargo bay 60 feet (18.3 m) long and 15 feet (4.6 m) wide. This can be used to carry artificial satellites into orbit, or to take up SPACE PROBES (such as Magellan which was carried up in the Shuttle *Atlantis* in 1989 and then launched into space). A LABORATORY or workshop called Spacelab can also be carried in the cargo bay.

The *Challenger* explosion in 1986, in which all seven crew members died, caused a delay while the design was improved. The reusable Shuttle craft are more efficient and economic than rockets that are only launched once.

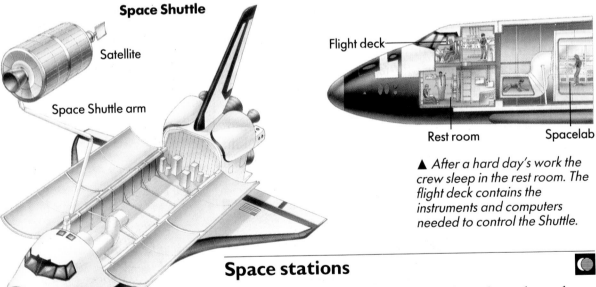

Space Shuttle

Satellite

Space Shuttle arm

Flight deck

Rest room

Spacelab

▲ After a hard day's work the crew sleep in the rest room. The flight deck contains the instruments and computers needed to control the Shuttle.

▲ The Space Shuttle can carry various payloads in its wide cargo bay. It can put a satellite into orbit (or bring one back), or carry a complete laboratory called Spacelab.

Space stations

At the present time all space stations have been large Earth SATELLITES, with enough room for several ASTRONAUTS. The astronauts may stay in the station for several months before another crew takes their place. A space station must have enough room for people to exercise and feel reasonably comfortable. Long-term experiments and astronomical observations can then be carried out. There must be at least one "docking port" so

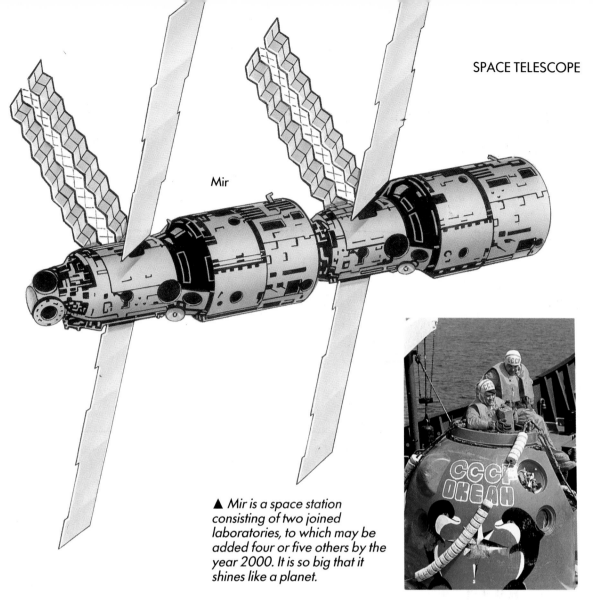

Mir

▲ Mir is a space station consisting of two joined laboratories, to which may be added four or five others by the year 2000. It is so big that it shines like a planet.

▲ Russian cosmonauts hold the record for having spent the longest time in space. Here two of them leave their escape module after 400 days in orbit on the Mir space station.

that crews from visiting spacecraft can pass in and out without air escaping.

The largest and most important space station launched so far is Mir. The first section was launched from Baikonur, Kazakhstan, in February 1986, and the first of four "laboratories," each weighing 21 tons, was launched a year later. Before the end of the century, the United States will have launched the space station Freedom, which will also be assembled in orbit. This will have living quarters for eight people, and in addition to being a zero-gravity laboratory it may be used as a stepping-stone for manned flights to the planets.

Space telescope

Telescopes on the Earth's surface have to observe through the ATMOSPHERE. Air currents make images tremble, and the gases block out important RADIATION.

The first manned space station was Salyut, launched by the USSR in 1971. Skylab 1 was the first American space station, launched in 1973. Over the next two years it was visited by several astronauts while it orbited 270 miles above the Earth. It reentered the Earth's atmosphere and disintegrated in 1979.

▶ *The Hubble Space Telescope was launched in early 1990 from the Space Shuttle. It has a huge reflecting mirror which had to be carefully cleaned before it left the Earth. The telescope was designed to allow astronomers to observe the stars without the distortion of Earth's atmosphere.*

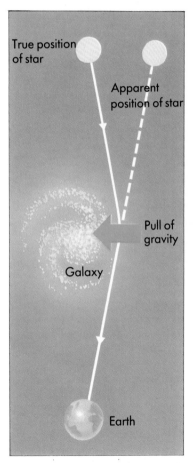

▲ *A strong gravitational field can divert a beam of light, which normally travels in straight lines. The pull of gravity from something as massive as a galaxy can bend a beam of light from a distant star. As a result, the star appears to be in a different position in the sky.*

Therefore the same size TELESCOPE in space should be far more effective than one on the ground. Several telescopes for special purposes had been put into orbit before the Hubble Space Telescope, with a mirror 2.5 m (8.2 feet) across, was launched aboard the Space Shuttle *Discovery* on April 24, 1990. It weighs 11 tons, and focuses images of the sky onto a CCD (charge coupled device). These images are radioed to Earth, where they are viewed on a screen or printed like photographs.

However, after the launch the mirror was found to be the wrong shape, so the telescope cannot work properly until new mirrors are taken up in another Shuttle flight.

Space-time

Space-time is the combination of space and TIME. We usually think of space as having only three dimensions. These can be represented by three lines which are at right angles to each other. However, the theory of RELATIVITY tells us to think of space and time together. Time is like an extra dimension, so space-time has four dimensions, not three. This is very hard to imagine! More difficult still, the theory of relativity also tells us that the combined space-time is curved by MASS or ENERGY. This curving produces the force of GRAVITY. The theory of relativity shows that if another person moves past you traveling very fast, his idea of time turns out to be a combination of your space and your time. Things look different depending on your vantage point and how fast you are traveling.

Species

A species is a particular kind of organism. There are about 1,000,000 known animal species and over 350,000 known plant species. All members of a species have the same general appearance and BEHAVIOR. The members of a species breed among themselves and, because the same mixture of CHROMOSOMES AND GENES is passed to the new generation, the offspring are of the same kind. Differences in structure and behavior usually prevent breeding between different species, but it can happen.

In a species, there can be a lot of variation between individuals. If you look at your friends, they are all slightly different though they are all members of the human species. A species stays much the same for long periods. But species can change. Suppose a chain of mountains or some other barrier, such as different

Fox terrier

Cocker spaniel

▲ All breeds of domestic dogs belong to the same species. They can interbreed to produce crossbreeds, or mongrels.

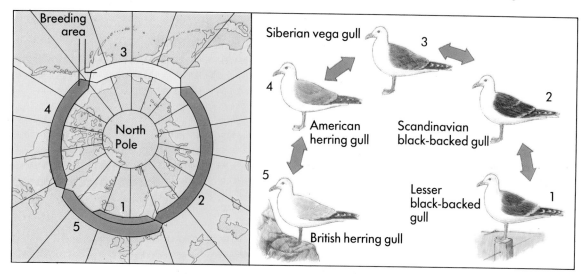

migratory patterns, prevented two populations of an animal or plant species from mixing. Small changes would spread throughout each population and may eventually prevent the two populations from breeding together if they met again. There would then be two species instead of one. This has happened many times in the past and is an important factor in EVOLUTION.
See also CLASSIFICATION; MUTATION; REPRODUCTION.

Specific gravity

The specific gravity of a material, also called its *relative density*, is its DENSITY compared with the density of

▲ The Lesser black-backed gull and the herring gull are clearly distinct species. They both occur in the same place, but they do not interbreed. They are, however, linked by a series of interbreeding subspecies of gull in a ring. This chain of subspecies is slowly changing in characteristics. Each one can and does breed with the subspecies next to it, but where the two extremes overlap, in northern Europe, the gulls do not interbreed.

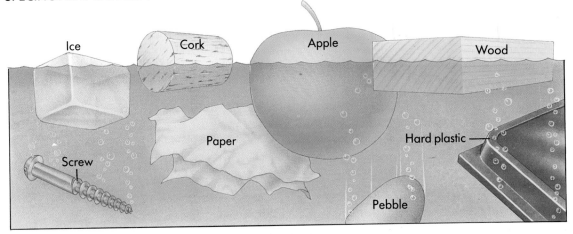

▲ The specific gravity or relative density of water is one. Anything with a lower specific gravity (less than one), such as ice, cork, and most kinds of wood, floats in water. Anything whose specific gravity is more than one, such as metals and stone, sinks in water. Dry paper floats, but when it is waterlogged it sinks.

Density depends on both weight and size. If two bodies of different materials weigh the same, the smaller body is the denser. Iron is denser than cork because a pound of iron takes up less space than a pound of cork. Because of differences in density, one liquid can float on another. Oil is less dense than water. You can test this by carefully pouring a little salad oil into a glass of water.

▶ Specific heat capacity is measured in joules per kilogram per degree kelvin (J/(kg K). Copper has a much lower specific heat capacity than water. It takes less heat energy to raise the temperature of a piece of copper than it does to raise the temperature of the same mass of water by the same amount.

water. The specific gravity of a LIQUID is measured by taking a carefully made float (HYDROMETER) and seeing how much of it is above the surface of the liquid when it floats. Whether or not something will float in water depends on its relative density. Water has a density of one and so anything that has a density greater than one will sink, but anything with a density less than one will float. For example, a SUBMARINE is controlled by pumping water in or out to raise or lower the relative density just above or below one.

See also BUOYANCY; FLOTATION.

Specific heat capacity

In order to increase the TEMPERATURE of an object, it is necessary to supply HEAT. The amount of heat depends on the MASS of the object and what it is made of. The specific heat capacity of a substance is the amount of heat needed to raise the temperature of 1 kg of the substance by 1 degree kelvin. Different materials have different specific heat capacities; for example, water has a specific heat capacity of 4,200 joules per kilogram per

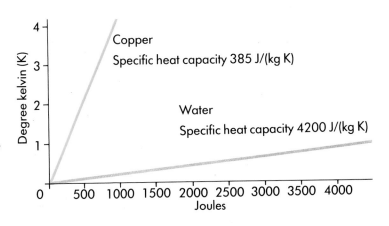

degree kelvin (J/(kg K)). The specific heat capacity can be measured by surrounding the material with some sort of thermal INSULATION so that it cannot lose heat easily. It is then heated using an electrical heater. The amount of electrical ENERGY supplied to the heater is known and the temperature change is measured with an accurate THERMOMETER such as a THERMOCOUPLE.

Spectroscopy

Spectroscopy is the analysis of RADIATION and matter using instruments called spectroscopes. A spectroscope distinguishes one substance from another by the LIGHT it gives out when it is hot. The radiation, which may be light from a star, is passed through a PRISM to separate it into its constituent WAVELENGTHS or colors. The colors are called the visible SPECTRUM and represent the ELEMENTS in the material that sends out the light. So, by studying the spectra of distant stars, scientists can learn what materials are present in the star. If a sample of an unknown material is burned, analyzing the spectrum of the light produced can reveal its chemical makeup. In MASS SPECTROSCOPY, magnets are used instead of prisms to separate IONS according to their different MASSES.

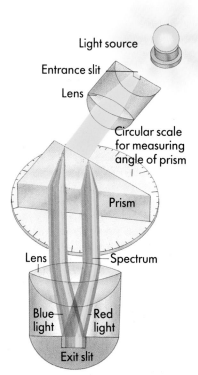

▲ One type of spectroscope uses a glass prism to split light into a spectrum. A lens produces a parallel beam of light from a slit, and a second lens focuses the spectrum onto an exit slit. The prism can be rotated so that only one color at a time can pass through the exit slit.

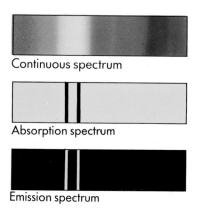

Continuous spectrum

Absorption spectrum

Emission spectrum

◀ Light from the Sun is a mixture of wavelengths and gives a continuous spectrum. To find out what wavelengths other substances use, their absorption or emission spectra are taken. In absorption the substance under test absorbs certain wavelengths shown by dark lines. For emission the substance is made to radiate light by being heated, giving the colored lines of an emission spectrum.

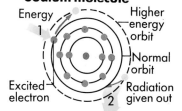

▲ Adding energy to the atoms of an element, perhaps by heating it, makes an outer electron move up to an orbit of higher energy 1. When this excited electron jumps back to its normal orbit, it gives out its extra energy as light 2. This light gives a characteristic emission spectrum. This is the source of the yellow light of sodium lamps.

Spectrum

The spectrum is the total range of ELECTROMAGNETIC RADIATION with different WAVELENGTHS and FREQUENCIES. The first part of the spectrum to be discovered was the visible spectrum of the different COLORS of LIGHT which we can see. It goes from violet light at the high-frequency end, with a wavelength of about 400 nanometers (billionths of a meter), to red at the low-

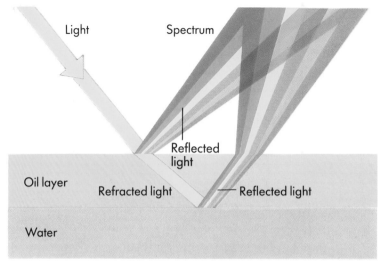

▲ A thin film of oil floating on water creates patterns of shimmering spectral colors (above). The colors are produced when light reflected from the surface of the oil film interacts with light reflected from the surface of the water underneath it (right).

frequency end, with a wavelength of about 650 nanometers. You can see the visible spectrum in a RAINBOW or with a PRISM. Electromagnetic radiation whose wavelength is shorter than the violet end of the visible spectrum is called ULTRAVIOLET LIGHT; beyond this lie X-RAYS and gamma rays. Beyond the red end of the visible spectrum, we find INFRARED RADIATION, MICROWAVES, and RADIO waves, which may be miles long.

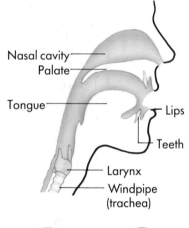

Speech

The power of speech is one ability that divides humans from other animals. Many organisms have ways of communicating simple messages to each other, to advise or warn about matters important to survival. The human ability to communicate exact information by speech (and in writing) is unique, allowing us to develop a complicated society. Speech is produced by AIR expelled from the LUNGS vibrating the vocal cords, which are located in the larynx. Changes in the tension of the vocal cords, and alterations in the speed of the air flow over them affect the pitch and volume of the sound produced. The lips, tongue, and palate combine to convert this SOUND into speech. Speech production requires complex BRAIN control, in order to construct words and sentences. Speech begins with a baby babbling simple words, and builds up gradually. The child's brain development controls the ability to use proper grammar in speech. Some of the ability to construct and use language is thought by some authorities to be built into the brain, rather than learned.

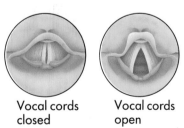

▲ The basic sounds of speech are produced when air passing up the windpipe from the lungs vibrates the vocal cords in the larynx. But recognizable words are formed by modifying the sounds in the nasal cavity and in the mouth by moving the tongue, teeth, and lips.

Speech recognition

Speech recognition describes the process by which a COMPUTER interprets information and commands that are spoken to it. It is relatively easy to make a computer create voicelike sounds. It is much more difficult to program a computer to understand human SPEECH. People speak with different accents, form words differently, and speak at different speeds. The words flow in a continuous stream of SOUND. It is difficult to program a computer to make sense of this. The English language contains about 300,000 words. Existing computers are not powerful enough to cope with this; instead, they are programmed to recognize a much smaller number of words. The chance of a computer recognizing words is increased if it can compare the sounds to stored copies of words to find sounds that match.

No two people speak in exactly the same way. As a result, everyone has a unique "voice print" which is different from everyone else's. Security systems can use computers to recognize people by their voice prints. A person who wants to enter a building speaks his or her name into a microphone, and the computer checks the identity by comparing the voice print with those in its memory.

◄ People with disabilities have been helped a great deal by computer technology. This computer has been programmed to recognize the user's voice, and he gives the machine instructions by talking to it through the tiny microphone in front of his face.

Speed *See* Velocity

Spontaneous combustion

Burning paper is a type of COMBUSTION. When something suddenly catches fire by itself, without the help of a match or other flame, it undergoes spontaneous combustion. In normal burning, intense HEAT, such as from a flame, is needed to start the process. In spontaneous combustion no external heat is applied. This can occur in damp haystacks where the damp hay ferments. This reaction produces HEAT, which cannot escape from the material. Its TEMPERATURE gradually rises and eventually it gets so hot that it bursts into flame. Spontaneous combustion has caused dangerous fires in piles of straw, paper, and rags.

Spontaneous combustion usually happens in piles of papers, oily rags, hay, or coal where there is little air movement. To prevent spontaneous combustion, crops are usually dried before or during storage by forced circulation of air. Coals are wetted to stop oxidation.

Stainless steel is unique in its general resistance to weather and to most corrosive materials. It is the chromium in the steel which helps it to resist corrosion. However, carbon reduces the ability of chromium to provide corrosive resistance, and because of this most stainless steels have very little carbon in them at all.

Spring balance *See* Scales and Balances

Stainless steel

Stainless steel is a METAL which is a type of strong, hard steel that does not easily corrode or rust. It is an ALLOY of iron and carbon, also containing nickel and a high proportion of chromium. It can be polished to a bright shine and is used in the home for knives and forks, saucepans, kitchen utensils, and sinks. It is made into pipes and containers for oil refineries and chemical plants because it resists attack by corrosive chemicals. It has largely replaced chromium-plated steel for the shiny parts of vehicles. Some vehicles have stainless steel exhaust pipes. Stainless steel is also used to make ball BEARINGS and TURBINE blades for jet engines.
See also CORROSION; IRON AND STEEL.

▶ *Stainless steel commonly used for cutlery is called 18-8 because it contains 18 percent chromium and 8 percent nickel.*

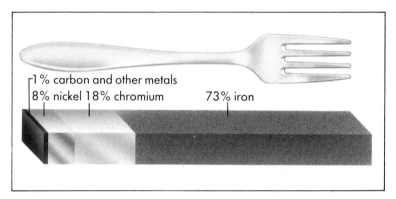

1% carbon and other metals
8% nickel 18% chromium
73% iron

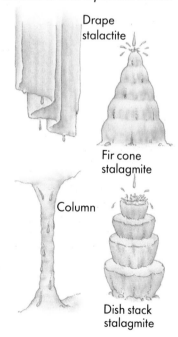

Drape stalactite

Fir cone stalagmite

Column

Dish stack stalagmite

▲ *Different types of stalactites and stalagmites are named after their shapes. Remember that stalactites (with a c) hang down from the ceiling, and stalagmites (with a g) grow up from the ground.*

Stalactites and Stalagmites

Stalactites and stalagmites are like icicles made of stone. They are formed in limestone caverns or in other places where water is able to drip. Stalactites are those that hang down from the roof of the cave, while the ones that grow upward from the floor are the stalagmites.

Water which flows through limestone country dissolves some of the CALCIUM carbonate (chalk) from the limestone and carries it in SOLUTION. If this water then drips into a cavern, some of the calcium carbonate comes out of solution as some water evaporates and carbon dioxide is released to the atmosphere. The carbonate builds up as a stony deposit. Slowly, the stalactite builds up and hangs from the roof of the cave. Where the water falls, more chalk comes out of solution as the drops hit the floor to form a growing pinnacle. The

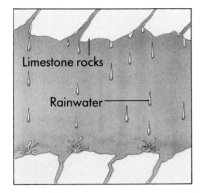

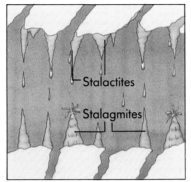

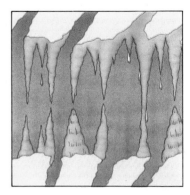

▲ *Stalactites and stalagmites are made of calcium carbonate. Rainwater draining through limestone rock dissolves calcium carbonate, which comes out of solution as the water evaporates after dripping through caves and caverns.*

◄ *Sometimes stalactites and stalagmites grow together and join up to form knobbly columns joining the ceiling and floor of a cave.*

world's longest stalactite is at least 23 feet (7 m) from top to bottom and is in a cave in County Clare, Ireland.

Starch

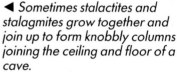

Starch is a white substance produced by plants. They make it by PHOTOSYNTHESIS, and store it in their tissues as a source of energy. Starch is the main CARBOHYDRATE food in our diet, and is the chief component of rice and flour (and foods made from flour such as bread and pasta). It is a POLYMER of the SUGAR glucose, and during DIGESTION starch in the food we eat is broken down into glucose, which our bodies use for ENERGY. Commercially starch is made from potatoes or CEREALS such as corn or rice. It is used in making paper and for stiffening cloth. Starch is used extensively in the food industry. A solution of iodine turns blue-black in the presence of starch. This CHEMICAL REACTION is used as a test for starch or for iodine.

SEE FOR YOURSELF
Many foods contain starch, which is the principal carbohydrate in foods such as bread, pasta, and potatoes. You can test for starch using iodine solution which turns dark blue in the presence of starch. Try testing a variety of different foods. Anything with a skin you will have to slice into. Can you find any fruits that contain starch? You only need a few drops of iodine on each food.

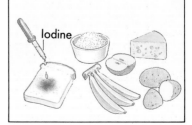
iodine

STARS

Stars are shining globes of gas. Their heat comes from deep inside, where hydrogen is turned into helium, giving out nuclear energy. Many stars, like our Sun, shine steadily for thousands of millions of years before they run out of "fuel."

By studying many stars, astronomers have found that they belong to different groups. Some are very hot and shine with a bluish light, while others are much cooler and look reddish. These tints can be seen in many of the naked-eye stars (stars that can be seen without a telescope) that form the constellations. For example the brightest star in the sky, Sirius, is much whiter and hotter than the Sun, while the closest known star after our Sun, Proxima Centauri, is small, dim, and red. The Sun is a medium hot yellow star.

Many of the star names, like the constellations, are thousands of years old, and are Arabic or Greek. Although stars are moving through space at many miles per second, they are so far away that the star patterns look no different from when they were first recorded.

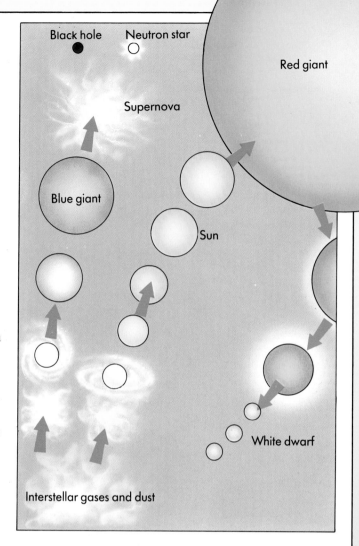

Black hole   Neutron star

Red giant

Supernova

Blue giant

Sun

White dwarf

Interstellar gases and dust

▲ Stars are born and may shine for thousands of millions of years before they die. A cloud of gas and dust condenses to form a young star. Some grow into blue giants that explode as supernovas and could become black holes or neutron stars. Smaller stars at the end of their life, expand into red giants and then shrink into white dwarfs that shine dimly.

Ejnar Hertzsprung (1873–1967)
Hertzsprung was a Danish astronomer who studied the brightness of stars and found that stars could be arranged in a family from hot bright stars to cool dim ones. This family is called main sequence, and our Sun lies about in the middle. The American Henry Russell did similar work, and a graph of star types is called a Hertzsprung-Russell diagram.

Distance in light years	
	225
	200
	175
	150
	125
	100
	75
	50

Earth

Big Dipper

Constellations
We think of the seven stars in the constellation called the Big Dipper as being the same distance away. But, as you can see on the left, the star on the extreme left is in fact twice as far away from Earth as most of the others.

See also BINARY STARS; CONSTELLATION; COMET; LIGHT-YEAR; NEUTRON STAR; PROXIMA CENTAURI; RED GIANT; SUN; WHITE DWARF.

States of matter

The states of matter are the different forms that substances can take. Matter normally exists in three states: SOLID, LIQUID, and GAS. For example, at low TEMPERATURES water is solid (ice). When heated it melts to form a liquid (water), and when boiled it becomes a gas (steam). The different states are sometimes called "phases." Another less familiar state is the "plasma" which is formed when a gas becomes so hot that the ELECTRONS become separated from their ATOMS. This gas behaves quite differently from ordinary gas, so it is given another name, plasma.
See also ANTIMATTER; MATTER.

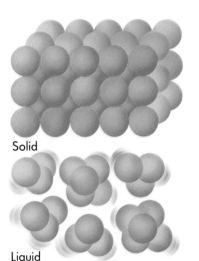

◀ *Whether a substance is a solid, liquid, or gas depends on how far apart its atoms or molecules are, and how fast they move. In a crystalline solid they form a pattern; in a liquid they are bound together more loosely; and in a gas they are free to move in all directions.*

Solid

Liquid

Gas

▼ *The electric charge of static electricity builds up on a comb that is pulled repeatedly through dry hair. The charged comb will induce an opposite charge on small pieces of paper, attract them, and pick them up.*

Static electricity

Static electricity consists of an electric charge which remains still in one place, rather than flowing around to form an electric current. The study of static electricity is known as electrostatics and one of the simplest and most useful instruments in electrostatics is the GOLD-LEAF ELECTROSCOPE. Static electricity was the first type of ELECTRICITY to be discovered. It can be produced by FRICTION; when two materials are rubbed together, ELECTRONS may be transferred from one to the other. The electrons carry a negative electrical charge, so one material develops a positive charge and the other a negative charge. The materials have to be electrical INSULATORS, so that the electric charge does not flow away.

Static electricity produced by friction causes the

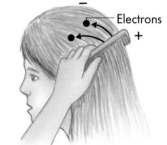

–

Electrons

+

Hair negatively charged after combing

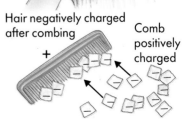

Comb positively charged

+

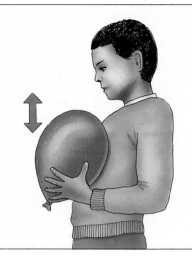

electric shocks one can sometimes get from nylon clothes when the charge is suddenly able to flow through you to the Earth. The crackling sound sometimes heard when folding the clothes is caused by an electrical charge traveling through the air and producing sparks. Static electricity in the ATMOSPHERE produces LIGHTNING.

Statistics

Statistics is the science of collecting and classifying data. It can be used for many purposes, from finding out the won-and-lost record of a football team to forecasting the weather. The theory of statistics is part of MATHEMATICS which uses PROBABILITY as the basic tool. *See* pages 660 and 661.

Steady State theory *See* Cosmology

Steam

Steam is the GAS or VAPOR formed from water when it evaporates. Pure steam is invisible; it is the clear region that you can see just above the spout of a kettle that is boiling rapidly. The cloud we usually call "steam" only occurs farther away from the spout, when the steam has mixed with the cold air so that tiny drops of water have condensed like a CLOUD. Steam can easily be produced at high PRESSURE by heating water in an enclosed container. This makes it the easiest working substance to use to drive machinery and this is probably why the STEAM ENGINE was the first engine to be invented.

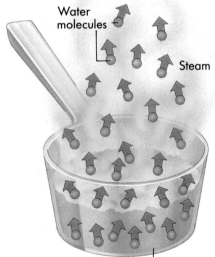

Water molecules

Steam

Boiling water

▲ Steam is water vapor. It is a gas that forms when molecules of water are given enough heat energy to break free from the surface of liquid water. In cold air the vapor soon condenses back to a liquid to form tiny water droplets, which we see as a white cloud over a pan of boiling water.

STEAM ENGINE

The steam engine is a machine that converts the energy stored in fuel into useful work using steam. Thomas Newcomen's steam engine of 1712 improved on earlier steam pumps. It was used to pump water out of mines. In 1769 James Watt invented a more efficient machine which used a separate condenser that achieved the same power from less fuel.

In these early steam engines water was heated to produce steam, which flowed through pipes to a second tank where it pushed a piston along a cylinder. The steam was cooled by a cold water spray. When it condensed, the pressure in the tank fell, sucking the piston back through the cylinder.

In 1784 James Watt built a new steam engine that could power other machines as well as pump water. Steam engines dominated industry and transportation until the internal combustion engine replaced them at the end of the 19th century.

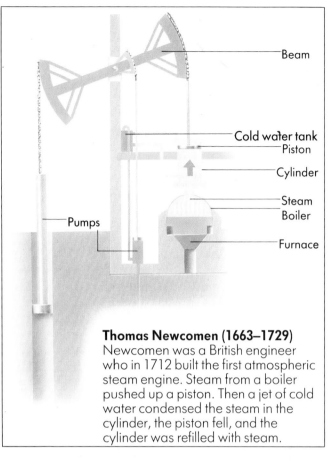

Beam

Cold water tank
Piston

Cylinder

Steam Boiler

Furnace

Pumps

Thomas Newcomen (1663–1729)
Newcomen was a British engineer who in 1712 built the first atmospheric steam engine. Steam from a boiler pushed up a piston. Then a jet of cold water condensed the steam in the cylinder, the piston fell, and the cylinder was refilled with steam.

SEE FOR YOURSELF
You can build a steam-propelled boat. Put three small candles in a metal foil food container. Find a long narrow can, such as a cigar tube or something similar, with a tight fitting lid. Make a small hole in the lid. Put a spoonful of water in the can and use modeling clay to mount it on the "boat" as shown, with the hole near the top. Light the candles and wait for the steam to build up.

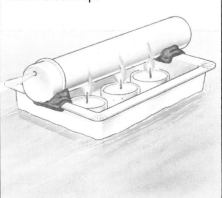

George Stephenson (1781–1848)
Stephenson was a British engineer who in 1813 built the first successful steam locomotive. His 1821 locomotive for the Stockton–Darlington line ran at 15 mph (24 km/h). A replica of his 1829 *Rocket* is shown below.

See also COAL; COMBUSTION; ENGINE; HORSEPOWER; INDUSTRIAL REVOLUTION; INTERNAL COMBUSTION ENGINE; POWER; STEAM.

STATISTICS

Mathematical statistics allows a study of data using probability models. Statistics grew out of methods for dealing with data obtained in repetitive operations such as those in games of chance or industrial processes. These methods are now applied to many diverse fields such as agriculture, insurance, chemistry, and medical research.

In statistics, complete certainty is never possible, but with enough data about a particular question the probability of a particular answer being right can be calculated. For an insurance company the question might be "will a client die in twenty or forty years' time?" Nobody knows, but with records of thousands of men and women an insurance company can make an estimate.

The whole universe is ruled by probability because although the action of atoms and molecules is random, when considered in their millions, their behavior is predictable.

Statistics help clothing and shoe manufacturers to group a population's varying body sizes into certain average size categories. Public opinion polls take a small sample of people (usually about 1,000) and from that sample draw conclusions about how the population as a whole might answer a certain question such as how votes will be divided in an election. One of the important considerations of statistics is that figures can be misinterpreted accidentally or deliberately.

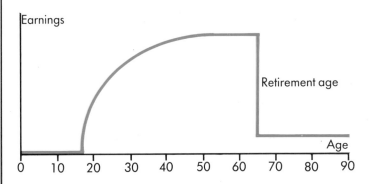

◄ Statistics can be presented in the form of a graph. This graph shows how a person's earnings might change with age. Until a person starts work they will only receive a small income from their allowance. When they are employed, earnings increase rapidly at first and then more slowly, until age 50. At age 65 (retirement age) income falls rapidly to a steady level that represents a pension.

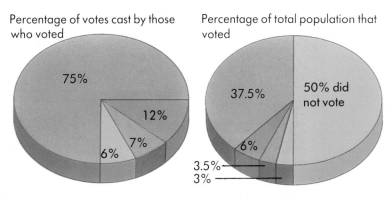

◄ Pie charts are a good way of comparing statistics. The chart on the left shows how voters in an election cast their votes. One candidate got 75% of all the votes cast—a great victory, you may think. But the right-hand chart shows that, because only half the people who could vote actually did so, that same candidate got only a little over a third of all the possible votes.

SEE FOR YOURSELF

Find a newspaper advertising cars for sale. Pick out 50 cars, noting the type of car, year, and price. Use the results to plot a bar chart like the one below. From this you can tell right away how many cars of each make are being advertised. If you make a bar chart of price figures you can also find the average price of a car of any particular year.

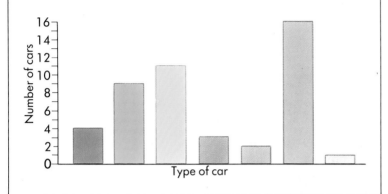

Type of car / *Number of cars*

▶ *Old stone steps have worn in the shape of an upside down normal distribution curve. Over the years, most people have walked near the center.*

SEE FOR YOURSELF

You can make a normal distribution curve by plotting the results of throwing 2 dice and adding the scores together. Throw the dice at least 50 times. Plot the number of times you throw each combination (from 2 to 12). You will find that the numbers near the middle occur most often, and so they are the most likely outcomes of throwing 2 dice. What is the most likely number of all?

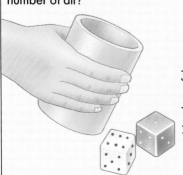

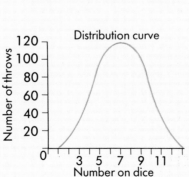

Distribution curve

Number of throws / *Number on dice*

Signs and Symbols

Statisticians have their own mathematical language to communicate ideas and findings. Here are a few of the special symbols used in statistics.

$\approx$ Means is approximately equal to.

Σ This is called "sigma." It means "the sum of" and simply means add up all the numbers in the group indicated. For example, if x is the group (8,5,13,2,7) then $\Sigma x = 8+5+13+2+7 = 35$

: Means ratio, the proportion of one thing to another.

$\propto$ Means proportional to; if one thing increases the other will as well.

> Means greater than.

< Means less than.

Karl Friedrich Gauss (1777–1855)

Gauss was a German mathematician who also studied electricity and magnetism. He worked on number theory, series, and the variations in the orbits of planets. In statistics he studied probability distributions and discovered the bell-shaped normal distribution curve, which is also known as the Gaussian distribution curve.

See also AVERAGE; ARITHMETIC; CALCULATOR; EXPERIMENT; GRAPH; MATHEMATICS; MEASUREMENT; NUMBERS; PROBABILITY.

▼ *The stem supports a plant and carries substance to and from the leaves and roots. Its internal structure is designed for these functions. Tough fibers provide support, and various microscopic tubes, or vessels, transport fluids up and down the stem. This so-called vascular tissue is made of xylem and phloem, which become the woody part (cambium) in stems and trunks of trees.*

Steel *See* Iron and Steel

Stem

The stem is that part of a plant that carries the LEAVES and arranges them so that they get the maximum amount of light. It also carries the FLOWERS and displays them so that they have the best chance of POLLINATION. It is often branched and it may be herbaceous (soft) or woody. The biggest stems are the trunks of the giant Californian redwood trees, some of which are more than 300 feet (100 m) high. Water flows up the stem in thousands of narrow, but tough-walled tubes. Food materials flow down to the ROOTS in another series of tubes. These tubes are arranged in scattered bundles in a young stem, but as the stem gets older the bundles usually join up to form a ring. Woody stems consist almost entirely of tough tubes and fibers, and they add an extra ring around the outside every year. Some stems, including those of most cacti,

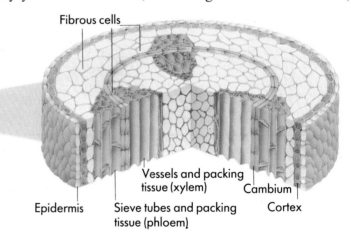

Fibrous cells

Vessels and packing tissue (xylem)

Cambium

Epidermis

Sieve tubes and packing tissue (phloem)

Cortex

SEE FOR YOURSELF
You can show how the vessels within the stems and stalks of a plant carry liquid along it. Take a leafy shoot off a celery plant and put it in a jar containing water which has had some red food coloring added to it. After an hour or two the color will have risen up the stem. Leave it long enough and the leaves will turn pink. Cut through the stalk and you will see the red dye in the vessels that carry liquid.

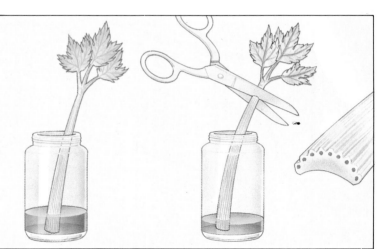

◀ *Irises have fat underground stems called rhizomes. They grow horizontally above the ground (though not all plant rhizomes grow above the ground). The plants use them to store food for the winter. Then in spring, new shoots sprout from the rhizomes.*

Plant stems are usually tough and stringy, because they have to be strong enough to support the plant. However the tender young stems of the ginger plant are used as food. Underground stems include rhizomes and tubers, which provide such starchy foods as potatoes and yams.

are specialized for storing water, and some such as the potato are used for storing food. Most stems grow upright, but some grow horizontally on or under the ground.

See also DENDROCHRONOLOGY; TRANSPIRATION; WOOD.

Stephenson, George *See* Steam engine

Stereophonic sound

Stereophonic sound is SOUND reproduction using two independent sound channels. Stereo sound has a directional quality that single channel or monophonic sound does not. Stereo sound is recorded using at least two MICROPHONES, one pointing at each side of the performers. When the sound is reproduced through at least two LOUDSPEAKERS placed on either side of the listener, they recreate the sounds received by the microphones. Each

▼ *The pickup of a stereo record player produces two signals, corresponding to right and left sound channels, picked up from the left and right sides of the groove in the record. These signals are amplified separately and fed to two loudspeakers.*

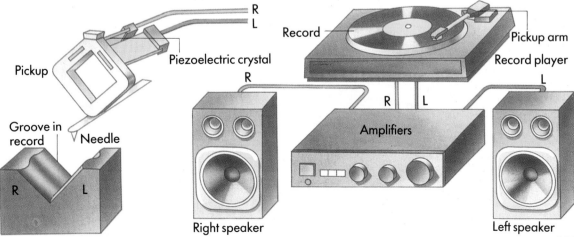

Record

Pickup arm

Record player

L

R

L

Piezoelectric crystal

Pickup

R

Amplifiers

R L

Groove in record

Needle

R L

Right speaker

Left speaker

One hundred years ago, people took stereoscopic photographs using roll-film cameras fitted with two lenses. The lenses were spaced about 2½ inches apart —the same as the distance between your eyes. The black-and-white prints were viewed with a stereoscope. Favorite subjects were landscapes and views of buildings, which kept still long enough for lengthy exposures.

ear hears slightly different sounds. There are other multichannel sound systems. A quadraphonic system has four channels. Most movies are made with four channels of sound: left, right, center, and rear. Dialogue is routed to the center channel. Music and special effects are steered to the other channels to surround the viewer with sound.

Stereoscope

A stereoscope is an instrument invented by Charles Wheatstone for viewing two pictures simultaneously so that each picture is seen by one EYE only. The two pictures show the same scene from slightly different angles. When they are viewed in a stereoscope, the BRAIN combines the two flat images into a single, apparently three-dimensional, image. Stereoscopy is made possible by BINOCULAR VISION. Because of the positions of our eyes, each eye sees everything from a slightly different angle. The differences between the two images, called PARALLAX, are interpreted by the brain as depth. Different points in the combined image appear to be at different distances from the viewer. Aerial photographs are sometimes taken in stereoscopic pairs to reveal more information than they could as ordinary ones.

▼ A modern stereoscope uses pairs of colored slides, one viewed by the left eye and one by the right eye. The brain merges the two views to give the impression of a three-dimensional image in the same way that our brains take information from our two eyes so that we can see objects around us in three-dimensions and judge distances.

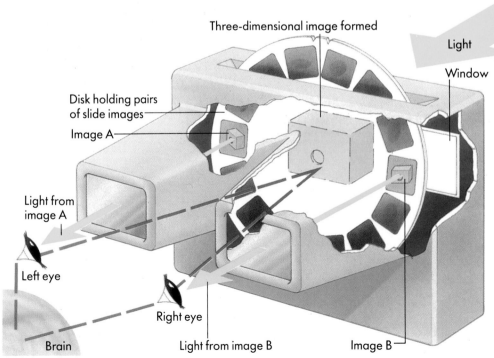

Three-dimensional image formed

Light

Window

Disk holding pairs of slide images

Image A

Light from image A

Left eye

Right eye

Brain

Light from image B

Image B

Sterilization

Sterilization is the technique used to kill MICRO-ORGANISMS that could cause INFECTION or contaminate food. Disinfectants are used to sterilize work surfaces or floors, killing most of the organisms on contact. The most effective sterilization involves the use of HEAT or RADIATION to kill every organism present. In hospitals and dentists' offices, an autoclave is used to sterilize

◄ *To control infection, hospitals have, for many years, used steam cabinets to sterilize their instruments.*

instruments and produce sterile dressings. This uses steam, held under pressure so that it reaches a very high temperature. The combination of heat and moisture, over a long time, kills disease organisms. Food can be sterilized in the same way, by cooking it in a sealed can. The technique of IRRADIATION is being developed for the preservation of foods such as fruit and meat for long periods.

Steroids

Steroids are a group of COMPOUNDS that occur in the body naturally, or can be made artificially. They resemble FATS. Bile salts and CHOLESTEROL are steroids, but the term is most commonly used for a group of important HORMONES. These control the levels in the body of minerals such as sodium and potassium, blood sugar levels, and sexual functions. Steroid hormones are produced in the adrenal glands near the KIDNEYS, and by the testes or ovaries. Some of these hormones have valuable

Heat from candle

Boiling water

Alcohol (spirits)

▲ *Objects may be sterilized using dry heat, the heat of prolonged boiling in water, or an antiseptic or disinfectant such as alcohol.*

665

A type of steroid called an anabolic steroid has been used by athletes to help them put on weight and build up muscles. Bodybuilders, weightlifters, and athletes in "power" events such as the shot put, javelin, and sprinting have been known to take steroids. The use of these drugs is banned in nearly every sport. Their prolonged use can also be dangerous, leading to heart conditions and other health problems.

effects, and are produced synthetically for use as DRUGS. Steroids similar to cortisone reduce inflammation, and are produced for treating arthritis and ALLERGIES. Steroids are powerful drugs. Steroid creams can be bought to treat rashes, but must only be used as directed, or they could damage the skin.

Stimulant *See* Tranquilizers and Stimulants

Stomach

The stomach is a muscular bag which receives food passing down the esophagus. In humans it has a capacity of about one quart. It churns and mixes the food with digestive ENZYMES and hydrochloric acid to begin the breakdown of protein in DIGESTION. Food remains in the stomach for three to four hours, and when it is liquefied it is passed on to the next stage of digestion in the INTESTINE. The stomach wall is protected from being digested by its corrosive contents because it is lined with thick

▶ *The stomach wall has three layers of muscle: lengthwise, circular, and slanting (oblique) which churn up food before moving it along to be digested. The enlarged cross section shows circular and lengthwise muscles as well as blood vessels which bring nutrients and oxygen to the stomach. The stomach wall also contains glands that secrete gastric juice, a liquid that contains acid and enzymes that digest food.*

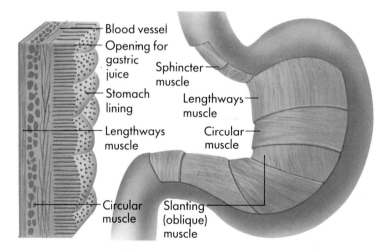

Many Stomachs
To digest the tough cellulose in grass, cattle and other ruminants have special stomachs. Food is swallowed and partly digested in the rumen. It is passed back to the mouth, rechewed and swallowed again. It then passes through the reticulum, omasum and the true stomach, which break the food down more so it can be absorbed.

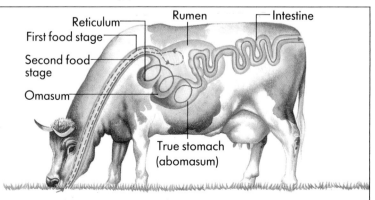

mucus. If the stomach juices do come into contact with the stomach wall, they attack it and cause a painful ulcer. The stomach in other animals suits their diet. Carnivores such as cats and dogs have large stomachs, because they bolt their food all at once and must store it for a long time while digestion takes place. Herbivores must digest tough CELLULOSE from the CELL walls of their plant food. Their intestines are long to allow this slow digestion to take place, and the stomach is usually in several parts.

Stratosphere

The stratosphere is the layer of the ATMOSPHERE above the TROPOSPHERE, but nearer the Earth than the mesosphere. It stretches from 6 miles (10 km) to 30 miles (48 km) above the Earth's surface. The temperature throughout the lower stratosphere is relatively constant though it becomes warmer (about 32°F/0°C) toward the top. The OZONE LAYER is within the stratosphere at between 10 and 20 miles (15 and 30 km) from the Earth. The OZONE absorbs the Sun's ULTRAVIOLET radiation, increasing the temperature of the upper stratosphere.

Because the stratosphere is stable, and because it is cooler at the bottom than at the top, clouds rarely rise beyond the troposphere. Instead, high clouds spread out at the base of the stratosphere to form the anvil-shaped clouds which may be seen at these heights.

Streamlining

Streamlining describes the shaping of an object so that it can travel through a FLUID with the least resistance (drag). This is done by giving the object smooth sides and a rounded outline. Anything that sticks out into the fluid breaks up the flow and causes turbulence. A teardrop shape traveling thick end first is streamlined. Most fish are streamlined. The study of objects moving

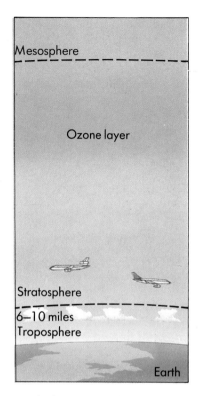

▲ The beginning of the stratosphere varies in different parts of the world. Near the poles it is about 6 miles (10km) above the Earth, but at the equator it is about 10 miles (16km) up. The stratosphere contains the ozone layer which protects the Earth from many of the Sun's harmful radiations. Pilots like to fly in the stratosphere because there is very little disturbance in the weather and almost no clouds at this height.

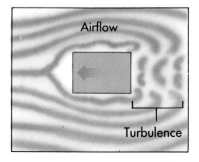

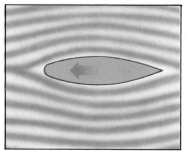

◄ The lines show the way in which air flows around differently shaped objects. A square shape disturbs the airflow and causes turbulence behind the object. This turbulence would cause drag in a vehicle. Compare this to the way that air flows around a smoothly shaped object.

▶ *This Alpine swift is almost as streamlined as a modern aircraft. The body of the bird is rounded and narrows toward the rear. The wings are curved so that air will flow over them smoothly.*

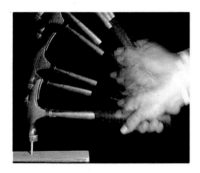

▲ *Pictures like this one of a hammer striking a nail can be taken using a stroboscope. The shutter of a camera is left open while a stroboscopic lamp flashes.*

▼ *The same effect as that of a flashing lamp can be obtained by looking through a rotating disk with holes in it. The light is steady, but the person looking only sees the fan when a hole in the disk comes around, so the blades appear stationary. The fan and disk must be rotating at the same speed to achieve this effect.*

through liquids is part of hydrodynamics. The study of gas flow (usually air) around objects is called AERODYNAMICS. Designers of vehicles and aircraft use hydro- and aerodynamics to produce streamlined boats, cars, trains, and planes. The efficiency of designs are tested by COMPUTER and by models in WIND TUNNELS or water tanks. A streamlined vehicle wastes less FUEL and engine power in overcoming fluid resistance.

Stroboscope

A stroboscope is an instrument that uses a flashing LIGHT to make spinning or vibrating objects appear to be stationary. For example, if a light flashing 10 times per second is pointed at a fan spinning at 10 revolutions per second, the fan appears to be stationary. Every time the fan is lit up by a flash of light, it is at the same position in each REVOLUTION. Examining a spinning or vibrating object such as a propeller or part of an ENGINE in slow motion like this can reveal possibly dangerous motions that would normally be invisible. If the frequency of the flashing light is known accurately, it can be used to

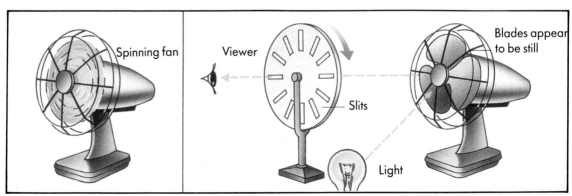

measure or set the speed of the spinning or vibration. The ignition timing of a car engine is set using a flashing light so that the electric spark that ignites the fuel occurs at precisely the correct moment.

Strontium

Strontium is a silvery yellow ELEMENT, found only in COMPOUNDS in various ores and in the water of some mineral springs. It is a soft, light metal, and is so reactive that it has to be stored away from air and water. It is used with iron to make strong magnets. Strontium compounds are used in making glass and pottery, and for giving a bright red flame to flares and FIREWORKS. The metal has a radioactive ISOTOPE called strontium-90, which is produced by the fission of URANIUM and occurs in FALL-OUT from nuclear explosions. Strontium-90 is very dangerous because it is absorbed into the body's bones in preference to calcium.

Subatomic particles

Subatomic particles are particles that are smaller than ATOMS. Three types of particles occur in atoms all around us; these are the PROTON and the NEUTRON, which make up the nucleus at the center of the atom, and the lighter ELECTRON outside the nucleus. Atoms can give off subatomic particles; this is called RADIOACTIVITY. Subatomic particles also have opposite, antiparticles which are called ANTIMATTER. For example, the POSITRON has the same MASS as the electron but the opposite electrical charge. If a positron and an electron collide they destroy each other and produce other particles. These collisions

Strontium was discovered in 1790 by Adair Crawford in Ireland. It was first extracted as an element on its own by Humphrey Davy. Strontium was named after a parish in Scotland called Strontian. It was in this area that strontium oxide was first found as a mineral.

Richard Feynman (1918–1988)
Feynman was an American physicist who discovered some of the rules that govern the interactions of subatomic particles. He determined how particles can interact by exchanging photons (quanta of light). He shared the 1965 Nobel Prize in Physics. After the explosion of the Space Shuttle *Challenger* in 1986, he was one of the scientists who investigated the disaster.

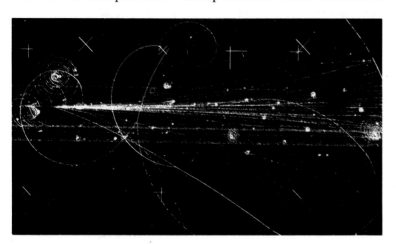

◀ *Electrically charged subatomic particles leave tracks of their paths in a bubble chamber. These tracks were formed when a fast-moving proton collided with a stationary particle.*

The Neutrino
The neutrino is a very unusual subatomic particle. It does not carry an electric charge and has no measurable mass. It travels at or near the speed of light and can pass right through the entire Earth with hardly any loss of strength. Neutrinos are produced when unstable atomic nuclei disintegrate. They reach us from the Sun and exploding stars in space. Scientists first detected a neutrino in 1956.

are observed in large PARTICLE ACCELERATORS.

Physicists now believe that the proton and the neutron are each made up of other particles called quarks which are bound together so strongly that they cannot be separated. It is thought that a proton is made up of three different kinds of quarks. Scientists also believe that there are altogether six kinds of quarks. However, in spite of much searching, no quarks have yet been observed.

Submarine

A submarine is a seagoing vessel designed to operate for long periods underwater. Almost all submarines are military vessels. The others are used for scientific research or tourist trips. The first submarine was built by a Dutchman called Cornelius Drebbel. He sailed it along the river Thames through London in 1620. In 1776, during the American Revolution, the American David Bushnell built an unsuccessful submarine called the *Turtle* to attack British ships. In 1800 another American, Robert Fulton, built the first submarine with a metal hull. The first successful long-distance submarine was built by the Irish-American John P. Holland in the

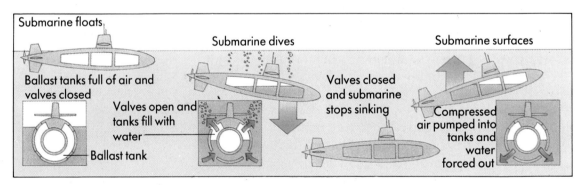

Submarine floats
Ballast tanks full of air and valves closed
Ballast tank

Submarine dives
Valves open and tanks fill with water

Valves closed and submarine stops sinking

Submarine surfaces
Compressed air pumped into tanks and water forced out

▲ A submarine floats or sinks depending on the amount of sea water in its ballast tanks. Compressed air is used to force out the water to make the submarine surface.

▶ It is difficult to imagine what it is like living in the small spaces of a submarine. Often people, especially friends and families of the crew, can look around a submarine on display.

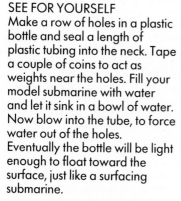
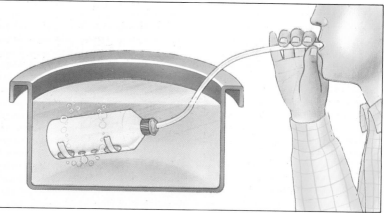

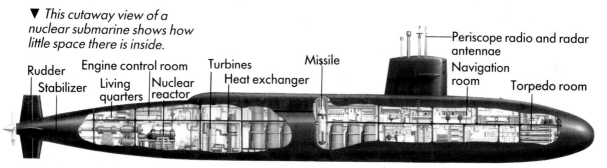

▼ *This cutaway view of a nuclear submarine shows how little space there is inside.*

Rudder Engine control room Turbines Missile Periscope radio and radar antennae

Stabilizer Living quarters Nuclear reactor Heat exchanger Navigation room Torpedo room

1890s. It was powered by a car engine when on the surface and an electric motor when submerged.

World War I was the first war in which submarines were used in large numbers. German *Unterseeboote* or U-boats were successful in attacking enemy shipping. In World War II, submarines were used once again to attack enemy ships. Nuclear submarines can remain submerged for thousands of miles. Diesel submarines have to surface to charge their batteries.

Sugars

Sugars are important sweet-tasting substances occurring naturally in many foods. They are CARBOHYDRATES. In the body, many natural sugars are converted into glucose, which is in turn broken down to provide ENERGY during RESPIRATION.

When people speak of sugar they usually mean *sucrose*, the sugar that comes from sugarcane and sugar beets. But there are other kinds of sugar. In addition to fruit and vegetables, other sources of sugar include maple syrup, honey, cornstarch, and milk. There are more than a hundred sweet-tasting substances, made up of the chemical elements carbon, hydrogen, and oxygen,

Monosaccharides

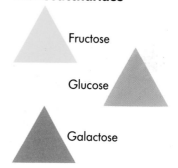

Fructose

Glucose

Galactose

Disaccharides

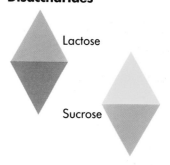

Lactose

Sucrose

▲ *Monosaccharides are sugars made up of single molecular units. Disaccharides have two sugar units joined together.*

▶ *A hummingbird hovers by a tropical flower to suck up nectar. Nectar is a solution of sugar and other nutrients. The hummingbird's beak is specially adapted to fit right down inside the flower of its chosen food plant.*

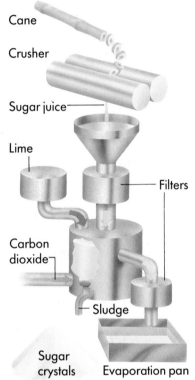

Cane

Crusher

Sugar juice

Lime

Filters

Carbon dioxide

Sludge

Sugar crystals

Evaporation pan

▲ *To make sugar from sugar-cane, which grows in tropical regions, the stems of the plant are crushed and the juice filtered and purified. The sugar solution is evaporated to produce sugar crystals. Sugar is extracted in a similar way from sugar beets, which grow in cooler climates.*

that are known as sugar. Next to sucrose, the most commonly used sugar is *dextrose* or *glucose*, sometimes called grape sugar. The blood normally contains about 0.1 percent glucose. Lactose or milk sugar makes up about 5 percent of cow's milk. Maltose, malt sugar, remains after the brewing process. Fructose is sugar produced by nearly all fruits and vegetables. It is also known as levulose. It is the chief sweetener in honey and is nearly twice as sweet as sucrose.

Sulfa drugs

Sulfa drugs are used to treat people suffering from some DISEASES caused by bacteria. The drugs are based on synthetic chemicals called sulfonamides. They do not kill bacteria but work by preventing bacteria from growing and multiplying, so that the body's natural defenses can deal with them easily. Sulfa drugs were discovered in the 1930s and were among the first really effective drugs to be made in the LABORATORY. They are mainly used to treat INFECTIONS of the stomach and bladder; other bacterial disorders are generally treated using ANTIBIOTICS such as penicillin. Neither sulfa drugs nor antibiotics are effective against VIRAL DISEASES.

Sulfates

Sulfates are SALTS of SULFURIC ACID. Several sulfates occur as deposits that can be dug up out of the ground, such as the MINERALS alabaster and gypsum, which are forms of calcium sulfate. Gypsum can be heated to make plaster of Paris, and it is the white substance used as school chalk. Other important sulfates include magnesium sulfate, also known as Epsom salts, used in medicines and for fireproofing cloth, and sodium sulfate which is used in making glass and in wood pulp for paper making. Sulfates can be made by dissolving a metal, a metal OXIDE, or a metal HYDROXIDE in sulfuric acid. Most sulfates dissolve in water. An exception is BARIUM sulfate, used in a barium "meal" which is swallowed by people having X-RAYS taken of their stomach. X-rays do not pass through barium and so the stomach shows up on the X-ray.

$$SO_4^{2-}$$

▲ A sulfate, SO_4 is a salt of sulfuric acid. One of the most important sulfates is probably calcium sulfate, used in making plaster.

Sulfides

Sulfides are compounds of SULFUR and another element. One of the best known is hydrogen sulfide, a gas that smells like rotten eggs. It is made by treating a METAL sulfide with dilute ACID. Metal sulfides can be prepared by bubbling hydrogen sulfide into a solution of the metal salt. They can also be made by direct reaction between the metal and sulfur. Most metal sulphides are colored substances, used as PIGMENTS in making paint. They also occur naturally in various MINERALS which are important sources of metals such as iron, lead, mercury, and zinc.

▲ The mineral form of arsenic trisulfide, As_2S_3, is called orpiment. It is powdered and used as a yellow pigment, but must be used with extreme care because it is very poisonous.

Sulfur

Sulfur is a bright yellow ELEMENT. It is a nonmetal, that is found as deposits on and under the ground in volcanic regions. It also occurs deep underground in places such as Texas, often near deposits of PETROLEUM (crude oil). It is "mined" by pumping superheated water and air down pipes into the sulfur deposits, which form a froth

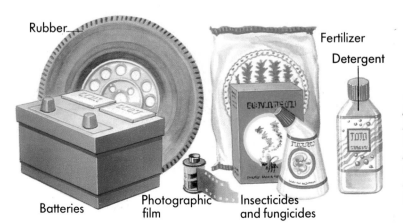

Rubber
Fertilizer
Detergent
Batteries
Photographic film
Insecticides and fungicides

◄ Sulfur is one of the most important nonmetallic elements. Its main uses are in vulcanizing (hardening) rubber and in the manufacture of sulfuric acid, which is used in car batteries and in the production of fertilizers and detergents.

▲ *In some volcanic regions, sulfur can be dug out of the ground. Here workers on the Indonesian island of Java load mined sulfur onto ponies.*

SO₂

▲ *Sulfur dioxide, SO₂, can be made by burning sulfur in air. It is used as a bleach and to make sulfuric acid.*

▼ *In the contact process for making sulfuric acid, sulfur is roasted in air to produce sulfur dioxide. This reacts with oxygen in air, in the presence of a catalyst, to form sulfur trioxide, which dissolves in sulfuric acid to make oleum. Water added to oleum converts it to sulfuric acid.*

of molten sulfur and hot water that is passed up another pipe to the surface. Sulfur also occurs combined with metals as SULFIDES, and as impurities in coal and oil. The major uses of sulfur are in vulcanizing rubber and making SULFURIC ACID; it is also an important component of SULFA DRUGS. When sulfur, or fuels containing sulfur burn, it forms SULFUR DIOXIDE, an acidic compound that causes AIR POLLUTION and ACID RAIN.

Sulfur dioxide

Sulfur dioxide is a colorless, poisonous gas with an acrid, choking smell. It is made by treating a sulfite with dilute ACID or by burning SULFUR or COMPOUNDS containing sulfur. The gas is used for BLEACHING wood pulp for making paper, as a food preservative, and as a fumigant (a disinfectant used in smoky form). Its main use, however, is in making SULFURIC ACID. Coal and oil contain traces of sulfur, and when they are burned as fuels, sulfur dioxide is formed and released into the air. As a result, sulfur dioxide is a major cause of AIR POLLUTION and is largely responsible for the formation of ACID RAIN which is damaging to trees and buildings.

Sulfuric acid

Sulfuric acid is probably the most important chemical COMPOUND produced. It has dozens of uses from making fertilizers and fibers to the production of drugs and explosives. It is the ACID in car batteries diluted with water. Sulfuric acid is made by the contact process. Ores containing metal SULFIDES or SULFUR are roasted in air

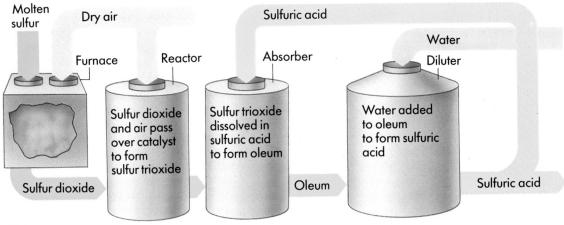

Molten sulfur

Dry air

Sulfuric acid

Water

Furnace

Reactor

Absorber

Diluter

Sulfur dioxide and air pass over catalyst to form sulfur trioxide

Sulfur trioxide dissolved in sulfuric acid to form oleum

Water added to oleum to form sulfuric acid

Sulfur dioxide

Oleum

Sulfuric acid

to produce SULFUR DIOXIDE. This gas is heated in the presence of a CATALYST (an oxide of the metal vanadium) to make it react with more air to produce sulfur trioxide. The trioxide is dissolved in concentrated sulfuric acid to form an acid called oleum, which is carefully diluted with water to produce more sulfuric acid. Sulfuric acid SALTS are called SULFATES, and these include many useful compounds.

H_2SO_4

▲ *Sulfuric acid, H_2SO_4, has a strong chemical attraction to water H_2O. This enables it to remove hydrogen and oxygen from many substances (including skin) and makes it a dangerous chemical to handle.*

Sun

The Sun is a globe of gas, mostly HYDROGEN, measuring 865,000 miles (1,392,000 km) across, over 100 times the diameter of the Earth. It is the center of the SOLAR SYSTEM and gives the Earth and other PLANETS their light and heat. The temperature of the surface is about 11,000°F (6,000°C), but at the center, where the nuclear reactions that keep it shining are going on, the temperature is believed to be about 27 million°F (15 million °C).

The Sun was born about 4.6 billion years ago, out of a vast dark gas cloud in one of the arms of the MILKY WAY. The planets formed at the same time. There are probably other stars like the Sun, with planets revolving around them, but they are too far away to be seen.

▼ *Below the surface of the Sun, called the photosphere, are layers of hydrogen. Near the Sun's center, nuclear fusion reactions, in which hydrogen atoms combine to form helium, produce the vast amounts of heat energy which keep the Sun shining.*

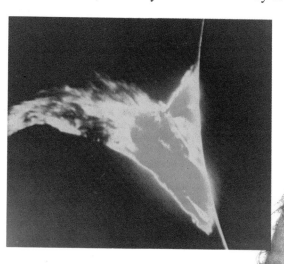

Earth

Sunspot

Photosphere

Helium core
Hydrogen layer

Heat rises through outer layer of hydrogen to photosphere

Prominence

▲ *Prominences are huge streamers of glowing gas that leap up from the Sun's surface. Some curve over to form an arch of fire.*

675

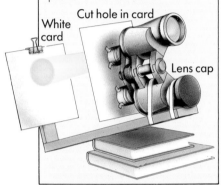

White card
Cut hole in card
Lens cap

The shining surface is called the photosphere, and this is where SUNSPOTS occur. Glowing hydrogen clouds known as prominences rise from it. Some of these clouds are larger than a hundred Earths. Atomic particles fly into space, causing the SOLAR WIND. There is also a thin cloud of atoms around the Sun, the CORONA, which can only be seen if the Sun is hidden during a total ECLIPSE.

Even a small change in the Sun would have disastrous effects on life on Earth. The Sun will shine for thousands of millions of years. Eventually it will expand and become a RED GIANT, causing the Earth's oceans to boil, and finally the Sun will shrink to a WHITE DWARF.

Sunspots

Beneath the SUN's brilliant surface, the churning gases can produce strong magnetic fields. Where these occur, the MAGNETISM "siphons" away HEAT, forming a cooler, darker area known as a sunspot. Sunspots range in size from a few thousand miles across to tens of thousands of miles (far larger than the Earth). Most last for less than a month. They increase in frequency about every 11 years, a period known as the sunspot cycle. A dozen sunspots may be visible when the cycle is near its peak. Vast explosions known as flares sometimes occur near or inside sunspots. These send out extra bursts of particles that upset the Earth's magnetic field and cause AURORAS.

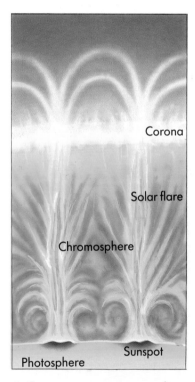

Corona

Solar flare

Chromosphere

Sunspot

Photosphere

▲ *Sunspots are regions on the Sun's surface (photosphere) that are cooler than the rest. Sometimes they send up solar flares into the Sun's atmosphere, or chromosphere, reaching beyond the Sun's corona or outer atmosphere.*

George Ellery Hale (1868–1938)
Hale was an American astronomer who studied the Sun and sunspots. In the 1890s he supervised the construction of the world's largest refracting telescope (using lenses) in Chicago. In 1929 he built the then largest reflecting telescope (using mirrors), the 5-meter (200-inch) Mount Palomar telescope which was finally commissioned in 1948.

Superconductor

A superconductor is a material that can carry an electrical current with very little RESISTANCE. This means that the ELECTRICITY is not used up, or wasted as heat as it

◀ A magnet floats in midair over a disk of superconducting ceramic material whose temperature is kept low with liquid nitrogen.

circulates. Superconducting solenoids are used in some large ELECTROMAGNETS, since they allow large currents to flow without the need to supply large amounts of ENERGY. Many metals, for example LEAD and ALUMINUM, become superconductors if they are cooled down to a low enough temperature, usually only a few degrees KELVIN above absolute zero. Recently new materials have been discovered which become superconducting at much higher temperatures. However, even these materials still need special cooling equipment using liquid (very cold) nitrogen to produce superconductivity. Some of these new materials are CERAMICS.

In 1975 scientists in the United States started an electric current moving around a circuit of superconductors, and then removed the source of the current. Years later the current was still flowing.

Supernova

A supernova is the result of the violent death of a massive STAR, larger than our SUN. A star shines as a round ball because it is "blown out" by the RADIATION coming from its center. When the center cools down, it collapses producing, for a short time, as much energy in the supernova explosion as a galaxy containing billions of

When a supernova collapses to become a neutron star it is one of the strangest objects in the universe. It becomes totally solid matter, a million million times heavier than lead. A pinhead-sized piece of a neutron star would weigh as much as a large skyscraper! All the atoms in the star are squashed together until the protons and electrons in each atom become one.

◀ The latest supernova, first sighted in 1987, is the bright "star" at the lower right of this photograph. It is 170,000 light-years away in the Large Magellanic Cloud.

677

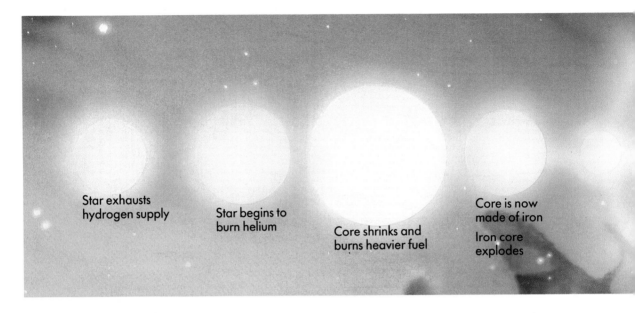

Star exhausts
hydrogen supply

Star begins to
burn helium

Core shrinks and
burns heavier fuel

Core is now
made of iron

Iron core
explodes

▲ *A supernova occurs when the core of a shrinking massive star suddenly explodes. In the first 10 seconds of the explosion, it produces 100 times more energy than the Sun has during the whole of its 4.6 billion year lifetime.*

stars. All that remains after the explosion is an expanding cloud of gas and a NEUTRON STAR a few miles across, containing what is left of the star. The last supernova in our own MILKY WAY galaxy was observed in 1604, but one was seen in the nearby large MAGELLANIC CLOUD in 1987.

Supersonic flight

Supersonic flight is faster than the speed of SOUND. Speeds greater than five times the speed of sound are described as *hypersonic*. The first supersonic flight was made by Captain Charles Yeager in a Bell XS-1 rocket-powered aircraft on October 14, 1947. Yeager passed through the SOUND BARRIER, and reached MACH 1.015 at Muroc, California. Mach 1 equals the speed of sound. The first civilian supersonic aircraft to fly was the Soviet

▼ *As an aircraft flies faster than the speed of sound, a shock wave reaches the ground to be heard as a sonic boom after the aircraft has passed overhead.*

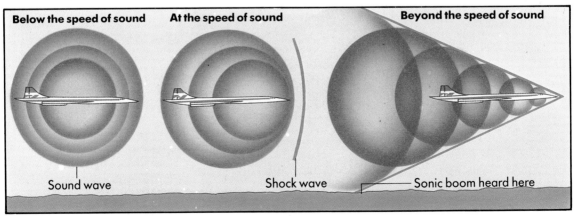

Below the speed of sound   **At the speed of sound**   **Beyond the speed of sound**

Sound wave   Shock wave   Sonic boom heard here

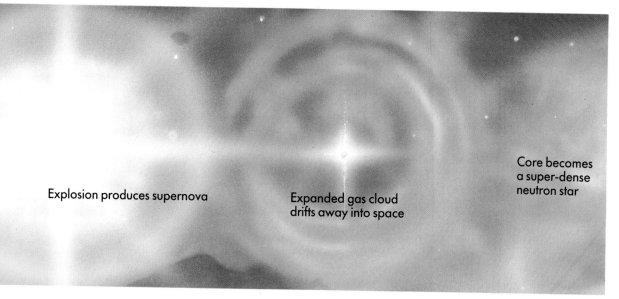

Explosion produces supernova

Expanded gas cloud drifts away into space

Core becomes a super-dense neutron star

◄ *The* Concorde *is the only supersonic aircraft still in commercial service, although there are many military aircraft that can fly faster.*

Tupolev Tu-144 on the last day of 1968, two months before the Anglo-French *Concorde*. To reduce drag at supersonic speeds, the aircraft wings are swept back into a triangular shape called a delta wing.

Surface tension

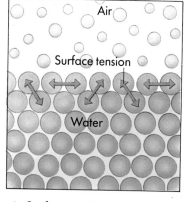

Air

Surface tension

Water

▲ *Surface tension is caused by the attraction between molecules of a liquid at its surface, giving the effect of an elastic skin on the liquid. This skin is also known as the meniscus.*

Surface tension is the FORCE that keeps drops of LIQUID such as water together. The MOLECULES that make up the liquid are pulled toward each other, so molecules at the surface are pulled back into the liquid. This causes the liquid to change shape to keep its surface as small as possible. This is why drops are round.

When a drop of liquid touches a SOLID, the shape that the drop takes up depends on the adhesive force between the liquid and its contact surface, or container, compared to the cohesive forces in the liquid itself. If the

▶ *Surface tension makes the water drop on the left dome upward. Detergent has been added to the drop on the right, reducing surface tension so that the water spreads out and wets the surface.*

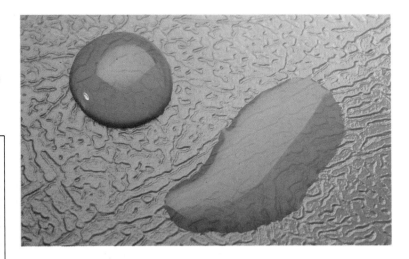

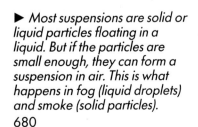
liquid molecules are not pulled toward the solid, the drop will remain as a drop, as when water comes into contact with a waxy or greasy surface. If, however, the liquid molecules are attracted strongly toward the solid, the drop will spread out and wet the solid surface so that as many molecules as possible can be near the solid, as in CAPILLARY ACTION.

The surface tension of water can be reduced by adding soap or detergent to it. This makes it better at wetting greasy surfaces and so better at cleaning them.
See also MENISCUS.

Suspension

A suspension is a MIXTURE containing particles suspended in a LIQUID or GAS. The particles may be MOLECULES of another liquid or be SOLID. The particles or drops are so small that you cannot see them individually but are larger than the particles in a COLLOID. Suspensions are almost always cloudy because LIGHT is scattered and reflected from the particles or drops.

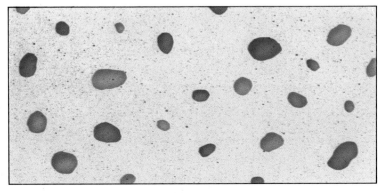

▶ *Most suspensions are solid or liquid particles floating in a liquid. But if the particles are small enough, they can form a suspension in air. This is what happens in fog (liquid droplets) and smoke (solid particles).*

A suspension is formed when the two substances will not form a SOLUTION. This happens because the molecules which form the tiny drops or particles are not attracted very strongly to the molecules in the rest of the liquid, so they stay together rather than separating out and dissolving. An everyday example of a suspension is sand or soil particles in water.
See also EMULSION.

Symbiosis

Symbiosis is a partnership between two different SPECIES in which both partners get some benefit. An example of a symbiotic relationship is between the crocodile bird and the Nile crocodile. The crocodile usually eats any animal that it can catch, but it allows a small black and white plover, commonly called a crocodile bird, to walk in and out of its mouth. The bird cleans the great reptile's teeth, by removing and eating scraps of food. It also eats the leeches and other PARASITES that feed there, doing the crocodile a favor.

▲ *Lichen, seen here growing as a blue green patch on the bark of a tree, is a symbiotic combination of two types of simple organisms: an alga and a fungus.*

Hermit crab and sea anemone

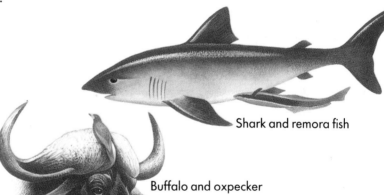

Shark and remora fish

Buffalo and oxpecker

◄ *Three symbiotic partnerships from the animal kingdom: sea anemones get scraps of food left by the foraging hermit crab while they protect the crab from predators; an oxpecker bird eats ticks and other parasites off the skin of a buffalo; and a remora fish performs the same service for a shark (and gets leftovers from the shark's meals).*

Many fish, called cleaner or barber fish, are symbiotic. The brightly colored cleaners commonly stay in a particular place and larger fish actually come to them to be cleaned, just as we might visit the hairdresser. The cleaner fish eat the scraps and parasites that they peck from their partners. Symbiosis is also found among plants. The slow-growing plants called lichens are made up of fungi and algae living in partnership. Neither of these could survive on its own. Parasites are not symbiotic because they cause harm.

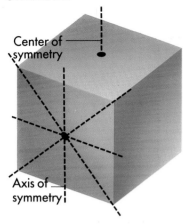

▲ *A cube has several planes of symmetry, shown by the axes (lines) above. For example, it is symmetrical around a plane that cuts one of its faces in half. All the symmetrical planes cut through the center of symmetry.*

▶ *Most starfish have five limbs and have radial symmetry, in other words they are symmetrical from the center point. The same plan applies also to sea urchins. A lizard, on the other hand, has axial symmetry because it is symmetrical along a line down the center of its body.*

Symmetry

Many two-dimensional or plane shapes around us have a line of symmetry. Either side of this line the two halves are identical and would match one another exactly if folded along the line of symmetry. If we placed a mirror along this line we would see the complete original shape. This type of symmetry is called reflective symmetry.

Many POLYGONS have lines of symmetry. A circle has an infinite number of lines of symmetry. Many things around us such as leaves, snowflakes, and aircraft have lines of symmetry. Three-dimensional shapes have more than one plane of symmetry. Another form of symmetry exists in ROTATION. Some shapes can be turned through less then 360° and still look as if they hadn't been turned. This is called rotational symmetry. Shapes that have no symmetry are said to be asymmetric.

Starfish

Lizard

SEE FOR YOURSELF
Fold a piece of paper and cut out any shape from the folded edge. Open the shape flat and you will see it has an axis of symmetry at the line of the fold. Now try folding a piece of paper in half twice and cutting out another shape from the folded corner. Does this piece of paper have two axes of symmetry?

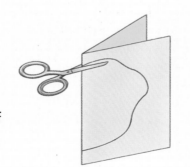

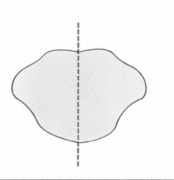

Synthesizer

A synthesizer is a musical INSTRUMENT used to make, or synthesize, SOUNDS electronically. A synthesizer may produce electronic copies of the sounds of musical instruments or it may produce entirely artificial sounds that are not based on any existing instrument. The

◀ *A modern synthesizer resembles a keyboard instrument such as an electronic organ, but it can produce a much wider range of sounds and effects.*

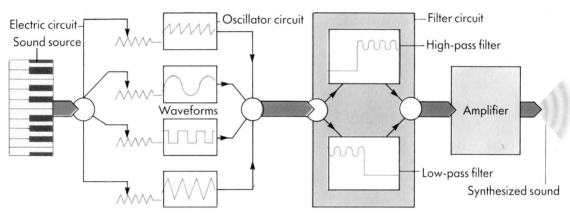

sounds are made by circuits called OSCILLATORS and shaped by other circuits called FILTERS. The first synthesizers were made in the 1960s. The Moog synthesizer, developed by Robert Moog in 1965, played one note at a time. Developments in ELECTRONICS and COMPUTERS in the 1970s and 1980s have resulted in more advanced synthesizers. Today's synthesizers are DIGITAL. They store and reproduce sounds from the same digital code that computers use. Computerized synthesizers can produce very complex arrangements of sounds.

▲ *Electronic oscillators in a synthesizer produce notes with various sound qualities. These can be blended and "shaped" by filter circuits to imitate a musical instrument or make an entirely new sound. High pass filters only allow high frequencies (high pitched sounds) to pass through while low pass filters only allow low frequencies (low pitched sounds) to pass through. Together they allow a particular frequency and therefore pitch to be used.*

Synthetic fibers

The common natural fibers are wool, cotton, and silk, used for making cloth. Nearly all other kinds of cloth are made from fibers produced using large MOLECULES in chemical compounds, and these are collectively known as synthetic, artificial, or manufactured fibers.

The first synthetic fibers were made from CELLULOSE early in the 20th century. The chief of these is rayon. It is

▶ *This circular jet contains 10,000 tiny holes through which a sticky solution of cellulose, called viscose, is squirted into a bath of acid. The viscose hardens to form fine strands of rayon, which are dried and spun into yarn to be woven into cloth.*

▼ *Synthetic fibers are manufactured by squirting molten plastic through tiny holes in a jet and letting the strands harden in air. Nylon is made in this way.*

Types of Synthetic Fibers
Cellulose
Rayon (viscose fiber)
Polyacrylics
Acrilan
Courtelle
Orlon
Polyamides
Aramid
Nylon
Polyesters
Melinex
Terylene (Dacron)

produced by dissolving wood pulp in an alkaline solution and squirting the sticky liquid produced through tiny holes into a bath of SULFURIC ACID. This hardens the fibers, which are then spun into yarn and woven into cloth. Cellulose itself is a natural POLYMER.

Other synthetic fibers are made from artificial polymers, which are products of the PLASTICS industry. There are dozens of different types, used on their own and in combination, including polyamides such as NYLON, polyesters such as Dacron, and polyacrylic fibers such as Acrilan and Orlon. Nylon was one of the first to be produced (in the mid-1930s), and was used during World War II to make parachutes. The first artificial silk stockings were made of nylon.

Most synthetic fibers are stronger than natural fibers and can be woven into crease-resistant cloth or fabric, although some are difficult to DYE and have to be washed and ironed at low temperatures. Their other major uses include making carpets and ropes.
See also FIBERS, NATURAL.

TAPE

Tannin

Tannin is a yellow COMPOUND that occurs in parts of many plants, such as the bark of trees, oak galls, walnuts, and even tea leaves and coffee beans. Its chemical name is tannic acid. Tannin is used in tanning animal skins and hides to make leather. After the skins have been soaked in water and treated with lime, they are treated with tannin. This reacts with PROTEINS in the skins to keep them supple and prevent them from rotting. Tannin is also used in dyeing and in making ink. *See also* CAFFEINE.

◀ *Tea leaves being churned and chopped on the Indian Ocean island of Mauritius. The leaves are boiled to extract the tannin. Tea is rich in tannin, which gives the drink its brown color.*

Tape, magnetic

Magnetic tape is a material manufactured to record pictures or SOUND. It is usually in the form of a long flexible PLASTIC strip with a coating of magnetic particles. Recordings are made by magnetizing the tape in a recorder. The tape is usually wound around two reels inside a cassette to make it easier to load into the recorder. When a recording is made or played back, the tape is threaded from one reel to the other by an electric motor. Tape used for

▼ *There are two main types of machines for recording and playing magnetic tape: reel-to-reel and cassette. A cassette can play either stereo or mono tapes because the tracks for left and right are together. A reel-to-reel either has to be mono playing or stereo because the tracks are apart.*

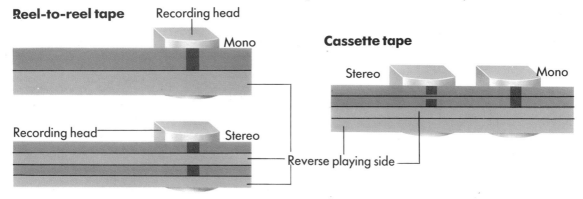

Reel-to-reel tape — Recording head — Mono — Recording head — Stereo — Cassette tape — Stereo — Mono — Reverse playing side

685

SEE FOR YOURSELF
Can you identify flavors by taste alone? Blindfold yourself, pinch your nostrils together and get a friend to put small pieces of various foods on your tongue. You will be unable to tell the difference between raw potato and apple, or between coffee and tea. This is because you also need your sense of smell in order to taste things.

recording sound only is called *audio tape*. Tape used to record pictures and sound is called *video tape*. The tape is manufactured in wide rolls which are then slit to produce narrower strips of tape for cassettes. Audio cassette tape is usually 0.15 inch (3.8mm) wide and video cassette tape is usually a half inch (12.65mm) wide. Audio cassette tape can have up to eight tracks recorded onto it. Tape can be used many times and can be easily edited by cutting out unwanted sections and binding the tape together again. This is called splicing.
See also CASSETTE RECORDER; VIDEO RECORDER.

Tape recorder *See* Cassette recorder

Taste

Taste is one of our five SENSES. We can only sense four different groups of tastes. These are sweet, sour, salt, and bitter, and we sense these by means of patches of sensory cells grouped into taste buds on the tongue and the sides of the mouth. Each taste is detected in a slightly different area. The tastes we experience in food are combinations of these simple tastes. We add to our sense of taste by our sense of smell. Tiny particles of food rise in the air at the back of the mouth and enter the NOSE where they stimulate the organs of smell. We have only about 3,000 taste buds, so compared to many animals, our sense of taste is quite crude. Substances only have a taste if they dissolve slightly in saliva, so insoluble substances, such as a glass, have no taste at all.

► *The four main flavors — sweet, salt, sour, and bitter — are detected by taste buds on different areas of the tongue. You can test this by dipping cotton balls in solutions of sugar, salt, vinegar, and coffee and applying them to your tongue.*

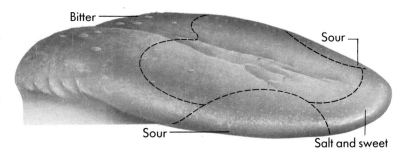

Bitter — Sour — Sour — Salt and sweet

Technology

Technology is the practical use of science in industry and everyday life. The most ancient technology was the making of stone tools by primitive people about one million years ago. *See* pages 688 and 689.

Teeth

Teeth are important for tearing, cutting, and grinding food to prepare it for swallowing and digestion. Teeth are living parts of animals, and are composed mostly of material resembling bone. In mammals, the outer part of a tooth is made from enamel, the hardest material in the body, which resists wear and decay. The shape and type of teeth depends on an animal's natural diet. Herbivores have large, ridged, grinding teeth; carnivores have sharp, cutting teeth. Rabbits' teeth grow all their lives, unlike ours. They must wear away their front teeth to keep them sharp, otherwise the teeth grow too long.

In humans, milk teeth are produced first and these are pushed out gradually as the adult teeth develop beneath them. Humans have 32 adult teeth, and their shape varies depending on their use. At the front of each jaw are chisel-shaped incisors to cut the food. Behind these are the pointed canine teeth to tear food and behind these are premolars and molars, which have uneven surfaces to grind the food as we chew.

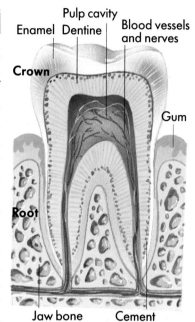

Pulp cavity
Enamel Dentine   Blood vessels and nerves
Crown
Gum
Root
Jaw bone   Cement

▲ *A tooth consists of three main layers: soft pulp at the center, covered in harder dentine overlaid with a coating of very hard enamel. At the center of the tooth is a space containing pulp, the living part of the tooth with the nerves and blood vessels. The gum seals the side of the tooth to prevent infection.*

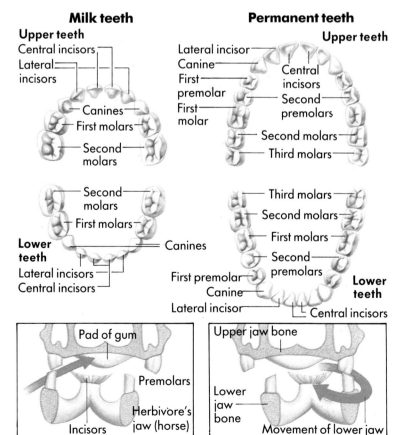

Milk teeth
Upper teeth
Central incisors
Lateral incisors
Canines
First molars
Second molars

Permanent teeth
Upper teeth
Lateral incisor
Canine
First premolar
First molar
Central incisors
Second premolars
Second molars
Third molars

Second molars
First molars
Lower teeth
Lateral incisors
Central incisors
Canines

Third molars
Second molars
First molars
Second premolars
First premolar
Canine
Lateral incisor
Lower teeth
Central incisors

Pad of gum
Premolars
Incisors
Herbivore's jaw (horse)

Upper jaw bone
Lower jaw bone
Movement of lower jaw

◀ *Children have 20 first (or milk) teeth. From about the age of six they are gradually replaced by 32 second (or permanent) teeth. An adult has 12 molars instead of a child's 8, and has, in addition, 8 premolars (a child has no premolars).*

◀ *In plant-eating animals such as a horse, the premolars and molars are used for grinding food with a circular movement of the lower jaw which we call chewing. You can see this action by watching plant-eating animals such as cattle or sheep.*

TECHNOLOGY

Until about 7,000 years ago, there was almost no technology apart from simple tools. From then on, human civilizations needed new farming tools, more housing, and new materials to make them. The most important development was the wheel, in use from about 5,000 years ago.

Ancient people learned how to make metals by heating ores found in the Earth's surface and to work the metals into useful objects. Much of the early technological development occurred in the Middle East and Far East. The Egyptians and Indians were advanced in making things from pottery, glass, and different metals.

Europe did not begin to catch up until the 14th century, when the Church's opposition to new scientific ideas began to decline. Developments in printing, mining, processing materials, and scientific instruments made Europe the most advanced technological region.

Technology was transformed by the production and control of energy to power machinery during the Industrial Revolution. The steam engine and later the internal-combustion engine provided reliable sources of power for manufacturing, transportation, agriculture, and processing. The development of electrical systems and later electronics made communications and small powerful computers possible and triggered a new revolution in the 20th century.

▶ *The first applications of technology were in making homes, and carts from stone, wood, and simple metals* **1**. *With the development of simple machines like levers and pulleys, people could build larger structures several stories high using the wider range of materials they had discovered* **2**. *The breakthrough in communications that enabled knowledge to travel widely came with the invention of printing* **3**.

4

5

6

◄ *The key to the Industrial Revolution was the development of the steam engine. It was used first to power pumps in mines and machines in factories, and later adapted to power steam locomotives* **4**. *The steam engine remained supreme until the invention of internal-combustion engines: gasoline engines, diesel engines, and later gas turbines* **5**. *Electronics revolutionized communications and made computers possible* **6**.

Some Milestones in Technology

c.100	Paper
1100	Magnetic compass
1440s	Printing press
1590	Compound microscope
1592	Thermometer
1608	Telescope
1620	Submarine
1650	Air pump
1656	Pendulum clock
1712	Steam engine
1735	Chronometer
1785	Power loom
1800	Electric battery
1804	Steam locomotive
1816	Bicycle
1826	Photography
1834	Harvesting machine
1837	Electric telegraph
1855	Celluloid
1858	Refrigerator
1864	Dynamite
1868	Typewriter
1876	Telephone
1877	Phonograph
1879	Light bulb
1885	Gasoline-engined car
1888	Pneumatic tire
1895	Radio
1898	Tape recorder
1903	Airplane
1907	Helicopter
1925	Television
1930	Jet engine
1935	Radar
1943	Electronic computer
1955	Fiber optics
1956	Video recorder
1957	Artificial satellite
1960	Laser
1971	Microprocessor
1987	High temperature superconductors

See also ELECTRONICS; INDUSTRIAL REVOLUTION; INSTRUMENTS, SCIENTIFIC; MACHINES, SIMPLE; MINING; PRINTING; STEAM ENGINE.

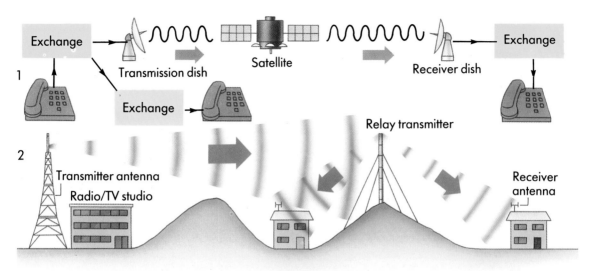

1

Exchange → Transmission dish · Satellite · Receiver dish → Exchange

Exchange →

2

Transmitter antenna
Radio/TV studio

Relay transmitter

Receiver antenna

▲ *The most used forms of telecommunications are telephones, radio, and television. Except for short-range telephone calls, all three employ radio waves and use antennas (dishes) to send and receive signals to and from satellites over large distances.*

Charles Wheatstone (1802–1875)
Wheatstone was a British scientist and inventor who in 1837, with William Cooke, made the first practical electric telegraph. He also invented a stereoscope (for viewing three-dimensional pictures). The Wheatstone bridge circuit was not his invention, but he used it extensively.

Telecommunications

Telecommunications describes the transmission of information over long distances by electric signals, RADIO waves, or LIGHT. The information, which might include speech, COMPUTER data, radio signals or, television programs, may be sent in one of two ways. It may be in the form of an electromagnetic copy of the information, called an ANALOG signal, but increasingly telecommunications signals are DIGITAL. They consist of a stream of electrical pulses that contains all the original information but in a coded form.

The signal is added to a high frequency radio signal, called a carrier wave, before transmission. This process is called modulation. At the receiver, the carrier wave is removed by a filter. A large number of transmitters and receivers linked together is called a network. The telephone system is an example of a network.

Telegraph

A telegraph transmits messages by cable or RADIO waves. The first electric telegraph was made by Georges Lesage in 1774. The transmitter and receiver were connected by a separate wire for each letter of the alphabet! In the 1830s two British physicists, William F. Cooke and Charles Wheatstone, worked on the telegraph and by the 1850s telegraphy had developed until information could be sent along a single wire as pulses of electric current. Each letter of the alphabet was represented by a different code of pulses. Samuel MORSE's code became the standard. The telegraphy network had spread

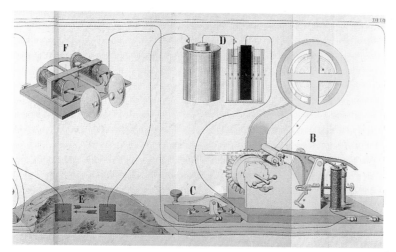

◄ *Samuel Morse's telegraph became the most widely used. The key labelled **C** was used to send messages in Morse code. The recorder **B** registered the incoming signals as dots and dashes on paper tape. A bell would ring to alert the operator that a message was coming through. **D** shows how batteries were wired to power the circuit, one side being grounded, **E**.*

throughout Europe and the United States by the end of the 19th century. Cables laid on the ocean floor connected the continents. Telegraphy lasted until the 1950s when international telephone links were established.

Telephone

The telephone is a device designed to transmit speech in the form of electric currents or RADIO waves. It enables people to talk to each other over long distances. It was invented by the American inventor Alexander Graham BELL in 1876, while he was working on improvements to the TELEGRAPH. In that year Bell transmitted human speech for the first time—to his assistant in another room. Rival services using different telephone systems were set up, including one designed by the inventor Thomas EDISON. At the beginning of this century it was decided to make all telephones in a standard way so that they could all be connected together.

▲ *An early telephone made in France in about 1900.*

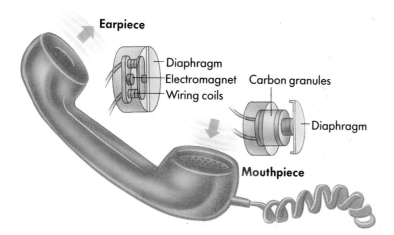

Earpiece
— Diaphragm
— Electromagnet
— Wiring coils
Carbon granules
— Diaphragm
Mouthpiece

◄ *The earpiece of a telephone contains a tiny loudspeaker, while the mouthpiece has a tiny carbon microphone. When the caller talks, sound waves of his or her voice vibrate a metal diaphragm which squeezes carbon granules and alters their electrical resistance. These changes vary an electric current along the telephone line. At the receiver's earpiece, the varying current makes an electromagnet vibrate another diaphragm, generating the sounds of the caller's speech.*

Hans Lippershey (1570–1619)

Lippershey was a Dutch eyeglass maker who in 1608 used two of his eyeglass lenses to make what was probably the first telescope. The design was copied by Galileo to make an astronomical telescope.

▶ Optical telescopes can be very large and powerful but interference by the Earth's atmosphere limits how much astronomers can see through them.

▼ The two main types of astronomical telescopes are called refractors and reflectors. A refracting telescope uses lenses to form an enlarged, upside down image. Reflecting telescopes have a large curved mirror to gather light, which is reflected off a second mirror into the eyepiece.

All calls were connected by people called telephone operators until the 1890s when automatic switches were invented. In the 1920s, radio was used to transmit some telephone calls. Since the 1960s, an increasing number of telephone calls have been relayed around the world by SATELLITES. During the 1960s the first DIGITAL telephone equipment was made. Now, many calls are transmitted as LASER beams along OPTICAL FIBERS.

Telescope

A telescope works by focusing the light from a distant object to form a magnified image. The image is examined with a powerful magnifying LENS, so the object is seen in close-up. Binoculars consist of two telescopes side by side. A reflecting telescope uses a MIRROR. Large astronomical telescopes always use mirrors, because mirrors are easier to make and to mount than lenses.

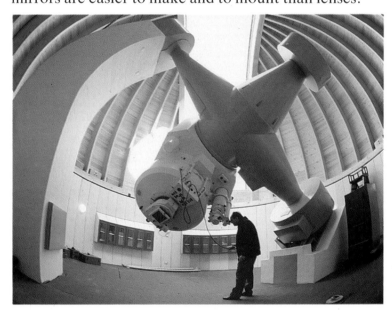

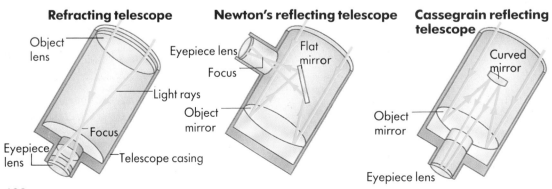

Refracting telescope

Object lens
Light rays
Focus
Eyepiece lens
Telescope casing

Newton's reflecting telescope

Eyepiece lens
Focus
Flat mirror
Object mirror

Cassegrain reflecting telescope

Curved mirror
Object mirror
Eyepiece lens

The first astronomical telescopes were refractors, and in 1609 GALILEO made important discoveries with a hand-held instrument. The Keck telescope, nearing completion in Hawaii, is the largest in the world, with a 10-meter (400-inch) mirror made up of 36 separate pieces. It will collect four times as much light as the famous 5-meter (200-inch) telescope on Mount Palomar, California. *See also* REFLECTION; REFRACTION.

▲ *Technicians in a television studio control room select pictures for transmission. The screens show the pictures being taken by each of the cameras.*

Television

Television is a system used to broadcast moving pictures and SOUND by RADIO waves or by cable. Pictures are converted into electrical signals by cameras. Sounds are converted into signals by MICROPHONES. Prerecorded TAPE such as a film, has sound and pictures in signal form. When the program is broadcast, the signals are sent to transmitting antennas. Receiving antennas pick up the signals and feed them to television sets which change the signals back into pictures and sound.

In the U.S. and Japan, the picture is composed of 525 lines and shown at the rate of 30 pictures per second.

▼ *At a television transmitter the video signal from a TV camera with the sound signal from a microphone are made to modulate continuous carrier waves. These are picked up by the receiver's TV antenna, demodulated and amplified to work the picture tube and loudspeaker of the TV set.*

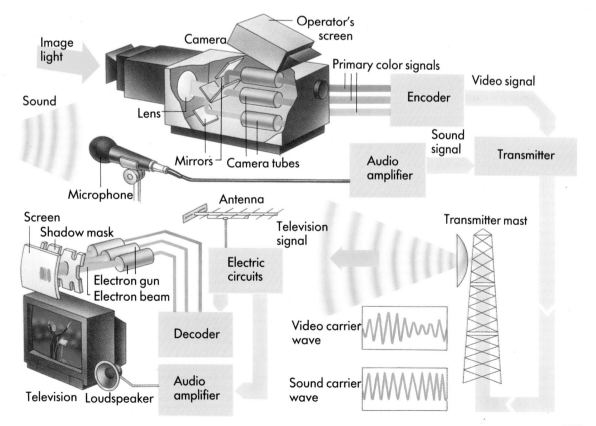

Image light — Camera — Operator's screen — Primary color signals — Encoder — Video signal — Sound — Lens — Mirrors — Camera tubes — Microphone — Audio amplifier — Sound signal — Transmitter — Antenna — Television signal — Transmitter mast — Screen — Shadow mask — Electron gun — Electron beam — Electric circuits — Decoder — Video carrier wave — Television — Loudspeaker — Audio amplifier — Sound carrier wave

Temperature Scales
There are three main temperature scales. The Fahrenheit scale is being replaced internationally by the Celsius scale. Scientists use the kelvin scale. Here the three are compared at the freezing and boiling points of water:

Freezing point	Boiling point
32°F	212°F
0°C	100°C
273 K	373 K

SEE FOR YOURSELF
In speech we use "hot" and "cold" to make comparisons of temperatures rather than as any sort of measurement. Get three bowls of water. Put hot water (as hot as you can stand) in the right-hand bowl, warm water in the middle one, and cold water in the left-hand bowl. Put your right hand in the hot water and your left hand in the cold water. After about a minute, put both hands into the warm water. To your right hand the warm water feels cold, but to your left hand it feels hot!

In Europe, broadcast television pictures are composed of 625 lines and 25 pictures per second. Because the pictures are shown in rapid succession, they give the impression of smooth movement. Closed circuit television (CCTV) conveys pictures from a camera directly to a CATHODE-RAY TUBE screen by cable. CCTV is used in security and surveillance to watch doors, stores, and banks for intruders or thieves. Broadcast television is used for entertainment and educational purposes.

Temperature

Temperature measures how hot something is. The higher the temperature of a material becomes, the more the ATOMS it is composed of move around. Do not confuse temperature and HEAT; heat is the ENERGY stored in the vibrations of the atoms. Heat added to an object produces a change in its state or temperature.

The second law of THERMODYNAMICS says that heat tends to flow from an object at high temperature to one at a lower temperature and never the other way around. The lowest possible temperature is absolute zero, where the atoms have lost all their vibrational energy. The SI UNIT of temperature, measured from absolute zero, is the KELVIN, but temperature is also measured in degrees FAHRENHEIT and CELSIUS.
See also SPECIFIC HEAT; THERMOMETER; THERMOCOUPLE.

Tempering

Tempering is a process used to toughen, or harden, METAL or GLASS by heating, drawing, or rolling. The material is heated to a high TEMPERATURE and then cooled

▶ *A blacksmith heats a horseshoe in his forge to temper the metal after it has been beaten into shape.*

very quickly. The heating allows the material's structure to move and this relieves the stresses inside that make it brittle. Steel often undergoes two heating cycles. It is heated to about 1,650°F (900°C) and cooled rapidly in water or oil. This is called quenching and it toughens the steel, but makes it brittle. Reheating it to 570°F (300°C) and cooling slowly makes it less brittle and produces hard, springy steel.

Tensile strength

The tensile strength of a MATERIAL is a measure of its ability to resist a FORCE that tries to pull it apart. It is equal to the greatest force the material can withstand before it breaks. Tensile strength is measured by stretching a bar of the material in a machine called a tensiometer until it breaks. A dial or display on the machine shows the force applied to the bar at the moment when it broke. The tensile strength is then calculated from this force divided by the bar's cross-section area. A material's tensile strength is affected by the way the material is manufactured and by treatments or processing after manufacturing.

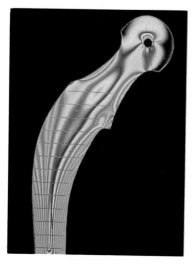

▲ Scientists check the strength of a design for an artificial hip joint. The actual joint is made of high-tensile steel, but here a plastic model is lit with polarized light. The rainbow patterns show where there are strains in the shape.

Terminal velocity

The terminal velocity of an object falling through a LIQUID or a GAS is the maximum VELOCITY that it reaches. The FRICTION force that pulls the object back as it moves through the fluid (liquid or gas) gets larger as the object moves more quickly. Eventually, the upward friction force, sometimes called the resistance or drag, becomes equal to the downward WEIGHT of the object. When this happens, the object does not ACCELERATE any more and its velocity stays the same; this velocity is the terminal velocity of the object.

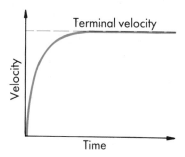

▲ A falling object accelerates until it reaches its terminal velocity, after which time it falls at a constant speed.

◀ Skydivers fall at their terminal velocity (up to 100 mph 160 km/h) for 3,000 feet (1,000 m) or more before opening their parachutes to slow their descent.

▲ *A modern laser theodolite can measure angles and distances with great accuracy using a concentrated beam of light.*

► *By knowing the precise length of a baseline, a surveyor can use a theodolite to measure the angles of a triangle and then calculate the lengths of its sides.*

Theodolite

A theodolite is an instrument that measures vertical and horizontal angles and which is used to survey a large area of land accurately. A theodolite is used in the original surveys from which MAPS are drawn. Traditional theodolites have a kind of TELESCOPE mounted on a tripod in such a way that it can be rotated horizontally as well as tilted up and down. The angles of rotation or tilt are indicated by means of accurate angular scales on the instrument. The theodolite is used to determine the precise positions of different points in the area. Today, even more accurate instruments with laser beams are used to measure angles and distances.

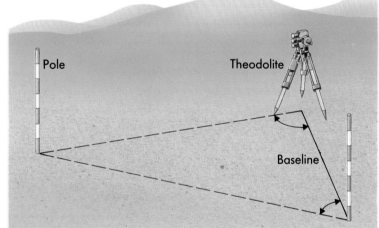

Thermocouple

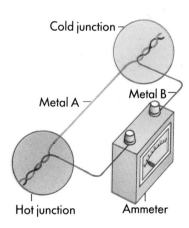

▲ *If the junctions between two dissimilar metals are kept at different temperatures, an electric current flows in the circuit. This is the principle of the thermocouple, used to measure temperature.*

A thermocouple is a loop made of two different materials, usually METALS. It is used to measure TEMPERATURE or to transfer HEAT. The two places where the different metals join are called junctions; when the two junctions are kept at different temperatures, an electrical voltage appears around the loop. This happens because the ELECTRONS in the metals move around slightly because of the difference in temperature of the two ends. The electrons carry electrical charge, so this movement of the electrons produces a voltage. The movement of the electrons in the two metals is different, so the voltages appearing along the two halves of the loop are different. The size of the voltage produced depends on the temperature difference of the junctions, so the thermocouple can be used with a VOLTMETER as an accurate THERMOMETER.

Thermodynamics

Thermodynamics is the study of HEAT and the way it flows from one place to another. Many processes involve heat; not just HEATING SYSTEMS, but ENGINES and machines of all kinds. There are three laws of thermodynamics. The first says that heat is just a form of ENERGY and that the total amount of energy in the world always remains the same. Heat engines such as a GAS TURBINE or NUCLEAR REACTOR change energy from FUEL into heat energy. Therefore, if heat is produced, exactly the same amount of some other form of energy must have been supplied. For example, the heat produced by an electric heater is equal to the electrical energy supplied to it.

The second law says that heat energy will always flow from a hotter object to a colder one, rather than the other way around. For example, we never see heat flowing from a cold cup into the hot coffee inside, making it

▼ *Any system involving changes in heat energy makes use of the principles of thermodynamics: literally the movement of heat. This sequence shows how heat is converted to work to move a rocket. In all thermodynamic systems, energy is conserved: it may change from one form to another but none is ever lost. However, the second law of thermodynamics means that an engine of this kind can never be totally efficient – some of its heat energy will be absorbed by colder objects surrounding the engine.*

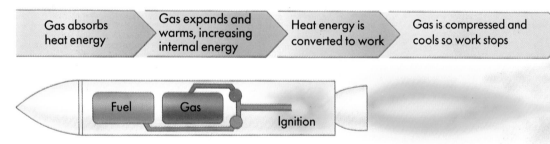

even hotter! The third law says that it is impossible to go on taking heat from an object so that it reaches zero on the KELVIN scale.

There is in fact a fourth law, the zeroth law. It depends on the other laws and was formulated after them. This says that if two objects are both at the same temperature as a third, then all three are at the same temperature. The three objects are described as being in thermal EQUILIBRIUM with each other.

See also ENTROPY; PHYSICS; TEMPERATURE.

Thermometer

A thermometer is an instrument that measures TEMPERATURE. To do this it may use any material that changes with temperature. The most common type of thermometer is a mercury thermometer. Some MERCURY is contained in a bulb and expands or contracts along a narrow tube as the temperature changes. Alcohol is used

▼ *A clinical thermometer measures body temperature. Usually the bulb of the thermometer is placed under the patient's tongue for a minute or two. When the thermometer is removed, the mercury thread breaks at a kink above the bulb so that the reading does not fall. That is why the thermometer has to be shaken before use (to rejoin the mercury thread).*

–Bulb

–Mercury

► *One type of maximum and minimum thermometer is really two thermometers, one filled with mercury and the other with alcohol. As the mercury column rises, it pushes a metal index inside the tube which stays at the maximum temperature reached even after the mercury falls again. An index in the alcohol thermometer records the lowest (minimum) temperature.*

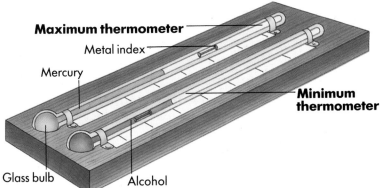

Maximum thermometer
Metal index
Mercury
Minimum thermometer
Glass bulb
Alcohol

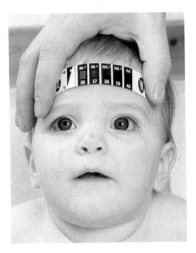

▲ *A temperature can be taken using a strip with a row of liquid crystal patches. One patch turns blue, indicating the temperature, while the others remain black.*

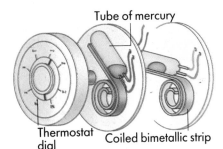

Tube of mercury
Thermostat dial
Coiled bimetallic strip

▲ *A common type of thermostat uses a coiled bimetallic strip which tilts a tube containing a blob of mercury. The mercury completes the circuit between two contacts. The circuit is broken when the tube tips the mercury away.*

698

when the temperature can drop below the FREEZING POINT of mercury (–38°F/–39°C). The glass walls of the bulb and the tube also expand and contract, so the thermometer must be carefully "calibrated" to find out which temperature a particular position of the mercury (or alcohol) corresponds to.

Dial thermometers, used in ovens, measure temperature by sensing the different EXPANSION of two metals. *See also* BIMETALLIC STRIP; CONTRACTION; THERMOCOUPLE.

Thermoplastics *See* Plastics

Thermos *See* Vacuum bottle

Thermostat

A thermostat is an automatic TEMPERATURE control device. The temperature sensitive part of a thermostat is usually a BIMETALLIC STRIP. This is a strip made from two different metals welded together which expand and contract at different rates so that as one side expands more than the other, the strip bends. This is used to complete or break an electric CIRCUIT. By using a screw to move a contact closer to or farther from the control, the thermostat's switching temperature can be varied. In a HEATING SYSTEM if the room cools down, the thermostat's bimetallic strip bends and completes a circuit, switching the system on. As the room warms up, the strip bends in the opposite direction, breaks the circuit and turns the system off. Thermostats are used in REFRIGERATORS to ensure food is stored at the right temperature and as safety devices to prevent equipment from overheating.

Thomson J. J. *See* Electron

Thomson W. M. *See* Kelvin, Lord

Thunder

Thunder is the name given to the sometimes loud rumbling or crashing sounds following a flash of LIGHTNING during a storm. So-called "thunderstorms," should really be called "lightning-storms" because the electrical discharge comes first and gives rise to the NOISE.

The thunder is caused because the air is heated very rapidly by the lightning and expands at speeds greater than the speed of sound. Because LIGHT travels much faster than SOUND waves, you will see the flash of lightning before you hear the thunder. Sound travels at about 758 mph (1,220 km/h), or just under 0.2 miles per second (0.33 km/s). Light travels so fast that you can see the lightning at the instant it occurs. If you see a flash of lightning but you do not hear any thunder until 5 seconds later, you will know that the storm is a mile away.

Tidal power

Tidal power is the ENERGY generated by the movements of the sea caused by the TIDES. Tidal power stations are built as part of a dam across a river's mouth where the tides cause a large movement of water. Channels in the dam allow water to pass through when the tide rises, and flow back as the tide falls. The water flow turns TURBINES in the channels which operate GENERATORS to produce ELECTRICITY. The main disadvantage of tidal power is that it can generate energy only at certain times. This disadvantage can be partly overcome by using the

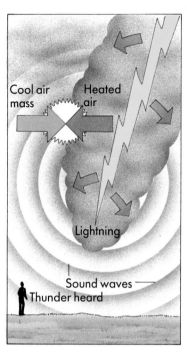

▲ The light from a lightning flash travels to an observer at 186,000 miles (300,000 km) per second. But the sound of thunder travels at only 1,085 feet (330 m) per second, which is why we hear thunder some time after seeing the flash.

The buildup of static electricity in a thundercloud may last for more than an hour. During this time, the voltage difference between the top and bottom of the cloud may reach 100 million volts. The pressure becomes too great and the lightning flashes and thunder rolls.

◄ A dam across the mouth of the Rance River in France contains 24 turbines which are turned by the flow of water as the tide comes in and out. The turbines generate electricity.

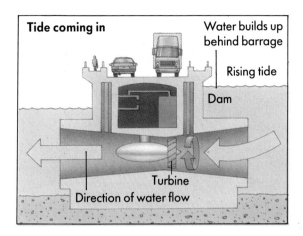

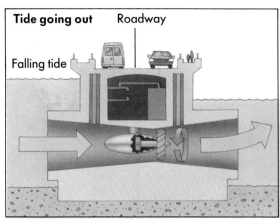

Tide coming in — Water builds up behind barrage / Rising tide / Dam / Turbine / Direction of water flow

Tide going out — Roadway / Falling tide

▲ *Dams called "tidal barriers" are used to harness tidal power. They are built across the estuaries of rivers. When the tide rises, water flows into the estuary through holes in the dam. The moving water turns the blades of turbines. When the tide falls, the water in the estuary flows out, again turning the turbines.*

▼ *Volcanic explosions under water often cause a series of powerful waves. Like ordinary waves, when tsunamis reach shallower water they react with the sea bed and become higher, slower, closer together, and more turbulent.*

energy produced at nonpeak demand times to operate pumps that pump water from one side of the dam to the other. This water can then be released at peak demand.

In most places the tides are not strong enough to be used to power modern turbines, but in a few places tidal power stations have been built. The first such station was opened in 1966 on the Rance River in France. The first tidal power plant in the Americas began operating on the Annapolis River in Nova Scotia in 1982.

Tidal waves and Tsunamis

Tidal waves are the large wavelike upwellings of water which move regularly around the EARTH and cause the TIDES. Freakishly high waves, caused when the seabed is disturbed by a major EARTHQUAKE or by volcanic activity, are incorrectly called tidal waves. They have nothing to do with tides and should be called tsunamis (pronounced soo-**nah**-mees).

In August 1883, the volcanic island of Krakatoa in Southeast Asia between Java and Sumatra blew to pieces in one of the world's most violent natural

125 miles ↕3 ft 80 ft

Volcanic eruption   Ocean floor   Friction with ocean floor increases as depth decreases

EXPLOSIONS. It is thought that the explosion was at least as powerful as detonating more than 100 fifty-megaton nuclear bombs! The eruption caused tsunamis more than 120 feet (36 m) high across the coasts of Java and Sumatra and at least 36,000 people drowned.

Tides

A tide is the regular rise and fall of the water which occurs about every 12 hours 26 minutes throughout the OCEANS and inlets of the world. Tides are caused by the pull of GRAVITY of the MOON and, to a lesser extent, the SUN, on the water. The force of gravity acts between two objects and is related to their mass and the distance between them. The Sun is so much bigger than the Moon that even though it is much farther away it can still exert some gravitational attraction.

At any moment in time the ocean closest to the Moon is attracted toward it more than the Earth beneath it and so wells up into a kind of giant wave. On the opposite side of the planet, it is the Earth rather than the water that is attracted more strongly toward the Moon because it is closer to it. This leaves behind another

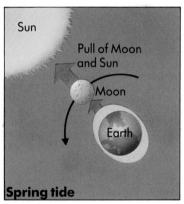

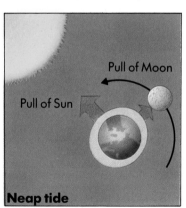

Spring tide

Neap tide

◀ Spring tides occur when the tide rises particularly high. Neap tides are when the tide does not rise as high as normal. Spring tides occur when the Moon and the Sun are directly in line, with the Moon either in front of or behind the Earth. Their gravities then pull in the same direction. At neap tides, the Moon is at right angles to the Earth when compared with the Sun.

wave of water similar to that attracted to the Moon. As the Earth spins on its axis, the waves of water travel around the world and cause the tides.

When the Earth, Moon, and Sun are in line, the Sun's gravity reinforces that of the Moon and the so-called spring tides are particularly high. This happens when the Moon is new or full and has nothing to do with the season. Where the Sun and Moon form a right-angle with the Earth, the Sun's gravity reduces the effect of the Moon's gravity and low or neap tides occur.

All bodies of water have tides, but only in very large bodies of water are they noticeable. For example, Lake Superior is the world's largest freshwater lake, but the tide only rises and falls by about 2 inches (50 mm). In the Bay of Fundy the difference between the high and the low tides can be as much as 70 feet (21 m).

One day

Earth

Earth turned once on its axis

One year

Sun

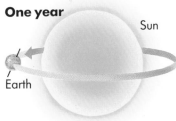

Earth

Earth once around Sun

One lunar month

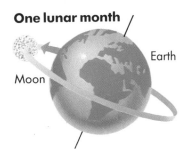

Earth

Moon

▲ One day is exactly the time it takes for the Earth to revolve once. A year is about the time it takes for the Earth to go around the Sun. But this is not quite accurate and we have leap years with an extra day every four years to even things out. A month is only approximately based on the time it takes the Moon to go around the Earth.

► People have kept time in various ways. A sundial uses the apparent movement of the Sun. An hourglass and a water clock use the rate at which sand or water flow from one vessel to another. In a pendulum clock, the swinging pendulum keeps time. A quartz watch and an atomic clock use the vibrations of a crystal or of individual atoms.

Time

People have always had to understand the passing of time. There are two natural units of time: the day, which is the time taken for the EARTH to turn around on its axis; and the year, which is the time taken for the Earth to travel once around the Sun. To measure times shorter than one day, a number of devices were invented. The sundial used the shadow cast by the Sun to measure the time, while the hourglass and the water clock used the flow of sand or water. With the invention of the PENDULUM, it became possible to make more accurate mechanical CLOCKS AND WATCHES. Very accurate measurements of time are now possible using "quartz clocks," which work by counting the regular vibrations of a small CRYSTAL of quartz, and "atomic clocks" which work by counting the regular vibrations of the LIGHT given out by ATOMS. The SI UNIT of time is the second.

The theory of RELATIVITY tells us that space (length, width, and height) and time are not really separate things, but are joined together to make up SPACE-TIME, sometimes called the fourth dimension.

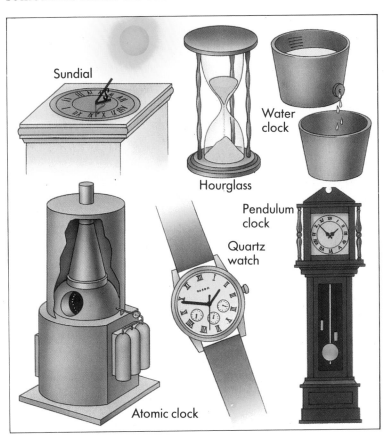

Sundial

Water clock

Hourglass

Pendulum clock

Quartz watch

Atomic clock

Tin

Tin is a silvery white ELEMENT. It is a soft METAL, which occurs in the form of its OXIDE in ores that have been mined since prehistoric times. Malaysia is the world's main producer of tin. It is easily extracted by roasting the ore with carbon. Its main use is for coating sheet steel to produce tinplate for making food cans. The steel is coated either by dipping it in molten tin or by ELECTRO-PLATING. Tin forms many useful ALLOYS with other metals, including bronze (an alloy of tin and copper, used for machine BEARINGS and coins), solder (an alloy of tin and lead, used for joining metals in plumbing and electrical circuits), and typemetal (a different tin-lead alloy that was used for casting type for printing). Tin compounds are employed in dyeing cloth, as PIGMENTS, and in fluoride toothpastes.

Tin Cans?
Tin is used to coat cans because it resists corrosion by the acids that are found in many foods. If tin does start to react with anything, it tends to form a resistant layer of oxide that prevents further reaction. However, tin is not resistant to alkalis and so is not good for canning certain foods.

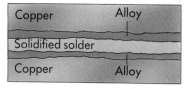

▲ Soldering makes a joint by using a layer of tin alloy that melts more easily than the metals to be joined.

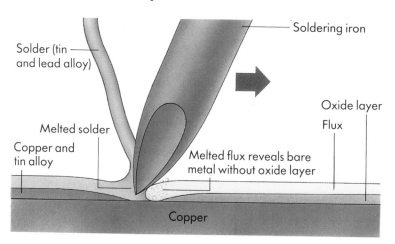

◄ In soldering, flux is used to remove any oxide from the metals to be joined. This allows the solder (an alloy of tin and lead) to come into contact with the parent metals and make a lasting joint.

Titanium

Titanium is a silvery white ELEMENT. It is a strong, light metal which can withstand high temperature and does not corrode. Together with its ALLOYS, it is used in the aerospace industry for aircraft and ROCKETS, and for making parts of chemical plants, naval ships, and missiles. Titanium is widely distributed in the Earth's crust, and has been found in METEORITES and even on the Moon. Its chief compound is its OXIDE, which occurs as the mineral rutile from which the metal is extracted. Titanium oxide is used as a white PIGMENT in paints and as a filler in making paper, rubber, and plastics. A compound of titanium and barium, barium titanate, is made into crystals for the PICK-UPS of record players.

▲ Titanium is found in many forms. These are crystals of the naturally occurring mineral called titanite. Titanite also contains calcium and silicon, and is found in various types of rock.

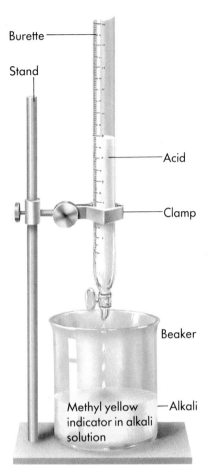

Burette

Stand

Acid

Clamp

Beaker

Methyl yellow indicator in alkali solution

Alkali

▲ *In a typical apparatus for doing a titration, the burette is held by a clamp and stand. The burette has accurate marks, and the stopcock on it can control the flow of liquid to the nearest drop. There are many different indicators, but methyl yellow is often used in alkaline solutions. It turns from yellow to red when the solution becomes acidic.*

Titration

Titration is a technique used in chemical ANALYSIS. It measures the exact volumes of two SOLUTIONS that react together. If the CONCENTRATION of one of the solutions is known, the concentration of the other one can be determined. A measured volume of one solution is put into a flask. The other solution is put into a tall graduated tube called a burette. The burette has a stopcock at the bottom so that the solution can be slowly added to the flask. The completion of the chemical reaction between the solutions, called the end point, is usually found by adding a chemical INDICATOR to the solution in the flask. For example, LITMUS can be used as an indicator in a titration between an ACID and an alkali. The end-point occurs when the litmus just changes color from red to blue (or blue to red).

SEE FOR YOURSELF
You can do your own simple titration at home. First make an indicator solution. Boil some red cabbage in water, then sieve out the pieces of cabbage. Put some of the indicator solution into a glass. Add baking soda (sodium hydrogen-carbonate) until it turns blue. The solution is now alkaline. Then add drops of vinegar (a weak acid) until the solution turns red again. Just at the point when the solution turns red, it is neutral (neither acidic nor alkaline).

Baking soda (alkali) in red cabbage indicator

Vinegar

Vinegar (acid) in red cabbage indicator

TNT

TNT is a powerful high EXPLOSIVE with the full name trinitrotoluene, sometimes called methyl trinitrobenzene. It is used in bombs and bullets, often mixed with other explosives, such as ammonium nitrate. It is also used in the warheads of guided MISSILES. TNT is a yellow solid, made by treating toluene, also known as methylbenzene, obtained from coal or oil, with a mixture of NITRIC

Although TNT is a very powerful explosive, it can be handled safely and may even be melted without igniting. It looks like pale yellow crystals.

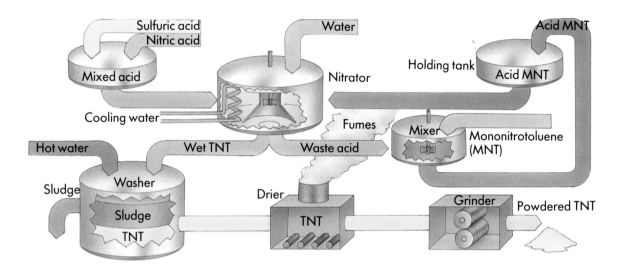

ACID and SULFURIC ACID. TNT is more stable than explosives such as NITROGLYCERIN and picric acid (trinitrophenol), which are very sensitive to shocks and therefore more dangerous to handle. TNT needs a small explosive charge or detonator to set it off.

Tornado

A tornado, or "twister" as it is sometimes called, is a violently spinning, funnel-shaped whirlwind which travels across the surface of the land or sea causing considerable destruction as it passes. Tornadoes are associated with the same kind of weather conditions that cause THUNDER storms. Tornadoes may occur in large numbers in areas around the Gulf of Mexico where the ATMOSPHERE is very unstable as warm humid air meets cold polar air. The wind speed in a tornado may reach 370 mph (600 km/h), and vehicles may be lifted completely off the

▲ In the manufacture of TNT, toluene is first converted to mononitrotoluene (MNT). This is then made acidic. The acid MNT passes into the nitrator where it is mixed with strong acid. This reaction generates heat and could be dangerous if the temperature became too high, so the reaction is kept cool by cold water in pipes.

Tornadoes cause much damage from the sheer force of wind. There is also a strong updraft inside a tornado which sometimes lifts vehicles and trees, and carries them several hundred yards. Tornadoes can cause extensive damage to buildings. When a tornado passes over a house, it sucks up air from around the building. This makes the pressure on the outside of the house much lower than that on the inside, and the building can explode.

◄ A tornado can pick up water and form a waterspout. Like most tornadoes, it will last for less than an hour and travel about 20 miles (30 km).

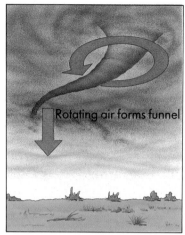

▲ *Before a tornado starts, large thunder clouds appear in the sky. One area of cloud becomes especially dark and dense. The air in this area is rotating quickly. A funnel-shaped cloud begins to form and extend downward. There are often lightning, rain, and hail. If the funnel of wind reaches the ground it raises a great cloud of dust and other material.*

Torque was a problem for early helicopter designers. When the rotor blades were turned, the helicopter's fuselage tried to turn in the opposite direction (called reactive torque). The problem was solved by placing a small set of rotor blades facing sideways at the back of the aircraft. This countered the twisting effect of the main rotor.

▶ *These two people are pushing a revolving door, as described in the text. The diagram shows that the woman is exerting a greater torque. The pivot is the point the door revolves around. The force is how hard the person is pushing. The distance is the distance between the pivot and the person's hand. The torque is then the force multiplied by the distance.*

ground. Tornadoes occurring over the sea may cause a waterspout; if they pass over desert areas, the columns of sand lifted up may be called sand devils. In 1925 a tornado passing across the southern United States caused the deaths of almost 700 people.

Torque

Torque measures the twisting effect of a FORCE. For example, imagine two people pushing in opposite directions on a revolving door. If they can both push with the same force, the person who is standing farther away from the center of the door will be able to turn the door in the direction he or she is pushing. This person is exerting a greater torque on the door. Torque is defined as the strength of the force multiplied by the distance between the force and the fixed axis of the ROTATION. Torque is used, for example, to give an indication of the performance of a car engine; it measures the twist force which the engine applies to the crankshaft.

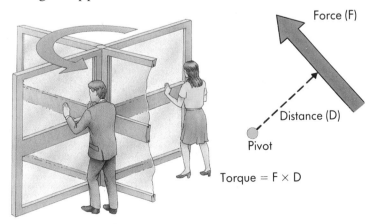

Force (F)

Distance (D)

Pivot

Torque = F × D

Torricelli, Evangelista *See* Barometer

Torsion

Torsion is used in science to mean twisting. An object is "in torsion" when one end of it is twisted relative to the other end. In PHYSICS, the torsion is the amount of turning of one end relative to the other, divided by the distance between the ends. Torsion can be produced by a twisting force or TORQUE. The word is also used in BIOLOGY to describe animals or plants that do not develop in straight lines but twist as they grow.

Snails grow with torsion. A snail starts off as a larva with a straight body. But as it grows the larva starts to coil and undergo torsion so that it will be able to fit into a spiral-shaped shell. One side of a snail's body grows faster than the other, giving rise to the body's torsion.

Touch

Touch is one of the SENSES. It helps to protect the body from accidental damage. It consists of five separate senses: pressure, touch, heat, cold, and pain. These combine to produce the sense of touch. The different receptors are grouped in the dermis layer of the SKIN, and pass their signals to the BRAIN along NERVES. In areas where it is important for the senses to be very sharp, the receptors are very close together. Touch and pressure receptors are clustered together closely in our fingertips and lips, which are among the most sensitive areas of the body. On the back, arms, and legs, however, these receptors are scattered thinly, because these areas are not important to our sense of touch. Tiny HAIRS covering the skin also add to our sense of touch, since we can feel a movement of the air by the stirring of these hairs.

SEE FOR YOURSELF
You can try a game using the sense of touch. Blindfold a friend. Then put a number of familiar objects on a table. How many of them can he or she recognize using touch alone? Now try the game with you blindfolded and your friend choosing the objects.

▲ *Touch is not only a way of detecting what is around us, but can also be an important way of communicating.*

Trace elements

Trace elements are chemical ELEMENTS that are needed in very small quantities by plants and animals to keep

Trace element	Use in the human body	Food sources
Calcium	Bones, teeth	Milk, cheese, bread (if chalk added)
Phosphorus	Bones, teeth, energy transfers	Milk proteins
Iron	To carry oxygen in blood	Eggs, liver, green vegetables
Sodium	Nerve and muscle control	Table salt
Potassium	Nerve and muscle control	Vegetables, fruit
Iodine	Hormonal control of metabolism	Seafood, table salt (if iodine added)
Fluorine	Tooth enamel	Toothpaste and water (if fluoride added)

Animals and Plants
A list of trace elements required by animals and plants would include: calcium, sodium, phosphorus, potassium, chlorine, sulfur, magnesium, iron, chromium, manganese, zinc, copper, iodine, cobalt, silicon, selenium, and molybdenum.

▶ *These potato leaves are suffering from a serious deficiency of the trace element magnesium.*

Human beings and all animals need the same trace elements to keep healthy. But they are needed in very small amounts. Cobalt in vitamin B_{12} protects against anemia, but only 0.000002 gram of this each day is needed by the body.

People can become psychologically dependent on tranquilizers as well as physically addicted. For example, a person may have been taking tranquilizers for several months for help getting to sleep. This person may then not be able to sleep without the tranquilizers simply because of worry about not having them.

them healthy. The most important trace elements for humans are the metals iron, copper, cobalt, zinc, and manganese, and the nonmetals iodine and boron. All of these elements need to be obtained from our food.

Iron, for example, is essential for the formation of hemoglobin, the red color in the BLOOD. Lack of iron can cause anemia. Foods rich in iron include meat (particularly liver) and eggs. Iodine is found in fish and other kinds of seafood. In small quantities it is essential for the proper functioning of the thyroid GLAND in the

neck, which controls METABOLISM. Lack of iodine in the diet can lead to goiter, a condition in which the thyroid gland becomes very swollen. In many countries, an iodine compound is added to table salt to make sure that everyone gets enough iodine. A balanced diet contains sufficient quantities of all trace elements, and normally there is no need to take supplements. In larger quantities most trace elements are poisonous.

Tranquilizers and Stimulants

Many DRUGS have an effect on the nervous system, and some drugs can change our moods and emotions. Tranquilizers and stimulants are drugs of this type. They work by affecting the way in which NERVES communicate, blocking or increasing the very small amounts of neurotransmitter substances which carry signals from one nerve cell to another in the BRAIN. Tranquilizers act by calming and relaxing, so they are often given to people just before an operation. They are also some-

◄ In parts of northern Canada, polar bears sometimes wander into the edges of towns. This bear has been put to sleep using a dart containing a powerful tranquilizer so that it can be taken back and released into the wild.

times given to people who worry and become very agitated, or who are feeling depressed. However, it has recently been found that, although these tranquilizers are very effective, most are also strongly addictive drugs if they are taken for more than a short time. Doctors are now discouraged from prescribing them except when they are really needed. Sleeping pills or hypnotics are drugs of the same type, but are taken in larger doses to produce sleep.

Stimulants have the reverse effect, making people feel mentally alert and active. Coffee and tea contain the substance CAFFEINE, a stimulant which is harmless in normal amounts, but can keep you awake if taken in large quantity or late at night. Unfortunately, powerful medical stimulants are often abused, so they are now seldom prescribed by doctors.

Transformer

A transformer converts an electrical signal from one voltage to another. It works only with an alternating current (which flows first in one direction, then in the other) and not with a direct current (which always flows in the same direction). This is because the transformer works using electromagnetic INDUCTION. A magnetic field is produced by the current in a "primary coil" (or solenoid) which is connected to the input of the transformer. The magnetic field passes through the middle of another solenoid, the "secondary coil." As the magnetic field changes with the alternating current, it creates an

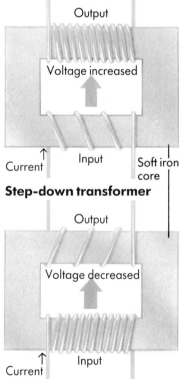

Step-up transformer

Output

Voltage increased

Current   Input   Soft iron core

Step-down transformer

Output

Voltage decreased

Input

Current

▲ In both of these transformers, a current flows through the input coil and induces a current with a different voltage in the output coil. In the step-up transformer, there are more turns of the output coil than of the input coil so the voltage is increased. In the step-down transformer, there are more turns of the input coil than of the output coil so the voltage is decreased.

709

William Shockley (1910–1989)
Shockley was an American physicist who in 1947, with John Bardeen and Walter Brattain, developed the point-contact transistor. A year later, Shockley devised the junction transistor. For this work the three scientists shared the 1956 Nobel Prize in Physics. Some time later Shockley became interested in inherited characteristics.

▶ *The transistor has a special circuit symbol. A transistor (right) is made of a sandwich of a specially treated piece of silicon between two differently treated ones. The three layers are called the emitter, the base, and the collector. A weak, electric current connected to the base causes a larger variation in the electron flow across the emitter and the collector. The transistor amplifies the current.*

alternating voltage in the secondary coil. If there are more turns on the secondary coil than the primary, the secondary (output) voltage is higher than the primary (input) voltage and the transformer is a *step-up transformer*, and in the opposite case, it the output voltage is lower, the transformer is a *step-down transformer*.

Electrical POWER is transmitted at very high voltages, because this reduces the loss of ENERGY due to the RESISTANCE of the wires; step-down transformers reduce the voltage before it enters people's homes.

Transistor

A transistor is an electronic device used as a switch or to amplify an electric current or voltage. It is a SEMICONDUCTOR device made from p-type and n-type semiconductors arranged as a p-n-p or n-p-n structure. The three layers are called the emitter, base, and collector. A small current flowing into the base causes the emitter-collector resistance to drop and allows a larger current to flow between them, so the emitter-collector current is an amplified copy of the base current. The transistor was developed in 1948 by William Shockley and others. It replaced the tube. Transistors are smaller than tubes, enabling electronic equipment to be smaller. Also they generate very little heat so they can be packed closer together than tubes, further reducing the size of the equipment. Electronic equipment such as transistor radios became portable because the transistor's low power requirement meant that they could be powered by small BATTERIES. In the 1970s, single transistors began to be replaced by INTEGRATED CIRCUITS containing large numbers of electronic components.

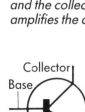

Transistor

Electrical symbol for transistor

Collector
Base
Emitter

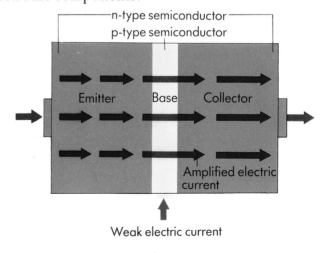

n-type semiconductor
p-type semiconductor

Emitter   Base   Collector

Amplified electric current

Weak electric current

Transpiration

Transpiration is the EVAPORATION of WATER from the parts of a plant above ground and occurs mostly through the LEAVES. Evaporation takes place through thousands of tiny pores, called stomata, on the undersides of the leaves. Water is taken into plants through their ROOTS then moves up the STEM into the leaves. This movement is called the transpiration stream. Although evaporation from the leaves will draw more water from the veins of the leaf and so pull water up in the transpiration stream, this alone does not account for the effect. The plant needs the water for PHOTOSYNTHESIS.

In hot, dry weather transpiration takes place faster than the plant can draw water from the soil. The plant then has to close its stomata, otherwise it will lose too much water and start to wilt.

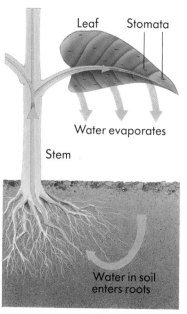

Leaf   Stomata

Water evaporates

Stem

Water in soil enters roots

▲ The water that exudes from a plant's leaves during transpiration comes originally from the soil. It is taken in by the roots and travels up the stem to the leaves where some of it evaporates through pores in the leaves called stomata.

SEE FOR YOURSELF
You can show that a plant transpires by putting a potted plant inside a closed plastic bag. After a while the bag will steam up and eventually drops of water will form on the inside. Remember to water the plant when you have finished your experiment.

Transplants

Transplants are grafts of living tissue from another organism, which are used to correct or replace a diseased part. Corneal grafting was the first transplant technique to be widely used in humans. Because the cornea of the EYE has no BLOOD supply, the IMMUNE SYSTEM of the body cannot recognize and attack the foreign or grafted tissue. Corneal grafts are used to restore sight when the surface of the eye has been burned or scarred. In other parts of the body, such as the kidney, lungs, heart, and liver, transplants can also be carried out successfully. The problem is that the body sometimes attacks or

Medical treatment of the form of cancer called leukemia involves radiation. This not only kills the cancer but also destroys the patient's bone marrow, the part of the body in which blood cells are made. The condition can be corrected by giving the patient a bone marrow transplant, using marrow from a healthy donor.

▶ *Many transplant operations are undertaken now. Once-complicated operations are now considered routine. The operation begins with an anesthetic to put the patient to sleep so that he or she does not feel a thing.*

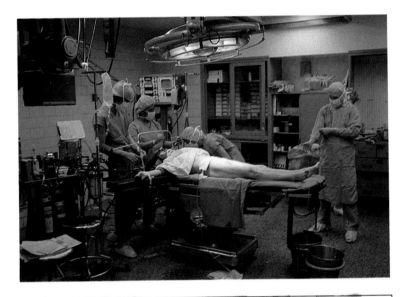

SEE FOR YOURSELF
To make a transplant on a plant, first take a cutting of a strong-growing shoot. Cut it at an angle just below a leaf bud **1**. Then on another plant of the same kind, called the stock, make a T-shaped cut through the bark **2** and peel it back. Insert the shoot (the graft) **3** and bind it with adhesive tape **4**. After a few weeks it will join the stock and continue to grow.

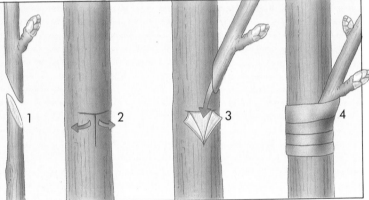

rejects the donor organ (unless the organ comes from an identical twin). Tissues can be matched so that the organ is less likely to be rejected, but powerful DRUGS such as STEROIDS must be given to prevent rejection. Transplants have become very successful in recent years, since the introduction of a new drug called cyclosporine, and many of the major body organs can now be transplanted.

Parts of plants can also be transplanted or grafted. Often a vigorously fruiting stem is grafted onto a sturdy rootstock to improve the fruit yield of a plant.

Tropics

The tropics are the two parallel lines of LATITUDE at an angular distance of 23.5° from the equator. The tropics also describes the broad zone that circles the Earth between the tropics of Cancer (northern) and Capricorn

Most places in the tropics are hot all year, and they have some of the world's greatest rainfall. But at the tops of high mountains it can be very cold even in the tropics: the temperature falls by about 11°F (6°C) for every 3,300 feet (1,000 m) of altitude. The top of Mount Kilimanjaro in Tanzania is covered in snow all year.

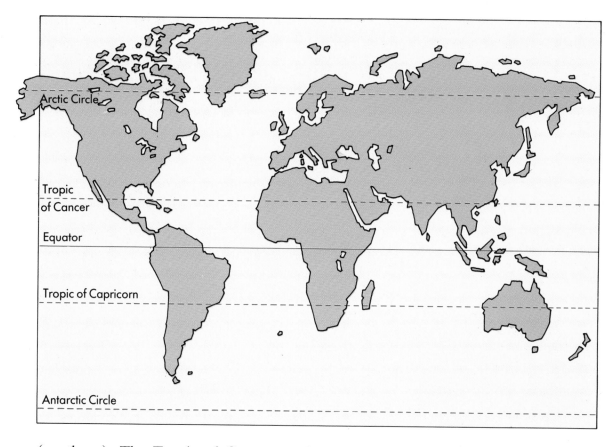

(southern). The Tropic of Cancer marks the farthest limit north of the equator where the Sun can appear directly overhead. The Tropic of Capricorn is the Sun's overhead limit south of the equator. Most places in the tropics have warm to hot temperatures because the amount of daylight differs little from season to season. In the tropics the Sun always rises and sets at around 6 o'clock and there is no long twilight before dawn or after sunset. The tropics give rise to two important air masses which move toward the poles and affect the CLIMATE of the areas in between.

▲ The region known as the tropics lies astride the equator between the Tropics of Cancer and Capricorn. The tropics include all the world's tropical forests as well as some of the hot deserts.

In tropical regions the main airflow is upward and the surface winds are often very light. In the days of sail, ships often used to lie becalmed in the glassy seas. Sailors called this being in the "doldrums" meaning that they felt gloomy. Today, this region is still referred to as the doldrums.

◄ Dense jungle, known as rain forest, is one of the typical types of vegetation in a tropical country such as Nigeria. The forest is home for hundreds of kinds of birds and animals.

▲ *The troposphere is the part of the atmosphere, above the Earth's surface, where weather movements occur.*

Troposphere

The troposphere is the layer of the ATMOSPHERE that extends from the surface of the EARTH to a height of about 6 miles (10km) at the North and South Poles and about 10 miles (16km) at the equator. It is the layer in which we live. In the troposphere, the temperature gradually falls with increasing height at a rate of about 3.5°F for every 1,000 feet (6.5°C for every kilometer). The boundary between the troposphere and the STRATOSPHERE is referred to as the tropopause, and its actual height varies considerably.

Almost all of the water VAPOR in the atmosphere is found in the troposphere so that it is here that CLOUDS form. Here, too, most of the disturbances that we call WEATHER occur because of the movements of air masses through CONVECTION. The troposphere contains most of the oxygen, other gases, and solid or liquid particles, such as smoke or fog.

Tsunami *See* Tidal waves and Tsunamis

Tube *See* Vacuum tube

Tungsten

Tungsten is a silvery white ELEMENT sometimes called wolfram. It is a tough METAL that does not easily corrode, used for filaments in electric lamps and heating elements

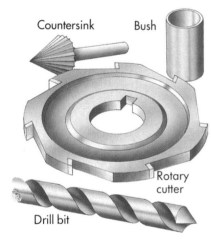

▲ *Tungsten carbide, a compound of tungsten and carbon, is an extremely hard substance. It is used for the cutting edges of power tools and to make objects that have to withstand a lot of wear.*

▶ *The filament in an electric lamp is made of tungsten. The metal has a high resistance and becomes very hot when an electric current flows through it. The lamp is filled with an inert gas such as nitrogen so that the hot filament does not oxidize and burn away.*

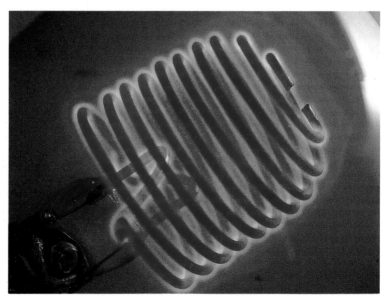

714

in electric toasters. Its main use is in various ALLOYS, particularly tungsten steels for making tools for cutting other metals. Alloys of tungsten and copper or silver are made into contacts for electric switches that have to control very large currents. A compound of tungsten and carbon, called tungsten carbide, is one of the hardest substances known. Only DIAMOND is harder. Tungsten carbide is used to make the tips of drills and edges of saws for cutting rock and concrete.
See also CORROSION; HARDNESS.

Tunnel

A tunnel is a passage cut under the EARTH's surface. Tunnels allow roads, canals, and railroad lines to pass through mountains and under roads. Tunnels called sewers carry waste materials away from houses.

People have dug into the ground since prehistoric times to look for MINERALS. The Romans built tunnels to carry water to their cities. During the INDUSTRIAL REVOLUTION tunnels were built for canals. Tunneling through ROCK used to be done by drilling holes in it and filling them with EXPLOSIVES. The blast shattered the rock. When this was cleared, the new rock face was drilled and blasted. Tunneling is now done by machines called moles which tunnel continuously. A circular cutting disk at the front of the mole is driven against the rock face by powerful hydraulic rams.

> **LONGEST VEHICLE TUNNELS:**
> **Seikan Rail Tunnel** between Fukushima and Honshu, Japan 33 miles.
> **Channel Tunnel** between Britain and France 30 miles.
> **Moscow Metro underground railroad tunnel** between Belyaevo and Medvedkovo 19 miles.
> **St. Gotthard Road Tunnel**, Alps, Switzerland 10 miles.

> The Romans built the first-known road tunnel over 2,000 years ago, in 36 B.C. It was near the city of Naples and was nearly a mile long. The West Delaware water supply tunnel in New York is the world's longest tunnel. It is 106 miles (170 km) long.

◀ *Automatic tunneling machines, or moles, are used today. They have large rotating cutting heads which are pressed forward by hydraulic jacks to force the mole onward. A conveyor belt inside the machine carries away the rock and soil as it is cut. Moles can be powered by electricity and hydraulic motors.*

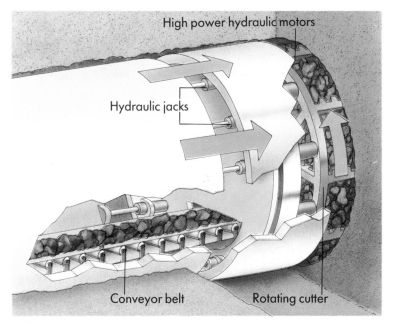

High power hydraulic motors

Hydraulic jacks

Conveyor belt

Rotating cutter

▶ This huge set of turbine blades is from a steam turbine of the kind used in power stations for making electricity.

Turbine

A turbine is a device used to convert the motion of a FLUID into mechanical ENERGY. It consists of a number of blades fixed to a central hub. The FORCE of the fluid pushing against the blades pushes them around. When the turbine rotates, the shaft rotates and this can be used to drive other machinery. The simplest turbine is a water wheel. The wheel may be dipped into flowing water or the water may be directed over the top of it.

The steam turbine was demonstrated by HERO OF ALEXANDRIA nearly 2,000 years ago, but the first practi-

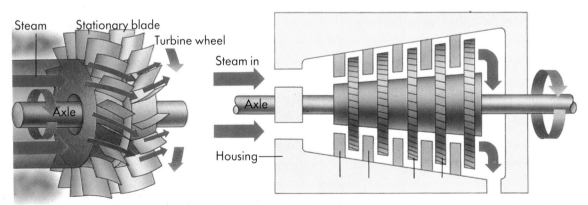

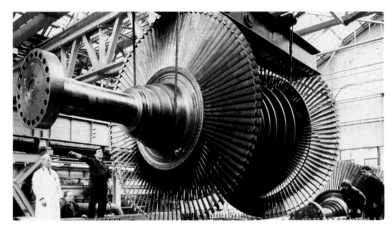

▲ The efficiency of a turbine is increased by directing the gas or steam with stationary blades before it passes between the turbine blades to make them rotate. Steam turbines have several sets of blades (seen in section, right), which are larger where the steam becomes cooler and loses some of its pressure.

cal steam turbine was not made until 1884, by Charles Parsons. The steam turbine quickly replaced the STEAM ENGINE in electrical power GENERATORS. This in turn was later replaced by the GAS TURBINE, which is also used to power some boats and aircraft.

Turbojet *See* Jet propulsion

Turtle *See* Computer

Ultrahigh frequency (UHF)

Ultrahigh frequency (UHF) is the name given to ELEC-TROMAGNETIC RADIATION that has an even higher FREQUENCY than VERY HIGH FREQUENCY (VHF) radio waves. A UHF wave has a frequency between 300 and 3,000 megahertz (a MHz is one million cycles per second). Because of its frequency, a UHF radio wave can carry much more information every second than an ordinary radio wave or a VHF signal. For example, UHF radio waves are used to broadcast TELEVISION signals. These contain a great deal of information because one of three colors has to be given to each spot on the screen each time the beam of the CATHODE-RAY TUBE in the television set passes over it. Hundreds of thousands of spots are scanned 25 or 30 times every second, so tens of millions of pieces of information have to be carried.

UHF signals are used to communicate with artificial SATELLITES and other spacecraft. They allow a lot of information to be transferred and they can pass easily through the IONOSPHERE, the layer of the upper ATMOSPHERE that reflects ordinary radio waves.

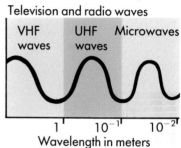

Television and radio waves

▲ *Ultrahigh frequency waves have frequencies greater than very high frequency waves but lower than microwaves.*

◄ *UHF waves travel in straight lines and pass through all the layers of the Earth's atmosphere without being bent or reflected (unlike radio waves of lower frequencies). They are used to send telephone messages, television signals, and computer data over long distances via communications satellites.*

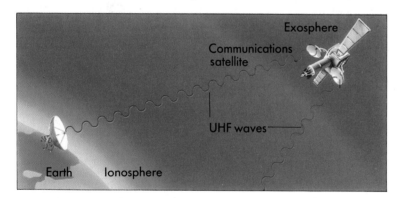

Ultrasound

Ultrasound is SOUND that cannot be heard because its FREQUENCY is greater than the highest frequency that the human EAR can detect. Sound with a frequency greater than 20 kilohertz (a kHz is one thousand cycles per second) can be described as ultrasound or ultrasonic. Ultrasound has a wide variety of uses. If the sound vibrations are strong enough, they can shake objects clean. If a dirty object is dipped into water and the ultrasound is switched on, the dirt is vibrated loose and falls from the object. The vibrations can also be used to break

An ultrasonic wave passed through a liquid or a solid makes the liquid or solid vibrate at a very fast rate. These vibrations can be used to mix paint thoroughly, clean tools, and homogenize milk by breaking up the fat particles. In dentistry, a drill controlled by ultrasonic vibrations can penetrate tooth enamel with very little friction or heat.

▶ *An ultrasound scanner builds up a picture of an unborn baby in its mother's womb. This technique, which is painless for the mother and harmless for the baby, is used to check the progress of pregnancy.*

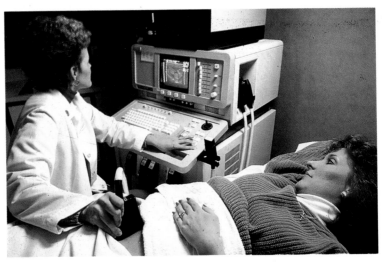

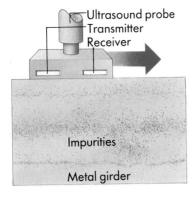

Ultrasound probe
Transmitter
Receiver

Impurities

Metal girder

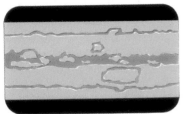

▲ *Ultrasound scanning is used to detect flaws and impurities in metals. The ultrasound probe is moved along the surface of the metal to be tested. The probe has a transmitter to produce ultrasound and a receiver to detect it. The main reflections, or echoes, come from the top and bottom surfaces. But any impurities also reflect the ultrasonic waves and show up as a trace on a screen or print-out.*

▶ *The eyes of some insects, such as bees, are sensitive to ultraviolet light. To a bee, these lobelia flowers look dark with pale lines down the middle of the petals. This encourages it to visit the flowers and pollinate them. Humans cannot see these lines (right) because in visible light the petals appear pale all over.*

up painful growths in the kidneys called kidney stones.

Ultrasound can be used to reveal details that cannot normally be seen. Ships and submarines have SONAR systems that use ultrasound to "see" under water. Scanners used in hospitals to check on the progress of unborn babies also use ultrasound. A scanner transmits ultrasound into the mother's body and receives reflections from inside. The reflections are displayed as a picture on a screen. Ultrasound is used because it is safer for the developing baby than X-rays.

Ultraviolet radiation

Ultraviolet radiation is ELECTROMAGNETIC RADIATION that has a higher FREQUENCY than the LIGHT we can see. It lies beyond the blue or violet end of the visible SPECTRUM. Each PHOTON (particle) of ultraviolet light carries more ENERGY than photons of visible light, so

MOLECULES that absorb ultraviolet radiation receive a large amount of energy. This extra energy can cause the molecule to break apart. This means that in ultraviolet light CHEMICAL REACTIONS can take place which would not otherwise occur. Ultraviolet light in sunlight can cause people's skin to burn. Large amounts of ultraviolet radiation can be dangerous. The OZONE LAYER is important because it absorbs most of the ultraviolet radiation from the Sun before it reaches the Earth. *See also* INFRARED RADIATION; PHOTOCHEMISTRY.

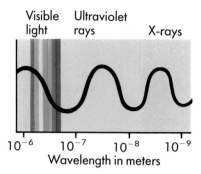

▲ *Ultraviolet rays have shorter wavelengths than visible light and lie beyond the violet end of the spectrum. (10^{-6} meters is 400 thousandths of an inch.)*

Universe

The universe is the whole of space and everything in it. Astronomers believe that it was formed after the BIG BANG, which probably took place about 15 billion years ago. The universe has been expanding ever since, and the clusters of GALAXIES in it (including the cluster containing the MILKY WAY, where our SOLAR SYSTEM is located), are flying farther apart. Although the universe is getting larger, this does not mean that it has an "edge" like an expanding balloon. This is because the force of GRAVITY in the space between the clusters of galaxies makes anything traveling through it follow a curved path, even though it seems to be straight. Trying to find

Edwin Hubble (1889–1953)
Hubble was an American astronomer whose work provided evidence for the theory that the universe is expanding. In the 1920s he studied hundreds of distant galaxies and, by measuring the red shift in their spectra, showed that they are moving rapidly away from each other. He also classified galaxies into various types.

◀ *The universe is made up of all the galaxies, stars, planets, moons, asteroids, and other bodies scattered through the emptiness of space.*

Edwin Mattison McMillan (1907–1991)
McMillan was a U.S. physicist who in 1940 made the first element heavier than uranium (element 92). He used neutrons accelerated in a particle accelerator to bombard uranium atoms and produced atoms of element 93, which he called neptunium. For this work, he shared the 1951 Nobel Prize in Chemistry.

▲ *These hands hold a piece of uranium-235, the isotope that is used as a fuel in nuclear reactors. Uranium is one of the densest metals; this small piece weighs 10 pounds and is worth over 200,000 dollars. Before holding the uranium the hands have to be protected with special gloves.*

720

the edge of the universe is like trying to find the "end" of a circle.

The visible universe contains millions of galaxies, collected into clusters and superclusters. These clusters are arranged in a clumpy way instead of being scattered evenly through space. Explaining this "clumping" is a major task in COSMOLOGY.

Astronomers have detected remote galaxies and QUASARS many thousands of millions of light-years away. Even these distant objects are made of the same ATOMS as the ones familiar to us, and obey the laws of physics. We are now used to the idea of the universe being similar everywhere, or "homogeneous," but it was only about a hundred years ago that the law of gravity was proved to operate beyond the Solar System.

Uranium

Uranium is a white METAL. It is an ELEMENT that exists in several varieties, or ISOTOPES, all of which are RADIOACTIVE. One of the isotopes, uranium-235, can undergo nuclear fission to release large amounts of ENERGY. It is used in atomic weapons and as the fuel in most types of NUCLEAR REACTORS. Uranium-238 is the fuel in another type of power station, a breeder reactor, which turns it into PLUTONIUM. Uranium occurs in ores such as pitchblende, but is difficult to extract and even more difficult to separate into its isotopes. The mining and extraction of uranium, and its use as a nuclear fuel, create large amounts of radioactive waste products which are difficult to get rid of safely.

See also NUCLEAR PHYSICS; NUCLEAR WASTE.

Glenn Theodore Seaborg (1912–   )
Seaborg is an American chemist who specializes in the transuranic elements (the radioactive elements that are heavier than uranium). From 1940, Seaborg and his team produced nine new elements, from plutonium (element 94) to nobelium (element 102). They described the elements' chemical properties. Seaborg shared the 1951 Nobel Prize in Physics.

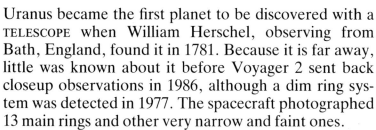

Earth

Uranus

URANUS FACTS
Diameter at equator
32,300 miles
(52,000 km)
Diameter at poles
31,200 miles
(49,900 km)
Average distance from Sun
1,783,000,000 miles
(2,870,000,000 km)
Year length 84 years
Day length 17 hours 18 min.
Mass 14.6 Earths
Density 0.22 Earth
Surface temperature
−328°F (−200°C)

◀ *Uranus has a faint ring system and 15 moons, 5 large ones and 10 small. Its diameter is four times that of Earth.*

Uranus

Uranus became the first planet to be discovered with a TELESCOPE when William Herschel, observing from Bath, England, found it in 1781. Because it is far away, little was known about it before Voyager 2 sent back closeup observations in 1986, although a dim ring system was detected in 1977. The spacecraft photographed 13 main rings and other very narrow and faint ones.

Five satellites have been known for many years, the largest being Titania 1,000 miles (1,600 km) across and the smallest, Miranda, 300 miles (480 km) across. They are all airless, icy-surfaced bodies with craters where flying fragments crashed into them. The satellite Ariel, has immense valleys, while Miranda is a patchwork of completely different markings. One suggestion is that an old satellite was shattered in a collision, and the fragments drifted together to form Miranda. Voyager discovered 10 new satellites.

Uranus itself is surrounded by a thick ATMOSPHERE of hydrogen, helium, and methane. But unlike the other "cloudy" outer planets it has hardly any cloud markings. The most curious thing about Uranus is the tilt of its axis, which is so tipped over that during its "year" the Sun can shine almost overhead at each pole, and parts of its surface are in continuous day, and then continuous night, for almost 42 of our years.

William Herschel (1738–1822)
Herschel was a German-born British astronomer who in 1781 discovered the planet Uranus using a telescope he had built. He went to Britain as a musician when he was 19, and took up astronomy when he was 36. As well as discovering Uranus, he identified nearly 2,000 nebulae and cataloged 800 double stars. He became astronomer to King George III.

Edward Jenner (1749–1823)
Jenner was a British doctor who in 1796 performed the first successful inoculations against disease. He inoculated people with cowpox (a disease of cattle) to protect them against deadly smallpox. The technique was widely adopted and over the next 100 years deaths from smallpox fell dramatically (from 40 per 10,000 people to 1 per 10,000).

▶ *Vaccination gives active immunity to a disease. It uses killed or weakened germs that have been "grown" in hen's eggs or laboratory animals. Passive immunity results from inoculation with a serum, usually from an animal that has developed immunity to the disease. It can also be given by using a similar, but less dangerous, live germ.*

722

Vaccination

Vaccination is a medical technique that causes the body to produce substances called ANTIBODIES, which fight DISEASE. Substances that do not naturally belong in the body are called antigens. These cause the IMMUNE SYSTEM to react by producing antibodies which make the antigens harmless. Antigens are carried on the surface of bacteria and viruses.

In vaccination, the antigens that enter the body, through injection or by mouth, are harmless. The vaccine has been treated to weaken the bacteria or virus, and in some cases, dead bacteria or viruses, or even extracts of the antigen substances, will cause the protective antibodies to be produced. Sometimes further vaccinations or boosters are needed to provide continuing protection against infection. To protect against tuberculosis (TB), a similar live but less dangerous bacterium is used to create an infection that causes the body to develop immunity to TB. This is called *inoculation*, and was first used to protect against smallpox, when people were injected with a milder disease called cowpox.

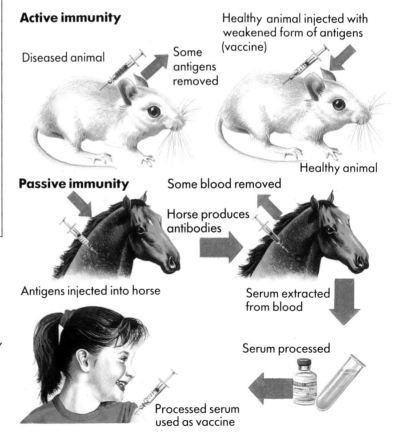

Active immunity

Diseased animal — Some antigens removed

Healthy animal injected with weakened form of antigens (vaccine)

Healthy animal

Passive immunity

Antigens injected into horse

Some blood removed

Horse produces antibodies

Serum extracted from blood

Serum processed

Processed serum used as vaccine

Vacuum

Most of the spaces on Earth which we usually think of as empty are filled with MOLECULES of AIR. A vacuum, on the other hand, is a space that really is empty; a perfect vacuum contains no molecules of any sort. Interstellar space, the open space between the STARS, is almost a perfect vacuum. It is difficult to make a vacuum. It is necessary to pump out all the air from inside a container. However, molecules of air can leak in through very tiny

holes in the container and molecules on the surface of the container evaporate into the empty space. The container must also be strong enough to withstand the inward PRESSURE of the air outside. Something that is nearly a vacuum is called a *partial vacuum*. A vacuum is useful as thermal INSULATION because it prevents heat flow by CONVECTION. Foods such as coffee which become stale when exposed to air, are packed in a "vacuum pack" from which the air has been removed.
See also EVAPORATION; MAGDEBURG SPHERES.

Vacuum bottle

A vacuum bottle is a container used to keep liquids or gases hot or cold. It is also known as a Thermos bottle or a Dewar flask after the Scottish scientist, Sir James Dewar, who invented it in the 1890s. It is made from a double-walled glass bottle. The air in the gap between the two glass walls is pumped out to create a VACUUM. The walls facing into the vacuum are silvered like a MIRROR. The vacuum prevents HEAT from passing across the

The best vacuums so far produced measure approximately 0.0000000001 pascal (one pascal equals a pressure of about 0.00015 pound per square inch). Even at this very low pressure, 1 cubic inch (16 cc) of gas contains over 500,000 molecules. A cc of normal air contains about 400 billion molecules.

◀ *Any container with a lower pressure on the inside than on the outside must be very strong. If a little water is boiled in a metal can, the water produces steam which expands. If the can is taken off the heat and the cap screwed on, the steam will cool and condense lowering the pressure inside the can, forming a partial vacuum. After a short time, the air pressure will crush the can inward.*

▼ *An upright vacuum cleaner has an electric motor that sucks air from the bottom of the dust bag. This leaves a partial vacuum which causes dust to be pushed up by the outside air pressure into the bag.*

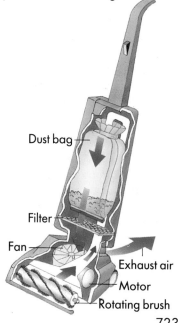

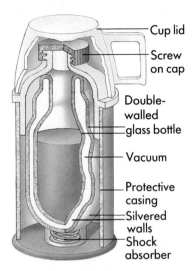

A vacuum bottle keeps hot liquids hot or cold liquids cold by preventing the transfer of heat between the contents and the outside. The vacuum prevents heat flow by convection, and silvering on the bottle's walls prevents heat flow by radiation.

Cup lid
Screw on cap
Double-walled glass bottle
Vacuum
Protective casing
Silvered walls
Shock absorber

Sir James Dewar (1842–1923)
Dewar was a British chemist and physicist who in about 1892 invented the vacuum bottle, also called a Dewar flask. It is sometimes known by its trade name, Thermos bottle. Dewar used the bottle in experiments with liquid oxygen, hydrogen, and other gases at very low temperatures. In 1891, with Frederick Abel, he developed cordite, a smokeless propellant explosive for cartridges and shells.

The American inventor Thomas Edison produced the first vacuum tube, but he did not realize its importance. Early in the 1880s, Edison sealed an extra electrode into a light bulb. He noticed that a current flowed from the bulb's filament to this electrode if it was positively charged. Edison had made a diode vacuum tube, but he could see no use for his invention.

▶ In a diode tube, electrons travel from the heated cathode (negative electrode) to the anode (positive electrode). A triode has a similar arrangement of electrodes but in addition has a control grid. This is between the cathode and anode, and its voltage is adjusted to control the flow of electrons.

gap by contact with air molecules. This transfer of heat is called CONVECTION. The silvering reflects heat, preventing it from crossing the gap by RADIATION. In 1925 a vacuum bottle enclosed in a case for protection first went on sale to the public for carrying hot or cold drinks.

Vacuum tube

A vacuum tube is a device that works by the action of ELECTRONS traveling through a gas or a VACUUM. Inside the tube's glass body, electrons flow from an electrically-heated electrode (the cathode) through the gas or vacuum to a second electrode, (the anode). There may be other electrodes between the cathode and anode which control the flow of electrons.

There are different types of vacuum tubes. The first,

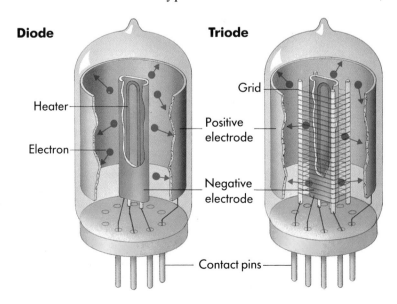

Diode
Heater
Electron

Triode
Grid
Positive electrode
Negative electrode

Contact pins

724

the diode, was invented in 1904. Electrons travel through it in one direction only, enabling it to convert alternating current to direct current. The triode, invented in 1910, is used to amplify electrical signals. Other types of tubes include the tetrode and pentode. Vacuum tubes have now been largely replaced by the semiconductor DIODE, TRANSISTOR, and INTEGRATED CIRCUIT.

Valency

Valency is the combining power of a chemical ELEMENT. It tells us how many chemical BONDS an element can form when it combines with other elements in COMPOUNDS. These bonds involve ELECTRONS, and so the valency is the number of electrons an element can give, take, or share in forming bonds. Some elements always have the same valency. For hydrogen it is always one, for oxygen it is two, and for carbon it is four. Other elements have more than one valency. Iron, for example, can combine to form compounds in two ways and so has a valency of two in some of its compounds, and in other compounds its valency is three.

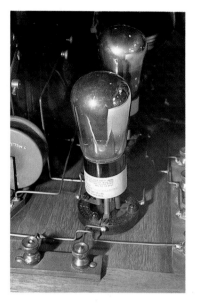

▲ Special vacuum tubes are used to generate radio waves. These tubes were the key components in an early short-wave radio transmitter.

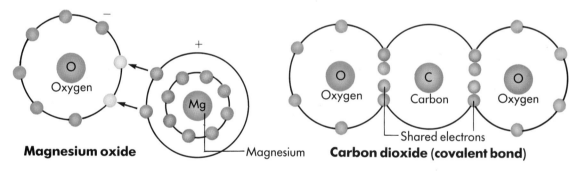

Magnesium oxide   Magnesium   **Carbon dioxide (covalent bond)**

Shared electrons

Van Allen belts

Van Allen belts are two "shells" of atomic particles sent out by the SUN, trapped in space around the EARTH by its magnetic field. They consist of ELECTRONS and PROTONS, and the inner one is about 2,000 miles (3,000 km) above the Earth, the outer one is about 10,000 miles (16,000 km) away.

The Van Allen belts are denser places in the Earth's magnetosphere. The magnetosphere is a huge volume of space, pushed into a comet shape by the SOLAR WIND, extending about 60,000 miles (100,000 km) toward the Sun and about a million miles away from it.

These two magnetic fields are like a vast generator

▲ Magnesium and oxygen both have a valency of two. The left-hand diagram shows how magnesium can give its two outer electrons to fill oxygen's outer shell (to give it eight electrons), forming the compound magnesium oxide. Carbon has four outer electrons and a valency of four. The right-hand diagram shows how one atom of carbon can combine with two oxygen atoms to form carbon dioxide.

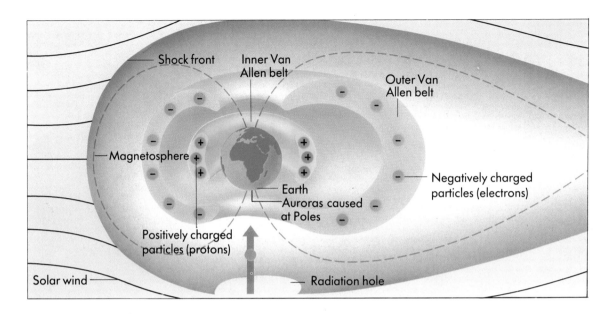

▲ *The Van Allen radiation belts around the Earth are part of the magnetosphere. The belts are distorted by the solar wind so that they are much closer to the surface of the Earth on the side of the Earth that faces the Sun.*

creating ELECTRICITY. The ENERGY is carried down by particles into the Earth's atmosphere, causing the glows known as AURORAS. These two belts were discovered in 1958 by the American physicist James Van Allen.

Van de Graaff generator

A Van de Graaff generator is a machine used to produce very high voltages. It was invented in the 1930s by the U.S. physicist, Robert Jemison Van de Graaff. It consists of a hollow metal hemisphere or dome supported on top of an insulated pillar. A belt made from an electrical INSULATOR is wound around two rollers, one at the top of the pillar inside the dome and one at the bottom. The

Scientists planning the first Apollo trips to the Moon were worried about the effects of the radiation in the Van Allen belts on the astronauts. It turned out that there was less danger than had been feared. The thickness of the spacecraft's outer layer was enough to protect the astronauts.

▶ *At a science demonstration, a high-voltage charge of static electricity from a Van de Graaff generator makes this girl's hair stand on end. Each hair tries to push away from the next one because the like charges repel and the hairs all have the same static charge.*

726

belt is driven around the rollers. As the belt travels past a row of metal points next to the bottom roller, it acquires a positive charge. The belt carries the charge up inside the dome where it is transferred to the dome and moves to the dome's outer surface. The charge continues to build up on the dome, which may reach an electric potential of up to 13 million volts.
See also STATIC ELECTRICITY.

Vapor

A vapor is a GAS that can exist at the same TEMPERATURE as the LIQUID or SOLID from which it comes. Unlike a gas above a certain temperature, a vapor can be liquefied by PRESSURE alone without being cooled.

After it has been raining and the Sun comes out, any puddles soon dry up. This is because when a liquid such as rainwater evaporates, ATOMS or MOLECULES leave its surface and form a vapor. When a liquid is heated, it changes to a vapor more rapidly than when the surroundings are cold. For example when water boils, it changes to a vapor, in this case STEAM, very quickly. If a vapor is cooled, it changes back into a liquid. In a steamy room, water vapor (steam) condenses on the window to form water. Sometimes when the temperature drops at the end of the day, water vapor in the air condenses as droplets of water that form mist or fog.

If a vapor is compressed, it changes back into a liquid. This cycle of changes is used in REFRIGERATION. A vapor is compressed to make a liquid, and then the

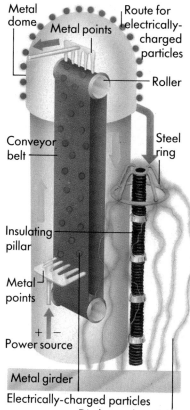

▲ A Van de Graaff generator uses a conveyor belt to carry electric charge and store it on a metal dome. The charge is picked up from a metal comb connected to a high-voltage electricity supply. A large enough charge of discharged particles (at millions of volts) can jump from the steel ring, ionizing the surrounding air and flashing to the ground like artificial lightning.

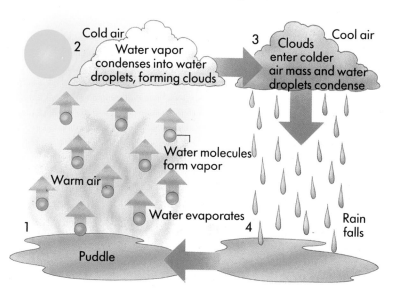

◀ *1.* Puddles dry up in the Sun as the water in them is changed to vapor. *2.* High in the sky, the vapor forms clouds of water droplets *3.* These droplets combine to form drops of rain when the cloud is cooled *4.* The rain falls and the water that lies on the ground forms puddles.

▲ *Clouds of vapor form around a horse's nostrils. In the cold air, water vapor in the animal's breath condenses to form minute droplets of water.*

▶ *Variable stars change in brightness. Sometimes this is not because the star flares up or dims. For example, a binary star consists of two stars orbiting each other. It appears bright when both stars are visible and less bright when one is hidden behind the other.*

▼ *The brightness of a variable star changes as the star swells and shrinks. Many of these stars pulsate regularly at a rate of a few hours or days.*

liquid is allowed to evaporate back into a vapor. This stage requires HEAT and the heat is taken from the inside of the refrigerator, thereby keeping the contents cool. *See also* CONDENSATION; EVAPORATION.

Variable stars

Most stars shine with a steady light, but some vary in brightness over periods from hours to years. A few of these "variable" stars do not actually change in light output at all, but appear to do so because they are twin or BINARY STARS. As they orbit each other, the light from one is blocked out for a time, and they are known as eclipsing binaries. True variables are usually unstable single stars that swell out and shrink, or binary stars where gas passes from one to the other and suddenly flares up. The unstable stars usually repeat this cycle of

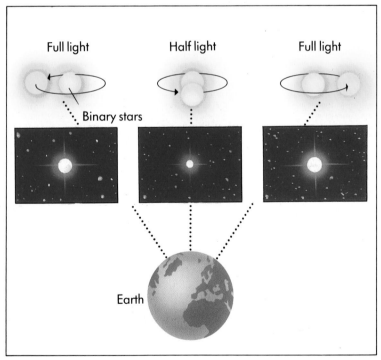

Full light   Half light   Full light

Binary stars

Earth

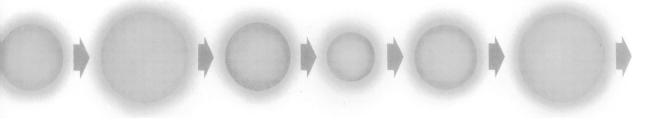

brightening and fading at regular intervals, while the explosive binaries are unpredictable. Other types of variables include flare stars (single stars that have brilliant surges of light), and the rare stars that are usually bright, but become dim as clouds form around them.

Velocity

Velocity is the rate at which an object's position changes. Velocity involves two pieces of information: the first is the speed at which the object is moving, and the second is the direction in which it is moving. If either of these two things changes, then the velocity changes, so two objects traveling with the same speed in different directions have different velocities. It is important not to confuse speed and velocity: speed refers to how fast an object is moving while velocity refers not only to the object's speed but to the direction it is moving in as well. The rate of change of the velocity is called the ACCELERATION, and the rate of change of position of an object is called speed. Velocity and acceleration are important in MECHANICS, the study of moving things.

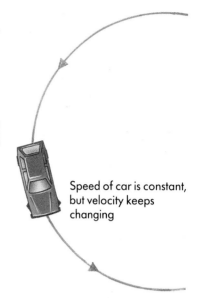

Speed of car is constant, but velocity keeps changing

▲ *Speed is the rate of change of position — how far something goes in a given time. Velocity is the speed in a particular direction. So a car driving in a circle can have a constant speed, but its velocity keeps on changing because the car keeps pointing in a different direction.*

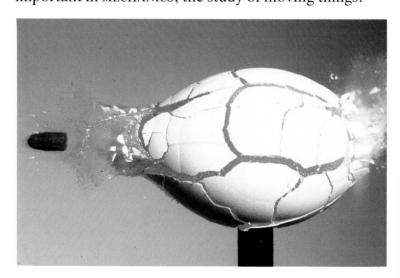

◄ *A camera freezes the action as a bullet traveling at a velocity of 1,480 feet per second (450 m/s) (nearly one and a half times faster than sound travels) hits a raw egg.*

Velocity is measured in units such as miles per hour or meters per second (m/s). The theory of RELATIVITY tells us that the largest possible velocity is the velocity of light, which is about 186,000 miles (300 million meters) per second.

See also CENTRIFUGAL FORCE; MOVEMENT AND MOTION.

Vein *See* Circulation

Stopping Distances
The faster vehicles are traveling, the greater the distance of road they need to stop. An ordinary car traveling at 30 mph (50 km/h) needs about 75 feet (23 m) to come to a stop, whereas a car traveling at 50 mph (80 km/h) needs 174 feet (53 m). This is because of the momentum of the vehicle, which combines its velocity and its mass. A large truck needs more room to stop in than a car.

VENUS FACTS
Diameter
7,545 miles (12,142 km)
Average distance from Sun
67,000,000 miles
(108,000,000 km)
Year length 225 days
Day length 117 Earth days
Mass 0.82 Earths
Density 0.89 Earth
Surface temperature
896°F (480°C) (maximum)
Atmosphere mainly carbon
dioxide gas.

▶ *The hot surface of Venus is hidden behind the dense clouds of its thick, poisonous atmosphere.*

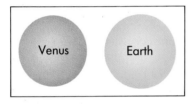

▲ *Venus is about the same size as Earth. Unusually, Venus takes longer to spin on its axis (243 days) than it takes the planet to orbit the Sun (225 days).*

▼ *The space probe Magellan has sent back to Earth the best pictures yet of Venus. The planet is possibly the most unpleasant place in the Solar System.*

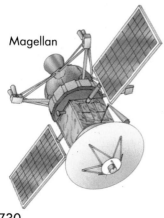

Magellan

Venus

Venus is a PLANET that orbits the SUN between the EARTH and MERCURY, and is almost exactly the same size as the Earth. But it is very different from our planet. The surface of Venus is the hottest place in the SOLAR SYSTEM, with a temperature reaching 896°F (480°C). It is a rocky windswept planet with an "atmosphere" that would feel thicker than ocean water at a depth of several hundred feet. This atmosphere contains carbon dioxide, sulfuric acid and other poisonous compounds, and lightning flickers between the clouds.

Sunlight falls on the rocky surface that warms up and gives out heat RADIATION. The carbon dioxide surrounding Venus lets in enough sunlight to heat the ground, but does not let out the heat radiated from the ground. The heat is trapped, releasing more carbon dioxide from the rocks and making the heat blanket even more efficient. This "runaway GREENHOUSE EFFECT" has turned Venus into an oven.

The invisible surface has been mapped by RADAR from Earth and from SPACE PROBES. Mountain peaks up to 7 miles (12 km) high have been charted. Some features look like Earth-type VOLCANOES. From measurements of the sulfur dioxide gas in Venus's atmosphere, it appears that one or more of the volcanoes may still be active, throwing out sulfur dioxide when it erupts.

Very high frequency (VHF)

Very high frequency (VHF) is the name given to RADIO waves whose FREQUENCY is higher than the frequency of other radio waves but not as high as ULTRAHIGH FREQUENCY waves (UHF). VHF waves have frequencies of around 100 MHz (one hundred million cycles per second), while other radio waves have frequencies of up to only a few hundred kHz (a few hundred thousand hertz). The higher frequency of VHF means that the signal can carry much more information than ordinary radio waves. The disadvantage of VHF signals,

Television waves **Radar waves**

Short wave | VHF | UHF

10   1 10^{-1}

Wavelengths in meters

▲ *VHF radio waves, which lie between short waves and radar waves in the electromagnetic spectrum, are mainly used for television and high-quality radio broadcasting.*

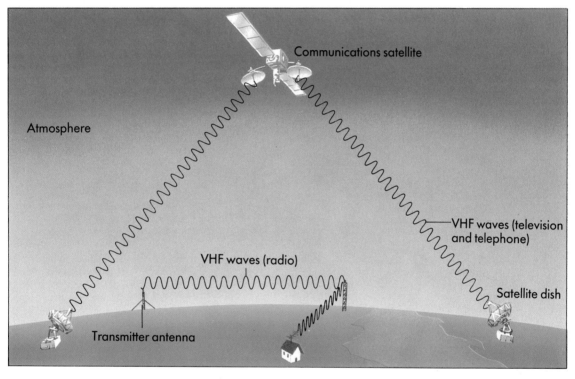

Communications satellite

Atmosphere

VHF waves (television and telephone)

VHF waves (radio)

Satellite dish

Transmitter antenna

however, is that they are not diffracted very easily over hills and, unlike lower-frequency radio waves, they are not reflected from the IONOSPHERE. This means that they are not very effective in transmitting radio signals over very long distances or in mountainous areas.

VHF radio signals are usually different from others because the frequency, rather than the amplitude, of the radio wave is changed when the sound signal is added to the carrier wave. This is called frequency modulation (FM) rather than amplitude modulation (AM).

▲ *VHF radio waves can be used for communication only between places that are within sight of each other. Even with a very tall mast for the transmitting antenna an effective range is only about 50 miles (80 km) overland. But communications satellites allow much greater ranges, and VHF signals to and from a satellite can span an ocean or a whole continent.*

Vesalius, Andreas *See* Muscles

VETERINARY MEDICINE

Veterinary medicine is concerned with the health and treatment of animals. Experiments and surgery on animals have been used for centuries to train doctors, but now veterinary medicine is a highly specialized science in its own right. The training is similar to that for medical doctors, but is in some ways more complicated, because of the many different animals that must be studied. The veterinarian must be highly skilled at making a diagnosis because, unlike humans, animals cannot help the diagnosis by describing how they feel.

Veterinary medicine can be divided into two groups. Small animal veterinary medicine is concerned with the health and treatment of domestic animals such as cats, dogs, and other small pets. A large animal veterinary practice looks after farm livestock and horses, and is generally concerned with preventing illness in these animals, as much as treating them once they are sick. Veterinarians routinely treat farm livestock to remove worms and other parasites which slow their growth or reduce milk production. Vaccines are available to immunize domestic pets and farm livestock against common diseases.

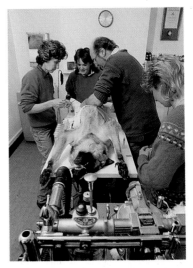

▲ In towns and cities, veterinarians see mainly domestic animals kept as pets. They treat animals that are ill or injured and also immunize them against common diseases and administer other preventative care. Here a dog is undergoing surgery.

◄ In agricultural communities, veterinarians treat farm animals to keep them healthy and prevent the outbreak of diseases. Herds of cattle or other groups of animals are at danger from epidemics of animal diseases because the disease can spread very quickly. Whole herds of animals could die and infect the animals belonging to other farmers nearby. On this farm, the cattle are being given an injection of a drug to combat internal parasites.

Some Common Animal Diseases

Animal diseases need to be treated before the disease can spread to other animals. Many animal diseases can be transmitted to humans.
Brucellosis an infectious disease of cattle, goats, and pigs which causes fever.
Psittacosis a viral disease of parrots and other birds that is similar to pneumonia.
Rabies a very infectious viral disease which affects the nervous system and in dogs, causes foaming at the mouth.
Tuberculosis an infectious disease which mostly affects the lungs. Tuberculosis in cattle can be passed to humans.

Some exotic animals such as gorillas, lions, and tigers, are treated by veterinarians. All of these animals need dental care in captivity. Special techniques are used to help breed some endangered species that are dying out in the wild. Veterinarians are employed by zoos to keep rare animals healthy.

See also AGRICULTURE; BIOLOGY; BREEDING; DISEASE; ENDANGERED SPECIES; PARASITE; PATHOLOGY; VACCINATION; ZOOLOGY.

Video camera

A video camera is used to convert an image into an electrical signal that can form a picture on a TELEVISION screen or be recorded on video TAPE.

Light enters the camera through a LENS. This bends the light rays together so that they form a sharp image on a light-sensitive plate called a target. The target is normally charged up to about 30 volts. When light falls on it, the voltage leaks away. A brightly lit part of the target may fall to zero volts. The pickup tube produces an ELECTRON beam that scans across the target. It restores each part of the target to its fully charged state. The bright parts of the target require greater charging than the darker parts. This charging current forms the video signal from the camera.

Although many cameras used in television studios still have pickup tubes, most home video cameras and camcorders (a camcorder is a combined camera and recorder) use a different light sensor called a charge coupled device or CCD. This SEMICONDUCTOR device is much smaller than a pickup tube, is less fragile than the glass tube and it is not damaged by exposure to very bright light as the pickup tube can be.
See also VIDEOCASSETTE RECORDER.

All cameras have to be held steady so that the pictures produced will be clear. Originally, movie cameras had to run on rails similar to those used by trains to keep them steady. Steadicam is a system that allows a video camera operator to move around freely without the picture becoming wobbly and unsteady. It has a harness for the camera operator and a system of springs and levers to absorb any sudden movements. It works somewhat like the suspension of a car in flattening out bumps.

Camcorder

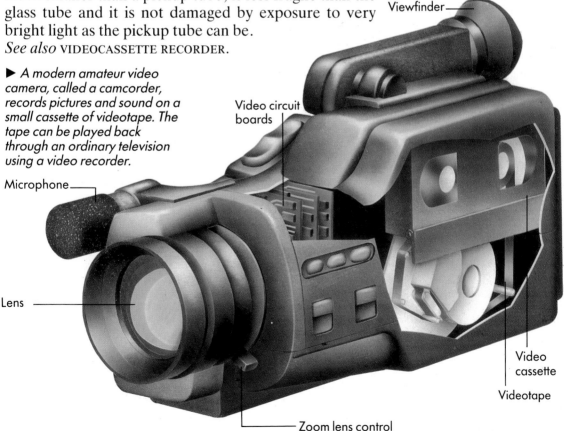

▶ *A modern amateur video camera, called a camcorder, records pictures and sound on a small cassette of videotape. The tape can be played back through an ordinary television using a video recorder.*

Viewfinder

Video circuit boards

Microphone

Lens

Video cassette

Videotape

Zoom lens control

▲ *Modern home videocassette recorders often have a wide variety of features to control both recording and playback. Many now have remote control devices that send infrared signals to the recorder to operate these features.*

Videocassette recorder (VCR)

A videocassette recorder is a machine used to store moving pictures on magnetic TAPE. It receives signals through a cable connected to the TELEVISION antenna. As in an audio CASSETTE RECORDER, the tape is held against a spinning metal drum containing the recording heads. The drum is set at an angle to the tape. Each revolution of the drum records a single television picture across the width of the tape. To record, an erase head removes any existing magnetic pattern from the tape and a video head records new picture signals as a diagonal pattern on the magnetic tape. Sound signals are recorded along one edge of the tape by the audio head.

The first video recorder was developed in 1956 by the U.S. Ampex Corporation. It recorded television pictures a line at a time across the width of 50mm (2-inch) wide magnetic tape. The first video recorder for home use was developed by the European Philips company in 1972. The most popular home video system or format is now VHS, the Video Home System developed by JVC in Japan in the mid 1970s.

How a Videocassette Recorder works

A VCR stores signals for sound and pictures, received by the television antenna, on separate tracks on the videotape. An audio head records the sound on a narrow track, and an angled video head records the pictures on a zig-zag track that occupies most of the rest of the tape. There is also a narrow control track.

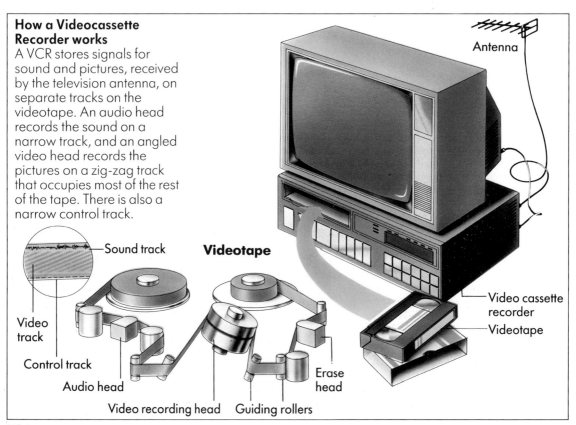

Sound track

Videotape

Video track

Control track

Audio head

Video recording head

Guiding rollers

Erase head

Antenna

Video cassette recorder

Videotape

VIRUSES AND VIRAL DISEASES 🗚

Viruses are tiny organisms that nearly always produce diseases in animals and plants. All viruses are parasites which can live only in other life forms. Technically, they are not living creatures at all, because they can reproduce and carry out the normal processes of life only when they are inside a cell, and forming a part of the cell's structure. Viruses invade cells and take over the genetic material (DNA and RNA), changing its function so that the whole cell becomes a "factory" producing viruses. Eventually the cell bursts and dies, releasing the new viruses to spread.

Because the function of the cell is affected, infection with viruses nearly always causes disease. The body's usual defenses cannot easily fight the virus, because once the virus is inside the cell, the body's immune system is unable to recognize the invader. Antibodies can attack the virus only when it bursts out of the cell ready to infect other cells. Drugs such as antibiotics do not work against viruses, and the immune system must be relied upon to fight the infection. The HIV virus, which can cause AIDS, is particularly dangerous because it infects and kills the cells of the immune system which normally fight diseases. Virus particles, or virions, are very tiny. Viral diseases are usually spread by viruses carried in water droplets in the air, which are inhaled into the lungs. Colds and influenza are common infections caused by viruses.

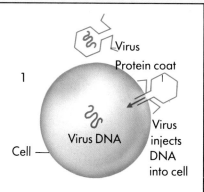
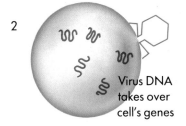

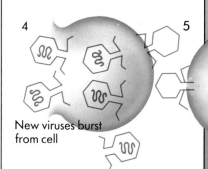

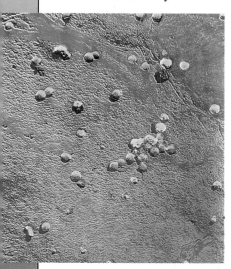

▲ A false-color picture taken with an electron microscope shows particles of the virus adenovirus (yellow), similar to the type that cause the common cold. The tiny organism is magnified here 25,000 times.

Viral Diseases

Diseases caused by viruses include some of the most dangerous and most annoying of all illnesses. Some of them (but by no means all) can be prevented by vaccination, but treatment is usually limited to relieving the symptoms. Antibiotics, effective against most bacterial diseases, are useless against viruses. Viral diseases include:

AIDS (acquired immune
  deficiency syndrome)
Chicken pox
Common cold
Influenza
Measles
Mumps
Polio
Rabies
Rubella (German measles)

▲ 1. A virus consists of a strand of genetic material (DNA or RNA) inside a protein coat. It infects a cell by injecting its DNA into the cell 2. The viral DNA takes over the cell and 3. makes the cell produce more viruses 4. Eventually the infected cell bursts, releasing the new viruses that go on to attack more cells 5.

See also AIDS; ANTIBIOTICS; ANTIBODIES AND ANTIGENS; CELL; DISEASE; IMMUNE SYSTEM; INFECTION; PARASITE; VACCINATION.

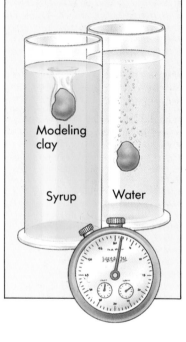

Modeling clay

Syrup   Water

Viscosity

Viscosity describes the ability of FLUIDS (GASES or LIQUIDS) to flow. The property of flowing is called the fluidity, resistance to flow is the viscosity. It is a type of FRICTION force. If an object is moved through a fluid, the fluid next to the object is carried along with it. The nearby fluid is therefore moving relative to the fluid farther away from the object and the resistance which is produced pulls the object back. This backward force from the viscosity can be reduced by STREAMLINING. Different fluids have different viscosities; a gas such as air has a very low viscosity, since the MOLECULES in it do not pull on each other very much. Liquids lose some of their viscosity as they are heated because their molecules do not interact as much as they grow hotter. However, hot gases have a higher viscosity than cold gases.

Visual display unit (VDU)

A visual display unit or VDU is part of a COMPUTER. It shows visual information such as text and COMPUTER GRAPHICS on a screen. The most common type of VDU is the CATHODE-RAY TUBE or CRT. A CRT works like a TELEVISION screen. It builds up the picture from hundreds of lines of glowing phosphor dots. It may be monochrome (single-color) or color. Alternatives to the CRT include the plasma panel, LIQUID CRYSTAL DISPLAY (LCD), and electroluminescent display. They use glowing NEON gas, LIQUID CRYSTALS, and glowing phosphors respectively to form images. These flat panel displays are more compact and less fragile than the glass CRT.

▶ A visual display unit, or VDU, connected to a computer can show alphanumeric characters (letters and numbers) so can be used with word processing software to display text. VDUs can also be used with computer graphics programs to display graphs and charts.

Vitamins

Vitamins are substances that our bodies need to help the many CHEMICAL REACTIONS that take place inside the CELLS. Vitamins cannot be made inside the body (except some vitamin D which can be made in the skin), so they must be obtained from the food we eat. There are several types of vitamins, which are found in a very wide range of foods. Some vitamins dissolve in body fat and can be stored in this way, so they are needed only in very small amounts in our food. Others such as vitamin C dissolve in water, and are flushed out in our urine, so we constantly need to supplement the amounts in our body. Vitamins and MINERALS are important nutrients which help to build cells.

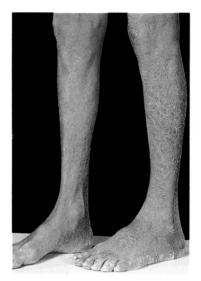

▲ This person is suffering from pellagra. The disorder results from a lack of one type of vitamin B in the diet and causes broken skin and weakness in the muscles. The type of vitamin B missing is needed by the body to obtain energy from glucose. Without it the tissues of the body lose a lot of energy.

Vitamin	Usual Sources	Action in Body
Vitamin A	Liver, fish oils, dairy products, fruit, and vegetables	Needed for healthy eyes, skin, and tissues
Vitamin B (several types)	Meat, dairy products, whole grains (as in wholemeal flour and bread), vegetables	Used by cells in the release of energy, and in red blood cell production
Vitamin C (ascorbic acid)	Oranges, lemons, many other fruits, and vegetables	Needed for healthy bones and teeth, and for tissue repair
Vitamin D	Oily fish, dairy products, and eggs. Some vitamin D is made in the skin by sunlight.	Needed for bone growth
Vitamin E	Brown flour, wheat-germ, liver, green vegetables	In humans no proved function
Vitamin K	Leafy vegetables. Also made in the intestines by harmless bacteria	Helps with blood clotting

In Western countries, the type and amounts of food available mean that people are rarely deficient in vitamins. Where famine and malnutrition are common, vitamin deficiency can be serious, particularly in children. Deficiencies of vitamin D cause rickets, a disease in which the bones do not harden properly, so the legs become deformed. This often affects children where the diet consists mainly of rice, even though some vitamin D is made when sunlight falls on the skin. Vitamin supplements are not necessary if a balanced diet is eaten.

▲ A properly balanced diet will contain all the vitamins that a person needs. It should include milk and dairy products, bread, meat and fish or legumes, and plenty of fresh fruit and vegetables.

737

▶ *An erupting volcano can produce thousands of tons of lava. Red-hot lava can have a temperature of over 1,800°F.*

The world's most devastating volcanic eruption took place at Tambora, Indonesia in 1815 when 12,000 people were killed. The volcano threw out about 36 cubic miles (150 cubic km) of ash and dust. Later in the 19th century when Krakatau, also in Indonesia, exploded, more than 35,000 people were drowned by a giant ocean wave (tsunami).

Volcano Facts
There are about 850 active volcanoes in the world, of which 75 percent are part of the "Ring of Fire." The word "volcano" comes from the Latin name *Volcanus* for the ancient god of fire. Near Sicily, Italy, there is an island called Vulcano with an active volcano on it.

The best-documented volcanic eruption was that of Mount St. Helens in the state of Washington in 1980. For several weeks before the eruption the volcano's activity was monitored by scientists. Despite all this care 60 people died, one of whom was one of the observing scientists. He was too close because the eruption was more powerful than expected. The volcano has erupted several times.

▶ *Most volcanoes are found along or close to the edges of the plates that make up the Earth's crust. The plates float on the Earth's red-hot core. Their movements cause the flow of hot material to the surface that leads to volcanic eruptions.*

Volcanoes

Volcanoes are the various vents or cracks in the crust of the EARTH through which molten rock or LAVA, gas, steam, ash, and even solid ROCK material may be forced out to the surface. The shape of a volcano depends largely on the type of material forced out.

Volcanic eruptions take place in those parts of the Earth's crust where there is a large flow of heat from within the mantle. This is usually along the margins of plates that carry the land and sea. Some volcanoes, such as those that make up the Hawaiian islands, occur within a plate itself and these tend to be less violent than those

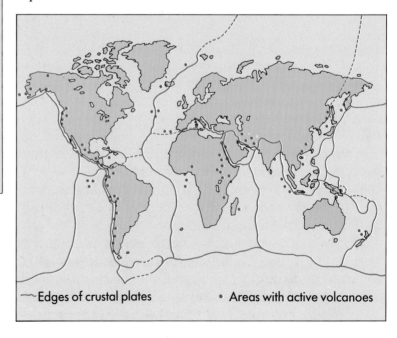

⎯ Edges of crustal plates   • Areas with active volcanoes

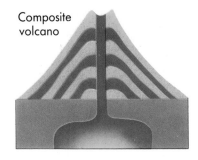

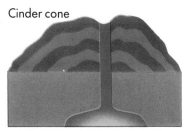

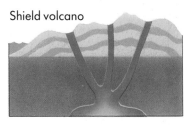

▲ *The three main types of volcano each have distinctive cones. A composite volcano erupts regularly, spilling out* *lava and cinders that flow down the sides and cool to form a cone-shaped mountain. A cinder volcano throws out ash* *and builds a flatter cone. A shield volcano is flatter still and has several openings where lava wells up to the surface.*

that occur at plate margins. There are so many volcanoes around the boundary of the Pacific plate that it is known as the "Pacific ring of fire."

Volcanoes, such as those of the Hawaiian islands, force out large amounts of thin lava so that the volcanic cone is low and spreads out to cover a wide area. Layer after layer of lava, ash, and debris builds up gradually to form the elegantly shaped cone.

In some volcanoes, the vent becomes blocked between eruptions by a plug of rock. Slowly, the pressure under the plug builds up and the volcano erupts with such force and speed that no one has any time to escape. For example, the ancient city of Pompeii in southwest Italy was buried by an eruption of Vesuvius in A.D. 79.

Volt

The volt is the SI UNIT that measures voltage. Voltage is also known as electromotive force (e.m.f.) or "potential difference." This is the difference in the ENERGY of an electric charge at two different points. Work must be done to push an electric current through a wire. To do this work there must be a voltage — a difference in potential — between one end of the wire and the other. An ordinary flashlight battery produces $1\frac{1}{2}$ volts. Most household appliances run on 110 volts. One volt of potential difference across a RESISTANCE of one ohm produces a current of one AMPERE.

Voltages are measured using a voltmeter; these can work by using the voltage to be measured to send an electric current through a resistance. The magnetic field of this current then moves the needle on the voltmeter's scale to show how many volts are flowing. More accurate

SEE FOR YOURSELF
The molten rock called magma moves through the Earth's crust under pressure. You can produce a similar effect if you roll up a nearly-finished tube of toothpaste. The pressure squeezes the paste toward the cap. Make a small hole near the cap and keep squeezing, toothpaste will ooze out of the hole like lava from a volcano.

▶ *The voltage between two points in a circuit is measured using a voltmeter. The voltmeter has a high internal resistance. It works by using the magnetic effect of the small current flowing through it to produce movement which makes a needle move around a scale. The size of the current affects the amount the needle moves against the scale and this indicates the size of voltage.*

The discovery of vulcanization in 1838 was a turning point in the rubber industry. Before then, rubber products were of little use because they stiffened in winter and became soft and sticky in summer. Then, one day, Charles Goodyear accidentally dropped a rubber sulfur mixture he was experimenting with onto a hot stove. Instead of melting, the rubber became firm and strong.

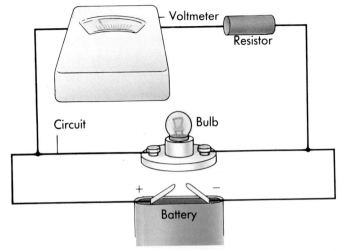

DIGITAL voltmeters are often used today. The volt is named after the Italian scientist Alessandro Volta. *See also* ELECTRICITY; GALVANOMETER.

Volta, Alessandro *See* Electricity

Volume *See* Measurement

Vulcanizing

Vulcanizing is a process for hardening rubber. The RUB-BER extracted from the tree is sticky and plastic. It is vulcanized by heating with SULFUR or sulfur compounds. The MOLECULES in unvulcanized rubber have a long zig-zag shape. They straighten when the rubber is stretched and break fairly easily. Vulcanizing causes the long molecules to form chemical BONDS that join them side to side. This makes the rubber tougher and stronger. It still stretches when pulled, but snaps back to its former shape when the force is removed.
See also ELASTICITY.

▼ *Unvulcanized rubber is soft and easily broken. It is used in erasers for removing pencil marks. Heating rubber with sulfur causes chemical bonds to form between the rubber's long hydrocarbon molecules. The resulting vulcanized rubber is very much harder and stronger, and is used for making vehicle tires.*

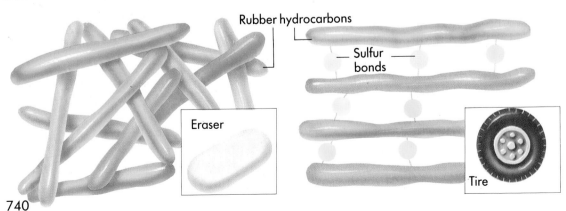

Rubber hydrocarbons

Sulfur bonds

Eraser

Tire

Wankel engine

The Wankel engine is a type of INTERNAL-COMBUSTION ENGINE. It was invented by the German engineer, Felix Wankel, in the 1950s. In an ordinary engine, the up and down motion of the pistons has to be converted into a rotary motion to drive the wheels. The link between the engine and wheels could be simplified if the pistons themselves rotated. In the Wankel engine, a triangular piston rotates inside a chamber shaped like an eight. As it rotates, FUEL and air are sucked in through a valve, compressed, and ignited by an electrical spark. The burning gases expand and drive the piston around.

The first car powered by a Wankel engine was the NSU Wankel Spyder. Despite the small size of the engine (500cc), the car had a top speed of 94 mph (152 km/h). The early engines suffered from several problems. The seals between the rotating piston and the chamber wore down, allowing gases to leak from one side of the piston to the others. It used fuel more quickly than other engines and produced high levels of exhaust.

▼ As in most internal-combustion engines, the Wankel engine works using a cycle of four stages: drawing in fuel and air (intake), compressing the fuel/air mixture (compression), igniting the mixture to generate power (power), and getting rid of the burned gases (exhaust). It does this with a single rotating piston and two spark plugs.

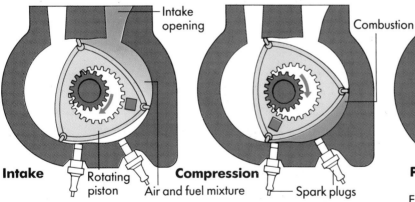

Intake — Intake opening, Rotating piston, Air and fuel mixture

Compression — Spark plugs

Power — Combustion, Ignition, Exhaust opening

Waste disposal

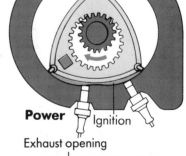

Waste disposal refers to the methods people use to get rid of materials, often called refuse, which they no longer need. Humans have become a problem for the ENVIRONMENT because of their rapidly increasing population. Human waste or sewage, for example, needs treatment to make it harmless. Sewage is sometimes disposed of into the sea. This can lead to overloading of the natural processes of decay which can spread disease or cause rapid growths of possibly harmful algae.

People produce huge quantities of waste. Containers,

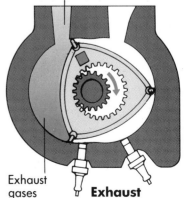

Exhaust gases

Exhaust

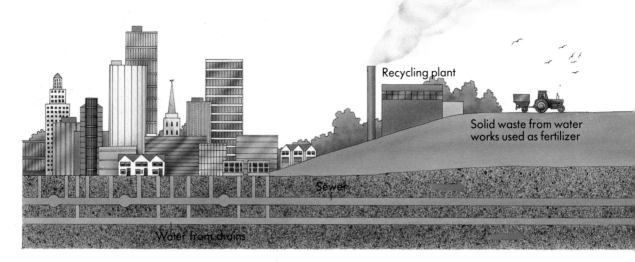

Recycling plant

Solid waste from water works used as fertilizer

Sewer

Water from drains

▲ Most wastes have to be treated to make them safe before they are released into the environment. An exception is rainwater that runs off the surface of the land, and can be piped into a river. Water waste from our homes has to be treated at a sewage plant before it can be released.

such as bottles and cans, which once filled garbage cans, can now be recycled. Much of our waste is buried and these sites are then used for construction. Other waste is burned in incinerators, usually in large cities. The by-products of many industries can be very poisonous and, in recent years, strict controls have been introduced to prevent companies from releasing untreated waste into rivers, seas, or the atmosphere. The NUCLEAR WASTE from nuclear power stations produces separate problems.

▲ At a well-managed landfill site, waste is compacted together and then sealed off by being covered with soil. It is important that the waste is covered to prevent smells and to stop animals such as rats from living in it.

Water

More than two-thirds of the human body is made of water, and some animals, such as jellyfish, are almost 100 percent water. The very first forms of life which appeared on EARTH evolved in a watery ENVIRONMENT and this transparent LIQUID is vital to every living thing on our planet. *See* pages 744 and 745.

Water pollution

Water in rivers, lakes, and streams almost always contains dissolved chemicals or carries debris suspended in it. Water is described as polluted if the amounts or kinds of substances contained in it are likely to cause harm to humans, other animals, plants, or the ENVIRONMENT.

Rivers and seas have traditionally been used for WASTE DISPOSAL. Fast-flowing rivers are able to transport sewage and other waste away to the oceans where the natural processes of decay can usually cope with the waste. But, in slower-flowing waters or where more

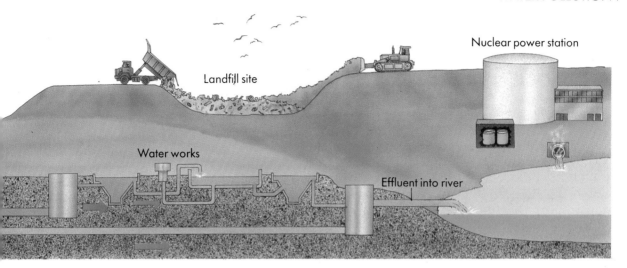

▲ Although many materials, such as paper, glass, and metals, can be separated from wastes and recycled, a lot of waste is still disposed of in landfill sites. Waste from nuclear power stations is reprocessed and stored in sealed containers.

◀ One of the major sources of water pollution is chemical waste from factories being discharged into rivers or lakes.

▼ Sewage, animal waste, and fertilizers can eventually kill off life in a river. Bacteria in the water use oxygen to break-down this organic waste into nutrients. The nutrients encourage the rapid growth of algae. As these die, they add to the organic waste present in the river. The bacteria use so much oxygen to break down all the organic waste that fish cannot breathe and they die.

waste is put into the water than can decay naturally, the water can become polluted with disease-carrying sewage or with products that may be poisonous to the animals and plants living in it.

Sometimes, water can be polluted by becoming too rich in nourishment, possibly from FERTILIZERS draining from agricultural land. If this happens, certain plants grow rapidly and use up all the oxygen in the water.

In many countries, waste products must be treated before they are released into seas and rivers.

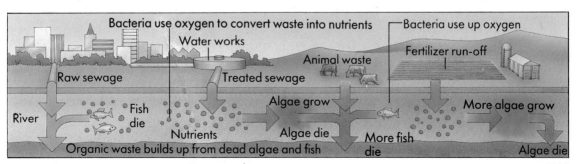

WATER

Chemically, water is a molecule consisting of two atoms of the gas hydrogen linked by chemical bonds to one atom of the gas oxygen. Pure water, at normal temperatures and pressures, is a tasteless and colorless liquid which lacks any kind of smell. The water we drink, which comes from the water supply, does have a taste because it contains minerals which have dissolved in it when it passed through rocks as groundwater. Water is a very good solvent and is able to dissolve more solids than many other liquids. Water is also good for cleaning because it dissolves dirt. Heating it and adding soap or detergent increases its efficiency. Water is the main component of blood and many substances are carried around the body in this watery liquid. Water also helps to remove some body wastes in the form of another liquid, urine. Water helps animals to keep cool because when animals sweat or pant, water evaporates, and removes some of their body heat.

Temperature changes the state of water. At temperatures above 212°F (100°C) it becomes water vapor or the gas, steam. At 32°F (0°C) water freezes to form solid ice. Most solids become denser than their liquid form when they freeze but water is at its most dense at 39°F (4°C).

Flowing water can be used to turn water wheels to provide power and in hydroelectric schemes is used to provide electricity. It circulates between the atmosphere and the Earth in a process known as the water, or hydrological, cycle.

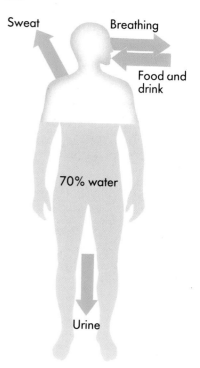

▲ Water probably has the best known chemical formula: H_2O, that is one oxygen atom and two of hydrogen. It is a remarkable substance, needed for all forms of life.

▲ A person can go without food for several weeks if necessary, but without water life cannot last more than a few days. The human body is 70 percent water. We take it in with food and drink, and lose it in urine, in sweat, and in our breath (as water vapor).

▲ Deserts have no free water in streams or lakes, and rain is very rare. There are occasional wells and wet places even in deserts and these are called oases. An oasis is therefore a welcome source of life-giving water to people and animals in these dry environments.
Depending on the amount of water, an oasis may support a few families and their animals or it may support a big city.

◄ Over thousands of years, flowing water can find its way through even the hardest rocks, carving out deep canyons and gorges with its constant pressure. Here the Yellowstone River flows out of the lower (downstream) end of the Grand Canyon.

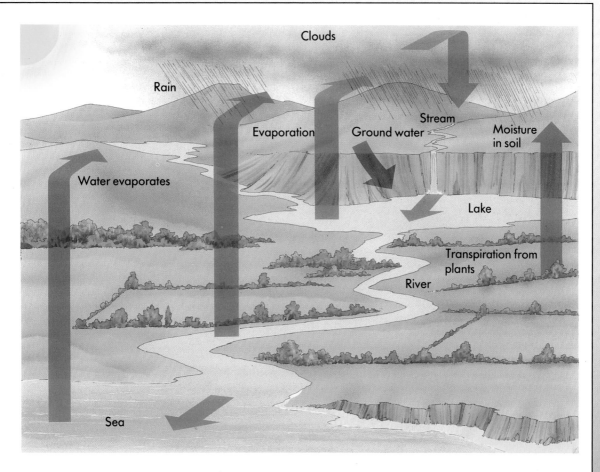

Clouds

Rain

Evaporation

Stream

Ground water

Moisture in soil

Water evaporates

Lake

Transpiration from plants

River

Sea

▲ All the water in the world goes around and around in a great cycle. Water that falls as rain soaks into the ground and is taken up by plants or runs off and forms rivers, which flow to the sea. Plants give off water vapor from their leaves, and water in rivers and the sea also evaporates as vapor. The vapor condenses in the atmosphere to form clouds, which produce rain to keep the cycle going.

Water is unusual in that most liquids contract as they cool and freeze, but water contracts to 39°F (4°C) and then expands as it freezes. This is important for animals because if a pond or river freezes over, the less dense ice floats, leaving liquid water beneath in which fish and other animals can survive.

SEE FOR YOURSELF
Water pressure depends on the "head" of water — the height of the top of the water supply above the level at which it is used. This is because of the pressure exerted by the volume of water above the outlet. You can show this by making a series of holes down the side of a plastic bottle. Cover the holes with tape and fill the bottle with water. Remember to place a bowl on the floor to catch the water before quickly removing the bits of tape. The jet of water where the pressure is greatest (at the bottom of the bottle) squirts out farther than water from near the top.

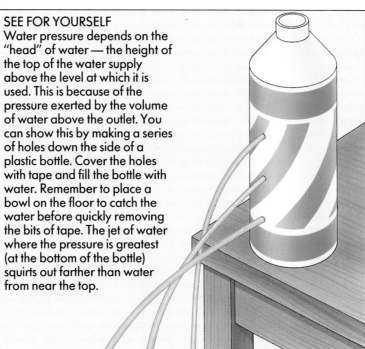

See also CLOUD; EVAPORATION; GROUNDWATER; HEAVY WATER; HYDRO-ELECTRICITY; HYDROGEN BONDS; ICE; PRECIPITATION; SOLVENT; STEAM.

▲ *In times of drought or in parts of the world where water is in short supply, it may not be possible to pipe water to people's homes. These people have to carry all the water they use from a communal pipe.*

Water supply

A supply of unpolluted fresh WATER is vital for humans. Various methods are used to supply and purify water. Water may be piped from rivers that are reasonably free of POLLUTION. Such water must be filtered and treated to ensure that it is clean. For small-scale supplies, water may be obtained by drilling a well in the ground to below the level of the WATER TABLE. Sometimes GROUNDWATER may be under pressure because of the rock structure. If a well is dug into the water-bearing rocks, the water is forced to the surface under its own pressure as an ARTE-SIAN WELL. In areas where the population is large, hollows or river valleys may be dammed and flooded to provide reservoirs. In dry parts of the world, water may be piped, or carried in channels, over long distances to irrigate growing crops.

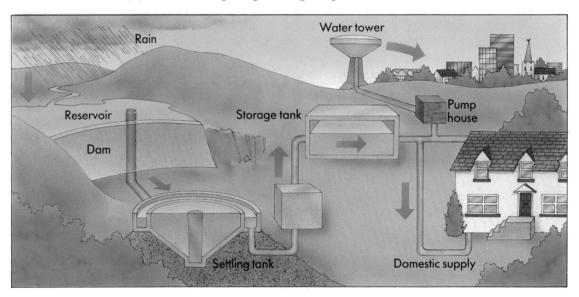

▲ *Water for use in homes and factories is stored in a reservoir, often behind a dam, before being piped to a water works. At the water works, any particles in the water are allowed to settle out in settling tanks and then the water is filtered and treated with chlorine to kill any germs. In some places the purified water is supplied from tall water towers. When water needs to be moved uphill it has to be pumped to overcome gravity.*

Water table

The water table is the top surface of those porous ROCKS that are saturated with GROUNDWATER. In general, the line of the water table follows that of the land surface but it rises and falls depending on the amount of PRECIP-ITATION that filters into the rocks and on how much WATER is drawn from them. Rock which is saturated with water is referred to as an *aquifer*. The aquifer is not a kind of underground pool. The water is held in the pores and cracks in the rocks.

The SOIL and rocks can be divided into three zones:

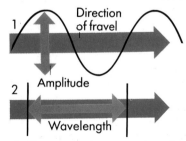

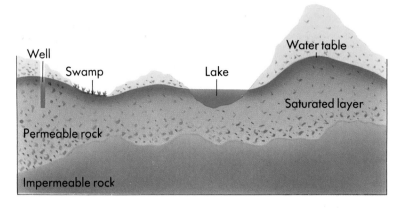

◄ *Water soaks into the ground until it reaches rock that is impermeable to water. The permeable rock above this becomes "filled" with water up to the level known as the water table. If this level is at the surface, the ground will be wet or swampy. A lake will tend to soak the ground beneath it and raise the water table. A well must be dug deep below the water table to stop it from drying out in a drought.*

the zone from the surface down through which water passes to reach the aquifer; the zone that is sometimes saturated; the zone that is permanently saturated, and may be 3,000 feet (1,000 m) deep. A well that will not run dry in a drought must be drilled into this last zone.

Watson, James *See* DNA

Watt

The watt (W) is the SI UNIT of POWER. One watt corresponds to the conversion of one JOULE of ENERGY from one form into another every second. For example, a light bulb uses about 100 watts of power, so it turns 100 joules of electrical energy into heat and light every second, while an electric toaster may have a power of about 1,000 watts or 1 kilowatt (kW), so it converts 1,000 joules of electrical energy into heat every second. The ENGINE of a medium-sized car produces about 50,000 watts (50 kW), while a large electrical power station produces several hundred million watts.
See also KILOWATT-HOUR.

Watt, James *See* Power

Wave

A wave is a disturbance or displacement that repeats itself. Both ELECTROMAGNETIC RADIATION, which includes LIGHT and RADIO waves, and SOUND travel as waves. The simplest kind of wave is called a sine wave. A sine wave is described by its amplitude (the height of the wave) and its WAVELENGTH. In many WAVE MOTIONS, a sine wave travels along without changing its shape at a particular VELOCITY. The number of peaks or troughs of the wave

Powerful Electricity
An electric heater converts electrical energy into heat energy. The rate at which it does this is its power. For example, if it converts 1,000 joules of electricity into heat in 1 second, its power is 1,000 joules per second or 1,000 watts (equal to 1 kilowatt).

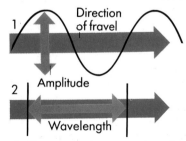

▲ *The two main properties of a wave are its amplitude and wavelength. The amplitude is the maximum displacement — the height from the crest of a wave to a trough. The wavelength is the distance between two consecutive waves. The number of waves that pass a particular point in a given time gives the frequency of the waves.*

▶ *Refraction, reflection, and diffraction are all important properties of waves. Waves are refracted, or bent, when they pass from one substance into another of different density. For example, when sound waves travel from air into a brick wall, they are refracted. They are refracted back to the same original direction when they pass out of the brick and into the air again. Reflection and diffraction are other ways in which waves can be bent (see diagram). In reflection, the waves bounce off a barrier, just as a light beam bounces off a mirror. Sound echoes are produced when sound waves bounce back off a wall or cliff. In diffraction, the waves spread out after they have passed through a narrow gap in a barrier.*

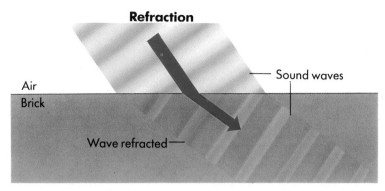

Refraction

Air
Brick

Sound waves

Wave refracted

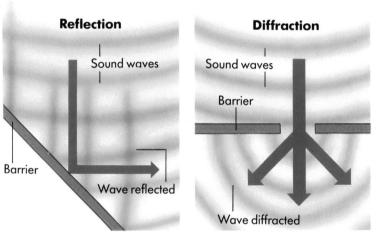

Reflection

Sound waves

Barrier

Wave reflected

Diffraction

Sound waves

Barrier

Wave diffracted

SEE FOR YOURSELF
If you take hold of the end of a length of rope and give it a quick up-and-down flick, a transverse wave will run along the rope. You can keep the waves going by keeping the end moving. You can also make waves by dropping a light ball into a bowl of water. The ripples that spread out are longitudinal waves.

Standing wave

Transverse wave

---

passing a point each second is the FREQUENCY of the wave.

One important property of waves is that they can "interfere;" if two waves are present in the same place at the same time, their effects add up. If the peaks of two equal waves arrive at a point at the same time, then they combine to give a peak twice as high. However, if the peaks of one wave arrive at an observer at the same time as the troughs of the other, they cancel each other out. Interference is important in DIFFRACTION, the way waves spread out as they pass through a narrow opening or around an obstacle.
See also REFLECTION; REFRACTION.

Wave motion

A wave motion is a pattern of disturbance that changes regularly as time passes and the wave moves from one place to another. The disturbance might be in the position of the surface of a liquid, as in waves on the sea, or in the PRESSURE of a gas, as in a SOUND wave in air, or in the electrical and magnetic fields, as in a LIGHT wave. Waves can be divided into traveling waves which move

◄ *A water droplet hitting the surface of water causes longitudinal waves that travel out in widening circles from where the drop landed. Two drops of water will each produce waves or ripples which will interfere with each other when they meet.*

Waves can also travel through solid material. If something is hit or twisted, it vibrates. The vibrations are waves that travel through the material. Earthquakes are waves traveling through solid rocks of the Earth. The denser the rocks, the faster the waves travel. Such waves can travel at several miles per second.

along with time, like a sound wave in the open air, or standing waves which stay in the same place like the waves on a drumhead when it is struck. They can also be divided into longitudinal waves, such as sound in a FLUID, where the wave disturbance flows in the same direction as the wave, and transverse waves such as light where the disturbance flows at right angles to the direction of travel.

See also FREQUENCY; WAVE; WAVELENGTH.

Wave power

Where the vibration is at right angles to the direction the wave is moving, the wave is a **transverse wave**. When the vibration is in the same direction as the direction of the wave, the wave is a **longitudinal wave**.

Wave power describes the production of ELECTRICITY from the motion of waves at sea. As waves travel along the sea's surface, the water at any point on the surface does not travel with the wave. It moves up and down. This motion can be used to drive GENERATORS. Several types of wave-power generator have been designed and built. The best-known is the "nodding duck." A line of floats are each pivoted at one side, allowing the other side to nod up and down with the waves. The hub where each float pivots contains a water pump. The pump, driven by the nodding action of

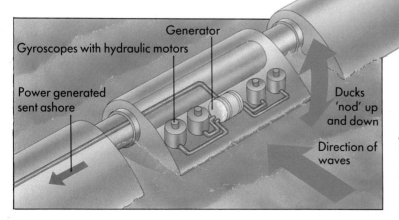

Gyroscopes with hydraulic motors

Generator

Power generated sent ashore

Ducks 'nod' up and down

Direction of waves

◄ *One method of generating power from sea waves uses rows of floats called nodding ducks. As the floats bob up and down, the energy in their movement is used to generate electricity.*

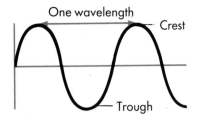

One wavelength

Crest

Trough

▲ *Wavelength is the distance between two waves.*

SEE FOR YOURSELF
To make a wax candle, tie a weight to some string passed through a hole in the bottom of a small carton. Tie the upper end of the string to a pencil, as shown. Carefully melt some wax crayons or ends of candles in an old pan on a gentle heat and pour the wax into the carton. Tear away the carton when the wax has set.

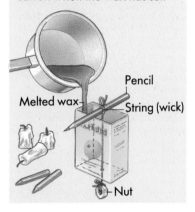

Pencil

Melted wax

String (wick)

Nut

▼ *Honeybees make wax to build the comb in which they raise their grubs inside the hive.*

the float, pumps water through the float. The flow of this pumped water is used to power a TURBINE which drives a generator.
See also ENERGY; TIDAL POWER.

Wavelength

A wave is a disturbance that repeats itself in space; the wavelength is the distance between two similar places on the wave at one TIME; for example, it is the distance between one wave peak and the next. The wavelength, multiplied by the FREQUENCY of the wave, gives the wave's VELOCITY. This means that if two different sorts of ELECTROMAGNETIC RADIATION travel at the same velocity, the waves with higher frequency have shorter wavelengths and the waves with lower frequency have longer wavelengths. For example, a RADIO wave might have a frequency of 200 kHz (a kHz is one thousand cycles per second) and a wavelength of 1,500 m, while a light wave might have a frequency of 600 THz (600 trillion hertz) and a wavelength of 500 nm (500 millionths of a millimeter). Both have the same wave velocity.

Wax

A wax is a solid or semisolid substance obtained from living things or from MINERAL sources. Examples include beeswax from the honeycomb of a beehive; tallow made from suet, which is the FAT inside animals such as cattle and sheep; and paraffin wax made from crude oil. Waxes are characterized by being insoluble in water, and by softening or melting when heated. Today, synthetic waxes are manufactured by the PLASTICS industry. Waxes repel water and have many uses. They are used to coat paper and leather to make them waterproof. They are also made into furniture polishes, candles, crayons, cosmetics, and ointments, and used in making matches and electrical INSULATORS.

Weather

Weather is the name given to the combination of the changing conditions of the ATMOSPHERE, including temperature, PRECIPITATION, atmospheric pressure, HUMIDITY, hours of sunshine, the amount and type of CLOUDS, and the speed and direction of the WIND. In some parts of

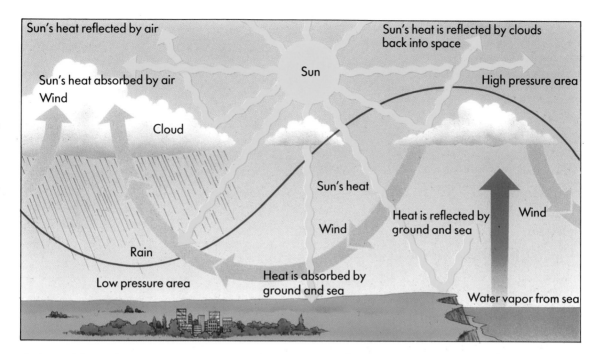

Sun's heat reflected by air

Sun's heat is reflected by clouds back into space

Sun's heat absorbed by air
Wind

High pressure area

Sun

Cloud

Sun's heat

Heat is reflected by ground and sea

Wind

Wind

Rain

Low pressure area

Heat is absorbed by ground and sea

Water vapor from sea

the world, such as western Australia, the weather may be the same week after week and month after month. Elsewhere, the weather is very unstable, and may change from hour to hour.

Weather is not the same as CLIMATE. Climate is the average weather of an area over a long period of time. The weather may change from day to day and is a mixture of many things. Some of these scientists understand, others are still a mystery. Nearly all weather occurs in the lowest layer of the atmosphere — the troposphere — and depends on four elements — temperature, wind, air pressure, and moisture. The boundary between two different air masses is called a FRONT and it is these fronts, moving across a region, which give rise to the type of weather.

Weather forecasting *See* Meteorology

Weathering *See* Erosion and Weathering

Weight

Weight is the downward FORCE that acts on all objects because they are attracted by GRAVITY toward the center of the EARTH. The weight of an object depends on its MASS; an object with twice the mass has twice the weight, so an object's weight can be used to measure its

▲ *Weather is produced by the heat of the Sun and the effects it has on the atmosphere. The Sun's heat causes water to evaporate. The water vapor forms clouds in the atmosphere, which give rain or snow. Heat from the Sun warms the air, which rises, creating areas of low pressure. Wind is air moving from high-pressure areas to low-pressure areas.*

Weather Facts
The heaviest **rainstorm** occurred on the island of Réunion which in 1952 had 74 inches (1,870mm) of rain in 24 hours. The driest place on Earth is Arica in Chile which averages only three-hundredth inch (0.76mm) of rain per year. The highest **temperature** recorded was 136°F (58°C) in the shade in Libya in 1922. The lowest temperature was −129°F (−89.2°C) at Vostok in Antarctica in 1983. The strongest wind was 231 mph at Mt. Washington in 1934.

SEE FOR YOURSELF
SEE FOR YOURSELF
Weight is a force. You can prove this by using a spring balance to weigh an object such as a banana. Weigh it in air and then weigh it again submerged in water. It weighs less in water because the water exerts an upward force (upthrust) that effectively lessens the force of gravity. The amount of upthrust is equal to the weight of water displaced by the banana.

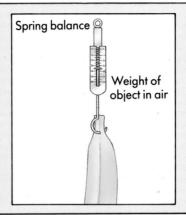

Spring balance

Weight of object in air

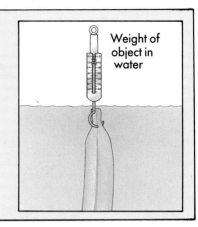

Weight of object in water

► The mass of an object is constant but its weight depends on the force of gravity. *1* A person who weighs 150 pounds (68 kg) on Earth weighs only 24 pounds (11 kg) on the Moon *2*, because the Moon's gravity is one-sixth of Earth's. The same person in a spaceship accelerating through space would feel weightless *3*.

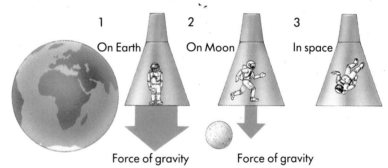

1   On Earth   2   On Moon   3   In space

Force of gravity   Force of gravity

SEE FOR YOURSELF
Can you judge an object's weight by its size? It is not always possible. Of these three objects, the ball is the largest but it is also the lightest. The brick, the smallest, is the heaviest. This is because the objects have very different densities. Only if objects have the same density are their sizes a guide to their weights.

mass. However, the mass and the weight are not the same; the mass depends only on the amount of material in the object and would be the same no matter where the object was taken in the universe. The weight, however, depends on which other masses are nearby. For example, at the surface of the Moon the weight of an object is about one-sixth of its weight on the Earth because the force of gravity on the MOON is much less than that on Earth. Astronauts in a spacecraft orbiting the Earth feel no weight. They are free of the effects of the pull of the Earth's gravity. There is no up or down. This is just like the sudden lessening in your weight that you feel when you stand in an elevator which starts to move downward. But your mass remains constant.

Weights and Measures   √

Many things in life depend on our ability to measure things accurately and meaningfully. Think of all the different things that you do that require some form of MEASUREMENT. Going on a trip requires a knowledge of distance and time, buying a rug requires a knowledge of area, drawing a triangle requires a knowledge of angles, etc. But it is not just the measuring that is

◄ The best way of selling similar things of different sizes is by weight. Simple balances like this one have been used for thousands of years to weigh objects for sale.

METRIC CONVERSIONS
Multiply by

Inches	25.4	Millimeters
Inches	2.54	Centimeters
Feet	30.5	Centimeters
Yards	0.91	Meters
Miles	1.61	Kilometers
Square inches	6.5	Square centimeters
Square feet	0.09	Square meters
Square yards	0.8	Square meters
Square miles	2.6	Square kilometers
Acres	0.4	Hectares
Ounces (fluid)	29.6	Milliliters
Pints	0.47	Liters
Gallons	3.8	Liters
Cubic inches	16.4	Cubic centimeters
Cubic feet	0.028	Cubic meters
Cubic yards	0.76	Cubic meters
Ounces (avoirdupois)	28.3	Grams
Pounds	0.45	Kilograms
Short tons	0.9	Metric tons

important, it is the use of the most sensible units that matters. You would not measure the distance between two towns using a 12in ruler, but you might if the two towns were on a MAP.

Scientists throughout the world use the same units of length, time, mass, and so on. These are called SI UNITS after the French for International System of Units. Using this system, a measurement made in any country uses the same units as those used in any other country.

Today, nearly the whole world uses the metric system. In 1901 the U.S. National Bureau of Standards was established to regulate standard measure. But it was only in the 1970s that the United States and Canada began introducing the metric system.

Weismann, A. *See* Chromosomes and Genes

Welding

Welding is used to join METAL objects by melting their edges so that they fuse together. There are several welding methods: forge welding, OXYACETYLENE WELDING, ELECTRIC ARC welding, seam welding, and spot welding. In forge welding, the parts are heated and then hammered together. Oxyacetylene welding uses a gas flame to heat the parts. In electric arc welding, the metal forms one electrode of an electric CIRCUIT and a metal rod called a filler rod forms the second electrode. When the two electrodes are held close together a spark jumps

▲ Construction workers use oxyacetylene torches to cut and weld steel girders. Joints in sheet metal, such as for car body repairs, are usually made by electric arc welding.

753

▲ *George Westinghouse is best known for his invention of the air brake used in railroad locomotives and vehicles.*

from one to the other, melting both the metal parts and the filler rod. Spot and seam welding are both electrical methods. The joint is clamped between two electrodes and a current is passed through it. The electrical RESISTANCE of the metal causes it to heat up until it melts.

Westinghouse, George

George Westinghouse (1846–1914) was the U.S. inventor and industrialist responsible for the use of alternating current (AC) for electrical supply in the United States. Westinghouse imported an AC system from Britain and developed it further. He employed the engineer Nikola Tesla to perfect it. After a struggle between AC and DC supporters, AC was eventually adopted.

In the 1860s Westinghouse produced a series of INVENTIONS ranging from a rotary STEAM ENGINE to his first major invention in 1869, the air brake. The Westinghouse air brake was widely used by railroads in the United States. He went on to improve the design so that it worked automatically. He later developed a new railroad signaling system and then patented several dozen original ideas for piping NATURAL GAS.

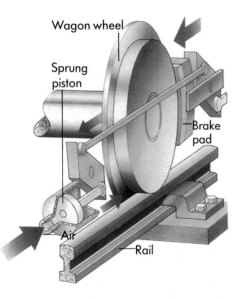

Wagon wheel

Sprung piston

Brake pad

Air

Rail

▲ *The Westinghouse brake uses air pressure to move a piston against the pressure of a spring. Movement of the piston works a lever that forces the brake pad against the edge of the wheel.*

▶ *A white dwarf is a star in the final stage of its life. A medium-sized star, like our Sun, gradually swells as it ages to become a red giant. The giant's outer material escapes into space, and its core shrinks to form a white dwarf.*

White dwarf

A white dwarf is the final stage of a normal STAR like our SUN, before it fades into blackness. It is the remains of the star's core, where the NUCLEAR ENERGY that made the star shine was generated. A white dwarf is made when a RED GIANT collapses at its center. Although made of hydrogen and helium, which we know as gases, the atoms in a white dwarf are compressed so tightly that they are hundreds of times denser than lead. The surface is about 14,000°F (8,000°C), but white dwarfs are so small they send out little light, and are hard to detect.

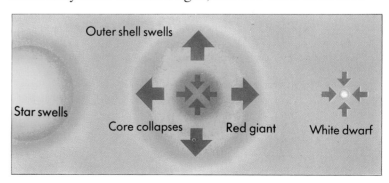

Star swells

Outer shell swells

Core collapses

Red giant

White dwarf

Whittle, Frank *See* Jet propulsion

Wind

Wind is the movement of AIR that depends upon variations in atmospheric PRESSURE. Air normally flows from areas of high atmospheric pressure to areas of low atmospheric pressure. In other words, if the EARTH did not spin on its axis, wind would normally blow from high to low pressure areas. But because the planet spins from west to east the winds are deflected to the right in the Northern HEMISPHERE and to the left in the Southern Hemisphere. This is the Coriolis effect and, in the north, it means that the airflow is clockwise around an area of high pressure and counterclockwise around an area of low pressure and in the South, the other way around.

The speed of the wind depends on the differences in the air pressures. If you look at a weather map, the winds

▲ Trees that grow in places where there is a strong wind that usually comes from one direction grow crookedly, leaning away from the wind. The wind on the seashore usually comes from the sea.

Beaufort Wind Scale
The force of the wind can be expressed on the Beaufort wind scale, which defines wind strength in terms of the wind's effects on objects in its path. The scale was devised by the British admiral Sir Francis Beaufort in 1805. The Beaufort scale is a series of numbers from 0 (no wind) to 12 (a violent hurricane). The steps on the scale are:
0 Calm (less than 1 mph). Smoke rises straight up.
1–3 Light wind (up to 12 mph). Leaves and twigs move, flags blow out.
4–5 Moderate wind (up to 24 mph). Small trees sway, waves on lakes.
6–7 Strong wind (up to 38 mph). Large trees sway, and walking is hard.
8–9 Gale (up to 54 mph). Shingles fall off roofs.
10–11 Storm (up to 73 mph). Widespread damage is caused to buildings and property.
12 Hurricane (over 73 mph). Devastation.

Force 0
Force 1–3
Force 4–5
Force 6–7
Force 8–9
Force 10–11
Force 12

▼ The general directions of winds around the world follow a simple pattern. The directions of these winds is affected by the motion of the Earth spinning on its axis. They tend to blow in a southwesterly direction in the Northern Hemisphere and northwesterly in the Southern Hemisphere. There is little wind in the doldrums on either side of the equator.

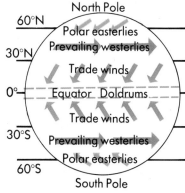

North Pole
60°N Polar easterlies
Prevailing westerlies
30°N
Trade winds
0° Equator Doldrums
Trade winds
30°S Prevailing westerlies
Polar easterlies
60°S
South Pole

▲ *One design for a modern windmill has two curved blades that spin on a vertical axis. Strong cables act as guy ropes to anchor the mill and keep it upright.*

▶ *Windmills called bonnet mills, which have a "cap" that moves around so that the sails always face the wind, were once common in the Netherlands. Most of them were used for pumping water, not for grinding corn.*

will be strongest where the ISOBARS (lines of equal pressure) are closer together. Wind speed is measured using an ANEMOMETER. The speed or force of the wind may be measured by a scale of numbers from 1 to 12. This is referred to as the Beaufort scale.

Wind power

Wind power describes the ways in which the ENERGY of the WIND can be harnessed, usually to generate ELECTRICITY. It is one of the various kinds of alternative energy sources. One of the benefits of wind power is that it generates energy without any POLLUTION.

In flat countries such as the Netherlands, where the wind can blow without interruption, people have used windmills to grind their corn or to pump water from the ground for many years. Some countries build very large wind generators called wind turbines, where one GENER-

SEE FOR YOURSELF
You can make a pinwheel from thin cardboard to show how a windmill works. Cut out a four-pointed star as shown, making sure that the hole is exactly in the middle. Fold over the edges to form vanes, and use a thumbtack to fix the cardboard to a wooden handle. Either put the windmill upright in the ground or on a post, or swing it around at arm's length to create a flow of air over the vanes.

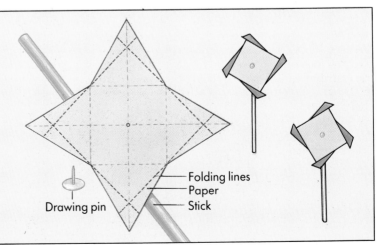

Drawing pin

Folding lines
Paper
Stick

◄ *A collection of modern windmills make up a "wind farm" in California. The windmills drive generators that produce electricity.*

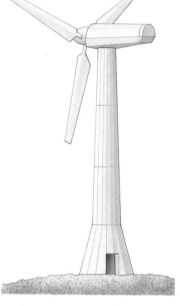

ATOR can generate enough electricity for the local people in rural areas. In other places "wind farms" of many wind turbines are constructed in isolated open areas. These turbines have large blades set on a horizontal shaft and mounted on a tall mast.

Wind tunnel

A wind tunnel is a device used to study the way that AIR flows around objects. Powerful engines generate a constant flow of air through the tunnel and around test objects inside it. Sensors attached to the objects reveal whether the airflow is smooth or turbulent and measures forces such as lift and drag generated by the airflow.

Aircraft manufacturers test models of new aircraft in wind tunnels as do car manufacturers because streamlined vehicles use less FUEL. Architects test models of bridges and buildings to make sure that they are stable in high winds.

▲ *The most efficient modern wind machines have two or three blades like the propeller of an aircraft. An electricity generator is located inside the "head" of the machine. The head can also rotate to keep the blades pointed into the wind.*

◄ *A model of a Tornado jet fighter aircraft is tested in a wind tunnel to observe the effects on its aerodynamics caused by hanging missiles and extra fuel tanks underneath it.*
If the aircraft is to carry heavy missiles it will need extra fuel, but it can only carry a certain amount of weight so it must be made as streamlined as possible.

▲ A cable contains many wires, all carrying different currents. Cables such as this are commonly used for carrying communications signals, such as telephone messages. Each separate wire in the cable is surrounded by insulating material, which is usually plastic. This is to stop the current from jumping from wire to wire.

All wood decay is caused by bacteria and fungi. They eat into the cells and leave rotting wood behind. If they were deprived of oxygen, heat, and moisture, they could not exist and the wood would last indefinitely. Some piles that Julius Caesar used in bridges in France were found to be sound after 2,000 years.

▶ The wood in a tree trunk forms in layers which appear as rings if the trunk is cut through. Beneath the outer bark is a layer of sapwood containing rings of phloem and xylem vessels. These are made up of tiny tubes and run the length of the trunk to carry food and water to the branches and leaves. A new ring of wood is formed each year and so it is possible to tell the age of a tree by counting the rings. The hard dry center of the trunk is called heartwood.

758

The largest wind tunnel in the world is operated by the U.S. space agency, NASA, in California. Its six engines can produce air speeds of up to 345 mph (555 km/h). *See also* AERODYNAMICS; STREAMLINING.

Wire

Wire is a flexible, fine strand of metal. A cable made from a number of metal strands twisted together is also called wire. Wire for electrical purposes is made from a good CONDUCTOR of electricity such as copper.

The electrical conductor is usually covered with a coating of plastic or enamel called a sleeve to insulate it from other conductors. A cable may contain a number of individual wires, each with its own plastic sleeve. The plastic sleeves may be color-coded to identify which wire does what in a CIRCUIT. Main electrical wiring, for example, is coded so that it can be connected correctly and safely to plugs and household appliances.

Wire is made by pulling metal rods through a series of progressively smaller holes in metal blocks called dies in a process called drawing.

Wood

Wood is the tough material that forms trunks and branches of trees. The same material also occurs in smaller amounts in the ROOTS and STEMS of other plants. It consists of tough-walled tubes and fibers in the plant's xylem. The tubes carry water and mineral salts up the trunk to the LEAVES, while the fibers provide the additional strength necessary to support the trunk and branches. The tubes and fibers start out as living CELLS, but a CARBOHYDRATE called lignin soon begins to build

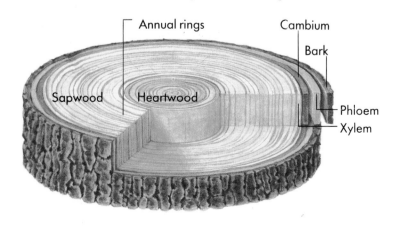

Annual rings · Cambium · Bark · Sapwood · Heartwood · Phloem · Xylem

up in their walls and make them hard. The cells then die, although they still work in the same way.

A tree trunk grows thicker by producing a new ring of wood just under the bark every year. The rings are clearly marked in trees growing in cool regions, where growth stops in the winter. They are called annual rings and are less obvious in tropical trees, which generally grow throughout the year. The oldest wood in the center of the trunk gradually gets crushed and cannot carry water. It is called heartwood and is usually harder and darker than the wood on the outside. This younger wood, which still carries water, is called sapwood.

Large areas of the world used to be covered with trees but today they are being cut down for FUEL, to make PAPER, and to clear land for farming.
See also DEFORESTATION; DENDROCHRONOLOGY.

Word processor

A word processor is a COMPUTER designed to be used for creating, editing, and storing text. At any time, the text may be retrieved from the word processor's memory and printed. A word processor consists of a keyboard similar to a typewriter keyboard, a VISUAL DISPLAY UNIT for displaying the text, a computer dedicated to processing text, a memory device such as a disk drive, and a printer. The disk drive stores the text on magnetic disks until it is needed again. A microcomputer with a word processing program can be used as a word processor.

Text is entered on the keyboard. After it has been

▼ *In many offices that deal with large amounts of text, several word processors can be linked to a central data bank as a network. In a network, several word processors can use the same printer.*

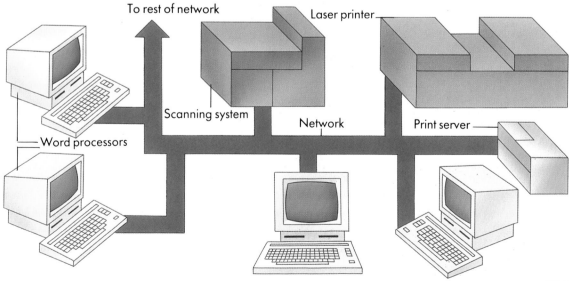

To rest of network · Laser printer · Scanning system · Network · Print server · Word processors

Work is done

Work is not done

▲ *Work is done when a force makes something move in the direction of the force. Pushing a car along involves work, but holding a book does not because the book is not being moved.*

▼ *In a steam locomotive, work is done by steam pressure because it makes the pistons move. The heat energy of the steam is converted into the mechanical energy of the moving piston. But some energy is wasted as work that has to be done to overcome friction in the moving parts.*

entered, it can be changed, corrected, and moved on the screen before printing. Some word processors can incorporate graphics to produce illustrated documents.
See also COMPUTER GRAPHICS; HARDWARE; SOFTWARE.

Work

In PHYSICS, work is said to be done when an object on which a FORCE is acting moves in the direction of that force. For example, if you are helping to push a car from the back and the car moves forward, you do work on the car. On the other hand, if you are standing still holding a heavy book in your hands, you do not do any work on it since the book is not moving. Similarly, if you are pushing the car from the side, even if the car moves forward (not sideways), you do not do any work because the car did not move in the same direction that you were pushing.

Work is the way in which ENERGY is changed from one form into another; having a certain amount of energy means that you are able to do a certain amount of work. Work and energy are both measured in JOULES. For example, when pushing the car, chemical energy stored in your body goes into doing work, which increases the kinetic energy of the car. Machines are designed to make the best use of the work that is done by reducing the FRICTION forces, the amount of kinetic energy lost or wasted as HEAT, and so on.

► *The work done in using a wrench is equal to the force applied to the handle multiplied by the distance the handle moves in the direction of the force.*

Work (effort)

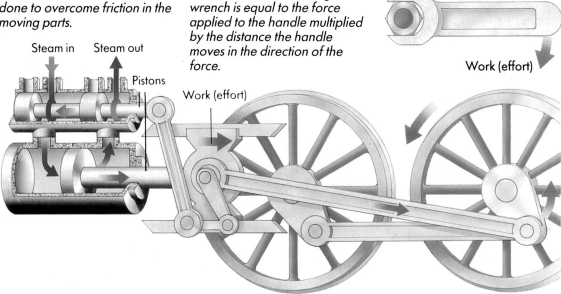

Steam in   Steam out

Pistons

Work (effort)

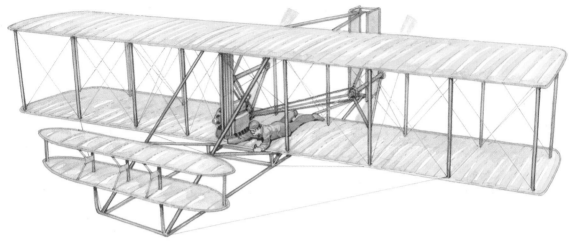

▲ *The world's first successful powered airplane, Flyer I* (above) *was built after experimenting with gliders* (left).

Wright, Orville and Wilbur

Wilbur Wright (1867–1912) and his brother Orville (1871–1948) made the world's first controlled flight of a powered airplane in 1903. The two brothers were interested in machines and designed and made printing presses and bicycles.

Between 1900 and 1902 they built a series of gliders to test the controls that would be used in their next venture, the powered airplane called Flyer I. Its historic flight on December 17, 1903 at Kill Devil Hills, Kitty Hawk, North Carolina lasted 12 seconds. They went on to build more airplanes, improving the design each time. They had to design and make their own propellers and ENGINES because none that was suitable existed at the time. Wilbur demonstrated their airplanes in Europe in 1908 and 1909, while Orville built the first airplane for the U.S. Army.

See also FLIGHT.

▲ *The Wright brothers, Wilbur* (top) *and Orville* (bottom) *played an important part in the development of aircraft.*

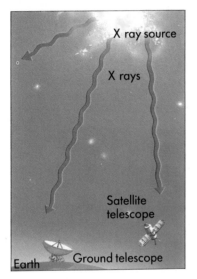

▲ *X rays from sources in space cannot be detected by telescopes on Earth. The first satellite to carry X-ray detectors was launched by the Soviet Union in 1958.*

Xerography *See* Photocopier

X-ray astronomy

All STARS send out a wide range of ELECTROMAGNETIC RADIATION from their surfaces, including X-RAYS, but the strongest radiation is in the visible part of the SPECTRUM. The hottest stars, however, send out large amounts of X rays, which cannot be seen and cannot penetrate the ATMOSPHERE. X-ray astronomy is carried out by SATELLITES, such as ROSAT, launched in 1990.

To produce X rays in a star, temperatures of at least a million degrees are needed. The Sun's core (about 27 million°F) produces them, and they would gradually destroy our CELLS if the atmosphere did not protect us.

There are many very bright X-ray objects in the sky: SUPERNOVAS, WHITE DWARFS, QUASARS, and NEUTRON STARS all send out X rays. Some PULSARS also emit them, as do BLACK HOLES such as Cygnus X-1.

X-ray diffraction

X-ray diffraction is used to discover how the ATOMS of a CRYSTAL are arranged. The atoms of a crystal lie in orderly rows. The spaces between the rows bend, or diffract, beams of X rays. In 1912 the German physicist Max von Laue used a crystal to diffract X rays, for which he received the NOBEL Prize in Physics in 1914. The pattern of intense spots made on photographic film by diffracted X rays gives information about the crystal's structure. The relationship between the spots and the

Sir William Henry Bragg (1862–1942) and Sir William Lawrence Bragg (1890–1971) The Braggs, father (left) and son, were British physicists who developed the technique of X-ray diffraction to investigate crystals. When they aimed a beam of X rays at a crystal, the regular arrangement of atoms in the crystal scattered the X rays to produce a characteristic pattern on a photographic plate. They shared the 1915 Nobel Prize in Physics.

spacing of atoms in the crystal was discovered by the two physicists, William and Lawrence Bragg. X-ray diffraction was used by Crick, Watson, and Wilkins to find the structure of the genetic material, DNA.

X rays

X rays are one kind of ELECTROMAGNETIC RADIATION. They have a very high FREQUENCY of about a million million million hertz (cycles per second), and so a very short WAVELENGTH. They were discovered in 1895 by Wilhelm Roentgen; he gave them their name because the letter X is often used to stand for something unknown. Materials that contain only light atoms do not absorb many X rays. For example, they pass easily through most living tissue, but not through BONES, which contain heavier atoms. This means that X rays can be used to find what is wrong with bones and teeth inside the body without surgery. Because X rays are a form of ionizing RADIATION, which can damage cells, the amount that a person receives has to be carefully controlled. X rays are used to study the structure of SOLIDS in X-RAY DIFFRACTION, and in X-RAY ASTRONOMY.

X rays can be produced by bombarding atoms with fast particles and knocking ELECTRONS out from the "shells" near the middle of the atom. Other electrons move in from the outer shells to take the place of the missing electrons, giving out ENERGY as X rays.

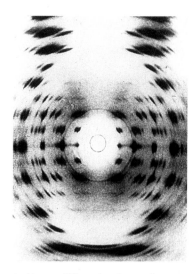

▲ X-ray diffraction is used to discover the structure of complicated molecules. This pattern is produced by DNA, which makes up genes and chromosomes in the cell nucleus.

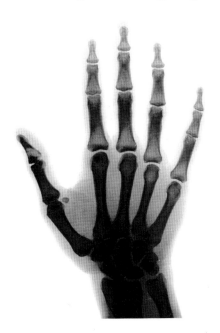

◄ Modern medical X-ray photographs, using carefully controlled doses of X rays, can reveal the structure of soft tissues as well as hard tissues such as bone.

▼ X rays form the part of the electromagnetic spectrum beyond ultraviolet rays. At very short wavelengths, they become gamma rays.

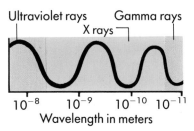

Ultraviolet rays   Gamma rays
X rays
10^{-8} 10^{-9} 10^{-10} 10^{-11}
Wavelength in meters

Wilhelm Conrad Roentgen (1845–1923)
Roentgen was a German physicist. In 1895 he noticed that rays from a covered cathode-ray tube (which would emit no cathode rays) caused a phosphorescent screen to fluoresce. He deduced that this was caused by a new type of radiation, which he called X rays. For this work, he received the first Nobel Prize for Physics in 1901.

Yeast

Yeasts are tiny single-celled MICROORGANISMS that are part of the group called fungi. They reproduce asexually, by budding off tiny CELLS which grow and eventually reproduce themselves. Some yeasts live naturally on the body, and they may cause DISEASE, such as thrush also known as candida, which can affect the mouth and sex organs. Yeasts also grow naturally on the surface of FRUIT, feeding on the SUGARS the fruit contains.

Some yeasts are essential in the process of FERMENTATION. When these yeasts grow in the presence of sugar, they break the sugar down to produce ethanol, a simple ALCOHOL, and release carbon dioxide. We make use of this property when making alcoholic drinks like wine and beer; the yeast ferments fruit sugars to make wine, or malt sugars, present in grain, to make beer. Yeast is also useful in baking, where the carbon dioxide gas it produces causes bread to rise. Yeast is a valuable source of PROTEIN and some VITAMINS of the B group. There are more than 600 species of yeasts.
See also BIOTECHNOLOGY; GENETIC ENGINEERING.

Dough fermented with yeast is called *leaven*. The name comes from the Latin word meaning "to raise," because fermented dough rises. Bread made of fermented dough is called leavened bread. The old English word for leaven is *yeast*.

SEE FOR YOURSELF
To watch yeast ferment, add a spoonful of sugar to a measuring cup of warm milk. Stir in some baker's yeast (or dried yeast), put the measuring cup in a warm place. A few hours later the milk will froth over as the yeast breaks down the sugar to release carbon dioxide gas.

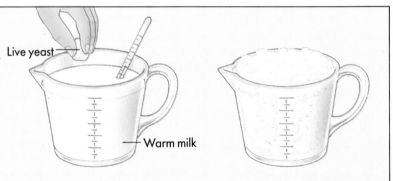

Live yeast

Warm milk

▶ *Seen using an electron microscope, baker's yeast is revealed as a single-celled fungus. It is used in making bread, where the carbon dioxide produced by fermentation makes the bread rise. Yeast is also used in the production of beer and wine, where it converts the sugar from the fruit, hops, or barley into carbon dioxide and alcohol.*

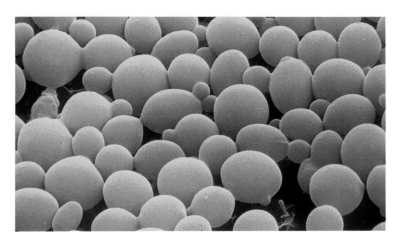

Zinc

Zinc is a bluish gray ELEMENT. It is a METAL, and has been known and used for hundreds of years. Its main use today is in GALVANIZING steel. The steel is covered with zinc either by being dipped or by ELECTROLYSIS to form a protective coating that prevents the steel from rusting. Galvanized steel is used in roofing and to make water tanks. Zinc is also used to make BATTERIES.

Zinc is a part of various ALLOYS, such as brass (zinc

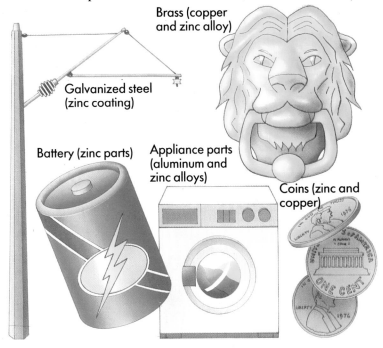

Brass (copper and zinc alloy)

Galvanized steel (zinc coating)

Battery (zinc parts)

Appliance parts (aluminum and zinc alloys)

Coins (zinc and copper)

◀ *Zinc is a metal with many uses, chief of which is in galvanizing steel. It is also made into the outer cases of dry batteries. The chief zinc alloy is brass, although other alloys are used in machines and to make coins.*

▲ *Zinc is a metal element. Like most metals it is shiny in its pure form but is only found in nature as zinc compounds.*

and copper) and the zinc-based alloy (with aluminum and copper) used for casting objects such as pots and door handles. Zinc oxide is the PIGMENT known as Chinese white and is used in antiseptic ointments. Zinc sulfide glows when hit by ULTRAVIOLET light or X RAYS and is used to coat the inside of TELEVISION screens and in luminous dials on clocks.

See also CORROSION; IRON AND STEEL; LUMINESCENCE.

Zoology

Zoology is the study of animals, from amoeba and other single-celled protozoans to humans and the huge whales. It covers the structure of the animals and their internal workings as well as the way in which they behave and how they live. *See* pages 766 and 767.

> **Zinc was used by the Romans more than 2,000 years ago, but because it is always found in combination with other elements, it was not identified as a separate metal until the 1500s by the Swiss doctor Paracelsus.**

ZOOLOGY

Zoology is a very large subject because there are over a million known animal species living all over the Earth. Most zoologists specialize in one particular topic, such as physiology, which is the study of the processes of the animals' lives, including their respiration, how they get rid of waste, how they reproduce, and so on. Others may study a particular group of animals. Entomologists, for example, study insects and ornithologists study birds. Many entomologists are involved with the control of insect pests, such as mosquitoes and locusts. Many other zoologists work in agriculture and in veterinary medicine, breeding animals for our farms and learning how to prevent and cure their various illnesses.

Ecology deals with the ways in which animals fit into their environments. It is very important for us to find out exactly what conditions the animals need if we are to conserve them in the wild. Sometimes animal species are threatened in their natural habitat and so a small population of them is preserved in a zoo or wildlife park. Some countries have game reserves or large national parks set aside for animals to live in without the interference of humans.

▲ *Some of the smallest of the world's animals make up the plankton that lives on and near the surface of the seas. This sample includes minute copepods and the larvae of crustaceans such as crabs and shrimps. Marine plankton are the starting point for a huge number of food chains. Many fish and birds eat plankton. Even some whales exist by sieving huge quantities of minute plankton from the Antarctic waters.*

▼ *There are more than 80,000 species of birds in the world, from flightless penguins to high-flying vultures, and aquatic ducks and geese.*

▼ *Frogs are amphibians. Like toads, newts, and salamanders, they lay their eggs in water but their tadpolelike larvae change into land animals.*

▼ *The blue whale is a mammal that lives in the sea and is the world's largest animal. It may grow to more than 100 feet in length and weigh over 100 tons.*

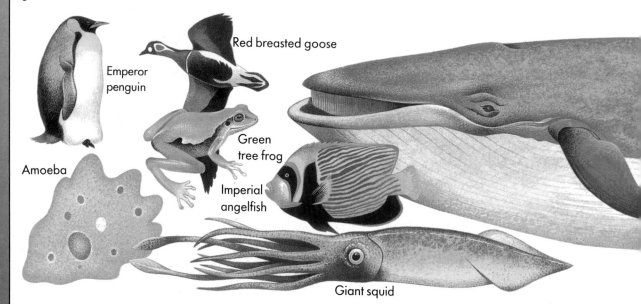

Emperor penguin

Red breasted goose

Amoeba

Green tree frog

Imperial angelfish

Giant squid

▲ *An amoeba is a microscopic single-celled animal whose jellylike body engulfs its food and pulls it inside to digest it. There are many other microscopic animals*

▲ *Fishes are the largest group of backboned animals (vertebrates), with about 20,000 different species varying in size from a tenth of an inch to 40 feet.*

▲ *The giant squid is the largest of the animals without backbones (invertebrates). It is a cephalopod which grows up to 50 feet long (including its tentacles).*

► Zoologists study the territories of birds, their population changes, and how they migrate by banding them. Here a sedge warbler is having a band put on its leg. Each band carries the address of the national organization that coordinates the information about birds that are found. A record card is filled in for each bird banded, with its weight, wing length, and species and the card is sent to the national organization and kept in case the bird is caught or found again.

Zoologists are always making fascinating discoveries. Until recently it was thought that insects blundered into spiders' webs by accident. But it was recently discovered that some spider webs reflect ultraviolet light which attracts insects to them.

▼ The goliath beetle is the size of a man's fist and is one of the heaviest insects in the world (some moths are larger). Insects are part of a larger group, the Arthropods.

SEE FOR YOURSELF
How many worms are there in a square yard of lawn? More than you think! To find out, use string to peg out a measured square yard and, toward sunset, water the grass with dilute dishwashing liquid. This will bring the worms to the surface. When it is dark, go out with a flashlight and collect the worms in a bowl. Release them after you have counted them.

Blue whale

Goliath beetle

Giant tortoise

African elephant

◄ The African elephant is the world's largest land animal, weighing about 7 tons (less than one-tenth of the weight of a blue whale).

▲ Giant tortoises are the longest-lived of all backboned animals. Some of these reptiles that have been kept in zoos have lived for more than 100 years.

See also AGRICULTURE; BIOLOGY; BOTANY; BREEDING; CLASSIFICATION; CONSERVATION, ENVIRONMENTAL; ECOLOGY; ORGANISM; SPECIES.

Zygote

When an ovum or EGG cell is fertilized by a sperm, it produces a zygote. This single CELL holds genes from both parents, and contains all of the instructions needed to make a complete organism, with all its organs and structure preplanned. The human zygote, for example, holds genes such as those that determine if the child will have blue or brown eyes, or dark or fair hair.

The zygote stays as one cell for only a very short time, because it begins to divide and this quickly leads to the next stage in development, called a blastula.

It is a zygote that is produced by test-tube FERTILIZATION when helping couples who have been unsuccessful in having children. The sperm fertilizes an ovum which has been removed from a woman's ovary. The blastula, consisting of several cells, is implanted back into the woman to continue its development normally.

▼ A zygote forms when the nuclei of two sex cells (one male, the sperm, and one female, the egg) join at fertilization. Once one sperm penetrates the egg, the egg's outer membrane thickens to prevent any more sperm from entering.

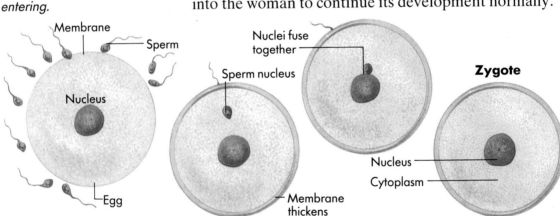

▶ A crowd of human sperm, (colored blue), try to penetrate the outer membrane of an egg, (colored yellow). The sperm look roughly spherical because their long tails do not show up on this electron microscope photograph. If a sperm gets through, fertilization takes place and the zygote formed eventually develops into a new individual.

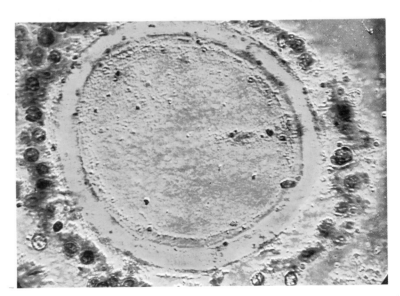

About Your Index

This index has been designed to help you find which articles will have information on the subject you are looking up. You may find that although there is no article on your subject, for example Aircraft, you will find a lot of information about it in other articles, such as Aerodynamics, Flight, Jet propulsion, and the Wright brothers.

The page numbers listed in this index are of different types. Those printed in **bold type** indicate where the main entry for the subject can be found, whereas page numbers in *italic type* refer to pages on which illustrations will be found. When you look up Acids and Bases, for example, you will see:

Acids and Bases 4, *4*
litmus 347, 407
pH 533, *533*

The main entry on this subject is on page 4, where there is also an illustration. Further information can be found under the articles on Litmus and pH.

After the main index you will find a Subject Index. In this, all the articles in the encyclopedia are divided up by subject. The entries are in alphabetical order within each subject. In addition there is an index of entries which are Special Features.

Subject Index

Map projections
Metamorphic rocks
Meteorology
Mica
Minerals
Mining
Monsoon
Mountains
Natural gas
Nuclear waste
Ocean
Oils
Ore
Ozone layer
Plate tectonics
Poles
Pollution
Precipitation
Rainbow
Recycling
Resonance
Resources
Richter scale
Rivers and Lakes
Rocks
Sedimentary rocks
Seismograph
Soil
Stalactites and
    Stalagmites
Stratosphere
Theodolite
Thunder
Tidal power
Tidal waves and
    Tsunamis
Tides
Tornado
Tropics
Troposphere
Van Allen belts
Volcanoes
Waste disposal
Water
Water pollution
Water supply
Water table
Weather
Wind
Wind power

Electronics

Bar code
Bit and Byte
Calculator
Capacitor
Computer
Computer graphics
Computer languages
Computer memory
Digital
Diode
Electronics
Feedback
Filter, electronic
Hardware
Information technology
Integrated circuit
Language translation by
    computers
Logic
Microchip
Microprocessor
Modem
Rectifier
Robots
Semiconductor
Software
Speech recognition
Synthesizer
Transistor
Vacuum tube

Visual display unit
    (VDU)
Word processor

Life Science

Adaptation
Adolescence
Aging
Agriculture
AIDS
Allergy
Anatomy
Antenna
Antibiotics
Antibodies and Antigens
Antiseptics
Behavior
Binocular vision
Biochemistry
Biological control
Biology
Bioluminescence
Biophysics
Biotechnology
Birth
Blood
Bone
Botany
Brain
Breathing
Breeding
Camouflage
Cancer
Carbohydrate
Carbon dioxide
Cell
Cell division
Cellulose
Cereals
Chlorophyll
Cholesterol
Chromosomes and
    Genes
Circulation
Classification
Clones
Conservation,
    environmental
Coordination
Cotyledon
Cytology
Dehydration
Dendrochronology
Digestion
Disease
Display
DNA
Dreams
Drug
Ear
Ecology
Ecosystem
Egg
Embryo
Endangered species
Environment
Enzymes
Evolution
Excretion
Experiment
Extinction
Eye
Fats
Feathers
Feedback
Feeding
Fermentation
Fertilization
Fertilizers
Fibers
Flowers
Food chain

Food poisoning
Forensic science
Fruit
Genetic engineering
Genetics
Gestation
Gills
Glands
Growth
Hair
Heart
Heredity
Hibernation
Homing
Hormone
Horticulture
Hybrid
Hydroponics
Hypothermia
Immune system
Infection
Instinct
Intelligence
Intestine
Joints
Kidneys
Laboratory
Lactic acid
Larva
Learning
Leaves
Liver
Lungs
Lymph system
Medicine
Memory
Metabolism
Metamorphosis
Microbiology
Microorganism
Migration
Milk
Monoclonal antibody
Movement and Motion
Muscle
Mutation
Natural selection
Nerves
Nicotine
Nose
Nucleic acid
Nucleus, cell
Nutrition
Oils
Organism
Osmosis
Pain
Paleontology
Pancreas
Parasite
Pasteurizaton
Pathology
Pesticides
Pharmacology
Photosynthesis
Physiology
Pigments
Plastic surgery
Poisons
Pollen and Pollination
Protein
Psychology and
    Psychiatry
Reflex
Reproduction
Respiration
Roots
Rubber
Seeds
Semipermeable
    membrane
Senses
SI Units

Skeleton
Skin
Sleep
Soil
Space medicine
Species
Speech
Starch
Stem
Sterilization
Steroids
Stomach
Streamlining
Sugars
Sulfa drugs
Symbiosis
Tannin
Taste
Teeth
Touch
Tranquilizers and
    Stimulants
Transpiration
Transplants
Vaccination
Veterinary medicine
Virus and Viral diseases
Vitamins
Water
Water supply
Wax
Wood
Yeast
Zoology
Zygote

Mathematics $\sqrt{}$

Abacus
Algebra
Arithmetic
Average
Binary numbers
Decimal
Geometry
Graph
Infinity
Latitude and Longitude
Light year
Logic
Map
Map projections
Mass
Mathematics
Measurement
Metric system
Numbers
Optical character
    recognition
Oscillator
Polygon
Probability
Ratio
Rotation
Scales and Balances
Statistics
Symmetry
Weights and Measures

Physics

Absorption
Acceleration
Acoustics
Aerodynamics
Aerosol
Ampere
Antimatter
Atomic number
Atomic weight
Balancing point
Ballistics
Battery

Bimetallic strip
Bioluminescence
Biophysics
Black body
Boiling point
Brownian motion
Bubbles
Buoyancy
Capacitor
Capillary action
Carbon dating
Cathode-ray tube
Celsius
Center of gravity
Centrifugal force
Circuit, breaker
Circuit, electric
Cold
Color
Compass
Condensation
Conduction, heat
Conductors, electric
Conservation
Contraction
Convection
Coulomb
Decibel
Density
Diffraction
Doppler effect
Echo
Efficiency
Elasticity
Electric arc
Electricity
Electromagnet
Electromagnetic radiation
Energy
Entropy
Equilibrium
Escape velocity
Expansion
Experiment
Fahrenheit
Fallout, radioactive
Filter, electronic
Flotation
Fluid
Focus
Force
Foucault pendulum
Frequency
Friction
Fuse
Galvanometer
Gas
Generator, electric
Gravity
Gyrocompass
Gyroscope
Half-life
Hardness
Harmonics
Heat
Hertz
Hologram
Horsepower
Hydroelectricity
Hydrogen bomb
Hydrometer
Hygrometer
Implosion
Inductance, self and
    magnetic
Induction coil
Inertia
Inertial guidance
Infrared radiation
Insulation, thermal
Insulators, electrical
Iridescence
Joule

Technology

Special Features Index

Acknowledgments

The publishers would like to thank the following artists for their contribution to this encyclopedia:

Marion Appleton, Craig Austin, Kuo Kang Chen, David Eddington (Maggie Mundy Illustrator's Agency), Dave Etchell, Chris Forsey, Mark Franklin, Jeremy Gower, Hardlines, Hayward Art Group, Christa Hooke (Linden Artists), Lisa Horstman, Ian Howatson, Industrial Artists, Ian Jackson, John James (Temple Rogers), Felicity Kayes (Design Associates), Elly and Christopher King, Terence Lambert, Steve Latibeaudiere, Mike Long (Design Associates), Chris Lyon, Janos Marffy (Jillian Burgess Agency), William Oliver, David Phipps (Design Associates), Malcolm Porter, Sebastian Quigley (Linden Artists), John Ridyard, Valerie Sangster (Linden Artists), Mike Saunders (Jillian Burgess Agency), George Thompson, John Woodcock (Jillian Burgess Agency), David Wright (Jillian Burgess Agency).

The publishers wish to thank the following for supplying photographs for this encyclopedia:

Cover Science Photo Library (SPL); page 1 SPL; 2 ZEFA; 5 VAG (UK) Ltd (top), Royal Albert Hall (bottom); 7 Paul Brierley; 9 ZEFA; 10 IVECO/Parlour Wood Ltd; 11 ZEFA; 12 SPL; 13 SPL; 15 ZEFA; 17 ZEFA; 18 Derby Museum & Art Gallery; 20 SPL; 21 McDonnell Douglas; 22 ZEFA; 23 SPL (left), ICI (right); 27 Ann Ronan Picture Library; 28 SPL; 29 SPL; 31 Ann Ronan Picture Library; 32 ZEFA; 34 Ronald Grant Archive; 36 Michael Holford (right), Paul Brierley (left); 37 Hutchison Library; 38 ZEFA; 39 SPL; 41 Istanbul University; 44 SPL (right), Grisewood & Dempsey (left); 45 ZEFA; 46 SPL; 48 ZEFA; 50 Science Museum; 51 Grisewood & Dempsey; 52 Mary Evans Picture Library; 53 ZEFA; 54 SPL; 58 ZEFA; 64 ZEFA; 65 SPL; 66 SPL; 67 Mansell Collection (top left), ZEFA (top right), Ann Ronan Picture Library (middle); 68 SPL; 71 F.R.Logan Ltd; 74 ZEFA; 75 SPL; 76 ZEFA (top), SPL (middle) 77 SPL; 78 SPL; 83 SPL; 84 SPL; 85 SPL; 87 ZEFA; 89 Robert Hunt Library (top), ZEFA (bottom); 95 Mike Potts (right), Beech Aircraft Corps (left); 96 Sony (UK) Ltd; 97 ZEFA; 103 Racal-Vodac Ltd; 104 SPL; 106 ZEFA; 108 D.Gardner (left), Isuzu Ceramics Institute (right); 110 SPL; 112 SPL; 115 Terry Cash; 116 Robert Hunt Library (right), ICI Chemicals & Polymers (left); 119 SPL; 120 Life Science Images; 121 SPL; 122 Lucas Film Ltd; 123 ZEFA; 131 ZEFA; 133 ZEFA; 135 NASA; 136 SPL; 139 Science Museum; 140 ZEFA (top), Atlas Copco (bottom); 141 The Moving Picture Co (top and left), Tektronik (UK) Ltd (right); 142 UNISYS; 143 Cray Research Inc; 146 ZEFA; 149 SPL; 151 Michael Hopkins & Partners; 152 ZEFA; 153 ZEFA; 154 ZEFA; 155 Ann Ronan Picture Library; 162 Popperfoto; 163 NASA; 165 National Museum of Photography, Film & Television; 166 Ann Ronan Picture Library (top), Michael Holford (bottom); 169 SPL; 170 SPL; 173 ZEFA; 175 De Beers (right), British Petroleum (left); 180 SPL; 181 ZEFA; 182 House of Seagram; 183 SPL; 185 Ann Ronan Picture Library; 186 SPL; 187 ZEFA; 191 NASA; 193 California Institute of Technology; 198 Bettmann Archive; 200 PSA; 201 ZEFA; 203 ZEFA; 204 SPL; 209 Cambridge Instruments Ltd; 210 PSA (right), ZEFA (left); 212 Ron Boardman; 214 Herberts; 215 NHPA/M.Tweedie; 218 ZEFA; 220 Paul Brierley; 223 ZEFA; 224 ZEFA; 231 Byrne Photography (right), ZEFA (left); 236 Jet Propulsion Lab, Pasadena, California (left), SPL (right); 239 Canon (UK); 240 Bruce Coleman; 241 NHPA/S.Krasemann; 242 ZEFA; 244 SPL; 245 BTTG; 249 ZEFA; 251 ZEFA; 252 NHPA/D.Woodfall; 253 Ann Ronan Picture Library; 254 ZEFA; 255 ZEFA; 257 Ron Boardman; 259 SPL; 260 SPL; 262 FBI; 263 ZEFA; 264 Dinosaur National Museum, Utah; 265 Ron Boardman; 267 Novosti; 270 Ferodo/ADS Group; 271 ZEFA; 273 ZEFA; 276 ZEFA; 278 VAG (UK) Ltd; 284 SPL; 285 SPL; 291 SPL; 292 ZEFA; 293 ZEFA; 294 ZEFA; 295 ZEFA, 296 Johnson Matthey plc; 298 NASA; 307 ZEFA; 308 Bull HN Information Systems; 312 ZEFA; 313 Allsport; 314 SPL (left), Michael Holford (right); 316 ZEFA; 325 SPL; 326 ZEFA; 329 SPL; 330 SPL; 332 NASA; 334 ZEFA; 336 ZEFA; 337 ZEFA; 339 SPL; 341 SPL; 343 Nestlé; 344 ZEFA; 345 SPL; 350 Science Museum; 351 Transport Road & Research Laboratory; 352 SPL; 354 SPL; 355 ICI Group Ltd; 357 ZEFA; 358 Hutchison Library; 359 ZEFA (left), Photographic Services Corp (top), SPL (bottom); 360 NASA; 361 SPL; 362 ZEFA; 363 Shell Research Ltd; 365 Science Museum (top), SPL (bottom); 368 ZEFA; 369 SPL; 370 ZEFA; 373 British Gas plc; 374 MoD; 376 Ron Boardman; 382 ZEFA; 383 SPL; 385 Beech Aircraft Corps; 386 ZEFA; 387 ZEFA; 389 ZEFA; 390 NCR (left), ZEFA (right); 391 SPL; 393 Ron Boardman (left), ZEFA (right); 394 ZEFA; 400 ZEFA; 401 ZEFA; 402 SPL; 403 ZEFA (top), SPL (bottom); 406 Casio Electronics Ltd; 412 SPL; 417 British Airways; 418 Ann Ronan Picture Library; 419 SPL; 420 SPL; 423 SPL; 428 NASA; 430 SPL (left), ZEFA (right); 432 Grisewood & Dempsey; 435 ZEFA; 437 SPL; 440 Biofotos (top), Ron Boardman (bottom); 441 SPL; 443 ZEFA; 444 ZEFA; 445 SPL; 448 Ron Boardman; 449 Hutchison Library; 450 ZEFA; 452 Ron Boardman; 453 SPL; 454 ZEFA; 459 ZEFA; 461 ZEFA; 463 ZEFA; 464 Spectrum Colour Library; 468 Grisewood & Dempsey; 469 Hutchison Library; 470 NASA; 473 ZEFA; 475 ZEFA; 478 SPL; 480 NHPA/M.Tweedie (top), SPL (bottom); 481 ZEFA; 484 ZEFA; 485 SPL; 486 SPL (left), ZEFA (right); 487 Frank Lane Picture Agency; 489 ICI Explosives; 490 Nobel Foundation; 492 SPL; 494 SPL; 495 SPL; 496 ZEFA; 497 SPL; 501 SPL; 502 SPL; 503 ZEFA; 506 ZEFA; 508 SPL; 509 Ron Boardman; 510 SPL; 511 Science Museum; 512 Paul Brierly (top), SPL (bottom); 513 ZEFA; 514 SPL; 518 ICI Paints; 519 IMITOR; 520 The Hutchison Library; 529 SPL; 531 ICI Chemicals; 533 Ann Ronan Picture Library; 534 IMITOR; 535 Durst; 537 SPL; 541 Terry Cash; 542 SPL; 543 SPL; 544 SPL; 545 Ann Ronan Picture Library; 546 SPL; 547 SPL; 548 ICI Group; 549 ICI Group; 551 Johnson Matthey; 553 UK Atomic Energy Authority Technology; 555 SPL; 556 Polaroid UK; 557 SPL; 558 ZEFA; 559 Exxon Company USA (left), SPL (right); 562 ZEFA (left), SPL (right); 570 Calor Gas Ltd; 571 SPL; 572 Ann Ronan Picture Library (left), ZEFA (right); 573 Mansell Collection; 574 Derek Widdicombe; 575 Pyrex; 577 SPL; 578 SPL; 579 Marconi Co. Ltd; 581 ZEFA; 583 SPL; 585 Polygram; 590 Ann Ronan Picture Library; 591 NHPA/S.Dalton; 592 Frank Lane Picture Agency; 593 NHPA/A.Banninster; 594 ZEFA; 598 ZEFA; 599 ZEFA (top), National Film Archive (bottom), Hunter (left); 600 ZEFA; 601 SPL; 604 Ann Ronan Picture Library (top), ZEFA (bottom); 606 ZEFA; 607 ZEFA; 611 NASA; 612 Science Museum; 613 Biofotos; 616 ZEFA; 619 Ron Boardman; 620 SPL; 621 SPL; 623 NHPA/A.Bannister; 624 ZEFA; 626 Derek Widdicombe; 627 SPL (top), D. Gardner (bottom); 629 ZEFA; 630 ZEFA; 633 ZEFA; 637 Marconi; 639 Ron Boardman; 641 ZEFA; 643 NASA; 644 NASA; 645 NASA; 647 SPL; 648 NASA; 652 NHPA/S.Krasemann; 653 SPL; 655 ZEFA; 659 Ron Boardman; 661 ZEFA; 663 NHPA/A.Bernard; 665 Ann Ronan Picture Library; 668 Frank Lane Picture Agency (right), SPL (left); 669 SPL; 670 J. Allan Cash; 672 ZEFA; 673 Ron Boardman; 674 ZEFA; 675 SPL; 677 ZEFA; 679 ZEFA; 680 Ron Boardman; 681 Ron Boardman; 683 Yamaha; 684 Courtaulds Ltd; 685 ZEFA; 691 ZEFA; 692 ZEFA; 693 ZEFA; 694 ZEFA; 695 SPL (top), ZEFA (bottom); 696 ZEFA; 698 SPL; 699 ZEFA; 703 Ron Boardman; 705 ZEFA; 708 MAFF; 709 NHPA/S.Krasemann; 712 J. Allan Cash; 713 ZEFA; 714 ZEFA; 716 CEGB; 718 ZEFA (top), NHPA/G.Bernard (bottom); 720 SPL; 725 Ron Boardman; 726 Ontario Science Centre; 728 ZEFA; 729 SPL; 732 ZEFA (right), J. Allan Cash (left); 734 Sony UK; 735 SPL; 736 Samsung; 737 St. Bartholomew's Hospital; 738 ZEFA; 742 Genet Group; 743 NHPA/D.Woodfall; 744 ZEFA; 746 Panos Pictures; 749 SPL; 750 NHPA/S.Dalton; 753 Mark Edwards/Still Pictures (top), ZEFA (bottom); 755 Dennis Gilbert; 757 SPL (top), British Aerospace (bottom); 758 ZEFA; 761 Musée de l'air; 763 SPL (top), Grisewood & Dempsey (bottom); 764 SPL; 765 SPL; 766 Biofotos; 767 NHPA/M.Leach; 768 SPL.